CLASSICAL GREEK OLIGARCHY

Classical Greek Oligarchy

A POLITICAL HISTORY

MATTHEW SIMONTON

PRINCETON UNIVERSITY PRESS
PRINCETON & OXFORD

Copyright © 2017 by Princeton University Press

Published by Princeton University Press,
41 William Street, Princeton, New Jersey 08540

In the United Kingdom: Princeton University Press,
6 Oxford Street, Woodstock, Oxfordshire OX20 1TR

press.princeton.edu

All Rights Reserved

First paperback printing 2019
Paper ISBN 978-0-691-19205-5
Cloth ISBN 978-0-691-17497-6

Classical Greek Oligarchy
Library of Congress Cataloging in Publication Control Number: 2016059885

British Library Cataloging-in-Publication Data is available

This book has been composed in Arno Pro

To my family

CONTENTS

Preface ix
Acknowledgments xiii
Abbreviations and Conventions xv

1 Problem, Background, Method   1
2 Oligarchic Power-Sharing   75
3 Balancing Coercion and Co-optation   107
4 The Politics of Public Space   148
5 The Manipulation of Information   186
6 Processes of Regime Breakdown   224

Afterword: The Eclipse of Oligarchia 275
Appendix 287
Works Cited 291
Index Locorum 323
General Index 343

PREFACE

"Oligarchy" is one of the many ancient Greek words that have continued to be employed as terms of political analysis centuries after they were first developed. Its staying power stems in part from the lasting appeal of the ancient Greek tripartite model of government. The idea of political regimes being defined according to whether they are ruled by the one, the few, or the many is simple, elegant, and (in theory, at least) easy to operationalize. Under this schema, a regime in which the few hold power—and those few are almost always the wealthy—ought to be readily identifiable as an oligarchy. In fact, as everyone knows, in states as large and as complex as modern representative governments, classification is a fraught enterprise. Everything depends on what we mean by "power" and how we propose to measure who has it. Nevertheless, in recent years a new focus on oligarchy has emerged. Several political scientists have proposed that the U.S. system, despite our constant talk of democracy, is best described as an oligarchy (Winters and Page 2009; Gilens and Page 2014). The concern that government of, by, and for the people is corroding under the influence of an unrepresentative few is growing stronger on both the left and the right ends of the political spectrum. Feelings of insecurity and suspicion toward the elite (however defined) are fueling resentment against what is perceived as an inequitable status quo. At the time of writing, the United States and Europe are entering a period in which largely taken-for-granted assumptions about what it means to be a liberal democratic society are being upended. Are we witnessing the takeover of government by narrow interests? A reassertion on the part of "the people" (or rather some portion of the electorate) against the elite? Both at the same time? No matter what constitutional labels we decide to apply to our political systems, current trends are disturbing to those who care about justice, equality, and human rights. It is very difficult to know what the future of our politics will hold. (See Cartledge 2016 for the story of democracy so far.) Whatever happens electorally, however, the increasing concentration of wealth will almost certainly continue.

Against this backdrop I hope it will prove rewarding to return to the origins of oligarchy in ancient Greece. Despite the persistence of the word, we have so far not understood very well what it meant in actual practice in its historical context. With any luck the present study will shed some light on that question. It does not presume to supply solutions to the problems alluded to above (assuming one considers them problems). In fact, I continue to vacillate on whether ancient Greek government—and in particular the constitutional type we tend to consider most familiar, democracy—can tell us much of anything about how we ought to conduct our political life today. It will become obvious, however, that I do believe we can better understand the historical events of ancient Greece through the use of contemporary theories and methods. In other words, this is a "positive" rather than a prescriptive work. It is intended to explain, not to advise. That mission statement will probably read as obvious to ancient historians, the book's primary audience, for whom value judgments do not usually enter into the equation. It might be more disappointing to political theorists, who are often interested in normative questions, and from whose work I have benefited greatly. Nevertheless, they may find the project worthwhile insofar as it better situates ancient thinkers such as Plato and Aristotle in their historical milieu. Most political theorists read Aristotle's *Politics* for the insights contained in the "theoretical" books (1–3); I hope to show that the "historical" or "empirical" books (4–6) also illuminate ancient political thought.

A warning to every potential reader: the patchy state of the evidence allows for extremely divergent reconstructions and interpretations. I have therefore often felt it necessary to indicate (at length) the place of the present study in historiographical debates. I have tried to confine these digressions to the footnotes, so that a more general audience can avoid being bogged down in scholarly arcana, while interested specialists are still able to check my reasoning. I also think—though this may turn out to be hubris—that Classical Greek oligarchy, as a topic, can be treated exhaustively (but I hope not exhaustingly) in a single monograph, with all relevant pieces of evidence cited. In any case, it seems like good practice in a work with a guiding theory to furnish all the evidence necessary for potentially disproving the argument. Likewise, understanding oligarchy requires the accurate interpretation of complicated passages and even of individual words in the original Greek. I have attempted, however, to limit the amount of Greek text in the book, and to provide English translations. This is all to say that while some of the notes may strike the eye as long and complicated, the book is meant to be approachable to nonspecialists. Those who have less of an interest in issues of Archaic Greek political development, and who require less convincing that Classical Greek oligarchy was a form of authoritarianism, may want to skip chapter 1, section 1.1.

The subtitle of this book is "A Political History." The "history" part has been explained above, as a way of distinguishing the study from normative political theory. The "political" part may seem redundant—of course a constitutional regime type is political. A growing trend in scholarship, however, has been to treat the Greek elite in social and cultural terms, as a group that exhibited relatively similar traits across space and time. Less energy has been devoted to investigating how different constitutional environments might have channeled, constrained, or otherwise affected elite behavior in distinctive ways. Often an underlying assumption of these studies is that our inherited political categories, like "democracy" and "oligarchy," stem from the idiosyncratic and overly schematic theorizing of Aristotle, and therefore are inadequate. (See, prominently, Duplouy 2006.) While I agree that the members of the elite were alike in certain respects across poleis (competitive, ostentatious, boastful, honor-driven), I would insist that constitutional differences were real, and that they mattered. This book is about the seizing and maintaining of political power. The struggle to hold on to power in the face of democratic resistance profoundly altered the actions of the ruling elite in oligarchies, in a manner that simply was not the case for the elite in non-oligarchically governed cities. As I explain in chapter 1, I find it useful to analyze these actions under the rubric of institutions. With this term, however, I do not restrict myself to political institutions conventionally and narrowly understood—voting bodies, magistracies, laws, and so on. The exercise of power in an oligarchy—as in a democracy—extended beyond formal rules, to broader communal practices, many of which will be familiar to scholars of Greek religion and poetry. I hope to show that such practices are no less amenable to institutional analysis, at least as I understand it. Observers of the Greeks have long recognized that power and culture were inextricably intertwined in the ancient world. The present book suggests how that connection affected the regime known as *oligarchia* in particular. In doing so it has tried to concern itself with what a stimulating piece calls "the places of the political" in ancient Greece, as opposed to simply "politics" (Azoulay and Ismard 2007). By "political" in the subtitle, therefore, one should understand "dealing with the workings of power and institutions, broadly conceived, within societies (oligarchic poleis) characterized by a common constitutional system."

ACKNOWLEDGMENTS

Writing this book would not have been possible without the help of many people. It began its life as a dissertation under the direction of Josiah Ober, to whom I continue to owe profound thanks for his insight, inspiration, encouragement, and friendship. Richard Martin, Ian Morris, and Andrea Nightingale also provided valuable feedback. A Stanford Interdisciplinary Graduate Fellowship allowed me to develop the theoretical framework employed in the book.

Since 2012, I have benefited from many intellectual communities and sources of support. Nicholas Boterf and James Kierstead graciously read the entire manuscript and offered thoughtful comments. I owe thanks to the obliging staff at several libraries: the Art History/Classics Library at the University of California, Berkeley; the Blegen Library at the American School of Classical Studies at Athens; the Center for Hellenic Studies Library; and the Fletcher Library at Arizona State University. A Scholarship, Research, and Creative Activities grant from Arizona State University in 2015 greatly helped in the completion of the manuscript, while a subvention grant from the Center for Critical Inquiry and Cultural Studies has helped with its production. My colleagues at the New College of Interdisciplinary Arts and Sciences have afforded me a welcoming and intellectually stimulating community in which to pursue my research. I have also profited over the years from conversations with Ryan Balot, Matt Christ, Eric Driscoll, Al Duncan, Brooks Kaiser, Foivos Karachalios, Melissa Lane, John Ma, Derin McLeod, Sarah Murray, Roland Oetjen, Mark Pyzyk, Eric Robinson, Steve Johnstone, Claire Taylor, and Dave Teegarden. A special note of thanks is due to James Kierstead, φίλος, συμπότης, δημοτικώτατος.

The expert editors and staff at Princeton University Press—Ryan Mulligan, Rob Tempio, Leslie Grundfest, and Eva Jaunzems—have made this an ideal book publication experience. I thank my (at the time) anonymous readers, Peter van Alfen and Paul Cartledge, who saved me from many errors and greatly improved the project.

Finally, I wish to extend my gratitude to the courteous and patient staff at Lux Central and Giant Coffee in Phoenix, Arizona, where I wrote much of this book. A cup of coffee has often purchased me hours of invaluable work time at those establishments.

This book is dedicated to my family: Allison Jones, Greer Simonton, and Mary Greer Simonton. Their love and support have sustained me over the years, during both happy and difficult times. I love y'all dearly.

November 28, 2016
Phoenix, Arizona

ABBREVIATIONS AND CONVENTIONS

Classical authors are cited according to the abbreviations found in S. Hornblower, A. Spawforth, and E. Eidinow, eds., *The Oxford Classical Dictionary*, fourth edition (Oxford 2012), except that I use "Plat." for Plato and "*Rep.*" for his *Republic*. I use Latinate spelling for ancient names, with a few exceptions (e.g., Kerameikos). The Greek word *dikastēs* is translated as "judge" or "dicast," never "juror." Unless otherwise noted, all dates are BCE and all translations are my own.

Arnaoutoglou Arnaoutoglou, I. 1998. *Ancient Greek Laws: A Sourcebook*. New York.
Bull. ép. *Bulletin épigraphique*. Produced annually in *Revue des études grecques*. Cited by year and entry number.
DK Diels, H. and W. Kranz, eds. 1951–1952. *Die Fragmente der Vorsokratiker*. 3 vols. 6th ed. Berlin.
FGrH Jacoby, F. et al. 1923–. *Die Fragmente der griechischen Historiker*. Berlin and Leiden.
Fornara Fornara, C., ed. 1983. *Translated Documents of Greece and Rome I: Archaic Times to the End of the Peloponnesian War*. 2nd ed. Cambridge.
Gehrke *Stasis* Gehrke, H.-J. 1985. *Stasis: Untersuchungen zu den inneren Kriegen in den griechischen Staaten des 5. und 4. Jahrhunderts v. Chr.* Munich.
HCT Gomme, A. W., A. Andrewes, and K. J. Dover, eds. 1945–1981. *A Historical Commentary on Thucydides*. 5 vols. Oxford.
Hornblower Hornblower, S. 1996–2008. *A Commentary on Thucydides*. 3 vols., Oxford.
IACP Hansen, M. H. and T. H. Nielsen, eds. 2004. *An Inventory of Archaic and Classical Poleis*. Oxford.
IG *Inscriptiones Graecae*. 1873–. Berlin.
IK *Inschriften griechischer Städte aus Kleinasien*. Bonn.
IPArk Thür, G. and H. Taeuber. 1994. *Prozessrechtliche Inschriften der griechischen Poleis: Arkadien (IPArk)*. Vienna.
IvO Dittenberger, W. and K. Purgold, eds. 1896. *Die Inschriften von Olympia*. Berlin.
K-A Kassel, R. and C. Austin, eds. 1983–. *Poetae Comici Graeci*. 8 vols. Berlin.
Koerner Koerner, R. 1993. *Inschriftliche Gesetzestexte der frühen griechischen Polis*. K. Hallof, ed. Cologne.
ML Meiggs, R. and D. M. Lewis, eds. 1989. *A Selection of Greek Historical Inscriptions*. Revised ed. Oxford.

Nomima van Effenterre, H. and F. Ruzé, eds. 1994–1995. *Nomima: Recueil d'inscriptions politiques et juridiques de l'archaïsme grec.* 2 vols. Rome.

PEP McCabe, D. F. et al., eds. 1984–1989. *Princeton Epigraphical Project.* Princeton.

PMG Page, D. L., ed. 1962. *Poetae Melici Graeci.* Oxford.

RO Rhodes, P. J. and R. Osborne, eds. 2003. *Greek Historical Inscriptions, 404–323 B.C.* Oxford.

S-M Snell, B. and H. Maehler, eds. 1984. *Pindari Carmina cum fragmentis.* Leipzig.

SEG *Supplementum Epigraphicum Graecum.* Leiden.

Syll.[3] Dittenberger, W., ed. 1915–1924. *Sylloge Inscriptionum Graecarum.* 3rd ed. Leipzig.

Tit. Cal. Segre, M., ed. 1952. *Tituli Calymnii. ASAtene* 22–3, n.s. 6–7 (1944–1945).

CLASSICAL GREEK OLIGARCHY

Map. The Greek Aegean ca. 400 BCE.

1

Problem, Background, Method

Oligarchy, the harsh and unjust greed of a few rich and wretched men arrayed against the poor majority.

—DIO OF PRUSA[1]

1.0 The Problem of Oligarchy

At least since the time of the poet Pindar in the mid-fifth century BCE, the ancient Greeks understood that political regimes could be classed according to rule by the one, the few, or the many.[2] Twenty-five centuries later, if one were to press Classical historians on how much attention they have paid to each type, they might respond, with some sheepishness, that two out of three ain't bad. Work has proliferated on the study of the rule of the many, *dēmokratia* (democracy). While Classical Athens has usually been the focus, scholars are starting to venture beyond the territory of Attica and beyond the constricting temporal boundaries of 508–322 as well.[3] A less intensive, but still impressive, amount of work has gone into understanding the rule of one. Scholarship has traditionally been interested in the Archaic tyrants, but more recently attention has expanded to encompass multiple forms of sole rulership in ancient

---

1. 3.48: ὀλιγαρχία, σκληρὰ καὶ ἄδικος πλεονεξία πλουσίων τινῶν καὶ πονηρῶν ὀλίγων ἐπὶ τοὺς πολλοὺς καὶ ἀπόρους συστᾶσα.

2. *Pyth.* 2.86–88.

3. For the Classical Athenian democracy, see especially the work of Ober (1989, 1996, 1998, 2008, 2015). For earlier studies, see, e.g., Jones 1957; Finley 1983, 1985; and the institutional studies of Hansen (e.g., his 1999). Recent work on the Athenian democracy, from a variety of methodological approaches, includes Balot 2001; Wohl 2002; Lanni 2006; Herman 2006; Christ 2012; Gottesman 2014. For ancient democracy beyond Athens, see O'Neil 1995; Robinson 1997, 2011; Gauthier 1993; Mann and Scholz 2012.

Greece, including Classical-era tyrants, Hellenistic kings, and longstanding dynasties.[4]

Studies devoted to the rule of the few, *oligarchia* (oligarchy), by contrast, are practically nonexistent. The last comprehensive treatment in English, by Leonard Whibley, was published one hundred and twenty years ago.[5] Subsequent studies, while adding to our knowledge of oligarchy, have not attempted to replace Whibley's work.[6] Moreover, historians have typically focused on the Athenian oligarchies of the late fifth century, and in particular on the oligarchic ideology that inspired them, rather than on the concrete actions of historical oligarchs from across the Greek world as they appear in the ancient sources.[7] It has rarely been asked what oligarchs in the Classical period actu-

---

4. For Archaic tyranny, see Andrewes 1956; Berve 1967; Mossé 1969; Barceló 1993; Steiner 1994; de Libero 1996; McGlew 1993; Kurke 1999; Anderson 2005; Lewis 2006; Morgan 2015. Studies on early Greek kingship include Drews 1983; Carlier 1984. For "sole rulership," see the articles collected in Luraghi 2013a. For Hellenistic kingship, see recently Hatzopoulos 1996; Ma 1999; Monson 2012; Kosmin 2014; Fischer-Bovet 2014. For ruling dynasties, see Mitchell 2013.

5. Whibley 1896. (Treatments of oligarchy can be found in the nineteenth-century handbook tradition, e.g., Busolt 1920: 341–69.) By bringing together many disparate scraps of evidence and organizing the little constitutional information we have, Whibley's study remains indispensable. It utilizes, however, a different definition of oligarchy from the one adopted here.

6. The other major study of oligarchy is Ostwald 2000, but it is focused more on Aristotelian terminology than on the historical practice of oligarchy. Brock and Hodkinson (2000: 16–20) briefly discuss oligarchy, making excellent points but giving too much weight to the idea of a "hoplite republic" (see below). De Ste. Croix (1981) treats class struggle in ancient Greece but spends comparatively little time on matters of oligarchic constitutional detail (283, 287–88, 291–92). See also Cartledge 2009: 52–54.

7. On the oligarchic interludes at Athens in the late fifth century and the ideology behind them, see, e.g., Krentz 1982; Raaflaub 1983, 2004: 235–47; Ostwald 1986: 337–496; Brock 1989; Lewis 1993; Lehmann 1997; Leppin 1999; Bultrighini 1999; Blösel 2000; Rhodes 2000; Heftner 2001, 2003; Németh 2006; Shear 2011; Bearzot 2013. Increasingly, historians are examining the oligarchies of the late fourth century in Athens as well: Williams 1985; Poddighe 2002; Oliver 2003b; Bayliss 2011. The oligarchic *koinon* of Boeotia has also been studied, e.g., by Larsen 1955; Cartledge 2000b. Surprisingly, studies of Aristotle's treatment of oligarchy are few, and include Mulgan 1991; Simpson 2011; Skultety 2011. The papers in Tabachnick and Koivukoski 2011 tend to treat oligarchy (both Greek and Roman) using a political thought-based approach; Cooper 2011, however, is more historical and quite in line with many of the arguments of this book. Teegarden 2014 explains how democratic anti-tyranny legislation defended against both tyranny and oligarchy, but it contains no comprehensive treatment of the nature of the oligarchic threat to democracy. Gray 2015 describes late-Classical and early-Hellenistic *stasis*, often between democrats and oligarchs, but does not attempt a new conceptualization of oligarchy. Caire 2016, on the development of the concept "oligarchy" in Athens in the fifth and fourth centuries, appeared too recently to be taken into consideration.

ally did in their capacity as oligarchs.[8] What was the relationship between the rulers and the wider male citizenry (the demos) of an oligarchically governed polis? To what extent was oligarchic rule contested by popular movements? And how might oligarchs have collectively responded in an attempt to retain their power? All of these questions will be concerns of this study, which, as the title states, is primarily a political history (one that treats of the development and functioning of political institutions over time) rather than an intellectual history or a study in political thought.

It is worth asking why historians have attempted so few studies of Classical Greek oligarchy. One reason is that the evidence for oligarchic governance is so lamentably thin. Finley, for example, despaired of being able to say anything systematic about oligarchies: "Unfortunately, the information is lacking for a meaningful discussion of politics in the oligarchic Greek ... states."[9] This claim is disputable. First, although there is admittedly much less evidence for oligarchy than for democracy, the sources that do exist—which include many important epigraphic discoveries not available to Whibley—have not been systematically collected. Second, the evidence has not been analyzed through the most productive methodological lens. When we view Classical Greek oligarchy as a species of authoritarianism, as I propose to do here, we are better able to organize and make sense of the available historical evidence.

More importantly, however, it is clear that scholars consider the topic of oligarchy less interesting because the political phenomenon is (supposedly) so overwhelmingly common. Wherever we look, whether in ancient Greece or in the modern world, we are apt to find a relatively small number of people doing the active work of governing in any given state. The early-twentieth-century political theorist Robert Michels designated this the "Iron Law of Oligarchy" (1962), from which no political organization could escape. Ober

---

8. Although I use the word "oligarch" throughout, there is actually no attested instance of the Greek noun *oligarchos*, on the model of *monarchos* (monarch). (One exception: Walbank would restore a genitive plural "*oli[garchōn]*" at *SEG* 32.161, line 5. Langdon is more cautious, leaving the space blank: Lalonde, Langdon, and Walbank 1991: 71.) The usual designation for an oligarch is the adjective *oligarchikos*, "oligarchically minded person" (e.g., Lys. 25.8), or a participial construction (e.g., "those ruling in an oligarchy," Arist. *Pol.* 4.1300a8). I do not assume that every wealthy man in a Greek polis was an oligarch. Ancient democracies allowed (in fact, required) the political participation of the wealthy, and many of them were sympathetic to the rule of the demos. In what follows I attempt as much as possible to restrict the use of "oligarch" to those ruling in an oligarchic regime or actively working to establish one.

9. Finley 1983: 63. Cf. the comments of Cartledge 2000b: 401; Forsdyke 2009: 201. Note Finley's further claim that "bits in Aristotle's *Politics* or in the Greek historians indicate that [oligarchies'] politics could be sharp and nasty." The present book would seem to support that judgment.

(1989) has decisively shown that Classical Athens defies the Iron Law, but all other Greek states remain potentially open to the charge. Some historians, therefore, might consider the ancient distinction between *oligarchia* and *dēmokratia* unhelpful and potentially misleading, since in fact all poleis were governed by a few.[10] At the same time, scholars tend to overestimate the conservatism of the Greeks outside of Classical Athens, and thus to overestimate the total number of oligarchies as well. Indeed, some assume that oligarchy was the most common type of constitution.[11]

This book takes a very different view. It contends that by confusing the "oligarchy" of Michels's "Iron Law of Oligarchy" with *oligarchia* in ancient Greece, we are in danger of misunderstanding much of ancient Greek politics. The "Iron Law" threatens to blur differences between regimes that were clear and often extremely important to political actors at the time. As much as we may want to conflate ancient Greek democracy and oligarchy—because ancient democracy seems unjustifiably exclusionary to our modern sensibilities—the labels were crucial for many contemporaries. To quote Finley once again: "'Rule by the few' or 'rule by the many' was a meaningful choice, the freedom and the rights that factions claimed for themselves were worth fighting for."[12] It would be presumptuous, therefore, to ignore or second-guess the claims of the sources. By the same token, we should not foist untested assumptions about the frequency of oligarchy onto the ancient evidence. New resources, such as the Copenhagen Polis Center's *Inventory of Archaic and Classical Poleis* (*IACP*), are enabling us to begin the process of tracing constitutional developments over time.[13] Teegarden has recently demonstrated, using data taken from the *Inventory*, that "the ancient Greek world became increasingly more densely democratic during the Classical and early Hellenistic periods."[14] As this book will show, democracy not only increasingly coexisted with oligarchy in the Greek world, it also largely replaced it during the

---

10. Another possible interpretation is to suppose that democracies and oligarchies existed along a spectrum, at the center of which the two regimes blurred together and were largely indistinguishable. Thus proposes Leppin (2013: 147): "[T]heir genesis and their reality put democracy and oligarchy much nearer to each other than their proponents would have wished." Blösel 2014 likewise sees "moderate oligarchies" as differing little from democracies (but he assumes the widespread existence of hoplite constitutions, on which see below). I show in this book that such views are mistaken and that (in the sources, at least) most democracies are readily distinguishable from most oligarchies.

11. e.g., Morris 1996: 41.

12. Finley 1983: 9.

13. See further the data collected by Josiah Ober's POLIS project (polis.stanford.edu) and utilized in his latest book (2015).

14. 2014: 2, with appendix.

Hellenistic period. Oligarchy, as it turns out, was not "inevitable" for the Greeks—in fact, it became *less* and not *more* common over the course of the Classical period.

The next section of this introductory chapter argues for a new and distinctive historical understanding of ancient Greek *oligarchia*, based on a careful reading of the ancient sources. According to this view, *oligarchia* does not refer to just any regime in which a small number of people govern, but to a specific constitutional alternative that arose as a reaction to *dēmokratia* between the late sixth and mid-fifth century. Thus, the meaning of *oligarchia*, both as a concept and as a form of political practice, cannot be understood apart from *dēmokratia*, alongside which it developed *pari passu*.[15] Once the Greek elite perceived *dēmokratia* as a potential threat to their interests as a class, many members of the elite, working in different poleis and under differing local conditions, created what nevertheless became a broadly similar repertoire of political and social institutions designed specifically to avoid the danger of democracy.[16] The term for this bundle of defensive and reactionary techniques was *oligarchia*.[17]

---

15. Leppin (2013: 149–50) has similar remarks on the "twin birth" of democracy and oligarchy, but the rest of his analysis differs sharply from mine.

16. Here I should address the question of class, which has been reopened recently by the neo-Marxist account of Rose 2012. The sources cannot fail to make apparent that political struggle in the ancient Greek world could be and indeed often was organized along class lines, if by "classes" we mean those wealthy enough to live without laboring and those who had to labor for their livelihood; moreover, these "classes" exist within the larger group of free citizen males and do not, except on rare occasions, extend outside of it (i.e., to metics and slaves). This definition in itself contains distinctions from traditional Marxism, which views class as a relational marker determined by location within the mode of production. I also do not suppose that political conflict always and everywhere in history is determined in the last instance by economic forces: other factors (ethnic identity, religious belief) frequently play an important, independent role (often the determinative role). It is the historian's job to determine what the central motivations are in a given historical period, or even in a specific historical episode. The politics of Classical Greece have a strongly class-based character, but politics need not always be like that. Cf. the remarks of the non-Marxist sociologist Michael Mann, discussing different forms of conflict in history (1986: 217): "[Greece] is the first known society to have moved fully into the third level of class organization, exhibiting to us *symmetrical, political class struggle*" (emphasis in original).

17. The present view of oligarchy is therefore to be distinguished from two common alternatives. Some take the term "oligarchy," which developed in the fifth century, and project it back onto the Archaic period. The ancients themselves, including Aristotle (*e.g.*, *Pol.* 4.1289b36–38), did this. Thus Whibley (1896: 72–83) discusses the replacement of aristocracy by oligarchy during the Archaic period as regimes of wealth replaced regimes of "nobility." I would speak instead in a rather undifferentiated manner of "Archaic elite-led regimes" (see further below).

This book therefore attempts to "de-naturalize" our inherited and largely taken-for-granted ideas about oligarchy. Once we see that *oligarchia* was a specific historical reaction to another concrete phenomenon, that of *dēmokratia*, we can begin to wonder afresh at how Classical Greek oligarchy managed to sustain itself as long as it did. For if, as I will argue, oligarchy was never intended to be popular with the mass of the demos, and if the average Greek citizen of the Classical period preferred democracy to oligarchy, we may well be puzzled by how anything so unpopular managed to survive for any length of time, let alone several centuries.[18] With the situation framed in this way, the central question of this book is the following: *Given the general unpopularity of oligarchy and the widespread appeal of democracy as a constitutional alternative, what accounts for the survival of oligarchy during the Classical period?* The answer, in brief, is institutions. The understanding of institutions employed here stems from engagement with the scholarship of political scientists working within the tradition of the "New Institutionalism." New Institutionalism, in contrast to older variants, recognizes that institutions, far from simply being either instruments of raw coercion or mere reflections of existing ideology, structure behavior by influencing individuals' expectations of others' actions. Its choice of institutions strongly affects the future stability of a given political regime, in that institutions tend to produce certain "equilibrium" states of behavior. When political actors design institutions effectively, they can engender equilibria in the aggregate that no individual would have chosen left to his or her own devices. In the case of authoritarian institutions, this can mean that populations acquiesce to an unpopular regime, even in the absence of thoroughgoing coercion or a legitimating ideology. Institutions in this scenario represent a particularly effective instrument in the toolkit of the authoritarian ruler.[19]

I am also interested in this study in when precisely the concept of *oligarchia* first arose, rather than in regimes we wish to label oligarchies in hindsight. Second, some scholars believe the concept of *oligarchia* emerged relatively late in the fifth century, perhaps as a reaction to the Athenian empire or in the crucible of the Peloponnesian War (see the bibliography cited below). I locate the emergence of *oligarchia* earlier than this in the fifth century, and in a broad array of independent contexts, not simply as a result of Athens.

18. Hansen has already drawn attention both to the unpopularity of oligarchy and to the correspondingly surprising frequency of it as a historically attested constitutional type: "*Tyrannis* and *oligarchia* in the classical period almost invariably are criticized as bad constitutions ... yet ... the rule of few [was a] rather common form of constitution in the age of Plato and Aristotle" (*IACP*, p. 83). Cf. his 2006b: "What we really lack today is sources for a positive evaluation of oligarchy."

19. For bibliography, see section 1.3 below.

Thus, to the question of why and how *oligarchia* persisted for so long in the face of *dēmokratia*, I answer that it was likelier to survive, all else being equal, when oligarchs implemented specialized social and political institutions that kept the elite united while discouraging the demos from collective action. These institutions, which comprise the "rules" that characterized the "rule of the few," are treated extensively in chapters 2 through 5. So long as the equilibria promoted by the various institutions obtained, the oligarchic polis was stable, even when large numbers of people among the demos individually preferred democracy to oligarchy. The focus throughout is not on what ancient oligarchs and their critics said about them, or how elite thinkers theorized about them, but what they actually did. The book is thus the first attempt to collect and analyze the characteristic actions of Classical-era oligarchic states. To make these processes clearer, I frequently adduce examples from "New Institutionalist" political science literature, especially from recent studies devoted to authoritarianism. Although the parallel is by no means perfect, modern authoritarian regimes, like Classical Greek oligarchies, have also discovered institutional means of staving off democracy and shoring up their own minority-run rule.

Chapter 6, by contrast, explores what happened when these same institutions broke down. Using examples from throughout Classical Greek history, I show that oligarchic *stasis* (civil war) and regime breakdown were not haphazard but resulted from a circumscribed set of scenarios that represented institutional failure. Here, in addition to surveying the contexts most conducive to democratic revolution, I use some basic game theory to illuminate the strategic choices at play in scenarios of oligarchic collapse. Oligarchs were often incapable of cooperating in high-risk, uncertain situations. Their need to save themselves frequently outweighed the benefits that would have accrued from maintaining unity against challenges to the oligarchic status quo. Over time, these tendencies fatally undermined the oligarchic project.

Thus, in a brief afterword, I look forward to the early Hellenistic period, when *oligarchia* ceded ideological ground to *dēmokratia* and shed all pretense of being a legitimate constitutional alternative. Hellenistic Greece, despite being cast sometimes as the graveyard of democracy, in fact became the high tide of democracy in the ancient world. Recent revisionist arguments about the survival of democracy beyond the fourth century show that democracy was the institutional "rules of the game" after the conquests of Alexander.[20] By the same token, the foregoing Classical period represented the apex, not of democracy, but of oligarchy. It was the period when oligarchy was created,

---

20. For the revisionist stance on democracy in the Hellenistic period, see the literature cited in the afterword.

developed, but was largely abandoned as a potential rival to democracy. The arguments of this book allow us to see more clearly why and how democracy was able to step into the constitutional space abdicated by oligarchy in the late Classical period.[21]

The remainder of this introductory chapter is taken up with three tasks. First (1.1), I present the evidence for the conception of oligarchy sketched above, as a reactionary form of government concerned to prevent democracy. To put this development in context I begin by surveying the Archaic period, when it would be more accurate to speak of "elite-led regimes" rather than "oligarchy" proper.[22] It will become clear that, although the Archaic elite could assume a hostile and snobbish pose toward the common people, the demos nonetheless played a significant role in the political life of the period. Archaic elite-led government did not define itself, as Classical oligarchy later did, as a united front of the elite against the demos. At the same time, many of the institutional techniques used by Classical oligarchs *were* forged in the political furnace of the Archaic period, particularly those designed to prevent the emergence of a tyrant from the ranks of the elite. I then discuss the development of a distinctly oligarchic mindset following the advent of *dēmokratia* in

---

21. The book is thus in part an argument for the continuing relevance of the periodization "Classical-Hellenistic." Gray speaks of the "long fourth century" between ca. 404–146 BCE (2015: 5); Fröhlich likewise argues that a volume on "approaches to the post-classical polis" ought simply to have been called "approaches to the Greek poleis" (2014: 755, reviewing Martzavou and Papazarkadas 2013). While I agree that the term "post-Classical" is unhelpful (because it establishes the Classical period as the standard against which all subsequent ages are measured), I would insist on a turning point in constitutional history around the death of Alexander in 323.

22. I call Archaic regimes "elite-led" constitutions for lack of a better term. "Aristocracy" is too freighted with Aristotelian (but also medieval European) connotations (Duplouy 2006; Fernoux and Stein 2007; Fisher and van Wees 2015). The Archaic Greeks themselves do not seem to have known the word *aristokratia* (its earliest attestation is Thuc. 3.82.8, in the year 427; Ar. *Av.* 125 points to its being a familiar term in 414). "Timocracy," while it helpfully combines notions of honor and status, is also a later terminological invention. (In its original usage in Plato's *Republic*, it refers to a Sparta-like regime, not an Archaic elite-led constitution.) *Eunomia* is the best attested term in the Archaic period: Hom. *Od.* 17.487; Hes. *Th.* 230, 902; Solon fr. 4.32 West; Xenophanes fr. 2.19 West; cf. Arist. *Pol.* 5.1306b39–1307a1, giving the title *Eunomia* to the poem of Tyrtaeus containing frr. 1–4 West. "Elite," which has gained currency in scholarship recently (e.g., Savalli-Lestrade 2003), remains usefully open and vague (although see the complaints of Gagarin and Perlman 2016: 55n144). Although I agree with his contention that elite status in ancient Greece was more performative and merit-based than hereditary, Duplouy (2006) downplays the importance of wealth among the Archaic and Classical elite. Here "elite" always connotes the leisured wealthy, even if such people always had to perform certain actions in the eyes of the community in order to maintain their position.

several poleis in the late sixth and early fifth centuries. Here the most important arguments will be three: that the opposition between oligarchy and democracy developed relatively early in the fifth century; that democratization, and the oligarchization that emerged in reaction to it, was a Panhellenic process, encouraged by but not solely reliant on the growth of democracy at Athens; and, relatedly, that conflict between democrats and oligarchs predated the Peloponnesian War. The war may have exacerbated political tensions within the poleis, but it did not create them *ex nihilo*.

In the next section (1.2), I provide a synchronic overview of the key features linking oligarchies during the Classical period. I show that oligarchies defined themselves overwhelmingly by a wealth criterion, and that the threshold for full citizenship was usually set in such a way as to encompass the leisured wealthy. This section also demonstrates that the so-called "hoplite republic" was largely a myth. This concept, attested mainly in the political works of Aristotle, has entered numerous discussions as an explanatory *via tertia* between broad democracy and narrow oligarchic "dynasties" (*dunasteiai*), or juntas.[23] I show, by contrast, that attested instances of the "hoplite republic" are extremely rare, and that the arguments advanced for its widespread existence are unconvincing. An investigation into the actual makeup of the ruling groups in oligarchies mentioned in the historical sources reveals that they were quite small, including at most the wealthiest 20 percent of the free male adult population of a polis but more typically less, around 10 or 15 percent. More often than not, in fact, hoplites can be found fighting in support of democracy against oligarchy during the Classical period.

The final section of this chapter (1.3) lays out the book's methodological approach. It defines "institutions" and the "New Institutionalism" in greater detail and specifies the extent to which these ideas can be adapted and applied to the ancient world. I also introduce some concepts that will be crucial for the argument going forward, specifically "equilibrium," "common knowledge," "coordination," the "collective action problem," and a few elementary games from game theory. The proof of the legitimacy of these concepts is, of course, their usefulness for explaining the ancient evidence, which will become apparent in subsequent chapters.

1.1 From Archaic Regimes to Classical Oligarchy

To recognize the extent to which Classical-era oligarchy represented an unprecedented attack on the political participation of the demos, we must first acknowledge the considerable involvement of the common people in the

---

23. See, e.g., Hanson 1995 *passim*; Samons 2004: 44; Raaflaub 2007: 121.

poleis of the Archaic period.[24] Such a view, while fully supported by the available evidence, nevertheless runs counter to certain elitist theories of Archaic government that have recently gained prominence. Consider, for example, this particularly strong-worded claim by Anderson, describing the Greek poleis of the seventh and sixth centuries: "Poorer individuals as yet had no political presence whatsoever."[25] Other historians have similarly emphasized the outsize role of the elite in Archaic political life, in the process playing down or even denying any significant participation by the wider community of free male citizens.[26] There is no doubt that the elite played the leading role in the political communities of Archaic Greece. On the other hand, Greece did not have to wait until the emergence of *dēmokratia* to witness political participation by the demos. A survey of our earliest Greek texts, both literary and epigraphical, provides a corrective to the strongly elitist view.[27] What is striking is not the sudden and unexpected appearance of the demos in the late sixth century, but rather its consistent presence in the political systems of Archaic Greece, starting from the earliest times.[28] The members of the Archaic elite, while they could on occasion be extraordinarily harsh and even violent toward

---

24. I define the Archaic period according to convention, as the time between the eighth century and the Persian Wars in 480. The Classical period comprises 480–323.

25. 2005: 178. This blanket statement is undermined by some of Anderson's claims elsewhere, such as that many poleis of the time possessed popular assemblies (178n9).

26. See, e.g., Osborne 1996: 187; Foxhall 1997: 119; Forsdyke 2005: 19. These accounts also frequently portray the Archaic state as quite primitive. They were less developed than in Classical times, to be sure, but they were still states. Van Wees (2013a) has argued that Archaic Athens was actually quite advanced in terms of its tax-raising abilities. The thesis of Berent (1996) that the Greek polis was a "stateless society" is unconvincing certainly for the Classical period; see Hansen 2002. It may describe certain poleis of the Archaic period, but not all.

27. As Davies has observed, references to sophisticated Archaic institutions, including instances of popular participation, have been largely overlooked by "political theorists and historians of political thought, who ignore the antiquarian, and above all the epigraphical, evidence" (2003b: 326).

28. One potential problem when starting out is our definition of the term "demos." It is relatively clear that in Homeric epic, "demos" designates the entirety of the free male community apart from the elite *basileis*. I do not see why this should substantially change over the course of the Archaic period. Some scholars, however, following a basically Aristotelian line, believe that the meaning of "demos" first constricted, to comprise the "hoplites" (i.e., the wealthier part of the free population), then later shifted to mean "the poorer, non-hoplitic part of the free population." For uncertainty as to the identity of the Archaic demos, see, e.g., Koerner 1981: 204; Osborne 1996: 187; Foxhall 1997: 65; Gagarin 2008: 82. For the identification of the Archaic demos with the hoplites, see Gehrke 2009: 397; Raaflaub and Wallace 2007: 23; cf. Donlan 1999 [1970]: 225–36. Morris, however, has argued persuasively that "it is wrong to imagine a slow evolution across the archaic period from royal to aristocratic to hoplite to thetic

the common people, seem overall to have tolerated the presence of the demos in everyday political life. The mitigating factor was that that presence was limited. When democracy appeared in the late Archaic and early Classical periods, heralding a much more extensive political role for the common people, the stance of many members of the elite toward the demos hardened into what we know as oligarchy.

1.1.1 Elite and Demos in Archaic Sources

To begin with Homeric epic,[29] scholars have increasingly come to see the assembly (*agorē*) of the people (*dēmos, laos*) as an important institution in the political world depicted by the poems.[30] As Raaflaub and Wallace put it in a recent survey of "people's power" in Archaic Greece, "The assembly is a constant feature of Homeric society, embedded in its structures and customs, and formalized to a considerable degree." Although there is no formal counting of votes, no individual proposals are made from the floor, and leaders do not always keep to the decisions pronounced in the assembly, the Homeric *agorē* is nonetheless a crucial political institution. It possesses, as Raaflaub and Wallace go on to say, "an important function in witnessing, approving, and legitimizing communal actions and decisions regarding such matters as the distribution of booty, 'foreign policy,' and the resolution of conflicts."[31] The elites depicted in Homeric epic no doubt expected that the announcement of political decisions in the common space of the assembly would strengthen the resolve of individuals to uphold them, precisely because they gained normative authority through being openly announced and commonly shared.[32] Although the members of the demos are not expected to speak beyond making shouts and acclamations, their assent and even critical input are sought by the leadership, as when Agamemnon says he will "test the army with words."[33]

---

power ... from the earliest sources, 'the middle' includes all citizens" (1996: 40; for "middle" one could substitute "demos").

29. To give all of the following sources the attention they deserve would be impossible. The purpose is to establish the presence and influence of the demos.

30. Carlier 1984, 1998; Andreev 1979; Raaflaub 1997; Haubold 2000; Ruzé 1997: 68–74; Hammer 2002: 144–69; Hölkeskamp 2002; Wecowski 2011: 77–79; Werlings 2010: 47–107. For the difficulties involved in using Homeric epic as historical evidence, see Raaflaub 1998.

31. Raaflaub and Wallace 2007: 28–29. Cf. the similar role of the *laos* in Hesiod, which meets in the assembly (*Theogony* 89) and witnesses the decisions of the *basileis*.

32. Cf. Hölkeskamp 2002: 317, discussing the Homeric assembly: "Universal consent on a ruling as being 'just' may generate collective pressure on individual parties to accept and submit to it."

33. *Il.* 2.73.

The idea of the *vox populi*, although often shadowy and consigned to the dramatic background, exerts a powerful influence over the basileis.[34]

The most useful place to turn after Homer is the epigraphic record of Archaic laws inscribed on stone.[35] Werlings, who has studied the presence of the demos in Archaic law (2010), has concluded that the demos often plays an influential role in these texts, even if they are not the sole, sovereign authority of the polis.[36] For example, we possess a law from Tiryns dated to the seventh century specifying that a group of magistrates are to perform some action with respect to the public property of the polis "however the *damos* [= demos] decides [*dokei*] ... [in an] assembly [in the] theater."[37] The language recalls the customary opening enactment clause of Classical Athenian decrees, "decided by the people" (*edoxe tō dēmōi*). Here, however, it does not name the body on whose authority the decree itself was decided, but rather a procedural step to be taken in specified circumstances.[38] The demos is not yet the authoritative voice of the polis, but it is one—important—voice within it. As Koerner puts it, discussing this example, "It is certain ... that the *damos* could

---

34. See, e.g., *Il.* 9.460, *Od.* 14.239, 15.468, with Ruzé 1997: 73; Hammer 2005: 115.

35. If I spend more time on the epigraphic evidence that follows than on the literary evidence, it is because the inscribed laws may be less familiar. Important works of scholarship in the field of Archaic inscribed law include ML; *Nomima*; Koerner; Hölkeskamp 1999; Gagarin 2008. Fornara has English-language translations of several of these laws.

36. By contrast, Archaic Crete, while epigraphically rich, is impoverished in terms of mentions of the *dēmos/damos*. Nonetheless, the constitutions of the Cretan poleis seem to have been broadly in line with the picture of Archaic elite-led regimes developed here. Against a picture of Crete as exceptionally "aristocratic" (e.g., Willetts 1955; Whitley 1997), Gagarin and Perlman note that while the Archaic Cretan poleis were certainly not democratic, their governments "were composed of a mixture of elements, with the *kosmos* [an important magistrate] having clear authority in some respects but also being subject to constraints imposed by the broader community" (2016: 55). The regimes of Classical Crete, on the other hand, remain much more obscure to us, largely because the number of Cretan inscribed laws sharply decreases in the later fifth and fourth centuries. Given the paucity of evidence, I am unable to classify Classical Cretan regimes as "oligarchies" in the sense known from mainland Greece and other Greek-speaking regions. I therefore bracket the Cretan case for the remainder of the book. For Cretan political history, see Perlman 1992, 2004, 2014; Gehrke 1997; Chaniotis 1999, 2005b; Wallace 2010; Seelentag 2015.

37. Koerner no. 31 (see also *Nomima* I.78).

38. For further discussion, see Osborne 1997: 39–40; Gagarin 2008: 64–65; Hawke 2011: 186–87; Koerner 1985. For another early inscription containing similar language about "however the *damos* decides," see *Nomima* I.21, a law of the first half of the sixth century which is labeled a "*rhetra*" (ordinance) of the Chaladrians (perhaps a deme of Elis). For additional Elean inscriptions, see below.

have the right to decide upon important matters of the polis long before the onset of democracy."³⁹

Other documents likewise highlight the demos's role as a political agent. A seventh-century Corcyrean inscription manages to fit four "demos"-based words into six lines: "This is the tomb of Menecrates the son of Tlasias, an Oianthean by birth, and the *damos* made it for him; for he was the dear *proxenos* [Oianthean representative] of the *damos*, but he died at sea, and there was public [*damosion*] woe.... Praximenes, coming from his homeland, made this tomb for his brother with the *damos*."⁴⁰ The repeated use of the word in such an early text has occasioned much comment, with Wallace claiming that the precociousness of the "demos" language can be explained only by the existence of a "democratic" faction at Corcyra. The epitaph is thus a "propaganda document, part of whose intent is to stress the independence and authority of the people."⁴¹ The interstate nature of the epitaph, however, points to the possibility that it was meant especially for external consumption, and here Werlings has a more convincing interpretation: given Corcyra's antagonistic relationship with Corinth during this period, it is best to see in the use of the word *damos* "a willingness on the part of the Corcyreans to affirm themselves as an independent and autonomous city vis-à-vis Corinth."⁴² Thus the *damos* would again stand for the entirety of the citizen community inhabiting the territory of Corcyra.

Next we come to the so-called "constitutional law of Chios," dated by Jeffery (1956) to ca. 575–550.⁴³ This famous inscription, full of references to the demos, has given rise to much speculation about the constitutional development of Chios at this time. Several earlier interpreters believe that the qualified title of the *dēmosiē boulē* ("people's" or "popular council," C.2–3, 5–6) marked it as distinct from another, more traditional council (not named by our inscription). Larsen, for example, claimed that "the existence of a 'popular' council suggests that there also was an aristocratic council."⁴⁴ The specification *dēmosiē* in the case of the Chian council does not require, however, the existence of a counterpart *boulē*. The latter assumption springs from a

---

39. 1985: 456: "Es ist dadurch sicher ... dass der Damos lange vor Enstehung der Demokratie das Recht zur Beschlussfassung über wichtige Angelegenheiten der Polis besitzen konnte."

40. ML 4 (trans. Fornara 14; see also *Nomima* I.34).

41. 1970: 193, 191.

42. 2010: 126: "la volonté de la part des Corcyréens de s'affirmer comme une cité indépendente et autonome vis-à-vis de Corinthe."

43. ML 8 (trans. Fornara 19; see also *Nomima* I.62; Koerner no. 61). The label "constitutional" is misleading, as I explain in greater detail below.

44. Larsen 1949: 171. Cf. Jeffery 1956: 166; Ehrenberg 1950: 538; ML 8, p. 16; Rhodes 1993: 153.

translation of the word *dēmosiē* as "popular," but it could just as easily mean "concerned with the public business," as it usually does during this period.[45]

We still might ask how much power the demos had in Chios at this time. Again, a careful consideration of the available evidence suggests that it played an important, but not sovereign, part in the running of the polis. It was one institution among many, assigned delimited duties in special situations. Its most concrete action comes at A.7, where "the demos has been assembled." According to Jeffery's text and translation, this gathering comes after a previous string of actions dealing with official misconduct, and precedes several others. The demos thus constitutes one step in an ongoing process of dispute and resolution. Finally, although some have seen the *dēmosiē boulē* as probouleutic for the Chian assembly, this is highly speculative and, on balance, unlikely: the *dēmosiē boulē* is said to "conduct" or "exact" (*prēssetō*) "the other business of the demos" (*ta alla ta dēmo*, C.9–11), and so it likely executes decisions rather than refers or submits them to the demos.[46] Nevertheless, the demos may have played other roles in the running of Chios that this particular law leaves unspecified. As with much Archaic Greek law, the "constitution" of Chios is aimed at a particular set of problems arising around certain offices, in this case the *dēmarchos* and the *basileus*, and it outlines procedures to be followed by countervailing offices and political bodies; it does not offer an exhaustive list of the duties attached to each office. Thus it is not properly a "constitution" at all, but, as Robinson puts it, a "set of laws concerning the administration of justice, of which only a portion survives."[47] We therefore do not know what other functions the assembly of citizens might have served at this time. In any case, the Chian law does not enshrine the demos as the sovereign power of the polis.[48]

A final set of inscribed laws exhibits characteristics similar to those of the Chian law. Several inscribed bronze plaques from Olympia edited by Dittenberger and Purgold in their 1896 *Inschriften von Olympia* mention the *damos* or similar bodies.[49] None of these inscriptions is actually enacted in the name

45. See Werlings' "Annexes III: Tableau B," with thirteen entries, to which add *IPArk* 7.4. Especially pertinent is a phrase from *Nomima* I.109, ϝράτρα ἀ δαμοσία, which I interpret as also meaning "concerned with the public business"—see below. See further Werlings 2010: 158–65; Ampolo 1983; Ruzé 1997: 364–66.

46. Probouleutic: Wade-Gery 1958: 189–92, 198–99; Ehrenberg 1950: 138; Jeffery 1956: 164; Robinson 1997: 97. Executive (or the author is ambivalent): Larsen 1949: 170–71; ML 8; Rhodes 1993: 160n13; Ruzé 1997: 366; Werlings 2010: 165.

47. 1997: 90. See further Hölkeskamp 1999 *passim*, for the absence of "codes" in Archaic law.

48. Alexander the Great's letter to Chios, from two centuries later, does this unambiguously (RO 84A, lines 3–4).

49. See further O'Neil 1981b: 339–40; Walter 1993: 116–25; Rhodes with Lewis 1997: 93–96; Robinson 1997: 108–11; Hölkeskamp 1999: 99–107; Minon 2007; Werlings 2010: 130–4.

of the *damos*; the more common practice is for them to be labeled a *wratra* (= *rhētra*, ordinance) for the community in question—the Eleans, the Heraeans, the Chaladrioi, and so on. The *damos*, however, undeniably plays an important role in many of them. One forbids the alteration of the document by "private citizen or magistrate or *damos*."[50] Guarducci, followed by Minon and Werlings, sees in this word a reference to the assembly of citizens.[51] At the very end of one law, something is not to be done "without the council and the *zamos plathuon* [= *dēmos plēthuōn*], 'full assembly.'"[52] A version of this phrase recurs in another law, the meaning of which is much clearer: if someone wishes to change the writings (*graphea*), he can do it up to three times, but only with "a valid council of five hundred men and a full assembly."[53] A final law contains a clause in which the *damos* possibly has the power to confirm the penalties set in the legislation.[54]

The Elean texts ultimately yield nothing certain about the constitutional history of the region. Jeffery and now Minon have argued, based on letter forms, that these documents date to the late sixth or early fifth century. Since I, for one, detect democracies apart from the Athenian one emerging around this time, I would not rule out democracy *a priori*. We cannot, however, jump to conclusions. O'Neil thinks that *IvO* 9 and 7 "clearly refer to an already existing democracy," but he assumes that only a democracy would mention the demos, which as we have seen is incorrect. Robinson, after a careful consideration of the evidence, upholds O'Neil's judgment.[55] Rhodes, however, thinks "constitutional government" is a "safer term," and I agree.[56] Consideration of the *damos*'s judgment for certain decisions does not entail democracy, as we have seen several times already, in Tiryns and Chios. Robinson claims that the council of 500, and the *dēmos plēthuōn* in particular, "resemble organs of the Athenian democracy."[57] More precisely, however, they resemble bodies found in Athens going back to Solon. Athens had a council and a fully open assembly even then, yet few would call Solon's *politeia* an instance of *dēmokratia*.[58]

---

50. ML 17 (trans. Fornara 25; see also *Nomima* I.52), lines 7–10: αἰ δέ τιρ τὰ γράφεα : ταῖ κα(δ) δαλέοιτο : αἴτε ϝέτας αἴτε τελεστά : αἴτε δᾶμος : ἐν τ'ἐπιάροι κ' ἐνέχοιτο.

51. See Werlings 2010: 141–42 with bibliography cited, and ML 17; Walter 1993: 122.

52. *Nomima* I.108.

53. *Nomima* I.109: σὺν βολαῖ <π>εντακατίον ἀϝλανέος καὶ δάμοι πλεθύοντι, line 4.

54. *Nomima* I.36: αἰ κα] δόξε καὶ τοῖ δάμοι. See also *Nomima* I.21, discussed above in conjunction with the Archaic law from Tiryns.

55. 1997: 108–11.

56. Rhodes with Lewis 1997: 96n1.

57. 1997: 108.

58. Solonian institutions: [Arist.] *Ath. Pol.* 7.3. The fact that δάμοι πλεθύοντι resembles the *dēmos plēthuōn* of *IG* I³ 105, as has been pointed out by several commentators (Lewis 1967; Rhodes 1972a: 197; Ostwald 1986: 32; Robinson 1997: 108n157), is not of much help: we do not

Therefore, in the absence of other historical evidence, I would tentatively label late-sixth-century Elis a "constitutional regime" along the lines of the other Archaic examples studied above.

There are several other instances of the demos playing a role in Archaic inscriptions, but I shift now to the literary evidence.[59] We have already noted that an assembly and a council existed in Athens from the earliest times, with a more representative council of 400 accompanying Solon's reforms in the early sixth century. Assemblies could be called elsewhere, even if they did not predominate in the constitution. Alcaeus, who lived in Mytilene on Lesbos around 600, misses the sound "of the agora [*scil.* 'assembly'] being summoned by the herald," and elsewhere he criticizes his fellow citizens for "all" praising his rival Pittacus and establishing him as tyrant.[60] "One of the Olympians set this civil war in motion," he says in another fragment, "leading the *damos* into ruin and bestowing desirable glory upon Pittacus."[61] The *damos* thus seems to have had an institutionalized role at Mytilene, and to have intervened on occasion to make decisive choices about the direction of political life.[62]

Similarly, Archilochus, writing in the seventh century, was familiar with the presence of the demos at Paros (they are "gathered together for contests" in fr. 182 West) and with their influence: he consoles one Aesimides with the thought that "no one ever did experience much pleasure who gave a thought to the censure of the demos."[63] As with Alcaeus, however, the demos can also

---

know when the statutes recopied in I^3 105 were first enacted, but Ryan (1994) has argued convincingly that they go back to Solon. If that is the case, then again the phrasing is not in itself reflective of democracy.

59. See *Nomima* I.32 (Cyzicus, sixth century: the demos swears an oath to maintain a certain Manes's privileges); *Nomima* I.24 (see also Koerner no. 39; Elis ca. 500: *damos* is the direct object of indeterminable action by *damiorgia*, line 6); ML 20 (trans. Fornara 47; Locris ca. 460–450: "partake of the *damos*," line 4—this could mean "territory," or it could mean "assembly"); *Nomima* I.58 (treaty of Zancle from Olympia ca. 500: possible mention of *damos* at line 8); *Nomima* I.102 (Atrax in Thessaly, ca. 475: "thethmos [= 'thesmos'] for the *damos*"). For many of these attestations, see the discussions in Werlings 2010.

60. Frr. 130b.18, 348 Liberman.

61. Fr. 70. Cf. also fr. 129, where Alcaeus claims to ward off pains from the *damos*.

62. Page (1955: 177) supposes "*damos*" to comprise the wealthy, a contradiction in terms. Forsdyke (2005: 45–48), while noting that the "all" in question in fr. 348 need not refer to the Mytilenean demos (cf. Romer 1982), ultimately decides based on other evidence that it does; but comparing the Mytilenean case with Athens and Megara, she claims that the common people had no "self-consciousness" and that their role in electing Pittacus was orchestrated by elite patrons (47). Wallace (2009: 423) by contrast claims the lines "clearly document the early *demos*'s power."

63. Fr. 14. Bowie (2008), drawing our attention to the boastful epigram of the Parian/Thasian

be an object of ridicule and serve as an unflattering point of comparison. According to late sources, Archilochus insulted someone as a prostitute with the words "demos" and *ergatis* (worker).[64] Archilochus's fellow iambographer Hipponax, from sixth-century Ephesus, hopes that an enemy might suffer "a horrible fate by a pebble [*psēphis*] from the *dēmosiē boulē*": the phrase brings together the images of a vote in a popular body as well as a communally exacted death by stoning.[65]

From the corpus of elegy, Theognis, while providing plenty of sententious phrases about the difference between good and bad, high and low, does not actually say much about the political structure of Archaic Megarian society. An "agora" is mentioned, in conjunction with *dikai* (lawsuits?), and is said to be free of "poverty."[66] This is little to go on, but the collocation of the terms and their close resemblance to the picture painted by Hesiod suggest that certain cases were heard in the agora before a popular assembly.[67] The corpus says little about the demos or *laos*: a speaker fears that the *kakoi*, who are probably to be identified with the *hegemones* (leaders) from a few lines before, will destroy (or perhaps corrupt) the demos, giving rise to a tyrant.[68] There is, of course, also the famous passage where the *laoi* are said to be different.[69] Otherwise the "empty-headed" demos is mainly lambasted for not giving a good man, "an acropolis and a tower" of the demos, his due, and for being excessively slavish (*philodespoton*).[70] Yet there is one passage that suggests that the demos was a consolidated and even powerful political group: at lines 947–48,

---

magistrate Aceratus (*Nomima* I.80), who was perhaps elected by the demos, suggests that Archilochus is consoling (or even mocking) Aesimides over a recent political rejection at the hands of the demos.

64. Fr. 242 West.

65. Fr. 128.4 West. The phrase *dēmosiē boulē* appears in the "constitutional law" from Chios (ML 8), as we have seen, but I do not think its use by Hipponax can be pressed to illuminate the makeup or constitutional nature of the Chian institution.

66. Thgn. 266–69. The lack of constitutional specificity may be because the Theognid poetic tradition is Panhellenic rather than narrowly Megarian: Nagy 1985.

67. Cf. Hes. *Th.* 89. The absence of *Penia* from this scene could be celebratory of Megara as a whole (it is a flourishing city), or it could be more normative, in the sense that the agora is not a site where poverty-inducing penalties are inflicted upon members of the elite (most likely by each other, not by the demos).

68. Thgn. 45.

69. Thgn. 53–68. On these lines, see further chapter 4, section 4.1.

70. Thgn. 233–34, 847–50. The language of this section is extremely harsh ("kick the empty-headed demos, beat it with a sharp stick, and put a burdensome yoke on it"); one can imagine later Classical-era oligarchs reciting it at symposia with relish (cf. Lane Fox 2000: 45–51). We possess definite evidence for the reception of Theognidean poetry among Classical oligarchs:

the speaker vows to "beautify" (*kosmēsō*) his polis, "since I did not hand it over to the demos, nor do I obey unjust men."[71] Although the speaker does not make clear what he means by "handing over" the polis to the demos, it sounds as though there are two competing groups of citizens, the demos and the unjust. The speaker may have thought the demos was amenable to a tyranny.[72] If the lines are grouped with the ones immediately preceding them, the speaker then says that he belongs to the "middle path" and will not favor either group. While I am hesitant to say that *dēmokratia* was a viable alternative at the time, there is no denying that the demos represents a significant social and political force in this particular Theognidean passage.[73]

Finally, there is the thorny case of Sparta. Historians once thought that Sparta held first place in constitutional precociousness—as exemplified by the seventh-century Great Rhetra—before falling into a kind of self-imposed backwardness.[74] Thommen, however, has convincingly argued that the content of the Rhetra, despite its guarantee that the *damos* have *kratos*, is anything but radical: instead, the Rhetra serves to regularize the meetings of an assembly that is in many respects similar to the Homeric one. Thommen plausibly sees in the assembly's fixedness and institutionalization a mechanism for preventing the manipulation of the *damos* by individual members of the elite. Since the Spartan assembly could not originate policy or even override the veto power of the elders, its involvement represents a balanced arrangement of powers, as in other Archaic poleis, rather than the supreme power of the *damos*.[75]

In sum, by the late sixth century many poleis possessed complex political structures with local variations on the common pattern of assembly, council, and magistrates. It is likely that no significant discussion went on at meetings of the assembly, nor did the leaders expect the wider community to do much

---

the Athenian oligarch Critias adopted the Theognidean image of setting the "seal of one's tongue" on a song for his poem to Alcibiades (DK 88 B 5). Cf. Xen. *Symp.* 2.4.

71. πατρίδα κοσμήσω, λιπαρὴν πόλιν, οὔτ' ἐπὶ δήμωι / τρέψας οὔτ' ἀδίκοισ' ἀνδράσι πειθόμενος.

72. Cf. lines 39–52 and Solon frr. 9, 34, 36, 37 West.

73. As the Theognidean corpus contains poems from different times and places, this particular section may originate from a time when democracy had become a constitutional possibility, but there is no way of knowing.

74. For the Great Rhetra (Plut. *Lyc.* 6.1–4) as a possible early form of democracy, see Hornblower 1992: 1; Hansen 1994: 33; Raaflaub and Wallace 2007: 39.

75. Thommen 1996: 38–44, 2003: 39–41. Cf. Meier 1998, 2002. This perspective was largely anticipated by Cartledge, e.g., his 2001: 35. Van Wees's revisionist interpretation of the Rhetra (1999) is unduly insistent that the *damos* during this period must have experienced complete subservience to the elite. For the constitutional complexity of Sparta during the Classical period, and for its relationship to Classical oligarchy, see section 1.2.3 below.

other than approve their directives. The assembly served mainly as a means of communication by which elites attempted to disseminate their proposals to the widest possible audience. The involvement of the common people, who had an interest in seeing the elite cooperate, could also have served as a "commitment device," a potential source of sanction beyond the direct control of the elite that would allow them to "credibly commit" to one another in their intra-elite dealings.[76] Finally, the people themselves occasionally asserted their collective presence and demanded further political concessions when the elite overstepped their bounds, whether toward one another or toward the demos.[77] The sources suggest all of these developments. What is certain is that the demos was anything but a nonentity during the Archaic period.

But neither was it sovereign, *kurios*. Effective power seems to have resided in elite councils—*boulai*—with presiding officials, and in powerful magistrates.[78] Judging from the Solonian example, these offices were restricted to the wealthiest citizens. Moreover, scholars are right to insist that much— although not all—of the Archaic legislation we possess is concerned with power-sharing, limitation of centralized influence, and checks and balances among the elite, beginning with the prohibition against the same man serving as *kosmos* within ten years at Dreros (ML 2).[79] While I agree in part with those (e.g., Gagarin 2008, Papakonstantinou 2008) who think that the impetus for some of this regulation originated outside the ranks of the elite, it need not exclusively have come from there, and in many, perhaps most instances, the members of the elite themselves are likely to have arrived at power-sharing mechanisms that mitigated costly civic strife. The demos played a part in civic life, but except in extraordinary circumstances, the

---

76. For the idea of the demos as a commitment device, see Fleck and Hanssen 2006.

77. See van Wees 2008: 35, who speaks of the Archaic community's "long-established habit of intervening in elite *stasis* and its equally old habit of asserting its own interests, violently if necessary"; cf. Papakonstantinou 2002: 15.

78. Council (sometimes with presidents): *Nomima* I.44 (see also Koerner no. 47; Naupactus ca. 500: *preiga* [council of elders], line 10); *Nomima* I.107 (see also Koerner no. 27; Argos or Halieis ca. 480: council presided over by Ariston); "constitutional" law of Chios ML 8: *dēmosiē boulē*. Officials: *Nomima* I.101 (see also Koerner no. 24; Mycenae, sixth century: *damiorgia, hiaromnamones*); Koerner no. 25 (Argos ca. 575/500: *damiorgia, amphipolos*); Koerner no. 29 (Argos, mid-sixth century: *damiorgia*); *Nomima* I.78 (see also Koerner no. 31; Tiryns, seventh century: *platiwoinarchos, hiaromnamon*); Koerner no. 35 (Arcadia, sixth or fifth century: *damiorgia*); *Nomima* I.80 (Thasos ca. 500: *archon*); *Nomima* I.18 (Sicily, Casmenae ca. 500–450: *gamoroi, archai*); *Nomima* I.72 (Delphi, early fifth century: "the fifteen"). See further Harris 2006: appendix.

79. Foxhall 1997: 120; Osborne 1996: 174–85; Forsdyke 2005: 26; Harris 2006: 304–312; Hawke 2011.

elite's attitude toward the demos was not primarily one of fear or anxiety, but rather of paternalism or mild contempt. Attention was largely focused on conflicts among the elite themselves, which, as Forsdyke has shown (2005), could threaten to tear the community apart. It took a "perfect storm" of conditions in several poleis all around the same time to produce *dēmokratia*, which, by triggering elite unity and reaction, made the costs of abandoning sustained political participation too high to endure. In other words, once *dēmokratia* emerged, the members of the demos could not afford to relinquish power for fear of elite reprisals. Democracy helped create the reasons for its own perpetuation.

1.1.2 The Emergence of Democracy

Dēmokratia was not simply a spontaneous movement by the newly awakened masses, nor was it a gift from elite to demos. Instead, it had (at least) three necessary conditions: 1) times had to be bad enough to give the demos good reason to risk uniting for political change; 2) certain members of the elite had to be alienated from the status quo enough to ally with the demos against their peers; and, crucially, 3) the members of the demos had to form a mass movement powerful enough that renegade members of the elite in question felt they had no choice but to offer power to the common people. Elite and demos had interacted in the past, but only sporadically and usually with limited aims.[80] This was due to the demos's relatively weak bargaining position, which itself was a result of material conditions (relative poverty and thus greater need for risk management, for example; low levels of urbanization) that affected the likelihood of sustained collective action. With an increase in wealth and urbanization, however, the ability of the demos to demand more from the elite made significant political reform the only choice for a renegade member of

---

80. While I do not have space to discuss tyranny at length, I will point out that one such interaction might be for (at least some) members of the demos to help a member of the elite achieve tyrannical power. A strongly elite-centered view, which denies the common people any role in the "age of the tyrants," has gained prominence recently (Cawkwell 1995; Anderson 2005). This position can stand only by ignoring the evidence of Solon's poetry, and as Luraghi has recently suggested (2015: 80), popular support for tyranny may also be apparent in the story of Peisistratus's bodyguard. Cawkwell (1995: 81) cites low urbanization as a reason for the demos' not having an active role during the "age of the tyrants." By contrast, I consider low urbanization to be precisely the reason why demotic political action often took the form it did, as occasional support for tyrants. It was a principal-agent relationship in which the principal (the demos) had little time for politics and so entrusted a representative with the responsibility of reining in the elite. (And in keeping with principal-agent relationships, there was a potential problem that the tyrant might exploit his position.)

the elite.[81] Yet the elite leader still had an important role to play. When members of the elite fell out with one another, they produced just the sort of people who could serve to coordinate the demos and strengthen its chances of surviving conflict with the elite. The key variable for the emergence of *dēmokratia* was the demos, however. Simply put, no member of the elite would have offered the kinds of reforms promised by Cleisthenes of Athens unless he felt there was no alternative.[82]

To begin with Athens, like many I view the events that took place in 508/7 not only as a major turning point in the political history of Athens, but as the beginning of its democracy.[83] This is what Herodotus reports, and the author of the *Ath. Pol.* follows him.[84] Herodotus also points to multiple occasions post-508/7 on which people remembered the demos as having exercised sovereign decision-making power: the treaty with Aristagoras; the decision about the "wooden wall," where the ambassadors to Delphi came "before the demos"; and the lynching of Lycides, who as a member of the council wanted to introduce a peace treaty with the Persians "to the demos."[85] Herodotus also notes that the Spartans, after the counterrevolution led by Isagoras failed, grumbled that they had "handed over the polis to an ungrateful demos."[86]

Scholars have wondered whether Herodotus misunderstood Cleisthenes's role and its significance for democracy in particular. There are scraps of contemporary evidence, however, that point to the prominence of the demos after 508/7. For example, the phrase "*dēmou kratousa cheir*," "ruling hand of the

---

81. See Morris 2004; Ober 2015: 81–84, 87–88 (32 percent of the Greek population living in urban centers in the fourth century); Bresson 2016: 199–206 (and note esp. his claim that growth "accelerat[ed] during the Archaic period," 199). For the relationship between urbanization and democracy, see Arist. *Pol.* 3.1286b20–21.

82. My account is thus much more "bottom-up" than that of Fleck and Hanssen 2006, who see the extension of power to the demos as a rational measure taken by the elite in order to credibly commit to certain wealth-maximizing strategies. As I have shown, the Archaic elite were already perfectly capable of utilizing the demos as a commitment device, but without full democratization. *Dēmokratia*, at least when it first emerged in Greece, was not a peaceable agreement between elite and mass but instead a forceful, sometimes violent, usurpation of political power by the demos. By the same token, I take a different position from that of North, Wallis, and Weingast, who see the extension of political rights in history as a grant by the elite (2009: 25). This is not the case in Archaic Greece.

83. Argued for most vigorously by Ober 1993, 1998, 2007; cf. Forsdyke 2005: 133–43; Cartledge 2007: 164; Hansen 1994; Pritchard 2010: 1. *Contra* Raaflaub 2007; Anderson 2003: 80; Ostwald 1986: 15–19.

84. Hdt. 5.66.2, 5.69.2 [twice], 5.78, most explicitly at 6.131.1; [Arist.] *Ath. Pol.* 20.1, 20.4.

85. Hdt. 5.97.2, 7.142.1, 9.5.1.

86. Hdt. 5.91.2.

demos," from Aeschylus's *Suppliants* (line 604), points to the existence at the time (as early as 477) of the concept of *dēmokratia*.[87] Furthermore, we possess several Athenian decrees enacted in the name of the demos, conventionally dated to the period immediately following Cleisthenes's reforms. Here the demos not only plays a role in the political system, as in the earlier Archaic inscriptions studied above, but actively proclaims the polis's decision in its own name.[88] Finally, there is an overlooked piece of evidence in an epigram of Simonides, which praises Athens for a military victory (presumably Marathon): "If it is necessary to honor whoever is best, daughter of Zeus, the demos of Athens alone accomplished this."[89] Werlings thinks Simonides is being intentionally playful with his claim that the "demos" was "best" (*aristos*), normally a contradiction in terms in the minds of the elite.[90] From all these considerations, it seems highly likely that power in 508/7 was transferred to the demos.

How and why had this change come about? Interpretations range between the Cleisthenes-centered (Ehrenberg 1950; Lewis 1963) and the demos-centered (Ober 1993). The Cleisthenic view has its own set of internal debates about the relative altruism or opportunism of its central figure. As Ostwald has rightly pointed out, if Cleisthenes had been some sort of "ideological democrat" all along, he presumably would not, along with the rest of the elite, have at first rejected the demos (Hdt. 5.69.2). Likewise, a pure opportunist probably would have solidified his and the Alcmaeonidae's place in the new regime much more securely.[91] He thus appears to be neither of the two extremes. In any case, any view of Cleisthenes's actions must take into account that the ultimate outcome did not constitute business as usual: the new system was a constitutional breakthrough. A more demos-centric view acknowledges this point, but it in turn must come to terms with the fact that the revolution would not have happened without Cleisthenes's initial offer to the demos.[92] The demos had the numbers and the willpower to effect the revolu-

---

87. Ehrenberg 1950: 522; Raaflaub 2007: 108. Cf. also lines 368–69, 398, 517–18, 600–1, 605–7, 699. Scholars used to date this tragedy with near certainty to the year 463, but Scullion (2002: 90) has shown that the reasons behind this argument are weak and that the play could have been produced as early as 477.

88. *IG* I³ 1, 4, 5. See further Anderson 2003: 52.

89. Fr. 86 West: εἰ δ' ἄρα τιμῆσαι θύγατερ Διός, ὅστις ἄριστος, / δῆμος Ἀθηναίων ἐξετέλεσσα μόνος.

90. Werlings 2010: 169.

91. Ostwald 1986: 17–18. Cleisthenes's opportunism might have been limited by the circumstances, however: see below.

92. As is well known, Cleisthenes appealed to the demos when he was "getting the worst of it" in his struggle with Isagoras (*hessoumenos*, Hdt. 5.66.2; cf. [Arist.] *Ath. Pol.* 20.1, *hēttōmenos*).

tion, but they lacked the resources and political savvy that a figure like Cleisthenes could provide. Therefore someone (it need not have been Cleisthenes himself) had to play a Cleisthenes-like role in order to get any sort of revolution started, but that figure's initial moves would have been heavily circumscribed by his perception of the demos's strength at the time.[93] If an initial offer fell far short of the demos's minimum expectations, the renegade member of the elite risked activating a movement that he could not control.[94]

Thus I am convinced that both elite and demos played crucial roles in the revolution of 508/7. Without some signal by a member of the elite to set it in motion, the uprising would never have taken place, but the content of the "reform bill" (Andrewes 1977) offered by Cleisthenes was determined in large part by the power of the demos. The question then arises of how Cleisthenes gauged the strength of the people. Many have speculated that the experience of the Solonian constitution and of the civic reforms and festivals instituted by the Peisistratids consolidated the Athenian civic body and helped the common people to develop a collective political identity.[95] Several recent events had also likely created anxiety among the demos about the status of their citizenship in 508/7.[96]

The other factor that cemented the new political order was the interference of the Spartans. Their involvement elevated the struggle to the level of external war, thus further uniting the demos against perceived enemies of its constitution. The collective memory of the event given voice in Aristophanes's *Lysistrata* (lines 273–82), when a chorus member "recalls" besieging the Spartan king Cleomenes on the acropolis, confirms this.[97] Yet we should not overlook the effect Cleomenes's actions would have had on the decisions of the Athenian elite. By "playing favorites" and attempting to install Isagoras and three

---

For situations in which elites break with the oligarchic status quo to establish a democracy, see chapter 6, section 6.2.3.

93. Ober readily acknowledges these points (2007: 86): "Cleisthenes plays an important role in my story, but he is not the lead actor. [. . .] [Cleisthenes's] surprise move suggests that he was aware of a desire for political recognition on the part of the demos."

94. Cf. Solon fr. 37.7–8 West: "He [a tyrant] would not have restrained the demos, nor would he have stopped before he had taken the cream from the milk."

95. Snodgrass 1980: 115–18; Manville 1990: 162–73; Salmon 1997; Lavelle 2004; Hammer 2005: 121–23; Forsdyke 2005: 79–80, 125–27; Raaflaub and Wallace 2007: 42–43; Ober 2007: 89–90; Stahl and Walter 2009: 149–51. See also the point above that Athens was wealthier and more urbanized by this time.

96. It is tempting to think that there was active resistance to the *diapsēphismos* carried out in 510, which deprived certain people of citizenship ([Arist]. *Ath. Pol.* 13.5: see Fornara 1970; Manville 1990: 173–91; Anderson 2003: 4).

97. Ober 2007: 90.

hundred of his allies, Cleomenes likely split the elite and drove the remaining members of the upper classes into the open arms of the nascent democracy.[98] This interclass defensive partnership, as well as the stunning military success of Athens in its battle against Boeotia and Chalcis in 506, goes a long way toward explaining the stability of the Athenian democracy in its early years.[99]

Turning from Athens to other early democratizers, we often see similar dynamics at work. I do not suppose that Athens was the first example of democracy after which all future instances patterned themselves. Instead it appears that *dēmokratia* was an idea whose time had come in the late sixth century. After centuries of the Greek poleis experimenting with self-government, conditions were ripe in several places for the outbreak of a regime controlled by the demos. Robinson has emphasized this point in his indispensable book on early Greek democracy.[100] He examines the evidence for democracy in several poleis outside Athens, the most convincing cases being Argos, Mantinea, Naxos, and Syracuse.[101]

One factor not necessarily stressed by Robinson is the importance of external interference in the consolidation of democracies. As we saw in the case of Athens, Cleomenes's support for Isagoras and his faction was a crucial condition for strengthening the resolve of the citizens to support the new constitution. This was not the first or the last time Sparta attempted to install a pro-Spartan ruling elite. As both Yates and Bolmarcich have shown, already in the mid-sixth century Sparta was interfering in other poleis' sovereignty to bolster its own hegemony.[102] By the fifth century, Thucydides can say explicitly that Sparta maintained its power through the cultivation of oligarchies.[103] We can dismiss the idea that Sparta's sixth-century allies were known as "oligar-

---

98. Hdt. 5.72.1–2; [Arist.] *Ath. Pol.* 20.3. Note that one hundred years later, the involvement of the Spartans in the regime of the Thirty also allowed the Athenians to remember it in part as an external war: Loraux 2002; Shear 2011.

99. As Forsdyke (2005) has shown, the greater stability resulting from demotic control over the power of banishment (in the form of ostracism) also likely contributed to the consolidation of the democracy. The cult of the tyrannicides probably served as a source of unity as well: Anderson 2007: 120–24.

100. See esp. Robinson 1997: 65–73, 127–30.

101. As noted above, section 1.1.1, I do not think the Olympia bronze plaques definitively prove democracy in Elis in the late sixth century. The early fifth century, around the time of the synoecism of 471 (Diod. Sic. 11.54.1; Strabo 8.3.2), seems a more likely time.

102. Yates 2005; Bolmarcich 2005; de Ste. Croix 1972: 89–166 and 333–42. This is especially true in the case of Tegea, where internal interference by Sparta is attested in an early treaty, portions of which survive in Plutarch's *Greek Questions: Mor.* 292b, 277b-c = Arist. fr. 592 Rose; see Jacoby 1944; Braun 1994.

103. Thuc. 1.19.

chies," but Sparta, through its meddling, may have unwittingly created several of the early democracies against which oligarchy arose. It is striking that several early democratizers, such as Argos, Elis, and Mantinea, came from Sparta's periphery in the Peloponnese.[104] The late-sixth-century democracy at Eretria, spearheaded by an elite man named Diagoras, may also have arisen in part from Spartan interference.[105]

1.1.3 Early Elite Reactions to Dēmokratia

As much as the demos and (certain parts of) the elite might have at first cooperated in the new experiment known as *dēmokratia*, some members of the elite quickly came to oppose the phenomenon. This section argues that elite reaction to democracy, which would form the ideological basis for *oligarchia*, began simultaneously with the outbreak of *dēmokratia* in the late sixth and early fifth century. Many scholars, taking a very cautious approach to the sources, suppose that *oligarchia* was a rather late concept, arising in the latter half of the fifth century, and perhaps in specific opposition to the Athenian democracy.[106] By contrast, I show that resistance to the power of the demos appears early on in sources whose reliability we should not *a priori* discount.

104. For Argive democracy, see Piérart 2000; Robinson 1997: 82–88, 2011: 6–21. Mantinea: Gehrke *Stasis* 101–3; Robinson 1997: 113–14; *IACP* no. 261 (Nielsen), p. 519. Elis: Robinson 1997: 108–11. Certainly, Sparta interfered in those states in the later fifth and fourth centuries: in Argos in 418/17 (Thuc. 5.81.2; cf. Paus. 2.20.2; Diod. Sic. 12.80.2); in Elis around 400 (Xen. *Hell.* 3.2.27–29; Paus. 3.8.4; 5.4.8); in Mantinea in 385, when it dioecized the polis (Xen. *Hell.* 5.2.1–7; Diod. Sic. 15.5.4–12; the resulting dioecized community was not a normal oligarchy, however—see chapter 4, section 4.4).

105. Diagoras overthrew the oligarchy known as the *hippeis* because he had been unjustly treated in the matter of a marriage (Arist. *Pol.* 5.1306a35–36; for more on this episode, see chapter 6, section 6.2.3). As this oligarchy was allied with the Peisistratids of Athens ([Arist.] *Ath. Pol.* 15.2), Diagoras' *coup* probably came after the fall of the latter in 510. A fragment of Aristotle tells us that the Eretrians set up a statue to Diagoras after he died in Corinth, "in the course of being conveyed to Sparta" (fr. 611.40 Rose). Perhaps the Spartans, allying with the fallen *hippeis*, had arrested Diagoras on the grounds that he was a tyrant or enemy of Sparta (cf. Hdt. 5.70.1, 9.37.1; Xen. *Hell.* 1.3.19; Plut. *Pel.* 5.3). Knoepfler has shown that an early Eretrian proxeny decree, with democratic enactment formula, is not evidence for the early years of Diagoras's democracy, since it was inscribed in the third quarter of the fifth century (2001a: 73, analyzing *IG* XII Suppl. 549a). Nonetheless, he has elsewhere called Diagoras "a kind of Eretrian Cleisthenes [the democratic reformer of Athens]" (*Bull. ép.* 2014 no. 219). For the monument to a democratic founder, see the discussion in chapter 5, section 5.2.4.

106. Raaflaub 1989: 37–41. Ostwald (2000: 23 with n43) thinks a Periclean context is too late given the evidence of Pindar and Herodotus, but even he is willing only to say that oligarchy seems secure as an oppositional concept to democracy as late as 423, with the production of

For example, we already saw that Herodotus could put words into the Spartans' collective mouth to the effect that they had handed over Athens to an "ungrateful" (*acharistos*) demos.[107] Herodotus thought that resentment could be expressed toward the demos itself already in 507/6. Considering this fact, as well as the literary and now material evidence we possess for the predominance of the demos during the period between Cleisthenes's reforms and the Persian Wars, we should not be surprised when we read in Plutarch's *Life of Aristides* that already in 479 certain impoverished elites had plotted to overthrow the democracy.[108] Plutarch is our only source for this episode, but we should not therefore dismiss it out of hand.[109] As Rhodes has pointed out, the (likely) appearance of one of the conspirators, Agasias of Lamptrae, on ostraca of the period lends credence to the story.[110] Furthermore, claims that the phrase *katalusis tou dēmou* is "too early" beg the question.[111] While it is true

---

Euripides's *Supplices*. Bleicken (1979: 169–71) thinks *oligarchia* arose in the subject states of the Athenian empire; this does seem to be part of the story, especially in cases like Samos, where a democracy was briefly imposed in 440 (Thuc. 1.115.2–3), and Boeotia, which experienced democracy after Oenophyta in 457. There were likely "homegrown" oligarchs in Athens as well, however, beginning at least as early as the reforms of Ephialtes in 462 and perhaps going back to 479 or earlier (see n111).

107. Hdt. 5.91.2. The demos's lack of *charis* (grace, thanks) was an elitist commonplace later on: Theophr. *Char.* 26.4; [Plat.] *Axioch.* 369a; Plut. *Dion* 38.5, 42.1. Elsewhere in Herodotus, the tyrant Gelon describes the demos as the "most disagreeable living-mate" (*sunoikēma acharitōtaton*, 7.156.3). Andrewes (1956: 135), followed by (Kurke 1999: 132), supposes that this piquant phrase represents Gelon's *ipsissima verba*. This would constitute anti-populist discourse about 20 years after the remark about the "ungrateful demos" Herodotus attributes to the Spartans.

108. Plut. *Arist.* 13.1: *sunōmosanto katalusein ton demon*. For the important decisions undertaken by the demos during this period, see above, citing Hdt. 5.97.2, 7.142.1, 9.5.1; cf. [Arist.] *Ath. Pol.* 22.3 (*tharrountos ... tou dēmou*), 22.7, 23.1. Siewert et al. (2002) assemble the new ostraca from the Kerameikos, primarily from the 470s, and combine them with previously known examples: for these as evidence of demotic power in the early fifth century, see Forsdyke 2005: 175–77; Thomas 2009: 23; Mann 2007: 73–74; Kosmin 2015: 122. Elite dissatisfaction with democracy might also be seen in the positive portrayals of the conservative Cimon by his foreign contemporaries Stesimbrotus of Thasos *FGrH* 1002 F 4 and Ion of Chios *FGrH* 392 F 13, 15.

109. Doubted by Hignett (1963: 321 with n2), who ascribes the story to the historian Idomeneus of Lampsacus.

110. Rhodes (2000: 123) notes the possible identification of "Agasias of Acharnae," named by Plutarch, with the well-attested "Agasias of Lamptrae" from the ostraca (see Brenne 2002: 46: 17 instances).

111. Ostwald (1986: 177) asserts that the expression *katalusis tou dēmou* "cannot antedate the reforms of Ephialtes," but this assumes what it needs to prove. Many scholars situate the emergence of an explicitly oligarchic ideology at the earliest in the 440s, when Pericles and

that the democracy's immense success early on largely accounts for the elite's general acceptance of the new regime, pockets of resentment and resistance were still a persistent feature of Athenian life, reaching back to the earliest days of the democracy.[112]

If the powerful and successful polis of Athens could have its anti-democratic critics so early, we should not be surprised if smaller, more vulnerable poleis experienced more destructive pro- and anti-democratic *stasis* in the early days of democracy. Herodotus tells us of conflict between the demos and the elite in Aegina in the 490s, in Syracuse ca. 491, and in Naxos ca. 500.[113] The Ephesian philosopher Heraclitus might also represent an early example of an anti-democratic thinker: he is quoted as blaming "all" the Ephesians for banishing his friend Hermodorus, the "worthiest" man among them. He also chided certain people for "obeying the singers [*aoidoi*] of the common people [*dēmoi*] and making use of the crowd [*homilos*] as teacher, not knowing that the many are bad, but the few good."[114] On this basis many scholars have

---

Thucydides the son of Melesias were political rivals (Plut. *Per.* 11.1–3; [Arist.] *Ath. Pol.* 28.2; see, e.g., Connor 1992: 63n54). Ostwald (1986: 186) argues that Thucydides was the spokesman of the *oligoi* but that there is "no indication of antagonism toward the democratic institutions of Athens as such." Cf. Frost 1964; Hölkeskamp 1998. I do not see how these views are compatible with the clear statement of Thucydides on the aborted oligarchic conspiracy at Athens before the Battle of Tanagra in 457 (1.107.4); and if this stands, Plutarch's comment about 479 looks more plausible.

112. Cf. Mann 2007: 115.

113. Aegina: 6.88–91: Nicodromus of Aegina, a prominent member of the elite who held a grudge against the Aeginetan oligarchs for exiling him on a previous occasion, plotted with the Athenians to betray the island to them. He allied himself with the demos of Aegina, 700 members of which were supposedly killed by the "fat cats" (*pachees*) in retaliation. See further chapter 2, section 2.5, with literature cited. Syracuse: 7.155.2. The landholders (*gamoroi*) had been driven out by a coalition of the demos and the slave population, the so-called *Kallyrioi*. See further Marm. Par. *FGrH* 239A.52; Arist. fr. 586 Rose *apud* Phot. s.v. Καλλικύριοι. The polis had recently lost a battle near the river Helorus, and the members of the elite were further split by an internal dispute between two erotic rivals (Arist. *Pol.* 5.1303b20–26 and Plut. *Mor.* 825d, discussed below, chapter 2, section 2.5, and chapter 6, section 6.2.3). Further discussion: Robinson 1997: 120–22. Naxos: Hdt. 5.30.1, discussed above. Again, the pejorative label *pachees* is used. See Robinson 1997: 117–18.

114. DK 22 B 121: ἄξιον Ἐφεσίοις ἡβηδὸν ἀπάγξασθαι πᾶσι καὶ τοῖς ἀνήβοις τὴν πόλιν καταλιπεῖν, οἵτινες Ἑρμόδωρον <ἄνδρα> ἑωυτῶν ὀνήιστον ἐξέβαλον. Β 104: τίς γὰρ αὐτῶν νόος ἢ φρήν; δήμων ἀοιδοῖσι πείθονται καὶ διδασκάλῳ χρείονται ὁμίλῳ οὐκ εἰδότες ὅτι οἱ πολλοὶ κακοί, ὀλίγοι δὲ ἀγαθοί. (The last phrase may be a reuse of a famous saying of Bias, the "majority are bad": Diog. Laert. 1.88.) The Hellenistic philosopher Timon of Phlius remembered Heraclitus as *ochloloidoros*, "mob-abuser." See further Donlan 1978: 98n4, 106n19; Kahn 1981: 179.

posited a democratic revolution in Ephesus during Heraclitus's lifetime.[115] In these instances we see examples of the phenomenon noted by Donlan in his study of the changing uses of the word "demos," whereby Greek society gradually came to be divided into opposing social groups perceived as having distinct interests.[116] While it is likely that the actual term *oligarchia* was not yet in circulation during these early years, the idea that the wealthy elite could resist the encroachments of the demos and assert their own, exclusive claims to power seems certain.[117]

When we move to the Peloponnesian War, the next period for which we have good historical sources, we see that Athens and Sparta had not in fact "brought on and fostered violent ... political antagonism between the rich and the poor," but that intense *stasis* was a fairly common feature of polis life, which the two sides subsequently used to their advantage.[118] In a few places we do read that the warring powers interfered directly in the constitutional order of other states without invitation from a fifth column (e.g., the Spartans at Sicyon and Achaea, Thuc. 5.81–82), but there are many instances in which *stasis* enjoys an independent logic. For example, about the *stasis* at Epidamnus that begins Thucydides's war narrative we learn that "the demos expelled the powerful."[119] If we follow Aristotle on this (*Pol.* 5.1304a13–17), the conflict began when a quarrel over a marriage within the ranks of the oligarchs led to the weaker party reaching out to the demos.[120] Civil strife therefore had nothing to do with "great power" politics in this instance but with purely local

---

115. See Gehrke *Stasis* 57–58; *IACP* no. 844 (Rubinstein), pp. 1071–72. It is possible that the democratic regime Heraclitus complained about was introduced by the Persian commander Mardonius in 494 (Hdt. 6.43.3).

116. Donlan 1999: 225–36.

117. Note that Polyaenus records *stasis* between democrats and oligarchs at Corinth during the reign of Archidamus (probably the fifth-century king: *Strat.* 1.41.2) and at Tegea during the time of the Spartan Cleandridas (ca. 460, 2.10.3; see further Braun 1994: 44–45).

118. Bradeen 1960: 263. Many, including Bradeen, rely heavily on Thucydides' statement (3.82.1) that over the course of the war the whole Greek world was convulsed, with the demos bringing in the Athenians and the oligarchs the Spartans. But while the war made the situation more common in occurrence and worse in outcome, it did not initiate the basic phenomenon (see next note). Cf. those passages where Thucydides implies that citizens have often fought with each other regardless of the actions of Athens or Sparta (4.92.6, 6.17.4, 38.3).

119. 1.24.5. For the importance of this episode for the larger narrative, see Ober 1998: 70–73; Price 2001: 274–75. In its progression from provincial civil strife to widespread destruction, the Epidamnus *stasis* resembles the conflict between the demos and the *pachees* on Naxos (Hdt. 5.30.1, see above), which led to the Ionian Revolt.

120. See Gehrke *Stasis* 60–62; Robinson 2011: 128. For further discussion of the Aristotle passage, see chapter 6, section 6.2.3.

conditions. We learn of similar episodes of *stasis* at Plataea, Colophon, Megara, Rhegium, Leontini, Thespiae, and Samos.[121] Even in situations where factions appealed to one great power or the other, the initiative often originates on their end and not with an overture by Athens or Sparta.[122]

Elite attitudes toward the demos emerge from the sources of this time as increasingly hostile and implacable. Perhaps most famously, in Herodotus's so-called Constitutional Debate, the pro-oligarchic speaker Megabyzus delivers a tirade against democratic government that reads as a "greatest hits" of anti-populist invective.[123] Nothing is "more stupid" (*axunetōteros*) or "more hubristic" (*hubristoteros*) than the "worthless crowd" (*homilos achreios*).[124] To escape the hubris of a tyrant, only to fall victim to the hubris of the "unrestrained [*akolastos*] demos," would be intolerable.[125] The demos has "received

---

121. All of the following are treated in the relevant sections of Gehrke *Stasis*: Thuc. 2.2.2 (see Hornblower *ad loc.* for this episode as casting doubt on the extreme "Aussenpolitik" view of Ruschenbusch 1978: 31), 3.34.1 (cf. Arist. *Pol.* 5.1303b7–10; ML 47), 3.68.3, 4.66.1, 4.1.3, 5.4.2–3, 6.95.2, 8.21.

122. As Brock (2009) has shown (cf. Ostwald 1993, 2002), Athens had a spotty record of actively promoting democracy among the member states of the Delian League. Robinson (2011: 188–200) has a detailed discussion and refutation of the notion that the spread of democracy was due solely to Athens.

123. 3.81. For this passage, and for the "Constitutional Debate" in general, see esp. Bleicken 1979: 151–58; Robinson 1997: 48–50; Ostwald 2000: 14–20. It purports to describe a debate in the later sixth century between three Persian interlocutors, who advocate respectively for democracy, oligarchy, and monarchy. I do not believe that the "Constitutional Debate" took place; nevertheless, I am in agreement with Robinson (1997: 50) that the passage reveals that Herodotus considered it perfectly plausible that people in the late sixth century might speak in terms of tyranny, oligarchy, and democracy (or rather *isonomia*). Certainly, I think the tripartite model used by Herodotus was well developed before the Peloponnesian War.

124. At Thuc. 6.39.1, the Syracusan demagogue Athenagoras claims that oligarchic opponents of democracy will say that democracy is not *xunetos*, "intelligent." Critias's tombstone (see below) also labeled the "accursed people" (*kataratos dēmos*) hubristic: DK 88 A 13. For the worthlessness of the crowd, see the fragment of Heraclitus, DK 22 B 104, cited above. The so-called "Stadiasmus Patarensis" inscription from the first century CE describes the majority (*plēthos*) as undiscerning (*akriton*): SEG 51.1832, lines 25–29, and see the afterword.

125. The "mob" is similarly *akolastos* at Eur. *Hec.* 607. Other attestations of supposed democratic *akolasia* include [Xen.] *Ath. Pol.* 1.5 (where the demos also suffers from *amathia*); Plat. *Rep.* 8.555c; Isoc. 7.20; Theopomp. *FGrH* 115 F 62; Plut. *Mor.* 295d, 304e-f. Sometimes the antidemocratic language of "restraint" becomes more specifically equestrian: Plutarch says that oligarchs upbraided the Spartan king Pausanias for releasing the Athenian demos when it had been "bridled by oligarchy" (i.e., ruled by the Thirty) (*Lys.* 21.4); this may reflect late-fifth-century language. An anonymous comic poet also quoted by Plutarch (Comic. Adesp. 700 K-A apud *Per.* 7.6) compares the Athenian demos to a horse that has broken free of restraint: "it is

no education," it understands neither what is noble nor what is proper.[126] In a memorable image, the demos "rushes falling headlong into politics mindlessly, like a river swollen by winter weather."[127] Megabyzus's solution to the inveterate stupidity and vice of the demos is to "pick out a company [*homiliē*] of the best [*aristoi*] men and hand over power [*kratos*] to them." Megabyzus does not hesitate to point out that the interlocutors themselves, as Persian nobles, will be included among this group, and he predicts that a group of the best men would produce the best deliberations (*arista bouleumata*).[128]

The content of Megabyzus's speech, as well as its position in the order of the "Constitutional Debate," is highly significant. Notably, the debate does not begin with Megabyzus laying out the benefits of oligarchy on grounds of precedent. He does not say that oligarchy is the traditional way of doing things in many communities, that it is a tried and tested political method, or that it has a much longer track record of success than democracy.[129] In fact, his argument for the superior deliberations of oligarchy is based on probability rather than on empirical evidence. It is merely "likely" (*oikos*) that the best men will come up with the best policies. The bulk of his speech is devoted to lambasting the demos. Many scholars have thought that Herodotus does not give oligarchy its due; that he prioritizes Otanes's defense of democracy because he is more interested in it as a constitution, and in fact favors it; or perhaps that oligarchy is relatively uninteresting to Herodotus because, in its more "moderate" forms, at least, it was too similar to democracy to occasion much comment.[130] In fact, Herodotus has crafted a speech for Megabyzus

---

outrageous and no longer tolerates obedience, but bites at Euboea and rears up at the islands." The sophist Antiphon used the word "*euēniōtata*," "most obedient to the rein," in his treatise *On Like-mindedness (Homonoia)* (F 70 Pendrick = Harp. s.v. εὐηνιώτατα): "'Obedient to the rein' means gentle and moderate and not troublesome; the metaphor is from horses." Antiphon may have been thinking of an idealized, obedient demos, which would submit to oligarchs in a state of *homonoia*. See also Brock 2013: 121.

126. Cf. Eur. *Supp.* 420–22: the Theban herald criticizes democracy on the grounds that, even if a farmer managed not to be unintelligent (*amathēs*), his work would keep him from participating in politics.

127. 3.81.2: ὠθέει τε ἐμπεσὼν τὰ πρήγματα ἄνευ νόου, χειμάρρῳ ποταμῷ εἴκελος. The demos is similarly associated with a lack of *nous* by Heraclitus (DK 22 B 104). The hydraulic imagery finds parallels at Isoc. 15.172 and Xen. *Hell.* 2.3.18. See Brock 2013: 61–62, with additional examples cited.

128. Hdt. 3.81.3.

129. Megabyzus does not actually say "oligarchy," but Herodotus ascribes advocacy of it to him. The use of "*oligarchia*" by Herodotus is the earliest instance of the term we possess in the extant sources, unless the Old Oligarch predates the historian, which is unlikely.

130. See Ostwald 2000: 19; Raaflaub 2004a: 236; Osborne 2003: 252–53.

that picks out several salient points about oligarchy. Oligarchy is not the long-standing norm to which democracy stands as a late and irrational aberration. Instead, the oligarchic impulse first arises out of a sense of disgust toward democracy and its governing element, the people. In other words, the oligarchic frame of mind does not exist until the elite have experienced the concrete effects of the demos in power. Moreover, when they grow exasperated with the supposed defects of democratic governance, their preference is not merely for a return to the elite-led regimes of the Archaic period, where, as we have seen, the demos often played a significant role. Their new goal is a highly exclusionary system that takes the radical and unprecedented step of dispensing with input from the demos altogether. Oligarchy, in contrast to Archaic elite government, is the exclusive preserve of a narrow circle of the "best"; one of its defining elements is its refusal to "make use" (*chrasthōn*) of the demos in any way.[131]

Lest we think the ideology Herodotus puts in Megabyzus's mouth was an exclusively Athenian phenomenon, we have several sources that attest otherwise. The Old Oligarch, for example, states that "in every land, the best element [of society] is opposed to democracy."[132] The speaker, it is true, is an Athenian, and so he may be projecting his own local perspective onto the rest of the Greek world. He expects that his audience will readily assent to this and subsequent points, however. An even more decisive piece of evidence comes from the sophistic treatise, written in the Doric dialect, known as the *Dissoi Logoi* (Double Arguments).[133] The author is almost certainly not an Athenian, and therefore represents a non-Athenocentric view. The seventh section of the treatise discusses the use of the lottery for apportioning political offices. The speaker gives a counterintuitive argument that, despite its reputation as a democratic device, sortition is not democratic:

> They say also that it [the lot] is a good thing and exceedingly favorable to the common people [*damotikos*]. I consider it the least populist device imaginable. For in the cities [*poleis*] there are men who hate the common people [*misodamoi*], who, should the bean [*kuamos*] select them, will destroy the

---

131. "Let those who wish the Persians ill make use of the demos," Megabyzus says, "but we will pick out a group of the best men," etc. (3.81.3).

132. [Xen.] *Ath. Pol.* 1.5. "The Old Oligarch" is the name scholars use for the anonymous pamphleteer whose work (probably from the last quarter of the fifth century) is included in the manuscripts of Xenophon. On this work, see Rhodes and Marr 2008.

133. A reference to a Spartan victory over Athens and its allies in this text (1.8) has traditionally been taken to refer to the end of the Peloponnesian War. There are several good candidates, however, including Tanagra in 457. I consider the document no later than the end of the fifth century. See further Graham 2010: 877.

people [*apolounti ton damon*]. Seeing this, the demos itself ought to choose men who are all favorably disposed towards it. (DK 90 B 7.5–6)[134]

The author's statement is *prima facie* evidence that hatred of the people, rather than any positive program of rule, defined the oligarchic mindset in many cities other than Athens. Opponents of the people throughout the poleis of Greece wished not simply to be rid of democratic government but to destroy the common people wholesale.[135] The *Dissoi Logoi*'s statement bespeaks the deep-seated revulsion and hatred felt by many of the Greek elite toward democracy.

We can productively conceive of this increasingly rigid oligarchic mindset in terms of Bourdieu's notions of *doxa*, heterodoxy, and orthodoxy. For Bourdieu, *doxa* represents the unspoken rules of the game, the status quo that passes for "common sense" among both the rulers and the ruled. Then comes heterodoxy, a decisive and self-conscious break with the norm. Heterodoxy precipitates a rearguard attempt at reestablishing the *ancien régime*—orthodoxy—which, however, in its conscientious attack on a new political alternative, rapidly evolves into something unprecedented and innovative. In Bourdieu's suggestive formulation, "Orthodoxy, straight, or rather *straightened*, opinion, which aims, without ever entirely succeeding, at restoring the primal state of innocence of *doxa*, exists only in the objective relationship which opposes it to heterodoxy, that is, by reference to the choice—*hairesis*, heresy—made possible by the existence of *competing possibles*."[136] Archaic elite-led governance, on this reading, constitutes the state of *doxa* against which democracy, in times of crisis, emerges as a heterodoxical alternative. What begins as an emergency intervention of the common people into the elite's running of political affairs quickly takes on a life of its own, one with unpalatable consequences for the formerly ascendant elite. Their reaction, *oligarchia*, the explicit narrowing of the "rule of all" to "the rule of the few," is an attempt to impose an orthodoxy that is in reality a new way of dealing with a new problem.

Oligarchy was thus not simply Archaic government updated with Classical language. The engine driving Classical oligarchies was their opposition to democracy, which had characterized them *ab ovo*—more specifically, it was

---

134. "The bean" (*kuamos*) is literally a colored bean used for the purpose of selecting officers randomly: see Hdt. 6.109; Thuc. 8.66.1, 69.4; Andoc. 1.96.

135. One might suppose that *apolounti ton damon* means simply "put down the democracy," but the usual verb for this, in Athens and beyond, is *kataluein*, not *apollunai* (Thuc. 3.81.4, 5.76.2; Ar. *Eccl.* 453; SEG 51.1105B, line 6; IK Sinope 1, lines 27–28). Cf. [Xen.] *Ath. Pol.* 3.11, a list of times when oligarchs attacked the demos.

136. 1977: 169, emphasis in original.

oligarchs' shared fear of mass action on the part of the people. Oligarchs claimed many distinctions for themselves, but their most basic motive was defensive and reactionary, an attempt to prevent democracy or to overthrow it once established. This collective anxiety forged new forms of intra-elite cooperation.[137] The Archaic elite had been a particularly fractious lot. Classical oligarchs possessed, by contrast, a new nemesis against which to unite. Fear of the democratic enemy provided, in language that will be defined more precisely below, a focal point for pan-elite coordination.[138] The sources of the elite's anxiety were various: they included the threat of death or confiscation of wealth during times of political reform or revolution; taxes (in particular the *eisphora* or direct wealth tax) and liturgies; and the need to avoid demagogues, sycophants, and lawsuits.[139] Not all of these fears were always well founded, of course (in fact the risk of them was often exaggerated), and oligarchic action was frequently predicated not on stopping an impending danger but on removing even the possibility that such a danger might arise—

---

137. Many accounts focus too strongly on the perceived weakness of the Greek elite as a ruling group and on the competition and lack of cooperation among oligarchs. For example, Duplouy has recently argued against traditional analysis based on political regime type. He proposes instead to focus on the myriad ways in which the community witnessed, judged, and validated competing elite performance (see, e.g., 2006 *passim*). This approach may apply to the Archaic period, but it is less useful in the Classical period, when constitutions hardened into opposed regimes. It threatens to overlook changes in elite practice over time and to ignore the ways political and institutional context shapes behavior.

138. Intra-elite competition was always a problem for oligarchies (see, e.g., Hdt. 3.82.3 and the preceding note), but it was not for all that totally insurmountable. Fear of a common enemy could unite competitive elites: see Arist. *Pol.* 5.1304b23–24 (discussing oligarchs): "a common fear [*koinos phobos*] brings together even the bitterest enemies." On fear of enemies as a driver of authoritarian government, see Smith 2005; also Slater 2010: 12 (discussing Southeast Asia), citing Evrigenis 2007.

139. In the sources cited here I place an asterisk next to non-Athenian examples, in order to indicate the extent of this kind of oligarchic reasoning beyond an Athenian context. Death and/or confiscation of wealth: Thuc. 5.4.3*; [Arist.] *Ath. Pol.* 40.3. Taxes and liturgies: [Xen.] *Ath. Pol.* 1.13, 2.9–10; Ar. *Eq.* 924; Thuc. 8.48.1, 63.4; Xen. *Mem.* 1.2.45, *Symp.* 4.31–32; [Arist.] *Rhet. ad Alex.* 1424a24–25*, 34–35*, 1424b11–12*, 1446b24–25*; Arist. *Pol.* 5.1309a15–20*, 6.1320a20–33*; Theophr. *Char.* 26.5; Plut. *Arist.* 13.1. Demagogues, sycophants, and lawsuits: [Xen.] *Ath. Pol.* 1.14; Thuc. 3.70*, 8.54.4, 8.65.1; Xen. *Hell.* 2.3.12, 22, 25, 27, 5.2.7*, 5.3.10–12*; Lys. 25.27; Arist. *Pol.* 5.1302b23–25*, 1310a3–6*, 6.1318b35*, 1319b15*, 1320a4–16*; [Arist.] *Ath. Pol.* 9.1–2, 26.1, 28.3, 35.2–3, 41.2; Theophr. *Char.* 26.4. Note also that when it came to redistributing wealth to the community, oligarchies were not expected to pay for the maintenance of the orphans of fallen soldiers, while democracies were ([Arist.] *Rhet. ad Alex.* 1424a35–38; for historical instances of this practice, see Thuc. 2.46.1 [Athens]; *SEG* 57.820 [Thasos]).

it was, in other words, preventive rather than preemptive action.[140] Indeed, we can suspect that a prime motivator for oligarchs in overthrowing democracy was a feeling of powerlessness, to which they were not accustomed and which they felt was beneath their superior status. Oligarchs could not abide the feeling that they were at the mercy of their inferiors.[141] Their motives were thus both material and ideological, but in any case they stemmed from worries about what the common people might do and from a supposed need to prevent this.

1.2 The World of Classical Oligarchic Politics

Now that we have surveyed the historical origins of *oligarchia*, we can turn to broad trends in oligarchic governance across the Classical period. Research in this area has been made much easier thanks to efforts such as the Copenhagen Polis Center's *Inventory of Archaic and Classical Poleis*, the Stanford POLIS Project, and Teegarden's research (2014: appendix). A survey of these resources, combined with personal research and corrections, reveals just over 110 discrete oligarchic regimes known from the Classical period.[142] Although historians have traditionally lamented the limited evidence available to us on Classical oligarchies, this new, systematically catalogued dataset offers us the chance to study oligarchy in a manner unavailable to Whibley in the late nineteenth century.

In what follows I treat oligarchy as a generalizable type. Forsdyke has recently called for a study of oligarchies "to show the great range of constitutions that fit under this rubric."[143] My view, however, is that we should start with the essential unity of oligarchies before exploring their diversity. Aris-

---

140. The risk was exaggerated, but for all that not entirely outside the realm of possibility. As Pyzyk has shown (unpublished manuscript), liturgies could be financially ruinous for those in the lower tiers of the liturgical elite; only the biggest fortunes could survive successive years of liturgical service. On the costs of Athenian liturgies, see most recently Pritchard 2015.

141. For oligarchs' belief that they should have more political rights because they supposedly contributed more to the city's well-being, see Thuc. 3.65.3*, 6.39.2*. For their sense of dishonor or outrage at being governed by "inferiors," see Hdt. 3.81.1–2; Thuc. 8.89.3; Critias DK 88 A 13; Xen. *Hell.* 2.3.48; Arist. *Pol.* 5.1309a9–10*; Theophr. *Char.* 26.3. They could liken their status under democracy to that of a slave: Tamiolaki 2013. The ancient sources thus seem to me to provide a richer picture of oligarchic motivation than that given by the political scientist Jeffery Winters, viz. the defense of entrenched wealth (2011). (Note also that Winters' example of a Classical-era Greek oligarchy is—Athens. Regimes actually designated *oligarchiai* at the time do not receive treatment.)

142. See the appendix.

143. 2009: 201; cf. Leppin 2013: 157.

totle, of course, thought that there were several types of oligarchy (four, to be precise), just as there were four types of democracy.[144] Nevertheless, he admits that "some people think there is only one kind of [each]."[145] This may indicate that the notion was in fact quite widespread. Aristotle was a hyperanalytical philosopher with a tendency to complicate conventional discourse. Most people's notions were less nuanced. To get at the everyday reality of oligarchy, we should take seriously what others—perhaps a majority—said about oligarchy, rather than what an elite thinker with a unique teleological view of life and politics thought about it.[146] We can begin with the socioeconomic profile of oligarchic ruling elites.

1.2.1 The Rule of the Wealthy

Taken at face value, the term "oligarchy" is purely numerical. It states only that a "few" rule. The reality, as Aristotle and many others recognized, was that the identity of these "few" was almost without fail "the rich."[147] Xenophon describes the antagonists in a bout of *stasis* at Rhodes in the 390s as "the demos" and the "wealthier men" (*plousiōteroi*, Hell. 4.8.20); in Sicyon in the 360s the two constitutional options countenanced are "democracy" and "the wealthiest men in charge" (*plousiōtatoi enkrateis*, 7.1.44). Aeneas Tacticus, the author of a fourth-century manual on how to withstand a military siege, similarly describes attacks on democracy by "the rich," first in Argos (11.7–10), next in Heraclea Pontica (11.10bis), and finally in Corcyra (where they are called "the rich and oligarchic," 11.13–15).[148] The word "plutocracy" is rare in ancient Greek, but Xenophon's Socrates uses it to describe what are plainly

---

144. See esp. *Pol.* 4.1292a39-b10, 1293a10–34. Aristotle is an excellent witness for the characteristic actions and instituions of oligarchies, as well as for historical examples, but he is not necessarily correct that different kinds of action are representative of his four different forms of oligarchy. (Note also that none of Aristotle's forms of oligarchy, not even the most moderate, comprises a majority of the male citizen population. Brock and Hodkinson (2000: 17), however, mention that an oligarchy might potentially encompass a majority. There are no known examples of this.)

145. *Pol.* 4.1289a8–9; cf. 1290a13–16, 1296a22–23.

146. Aristotle's discussions of "final" democracy and oligarchy (*teleutaia*, e.g., *Pol.* 4.1293a1, 6.1319b1–2) stem from his teleological model. As Hansen points out (*IACP* 82–83), the nonphilosophical sources speak of a basic tripartite division between rule by one, few, and many, and do not introduce gradations.

147. Arist. *Pol.* 4.1290b1–3.

148. For Aeneas (perhaps the Aeneas of Stymphalus mentioned at Xen. *Hell.* 7.3.1), see Whitehead 2011. It is noteworthy that Aeneas never speaks explicitly of "the poor" or "the demotic" attempting to subvert a legitimate oligarchic regime.

oligarchies.[149] The remarks of the third-century CE rhetorician Menander of Laodicea (Menander Rhetor) on *ploutokratia* attest to several centuries' worth of association between oligarchy and wealth. Menander, whose immediate purpose is to explain to rhetoricians how to praise cities in speeches, lists three kinds of constitution: kingship, aristocracy, and democracy; to which correspond three corrupt types: tyranny, "oligarchy and so-called plutocracy," and "mob rule" (*laokratia*) (Menander Rhetor, p. 359 Spengel). Plainly oligarchy was a byword for rule by the wealthy.[150]

The notion of "wealthy," however, is culturally constructed and historically contingent, meaning different things at different times. The comparative nature of Xenophon's phrase "the wealthier men" hints that the *plousioi* might admit of different degrees and encompass several distinct socioeconomic groups. The Aristotelian corpus suggests that, at a minimum, the "wealthy" who ruled in an oligarchy would come from the very wealthiest, those who could afford to maintain horses. Thus in a fragment of the lost *Constitution of the Cymaeans*, we read that a reformer named Pheidon (date unknown, but almost certainly Archaic) defined full citizenship according to whether a man could "rear a horse" (*trephein hippon*).[151] The "equestrian" nature of many oligarchies is also reflected in the title of *hippeis* (cavalry) for the regime that ruled late Archaic Eretria, as well as the "horse-rearers," *hippobotai*, of neighboring Chalcis.[152] We might also point to the second-highest census class of *hippeis* under the Solonian constitution of Athens, which, whether it is eco-

---

149. *Mem*. 4.6.12: plutocracies are those regimes where the *archai* are determined "by property assessments," *apo timēmatōn*. If the magistracies are filled by those "who fulfill the lawful requirements [*nomima*]" rather than a property requirement, the result is *aristokratia*. In actual fact oligarchs more commonly used the term "aristocracy" as a euphemism for their own rule.

150. Instances of the *plousioi* favoring or participating in oligarchy in Aristotle (e.g., *Pol*. 4.1299b25–26) are too numerous to list in full. The instances from Xenophon and Aeneas are meant to show that association of the rich with oligarchy is not confined to Aristotle and his school. See also Eur. fr. 626 Nauck, where the opposite of endowing the demos with *kratos* (i.e., democracy) is making wealth the thing that is valued (*ploutos entimos*). Thucydides, while perfectly capable of speaking of the "rich" as being oligarchic (e.g., 3.70.4), prefers the terms *dunatoi/dunatōtatoi*, "powerful" and "most powerful" (5.4.3, 8.21, 47.2), and simply *oligoi* (5.82.2, 84.3—but see 3.70.4 and 8.63.4 for acknowledgment that the *dunatoi* are wealthy). The *dunatoi* are not necessarily coterminous with "oligarchs" *sensu stricto*. It is safe to say that all *dunatoi* were wealthy, but they might exercise power in a democracy as well as an oligarchy. Moreover, they did not necessarily favor oligarchy over democracy, but the great majority of those who did favor oligarchy tended to come from the ranks of the *dunatoi*. See further Lintott 1982: 92–94.

151. Arist. fr. 611.39 Rose.

152. *Hippeis* of Eretria: Arist. *Pol*. 4.1289b39, 5.1306a35–36; [Arist.] *Ath. Pol*. 15.2. Hippobotai

nomic or military, shows the connection, in some regimes at least, between wealth, horse-rearing, and political power. The cavalry continued to play a role in oligarchic government in the Classical period. Indeed they may be called the *sine qua non* of a "typical" oligarchic ruling elite. There were particularly narrow and "dynastic" oligarchies that comprised only a specific clique or a group of families, but normally oligarchies defined by a property requirement included, at the very least, the horse-owning upper crust.[153] The question is how much further down the socioeconomic scale they were willing to go, and what if any characteristics defined the overall group that typically made the cut. I will return to this point shortly, after examining the mechanism just mentioned, the property requirement according to which oligarchies selected their ruling body.

The Greek word for "property requirement," *timēma*, means in its most primary sense "property assessment." As such assessments became important for political office-holding; however, the term came to have the secondary meaning "property requirement." As we have just seen, Xenophon's Socrates associates property requirements with oligarchy, which he labels a "plutocracy." For Plato, oligarchic regimes are those in which the magistracies (*archai*) depend upon property requirements (*apo timēmatōn*, Rep. 8.550c, 553a). Aristotle also glosses them this way in the *Rhetoric*, where he has less time to devote to the topic than in the *Politics* (1.1365b33).[154] A closing passage of the *Rhetoric to Alexander* says oligarchies are of two main types: those defined by membership in a political club (*hetaireia*) and those *apo timēmatōn* (1446b25–26).[155] The oligarchy headed by Phocion, imposed on

---

of Chalcis: Hdt. 5.77.2, 6.100.1; Arist. *Pol.* 4.1289b39; Strabo 10.1.8 (= Arist. fr. 603 Rose); Plut. *Per.* 23.2; Ael. *VH* 6.1; cf. Thuc. 1.114.1–3.

153. Whibley 1896: 126–32; cf. Bugh 1988: 120–28 and Spence 1993: 216–24 for the role of the cavalry in the oligarchic regimes at Athens in the late fifth century. See also Diod. Sic. 15.79.3, for oligarchic *hippeis* from Boeotian Orchomenos.

154. The concern is again with the *archai*: democracies are those constitutions in which the citizens distribute magistracies by lot, oligarchies by property requirements, aristocracies "by education" (*paideia*). (Note the observation below that oligarchies could also distribute magistracies by lot, just within the ruling elite.) Aristotle has a more idiosyncratic discussion of constitutions in the *Nicomachean Ethics*, in which the three good forms are kingship, aristocracy, and a third defined *apo timēmatōn*, to be called timocratic or a politeia, while the three bad forms are tyranny, oligarchy, and democracy (8.1160a31-b22). This conceptualization, with its strange use of *timēmata*, makes a mess of oligarchy, aristocracy, *and* timocracy.

155. The section is bracketed by editors as spurious but still provides good evidence for the notion of oligarchy as defined by property qualifications. For the importance of the *Rhetoric to Alexander* for understanding Classical oligarchies see chapter 2, section 2.2.3.

the Athenians by Antipater in 321, was to be *apo timēmatōn*.¹⁵⁶ Oligarchy and wealth requirements remained so closely associated that Themistius in the fourth century CE can still speak of "oligarchies based *apo timēmatōn*" (Oration 2, p. 35b Harduin).¹⁵⁷

The process of actually assessing citizens to see if they met the property requirement tended to depend on private initiative. It was up to an individual citizen to provide the authorities with his own valuation of his property when he declared himself interested in a magistracy.¹⁵⁸ Depending on his measurement, a citizen then belonged to a specific *timēsis*, or rating.¹⁵⁹ In some regimes magistracies were distributed differentially according to the different ratings.¹⁶⁰ It seems that in most oligarchies, however, a single fixed *timēma* admitted one to the most authoritative offices.¹⁶¹ We have actual numbers in the cases of Phocion and Demetrius of Phalerum's oligarchies: 2,000 drachmas and 1,000 drachmas, respectively.¹⁶² We hear of no further gradations within those basic

---

156. Plut. *Phoc.* 27.3. Cf. Diod. Sic. 18.18.4: *apo timēseōs*.
157. For further examples see Paus. 7.16.9; Luc. *Jup. Trag.* 7; Hesych. s.v. γαμόροι.
158. See Johnstone 2011: 86–88.
159. Arist. *Pol.* 5.1308b2–6.
160. E.g., the constitution of Draco preserved at [Arist.] *Ath. Pol.* 4.2; that of Solon, 8.1.
161. See, e.g., Arist. *Pol.* 4.1294b10, 1297b2, 5.1303a23, 1306b7–16, 1307a27–29; but see 6.1320b22–25, where the author recommends two levels of assessment. Oligarchies might change the *timēma* if they thought overall wealth was increasing and too many citizens were meeting the qualification for full citizenship: Arist. *Pol.* 5.1308a35-b10. This practice suggests that some oligarchs did not think a specific amount of wealth actually guaranteed minimal political competence (see Thuc. 6.39.1), but instead wanted to keep the circle of the ruling elite narrow for its own sake. Interestingly, the passage of Aristotle also suggests that some poleis carried out their own public assessments instead of relying on individual initiative (or they at least required all citizens to provide assessments). These would have amounted to a kind of census. Aristotle specifies that oligarchies from smaller cities might carry out their assessments every year, those from larger ones every three or five years (not counting inclusively: every two or four years). Fourth-century Athens carried out large-scale assessments of its total wealth (Dem. 14.19; Polyb. 2.62.6–7), but this was probably only among members of symmories (and so members of the elite), and it was still by self-declaration, albeit under scrutiny (Christ 2007: 63–67). In the so-called *diagramma* (ordinance) of King Ptolemy for Hellenistic Cyrene, establishing an oligarchic constitution (*SEG* 9.1, on which see below), sixty officials called "assessors," *timētēres*, measure the citizens' wealth for political purposes. In other texts the word is *timētēs* and is the Greek translation of the Latin *censor* (e.g., Polyb. 6.53.7). A recently published Imperial inscription has been interpreted as showing a *timētēs* selecting members of the council, presumably according to wealth: *Bull. ép.* 2014 no. 603.
162. 2,000: Diod. Sic. 18.18.4. 1000 (10 *mnai*): 18.74.3. (Cf. the *diagramma* of Ptolemy for Cyrene, where the ruling body is nominally the "Ten Thousand" [*murioi*] but in fact those who possess at least 2,000 drachmas. Although the figure of ten thousand looks large, Cyrene was a

PROBLEM, BACKGROUND, METHOD 39

amounts. Similarly, Plato says that oligarchies set "an amount of property [*plēthos chrēmatōn*], greater where the constitution is more oligarchic, less where it is less so, and they decree that he is not to partake of the *archai* whose property does not equal the stated requirement [*timēma*]."[163] In the oligarchic Boeotian *koinon* of the mid-fifth to early fourth century, the chief decision-making bodies in each of the poleis of the confederacy were four councils, "in which it was not possible for all the citizens [*politai*] to participate [*metechein*], but only those who possessed a certain amount of property [*plēthos ti chrēmatōn*]."[164] The property requirement thus usually seems to have been single and consistent. What might change was the selection process according to which magistrates were chosen. According to the *Rhetoric to Alexander*, within oligarchies "the laws ought to distribute the magistracies [*archai*] equally to all of those who participate in the *politeia*, and of these the majority ought to be assigned by lot, but the greatest [magistracies] voted on by secret ballot accompanied by oaths and the strictest scrutiny."[165] It was crucial that all oligarchs be at least eligible for the same magistracies, even if in practice elective positions would favor the wealthiest and most influential.[166]

---

huge polis, and a *timēma* of 20 mnai might reasonably be expected to exclude two thirds of the demos, if we use Phocion's oligarchy as an example. The constitution outlined by the diagramma is definitely oligarchic: Robinson 2011: 132n204; Johnstone 2011: 102–107.) The requirements are relatively low, especially that of Demetrius's regime, for which see van Wees 2011. For Phocion's census, see Poddighe 1997. The regimes technically fall outside of the temporal boundaries established in the present study, but I hope to treat them at greater length elsewhere. It is worth noting that although there is a flurry of experimentation with oligarchic government at the end of the fourth century, the regimes listed failed after only a few years.

163. *Rep.* 8.551b. Cf. Thuc. 6.39.1; Arist. *Pol.* 4.1292a41; Diod. Sic. 18.18.4.

164. *Hell. Oxy.* 19.2 Chambers. The phrase *plēthos ti chrēmatōn* is partially restored, but the reading is convincing. For more on the *koinon* and its councils, see chapter 2, section 2.2.1.

165. 1424a40–24b3; cf. Arist. *Pol.* 4.1300b1–3. Elsewhere Aristotle suggests that it is a mark of oligarchies to make the highest magistracies the preserve of the highest census classes (*Pol.* 2.1266a12–14), but here he is describing the constitution of Plato's *Laws*, which may have been exceptional.

166. Despite the fact that a wealth requirement determined eligibility for the highest magistracies, individuals who fell below that threshold in oligarchies were not necessarily considered not to be citizens. See *Hell. Oxy.* 19.2 Chambers, just discussed; [Arist.] *Rhet. ad Alex.* 1424b3–6; Isoc. 10.32. Aristotle and his school, as in many other areas, appear to have been the first to change the usual understanding of *politēs* out of a need for greater conceptual clarity and consistency, e.g., at *Pol.* 3.1275a2–5. This usage is idiosyncratic, however, as Aristotle himself admits (*Pol.* 3.1275b5–7). See further Blok 2013: 162–63. There are no ancient terms that correspond precisely to the modern distinction between "active" and "passive" citizens (Mossé 1979); one can perhaps say, however, that *hoi politeuomenoi* are usually the "active" citizens, as they constitute the *politeuma*.

What emerges from the foregoing account is that *oligarchia* was a *politeia* in which access to the authoritative magistracies (*archai*) was restricted to those in possession of a certain (usually quite exclusionary) property requirement (*timēma*), who constituted the sovereign ruling element (*kurion politeuma*).[167] It is important to note what this definition does not say. Oligarchy is not the restriction of the "franchise" to a narrow body of men. There would be several problems with such a statement. In contrast to the modern period, in antiquity the mere possession of the ability to vote for office-holders (the "franchise") was not determinative of constitutional type.[168] In fact, as I explore below in chapter 3, oligarchies often retained a popular assembly open to all free adult male citizens.[169] What distinguished oligarchy from democracy was that the assembly's role in the former was highly circumscribed, retaining little independent authority. Authority was instead invested in the *archai*, which were both more powerful than in democracies and, crucially, available exclusively to the rich.[170] The office that was most commonly characterized as expressing the decision of the oligarchic *politeuma* was the council (*boulē*), notwithstanding recent attempts to argue otherwise.[171]

---

167. Cf. Arist. *Pol.* 3.1278b8–11 and the concluding statement of Ostwald 2000: 75. (I base this description on the most common type of oligarchy, but those based on family ties or specific political factions also existed.) The *politeuma* is not primarily the regime type (although see, e.g., Plut. *Mor.* 851f), but instead the circle of the adult male citizenry that is included in the authoritative magistracies. As Aristotle says, in democracies the *politeuma* is the demos, in oligarchies it is the few (1278b11–13). Inscriptions show that by the late fourth century the same terms were used in public discourse: in Alexander the Great's letter to Chios, he specifies that the *politeuma* is to be the demos (RO 84 A, lines 3–4; not "the constitution shall be a democracy" as in the translation of RO). In the *diagramma* of Ptolemy for Cyrene, by contrast, the *politeuma* is to be the "Ten Thousand" (*muroi*: SEG 9.1, line 6). The Ten Thousand are not some sort of "restricted" Cyrenaean demos; they are distinct from the demos altogether (the demos is never mentioned in the document).

168. See further the discussion in chapter 3, section 3.2, below.

169. A property requirement for the *ekklēsia* is mentioned as a possibility by Aristotle (e.g., *Pol.* 3.1282a29–31, 4.1294b3–4), but at 4.1298b30–31 he speaks as if the demos will participate in the assembly (see below, chapter 3, section 3.3).

170. Note the numerous mentions of the *archai* in the Classical sources cited above, to which add Thuc. 8.53.3, Hdt. 3.80.6.

171. On this point Whibley was correct (1896: 157); *pace* Wallace 2013: 193–99, who argues that policy within oligarchies was decided by a (restricted) citizen body in an assembly. While the *politeuma* was indeed exclusive in an oligarchy, it rarely if ever met in plenary session, but instead exercised power through magistracies, especially the council. As we have seen, councils held authority in the poleis of the fifth-century Boeotian *koinon*. We also possess extensive epigraphic evidence showing transfer of enactment authority from the assembly to the council

1.2.2 The Myth of the "Hoplite Republic"

We can now return to the question of who, other than those able to rear horses, were typically part of an oligarchic *politeuma*. One of the most influential answers has pointed to the so-called "hoplite class," constituting anywhere between one third to one half of the free male citizen population, the members of which might be determined by a "hoplite census."[172] Following Aristotle's remarks in the *Politics*, which trace the expansion of political participation and power in Archaic Greece according to a military-developmental logic, scholars have postulated that the newly emergent "middling hoplite class" of the seventh century came to occupy a hegemonic political and ideological position within the polis. Such regimes could be labeled "hoplite republics," "hoplite constitutions" (German, *Hoplitenpoliteia*), "moderate oligarchies," or even "democracies" (as Aristotle says), which came to look restrictive only when contrasted with the more "radical" version of democracy practiced by Athens and a number of other poleis in the fifth century. The growing power of the "middling" hoplite class, the moderately wealthy yeoman farmers, can supposedly be seen in the *zeugitai* census class of Solonian Athens, whose name "yoke-men" has been taken to mean infantrymen "yoked together" in the hoplite phalanx, as well as in any constitution in

---

following the introduction of oligarchic government (in these cases I do not rely on the language of the enactment formula alone, which would be question-begging—perhaps democracies sometimes enacted decrees in the name of the council only—but on additional independent evidence). Athens during the Four Hundred: ML 81, lines 14–15. Eretria after the introduction of oligarchy in 411 (see Thuc. 8.64.2–65.1): ML 82. Erythrae after the King's Peace: RO 56; *SEG* 31.969. Rhodes after the synoecism on the island in 408 that produced an oligarchic polis: *I Lindos* II 16, in contrast to the earlier democratic language of *I Lindos* II 16 appendix. Chios in the fifth century, when the city was known to be oligarchic (Thuc. 8.24.4 with O'Neil 1978/79 and *IACP* no. 840, p. 1067 [Rubinstein]), and again in the early fourth century: *PEP Chios* 76; *PEP Chios* 2; *SEG* 35.923. See further the power of the council in fourth-century oligarchic Heraclea Pontica (Justin 16.4.1; Polyaen. *Strat.* 2.30.2). In other literary sources the "*archai*" or "*archontes*" are considered authoritative in oligarchies (these might include the councilors, *bouleutai*): Thuc. 3.27.3, 5.84.3; *Hell. Oxy.* 18.2 Chambers. In the law against tyranny and oligarchy from Eretria, the worry for democrats is not that the assembly will become restricted but that conspirators will try to propose a *boulē* other than one "selected by lot from all of the Eretrians" (*SEG* 51.1105 B, lines 19–20, partly restored). The new council's members would likely come from a restricted *politeuma*, but the latter is not envisaged as meeting in an assembly (let alone constituting the demos).

172. For the numbers, see, e.g., Pritchard 2013: 202 (the Athenian hoplites constituted about 30 percent of militarily active citizens); van Wees 2013b: 240 (hoplite farmers as 40 percent of the population in many cities).

which the *hopla parechomenoi*, "those who provided their own armor," predominated.[173]

The idea of the *Hoplitenpoliteia* has proved attractive for a number of reasons. First, it assigns a place of central political importance to the hoplites, who were undoubtedly a crucial element both in Greek military success and in the social imaginary.[174] Second, the eminently "common-sense," stolid, moderate picture of the hoplite republic has afforded a conceptual third way between the two "extremes" of narrow oligarchy and supposedly "radical" democracy.[175] Assuming the existence of *Hoplitenpoliteiai* in long-standing oligarchies, such as those of Corinth and Thebes, helps to explain their stability; it helps the ancient Greeks live up to their reputation for "moderation in all things"; and it allows us to see democracy and oligarchy as two sides of the same coin of "republicanism," as regimes that were different in degree rather than in kind.[176]

Several considerations come together to dispel the notion of a hoplite republic, however, and to reveal it, ultimately, as an ideological fiction.[177] First, there was no seventh-century hoplite revolution. Snodgrass in 1965 had already suggested that the development of hoplite tactics and armor was gradual and piecemeal, but Frost put the point more bluntly (though no less truthfully) when he said that the so-called revolution was "one of the great non-events of history."[178] Problems beset the thesis at all levels, beginning with the earliest literary evidence. Several scholars have shown that the "Homeric way

173. For Aristotle's developmentalist military schema see *Pol.* 4.1297b16–28. For the notion of a "hoplite breakthrough" or "hoplite revolution" in the seventh century, see Lorimer 1947; Cartledge 1977: 20; Salmon 1977. "Hoplite republics" as the typical form of polis government in the Archaic period and beyond: Hanson 1995 *passim*; Samons 2004: 23; Raaflaub 2007: 121. Gehrke, in his seminal study on *stasis*, uses the *Hoplitenpoliteia* concept extensively, e.g., as a constitutional label for Andros, Erythrae, Corcyra, Mantinea, Samos, and Sicyon. *Zeugitai* as yoked in the hoplite phalanx: Cichorius 1894; Whitehead 1981. *Hopla parechomenoi*: Thuc. 8.97.1; [Arist.] *Ath. Pol.* 4.2.

174. See Hanson 1991, 1995; Schwartz 2009; Kagan and Viggiano 2013.

175. The term "radical" is modern, and no equivalent outside of Aristotle ("final [*teleutaia*] democracy") can be found in the Classical sources: see Strauss 1987; Robinson 2011: 218. Thucydides, for one, discusses democracies without introducing distinctions between them: Athens, Syracuse, Mantinea, and Argos are all "democratically governed," without qualification (*pace* Hornblower *ad* 5.29.1 and 7.55.2).

176. See, e.g., Raaflaub 1989: 46.

177. I cannot give the subject the space it deserves here. My position will be stated categorically, drawing upon the relevant evidence and supporting secondary literature, but each point is, I readily admit, highly contested.

178. Frost 1984: 293.

of war," far from placing emphasis exclusively or even primarily on the outstanding "fore-fighters," or *promachoi*, gives evidence of a massed form of fighting in which average soldiers have a crucial role to play.[179] Furthermore, as we have just seen in our survey of Archaic epigraphical and literary evidence, sources as early as the eighth and seventh centuries attest to the political involvement of the demos. The military and political involvement of the non-elite, in other words, did not have to await a revolution in armor and tactics.[180]

Second, the Solonian census classes do not show the newly ascendant power of the hoplites as represented by the *telos* of the *zeugitai*. The identification of the census classes with military groups has always been a modern thesis, based on the assumption that Aristotle is ignorant on this point.[181] If we take Aristotle's claims seriously, however, it becomes impossible to maintain that the *zeugitai* were in any way "middling small farmers."[182] Van Wees in particular has shown that the top three census classes must have constituted a rather narrow elite of the landed wealthy.[183] This view comports with the observation that the Athenian hoplite army was relatively meager until as late as the end of the sixth century.[184] Solon's constitution seems to have vested power largely in the leisured elite, rather than ceding significant authority to a broad hoplite group. It took the Cleisthenic revolution of 508/7 to transfer effective power in the polis to the demos, understood as the great majority of

---

179. On the importance of the masses in Homeric fighting, see Latacz 1977; Pritchett 1971–79, vol. 4; van Wees 1994; Raaflaub 2008.

180. Raaflaub 1997; Hawke 2011: 113–16; Foxhall 2013.

181. Aristotle (or rather his student) is insistent at *Ath. Pol.* 7.4 that the census classes were determined by a measurement of wealth rather than by military function. Against this thesis are the opinions of de Ste. Croix 2004; Rhodes 1993: 138; Guia and Gallego 2010.

182. Thuc. 6.43.1 has been taken to indicate that the census classes were based on military function, but Gabrielsen (2002a/b) has shown otherwise. In the same year Rosivach likewise twice demonstrated (2002a/b) that the arguments for going against Aristotle's economic interpretation are weak.

183. See van Wees 1995, 2001, 2002, 2004, 2006; cf. Foxhall 1997. There is ancient evidence that Aristotle himself considered the top three *telē* a leisured elite and, moreover, that he thought there were citizens outside of those groups who nonetheless served as hoplites. In the *Politics* (2.1274a18–21) he glosses the first three classes as the *gnōrimoi* and *euporoi*, while the *Ath. Pol.* (26.1) says that in the mid-fifth century, when hoplites were drawn "from a *katalogos*," many of the "better sort" of both the demos and the *euporoi* used to die in great numbers. The inescapable conclusion here, unless the author of the *Ath. Pol.* did not agree with his teacher, is that there were members of the demos among the hoplite army in addition to the top three census classes who comprised the *euporoi*.

184. Frost 1984; Singor 2000.

the hoplites as well as those below hoplite status.[185] These groups, despite the supposedly *infra dignitatem* station of the light-armed, do not seem to have been at odds, and they cooperated consistently in support of the democratic constitution.[186] The revolution of 508/7 is now increasingly being understood as a decisive break, rather than as the latest step in a gradual progression of power, with the supposed "hoplite constitution" of Solon's time paving the way for Cleisthenes's more inclusive reforms.[187] There was in fact no intervening hoplite constitution.

Finally, concrete, attested instances of regimes governed by the *hopla parechomenoi*—rather than "examples" which are nothing more than modern hypotheses—are exceedingly rare.[188] Whibley observed this already in his book on oligarchy (1896: 133), and on this point, at least, nothing has changed in the intervening century that would necessitate a reappraisal of his view. A reappraisal has nevertheless occurred, and, as we have seen, some scholars even believe that the *Hoplitenpoliteia* was an exceedingly common type of constitu-

---

185. See Ober 2007: 97, citing the work of Georges (1993), for the cooperation between hoplites and "subhoplites" in the new Cleisthenic dispensation.

186. Some scholars have posited a division between "thetic" and "hoplitic" ideology (Strauss 1996; Hanson 1996; Burke 2005), but Epstein (2011) shows convincingly that this conception is unsupported by the evidence.

187. See Pritchard (2010: 23–27) for arguments in favor of the position that the "association of Solonian classes and forms of military service needs to be abandoned entirely" (23). One further scholarly development that has argued against the military view of the census classes is the abandonment of the notion of a single "hoplite register," or *katalogos*. Instead, separate, *ad hoc katalogoi* were drawn up by the generals and taxiarchs every campaign: Hansen 1985: 83; Christ 2001: 400–403; Bakewell 2007: 91–93; Guia and Gallego 2010: 258–61 (against the old view of, e.g., Jones 1957: 163; Andrewes 1981; Burckhardt 1999). Military officials might have made use of the deme registers, or *lēxiarchika grammateia*, for conscription purposes, but there is no evidence that these contained information about citizens' Solonian census classes, or that those census designations were linked with military obligations (Jameson 1963: 399–400; Whitehead 1986: 35n130; Bakewell 2007: 92; *pace* Ostwald 1995: 378; Sickinger 1999: 55; Pébarthe 2006: 184).

188. See above, n164, for Gehrke's assignment of *Hoplitenpoliteia* status to many poleis. Several historians have also speculated that Opuntian Locris had a hoplite constitution in the mid-fifth century, based on two pieces of evidence: 1) an inscription (ML 20) contains the phrase hοπoντίον τε χιλίον πλέθαι (translated below), and 2) Diodorus's statement (11.4.7) that the Locrians provided 1,000 hoplites at Thermopylae (cf. Hdt. 7.203.1). Some put these two facts together to speculate that the Opuntians had a hoplite class of 1,000 men and that these formed "the assembly of the Opuntian Thousand" (ML; Rhodes with Lewis 1997: 147; Beck 1999; Nielsen 2000: 114–15; Hornblower 2004a: 167; Domínguez Monedero 2013: 459–60). But the Greek cited above, which lacks definite articles, should mean "a majority out of a thousand Opuntians" (cf. *plethus* in the sense of "majority" at *IG* IX 1² 3 717 line 18, with Ruzé 1984: 257).

tion during the Classical period. The evidence, however, is meager. There are four attestations: 1) The Draconian constitution described at [Arist.] *Ath. Pol.* 4.2; 2) the "intermediate regime" of 411–410 which followed the overthrow of the Four Hundred (Thuc. 8.97.1; [Arist.] *Ath. Pol.* 33.1); 3) the constitution of the Malians as described by Aristotle (*Pol.* 4.1297b12–16), the date of which, however, is unknown; and 4) the statement of the speech *peri politeias*, "on the constitution," included in the manuscripts of Herodes Atticus, to the effect that the oligarchic regimes imposed by the Spartans tended to comprise at least a third of the population, defined as those who were able to benefit the common good "either by arms or some other ability" (section 31).[189] In brief, we can observe that (1) has long been identified as an ideologically charged forgery; (3) may not apply to the time period under consideration here; and (4) is almost certainly an exercise in Second Sophistic rhetoric, with probably little connection to actual events in late-fifth-century Thessaly.[190]

The case of the intermediate regime of 411–10 requires more careful consideration. As Thucydides presents the events of 411, the original call was for a regime of those "most capable of benefiting the city with their possessions [*chrēmata*] and persons [*sōmata*]," and that these were to number no more than five thousand.[191] It is clear from Thucydides, at least, that the oligarchs considered five thousand a *numerus clausus*. Some hoplites would, for reasons of wealth, not be included in this number. Otherwise, the Four Hundred would not have laid so much emphasis on enrolling citizens in the list and determining thereby who was in and who was out.[192] Five thousand was clearly less than the total number of hoplites at the time, and in fact amounted

---

189. Additional evidence for the existence of hoplite constitutions might include Theramenes's statement at Xen. *Hell.* 2.3.48 that an ideal citizenry ought to comprise those who can benefit the polis "with shields and horses," i.e., the hoplites and the cavalry. As the Thirty never managed to enroll this group, however, Theramenes's remarks cannot serve as evidence that such a regime existed in practice. Furthermore, we will see shortly that this statement may reflect Xenophon's own personal ideology. Hansen (2006c: 81–82) detects a hoplite constitution behind the Eretrian inscriptions *IG* XII.9 245–47 (lists of names, but see the convincing rejoinder of Knoepfler in *Bull. ép.* 2007 no. 327, ascribing the lists to a democratic regime).

190. Draconian constitution as forgery: Rhodes 1993: 86. Van Wees (2011) thinks it dates to the period of Demetrius of Phalerum's oligarchy at Athens (late fourth century), which would further strengthen the view that the idea of the regime of the *hopla parechomenoi* did not predate Aristotle: see further below. Wade-Gery 1945 thought that Ps.-Herodes *peri politeias* might be a work of Critias, and many have cited it as evidence for hoplite regimes (Vlastos 1952: 191n7; de Ste. Croix 1972: 35n65; Cartledge 1977: 23 with n90; Brock 1989: 163). Russell, however, authoritatively assigns it to the second century CE on stylistic grounds (1983: 111).

191. Thuc. 8.65.3.

192. The closed nature of the number Five Thousand emerges from Thuc. 8.72.1, 92.11. The

to somewhere between 10 and 16 percent of the total male citizen population.[193] Van Wees has rightly emphasized this fact, observing that the Constitution of the Five Thousand as originally proposed was meant to divide the hoplites down the middle, between what he calls "leisure-class" and "working-class" hoplites.[194] Guia and Gallego make the attractive further suggestion that the Five Thousand were meant to correspond roughly to the total number of *eisphora*, or war-tax, payers.[195] This would make sense of the reference to the Five Thousand's ability to contribute with their possessions, *chrēmata*, first and foremost.[196] When the Four Hundred are overthrown, Thucydides is careful to specify that the constitution was handed over "to the Five Thousand," but that these were now to include "as many also as could furnish their own arms" (*hoposoi kai hopla parechontai*, 8.97.1). The *kai* (also) in particular signals that the intermediate regime included more people than were originally proposed by Peisander and the other oligarchs. We should therefore not think of the intermediate regime as the proposed Five Thousand put into practice but as a different, expanded constitution.

Here, then, was an actually existing *Hoplitenpoliteia*. It is noteworthy, however, that Thucydides does not label it an oligarchy. Instead he says that "oligarchy and *stasis* at Athens" came to an end with the defection of Aristarchus to Boeotia in 411 (8.98.4). The intermediate regime was, notoriously, a "mod-

---

names of the 5,000 were kept secret in order to manipulate the hoplites, who would have simply assumed they were included if the 5,000 were always meant to be "all of the hoplites."

193. Evidence for 5,000 being less than the total number of hoplites comes from Lys. 20.13, where it is said that the defendant, Polystratus, a *katalogeus* or "enrollment officer" under the Four Hundred (cf. [Arist.] *Ath. Pol.* 29.5), himself enrolled 9,000 men.

194. 2006: 374. The "leisure-class" half would include the first three Solonian census classes, while the "working-class" half would include thetes. Socrates would seem to be a famous example of a "working-class hoplite": he valued his property at only five *mnai* (Xen. *Oec.* 2.3). This would not have been enough to secure him full citizenship even in the moderate oligarchy of Demetrius of Phalerum, where the *timēma* was ten *mnai* (see above).

195. 2010: 263–64. The *eisphorai* had either increased or been first instituted in 428 (Thuc. 3.19.1). The total number of *eisphora* payers in the fifth century is unknown, but it was wider than the circle of liturgy-payers, who probably numbered fewer than 2000 (for discussion see de Ste. Croix 1953; Jones 1957: 23–38; Thomsen 1964: 14–23; Rhodes 1982a; Ober 1989: 128–29; Christ 2007).

196. Another piece of evidence, not adduced by Guia and Gallego, is that the original plotters of the oligarchic *coup* in 411 are described by Thucydides as being "the most imposed upon" (*talaipōrountai malista*, 8.48.1), presumably by taxes. These same men are later described as "willingly contributing [*eispherein*] money [*chrēmata*] from their own private households" now that they are paying for themselves and not others (8.63.4). The collocation *eispherein chrēmata* indicates members of the *eisphora*-paying class.

erate blending," a *metria xunkrasis*, in the interests of the few and the many (*es tous oligous kai tous pollous*, 8.97.2).[197] In my view, this designation stems in part from the fact that those in charge under the regime, the *hopla parechomenoi*, comprised both the few (the leisured wealthy) and (some) members of the many, those of the demos beneath leisured status. It was the status of the hoplite army as a mediating institution, one straddling both the rich (*plousioi*) and the poor (*penētes*), that made the intermediate regime of 411–10 a constitutional anomaly, an outlier, in the normal scheme of things. Indeed, the reader gets the impression from the larger narrative of Thucydides's history, not that the intermediate regime was one of many such regimes in the Greek world at the time, but that it was radically singular. Thucydides refuses to call it by one of the usual constitutional labels, while regimes like those of Thebes and Megara are straightforwardly called "oligarchies."[198] Not surprisingly, then, this *rara avis* did not last long: as the *Ath. Pol.* says, "the demos quickly took back the constitution from these men [the intermediate regime]."[199] The intermediate regime thus appears to have been an emergency measure that looked forward to the restoration of full democracy; it would serve as an armed caretaker of the polis until such time as the traditional democracy could be safely reinstated. With so many members of the demos (those who were hoplites) already included in the *politeuma*, it would just be a matter of time before the regime "tipped" back into encompassing the entire free male citizenry. The *Hoplitenpoliteia* was not the norm at all; it was an unsustainable equilibrium.[200]

---

197. For *sunkrasis* in a political context, see Eur. fr. 21 Nauck, where such a mixing is considered superior to a scenario in which the "entirety of the poor *laos* governed without the rich men [*plousioi*]."

198. Thuc. 5.31.6. For the importance of this statement in interpreting the nature of the Theban oligarchy, see below.

199. [Arist.] *Ath. Pol.* 34.1.

200. The literature on the Five Thousand and the intermediate regime of 411–10 is vast. Perhaps most famously, de Ste. Croix (1956) and Rhodes (1972b) disagree over whether the intermediate regime admitted the thetes. But if, as argued above, the Solonian census classes were never connected with military function, the question is instead whether the unarmed could attend the assembly. They likely could not, but for pragmatic rather than ideological reasons: meetings of the assembly at this time were perceived as under threat and required armed vigilance (Thuc. 8.93.1). It is also worth noting that the oligarch Antiphon's trial took place during the period of the intermediary regime (Craterus *FGrH* 342 F 5b; cf. Thuc. 8.68.2 [text uncertain]), but he spoke in his defense before the judges about democracy and oligarchy as though they were good and bad things, respectively (fr. 1a Nicole). For more on the intermediate regime, and on Thucydides' assessment of it as a *metria xunkrasis*, see Ostwald 1986: 395–411; Raaflaub 2006b: 189–90, 213–16.

Actually existing oligarchic regimes seem to have been much narrower than the *Hoplitenpoliteia*, and it is only modern scholars' attraction to the concept of the hoplite constitution that has caused them to see such regimes where there is no good evidence for them.[201] Take, for example, the constitution of Boeotia under the oligarchic *koinon* of the mid-fifth to early-fourth century. We have already seen that Thucydides explicitly calls it an oligarchy, without qualification (5.31.6). That he does not consider the intermediate regime at Athens from 411–410 an oligarchy (8.98.4) thus constitutes *prima facie* evidence that he did not think Thebes had a hoplite constitution, understood as a *metria xunkrasis*. Nevertheless, scholars have interpreted the Theban constitution along those lines. Whibley, we might note, did not, but he did not have the evidence of the *Hellenica Oxyrhynchia*, discovered in 1906. As we have already seen, a fragment of this text says that "it was not possible for all the citizens [*politai*] to participate [*metechein*], but only those who possessed a certain amount of money [*plēthos ti chrēmatōn*]."[202] For several reasons (none of which is very sound), numerous scholars have supposed that the *plēthos* of *chrēmata* referred to by the historian amounts to a "hoplite census," thus making the constitution a *Hoplitenpoliteia*.[203] In light of the arguments given above about military capacity and census classes, however, this point of near-orthodoxy has its problems. The very idea of an amount of money that "corresponded to" or was "the equivalent" of hoplite status is unattested in the ancient sources.[204] As we have seen, Hansen has demonstrated that the notion

---

201. If the "hoplite republic" has come to seem like such a hegemonic regime type, it is largely because Aristotle and his school wished it to be one, pressing the testimony of Thucydides into their model in the process. What was a *numerus clausus* for Thucydides becomes a minimum for the author of the *Ath. Pol.* (29.5). Later, in the lead-up to the institution of the Thirty, the author can speak of three groups vying for political power, the demos, the oligarchs, and a middle group in favor of the "traditional constitution" or *patrios politeia*. As Sancho Rocher has shown, however (2007), there is no additional evidence for the existence of such a "third way" group, which is better understood as reflecting an Aristotelian preference for the "mean" or "middle" way. Aristotle himself admits that "middle constitutions" are extremely rare: *Pol.* 4.1296a36–38.

202. *Hell. Oxy.* 19.2 Chambers.

203. See, e.g., Swoboda 1910: 318; Larsen 1955: 41; Bruce 1967: 158; Gehrke *Stasis* 170; Moore 1975: 129; Cartledge 2000b: 403; Hammond 2000: 84. One "moderate" measure that did feature in the constitution was the payment of councilors at the federal level. Pay for office in oligarchies was rare, but in this exceptional case it may have been because councilors had to travel from their districts to Thebes, an atypical expense.

204. Some have supposed that we know from Pollux (10.165 = Arist. fr. 566 Rose) that a measure of grain called the *achanē*, equivalent to 45 Attic medimnoi, was "the property requirement for those to serve as hoplites" in the Boeotian polis of Orchomenos (Hanson 1995: 208;

of a "hoplite census" is a modern construction (1985: 83.) Considering the matter logically, we should find it odd that there would have been, in addition to the simple ability to furnish arms, a separate monetary amount that would be calculated to correspond to this ability. On the other hand, there is a perfectly good Greek phrase for those who could provide their own hoplite arms, the *hopla parechomenoi* discussed in the preceding pages. The Oxyrhynchus historian says nothing along these lines, but the phrase he does use, *plēthos* of *chrēmata*, is the exact one used by Plato in his discussion of oligarchies in the eighth book of the *Republic*, where he is clearly referring to wealth and not military capability.[205] Since there is no other evidence that Thebes was a *Hoplitenpoliteia*, and since Thucydides considered Thebes an oligarchy, full stop, we should strongly consider the possibility that it set its property requirement higher than most hoplites could afford.[206]

How narrow oligarchies tended to be is made somewhat clearer by several scattered pieces of evidence. We have already seen that the *numerus clausus* of five thousand at Athens in 411 was at most 15 percent of the adult male citizen population. Consider, too, that one thousand oligarchic ringleaders were eventually arrested and sent to Athens as the chief instigators of Lesbos's defection from the empire.[207] Some have thought that this is quite large for an oligarchic class, but as Gomme and others have pointed out, the Athenian general Paches had arrested both Mytilineans and anyone else from the other cities of Lesbos he considered responsible for the revolt. The Mytilenean oligarchs within this group were probably a majority, but their numbers still could have been considerably fewer than one thousand.[208] Historians have

---

cf. Bruce 1967:158; Moore 1975: 129). But as Buckler points out (1980: 286), Pollux does not say he is giving us a "property requirement" for political participation—he is simply explaining what an *achanē* is. We have no good reason for thinking the *achanē* was used for political purposes (cf. Müller 2010: 227–28n14). The one attempt at calculating the monetary equivalent of being a hoplite may have been Demetrius of Phalerum's rate of 1,000 drachmas (van Wees 2011). This was likely undertaken under the influence of Aristotelian doctrine and was atypical practice.

205. 8.551b. Plato later implies that the excluded poor either retain their arms under an oligarchy (556d) or have them taken away (551d-e).

206. Swoboda (1910: 318n4), Gehrke (*Stasis* 170n31) and Hammond (2000: 84, 91) all draw attention to Xenophon's phrase "all the Thebans, both the cavalry and the hoplites" (*Hell.* 5.4.9). This would indeed count as crucial information, had Xenophon not also glossed "all the Athenians" as "both the hoplites and the cavalry" (5.1.22). Since clearly there were many non-hoplites among the ranks of the Athenian citizenry, this seems to be a verbal tic on Xenophon's part (cf. 3.5.19) rather than good evidence for regime type.

207. Thuc. 3.35.1, 50.1.

208. Gomme *HCT* 2: 325–26; Legon 1968: 207 with n11; Quinn 1971: 408n21.

guessed at a total adult male citizen population of about five thousand or more at Mytilene: thus the thousand oligarchs would represent, at most, 20 percent of the citizenry, and very probably much less.[209]

At the conclusion of the famous *stasis* at Corcyra, the entire oligarchic faction was wiped out (Thuc. 4.48.5). Thucydides does not give precise figures, but this amounted, on my calculations, to about 1,000 men at the absolute most out of a citizen population of between 7,000 and 10,000, or anywhere from 10 to 14 percent.[210] The democratic revolution at Corinth in 393 (see chapter 6, section 6.1.1) resulted, according to Diodorus, in 120 dead and 500 in exile (14.86.1). Xenophon says that the "majority and the best of the Corinthians" were on the losing side (*Hell.* 4.4.1). This probably means that the majority within the ruling class were victims of the revolution, while a minority of the Corinthian oligarchs allied with the demos to set up a democracy. We do not know how many were in the minority, but the two sides were probably closely balanced. Assuming a roughly equal pairing, there would have been about 1,240 full members of the Corinthian regime (120 + 500 = 620 x 2 = 1240). Even assuming that we can round up to about 1,500 to capture those from the oligarchic class who managed to stay out of the *stasis* completely, 1,500 out of an estimated adult male citizen population of 15,000 is 10 percent.[211]

At Tegea in 370, 800 pro-Spartan Tegeans went into exile.[212] An unspecified number had also been killed fighting with a pro-democratic faction. As-

---

209. For the number 5,000, see Gomme (previous n.). *IACP* no. 798, p. 1026 (Hansen, Spencer, Williams) estimates a total population of ca. 20,000.

210. Both Wilson (1987: 97) and Hornblower (*ad* 3.74.1) err in assuming that a large number of men *in addition* to the 400 who escaped to the temple of Hera (3.75.5) were enrolled as crews of ships (for Wilson, this would mean 200 additional men). In fact, Thucydides uses the inchoative imperfect *katelegon*, "they began to enroll" (75.3), to suggest that the *prostatai* of the demos started to enroll their enemies as crew members. We should not assume that the list was finished. When the oligarchs saw what was happening, the ones initially enrolled ran to the temple of the Dioscuri (75.3), while the rest, 400 in number, took shelter in the temple of Hera. I do not suppose that the total number of oligarchs here exceeded 450. These men were all killed (3.81), but 500 additional people fled (85.2) and were later killed. Counting the victims of the fighting at 3.74.1, we have about 1,000 oligarchs in all. For the total Corcyrean citizen population, see Wilson 1987: 90, implying 10,000.

211. 15,000: Salmon 1984: 168. If we use Hansen's preferred method for turning hoplite army numbers into population numbers (2011), then the 5,000 Corinthian hoplites fielded at Plataea (Hdt. 9.28.3) equate to around the same number, ca. 16,600. The 3,000 at Nemea in 394 (Xen. *Hell.* 4.2.17) would yield 10,000 adult male citizens, with the oligarchs at 15 percent. In either case the ruling class *per* Xenophon and Diodorus is much smaller than the total number of hoplites. For more on this episode, see chapter 6, section 6.1.1.

212. Xen. *Hell.* 6.5.10.

suming about 100 for this group, we have 900 in the oligarchic majority. We are not told how many were in the pro-democratic faction led by Callibius and Proxenus, but they were defeated in the oligarchic body of the *thearoi* and required the assistance of the Tegean demos. Assuming they were quite inferior, say about 300, we have 1,200 within the ranks of the oligarchs. Using Hansen's formula, the 2,400 Tegean hoplites at Nemea in 394 would translate into an adult male population of 8,000, giving an oligarchic class of 15 percent.[213]

Finally, the Phliasians are said to be a city of more than 5,000 men, with a group of a little fewer than 1,000 defecting to Sparta.[214] These oligarchs, too, would amount to less than 20 percent of the citizen total (1000/5000+).[215] In addition to these figures, which represent maximums, we know of even narrower oligarchies.[216] An oligarchic class of 10 to 20 percent is higher than the Athenian "leisure class" which numbered between 1,200 and 2,000 citizens, the richest 5 to 10 percent.[217] Yet there are ready explanations at hand for why oligarchs would typically constitute more than a bare minimum of the leisured wealthy—in particular the need to co-opt influential citizens outside of the narrow band of the economic elite.[218] I would therefore suggest that the typical oligarchies of the Classical period were based overwhelmingly on the leisure class, which provided the backbone of the regime, but that they also incorporated several of the richer hoplites from the demos, who might hope to aggrandize themselves via participation in the oligarchy to the point of

---

213. 2,400 hoplites at Nemea: Nielsen 2002: 327.

214. Xen. *Hell*. 5.3.16.

215. The democrats were in the habit of "holding their assemblies outside," to display their superior numbers to the Spartans and the Phliasian oligarchs. Very likely we are to understand many of these 5,000 as hoplites, since the point of the public display was to drive home to the Spartans the superiority of their own militia over that of the oligarchs. For the Phliasian constitution as democratic, see Legon 1967: 326–28; *IACP* no. 355, p. 614 (Piérart); Robinson 2011: 48–50.

216. Xenophon draws our attention to the very narrow nature of the oligarchy of Pellene: *Hell*. 7.4.18. Other narrow oligarchies: the Thousand of Acragas, supposedly put down by the philosopher Empedocles (Diog. Laert. 8.66); the Thousand, again, of Epizephyrian Locri (Polyb. 12.16.10, and see the rich treatment of Redfield 2003); the "very narrow" oligarchy imposed at Megara (Thuc. 4.74.4); the Three Hundred at Heraclea Pontica in the mid-fourth century (Polyaen. *Strat*. 2.30.2); the Six Hundred at Syracuse in the late fourth (Diod. Sic. 19.4.3); the Thousand of Cyrene (*SEG* 9.1, line 35). The Three Hundred at Thasos are ambiguous (ML 83)—they could represent the entire ruling group, or could be a subset thereof—as is the council (*sunhedrion*) of 600 men at Massalia (Val. Max. 2.6.7; Strabo 4.1.5).

217. Ober 1989: 28, citing Davies 1981: 28–35.

218. For co-optation within oligarchies see chapter 3, section 3.3.

achieving true elite-level self-sufficiency. In any case, the great majority of oligarchies were significantly narrower than the one third to one half of the population that comprised the hoplites. [219]

Confirming this assessment are numerous instances from the ancient sources in which it is only a subset of the hoplite army that favors oligarchy. In many cases, the majority of the hoplites can be considered members of the demos and broadly in support of democracy.[220] To begin with Athens, Thucydides claims that when Theramenes and the hoplites were tearing down the fortification at Eëtioneia in 411, "the call went out to the crowd that whoever wanted the Five Thousand to rule instead of the Four Hundred ought to join in the deed. They dissembled by using the name of the Five Thousand, rather than saying outright 'whoever wants the demos to rule,' fearing that they [the Five Thousand] existed and that they might, out of ignorance, say something to one of them and spoil the plan."[221] According to the historian, many of the hoplites, some of whom must have thought they stood a good chance of being included among the ranks of the Five Thousand, were ready for a return to full democracy, but they altered their language out of fear and uncertainty. Several readers have pointed out that Thucydides cannot have known what the hoplites were thinking, and that the passage represents his own personal interpretation of their actions.[222] Still, it is worth noting that he himself did not find it implausible that numerous hoplites would prefer a re-institution of the democratic regime to something closer to a "hoplite constitution."

Also in Thucydides we read about a small group of Argive hoplites—one thousand to be exact—who joined with the Spartans in campaigning against

---

219. An active citizenry of even 10 to 20 percent is of course exceptional in world history. Ancient Greek oligarchs were not the tiny ruling elite of most other world civilizations (including the Romans), nor were they quite as exclusive as the "one percent" discussed in contemporary political discourse. Nevertheless, when considered as a proportion of the total population of a given city-state, 10 to 20 percent of the citizen male group turns out to be quite narrow. The Five Thousand of Athens, if actually put into practice, would have represented two percent of the total population of Attica (5,000/ca. 250,000). The Corinthian oligarchy of 1,500 (see above) would represent slightly higher than two percent of the total population of 70,000 estimated by Salmon (1984: 165–69). One thousand Mytilinean oligarchs (in fact it was less—see above) out of a population of 20,000 is less than five percent. Greek oligarchies were relatively large for a ruling class—larger, typically, than the 150 members above which small, informal groups become unmanageable (Ober 2008: 88), and so large enough to require formalized, impersonal institutions—but that in no way makes them broad-based or "representative."

220. Plat. *Rep.* 8.551e implies that most oligarchies would be unable to field a complete hoplite army using the members of the oligarchic class alone.

221. Thuc. 8.92.11.

222. Rhodes 1972b: 115–16, 120; Andrewes in *HCT* 5 *ad loc.*

their polis and putting down the democracy there.²²³ These hoplites may be identical with the "thousand picked Argives who for a long time had been provided training in war at public expense," but Thucydides does not explicitly connect the two.²²⁴ In any case they were a small group and not representative of the larger army of Argive hoplites, who were probably among the demos that "regrouped" and overthrew the oligarchy at Argos later in the year.²²⁵ If Aeneas Tacticus is referring to this oligarchic *coup* in his description of Argive *stasis*, he lends further support to the idea that the oligarchs were a subset of the hoplites.²²⁶ A group of oligarchic conspirators uses an extramural festival as an opportunity to gain control of the polis. They confiscate a cache of weapons discarded by the broader group of Argives during a sacrifice—these were probably the arms of pro-democratic Argive hoplites.²²⁷ A second Argive episode reported by Aeneas likewise illuminates a passing remark in Thucydides and again shows the division between pro- and anti-democratic hoplites. In what he calls the "second attempt of the rich against the democracy," the oligarchs plot to bring foreign fighters (*xenoi*) into the city at night. The *prostatēs* (champion) of the Argive demos, however, learning of the plot, orders all the Argives to remain under arms all night according to tribe. As a result the rich are scattered throughout the tribes and unable to assemble and bring in the *xenoi*.²²⁸ The episode makes clear that the rank-and-file Argive hoplites greatly outnumbered the oligarchic conspirators among them.

Two final examples, this time from Xenophon's history, complete the picture. When a democratic faction seized the acropolis of Elis sometime before 362, the oligarchic opposition comprised not the cavalry and all of the hoplites, but the cavalry and the "Three Hundred," a select group of Elean infantry.²²⁹ And nothing better illustrates the fact that it was not being a hoplite *per se*, but one's wealth as a hoplite, that inclined one toward oligarchy than the

---

223. Thuc. 5.81.2. Cf. the 700 Argive hoplites who were killed at Mantinea (Thuc. 4.74.2), who, if they were killed proportionately with the rest of the allies at a loss of 13.8 percent, came from a total Argive hoplite army of over 5,000. Krentz estimates the total forces on the Argive side that day as "some 8,000" (1985: 16).

224. Thuc. 5.67.2; cf. 76.2. Later authors did connect them: Diod. Sic. 12.75.7, 80.2; Paus. 2.20.2; cf. Arist. *Pol.* 5.1304a25–27.

225. Thuc. 5.82.2; note that this uprising involved a "battle" [*machē*] within the city walls.

226. 17.2–4. For the identification, see Whitehead 2001 *ad loc.*, David 1986.

227. Aen. Tact. 17.3. For more on this revolutionary tactic of disarming the populace and occupying the polis, see chapter 4, section 4.3.

228. 11.7. Cf. the oligarchic plot of 417 mentioned by Thucydides (5.83.1). Stylianou 1998 *ad* Diod. Sic. 15.57.3 equates the two episodes.

229. Xen. *Hell.* 7.4.16. For this elite group, see also 7.4.13 (where they are paired with the otherwise unknown "Four Hundred") and 7.4.31, where their commander, Stratolas, is killed.

case of the *eparitoi* of the Arcadian *koinon* (confederacy). The *koinon*, which was founded as a democracy with an authoritative common assembly of "Ten Thousand," at first maintained its elite troops, or *eparitoi*, at public expense.[230] When, however, the leaders of Arcadia were accused of committing sacrilege by funding the army with the sacred funds of Olympia, the Ten Thousand decided to cut off pay to the *eparitoi*. The result, says Xenophon, was that "very soon those not able to be part of the *eparitoi* without pay [*misthos*] started to leave, but those who were able [sc. who were independently wealthy] encouraged one another to join the *eparitoi*, in order that they not be under the control of those men [the democratic leaders of the *koinon*], but those men under them."[231] This altered group of *eparitoi*, filled with oligarchs and Spartan sympathizers, is later seen sending an embassy to Lacedaemon suggesting that the two join forces.[232] It seems that when the elite hoplite body of the *koinon* was a paid position, it was manned by hoplites happy to serve a democratic constitution. With the elimination of pay, however, it was quickly taken over by wealthy oligarchs eager to use the powerful institution to undermine the democracy from within.[233]

1.2.3 The Spartan Constitution and Greek Oligarchies

A further topic that needs to be addressed when discussing the relationship between oligarchies and hoplites is Sparta. As was mentioned above, section 1.1, Sparta was an atypical regime in several respects. There is no doubt that it laid extreme emphasis on its hoplite army, which was also its citizenry. According to Plutarch, Agesilaus once illustrated this fact to Sparta's military allies in striking visual fashion. When the allies were complaining that they followed the Spartans everywhere and campaigned constantly, despite their soldiers being more numerous than the few Spartiates, Agesilaus assembled the allied army and had them sit down. He then had the herald first tell the

---

Three hundred "picked" Elean hoplites are also known from Thuc. 2.25.3, but their political views are unknown.

230. For the democratic nature of the *koinon*, see Schaefer 1961: 311–14; Trampedach 1994: 27–33; Roy 2000: 314; Robinson 2011: 42–43. Most scholars agree that "Ten Thousand" (*murioi*) was a nominal number, not a *numerus clausus*, and that there was no property requirement for participation. For the *eparitoi*, cf. Hesychius s.v.

231. Xen. *Hell.* 7.4.34.

232. Xen. *Hell.* 7.5.3.

233. See further Pritchett 1971–79 vol. 2: 223; Lintott 1982: 232–33; Roy 2000: 316–21; Nielsen 2002: 487–90; Hunt 2007: 144–45. For a final example of hoplites defending democracy see the case of Mende in 423, discussed in greater detail in chapter 6, section 6.1.2.

potters to stand up, then the smiths, then the builders, and so on, going through the various trades (*technai*), until virtually all of the allies were standing while the Spartiates remained sitting. He laughed and told the allies it was now clear how many more soldiers (*stratiōtai*) the Spartans had contributed than they had.[234]

The story brings out several important and idiosyncratic features of the Spartan regime. First, the Spartiates, uniquely among Greeks, were full-time professional soldiers.[235] Second, and relatedly, all Spartiates were hoplites. As Cartledge has pointed out, Sparta, instead of allowing all soldiers into the ranks of the citizenry, made certain all full citizens were soldiers.[236] This arrangement notoriously depended upon an exploitative conquest state that extracted surplus resources from its subject helot population. It was only by conquering its neighbors in Messenia that the Spartans could maintain all of their citizens in professional hoplite status. Thus, while Sparta was a kind of *Hoplitenpoliteia*, it was one of unusual and unparalleled size, whose insistence on making all of its citizens hoplites was both enabled by and directed toward its vast laboring class.

It was therefore unclear to the ancients themselves what kind of regime the Spartans had.[237] Herodotus says that in the Archaic period the Spartans had transitioned from being "the worst governed" (*kakonomōtatoi*) of nearly all the Greeks to enjoying *eunomia*, and he seems to assume that this trend toward good government continued down to his day. Otherwise he declines to provide constitutional labels for Sparta, despite being well aware of the polis's central institutions.[238] Thucydides echoes Herodotus's assessment of Sparta's *eunomia* and goes on to say that Sparta maintained its supremacy within the Peloponnesian League by "using oligarchy to maintain regimes that would

234. *Ages.* 26.5; cf. *Mor.* 214a; Polyaen. *Strat.* 2.1.7.

235. The episode also illustrates the fact that many hoplites from the poleis of the Peloponnese must have been relatively poor and practiced "banausic" trades. It is striking that Agesilaus does not ask the "farmers" to stand up. It is unusual to see a hoplite army with *no* small farmers in it. This is likely a distortion: Agesilaus wishes to contrast the Spartiates with the *banausoi* within the allied forces, but this does not mean that every last member of the allies was a *banausos*. Even if there were many farmers among the allies, however, their livelihood still would have been regarded as too menial for the Spartiate lifestyle.

236. Cartledge 2001: 165. As we have now seen, the former option was not actually practiced by many.

237. With the following discussion cf. Hodkinson 2005; *IACP* no. 345, pp. 591–92 (Shipley).

238. Hdt. 1.65.2, 65.5, listing *enōmotiai*, *triēkades*, *sussitia*, ephors and elders. Note however that Sparta's actions during the events at Athens in 508/7, when Cleomenes attempted to install his guest-friend Isagoras and 300 others as rulers, are in line with Sparta's later pro-oligarchic policy (Thuc. 1.19, discussed below, and see above, section 1.1).

govern themselves in a manner advantageous to themselves [the Spartans] alone."[239] He does not say explicitly, however, that the Spartans themselves are oligarchs. They possess a *politeia* (1.68.1) which the Theban and Megarian oligarchs consider to be more suited to themselves than the democracy of the Argives (5.31.6), and Thucydides comments that the Spartans, in addition to the Chians, were the only Greeks he knew of who "flourished" (*ēudaimonēsan*) at the same time as they "practiced moderation" (*esōphronēsan*) (8.24.4). In making these statements Thucydides carefully avoids labeling them as one regime type or the other. They are undoubtedly hostile to democracy, however: when the exiled Alcibiades argues in front of the Spartans, he evidently thinks they will respond positively to the statement that democracy is "acknowledged to be stupidity itself [*anoia*]."[240] Nicias also warns the Athenians, when they are debating the Sicilian expedition, that they are better off spending their time at home guarding against "a polis plotting against us through oligarchy."[241] This obviously refers to Sparta, but it is unclear what exactly he means by the Spartans attacking Athens "through" oligarchy: most likely Thucydides does not mean that the Spartans themselves were an oligarchy, but rather that they would conspire with pro-oligarchic elements within Athens to overthrow the democracy.[242]

Classical sources of the later fifth and fourth centuries are similarly ambivalent about Sparta. Xenophon in his *Politeia* avoids strict labels, focusing on specific institutions and Sparta's general mode of life without reference to constitutional terminology.[243] A Spartan interlocutor in Plato's mid-fourth century *Laws*, professes ignorance as to what to call his *politeia*, since different elements of it seem to him, in turn, tyrannical, democratic, aristocratic, and kingly.[244] Aristotle in the *Politics* continues the theme of Sparta as a constitutional anomaly, citing the Lacedaemonians as a people who enjoy a *politeia* that is "mixed [*memigmenē*] from all of the other constitutions."[245] Elsewhere

---

239. Thuc. 1.18.1, 19. For instances of them doing precisely this in the *Histories*, see 5.81–82 (Argos, Sicyon, and Achaea).

240. Thuc. 6.89.6. There is potentially further evidence here that hinges on a textual crux: at 4.126.2, Brasidas may tell the Peloponnesians that they have nothing to fear from a mob since they come, "not from cities where the many rule the few, but rather the fewer rule over the greater number." For debate on this passage, see Gomme 1951: 135–36; Hornblower *ad loc.*

241. Thuc. 6.11.7.

242. For other interpretations, see Hornblower *ad loc.* For Thucydides on Sparta, see Raaflaub 2006b: 216–20; Leppin 1999: 171–84.

243. *Ages.* 1.4, listing democracy, oligarchy, tyranny, and kingship, suggests Xenophon considered Sparta a kingship (*basileia*).

244. Plat. *Leg.* 4.712d-13a.

245. Arist. *Pol.* 2.1265b33–35. See further Pseudo-Archytas 34.15–20 Thesleff = Stob. 4.1.138.

in the same book, however, he says that due to the power of the ephors, who were elected from the whole demos, the *politeia* has deteriorated from an aristocracy to a democracy (1270b6–17). In book 4, meanwhile, the Lacedaemonians are an example of a "polity," (*politeia*), Aristotle's term for the intermediate category between democracy and oligarchy (1294b13–34). He is forthright, however, about the Spartans' hostility toward democracy, citing their practice of putting down democratic regimes during the Peloponnesian War (5.1307b22–24). In the corpus of Attic orators, Sparta is sometimes labeled an oligarchy outright (Dem. 20.108) or else is closely connected with oligarchy (Lys. 12.58–59).[246] A political dialogue from the period, preserved on papyrus, illustrates well the uncertainty surrounding what to call Sparta. One speaker asks whether the ability to speak well is more beneficial in a democracy or in an oligarchy. He then rephrases the question: Here, or in Lacedaemon? He goes on to say that the difference between the two constitutions (*politeiai*) is that "here" (in Athens, presumably, if the speaker is Socrates) the many are those *politeuomenoi* ("taking part in politics"), while there it is the few. In other words, "here there is a democracy, there an aristocracy" (Merkelbach 1949: 57). It is unclear whether the speaker equates "oligarchy," "the participating of the few," and "aristocracy" and applies them all equally to Sparta, or if he thinks the Spartan aristocracy is a special subcategory of oligarchy. In any case, the text indicates that the constitutional nature of Sparta was, in its own day, deemed quite complex.

Despite the fact that theirs was an atypical constitution, whose characteristic features were difficult if not impossible to replicate, the Spartans were emulated by oligarchs throughout the Greek world. Aristophanes has his chorus of elitist knights beg indulgence from the demos (represented by the theater audience) for their long hair, a typically Spartan trait.[247] In the *Wasps* the connection between Sparta, wearing one's hair long, and anti-democratic sentiment is even clearer. The chorus accuses Bdelycleon of being "hateful towards the people" (*misodēmos*) and (somewhat confusingly) "a lover of monarchy," "conspiring with Brasidas and wearing fringes of wool and growing out your beard untrimmed."[248] The laconizing tendencies of oligarchs within

---

246. Isoc. 3.24 straightforwardly labels Sparta an oligarchy.

247. Ar. *Eq.* 579–80.

248. Ar. *Vesp.* 474–76. The passage seems to conflate Sparta with tyranny rather than oligarchy (cf. 464–65 just preceding, where *turannis* is linked with "the long-haired Amynias"; also Ar. fr. 110 K-A, from the *Farmers*, in which a speaker refuses to plant a "Laconian fig" because it is *turannikon* and *misodēmon*). Already by this time, however, the two terms were becoming conflated: cf. Thuc. 6.60.1 and Raaflaub 2003: 83. For more instances of long hair, pro-Spartan sentiment, and elitist leanings in Aristophanes, cf. *Av.* 1280–85.

Athens really come to the fore, however, during the regime of the Thirty, in particular in the figure of Critias.[249] According to Xenophon, Critias said that the Thirty were working with the Lacedaemonians to set up "the present *politeia*," which, in contrast to the demos, would remain faithful to the Spartans; he is explicit, moreover, in calling the Thirty's regime an *oligarchia*.[250] Later he claims that the *politeia* of the Spartans is regarded as "the finest of all" and cites the example of the ephors as a reason to condemn his enemy Theramenes.[251] Critias is careful to specify the Spartan constitution as something other than a typical oligarchy, but also to draw attention to the close connection between Sparta and oligarchs and to the sense of emulation oligarchs had toward their patrons.[252]

The same is true in other poleis. Already during the Peloponnesian War, Thucydides had noted oligarchs' tendency to call in the Spartans during bouts of *stasis* with the demos.[253] This trend only accelerated during the period of the Corinthian War and the King's Peace. The Spartans receive requests for aid from wealthy oligarchs in Thasos, Rhodes, Phlius, Sicyon, Tegea, and the Arcadian *koinon*, who are frequently said to "laconize."[254] By the mid-fourth century it could be taken for granted that an oligarch, including one from outside Athens, would admire the Lacedaemonians: Isocrates assumes this when he says he ran his Panathenaic speech by a former pupil who had "taken part in politics [*politeuomenon*] in an oligarchy" and who had chosen to praise Sparta.[255] Sparta's *politeia* might be admired, praised, and theorized about by the oligarchic elite; Sparta itself might supply material aid and training to laconizing oligarchs throughout the Greek world; but no sympathetic oligarchy seems to have actually instituted the extensive hoplite regime for which Sparta was famous.[256]

---

249. Critias the son of Callaeschrus, an associate of Socrates, poet, political thinker, and extreme oligarch during the rule of the Thirty. For the fanatically anti-democratic imagery on his gravestone, see below; on his life and works, Bultrighini 1999.

250. Xen. *Hell.* 2.3.24–25.

251. For Critias's comments about the ephors, see chapter 2, section 2.2.

252. Critias wrote an entire prose *Politeia* of the Spartans, now lost except for a few fragments, presumably similar in style to that later composed by Xenophon (DK 88 B 32–37). He also wrote a separate treatise in verse on Sparta (DK 88 B 6–9).

253. Thuc. 3.82.1; cf. Arist. *Pol.* 5.1307b22–24.

254. Xen. *Hell.* 1.1.32 (*lakōnistai* and the Spartan harmost Eteonicus expelled from Thasos), 4.8.20, 5.3.10–13, 6.5.10 (and cf. 6.4.18, *lakōnizontes*), 7.1.44 (*lakōnizein*), 7.5.3. As we have seen already, such groups rarely if ever comprised the entire hoplite infantry.

255. Isoc. 12.220.

256. This is to say nothing of the fact that the Spartiate elite shrank rapidly in the fourth century and the ranks of the hoplite infantry had to be filled with various subordinate popula-

1.2.4 Public Perceptions of Oligarchy in the Classical Period

Finally, to round out this section, we may ask about the self-presentation and public perception of oligarchies during the Classical period. An extended discussion of oligarchs' practices of image projection can be found in chapter 5.[257] For now I wish to focus on the picture of oligarchs in Greek popular discourse and in inscribed decrees, which, as Hansen has pointed out, is almost uniformly negative.[258]

Tellingly, no Greek oligarchy ever advertises itself publicly as such, although oligarchs could speak within their own ranks about the desirability of *oligarchia* for themselves.[259] Oligarchs could opt for the neutral-sounding *politeia* (constitution),[260] and in more propagandistic moments they hailed their *eunomia* (good order)[261] or tried to appropriate *aristokratia*.[262] This latter

---

tions: *hupomeiones, perioikoi*, helots, and so on. For Sparta's resemblance to a "typical oligarchy" by the mid-fourth century, see Hodkinson 2000: ch. 13.

257. See esp. section 5.2.

258. *IACP* p. 83.

259. For oligarchs candidly using "*oligarchia*" when "among friends," see [Xen.] *Ath. Pol.* 2.20; Thuc. 3.62.3, 8.48.4–5; Xen. *Hell.* 2.3.17, 24, 26. Critias's grave monument supposedly showed a personified female *Oligarchia* setting fire to *Dēmokratia* (DK 88 A 13 = schol. ad Aeschin. 1.39); we should note that this was a private act undertaken by the friends of a rabidly anti-democratic individual and that it was erected safely after his death.

260. *Politeia*: at *Hell. Oxy.* 18.3 Chambers, the author describes democratic revolutionaries as putting down the "*politeia*" of the Rhodians and setting up a democracy. At Xen. *Hell.* 7.1.42, oligarchic Achaeans ask that Epaminondas and the Thebans not change their *politeia*. "*Politeiai*" has been restored at RO 41, lines 25–31, where it refers to the governments of oligarchic Arcadia, Elis, and Achaea.

261. Thuc. 8.64.5; [Xen.] *Ath. Pol.* 1.8, 9; Bacchyl. 13.186; Pind. fr. 52a.10 S-M; see Andrewes 1938. (A new authoritarian claim for "*eunomia*" can be found in a recently discovered statue base for Idrieus the son of Hecatomnus, which says that he led the people of Iasos from suffering to "good order": Nafissi 2015, esp. 79–81.) The virtue of *sōphrosunē* was also often stressed: Thuc. 3.65.3, 3.82.8, 8.24.4, 8.64.5; Xen. *Hell.* 3.2.23; Eur. *Hipp.* 983–1035; Plut. *Mor.* 295c; see North 1966. The elite were the *kaloi kagathoi*, the "beautiful and good": Bourriot 1995.

262. *Aristokratia*: Thuc. 3.82.8 (for which see Graham and Forsythe 1984), 8.64.3; Ar. *Av.* 125 (where it is a pun on the name Aristokrates but clearly refers to a non-democratic constitutional alternative); Xen. *Hell.* 2.3.47; Heniochus fr. 5 K-A (personified *Dēmokratia* vs. *Aristokratia* [clearly *Oligarchia* is meant]); Diod. Sic. 15.79.3. Despite the attempts by Aristotle and others to argue that aristocracy was a true form, to be distinguished from oligarchy by its lawfulness (e.g., *Pol.* 3.1279b5), in practice different people called the same basic regime different names according to argumentative need and political preference. Note that Menander Rhetor advises speakers to praise cities governed plutocratically as "aristocracies" (p. 360 Spengel).

term, however, was content-free and could be used to refer to democracies.[263] Over time, for various reasons, oligarchies lost the discursive battle with democracies over the idea of tyranny and were conflated with tyrants. The process started early—awareness of the fine line between tyranny and certain narrow forms of oligarchy probably begins in the mid-fifth century—and by the late fourth century was nearly complete.[264] An increasing number of inscribed decrees specify that the constitution of a polis is to be a democracy and that oligarchies and tyrannies are equally to be opposed.[265] Strikingly, no decree survives that takes the opposite tack, explicitly instituting oligarchy and conflating democracy and tyranny as illegitimate alternatives. Nor do we possess any inscription that describes episodes of unconstitutional revolution in which "the demos was in power" or the ringleaders were "those in control during the democracy," as we do in the case of Athens and Erythrae under oligarchy.[266] While we possess numerous attestations of cults devoted to both Demos and Demokratia, of statues depicting Demos and Demokratia, and even of ships named "Demokratia," both in Athens and beyond, no polis is known to have done the same with the concepts "Oligoi," "Oligarchia," or even "Aristokratia."[267] Oligarchy, from the time of its first appearance in our

263. Isoc. 12.131; Plat. *Men.* 238c-d. The only instance of *aristokratia* on stone, from Isyllus of Epidaurus's inscribed hymn to Apollo and Asclepius (*IG* IV² 1 128.3, Hellenistic), is compatible with democratic government, since the *damos* is mentioned multiple times. Other decrees of Hellenistic Epidaurus attest to a demos as well as a *boulē*, strongly indicating (but not guaranteeing) democracy.

264. For dynastic oligarchy as closest in form to tyranny, see Thuc. 3.62.3. For the conflation of oligarchs with tyrants, see Eur. fr. 275 Nauck (accepting the emendation of Hense); Thuc. 6.60.1; the tyrannicide-like assassination of the oligarch Phrynichus in 411 (Thuc. 8.92.2); *Hell. Oxy.* 18.2 Chambers (Rhodes in 395); Xen. *Hell.* 5.4.9 (the liberation Thebes in 379); and the decrees cited below. The philosopher Democritus labeled nondemocratic regimes (so, presumably, both oligarchy and tyranny) as "despots" (*dunastai*): DK 68 B 251. See also the afterword.

265. RO 41, lines 25–26 (terms of alliance specifying the demos rather than a tyrant or an oligarchy as the regime at Athens, 362); *SEG* 51.1105 (Eretria, mid-fourth century); *IK Ilion* 25 (early third century); *Tit. Cal.* test. xii (Cos/Calymna, mid-third century or earlier).

266. *IG* II² 448, line 61 (late fourth century, describing the regime of Phocion); *SEG* 28.60, line 81 (decree for Callias of Sphettus, 270/69); *IK Erythrai* 503, line 2 (probably early third century). Cf. the decree for Demosthenes proposed by his nephew Demochares *apud* Plut. *Mor.* 851c: Demosthenes "was in exile because of the oligarchy, when the demos had been put down."

267. For the cult of Demokratia in Athens, see *IG* II² 1496, lines 131–2, 140–1. Although the inscription dates to the 330s, the cult probably began with the restoration of democracy in 403. There was a statue to Demokratia in the agora by the time of Demetrius Poliorcetes in the late fourth century: *SEG* 25.149 with Raubitschek 1962. Demos and Demokratia appear together in the famous relief crowning the Eucrates law, RO 79. For other depictions of the personified Demos, see Glowacki 2003: appendix. In the Hellenistic period there was a cult for Demos and

extant sources, was unpopular, and it remained so. A remark of Aristotle's is revealing in this regard: He is discussing the issue of whether the polis remains the same when new political regimes come to power. The question is important in that newly installed democrats might refuse to fulfill contracts (*sumbolaia*) made under tyrannies or oligarchies; the basis of their refusal being, he says, that those regimes depend on force and are not established with the common good in mind.[268] Aristotle contests this democratic claim by arguing that many democracies, no less than oligarchies and tyrannies, are based on the domination of one class or faction over others. That he had to make the argument in the first place, however, suggests that the majority held to a "common-sense" notion that democracy much more than oligarchy or tyranny represented the will of the community, and that the other two were coercive regimes at base. In making a clever point, therefore, Aristotle reveals that most people took for granted the illegitimacy of oligarchy.[269] The description of oligarchy given by Dio of Prusa, which serves as the epigraph to this chapter, would therefore likely have found approval among the majority of Greek men at the end of the fourth century: "Oligarchy, the harsh and unjust greed of a few rich and wretched men arrayed against the poor majority."[270]

1.3 Methodology

This final section of the introductory chapter lays out the methodological approaches employed by the book, defines terms, and introduces several

---

the Charites (Mikalson 1998: ch. 6). For a ship named *Dēmokratia*, already "old" in 374/3 when its existence is recorded, see *IG* II² 1606, lines 59–60. For cults and personifications along these lines outside of Athens, see Isager and Karlsson 2008 = *SEG* 58.1220; *F. Delphes* III.4.163, lines 25–28l; *IK Kyme* 13, lines 2–4; *IG Bulg.* I² 320. See further Aubriet 2012: 202–4 and, for political personification generally, Messerschmidt 2003; Neils 2013. The only known personification of Oligarchia comes from the grave relief of Critias, discussed above, but cf. Heniochus fr. 5 K-A (personified *Aristokratia*, likely depicted as a prostitute along with *Dēmokratia*).

268. *Pol.* 3.1276a8–13.

269. The same thing applies to the conversation between Pericles and Alcibiades preserved in Xenophon (*Mem.* 1.2.40–46): it is assumed that democracy is legitimate and tyranny and oligarchy are not until Alcibiades cleverly argues that decisions of the democratic majority also constitute acts of force.

270. 3.48. He goes on to criticize democracy as well, of course, employing typical antidemocratic *topoi*: the demos is wild, variegated, and ignorant, and liable to be whipped into a frenzy by unscrupulous demagogues (3.49). Here, though, as with other criticisms of democracy, the demos is spared the charge of intentional malice. It is stupid and prone to viciousness, but this is not entirely its fault (the paternalistic tone is obvious). For the association of oligarchy with greed, see Balot 2001: 179–233.

important recurring concepts. The most fundamental concept used is "methodological individualism." This approach assumes that the basic unit of analysis, through and out of which large-scale political and social phenomena arise, is the discrete (human) individual, who makes purposeful choices.[271] Supra-individual entities, which in the present case include such important concepts as the demos and the polis, remain meaningful in the sense that contemporary actors endow them with cultural import and, crucially, base their own actions on belief in them. Ultimately, however, these entities depend upon the aggregate shared beliefs of individuals, which can change.[272]

Since I cannot address all of the reasons for adopting methodological individualism, I will emphasize here that it respects the important fact that individuals cannot read one another's minds, and that therefore collective action depends heavily upon individuals' anticipation of others' actions. This consideration is crucial when considering any group effort. It militates against the assumption that groups of individuals with a shared interest will necessarily act upon that interest. Quite often, as an extensive scholarly literature within the social sciences has shown, welfare-enhancing collective action fails to occur because of choices at the individual level.[273] This does not mean that collectivities do not exist—I take it for granted in this book, for example, that the group identity marker "member of the demos" was well defined, that it was embraced by certain individuals, and that it suggested to those individuals certain desirable ways of acting collectively. I do not for that reason assume, however, that "the demos" always and everywhere acted in its own self-interest. There was no supra-individual "collective consciousness" of the demos that determined its actions. If the members of the demos were to act together—to challenge an oligarchy, to establish a democracy, to enact policies within a constitutional structure—they had to make a sufficient number of individual decisions to produce group action in the aggregate.[274] Numerous

---

271. See Elster 2007: ch. 1; for a critical view, see Lukes 2006. Note that although I speak throughout the book of individual oligarchs, I am aware that they did not act in isolation but were members (usually the heads) of households (*oikoi*). Sometimes members of an elite *oikos* in an oligarchy quarreled, especially when only certain individuals in the family were able to participate in the regime (Arist. *Pol.* 5.1305b2–16). My working assumption, however, is that *oikoi* cooperated internally, and that we can still productively think of oligarchies as the result of choices made by individuals.

272. I do not mean that the relevant social actors are necessarily *aware* of the dependency of a concept like the polis on their aggregate beliefs—they do not typically operate under the assumption that their concepts are merely social conventions that can be dropped. What I do mean is that when such concepts change, it is because enough people have changed their minds about them, for whatever reason.

273. Olson 1965; Hardin 1982; Ostrom 1990: 5–6.

274. Thus methodological individualism maintains that human beings, rather than classes,

times, and for various reasons, they failed to do so. As will become clear, oligarchic stability and the institutions that produced this stability were premised on the assumption that the members of the demos could be induced *not* to act together.

It is important to say briefly what methodological individualism is not. It is not a theory of individual preference that posits selfishness as the motivation for all human action. Max Weber, who employed methodological individualism, was adamant that the approach did not entail psychological egoism or any other self-centered conception of the human mind.[275] Methodological individualism is not equivalent to treating individuals as the *homo economicus* known from some strong forms of neoclassical economics, in which individual utility, reducible to cash value, determines choice.[276] It leaves open the possibility that a person will act for reasons of self-sacrifice, love, duty, or honor—but insists that it is he or she who is acting, and not some collective entity.

Furthermore, the potential problems of collective action identified by a methodologically individualist approach are not intractable, and can in fact be mitigated by cultural ties, norms, and other forms of nonmaterial, ideological conditioning. In other words, the individuals considered by methodological individualism are not radically alienated from one another; are not self-seeking monads with no consideration of others' claims or interests; and are frequently able to overcome what would normally be barriers to collective action through socialization, communication, and solidarity. As a shorthand, we can subsume these factors under the concept—increasingly common in social science literature—of "social capital."[277] The Nobel Prize-winning economist Elinor Ostrom, for example, was beginning to incorporate considerations of social capital into the study of collective action toward the end of her life.[278]

---

nations, or other groups, have intention and make decisions. We can speak of "the few" doing something, "the demos" doing another—and I do speak this way in this book—as long as we recognize that these group efforts are the product of aggregate individual choices. The failure of collective action is the limit case that reveals the ultimate dependence of group action on individual decisions.

275. Weber 1978: 18: "It is a tremendous misunderstanding to think that an 'individualistic' *method* should involve what is in any conceivable sense an individualistic system of *values*." See further the *Stanford Encyclopedia of Philosophy* s.v. "methodological individualism."

276. For *homo economicus*, see, e.g., Becker 1976.

277. Coleman 1990; Putnam 1993; Fukuyama 1995; critical overview by Seubert 2009. See now Kierstead 2013 for an account of the Athenian democracy that utilizes the concept of social capital.

278. See her 1998 and 2000, building on her earlier work (1990) concerning "governing the commons"—on which see further below.

These trends, coupled with other attacks on the traditional economistic picture of human beings as purely rational utility maximizers, have only increased in recent years, and they conform to what the Greeks themselves tell us about how they conceived of motivation, group identity, and collective action.[279] As Aristotle notes, a community of citizens (in other words, a polis in the Greek context) is not merely an alliance, "a surety to one another of justice," nor a place established simply "for the prevention of mutual crime and for the sake of exchange," but a joint project undertaken for the sake of the good life.[280] In another famous passage, he notes that human beings, those "political animals," alone out of all animals possess speech (*logos*), which sets forth the expedient and the inexpedient, and thus the just and the unjust, which are claims upon others.[281] The Greeks thus well understood the importance to human beings of communitarian values, of identifying with others, and of coming to collective agreement through the mutual exchange of views.[282]

Several important models of group behavior follow from the premises of methodological individualism. Two of them are "coordination" and (what is a subset of group coordination) "collective action." Coordination describes a situation in which two or more individuals desire the same outcome but must align along a similar choice of action in order to bring it about. A standard example of a coordination problem in the literature is the decision of which side of the road to drive on. Left or right works equally well, but the drivers must arrive at a conventional agreement in order for traffic to proceed safely. Once agreed upon, moreover, neither party has a reason to change his or her side of the road unilaterally: this would greatly increase the likelihood of accident. Everyone's interests are served by adhering to the original agreement, even if it was arbitrary. They can do no better by changing their course of action.[283]

---

279. Attacks on *homo economicus* have come from prospect theory (Kahneman and Tversky 1979) and experimental psychology and economics (Henrich et al. 2005; Camerer and Fehr 2006), among others.

280. Arist. *Pol.* 3.1280b8–12, 30–32, 39.

281. Arist. *Pol.* 1.1253a9–15.

282. See further Balot 2006: 14–15: "We find within Greek political thought approval of individual autonomy, innovation, private freedom, and equality of opportunity," yes also the belief that "individuals were defined by their attachments to their families, religion, and communities and, furthermore, that individuals became happy through participating in the traditions and culture of their poleis." The work of Christ has demonstrated from the opposite direction that despite a strong communitarian streak in Greek thinking, the Greeks (and especially the Athenians) well understood self-interest and individual choice (see his 2006, 2012).

283. On coordination, see Lewis 1969; Sen 1967; Chwe 2001; Skyrms 2004.

The whole schema, however, hinges upon the ability of the players to signal their intentions to one another early on. Normally participants have no reason to hide their preferences, since everyone benefits from an open airing of views and communication costs nothing. If, for whatever reason, others' preferences remain unknown, however, coordination can fail to occur. People would rather do nothing than risk embarking on a course of action which others might be unwilling to undertake. The importance of this fact comes out especially in situations of anti-authoritarian revolutionary upheaval. Suppose that of the subjects of an authoritarian regime each is individually willing to join with the others in overthrowing the regime; he or she will openly oppose the regime, however, only if s/he is certain that others are willing to participate as well. Authoritarian rulers thus have an interest in maintaining their subjects in ignorance of one another's preferences.[284]

The ancient Greeks saw clearly that authoritarian rulers who wished to rule over unwilling subjects could attempt to undermine civic ties in order to weaken the opposition. Aristotle notes that the tyrant who wishes to preempt opposition to his rule must reduce the overall social capital of his subjects: by getting rid of "schools and other meetings for discussion," he undercuts public-mindedness and communal solidarity. "Familiarity [*gnōsis*]," Aristotle explains, "is what produces trust [*pistis*]," but the tyrant keeps his people ignorant of one another and therefore incapable of collective action, in the process strengthening his regime.[285] I argue that a similar dynamic obtained in oligarchies, where the ruling elite had to worry that the demos might come together and overthrow the constitution. Where oligarchs succeeded in decreasing the stock of social capital, we ought to expect increased difficulty in coordinating democratic revolutionary action.[286]

An important corollary to the problem of coordination, as well as a potential means of overcoming it, is the notion of "common knowledge."[287] Common knowledge is not simply the idea that two people both know the same thing. Common knowledge obtains in a two-person scenario when person A knows thing X, person B knows X, person A knows person B knows X, person B knows that person A knows X, and each knows that the other knows the

---

284. See Kuran 1995 on "preference falsification" under authoritarianism. Teegarden 2014 puts this point to excellent use in his study of ancient Greek anti-tyranny legislation.

285. Arist. *Pol.* 5.1313b5–6.

286. Thus I am not claiming that highly individualistic decision-making was always and everywhere the norm; instead, this kind of strategizing increased in high-risk authoritarian scenarios where the ruling powers purposefully engendered distrust among the populace.

287. For the connection between coordination and common knowledge, see Chwe 2001. Historians of ancient Greece who have already realized the importance of Chwe's work include Ober (e.g., his 2008: 114–15) and Teegarden (2014: 37–39).

same about him/her. If any link in this chain fails, there is no common knowledge. The importance of common knowledge for coordination comes through clearly in the authoritarian context described above. Subjects of an authoritarian regime may be individually willing to cooperate to overthrow the regime, but only if others are willing as well. Suppose an individual citizen receives a flyer in the mail calling for a protest against the regime. In the absence of confirmation that other citizens have received the same flyer, the individual is not likely to attend the rally, for fear of being the only one there. If, by contrast, a clandestine group manages to place a poster advertising the rally in a prominent public place where citizens are allowed to congregate, the poster becomes a matter of common knowledge: citizen A has seen the poster, but also knows that citizen B has seen it, and that they each know this about the other. In such situations, individuals may feel empowered to express their true feelings. By learning that at least some people share their opposition to the regime (in an environment that had previously been tightly monitored and controlled by the ruling group), citizens may more readily dare to speak out themselves. The result, well known from contemporary studies of revolution, can be a cascade of coordinated behavior powerful enough to topple the ruling power.[288]

A subspecies of the coordination problem is the collective action problem. Unlike coordination problems, in which the players are assumed to have no reasons to defect from cooperation so long as preferences are signaled clearly, the problem of collective action describes a situation in which self-interest ruins the possibility of shared gain.[289] The most famous example of a collective action problem is the so-called Prisoner's Dilemma, known from game theory.[290] Imagine two prisoners, A and B, brought in separately by the police on suspicion of a crime. The police lay out the following choices for each suspect: 1) if A informs on B, A will go free and B will face maximum jail time, and vice versa; 2) if A and B both inform on each other, they will both go to jail, but with reduced sentences; 3) if A and B both refuse to inform on each other, the police have no choice but to set them free after a year. Each prisoner must then make the decision whether or not to inform on the other. Their decisions occur in isolation of each other, with no knowledge of how the other is choosing; they must make their choice based on what they expect the other will do. The possible outcomes of the "game" can be repre-

---

288. Kuran 1989 (on the "sparks" that light the prairie fires of revolution; see further chapter 6, section 6.1.2); Lohmann 2000; Scott 1990: ch. 8.

289. The most famous statement of the problem is in Olson 1965.

290. Hardin 1982 first showed that the problem of collective action and the Prisoner's Dilemma are equivalent.

sented stylistically as follows (A's outcomes are listed first in the parentheses, B's second):

		Prisoner B	
		Tell	Don't Tell
Prisoner A	Tell	(-10, -10)	(0, -20)
	Don't Tell	(-20, 0)	(-1, -1)

FIGURE 1. The Prisoner's Dilemma

Here the numbers represent the amount of time spent in jail, but they also track the prisoners' preference ordering: each prefers 0 to -1 to -10 to -20.

For both players, the "dominant strategy" is to tell on the other person. Strictly speaking, this is because the "Tell" option always has a better outcome. If Player A is comparing his or her possible outcomes from choosing "Tell" over "Don't Tell" (top square over bottom square), -10 is better than -20 and 0 is better than -1. It is thus rational for both to choose a strategy of "Tell." The solution to the game is for both to choose "Tell" and renege on each other, but then both go to jail, in this case for ten years. But it was possible (just not rational) for both to choose "Don't Tell," so that they would go to jail for only one year. Individual rationality has led to a suboptimal group outcome.

Classical Greek oligarchs counted on their political institutions engendering Prisoner's Dilemma-like collective action problems among their subjects. If they could make the common people's livelihoods, or even their very lives, depend upon cooperation with the regime rather than cooperation with their fellow citizens, they could stymie collective action. So long as the members of the demos viewed the potential costs of collective action as outweighing the potential benefits of overthrowing the oligarchy and establishing a democracy, they would fail to initiate resistance. The targeted inducements utilized by the oligarchs included rewards for informants, positions of authority or material gain within the regime itself, and threats (explicit or implicit) against potential subversives.[291]

At the same time, the members of the oligarchy faced their own set of collective action problems, most of them stemming from the fact that (in most

---

291. See especially chapter 3.

cases, we might guess) an oligarch preferred the outcome of his being tyrant over cooperation with his oligarchic peers.[292] Oligarchic stability was constantly threatened by the possibility that some individual or subgroup within the ruling elite would discover a means of acquiring sole domination. I conceive of stable oligarchic government as the cooperative solution to an "iterated" Prisoner's Dilemma. Social scientists have found that the possibility of continued ("iterated") play creates an opportunity for sustained cooperation over time. If the game is going to persist indefinitely, cooperation makes rational sense.[293] Oligarchs resemble participants in such a game. Each member of the elite in a hypothetical two-person struggle for power would like to take advantage of the other's naïve trust, in the process becoming tyrant. Such an outcome is represented by the lower-left and upper-right quadrants in figure 1. In the upper-left quadrant, we have the equivalent of double defection, in the Greek case meaning ongoing *stasis*. Since the two members of the elite are going to be playing the game seemingly without end, however, it becomes rational to cooperate: why continuously harm one another if they can get by on their second-best option, represented by the lower-right quadrant? Oligarchy is thus a cooperative long-term equilibrium that represents the overcoming of short-term gain.[294]

292. The desirability of tyranny is a commonplace in the sources: Archilochus fr. 19 West; Solon fr. 33 West; Xen. *Hier.* 1.9; Ar. *Eq.* 1111–19; Plat. *Gorg.* 471a-d, 491e-92c, *Rep.* 8.568b-c. This positive assessment of tyranny might be critically interrogated by philosophers like Plato, who wished to show that it was incorrect, but it was taken for granted by the average Greek. This does not, of course, mean that Greeks desired to be *ruled* by a tyrant, only that they wanted to *be* one. (Anyway, it was beyond the reach of the vast majority of people.) Anderson argues that tyranny did not have a negative connotation during the Archaic period but that tyrants were instead de facto leaders who enjoyed "broad consent for their authority from among the governing class" (2005: 187); this is, in my view, to take too sanguine a view of the ability of the Archaic elite willingly to acknowledge superiority in another. If a man became tyrant, it was because he enjoyed access to some means of power over his rivals which they lacked. For oligarchic preference orderings, see further chapter 6, section 6.2.1.

293. See Axelrod 1984. It does not make rational sense if the precise number of games to be played is known: then it makes sense to defect rather than cooperate on the last game, since there is no further game to keep the players cooperative. But if one is going to defect on the last game, one should defect on the second-to-last game (since the last game is now a lost cause), then the third-to-last game, and so on, until one finally works back (through "backward induction") to the conclusion that one should defect on all the games after all.

294. We will see in chapter 6, section 6.2.1, how this equilibrium could easily break down with the introduction of new and unforeseen sources of power. Note also that oligarchs had to deal with their own version of the "tragedy of the commons"—the process whereby individuals deplete a common resource by acting self-interestedly. In a Greek oligarchy, the worry was that individual oligarchs would choose to exploit members of the demos, thinking that the conse-

The basic concepts of methodological individualism, coordination, common knowledge, and collective action problems have now laid the groundwork for an understanding of the present book's approach to institutions. As mentioned in the opening section of this chapter, a new and distinctive set of approaches to institutions has emerged under the title of the "New Institutionalism."[295] Older forms of institutionalism either catalogued the elements of political institutions in list-like fashion, or explained institutional variety as reflective of the underlying structures or values of society.[296] By contrast, the New Institutionalism focuses on the ways in which institutions are situated within a complex matrix of human intention, historical context, and relationships of power. Although there are several varieties of the New Institutionalism, this study adopts methods most closely associated with "Historical Institutionalism." In the words of sympathetic commentators, Historical Institutionalism

---

quences of their personal actions would be negligible. In the aggregate, however, their behavior might precipitate democratic resistance (see chapters 3 and 6, on scenarios when oligarchic abuse leads to revolution). Oligarchs had to monitor one another's behavior, but they were unwilling to establish a "Leviathan"-like central authority in order to do so (this would represent too great a diminution of their personal power). We can think of the institutions they devised instead as an interesting take on Ostrom's notion of "governing the commons" (1990), in which the users of a common resource maintain it through "self-government" rather than through either privatization of property rights or establishment of a powerful central state.

295. For the application of New Institutionalist methods to the study of ancient history, see already Frier and Kehoe 2007; Ober 2008: 8 with n12; Müller 2011: 356–60; Mackil 2013: 10–13; Bresson 2016: 15–27.

296. There is a longstanding tradition within ancient historiography of studying the political institutions of the Greek city-states. My promotion of New Institutionalism is in no way intended to downplay the importance of studies in this tradition, without which research on ancient politics would be impossible. Within this group of institutional studies, one strand, largely Anglophone, has examined the institutions of the Classical Athenian democracy (e.g., Hansen 1983 and 1989 on the assembly; Rhodes 1982b on the council). Another strand, this time largely Francophone, has documented the institutions of the Greek cities of the Hellenistic period and later, attested primarily through inscriptions. Publications in this vein are ongoing (e.g., Gauthier 1985 on civic benefaction; Fröhlich 2004 on *euthuna* or accountability procedures; Feyel 2009 on the *dokimasia* or scrutiny of officials; Chankowski 2010 on the ephebate or training of young men). Works in the French tradition tend to emphasize the diversity of institutions within the Hellenistic Greek world and their variation from polis to polis, as well as their gradual development over time. The sources necessary for conducting this sort of analysis of Classical Greek oligarchy, however, are lacking. A New Institutional approach allows us to pick out commonly shared features of Classical Greek oligarchies in general and, more importantly, to explain how oligarchic practices (institutions) kept oligarchs in power.

conceptualize[s] the relationship between institutions and individual behavior in relatively broad terms, ... emphasize[s] the asymmetries of power associated with the operation and development of institutions, ... emphasizes path dependence and unintended consequences [in institutional development], ... [and] integrate[s] institutional analysis with the contribution that other kinds of factors, such as ideas, can make to political outcomes. (Hall and Taylor 1996: 938)[297]

The appeal to the historian in this description should be clear. It remains to explain what it means by institutions and how they work.

In line with other practitioners of the New Institutionalism, I define institutions as "sets of action-guiding rules established to constrain behavior through controlling the sequence of action, the information available to participants, and the participants' perceptions of the expected outcomes from their actions."[298] Institutions are especially important for political regimes because they have the potential to induce equilibrium states of behavior among individuals in which no participant has a reason to alter his or her action unilaterally. When the equilibrium state in question is one of acquiescence, the regime enjoys basic stability. In other scenarios, of course, the purpose of an institution might be to produce an equilibrium state of cooperation. Several of the earliest exercises in New Institutionalism explained institutions as mechanisms for overcoming collective action problems, and thus for allowing people to enjoy the gains to be had from mutual cooperation. The result is democracy and the rule of law.[299] This is a particularly rosy picture of the purpose of institutions. As commentators have pointed out subsequently, institutions can just as easily be used by authoritarian rulers to oppress their subjects and consolidate their own power. Those in a position to establish new institutions at the onset of a regime enjoy an enormous advantage, and they can use it for autocracy as often as (perhaps more often than) for democracy.[300]

A more recent crop of New Institutionalist literature has therefore examined the effect of institutions under authoritarian political conditions. For these authors, institutions do not enable citizens to pursue their interests or to achieve common goals collectively, but instead restrict individual freedom of action for the purpose of promoting elite authority. Authoritarian institutions include elite councils, co-opted parliaments, rigged elections, patronage

297. Hall and Taylor 1996: 938. For other overviews of Historical Institutionalism, see Thelen and Steinmo 1992; Clemens and Cook 1999; Thelen 1999; and Pierson and Skocpol 2002.

298. Compare the definition of Weingast 2002.

299. Shepsle 1986: 74; Weingast 2002: 670.

300. Bates 1988; Knight 1992; Moe 2005. Much of the criticism of traditional New Institutionalist analysis involves the charge that it ignores asymmetries of power.

networks, censorship of the press and of civil society, and coercive state apparatuses such as the secret police.[301] As the political scientist Milan Svolik has argued, these institutions tend to address two central problems of authoritarian governance: the problem of authoritarian power-sharing (regulating relations among the ruling elite) and the problem of authoritarian control (managing a discontented and potentially unruly citizenry).[302] Political scientists studying the institutions in question have found that they provide a third way between the two extreme and often impractical measures of total ideological hegemony and total repressive violence. In other words, few authoritarian regimes possess the willpower or the resources necessary either to indoctrinate their subjects entirely or to keep them down by pure force. Well-crafted institutions afford authoritarians a much less time- and labor-intensive method of controlling unwilling populations.

I have made the decision to treat Classical Greek oligarchy as a kind of authoritarian regime along these lines (in fact a very early example of one), *mutatis mutandis*.[303] Various sources cited over the course of this chapter have made it clear that, despite appeals to greater "good order" (*eunomia*) and "moderation" (*sōphrosunē*), oligarchies were on the whole much more repressive than democracies. Aristotle straightforwardly labels them "more despotic" (*despotikōterai*), while Plato has Socrates say in the *Republic* that oligarchies are established either through force of arms or through terror, and that the rulers must henceforth forcibly restrain the discontented masses through "oversight" (*epimeleia*).[304] Most oligarchies throughout the Classical period seem to have operated on the notion that they had to struggle to survive against the popular tide of democracy.

---

301. For an overview of the New Institutionalist approach to authoritarianism, see Magaloni and Kricheli 2010. See further Barros 2002; Svolik 2012; Gandhi and Przeworski 2007; Magaloni 2006; Gandhi 2008; Brownlee 2007; Simpser 2013; Gandhi and Lust-Okar 2009; Stokes 2005; Blaydes 2010; Levitsky and Way 2010.

302. 2012: 2. Strikingly, Svolik uses Aristotle's statement about the twin dangers facing oligarchies (*Pol.* 5.1302a8–11, which serves as the epigraph to chapter 6 below) as the epigraph to his first chapter.

303. I do not consider oligarchies totalitarian regimes on the order of those that have existed since the twentieth century. Totalitarian regimes aim for complete ideological conditioning of the subject population and the minute control of every aspect of civil society, concepts that most Greeks, including oligarchs, would not even have understood (except perhaps Plato in the *Republic*). For the important differences between totalitarian and authoritarian states, see Linz 2000.

304. Arist. *Pol.* 4.1290a28; Plat. *Rep.* 8.551b, 552e (and cf. *Leg.* 4.710e, where oligarchy is said to contain "the greatest number of despots [*dunastai*]"). For the importance of the term *epimeleia* for understanding oligarchic relations of clientelism, see chapter 4, section 4.4.

If oligarchies were authoritarian states, however, they were a very specific historical variety of them. De Ste. Croix compares the holdings of Classical Greek landholders with the huge estates of later Roman senators in order to "place in better perspective the relatively mean little estates possessed by even the 'aristocracy' of Classical Greece."[305] Josiah Ober has likewise recently shown, using the available quantitative data, that wealth distribution was relatively egalitarian in Classical Greece, with Gini coefficients (a standard measure of inequality) falling well below the extremes found in other societies, including some modern liberal democracies.[306] The comparative paltriness of the Greek upper class's landholdings has crucial implications for our understanding of oligarchy. These regimes were weak, not only absolutely speaking, in the sense that all Greek poleis' state apparatuses were rudimentary, but also in that the Greek elite never amassed enough wealth so as to consolidate a stable and impenetrable state edifice against popular agitation. Several factors, both external and internal to the elite, mitigated against inequality: not only was there a strong ideology of citizen male egalitarianism, but the members of the elite themselves were also so suspicious of centralized power—that is, of a single man (tyrant) acquiring it—that they likely prevented too unequal a distribution of property.[307] Thus a combination of egalitarian economic institutions and political decentralization prevented the hoarding of wealth within a central ruling class, at least until later historical developments, including the rise of immense kingdoms and the involvement of Rome, changed the political and economic landscape.

Classical oligarchies thus lacked the raw coercive power exercised by more exploitative societies in later historical periods, such as European settler colonies or even the Roman Empire. On the other hand, they did little to ingratiate themselves to their subjects, and they eschewed any pretense of being "populist" authoritarian regimes such as existed in the twentieth century and continue to persist today.[308] While some oligarchs no doubt honestly believed that their preferred political arrangements were to the ultimate benefit of so-

305. De Ste. Croix 1981: 120.

306. See Ober 2015, esp. 90–93 with fig. 4.2. Cf. Bresson 2016: 149 (emphasis added): "In the democratic city-state, or at least in the run-of-the-mill city-states of the Classical period (*not all of which were democratic*), land ownership was relatively widely distributed."

307. Runciman 1990 stresses this point, esp. p. 364, where he calls the poleis (even the oligarchic ones) "far too democratic" to create "a close concentration of economic, ideological, and coercive power in the hands of a compact, self-reproducing elite." For the extensive spread of an ideology of egalitarian male citizenship throughout mainland Greece by the end of the Archaic period, see Morris 1996: 41.

308. Populist authoritarian regimes might include Mexico under the PRI (Magaloni 2006) and Argentina under Perón.

ciety, in that each "kind" of person under an oligarchy would get what he or she "naturally" deserved and the polis would be stable and well-governed, they were also aware that their goals were often most easily obtained, not by persuading the members of the demos of the rightness of their program, but by violent imposition.[309] This unpopularity, coupled with the severe (but not insurmountable) sense of competition felt between members of the elite, again impresses upon us the considerable feat achieved by stable oligarchies and the need to explain it. As I have indicated, their survival is best understood in terms of the operation of their political institutions within the context of the ancient Greek polis.

In the chapters that follow, I test the following theory: Given that Classical Greek oligarchies were authoritarian regimes, which faced internal pressure both at the intra-elite level and in relations between elite and demos, successful institutions should be those that a) kept the fractious elite in an equilibrium of unified cooperation, while b) engendering an equilibrium state of inaction among the members of the demos. In addition, a key feature underpinning the success of these institutions should be the greater organization afforded oligarchs by their smaller numbers. On the assumption that a smaller group can more easily overcome barriers to collective action than a larger one, we should see oligarchs taking advantage of both their own closer familiarity with each other and the greater size and disorganization of the demos.[310] The theory, while informed by the study of contemporary authoritarianism, is not

---

309. For overviews of oligarchic justificatory ideology see Raaflaub 1983: 524–34; Ostwald 2000: 21–30; Rhodes 2000: 128–35. The Thirty at Athens claimed at the onset of their regime that they were "purifying the city of unjust men and turning the rest of the citizenry toward virtue and justice" (Lys. 12.5), but what little good will, if any, they enjoyed from the demos was quickly squandered. According to Xenophon, Critias and other hardcore members of the Thirty were implacably opposed to the demos from the beginning (*Hell.* 2.3.24–26). It is true that Aristotle recommends that citizens of democracies and oligarchies be "acculturated and educated in the constitution" to ensure stability (*Pol.* 5.1310a16–17), but he does not indicate how often oligarchies actually practiced this (let alone achieved it). The rest of the *Politics* suggests that ideological differences between oligarchs and democrats were more often insurmountable.

310. Cf. Teegarden 2014: 172: "Nondemocratic regimes will have political institutions and practices that control common knowledge so that people raise their revolutionary thresholds [the point at which they are willing to engage in resistance] and thus become atomized." Note that my definition of "institution" encompasses social practices not typically included among political institutions more conventionally understood; this will become most apparent in chapters 4 and 5. Fröhlich has criticized the "purely institutional" approach to the Greek city represented by the *IACP*, saying that it gives us a picture of a "city without society" (2010: 667–75, quotation at 673). I hope to give some indication in this book of how power permeated the society and culture of oligarchic poleis in addition to the formal political bodies.

simply a modern import. The initial impetus for formulating the theory arises from the ancient sources themselves, which paint oligarchy in an almost uniformly negative light. If we take the sources seriously that oligarchy was unpopular, we should inquire into the sources of oligarchic regime stability, which become much more mysterious. A theory provides a rigorous means of both testing the evidence and explaining a puzzling phenomenon. If the theory helps to organize and to elucidate the extant evidence, the exercise in theory-building and -testing will have accomplished its task.[311]

I do not suppose that mine is the last word on Classical Greek oligarchy. I have, however, attempted to treat the phenomenon in a thorough and rigorous way, and to say something decisive about the general practice of oligarchy. No doubt others will dispute elements of the argument: its geographical and conceptual scope; its methodologically individualist approach; its focus on conflict instead of cooperation; and its elevation of institutions over ideology, just to name a few possibilities.[312] While parts of the book will read to some as traditional, others will seem radically novel. I consider it to be an invitation to consider an important topic of Classical Greek history using a particular methodological lens.

---

311. The book does not aim to be an exhaustive list of every last oligarchic institution. I focus on those that maintained oligarchic control in the face of potential resistance, which on my reading were the most important anyway.

312. The majority of the evidence comes from the best-known poleis of mainland Greece, the Aegean, Asia Minor, and the West. I have not given as much attention to what have traditionally been considered more "marginal" regions of the Greek-speaking world—Thessaly (Graninger 2011; Mili 2015), Crete (see above, n36), Macedonia (Hammond 1989; Hatzopoulos 1996)—nor on political entities beyond the polis, such as tribes, federations, and kingdoms (Morgan 2003; Mackil 2013; Mitchell 2013). With respect to ideology, I have downplayed its potential effects on oligarchic regime stability, both because I think the ideological appeal of oligarchy to the demos was weak, and because the effects of ideology are so difficult to measure. One of the chief methodological goals of this book is to indicate the extent to which political acquiescence can be explained by institutional success, without ideology having to enter into the picture.

2

Oligarchic Power-Sharing

The true statesman will administer an oligarchy well, harmonizing himself with men of equal power and like honor, gently compelling them to do as he wishes.

—PSEUDO-PLUTARCH[1]

2.0 Introduction

This chapter is devoted to institutions that governed relations among the elite themselves. The members of the ancient Greek elite were extraordinarily competitive, and their cooperation could not be taken for granted—it had to be achieved. This problem went back to the Archaic period, when elite Greeks found it necessary to develop institutions to prevent the rise of tyranny, but it took on a new life in the age of democracy, when the demos represented a novel threat to the oligarchic status quo. One danger was that relations between oligarchs would become so strained that a renegade member of the elite might choose to break with his peers and reach out to the demos.[2] Oligarchs thus had to forge methods for governing the polis that avoided excessive intra-elite confrontation while at the same time leaving open the possibility of successfully punishing transgressors. Thus, after establishing the strong need for egalitarian relations among oligarchs (2.1), I will examine political mechanisms that secured equality among the members of the oligarchy and satisfied their individual sense of self-worth, including the establishment of multiple veto points in the voting process, consensus-building, and the secret ballot (2.2). In the social sphere, strict regulation of expenditure through sumptuary

---

1. *Mor.* 827b: ὁ πολιτικὸς ἀνὴρ εὖ μὲν ὀλιγαρχίαν . . . μεταχειριεῖται, συναρμοσάμενος αὐτῷ τοὺς ἰσοκρατεῖς καὶ ὁμοτίμους ἄνδρας, ἡσυχῇ προσβιαζόμενος.

2. For historical instances of this, see chapter 6.

legislation prevented any one person from becoming preeminent and thus threatening to the egalitarian order (2.3). In judicial situations, oligarchs devised ways of keeping dispute resolution restrained, courteous, and respectful of one another's pride, thus avoiding escalation (2.4). Finally, I will examine the use of exile as an effective institution of oligarchic punishment (2.5). Although recent work has emphasized the ways in which exile frequently led to *stasis*, I show that exile could be a useful tool if it was unanimously agreed upon by the members of the oligarchic community. Exile temporarily excluded a problematic member of the elite from the polis while—and this was crucial—holding open the possibility that he might eventually be reintegrated.[3]

2.1 The Need for Equality among the Elite

Scholars often argue that equality was valued primarily by ancient democracies, with oligarchies and tyrannies being premised on hierarchy. If oligarchies acknowledged equality at all, it was a special, "geometric" form of equality, according to which people who were "worth" more (usually in terms of wealth) thereby deserved more representation in the political system. Democrats, who claimed to treat all citizens equally, practiced a contrasting "arithmetical" form of equality.[4] Others have acknowledged that even before the onset of democracy there was a strongly egalitarian current in Archaic Greek culture, but they do not tend to extend the analysis past the sixth century.[5] Less remarked upon has been the continued importance of equality among oligarchs during the Classical period. In fact, I will argue that oligarchs were much more sensitive to discrepancies in political power between any two members of the ruling class than democracies were to discrepancies between their citizens. In democracies, political power was diluted among a much greater swathe of the population, and the relative weakness of any one member of the demos was compensated for by the corporate power of the demos assembled in the *ekklēsia*.[6] In oligarchies, by contrast, a much smaller pool of

---

3. There are many additional power-sharing mechanisms that arguably stabilized oligarchy. Most of them were developed during the Archaic period, including the rotation of offices, overlapping powers, and short terms of office. See the discussion of Harris 2006: 301–312, citing numerous examples from *Nomima* and Koerner. Since scholars have covered these Archaic institutions elsewhere, I prefer to focus on Classical-era sources.

4. For democracy and equality, see Robinson 1997: 13–14, 36, 53–55, 2011: 223, 228; Hansen 1999: 81–85; Edge 2009 *passim*. Arithmetic vs. geometric equality: Harvey 1965.

5. Vernant 1982; Walter 1993; Morris 1996; Raaflaub 1996; Raaflaub and Wallace 2007; Ober 2015: 128–55.

6. See Dem. 21.140: "Because of this you should unite, that each one of you is weaker when

men shared effective power, with the result that each oligarch possessed comparatively greater influence. Since even minor swings in power among members of this group might inspire individuals to try to overthrow the regime, it was absolutely crucial that power be equalized as much as possible and that this arrangement be scrupulously maintained. These considerations had been overriding during the Archaic period, but they became even more important following the introduction of democracy as a constitutional alternative. After that point, the danger was no longer limited to the damage that might accrue from one man's (or one group's) increase in power, for a significant *decrease* in one oligarch's power might lead the disgraced individual to ally with the demos in order to restore lost face.[7]

Thus, unsurprisingly, the earliest statements of oligarchic theory acknowledge both the need for equality within the ruling elite and the dangers stemming from excessive competition among them. During the "Constitutional Debate," for example, Herodotus has Darius criticize oligarchy on these grounds: "In an oligarchy intense hatreds [*echthea*] arise when many are striving for preeminence [*aretē*] in political affairs [*to koinon*]; for each one wishes to be chief [*koruphaios*] and to be victorious with his proposals, and so they end up falling into great feuds [*echthea megala*] with each other."[8] Kurke has explored the importance of this statement for understanding relations among the elite in oligarchies, as evidenced, for example, by the ideological concerns of choral lyric poetry.[9] Athletic victors from oligarchic poleis are often exhorted in epinician song to shun hubris, enjoy moderation, and turn their minds toward civic peace.[10] Thucydides's oligarchic Thebans likewise emphasize their distance from tyranny and *dunasteia*, applying to their *oligarchia* a concept normally associated with democracy in the fifth century, *isonomia* or "equality under the law."[11] Another set of oligarchs in Thucydides falls prey to the tendencies outlined by Herodotus: the members of the Four Hundred, he

---

it comes to allies or resources or the like, but united you are stronger than each of these things and can put a stop to *hubris*." Cf. Arist. *Pol.* 3.1281a42-b7, b34-37, 1282a14-17, 34-38, 1283b30-33.

7. See chapter 6, esp. section 6.2.3.

8. Hdt. 3.82.3. For the "Constitutional Debate," see chapter 1, section 1.1.3.

9. Kurke 2007: 77–79.

10. See, e.g., Pind. *Ol.* 7.90–92 (oligarchic Rhodes), *Pyth.* 8.1–13 (Aegina), 11.50–58 (Thebes), *Isthm.* 6.71 (Aegina), fr. 52a S-M (Thebes), fr. 109 (Thebes). For the public presentation of these statements in oligarchic poleis, see chapter 5, section 5.2.

11. Thuc. 3.62.3. Most likely this word originated in democracies and was primarily associated with them (as at Thuc. 6.38.5), but the essence of the idea did look back to Archaic elite values. The point of applying *isonomos* to *oligarchia* in the immediate context is to show that the *dunasteia* in power during the Persian Wars did not represent the political community. Democracies can safely be assumed to fulfill such a requirement, and so the speaker feels no need to

says, "thanks to their private ambitions [*philotimia*], inclined toward the thing that most often destroys an oligarchy that arises out of a democracy: for they all immediately wanted, not to be equal [*isoi*], but that each one actually be foremost [*polu prōtos*]."[12] Had the Four Hundred been more experienced at controlling competition among themselves, they might have lasted considerably longer. As it was, their sudden ascension to power under an oligarchy unleashed the feelings of individual superiority that they had nurtured under democracy.[13]

Several sources from the fourth century and later underscore the equality required for stable oligarchy. Isocrates cites this characteristic of oligarchies as a reason why they, along with democracies, are in fact inferior to monarchies: "Oligarchies and democracies require equal relations [*tas isotētas*] for those that share in the constitution, and the idea that no one should be able to have more than another man takes precedence among them."[14] These comments ought to make us take seriously Demosthenes's description of the apportionment of power under oligarchies, which we might otherwise dismiss as ideologically biased: "Constitutions governed by a few people are made harmonious [*homonoein*] by the fact that those who have control over political affairs [*hoi tōn koinōn kurioi*] all possess equal power [*echein ison*] to one another."[15] As we see in the epigraph to this chapter, the author of the pseudo-Plutarchan treatise "On Monarchy, Democracy, and Oligarchy" observes that the ideal oligarchic politician must "harmonize" himself with his colleagues, men of "equal power" (*isokrateis*) and "like honor" (*homotimoi*). If there is ever the need to pressure the others to adopt his policies, he must do it "gently" (literally, with *hēsuchia*, a word commonly associated with oligarchy).

---

qualify *dēmokratia* with *isonomos*. Only certain kinds of oligarchy count as *isonomos*, however. See futher Ostwald 2000: 25; Vlastos 1953: 347; Brock 1991; 169.

12. Thuc. 8.89.3. For the importance of this passage in explaining oligarchic breakdown, see further chapter 6, section 6.2.2.

13. Thucydides explains that one reason they had a difficult time cooperating was that each man had an inflated sense of his own self-worth: if he was ever defeated in the awarding of honors under democracy, he attributed his failure to the fact that his judges, the demos, were inferior to him and incapable of recognizing true talent (8.89.3: the contest was "not fair"). Somewhat ironically, then, it seems that democracy was more stable than oligarchy in the sense that oligarchs took losses less bitterly under the former because they considered the results absurd. For the corresponding intensity of oligarchic political elections, see the passage from the *Rhetoric to Alexander* discussed below.

14. Isoc. 3.15. Isocrates also has Nicocles complain of the quarreling that goes on in oligarchies: 3.18, 19.

15. Dem. 20.108. Note that this statement follows a description of the Spartan ephorate, which Demosthenes considers an oligarchic institution.

The passage indicates clearly how sensitive some oligarchs could be to perceived insults to their equal status and honor. Intriguingly, the adjective *isokratēs* used here is extremely rare and connected exclusively with oligarchy in political contexts.[16]

Oligarchies thus possessed an intense need for equality (and for institutions that could secure that equality). Before examining these institutions in detail, we should note the special character of oligarchic equality. In the following sections it will become clear that the "equality" under discussion is not the sort that sees all citizens as essentially interchangeable and thus gives rise to the "one person, one vote" phenomenon, accompanied by simple majoritarianism.[17] Oligarchic equality is fiercely individualistic, with each oligarch viewing himself as indispensable *qua* concrete personality, as a man whose personal qualities bestow on him unique worth.[18] Moreover, the typical oligarch was a man who could retaliate violently if he felt his honor was slighted. Thus the institutions surveyed here were not necessarily implemented because they respected each and every individual out of principle, but because communal decision-making might devolve into bloody chaos. They were far more practical than ideological and concerned ultimately with controlling violence. Oligarchies lacked the positive, mediating input of the demos as a tool for arbitrating between elite disputes. To make matters worse, they vested power in the hands of precisely those men with the greatest capacity for aggression. The need for effective institutions as a constraint on elite action was thus acute.[19]

---

16. Plut. *Mor.* 827b. For *isokratēs/isokratia*, see also Hdt. 5.92α (describing oligarchic Corinth) and the discussion of Ostwald 1973, reprinted as 2009: ch. 2. It is not difficult to see why, in addition to the considerations cited in the present discussion, the concept of "equality of power" was associated with oligarchy. In a democracy, power (*kratos*) was imagined as belonging to a unitary entity, the demos. There was no need for this power to be "equal" since it was undivided. In an oligarchy, by contrast, the concern is to divide power among irreducibly multiple individuals.

17. For the emergence of majority voting in ancient Greece, see now the authoritative discussion of Flaig 2013; earlier studies include Larsen 1949; Ruzé 1984; Schwartzberg 2010.

18. Anderson's picture (2009 and 2015) of the Greek state, conceived of as a corporate personality in the form of "the Demos," is thus too Athenocentric. Athens may have believed in the existence of "a" supraindividual Demos, but the ruling individuals in oligarchies were distinctive personalities. This is probably one reason (outside of reasons of popularity) that oligarchy was rarely depicted in art, while the Demos was frequently represented as a single male figure (above, chapter 1, section 1.2.4).

19. For the similar problems faced by contemporary authoritarian regimes, see Svolik 2012: 86–88. According to Svolik, "authoritarian elites operate under distinctively toxic conditions . . . widespread secrecy, the absence of an independent authority that can enforce mutual agree-

2.2 Regulating Political Procedure
2.2.1 Veto Points

If oligarchs truly were insistent on their individual self-worth, we should expect a comparatively large number of *veto points* within their institutions. Veto points allow for the unilateral rejection, by a minority, of a policy favored by the majority, when the minority's numbers reach a certain threshold. Indeed, some veto points, like a filibuster in the modern-day United States Senate, invest a single individual with the power to nullify a proposal favored by fifty-nine Senators. Veto points thus have the effect of promoting "status quo bias": it is extremely difficult to change the reigning consensus except by a new, super majoritarian consensus. Political systems heavy in veto points will therefore exhibit greater overall conservatism, in the sense that they will not tend to pursue novel policies.[20] We can see immediately that veto points would serve the interests of competitive oligarchs quite well. When a minority can insulate itself from the decisions of the majority, each man will consider his personal position better protected.

The conscious employment of veto points appears in the oligarchic constitution of the Boeotian *koinon* that emerged after 447.[21] This federal oligarchy was created after the Boeotian defeat of Athens at Coronea; before this, following their military loss at Oenophyta in 457/6, the Boeotian cities had been under the control of the Athenian empire.[22] The available evidence suggests that the Athenians had at first installed democratic regimes in the poleis of Boeotia. At least some of these democracies proved "anarchic," however, and oligarchies took over, with Athenian consent. This partial re-oligarchization

---

ments, and the ever-present potential for violence generate commitment problems that may undermine the stability of authoritarian rule" (86). One solution is political institutions that foster "greater transparency" among regime members and "facilitate the detection of... noncompliance" (87). For institutions in most pre-modern states as being concerned with managing violence among the elite, see North, Wallis, and Weingast 2009.

20. For the importance of veto points in politics, see Tsebelis 2002.

21. There is a curious case of vetoing from (presumably) democratic Tarentum. Although the majority of the assembly was in favor of one proposal, the general, Dinon, apparently utilizing some kind of veto power, ratified the motion of the minority, saying in the process either "this [his hand] is stronger" or "these [hands] are better" (Plut. *Mor.* 301c = *QG* 42 = Theophrastus F 624 Fortenbaugh).

22. Thuc. 1.113.2–4. For the *koinon*, see esp. Glotz 1908; Cloché 1952; Larsen 1955; Roesch 1965; Bruce 1967: 102–109 and appendix II; Moore 1975: 125–34; Gehrke *Stasis* 164–72 and appendix VIII; Cook 1988; Buck 1994: 9–10; Hanson 1995: 207–10; Cartledge 2000b; Müller 2010: 226–28; Mackil 2013: 22–46.

inspired certain oligarchs who had been exiled from the democratic poleis to attempt to reclaim all of Boeotia. When they defeated the Athenians at Coronea, they got their wish.[23] Since the elites in this scenario effectively had carte blanche to institute their preferred policies, we should expect some constitutional innovation. Before the discovery of the fragmentary *Hellenica Oxyrhynchia* in 1906, comparatively little was known about the regime: it was an oligarchy, albeit one whose proponents, as we have seen, called it *isonomos*, and it had eleven officials called Boeotarchs, who could propose policies to the "four councils of the Boeotians, who held sovereignty."[24] The *Hellenica* now tells us substantially more. Not only the federal system, but each city within the *koinon* had four councils, "in which it was not possible for all the citizens to participate, but only those who possessed a certain amount of money; and each [of the four councils] would in turn convene and deliberate in advance [*probouleuousa*] about policy before introducing [*eispheren*] its proposals to the three, and whatever was decided [*doxeien*] by all of them [*hapasais*] became valid [*kurion*]."[25]

In chapter 1 I discussed the meaning of the phrase "certain amount of money," showing that it does not imply a so-called "hoplite census."[26] Here I wish to focus on the decision-making rules of the councils. It is worth noting at the outset that there is absolutely no mention in the *Hellenica* of an institution within the *koinon* corresponding to a popular assembly. When given the opportunity to remake their constitution with a free hand, the Boeotian oligarchs dispensed with a meeting-place for the demos entirely.[27] As we will see in chapter 3, oligarchies sometimes retained popular assemblies but manipulated their proceedings.[28] The Boeotians, by contrast, eliminated all opportunity for participation by the demos.

---

23. Democracies imposed: perhaps implied by Thuc. 1.108.3. Anarchic democracy at Thebes: Arist. *Pol.* 5.1302b29–30. Athenian toleration of restored oligarchies: [Xen.] *Ath. Pol.* 3.11. Emboldened oligarchic exiles: Thuc. 1.113.2; Hellanicus *FGrH* 4 F 81. Reconstructions by Gomme *HCT* 1: 317–18; Hornblower *ad locc.*; Cartledge 2000b: 403.

24. The information comes almost exclusively from Thucydides: 2.2.1, 3.62.3, 4.91, 5.31.6, 5.38.2, 7.30.3.

25. *Hell. Oxy.* 19.2 Chambers.

26. See chapter 1, section 1.2.

27. Cf. Andrewes in *HCT* 5: 325; Robinson 2011: 55. By contrast, a Theban *halia* (assembly) is known from an earlier time (Hdt. 5.79.2). Some have supposed that Boeotians who did not meet the property requirement could still vote on candidates for the council (e.g., Cartledge 2000b: 404; Moore 1975: 129). But the historian's words imply that meeting the property requirement sufficed for participation in the councils: it was not an elective but a rotation-based position.

28. Chapter 3, section 3.2.

It might be objected that an equivalent of an assembly remains within the constitution, in the form of a plenary session of the four councils. Some scholars believe that each of the four councils took its turn acting as a probouleutic body before delivering opinions to the other three councils gathered together. This assembled oligarchic body would then decide on measures by majority vote.[29] But if that were the case, we would expect there to be one body of oligarchs, within which one quarter served as *probouloi* or preliminary councilors for a portion of the year.[30] Instead, the insistence on four separate councils strongly suggests that they remained distinct throughout the process. The Oxyrhynchus historian's words "whatever seemed good to all of them" must mean that they proposed their policies to the other councils separately, and that what was decided by majority vote by each and every council was passed.[31]

In keeping the four councils separate, the Boeotian oligarchs seem to have been taking precautions against the potential danger of their own numbers, lest their meetings take on a "mob mentality." In this respect their actions are in line with the anxiety expressed by some members of the Four Hundred at Athens that a meeting of the Five Thousand would amount to an "outright demos."[32] Even oligarchs were in danger of becoming "democratic" in their disorder if too many of them assembled at one time.[33] Looked at in this way, the Boeotian rotating council scheme accomplished the same thing as other oligarchies, but by different means. In other oligarchic regimes, the norm seems to have been a single powerful council, which, however, could accommodate only part of the ruling class at any one time.

---

29. So Rhodes 1993: 393; Cartledge 2000b: 404.

30. Cf. Corinth as described by Nicolaus of Damascus (*FGrH* 90 F 60), with its council of 80 with 8 *probouloi*. (In this case, however, 80 presumably does not exhaust the total number of those eligible to serve, but is instead an office allotted from a group of all those meeting a property requirement. The similarity to the Theban case, however, lies in the fact that the deliberative body is not allowed to be too large.)

31. If the "constitution for the future" in the *Ath. Pol.* (30) is based on the Boeotian system, its lack of a plenary session (noted by Rhodes 1993: 396) is further evidence that the *koinon* lacked an assembly. For this interpretation of the probouleusis process, see Bruce 1967: 103, 158. The *diagramma* of Cyrene left a very few decisions to be decided by its *politeuma*, the Ten Thousand, presumably gathered in assembly (*SEG* 9.1, lines 29–30, 35). The *politeuma* of the Three Thousand at Athens in 404/3 met as a group only under emergency conditions; most of the time they were content to appoint plenipotentiary magistrates ([Arist.] *Ath. Pol.* 38.1).

32. Thuc. 8.92.11.

33. For oligarchic complaints about the disorder and ineptitude of democratic assemblies, see below, section 2.2.2, and chapter 5, section 5.1.

Oligarchs rotated in and out of the council by allotment or election. In Boeotia, the oligarchs figured out a way to be active citizens all of the time (with the probouleutic council being especially active), while avoiding the problem of large, chaotic meetings.[34]

Another important aspect of the four Boeotian councils is the extreme conservatism embodied in the institution of multiple veto points. Some scholars have considered it incredible that the Boeotians would be so cautious as to allow each council the chance to reject a probouleutic proposal.[35] After all, in a simple majority-vote system the so-called "median voter" has veto power, or rather pivotal importance.[36] In the Boeotian system, by contrast, there was a distinct chance that one of the councils, whether due to random allotment or self-sorting, would contain a much more conservative electorate than the four councils taken together. Legislation would thus have to be crafted with an eye to avoiding the veto power of a potentially much more conservative median voter. However, we should think of this not as an ideological preference for conservatism *per se* but, in line with what I said above, as a stabilizing measure. Boeotia had previously been torn apart by intra-elite *stasis*, which invited anarchy and foreign domination. The oligarchic *koinon* established after Coronea, however, seems to have been much more stable: it is praised by one of the Boeotarchs, Pagondas, as having afforded them "great security" (*pollēn adeian*) down to 424.[37] As an oligarchic regime that sat atop a discontented demos, the Boeotian *koinon* required both minimally satisfactory relations with the demos itself and harmony among the active members of the oligarchic class.[38] By requiring what were in effect super-majority votes for all policies, *koinon* institutions at the local level helped to secure this intra-elite consensus and decrease the likelihood of *stasis*.[39]

---

34. For oligarchic complaints about the boisterousness of democratic assemblies, see chapter 5, section 5.1.

35. See Moore 1975: 130: "to give the right of veto to one quarter of the legislative body would be very cautious."

36. For the importance of the "median voter" in an electoral system, see Black 1958; Krehbiel 1988.

37. Thuc. 4.92.6. See Hornblower *ad loc.*, who inclines towards Gehrke's view (*Stasis* 166n16) that the *stasis* meant is internal conflict, not inter-polis conflict (cf. Arist. *Rhet.* 3.1407a2–6, which allows for either possibility).

38. Evidence for democratic discontent within the oligarchic *koinon*: Thuc. 6.95.2 (an unsuccessful uprising of the Thespian demos against the ruling oligarchs in 414).

39. In the end, the institutional attempt at staving off *stasis* and democratization failed: see chapter 6, section 6.2.1.

2.2.2 Consensus-Building

Elsewhere we see safeguards that are not so much attempts to institute formal veto points as measures that use the potential afforded by small deliberative bodies to reach broader agreement through intensive discussion.[40] Throughout history, advocates of "representative" as opposed to bare "majoritarian" government have championed the ability of smaller, less directly accountable groups to set aside constituents' demands in order to compromise for the sake of the common good.[41] In many ways, this sentiment extends back to the small, oligarchic councils of Archaic and Classical Greece. In the ancient context, however, the practice of keeping debate closed to the public and of deliberating at length originated more from the need to preserve oligarchy than from any lofty political ideal.[42] To be sure, we see instances where oligarchic councils were sharply divided, resulting in *stasis*, but in the usual course of business, procedure allowed for a deliberative environment that encouraged greater assent.[43] That there was a normative assumption that oligarchic deliberation should proceed in this way comes through in Critias's statement that the Spartan ephorate was expected to arrive at consensus: "If one of the ephors, instead of obeying the majority, tried to find fault with the institution and oppose what was being done, do you not think that he would be considered worthy of the greatest punishment by the ephors themselves as well as by the entire city?"[44] Of course, in this instance Critias has an interest in painting Theramenes's lone opposition to the rest of the Thirty as a punishable offense. Yet his statement might contain a kernel of truth, in that through open-ended debate an oligarchic deliberative body might arrive at a decision

---

40. Recent works on consensus-building (as well as on dissent) in ancient Greece include Flaig 2013; Elmer 2013; Barker 2009; Johnstone 2011: 116–21.

41. Perhaps most famously, Burke says in his "Speech to the Electors of Bristol" that "Parliament is not a *congress* of ambassadors from different and hostile interests; which interests each must maintain, as an agent and advocate, against other agents and advocates; but parliament is a *deliberative* assembly of *one* nation, with *one* interest, that of the whole" (emphasis in original). In other words, elected officials must use their supposedly more refined judgment to arrive at policies they commonly think best, rather than decide among competing interests and visions of government by majority vote. See Manin 1997: 203–4.

42. For the need for secrecy in oligarchies, see chapter 5, section 5.1.

43. For divided oligarchies see, e.g., Corinth in the early fourth century (*Hell. Oxy.* 10.2–3 Chambers; Xen. *Hell.* 4.4.1–13; Diod. Sic. 14.86) and Thebes at the same time (*Hell. Oxy.* 17.1 Chambers; Xen. *Hell.* 5.2.25; Plut. *Pel.* 5.1–2); see further the discussions in chapter 6, sections 6.1.1 and 6.2.1, respectively.

44. Xen. *Hell.* 2.3.34. The example gains in credibility not from its use of Sparta, which was an atypical oligarchy, but from the fact that it is issued by the arch-oligarch Critias.

that satisfied a high number of participants—*all* in the case of the Spartan ephorate, but probably fewer (simply some super-majority) in a more typical oligarchy.⁴⁵

This was also the ideal held up by the symposium, which, like politics, was considered a form of speaking "to the middle" (*eis to meson*).⁴⁶ The communal drinking party, which took place almost exclusively between members of the Greek elite, was clearly an opportunity for socialization, trust-building, and the forging of political ties.⁴⁷ The poet of *Theognidea* 493–96 counsels his fellow symposiasts to "speak well as you wait beside the mixing bowl, holding off at length from quarrels [*eris*] with one another, speaking to the middle [*eis to meson*] to one and all alike: in this way the symposium turns out pleasantly." Similarly an anonymous elegist whose words are preserved on papyrus orders all to "let seriousness follow [*sc.* playfulness], and let us listen to the speakers in turn, for this is the highest form [*aretē*] of the symposium. And let us obey the symposiarch: this is what good men do, and it produces the best deliberation."⁴⁸ Here men of leisure are expected to prove their discretion and magnanimity by yielding time to all in turn. The aggregate result is a deliberation that pleases everyone. Conveniently, this ideal dovetails with the political need to avoid partisan decisions and protracted feuds. The official appointed to regulate procedure, the symposiarch, who comes from the ranks of the symposiasts themselves but serves only for a short time, even mirrors the presiding officials and eponymous magistrates familiar from Archaic Greek deliberative bodies.⁴⁹ The symposium and oligarchic governance are thus in several important ways mirror images of each other.

---

45. Cf. Barros 2002: 75–76, discussing consensus-based features of the authoritarian constitution of Pinochet's Chile (and cf. the remarks above, section 2.1, about oligarchic equality): "Historically, unanimous decision-making has been used in situations in which actors could not conceive of a general corporate unity apart from the individuals or units forming a given association; in these situations, no collective will could exist if any member dissented. In such contexts, where the strong sense of individuality among the constituent units precludes any use of majority rule, unanimity provides a mechanism that assures that outcomes do not violate the component individual interests."

46. For what follows, see especially Wecowski 2014; Hobden 2013; Corner 2010: 358–61; Schmitt Pantel 1990. As Vernant (1982: 47–48) and Detienne (1996: 91–102) have shown, "the middle" was an extremely important political and social concept for the Archaic Greek elite.

47. Fisher 2000b has argued for widespread access to the symposium even for lower-class members of the demos under the Classical Athenian democracy. The Athenians may in fact have achieved this, but the symposium certainly originated among the elite and was primarily an elite phenomenon across the wider Greek world.

48. Adesp. Eleg. fr. 27.7–10 West.

49. See, e.g., Koerner no. 27, line 2: "the council presided over by Ariston."

In the age of democracy, some members of the elite contrasted the symposium's form of speaking *eis to meson* with the extended demagogic harangues that rhetors bandied back and forth in the assembly.[50] We should note especially a strand of imagery along these lines from Plato's *Protagoras*. The participants and spectators in the debate between Socrates and Protagoras are first said by Callias to constitution a *sunhedrion*, or political gathering.[51] Later Socrates complains that Protagoras's long-winded speeches remind him of Pericles in the assembly.[52] Finally, the two agree to settle into a controlled debate. The sophist Hippias sets up the contest using sociopolitical terminology: Socrates and Protagoras should not "be at odds with each other like the lowliest scum [*phaulotatoi*]: I implore you and advise you, Protagoras and Socrates, to come together, as though we were arbitrators [*diaitēteis*] reconciling you in compromise [*eis to meson*] . . . take my advice and choose a referee [*rhabdouchos*] or chairman [*epistatēs*] or presiding officer [*prytanis*] who will ensure a moderate length for each of your speeches."[53] The political subtext here implies that the ideal for the philosophical participant who is not "lowly" (*phaulos*) is to mimic the practices of elite political bodies, which through their cloistered, controlled atmosphere avoid the clamor (*thorubos*) of the democratic assembly and allow "good" men with shared interests to hammer out their differences peacefully.[54] The *prytanis* appointed to monitor the debate completes the circle of oligarchic symposium (with its symposiarch), deliberative council, and elite philosophical discourse. The point in each case is to preserve order through the institutionalization of turn-taking and patience, as opposed to the boisterousness of the *ekklēsia*.[55]

50. Thus I would say the notion of "the middle" was politically contested; it was not the preserve of any one group but was claimed by competing ideologies.

51. Plat. *Prot.* 317d. Denyer *ad loc.* points out Callias's pretentiousness here, noting that *sunhedrion* "is generally restricted to the grander sorts of 'sitting together.'"

52. Plat. *Prot.* 329a.

53. Plat. *Prot.* 338b.

54. For a similar discussion of the sociopolitical origins of philosophical discourse, see Nightingale 1995: 55–59, on *banausia* and *philosophia*.

55. Thucydides's Melian Dialogue likewise establishes connections between democracy and lengthy speeches, oligarchy and back-and-forth debate: 5.84–85. There is an element of irony here, however, since the closed atmosphere of the dialogue cannot ultimately save the Melians, whose fate has been determined in advance (see Macleod 1974: 389). For the Melian Dialogue as "oligarchic," see further Geddes 2007:134, who compares it to Ion of Chios *FGrH* 392 F 6 and 13 (concerning Sophocles and Cimon, and both, coincidentally, occurring within the context of the symposium): "Thucydides, in his sympathy for these [Melian] oligarchs, is drawing particular attention to the difference in decision-making between oligarchy and democracy, exemplified by the calm private discussion as opposed to the oratory delivered in the assembly."

2.2.3 The Secret Ballot

A final method of maintaining equality and defusing tension in oligarchic political procedure was the secret ballot.[56] In chapter 3 I will show how oligarchs could take advantage of open voting in the assembly to intimidate the demos into accepting its proposals.[57] When it came to their own decisions, however, the position of oligarchs often seems to have been, "the secret ballot for me but not for thee." Because of their smaller numbers, the separate votes of individual oligarchs on issues were rendered more conspicuous. In some instances this fact could be taken by oligarchs themselves to be a good thing. The Old Oligarch, for example, notes with a certain class-based pride than in oligarchies "it is necessary to stick to one's alliances and oaths: if they do not abide by their agreements, the names of the few people who established them in the first place are known to the mistreated party."[58] In other words, the identifiability of the voting parties puts pressure on them to maintain their agreements, since there would be no point in trying to deny responsibility. In democracies, by contrast, even though the demos is ultimately responsible *qua* voting majority, its members can break treaties at will and transfer blame onto individual rhetors on the grounds that they did not personally agree with the decision at the time.[59] To some extent the Old Oligarch's statement about oligarchic fidelity to agreements is correct, but he neglects to consider what could happen to oligarchies in situations of higher risk. When individual oligarchs' names became strongly associated with specific policies, those individuals were often left with few means of extricating themselves from blame if changed circumstances rendered their positions unpopular within the oligarchy. When this fact was combined with the strong tendency of members of the elite to try to punish their personal enemies by any and all means possible, it could produce a situation in which an oligarch on the losing side of a policy position felt he had no other option but to orchestrate a democratic revolution in order to save himself.[60]

The secret ballot could lessen the chances of this outcome for the same reason that hidden voting set at ease the mind of the average Athenian democratic judge: secrecy removed the ability of bystanders and fellow judges to associate him with, and thus hold him accountable for, the result of the trial.[61]

---

56. For a slightly different perspective, this time on individual vote-counting (secret and otherwise), see Schwartzberg 2010.

57. See in particular section 3.2.

58. [Xen.] *Ath. Pol.* 2.17. The text is corrupt but the sense is clear.

59. [Xen.] *Ath. Pol.* 2.17; Thuc. 2.61.2, 8.1.1.

60. See chapter 6, section 6.2.3, but also 6.1.1 for the situation in Corinth in 393.

61. For "bystanders" and secret voting, see Lanni 1997, esp. 186–87. Demosthenes praises the

The actual evidence for oligarchies utilizing the secret ballot is slim but important. The relevant source here is the *Rhetoric to Alexander*, a fourth-century text attributed in antiquity to Aristotle but probably written by the sophist Anaximenes of Lampsacus.[62] The *Rhetoric* recommends that in oligarchies, "the majority of political offices should be assigned by lot, but the most important should be determined by the secret ballot [*kruptē psēphos*] accompanied by oaths [*horkoi*] and the utmost strictness [*akribeia*]."[63] Here we see the explicit differentiation between high- and low-stakes scenarios neglected by the Old Oligarch. The author recognizes that the more prestigious the office, the more likely it is that a disgruntled loser, seizing upon some perceived corruption in the vote-counting, will react violently to the result. The potentially deadly stakes of such a situation are indicated by the recourse to oath-taking and extremely strict procedure (presumably when it comes to counting). Voting by secret ballot, however, defuses the twin dangers that candidates will be able to pick out their enemies and that voters will feel exposed.[64] It allows oligarchs to register their preference, which they no doubt felt was indispensable, without having to worry that they might be targeted for recrimination. It is unclear to what extent oligarchies institutionalized the secret ballot, but we can see why the author of the *Rhetoric* considers it so important.[65]

---

anonymity of the secret ballot at 19.239. Another example of secret voting performed for similar reasons is the decision of Acanthus to secede from the Athenian empire: Thuc. 4.88.1.

62. For the attribution of this text to Anaximenes, see the *Oxford Classical Dictionary* (3rd rev. ed.) s.v. "Anaximenes (2)." The text thus represents a non-Aristotelian fourth-century political treatise. For the importance of this text for understanding Classical oligarchy, see *IACP* 83: "probably the most important impartial account of *oligarchia*, although it is mostly overlooked." I try to rectify this shortcoming in the scholarly literature by employing the *Rhet. ad Alex.* extensively: see further below, section 2.4; chapter 4, section 4.3. Every one of the handful of sentences of the *Rhetoric* devoted to oligarchy illustrates a crucial point about oligarchic institutions.

63. [Arist.] *Rhet. ad Alex.* 1424b1–3. The passage is admittedly about electing magistrates rather than voting for policy in a council, but an election held in an oligarchic deliberative body is itself a kind of vote on policy, in that one is choosing candidates who might favor specific positions. I assume that by "secret vote" the author means the vote of the oligarchs themselves, not that of the wider demos; this is confirmed by his earlier statement that in democracies the highest offices are to be elected specifically "by the vote of the multitude" (1424a15–16).

64. Recall that oligarchs living under democracy seem not to have cared which people voted for them, since they considered the whole contest a farce (Thuc. 8.89.3, discussed above).

65. The Spartan gerousia apparently did not utilize the secret ballot, since the individual votes of a trial against King Pausanias were known to Pausanias the periegete (3.5.2); cf. Plut. *Agis* 11.1.

2.3 Monitoring Private Expenditure: Sumptuary Legislation

Beyond strict political procedure, some oligarchies seem also to have implemented sumptuary legislation as a means of maintaining intra-elite equality. Laws of this kind include the curbing of "excess" mourning at funerals, the regulation of ostentation (including clothing), and the scrutinizing of private gatherings such as symposia.[66] Some historians have plausibly wondered whether such measures represented an attempt on the part of the common people to foist a more egalitarian lifestyle upon the elite.[67] Yet on this point I am in agreement with those scholars who have argued that sumptuary laws more likely originated from among the ranks of the elite themselves, as a form of self-regulation and equality-maintenance. Hawke, in particular, notes the enormous fortunes specified in the funerary law from Iulis on Ceos.[68] On this basis he convincingly argues that the law was meant to apply to the very wealthy alone, as a means of preventing them from sparking feuds among themselves as they buried their dead. Hawke sees a similar *raison d'être* behind Solon's funerary legislation:

> By turning the burial of the important dead into a public event, the members of an aristocratic family could have advertised the greatness of their household... and used an emotionally charged setting to proclaim their own importance and... slander their enemies.... Solon recognized the danger of these festivities to the *precarious equilibrium* among the groups who wielded power in Athens and sought to eliminate them.[69]

Sumptuary legislation, on this account, amounts to an effort on the part of the elite to protect themselves against their own worst excesses.

According to this study's understanding of the origins and development of oligarchy, sumptuary legislation ought to have become more important during the Classical era. Whereas Archaic-age elites sought to prevent tyranny and *stasis* alone, oligarchs of the fifth and fourth centuries also had to guard

---

66. See generally Bernhardt 2003; also Garland 1985, 1989; Morris 1987: 50–52; Toher 1991; Sourvinou-Inwood 1995; van Wees 2009: 462–63. Epigraphic instances include Arnaoutoglou nos. 109–110.

67. See esp. Morris 1987: 50–52; Osborne 1996: 84.

68. Koerner no. 60 (trans. Arnaoutoglou, no. 109).

69. Hawke 2011: 180, 181 (emphasis added); cf. Forsdyke 2005: 24–25; Blok 2006: 234–35 (although elsewhere she disagrees that Solon's funerary legislation had anything to do with reining in ostentation). For Solon's funerary legislation, see Plut. *Sol*. 21.4–5. An Archaic law from Arcadia prevents the wearing of bright clothes by a woman in public; the penalty is banishment (*SEG* 11.1112; see Osborne 1997: n19 for a translation). This also looks like an attempt at self-regulation, enforced by a magistrate, the *damiorgos*.

against the threatening specter of democracy. Aristotle does in fact give the impression that oligarchies, much more than democracies, employed magistrates for purposes along these lines. In his discussion of the different political offices, he asserts that some are clearly not "populist" (*dēmotikai*), including those having to do with the regulation of women (*gunaikonomia*) and of children (*paidonomia*). Other offices, which for Aristotle represent an attempt to maintain "good order" (*eukosmia*), are the guardianship of the laws (*nomophulakia*), the gymnasiarchy, and the regulation of the Dionysian games.[70]

These offices were by no means limited to oligarchies, especially during the Hellenistic period.[71] Nor is *eukosmia* a strictly oligarchic virtue, as numerous democratic sources attest.[72] Nonetheless, we do see the offices enumerated by Aristotle at work in a specifically oligarchic context: namely, the regime of Demetrius of Phalerum at Athens, 317–307.[73] Demetrius enacted a set of regu-

---

70. *Pol.* 6.1322b37–1323a6. Elsewhere he says that the *gunaikonomoia* is fit neither for democracies nor oligarchies: in the former poor women cannot be stopped from leaving the house due to economic necessity (but could they ever?), while in the latter the wives of oligarchs cannot be controlled because they live in luxury (4.1300a6–8). Sumptuary legislation may have been difficult to impose under oligarchy, but it does not seem to have been impossible (see below on Demetrius of Phalerum).

71. In the Classical period, we see *gunaikonomoi* at Samos in the first half of the fourth century: *IG* XII.6 461. (Note that this could potentially overlap with the oligarchic regime that worshipped Lysander, for which see chapter 5, section 5.2.3.) They are also present in Thasos during what was clearly a democratic period (Fournier and Hamon 2007 = *SEG* 57.820, publishing a new fragment of a Thasian democratic decree instituting public support for war orphans). In the Hellenistic period, we see *paidonomoi* and *gunaikonomoi* in Magnesia in the early second century: *IK Magnesia* 98.18–20. *Nomophulakes* appear in Aeolis in the late third/early second century: *SEG* 34.1238. *Gunaikonomoi* play a prominent role in the cult regulations from Andania, early first century: *IG* V.1 1390, lines 26–28, 32–33 (on this long inscription, see recently Deshours 2006 and Gawlinski 2012 [esp. 133–34]). On *gunaikonomoi*, see Piolot 2009 (although I disagree with the argument that the magistracy was not begun at Athens under Demetrius). For the gymnasiarchy, see the exhaustive commentary by Gauthier and Hatzopoulos 1993 on an inscription from Beroia in Macedonia from the mid-second century. *Paidonomoi* are infrequently attested during the Classical period, and usually in non-democratic contexts (Xen. *Lac. Pol.* 2.2, 10; Ephorus *FGrH* 70 F 149).

72. For *eukosmia* as a virtue in democratic Athens, see, e.g., Dem. 25.9; Aeschin. 1.8; *IG* II[3] 306, lines 25–26 (the council of 343/2 is praised for overseeing the *eukosmia* of the theater).

73. For its oligarchic status, see Plut. *Demetr.* 10.2; Ferguson 1911; Gehrke 1978; Williams 1985; Banfi 2010; Bayliss 2011: ch. 3; van Wees 2011. *Pace* Tracy 2000: 338 (moderate democracy); O'Sullivan 2009 (see further below). Gehrke 1978 convincingly shows that Demetrius's program was political rather than philosophical, despite the fact that he was a Peripatetic. My point is not that these magistracies need be exclusively oligarchic, only that they functioned in a specific way within oligarchies to maintain stability. Furthermore, the introduction of these offices

lations that almost certainly included *nomophulakes*, meant to regulate the business of the assembly (see below); funerary legislation; and, most importantly for our purposes, *gunaikonomoi*, magistrates who inspected and regulated symposia.[74] The latters' duties included fining extravagant women at drinking parties and limiting the number of participants to thirty people.[75] Lape has suggested that the *gunaikonomoi* were instituted to "inhibit civic solidarity (and therefore potential resistance) by limiting and regulating collective activities" (2004: 52). This may indeed have been one byproduct of the *gunaikonomoi*'s regulation, but their primary function may have been rather to prevent the elite from falling into jealous competition with one another, which in turn could lead to intra-elite *stasis* and the reemergence of democracy.[76] Under democracy, feuding elite symposiasts had no excluded demos to appeal to, and so no regulation was necessary. When the demos became an untapped source of power under oligarchy, however, potentially inflammatory situations like banquets and revels had to be much more strictly monitored.[77]

---

precisely in a moment of transition from democracy to oligarchy suggests that an oligarchy might feel the need for them, if they did not already exist, in a way that democracies did not.

74. For Demetrius' reforms, see Duris FGrH 76 F 10. *Nomophulakes*: Philoch. FGrH 328 F 64; Din. or. 6 fr. 12 Conomis (and see further below). Funerary legislation: Cic. *de leg.* 2.66. *Gunaikonomoi*: see next n.

75. Fining women: Pollux 8.112; Harp. s.v. ὅτι χιλίας. Overseeing symposia: Philoch. FGrH 328 F 65; Timocles fr. 34 Kassel-Austin; Menander fr. 208 K-A; Lynceus of Samos *apud* Athen. 6.245a-c. For the role of the *gunaikonomoi* in Demetrius's regime, see Ferguson 1911: 45–47; Habicht 1997: 55–56; Harding 2007: 169; Banfi 2007.

76. Cf. Wiles (1984: 172), whose focus is also on relations among the elite rather than between elite and demos: "Perhaps it was not the mob that Demetrius feared as much as the resentment of those who ruined themselves by their own extravagance." I argue that the worry was not so much that the rich would bankrupt themselves (although see Arist. *Pol.* 5.1305b39-a9; Antiphon F 73 Pendrick), but that their drinking parties might lead to quarrels between rival groups. Likewise, I find this explanation more likely than the idea that Demetrius's sumptuary legislation "kept the poorer elements of society quiet by restricting their social superiors" (Bayliss 2011: 88).

77. The *gunaikonomoi* raise the difficult question of the role of women in oligarchies, which I will address briefly here. The evidence is very thin and often ideologically charged to the point of gross inaccuracy. We saw that Aristotle thinks the wives of oligarchies are too luxurious (*Pol.* 4.1300a7–8). He also thinks women (along with slaves) prefer life under democracy, since they "live happily" under it, and even enjoy the "rule of women" (*gunaikokratia*) in the household (5.1313b32–38; cf. Plat. *Rep.* 8.563b). As Jameson 1997 has shown, these are tropes of antidemocratic discourse (1993). At the same time, if oligarchies did restrict women's freedom of movement in the name of maintaining order, as suggested here, some women may have

This particularly oligarchic emphasis on sumptuary legislation suggests a surprising generalization: despite the fact that oligarchy was a regime nominally established for the benefit of the elite who ran it, members of the elite may have been much less free in certain respects to do as they pleased with their money and their time under oligarchy than under democracy. Oligarchs' comprehensive need to check both their own behavior and that of the demos in order to decrease the likelihood of *stasis* appears to have forced them in many instances to curtail their private choices for the sake of public order. Oligarchs dreaded the possibility that under democracy their property would be expropriated (or worse), but in the case of a democracy like Athens, at least, the lowered stakes of day-to-day existence provided a secure environment in which investment, economic growth, and "open access" were more attainable than under alternative regimes, as Ober has shown.[78] Of course, not every democracy was like Athens, and the inability of many populations throughout the Greek world to commit credibly to a peaceful democratic transition kept elites on the defensive and committed to the ideal of oligarchy.[79] This wary and reactionary stance on the part of the elite drove them to focus more on the minutiae of decorum (breach of which might result in democracy) than on freely pursuing their own private ends, such as they were.[80]

---

preferred democracy to oligarchy. Women joined the side of the democrats during episodes of civil strife in Plataea and Corcyra (Thuc. 2.4.2, 3.74.1), and they helped in the effort to build democratic Argos's fortifications (Thuc. 5.82.6). On the other hand, the citizen women of oligarchic Phlius congratulate the men after their successful repulsion of democratic exiles (Xen. *Hell.* 7.2.9). Much must unfortunately remain unclear. One wants to know more, for example, about the "most beautiful woman" at Aulon (likely a perioecic community of Sparta) who was "corrupting" Lacedaemonian men who came there; the ephors order her arrest (Xen. *Hell.* 3.3.8). What is certain is that under oligarchy, *stasis* arising from private conflicts (including those concerning women) was much more common: see below, section 2.4, and chapter 6, sections 6.2.2–4.

78. Ober 2008: 257–58, 2015. Not everything is money, of course, and I find it perfectly feasible that many Greek elites were willing to forego the possibility of income growth under democracy for the sake of less tangible goods (honor, pride, class-based satisfaction) under oligarchy.

79. See [Arist.] *Ath. Pol.* 40.3: "in other poleis, those who come to power in a democracy do not continue to make contributions from their own property but instead make a general redistribution of the land." Elite uncertainty about the transition to democracy continues to plague efforts at democratization in the modern world: Acemoglu and Robinson 2006.

80. Oligarchs' closer monitoring of one another's behavior might be evidenced by the Old Oligarch's statement that a "bad man is better able to escape notice in a democratic polis than in an oligarchic one" (2.20; cf. Isoc. 7.47). This is not merely because democracy is "bad" and allows "bad men" to go free, but because people are generally more tolerant and less likely to

As emphasized above, one of the oligarchs' chief political values was equality; freedom, by contrast—or at least the freedom to "live as one liked"—was never their rallying cry.

2.4 Oligarchic Dispute Resolution, in and out of the Courts: Controlling Behavior, Controlling Rhetoric

It was not enough for oligarchies to patrol their citizens' personal behavior in the interest of maintaining equality.[81] They also had to keep a close watch on inter-citizen disputes, particularly those between fellow members of the elite.[82] Disputes that were left untreated threatened to escalate into constitutional crises. Of course, Greeks in general were averse to letting feuds metastasize, and all had been aware since the Archaic period that private quarrels had the potential to disrupt the larger political community.[83] As Herman has argued, Athenians living under the Classical democracy emphasized their willingness to submit personal disputes to the judgment of the demos, who would then ensure a peaceful outcome.[84] It is, however, precisely this fact—of the demos as arbitrator—that afforded the Athenian democracy a "safety valve" for dealing with elite disputes. As much as elites may have resented having to argue their cases in front of their social "inferiors," the existence of an institution like the democratic people's courts (*dikastēria*) provided a safe and largely neutral space in which they could settle their differences. In other words, the demos's role as umpire in elite disputes greatly stabilized democracies.[85]

Ruling elites within an oligarchy lacked such third-party enforcement. Since, in order to preserve their own power, they had to exclude the demos

---

focus on minute details of character when the regime is more stable and the political stakes are lower (cf. Thuc. 2.37.2; Arist. *Pol.* 4.1290a27–29, 6.1317b11–12). "Bad" behavior might also be more readily detected under an oligarchy because the members are few and so can more easily monitor one another.

81. Much of the following argument has been expounded in greater detail in Simonton 2017: 30–42.

82. Oligarchic attempts to regulate their interactions with the demos are treated in chapter 3, section 3.1.3.

83. For dispute resolution in Archaic Greece, see Karachalios 2013; Hawke 2011; Papakonstantinou 2008.

84. Herman 2006. While I think that Herman is correct that the Athenian democracy of the fifth and fourth centuries was extraordinarily stable, I do not follow him in attributing this to a special Athenian "moral and behavioral code." Instead, I locate the reasons for stability and breakdown in the different regime dynamics of democracy and oligarchy.

85. Cf. Ober 1989: 336; Cohen 1995: 193; Redfield 2003: 199.

from all but the most controlled political and judicial participation, oligarchs had no one but themselves to look to for dispute resolution. It was this fact that made the need to resolve disputes so pressing in oligarchies. Oligarchs did not trust the demos with adjudication, and they could barely trust themselves, so emergent struggles had to be identified and settled as quickly as possible.[86] The ancient sources reflect this comparatively greater need within oligarchies. Aristotle in the *Politics* states unequivocally that "it is necessary to be on the lookout for the beginning of such situations [*sc.* disputes], and to settle [*dialuein*] the quarrels [*staseis*] of leaders and powerful men."[87] A fragmentary Vatican manuscript attributed to the philosopher Theophrastus likewise says that "cases which last a long time [*chronizomena*] harm a constitution [*politeia*]."[88] The statement might be taken to apply to all different kinds of regimes, but we should consider a passage from the *Rhetoric to Alexander*: "It is necessary to settle [*dialuein*] the disputes [*diaphorai*] of the citizens as quickly as possible and not let them last a long time [*chronizesthai*]."[89] The language employed by the author of the *Rhetoric* is nearly identical to that of Aristotle and Theophrastus, but the position of this statement in the larger context of the argument is telling. The author conveys this warning in the section of his text on oligarchies, but there is no corresponding passage in the section on democracies.[90]

The particular weaknesses and needs of oligarchic regimes with respect to disputes were thus clear to oligarchs and to those who would advise them politically. The question then is what oligarchs actually did, at the institutional level, to address these concerns. The available evidence reveals several related approaches. One was to empower individual magistrates to intervene directly in citizen disputes in the hopes of quelling them. Cohen has labeled this the

---

86. Aristotle says (*Pol.* 5.1305b33–38) that when the law courts are composed of those outside the ruling political body, oligarchic litigants are forced to play the demagogue to the demotic judges. He has only one example, that of Heraclea Pontica, suggesting that this arrangement did not occur often. For members of the elite as sensitive to the possibility that one of their number will play the demagogue with the common people, see Xen. *An.* 7.6.4 (where, notably, the demos in question is an army of hoplite soldiers).

87. Arist. *Pol.* 5.1303b26–28; cf. 1308a31–35: "It is necessary to guard against the love of strife [*philoneikia*] and the quarrels [*staseis*] of the notables [*gnōrimoi*] using the laws." For *philoneikia* and related terms, which were particularly dangerous for oligarchies, see chapter 6, section 6.2.4.

88. Fr. A, lines 65–68. The text was first edited by Aly 1943 and is discussed by Keaney 1974 and Oliver 1977.

89. [Arist.] *Rhet. ad Alex.* 1424b6–7.

90. The closest he comes is to say that "the laws should restrain the many from making attempts upon the property-holders" (1424a22–24; cf. 1424b10–12), which is not the same thing as preventing disputes generally.

"censorial model" of the rule of law, after the censors of the Roman Republic.[91] As he explains, the censorial mode involved "the entrusting of magistrates with broad disciplinary authority to maintain the civic virtues on which the preservation of constitutional government depends."[92] Cohen sees this line of thought primarily in the writings of Plato and Aristotle, rather than in the concrete historical record. He draws attention to Aristotle's statement that "a magistracy [*archē*] must be set up that will monitor those whose lives are detrimental to the constitution," seeing in this institution the need on Aristotle's part to "detect and punish behavior which does not suit the interests of those whose dominance the constitution enshrines."[93] By contrast, Cohen notes, as have many others, that the Athenian democracy relied upon private citizen initiative, rather than state agents, to uphold the rule of law.[94] The difference between oligarchic and democratic conceptions of the rule of law, according to Cohen, comes down to ideology. Democrats valued freedom (*eleutheria*), the ability to "live as one liked," and so built respect for individual freedom into their judicial practices. Oligarchs despised the "anarchy" and "license" of democracy and prized "good order," an attitude reflected in their greater reliance on unilateral interference by powerful officials.

The present discussion allows for a modification of this conception. I locate the origins of the oligarchic "censorial mode" more in concerns of basic political order than in ideology.[95] Because oligarchies were structurally less stable than democracies—they were, to put it more precisely, more "brittle" and less capable of absorbing shocks to the system—they required greater

---

91. Cohen 1995: 35, 40, 53.

92. Cohen 1995: 35.

93. Cohen 1995: 40, discussing *Pol.* 5.1308b20–22.

94. Cohen 1995: 53. For similar conceptions of Athenian justice, see Christ 1998; Lanni 2006: ch. 2.

95. Oligarchs also seem to have enjoyed the sense of individual power that came with authoritative magistracies, especially when they were singular and not part of a board of multiple members. Note the preference of Theophrastus's Oligarchic Man for a single elected official to be "plenipotentiary," *autokratōr*: *Char.* 26.2; cf. Isoc. 19.38 (an oligarchic faction from Siphnos elects a single man *archōn autokratōr*); Arist. *Pol.* 5.1301b25–26. Oligarchic magistracies were also on the whole of longer tenure than democratic ones: Aristotle recommends six-month magistracies for oligarchies (*Pol.* 5.1308a15) and says elsewhere that short terms of office are characteristic of democracies (6.1317b24–25), and this may imply that in practice short oligarchic magistracies were atypical. (We now know that Classical democratic Argos, in addition to previously known examples, had several six-month magistracies: Kritzas 2006: 421 with n84, citing also Rhodes, Delphi, and Tenos.) However, magistracies with great concentrated power and long tenure were dangerous for oligarchies in that they might serve as a fillip for an oligarch's seizing tyrannical control: Arist. *Pol.* 5.1305a15–18, 1310b20–22).

overall policing, including policing of personal disputes. Oligarchs' recourse to powerful magistrates bespeaks not so much a personal preference for greater order as a greater practical need for monitoring and self-regulation. After all, as Aristotle says elsewhere, "democracies on the whole are preserved by populousness [*poluanthrōpia*] . . . but it is clear that oligarchy relies for its preservation [*sōteria*] on the opposite principle, good order [*eutaxia*]."[96] Here Aristotle implicitly denies that democracies require good order for stability. Simply having a lot of people is enough. Oligarchies, on the other hand, must maintain *eutaxia* for their survival.[97]

Beyond abstract theorizing on Aristotle's part, we can also find historical instances of oligarchic monitoring along these lines. To begin with a rather difficult source, Isocrates's pamphlet the *Areopagiticus*[98] recalls a time in Athenian history when the Areopagus Council was empowered to "punish the disorderly [*akosmountes*]."[99] It regulated not only those who had already committed wrongdoings, but also those who were on the verge of doing so, keep-

---

96. Arist. *Pol.* 6.1321a1–4.

97. Demetrius of Phalerum, discussed above, tried to put these prescriptions into concrete practice. By instituting *nomophulakes*, overseers of assembly and council procedure, he guaranteed through unilateral magistrate action that proceedings would not get out of hand (Philoch. *FGrH* 328 F 64; recall also Aristotle's claim that the office of *nomophulakia* is connected with "good order," *eukosmia*: *Pol.* 6.1322b37–1323a6). As Canevaro has written, the *nomophulakes* "replaced a democratic procedure based on voluntary action by the citizens and decision by the popular law courts with the discretionary power to block debate and legislation in the Council and the Assembly by a board of (probably elected officials)" (2011: 67).

98. For the politics of the *Areopagiticus*, see the sources cited in chapter 4, section 4.4, where the *Areopagiticus*' conceptualization of political space comes under review.

99. Isoc. 7.46. For a similar concern with *akosmia*, "disorder," see Plat. *Leg.* 6.764b: the market officials of Plato's idealized polis of Magnesia, the *agoranomoi*, are empowered to discipline those behaving in a disorderly fashion in the agora, with whipping stipulated for slaves and foreigners, and fines of one hundred drachmas (to be exacted on the spot) for free men. The flogging of slaves by *agoranomoi* is found even in democratic poleis (e.g. *IG* V. 1 1390, lines 110–11; see further Roubineau 2012), but the ability of the *agoranomos* unilaterally to exact fines rather than refer the perpetrator to a tribunal seems to be a mark of Magnesia's more oligarchic character. Actual oligarchic regimes may have engaged in similar practices. On Plato's authoritarianism on this point see also Migeotte 2005: 290, 294; Bresson 2016: 246–47. It is noteworthy that a decree enacted during the oligarchy of Phocion in 320/19 consolidates the powers of the *astunomoi* or "city officials" in the *agoranomoi*, who are to keep order during the procession for Zeus Soter and Dionysus (*IG* II² 380). The decree evinces a heightened need for policing and order under the oligarchy (Bayliss 2011: 224n16), and might also reveal oligarchic unease with the festival setting, for the revolutionary potential of which see chapter 4, section 4.2 and chapter 6, section 6.1.1. For officials and order at festivals, see Chaniotis 2011: 34–35.

ing tabs on their personal habits through "oversight" (*epimeleia*).[100] When the Areopagus was in charge and regulated private behavior in this way, says Isocrates, the polis of Athens experienced neither "lawsuits" (*dikai*) nor "accusations" (*enklēmata*), but the citizens were in a state of peace (*hēsuchia*) with one another.[101] Isocrates's ideal society is one in which a central authority enjoys jurisdiction over its subjects' private conduct, ensuring—by coercion if necessary—peaceful relations between citizens. The society of the pamphlet is a fantasy, but it may reflect the practices of contemporary oligarchic regimes. The Spartans of the early fourth century, for example, gave their ephors the authority to punish whomever they wished, to exact fines from criminals on the spot, and even to depose other magistrates from their offices. They thus exercised precisely the kind of censorial power Isocrates fantasizes about in the *Areopagiticus*.[102] Furthermore, a fragment of Aristotle's lost *Constitution of the Cyrenaeans* describes a board of ephors, much like those of Sparta, who "haled before themselves the excessively litigious [*poludikoi*] and the wicked [*kakopragmones*], punishing them and stripping them of their citizenship."[103] The reference is impossible to date precisely, but Robinson, in his recent study of Classical democracies outside Athens, suggests the mid- to late fourth century, during which time Cyrene was governed by an oligarchy.[104] Here we see what was presumably a quite small and restrictive political body with the authority to punish individuals simply for engaging in too much litigation. Examining it through the present theoretical framework, we can recognize that the institution of the ephorate at Cyrene was likely designed to restrain members of the oligarchic elite from engaging in destructive disputes with one another. While democratic Athens was notorious for its love of the law courts, the proclivity of the Athenian elite to take each other to court never actually undermined the constitution. Oligarchs, by contrast, could not afford the same level of litigiousness, and they restricted themselves accordingly.[105]

---

100. Isoc. 7.47. For the use of *epimeleia* by oligarchs, see Plat. *Rep.* 8.552e and the discussion of surveillance in chapter 4, section 4.4.

101. Isoc. 7.51. For the ideology of *hēsuchia*, see chapter 5, section 5.2, discussing Pindar fr. 109 S-M.

102. For these powers of the ephors, see Xen. *Lac. Pol.* 8.4. We must keep in mind that the Spartans were not a typical oligarchy, however: see chapter 1, section 1.2.

103. Arist. fr. 611.18 Rose. A similar set of procedures against *poludikia* appears in the oligarchic *diagramma* of Ptolemy for Cyrene, which just postdates Aristotle (*SEG* 9.1, lines 46–47).

104. Robinson 2011: 132.

105. For Athens' litigiousness, see Thuc. 1.77.1 (where the Athenians are said to "love litigation," *philodikein*—cf. *poludikoi* in the Aristotle fragment); Ar. *Vesp. passim*, *Av.* 40–41, *Pax* 505; Xen. *Mem.* 3.5.16; [Xen.] *Ath. Pol.* 3.6. As Ober 1998 has pointed out, conservative critics' com-

If oligarchs tended to nip incipient feuds in the bud, they also took a distinctive approach to cases that did manage to reach the courts. They had to worry that confrontational rhetoric in the courtroom (as elsewhere) might inflame passions and exacerbate disputes.[106] Aristotle gives vent to these concerns at the beginning of the *Rhetoric*, and suggests that some "well administered" poleis attempted to deal with them :

> For the arousing of prejudice, compassion, anger, and similar emotions has no connection with the matter at hand, but is directed only to the dicast. The result would be that, if all trials were now carried on as they are in some states, especially those that are well administered [*eunomoumenai*], there would be nothing left for the rhetorician to say. (*Rhet.* 1.1354a16–21, trans. Freese)

In particularly "well governed" poleis, he says, employing the oligarchic concept of *eunomia*, the laws leave no room for the skilled speaker.[107] Unfortunately, we lack direct evidence for Greek poleis that implemented rules along these lines, but we possess a few statements and allusions from the oligarchic interludes at Athens in the late fifth century. A fragment of the defense speech of the sophist Antiphon, for example, sees the participant in the regime of the Four Hundred relying on the following argument:

> My accusers say that I composed speeches for others' lawsuits and that I profited from this. But in an oligarchy this would not have been possible for me, whereas in a democracy I have power from my words. In an oligarchy I was not going to be worth anything, but under democracy I am worth much. So come now, how is it likely that I would have desired oligarchy? (fr. 1a.10–17 Nicole)[108]

---

plaints notwithstanding, the Athenian democracy was not, for all of its litigiousness, threatened by internal collapse.

106. It is noteworthy in this respect that the art of rhetoric seems to have been first developed in democratic Syracuse by Tisias and Corax (Cic. *Brut.* 46). Robinson argues convincingly that the sophists, who taught rhetoric, helped spread the idea of democracy (2011: 210–16).

107. Similarly, Plutarch states that "the magistrates within aristocracies do not allow speakers to arouse the emotions" (*Mor.* 447e).

108. Antiphon was the intellectual mastermind behind the oligarchy of the Four Hundred. Thucydides notes his skill at helping Athenians with both courtroom and assembly speeches (8.68.1). He delivered his own defense speech, which was much admired by Thucydides, when the Four Hundred had fallen (8.68.2 [text uncertain]). Despite (or perhaps because of) the cleverness of his defense speech, he was condemned and executed (Craterus *FGrH* 342 F 5b). For the identification of his Antiphon with the sophist Antiphon, see Gagarin 2002.

This passage has not received sufficient attention. The speaker of course has an interest in playing up the supposed contrast between democracy and oligarchy on the matter of speechwriting and courtroom rhetoric. Perhaps the two regimes' respective approaches to legal *logoi* were not as opposed as the speaker claims. Nonetheless, the passage is *prima facie* evidence that the public perceived *logographia* as a specifically democratic phenomenon; otherwise, Antiphon would not have tried to build an argument on it. Taken straightforwardly, his remarks imply that the Athenian oligarchy of the Four Hundred, and perhaps oligarchies more generally, prohibited the hiring of speechwriters for legal cases. The present discussion suggests why this strict prohibition would have existed under the Four Hundred. Not only would there have been fewer lawsuits, but the ruling oligarchs would also have been concerned to limit the ability of litigants to raise the emotional stakes of court proceedings through the hiring of skilled rhetoricians. A logographer like Antiphon would have seen his *métier* forbidden because it threatened to exacerbate destructive divisions among the members of the ruling class.[109]

2.5 Effective Elite Punishment: Exile

In an elite-run political community like a Classical Greek oligarchy, punishment, when it needed to be meted out, had to weaken the transgressor's ability to retaliate violently, while in cases where the infraction was not a capital crime, it should also hold out the possibility of his future reintegration into the exclusive community of equals. Striking this balance between punishment and reconciliation was a tricky business, however, since an oligarch's prickly sense of honor often provoked him to choose courses of action that foreclosed peaceful resolution. Nonetheless, elites in general, and oligarchs in particular, had to try to make the best of their situation, and here I argue that they often chose exile as a punishment that approximated to the isolation/reintegration ideal. By physically displacing a member of the elite from the institutions of the polis, banishment removed the threat of violence in the most literal way possible; yet by offering the hope of reintegration, it could also serve to forestall conflict until cooler heads prevailed and harmony was reestablished.

---

109. Cf. the story, found in Xen. *Mem.* 1.2.31, that Critias in his capacity as lawgiver during the period of the Thirty forbade "the art of speaking" (*technē logōn*). Xenophon claims that the law was crafted specifically to target Socrates. I suspect, however, that the Thirty were opposed to sycophants and slippery rhetoricians not only on principle (although Critias himself was a master prevaricator), but also with the more practical goal in mind of eliminating opportunities for dangerous disputes.

Before beginning, I must address one issue. The idea that the imposition of exile could have served as a source of stability for oligarchic regimes might at first appear counterintuitive. Forsdyke in particular has shown that certain Archaic poleis were riven by violent acts of murder and expulsion that destabilized the community. These episodes ceased only when tyrants or oligarchic factions gained unassailable predominance over the polis. Even then, however, a relapse into feuding and violence remained likely. For Forsdyke, it was only with the emergence in Athens of democracy and of the popular institution of ostracism that a polis was able to bring the elite-based "politics of expulsion" to a peaceful conclusion.[110]

There are two potential problems with this analysis, however. First, by focusing on well-known cases (Mytilene, Megara, Samos, Corinth, Athens) where elite competition definitely did lead to violence, Forsdyke overlooks more mundane instances in which exile did not upend the community. In other words, even if every crisis Forsdyke examines involves exile, not every instance of exile in the Greek world need have entailed a crisis for the polis.[111] Second, as Forsdyke acknowledges elsewhere, democratic Athens was not the only polis to discover a more permanent safeguard against Archaic-style crises. She views the post-Cypselid oligarchy at Corinth, for example, as one that "ruled moderately," as evidenced by "the extraordinary stability of [the] regime."[112] Forsdyke thus leaves open the possibility that non-democratic poleis might have successfully reined in the politics of expulsion.[113]

There are at least two varieties of exile.[114] In the first variety, exile is a permanent condition. An infraction might explicitly entail permanent exile, or—what we often find in the epigraphic record—authorities might declare someone an exile *ex post facto*, when a man had already fled to avoid punishment by

---

110. Forsdyke 2000, 2005 *passim*. See especially 2005: 78: "The case of Athens demonstrates that a permanent solution to the problem of exile in archaic Greece could be found *only* through the greater involvement of the non-elites in the allocation of political power between elites" (emphasis added).

111. The issue is that Forsdyke has "selected on the dependent variable," that is, looked only at outcomes that support the theory. A complete analysis would need to look at every known case of exile and see how it turned out, rather than begin with crisis episodes. (For the problem of selecting on the dependent variable, see King, Keohane, and Verba 1994: 129–37.)

112. Forsdyke 2005: 77; cf. 32.

113. Another difference between our analyses is that Forsdyke looks at elite-led regimes in the Archaic period, while I focus on the Classical. The sustained cooperation which Forsdyke sees Archaic elites as conspicuously lacking emerged more strongly in the Classical period as a response to the danger of democracy.

114. Past treatments of ancient exile include Seibert 1979; McKechnie 1989; Gaertner 2007; Garland 2014; Gray 2015.

death. In this latter case banishment is a next-best measure, since the community would kill the criminal if it could; often times death is indeed prescribed should the transgressor somehow fall into the hands of the polis.[115] In the second variety, exile is open to negotiation: either the criminal goes into self-imposed exile until he can settle his debt, or those inflicting punishment specify at the outset how long the period of exile is to last.[116] In practice, these two forms were more permeable than the schematized versions laid out here.[117] Nevertheless, in what follows I will treat the stated intention of those inflicting the punishment as important.

When executed properly, exile fulfilled the three related requirements of speed, impersonality, and communal involvement that were crucial for oligarchic stability. First, as we have seen, the literary sources are quite clear that unresolved conflict was especially dangerous for oligarchies. Thus oligarchs as a group possessed an interest in settling disputes among their ranks as quickly as possible.[118] This fact leads to the consideration of impersonality: if punishment was left to be inflicted on a man by his personal enemies, he might react much more violently than if it was perceived as emanating from the oligarchic community as a whole.[119] Not only would the responsibility be shared by many people, but a united front of oligarchs would also appear a much less

---

115. Presumably permanent exile: *Nomima* I.107 (see also Koerner no. 37; Argos or Halieis, early fifth century); *Nomima* I.100 (see also Koerner no. 29; Argos, mid-sixth century [the text is a plausible conjecture]); ML 32, line 37 (Halicarnassus, fifth century). Exile imposed *ex post facto*: ML 43 (Miletus, early-to-mid-fifth century, treated below). The oligarchic decree from post-411 Thasos recording confiscations (*IG* XII.8 263) probably entails exile too; so too the unpublished late-sixth-century Theban inscription showing the sale of (presumably confiscated) property (Matthaiou 2014: 216). Many people appear to go into permanent exile already in Homer, e.g. *Od.* 23.118–20.

116. See esp. Ajax's words to Achilles (Hom. *Il.* 9.632–36): "Someone takes the blood price from his brother's killer ... and the latter remains in the community, having repaid the debt." See also the law of Draco (ML 86), line 18: should certain conditions obtain, the phratry members are to receive the killer back into the community; protections are elsewhere established (lines 26–29) for the homicide while in exile.

117. King Pleistoanax of Sparta, for example, was exiled (Thuc. 2.21.1) but later allowed to return, although not without contention, since his enemies accused him of bribing the Delphic oracle (5.16.1–2).

118. For oligarchies as particularly endangered by protracted struggles, see the sources cited above, section 2.4.

119. See Arist. *Pol.* 5.1306a36-b2, discussing the dissolution of oligarchies at Heraclea Pontica and Thebes: two men were punished for adultery, and moreover were punished justly (*dikaiōs*), but because they were pilloried in the agora by their personal enemies out of spite (*philoneikia*), in a spirit of faction (*stasiastikōs*), the punished men staged revolutions. See further chapter 6, section 6.2.4.

easily assailable target than a single man or a few people. Thus communal involvement: by making private disputes a matter of common concern, oligarchs preempted broader conflict, depersonalized responsibility for the action, and deterred retaliation. Just as importantly, they made the fact of a man's punishment a matter of common knowledge: each member of the ruling group individually knew both the details of the case and that all others knew the same about him as he about them, *ad infinitum*. The condition of common knowledge greatly facilitated future collective action, because if the recipient of the punishment openly defied the terms of his sentence, each oligarch could be assured that others would also recognize the action as a violation and thus would be able to count on others' assistance in enforcing the ruling.[120]

Turning to the historical record, we see a mid-fifth-century decree from oligarchic Miletus (ML 43) that illustrates these facets of exile nicely.[121] The text reads:

> [The sons of] Nympharetus, and Alkimos and Cresphontes the sons of Stratonax, are to be in a state of exile [*pheugen* = Attic *pheugein*] as a result of bloodshed [*ep' haimati*], both they themselves and their descendants, and whoever should kill one of them, there is to be awarded to him one hundred staters from the property of the family of Nympharetus. The *epimēnioi* [monthly magistrates] during whose period of office the killers present themselves are to pay the money. If they do not, they themselves are to owe it. If the polis should get the men in its power, the *epimēnioi* during whose period of office the men are captured are to kill them. Should they not kill them, they are to owe one hundred and fifty staters. The *epimēnios*, should he not bring forward the motion, is to owe one hundred staters, and incoming boards of *epimēnioi* are to always act according to this decree [*psēphisma*]. If they do not, they are to owe the same fine.[122]

---

120. For the idea of "common knowledge," see chapter 1, section 1.3. For further instances of common knowledge playing an important role in oligarchic politics, see, e.g., chapter 3, section 3.2; chapter 5, section 5.2; chapter 6, section 6.1.1.

121. It used to be thought that this decree had something to do with Athens' involvement with oligarchs in Miletus (attested by [Xen.] *Ath. Pol.* 3.11), especially since *IG* I³ 21, an Athenian decree for Miletus, was once dated to 450/49 based on the criterion of the three-barred sigma (see the discussion at ML 43 and the bibliography cited). Some even countenanced the idea that ML 43 was enacted by a democracy. However, the redating of *IG* I³ 21 to 426/5 probably means, in Rhodes's words, that "there is no longer any reason to think that 450/49 was a crucial year in the history of Miletus" (2006: 116). Cf. Gorman 2001: 233, showing that the context for the Milesian exile decree is oligarchic.

122. The decree is sometimes referred to as recording "expulsions" from Miletus (ML 43; Fornara 66), but the named men are not being expelled: they have already fled. If the city of

The decree illustrates considerations outlined above in several ways. First, while we cannot know exactly how soon after the criminal acts this ordinance was issued, the harshness and decisiveness of the decree suggest that the men targeted have only recently fled the city. The command to future boards of *epimēnioi* at the end might indicate that the current board of magistrates is the one during whose period of office the men fled. The punishment was apparently swiftly decided on. Furthermore, there is little evidence for believing that Miletus continued to experience *stasis* during this period. Thus, while we cannot prove that the decree itself prevented further civil strife, it is tempting to think that it played a role in that stability.[123] Second, the language of the decree suggests impartiality and an absence of individual vengeance. The instructions are couched in terms of "the polis" generally and of the rotating, nameless boards of *epimēnioi*, every member of which must consider the rules to apply equally to him. Finally, the exiles' condition is definitely a matter of public concern. Two features of the decree are significant here: first, a complex chain of delegation and authority is built in, in order that the *epimēnioi* should not shirk their responsibility. The drafters of the decree (themselves potentially future *epimēnioi*) were apparently attempting to bind their future selves and others to their present decisions by laying down significant fines for dereliction of duty. Second, the Milesian oligarchs also entice the wider community to enforce their decisions through the offer of a cash reward. They thus create a means of co-opting the people by giving them a material stake in enforcing the decisions of the regime.[124]

It was also possible for exiles to be integrated back into the oligarchic community, although the détente did not always last.[125] Our chief example of this is the case of Nicodromus of Aegina, a distinguished member of the elite described by Herodotus as "having previously suffered a bout of exile [*exelasis*]," which he secretly "held against [*memphomenos*]" his fellow oligarchs.[126] We

---

Miletus had had them in its power at the time the decree was issued, it would have simply killed them, not exiled them.

123. This becomes especially impressive when we consider that blood had already been spilt in the *stasis*: the men are outlawed "as a result of bloodshed [*ep' haimati*]."

124. See the discussion on rewards for informants, chapter 3, section 3.4.

125. In addition to the case of Nicodromus discussed immediately below, cf. Asopodorus of Thebes, described by Pindar at *Isthm.* 1.34–40 as having retreated to his "ancestral estate" at Orchomenos following a "shipwreck." The language is clearly metaphorical for exile. At the time of the ode's performance, however, it seems clear that Asopodorus and his son are back in the good graces of the Theban oligarchy.

126. Hdt. 6.88. For this episode, see Figueira 1981: 306–10; Lintott 1982: 87; Gehrke *Stasis* 15–16; Hornblower 2004a: 221; van Wees 2008: 31–32; de Ste. Croix 2004: 376–77; Fearn 2010: 221–22. I treat the Nicodromus episode as a case of oligarchic *stasis* in chapter 6, section 6.2.4.

do not know why Nicodromus was banished, or how long after his rehabilitation he offered his help to the Athenians, but he was willing to team up with the demos of Aegina to betray the city to Aegina's rival. He was definitely living in Aegina again when he attempted his *coup*, since his part of the bargain was to seize the "old city" of Aegina and deliver it up to the Athenians.[127] Herodotus explains that the revolution failed when the Athenians arrived too late, but the concerted reaction of the Aeginetan oligarchs against Nicodromus's followers suggests that they were ready to respond to any misbehavior on his part.[128] I would argue that the swiftness and unity of their response was made possible in part by the fact that they had all participated in Nicodromus's previous banishment. They therefore possessed common knowledge of his status as a potential subversive. At the same time, they had initially been willing to let Nicodromus back into the fold, and all things considered this might have been the most stabilizing decision at the time. A permanently exiled Nicodromus might have attempted a more forceful return to the island even sooner, while the returning Nicodromus appears to have plotted revolution only when the Athenians appeared on the scene.

Like Nicodromus, oligarchic exiles frequently fail to avenge themselves on their persecutors. Ptoeodorus of Thespiae, an exile (*phugas*) from the Boeotian *koinon* and the chief instigator of an attempted democratic revolution in Boeotia in 424, lost his chance at revenge when a Phocian, Nicomachus, betrayed the plot to the Spartans.[129] Ptoeodorus's status as an exile likely weakened the plot substantially. Not only would he have been a person of interest to the Thespian oligarchs and their allies in Thebes, but it is likely that the oligarchs had offered rewards for information about any attempted conspiracies on his part. Perhaps Nicomachus of Phocis was induced to confess the plot to the Spartans for precisely this reason, that as time went on the temptation for people to inform and reap the rewards made the *coup* less and less likely to succeed, and he concluded that he should therefore make the first move himself and obtain the gains.[130] Herodotus also provides us with an Archaic example of an exile unsuccessfully returning home. This time, his fellow citizens are explicitly said to have prevented the return by presenting a

---

127. Hdt. 6.88.

128. Hdt. 6.91.1–2: Herodotus calls this a matter of "the fatcats [*pachees*] of Aegina overpowering the uprising of the demos led by Nicodromus." They killed 700 of the common people in reprisal.

129. Thuc. 4.76.2, 89.1. Ptoeodorus established contact with the Athenian generals Demosthenes and Hippocrates and plotted a complex, multi-city democratic uprising with them. See further chapter 5, section 5.2.1.

130. On rewards for informants, see the treatment in chapter 3, section 3.4.

united front of opposition. Gillus of Tarentum, banished from his homeland in the late sixth century, earns a favor from the Persian King Darius. Gillus requests that a Cnidian escort restore him to his polis, but the Cnidians cannot persuade the Tarentines to take him back, even when they threaten them with force.[131] It is likely that the publicly known fact of Gillus's exile strengthened the Tarentines' resistance to his return. Once again the ability of the elite to unite behind a policy of exile increased their resolve and made the polis less rather than more vulnerable to violent reprisal.

Finally, an episode that can be pieced together from Aristotle and Plutarch shows what could happen when oligarchs failed to impose exile when they had the opportunity to do so. In Book 5 of the *Politics*, Aristotle offers a historical example of when expelling specific members would have saved an oligarchic regime.[132] Two young men from the ruling elite of late-Archaic Syracuse quarreled "on erotic grounds" (*peri erōtikēn aitian*): despite being one another's "companions" (*hetairoi*), one of them won over the other's beloved (*erōmenos*), and the first man, outraged, seduced the second man's wife in revenge. They eventually draw all the members of the elite into their competing factions and destroyed the constitution.[133] Plutarch provides crucial further information about the incident. When the ruling oligarchs learned that the two men were quarreling, one of the older Syracusans came forward to speak in the council (*boulē*) and advised the councilors to exile (*elaunein*) both men.[134] He was unable persuade the council, however, and the constitution was overthrown. The other members of the old Syracusan elite (known as the *geomoroi*, or landholders) spectacularly failed to heed the old man's words, although it would clearly have been within their power to deal with the private quarrel through political means, by uniting themselves behind the decision to

---

131. Hdt. 3.138.1–3. Asheri thinks Tarentum was governed at the time by a tyrant, Aristophilides, called *basileus* by Herodotus (3.136.2; see Asheri et al. 2007 *ad loc.*). IACP (no. 71, p. 300), however, follows Malkin (1994: 132 with n87) in seeing Aristophilides as a Spartan-style king operating within an elite-led constitution.

132. Elsewhere he advises the expulsion of any threatening member of a community, whether in a democracy or an oligarchy: *Pol.* 5.1308b19.

133. Arist. *Pol.* 1303b20–26. (On this episode, see also chapter 6, section 6.2.3.) Presumably Aristotle is describing the onset of the democracy mentioned by Herodotus (7.155.2) and elsewhere by Aristotle himself (*Pol.* 5.1302b31–32), which involved the demos and the Kallyrioi, or local slave population. See further Berger 1992: 35. The "erotic grounds" of the *stasis* recall the conspiracy of Harmodius and Aristogeiton, which Thucydides labels an "erotic mishap" (*erōtikē xuntuchia*, 6.54.1).

134. Plut. *Mor.* 825c-d. The medical imagery is common in cases of *stasis*: see Brock 2013: 69–82.

expel the young men.[135] Thus we can see how the practice of exile, when utilized with due attention to the oligarchic needs of speed, impersonality, and common sanction, might serve to stabilize an oligarchy.

135. Incidentally, the passage is also evidence that it was possible, even expected, for oligarchs to monitor and regulate each other's private behavior for the sake the of wider political community.

3

Balancing Coercion and Co-optation

> Whoever denounces a revolt being plotted against Thasos and proves it to be true, let him have a thousand staters from the city.
>
> —LAW REWARDING INFORMERS, THASOS[1]

3.0 Introduction: Institutions Governing Relations between Elite and Demos

If treating each other well was important, the oligarchs' relationship with the demos, that politically excluded portion of the poorer male citizenry, was perhaps even more crucial. The demos's political disempowerment constituted the dirty secret of oligarchy, the deeper cause from which many of its characteristic weaknesses emanated. The exclusion of the demos, and the ensuing *de facto* creation of a "reserve army" of the disaffected, led to problems for oligarchies that were simply absent in democracies. As was suggested in the previous chapter, and as will be discussed at greater length in chapter 6, one major purpose of intra-elite regulation was to defuse the possibility that a renegade member of the oligarchic class would turn to the demos as a means of exacting revenge from his fellow oligarchs. Similarly, as this chapter will show, oligarchs had to worry that members of their class would mistreat the common people to the point of sparking a democratic uprising that could bring down the oligarchic regime.

This mistreatment came in the form of sins of both commission and omission. Straightforwardly objectionable were acts of hubris—haughty, disdainful treatment—that palpably conveyed to the common people the

---

1. ML 83, lines 1–2: ὃς ἂν ἐπανάστασιν βολευομένην ἐπὶ Θάσωι κατείπηι καὶ φανῆι ἐόντα ἀληθέα, χιλίος στατῆρας ἐκ τῆς πόλεως ἰσχέτω.

vulnerability of their position.[2] Acts of hubris were especially liable to catalyze resistance when they transpired in public, in open view of the outraged demos. In such situations, considerations of common knowledge and mass coordination came into play (see further chapters 4 and 5). A more subtle and difficult problem stemmed from lack rather than excess of attention, when the members of the demos felt themselves neglected by the oligarchy. Indifference could give offense just as much as assault or humiliation, since the common people felt that the constitution, however unequal, ought to give at least some weight to the opinion of the wider community. Much as the oligarchs might prefer it, then, utter disregard of the demos was not an option.

This chapter initiates the examination of oligarchic institutions governing relations between elite and demos, which were designed to overcome the twin challenges identified above of excessive repression and offensive negligence. The fourth and fifth chapters continue the analysis but cover material that is best grouped into the categories of public space and information, which warrant separate treatment. First (3.1), I survey the issue of repression under ancient Greek oligarchy. Like modern authoritarianism, Greek oligarchy was in the great majority of cases a political system initiated by an act of force against the wishes of the majority. Furthermore, the regime maintained itself after its instauration through violence, or at least the threat of it. Greek oligarchies, however, relied less on direct repression than modern autocrats do, because the oligarchic state had no real technological advantage over the demos in terms of the means of violence. State violence under oligarchy thus tended to take on one of two forms: either it was hidden from view, in the form of secret assassinations, nocturnal trials, and summary executions; or (more rarely) it was staged as spectacular punishments, *pour encourager les autres*.[3] The latter form also frequently had a participatory component, in which the members of the demos were implicated in the act. As for interpersonal violence, the evidence suggests that oligarchs recognized the need to restrain themselves. Extant sources thus paint a peculiar picture of oligarchic violence toward the demos: it constantly loomed but rarely materialized. The image we get in pro-democratic authors, of oligarchs wantonly abusing the people, is more an ideological construct, meant to tar oligarchs with tyrannical association, than a description of reality. It is important to see that oligarchic violence operated according to its own specific logic.

---

2. Fisher 1992 remains the authoritative treatment of hubris. See also his 2000a, discussed in chapter 6 below.

3. See now Riess and Fagan 2016 for a collection of papers on the relationship between space and violence in antiquity, although there is no chapter devoted to Greek oligarchy.

The remainder of the chapter explores the alternatives to outright repression within oligarchies. Violence was a blunt and potentially dangerous tool. Better were institutions that employed a combination of threats and inducements, what I call "co-optation." By this means, oligarchs minimally satisfied the demos's desire for inclusion while at the same time channeling that participation in directions that bolstered oligarchic stability. Assemblies (3.2), positions in the regime (3.3), and rewards for informants (3.4) exemplify institutions of this type.

3.1 Oligarchies and Violence

3.1.1 Juridical Violence

Ancient democrats liked to characterize oligarchy as remorselessly violent. The democratic refugee Chaereas, fleeing the Four Hundred at Athens, tells the fleet at Samos that the oligarchy was whipping free men like slaves, abusing women and children, and planning to arrest and kill the relatives of the crew members—all of which, Thucydides drily notes, was a lie.[4] The speaker of Isocrates's *Against Lochites* also remembers the actions of the Thirty as flagrantly hubristic.[5] Such statements were all part of a larger trend of associating oligarchy with tyranny, even when the comparison was sometimes strained.[6]

Oligarchies were in fact repressive regimes, but not in the public and blatant way insisted upon by many democrats. Understanding oligarchic violence (particularly juridical violence) will require rethinking many of our preconceptions about punishment in the ancient Greek world, most of which are based on the Athenian experience. A generation of scholars has demonstrated how punishment in Classical Athens amounted to a kind of public spectacle, in which the punishing parties, the victims, and the onlookers articulated and negotiated communal norms surrounding acceptable behavior.[7] The system was both private and public, in the sense that many actions were initiated by private individuals rather than state forces, while at the same time volunteer prosecutors were expected to act in plain sight, under the watchful eye of the

---

4. Thuc. 8.74.3.

5. Isoc. 20.11. Xenophon (*Mem.* 1.2.58–59) says that his fellow citizens accused Socrates of quoting approvingly the Homeric lines in which Odysseus beats and upbraids the common soldiers (*Il.* 2.198–202); they claimed he was saying the poet advocated beating the poor. Whether Socrates meant this or not, the episode shows that democrats suspected oligarchs of wanting to abuse them physically.

6. For examples of speakers drawing comparisons between oligarchy and tyranny, see, e.g., Aeschin. 1.4–5, 3.6. For the success of this rhetorical strategy in the long run, see the afterword.

7. See Hunter 1994; Fisher 1998; Allen 2000; Riess 2012.

community.⁸ Furthermore, punishments were frequently spectacular in nature: a criminal might be bound in the stocks or attached to a board in a form of exposure called *apotumpanismos*; convicted adulterers might be penetrated with humiliating and painful objects (a radish, a spiny fish).⁹ This is to say nothing of those caught trying to put down the democracy itself—for that, various anti-tyranny and anti-subversion laws, such as the oath of Demophantus and the law of Eucrates, enjoined killing the perpetrator on the spot with impunity.¹⁰ In sum, Athenian democratic justice was privately initiated, democratically judged (in a *dikastērion* or "people's court"), and publicly executed.

The historical record offers a very different picture of oligarchic justice. If courts under democracy could be thought of as a foundation of democratic power, then oligarchic courts were arguably even more political. They were composed of members of the ruling elite who knew each other more intimately than did judges in an Athenian law court, and they possessed a clear sense of their corporate interests. It seems, with perhaps a few exceptions, that most oligarchic courts were manned by full citizens of the oligarchy. Aristotle says that it is characteristically oligarchic for "some to judge about all" (*Pol.* 4.1301a12–13). Thus the few had practically exclusive control over all legal matters. Oligarchic courts likely exhibited some traits that could be construed as improvements over democratic legal procedure: as we saw in chapter 2, legal feuding was more strongly curtailed than under democracy and inflammatory rhetoric was kept to a minimum.¹¹ Oligarchs could boast, with some credibility, that their courts were much more orderly than those of their democratic counterparts.

What they gained in terms of *sōphrosunē* and *eunomia*, however, they lacked in accountability and equitability. It was a common criticism of oligarchic courts that they held power over life and death without providing a fair trial.¹² This position seems to underlie an episode from Athenian legal history. The

---

8. Harris (2007) assembles the evidence for the enforcement of the law by magistrates at Athens, but this is largely for public regulations, not intercitizen disputes.

9. Stocks: Hunter 1994: 176–71; Allen 2000: 200; Forsdyke 2012–148–49. *Apotumpanismos*: Gernet 1981: 52–76; Todd 1993: 141; Allen 2000: 200–202; Forsdyke 2012: 164. Punishment of adulterers: Roy 1991; Carey 1993; Forsdyke 2012: 153–54.

10. And. 1.96–98; RO 79. (Canevaro and Harris [2012] argue that the documents in Andocides 1 are forgeries, but we still get an idea of the content of the Oath of Demophantus from Dem. 20.159 and Lyc. 1.124–27.) For the public aspect of the tyrannicide ideology embodied in these kinds of laws, see Teegarden 2014: 52–53 and *passim*; Riess 2006.

11. See section 2.4.

12. Arist. *Pol.* 4.1294b33–34 says that the Spartan constitution is oligarchic insofar as "a few people are authoritative [*kurioi*] in matters of death and exile." See further Pseudo-Archytas

author of the Aristotelian *Athēnaiōn Politeia* claims that the Athenian *boulē* at some point in the past had the authority to fine, imprison, and kill. However, a citizen named Eumelides of Alopece disputed this prerogative in the case of one Lysimachus, who had been sentenced to death and was awaiting execution. Eumelides argued that no citizen should die without the decision of a people's court (*dikastērion*); in the ensuing trial, Lysimachus got off, earning himself the nickname "the man who escaped the rod." The assembly then passed a law depriving the council of its punitive powers and allowing appeal to a *dikastērion* for all verdicts.[13] Rhodes, in his commentary on the *Ath. Pol.*, finds no further evidence that the *boulē* ever had such authority. He suggests that the story is a useful fiction, retrojected into the past, which justified a legal system in which the council had no right to punish or kill.[14] This appealing interpretation opens up the possibility that the Athenians were contrasting their system with contemporary oligarchies, in which the *boulē* and other small legislative bodies did hold greater authority. Thus the Eumelides story is more a matter of democratic self-definition and self-distancing from oligarchic practices.

As a historical example of such practices, one could point to an inscription from late-fifth-century Thasos, which almost certainly comes from an oligarchic regime.[15] The decree orders that the confiscated property of several exiles be dedicated to Apollo, "by the decision [*hadon*] of the three hundred" (lines 6–7). The group is likely either a restricted council or a body of powerful magistrates, acting as a kind of court. Thus we are looking at an instance of an oligarchic political organ unilaterally exercising power over citizens' property, without the input or approval of a more inclusive democratic institution.[16] Here the three hundred merely dispenses with the exiles' possessions, since the men themselves were not present to stand trial.[17] Had the oligarchy gotten the democrats into their grasp, however, it would likely have resulted in a politicized trial and execution.[18]

34.11–13 Thesleff = Stob. 4.1.135: democratic justice distributes "punishments" (*kolaseis*) "equally" (*ex isou*), oligarchic justice, "unequally" (*anisō*).

13. [Arist.] *Ath. Pol.* 45.1.

14. Rhodes 1993: 538.

15. *IG* XII.8 263.

16. For the Thasian inscription and its historical and political context, see Pouilloux 1954: 145; Pleket 1963: 75–76; Avery 1979: 235–36.

17. We know the men listed in *IG* XII.8 263 are exiles thanks to two Athenian decrees from the later fifth and early fourth centuries, *IG* II² 6 and 33, which attest to the presence of the sons of one of the men, Apemantus, in Athens.

18. As happened on Chios in the winter of 412/11, when the Spartan-backed oligarchy killed Tydeus, the son of Ion, and his companions on a similar charge of *attikismos* (Thuc. 8.38.3). See

3.1.2 Extralegal Violence and Clandestine Killing

In other instances, oligarchs dispensed with the pretense of a trial altogether. In such cases political opponents were killed *akritoi*, "without trial" or "without a hearing."[19] It was a traditional criticism of tyrants that they eliminated their opponents *akritoi*, as Otanes in Herodotus's "Constitutional Debate" makes clear.[20] In point of fact, no form of government, democratic or oligarchic, was innocent of summary execution, especially in times of crisis. Often this involved killing prisoners seized during interstate conflict.[21] At the domestic level, however, oligarchs relied more on the practice than did democrats. At least one oligarch openly admits this fact. When the oligarchic conspirators of 411 are considering setting up oligarchies in the cities of the Athenian empire, one of their number, Phrynichus, presciently disapproves. He observes that the allied cities would be unhappy with oligarchic rulers, because under their control people "would die violent deaths, without trial [*akritoi*], while the demos had been their refuge and a check on [the oligarchs]."[22] Phrynichus's frank admission looks forward to the "reign of terror" at Athens under the Four Hundred themselves, in which anyone who spoke out against the regime "died in some convenient manner" (8.66.2; see further below). Similar methods were employed by the Thirty, whose practice of ordering enemies to drink hemlock without trial Lysias calls "customary" (12.17). The oligarchic use of extralegal killing was thus not an invention of democratic ideology but enjoyed an independent existence. It aligns well with the statement of Aristotle that "oligarchic constitutions are the more taut and despotic, democratic ones the more lax and soft" (*Pol.* 4.1290a27–29).

A brief examination of the nature of oligarchic extralegal violence will reveal both the strategic calculus that drove oligarchs to use it and the characteristic forms it took. The accusations of democratic critics notwithstanding,

---

also the episode at Phlius in 379: a Spartan-backed oligarchic commission of one hundred men was to "establish the laws [*nomoi*] according to which they would conduct their political life [*politeuesthai*]," much like the Thirty in 404 (Xen. *Hell.* 2.3.2); this group, however, would also determine "who was fit [*dikaion*] to live and who to die" (5.3.25). Note, too, that the commission was made up of fifty oligarchic exiles and fifty men who had remained in the city under democracy; the latter were likely oligarchic sympathizers who were in any case now co-opted into the new oligarchic regime (see below, section 3.3).

19. Previous treatments of political murder in ancient Greece include Bearzot 2006, 2007; Riess 2006; Teegarden 2014. Outside of work on the Athenian oligarchies of the late fifth century, few studies have been devoted to oligarchic political violence.

20. Hdt. 3.80.5; cf. Dem. 17.3.

21. See Thuc. 2.67.4 (Athenians kill prisoners *akritoi*; cf. Hdt. 7.137.3).

22. Thuc. 8.48.6.

oligarchs did not kill their opponents in this manner simply because they were "more immoral" or "more depraved." Oligarchic techniques of violence reflected the precarious political position the oligarchs found themselves in, a status inherent in their very name. As an embattled minority whose authority was highly contested, oligarchs could not afford to execute their justice in the public, spectacular manner employed by democrats. There were dangers on multiple fronts: that the majority male citizenry would reject decisions the oligarchs thought "best" or "expedient"; that the demos would react violently to the oligarchs' unpopular policies; that they would use their superior numbers to overwhelm and overthrow the regime. It is therefore no surprise that oligarchic justice was driven "underground," taking on clandestine forms.

We can see the roots of this oligarchic approach to extralegal violence as early as the *Odyssey*. When Penelope's suitors plot to kill Telemachus, they gather together in the place of assembly (*agorē*, 16.361), but allow no one else from the community to sit with them (361–62). Antinous then advises them (371–84):

> Let us now devise a terrible death for Telemachus, and let him not escape us. . . . But come, before that man summons the Achaeans to assembly— for I do not think that he will relent, but he'll be angry, and standing up he will speak among all of them, because we wove sheer death for him but did not catch him. . . . But let us destroy him, seizing him in a field far from the polis, or on the road.

The suitors' actions, and Antinous's proposal, bear all the marks of an unpopular, power-hungry minority that wishes to prevent concerted majority action against it. The suitors prevent the population from hearing their deliberations by commandeering the civic space of the agora.[23] Antinous then suggests that they assassinate Telemachus in a remote location, far from the gaze of the community, in order to avoid the popular outcry that would ensue. The suitors, on the advice of Amphinomus, ultimately decide not to adopt Antinous's proposal (400–408), but the possibility of their murdering Telemachus in the countryside makes clear already at this early point in Greek history the methods deemed suitable for small, illegitimate groups.[24]

In other accounts of Archaic and Classical assassination, the perpetrators successfully kill their target: Cimon the son of Stesagoras was ambushed by

---

23. Cf. chapter 4, on oligarchic use of space, and chapter 5, on secrecy of information, below.

24. Indeed, Rose has seen in the suitors a kind of proto-oligarchy: 1992: 99–102, drawing on Whitman 1958: 306–308. The ancient commentators on Homer also compared the suitors to oligarchs: ps.-Plutarch *peri Homērou B* lines 2272–73 Kindstrand. This is a retrojection of a later term onto the past, however.

the agents of Peisistratus at night by the prytaneion building (Hdt. 6.103.3); Cnopus, the Archaic king of Erythrae, was murdered at sea by oligarchic conspirators (Hippias of Erythrae *FGrH* 421 F 1); and, perhaps most notoriously, Ephialtes the populist Athenian politician was killed at night by oligarchic agents.[25] As in the Homeric example, usurpers (autocrats, oligarchs) eliminate popular figures in situations where the latter are powerless to call for aid.

To what extent was this expedient practiced by actual oligarchs during the Classical period? We have seen from Thucydides's Phrynichus that oligarchs frequently killed opponents *akritoi*. The issue now is whether the killings were also clandestine, taking place in out-of-the-way locations, in the dead of night, and/or at the hands of persons unknown. Here as elsewhere the evidence is scrappy, but it ultimately points to the use of secret assassination by oligarchs as a means of securing their rule. Certainly it was the preferred method when staging an anti-democratic *coup*. Oligarchs across multiple poleis consistently utilize it when coming to power. In Elis during the Elean-Spartan War (ca. 400), oligarchic plotters kill a man they mistakenly think is Thrasydaeus, the *prostatēs* of the demos. Their confusion, and the fact that the real Thrasydaeus is later found sleeping off the previous night's hangover, indicate that the murder took place in the pre-dawn hours.[26] Similarly, Dion of Syracuse allows his associates to murder the demagogue Heraclides in private, in his home.[27] Nepos reports that the killing created widespread terror and insecurity (*maximum timorem*, *Dio* 7.1); we will return to this effect shortly. Plutarch explicitly states, just before this episode, that Dion's goal was to introduce an oligarchic government to Syracuse, based on the Corinthian model (53.3). Heraclides, who was popular with the common people for his proposals to redistribute the land (37.5), had to be eliminated far from the eyes of his adoring public.[28]

---

25. Antiph. 5.68; [Arist.] *Ath. Pol.* 25.4 (where the assassin is identified as Aristodicus of Tanagra in Boeotia); Plut. *Per.* 10.6–7, citing Idomeneus *FGrH* 338 F 8; Diod. Sic. 11.77.6. Stockton (1982) unconvincingly doubts that Ephialtes was murdered: see Roller 1989: 258n3; Marr 1993: 13.

26. Xen. *Hell.* 3.2.27. Cf. Gehrke *Stasis*: 53: "im Schutze der Nacht bzw. der Morgendämmerung." Note that the oligarchic faction led by Naucleides at Plataea advises the invading Theban force of 431, which infiltrated the city at night (Thuc. 2.2.1), to head for the houses of their opponents (2.2.4).

27. Plut. *Dion* 53.5. (And for a similar act of murder, this time in Miletus, see Diod. Sic. 13.104.5.) Notably, Nepos writes that prior to the murder Dion quoted the Homeric line οὐκ ἀγαθὸν πολυκοιρανίη, "multiple rule is not a good thing" (*Il.* 2.203, said by Odysseus); this is the one line of Homeric poetry known to Theophrastus's "Oligarchic Man" (*Char.* 26.2) and seems to have been something of an oligarchic catchphrase (Arist. *Pol.* 4.1292a13–15).

28. An interesting historical parallel: Emmanuel Le Roy Ladurie, in his seminal study of a

Dion's consent to the murder illustrates perfectly Socrates's statement in the *Republic* that when the "holders of property discover they are unable to expel [the *prostatēs* of the demos] or kill him by slandering him to the populace, they plot to do away with him secretly [*lathrai*], by violent means."[29]

The most infamous example of oligarchic clandestine killing, however, comes from the "reign of terror" of the Four Hundred at Athens in 411. Thucydides observes that conspirators murdered Androcles, the foremost champion of the demos, "in secret" (*krupha*). Certain other "inconvenient" people were also done away with, again secretly.[30] The ensuing description of the demos's reaction (8.66) demonstrates the chilling effectiveness of clandestine murder and its suitability for oligarchs. The demos kept quiet out of fear, satisfied with merely being left alive. The few, selective killings were enough to convince them that the oligarchic conspiracy was much bigger than it was, and that people who had previously favored democracy were now on the oligarchic side. Fear and mistrust characterized relations within the democratic faction. As Teegarden has recently argued, the murders created an environment of "preference falsification," in which potential opponents were frightened into concealing their true beliefs.[31] Selective, secretive murder was thus an "economizing" tactic for oligarchs: with just a little effort, they could take advantage of the greater size and correspondingly poorer organization of the demos.

---

massacre during Carnival in the small town of Romans, France, in 1580, observes that the popular leader of the local revolt, Paumier, was murdered in his home, at night, by patrician assassins (1979: 219–20). The oligarch who ordered the assassination, the judge Guérin, did not himself carry out the deed but delegated it to retainers.

29. *Rep.* 8.566b (and cf. Eur. fr. 626 Nauck). See also the incident in which the Mantinean democrat Lycomedes just happens to land his ship at the very spot where oligarchic exiles were gathered; they quickly murdered him (Xen. *Hell.* 7.4.3). Xenophon lamely labels the killing an "act of the divine," a claim doubted by Roy 1971: 582n69. Beck (1997) straightforwardly labels the act an "assassination" (*Attentat*). By contrast, oligarchs in Oreus on Euboea succeeded in "slandering" a democrat to the populace in the way Plato describes. In Demosthenes's telling, oligarchic conspirators were able to arrest the pro-Athenian Euphraeus on a flimsy charge, with the populace putting up no resistance; in fact, the demos welcomed the arrest (9.60–61; cf. [Arist.] *Ath. Pol.* 35.3, in which the Athenians at first delight at the Thirty's killing of sycophants and flatterers of the demos). The conspirators later instituted a Four Hundred-like "reign of terror" (see below) and took over the city.

30. Thuc. 8.65.2. The demagogue Hyperbolus is similarly dispatched at Samos while living out his ostracism: Thuc. 8.73.3. A fragment of the historian Theopompus records that the murderers put Hyperbolus's corpse in a sack and flung it into the sea: τὸ δὲ νεκρὸν αὐτοῦ εἰς σάκκον βληθὲν ῥιφῆναι εἰς τὸ πέλαγος, FGrH 115 F 96a.

31. Teegarden 2014: 18–25.

There is additional evidence that oligarchs continued to employ these techniques once they were in power. For example, the Theban exile Androcleidas was killed abroad by agents of the *dunasteia* in charge of Thebes at the time. According to Plutarch, "When Leontiades and his comrades learned that the exiles were spending their time at Athens getting friendly with the masses and enjoying the esteem of the *kaloi kagathoi*, they secretly [*krupha*] plotted against them; and sending unidentified men they killed Androcleidas by treachery [*dolōi*], although they failed to get the others."[32] The Thirty at Athens, in the waning days of their rule, executed a leading citizen, Demaretus. Their goal was to "terrify the populace (in which they were successful)."[33] It is unknown whether Demaretus was killed in public or behind closed doors, but given the usual practice of the Thirty, his death likely took place in private, through forcing him to drink hemlock.[34]

The best evidence for the use of clandestine killing during "normal times," however, comes from Sparta. Chapter 1 dealt with the difficulties involved in using Sparta as an example of oligarchy.[35] Nevertheless, it is worth canvassing the Spartan evidence on this point, for the reason that the examples surveyed describe "justice" administered within the full Spartiate class itself. The Spartans' treatment of the helots I leave aside, even though their repressive actions—including ritualized humiliation, nocturnal killings, and large-scale forced disappearances—have frequently been likened by ancient historians to the practices of contemporary authoritarian governments.[36] Relations within the Spartiate class constitute better evidence for our purposes: if the Spartan

---

32. Plut. *Pel.* 6.2.

33. [Arist.] *Ath. Pol.* 38.2. The verb "terrify" (καταπλῆξαι) has the same root as the noun used by Thucydides to describe the state of the demos in Athens during the reign of terror of the Four Hundred (8.66.2, κατάπληξιν; cf. 6.38.2).

34. Allen (2000: 232–35) reviews the evidence for the use of hemlock in Athens and concludes that the oligarchs of the late fifth century introduced it to the city. Note especially her comment that "[h]emlock would ... have suited oligarchic methods in that it was a form of execution that could be carried out by the few against the many *because it could be carried out secretly and beyond the purview of the public*" (235, emphasis added).

35. See further the comments in chapter 1, section 1.2.

36. The evidence for the Spartan *krupteia*, the "secret service" of young Spartiates in training whose duties including murdering helots, has been collected and analyzed by Ducat (1997a and b). The *locus classicus* for the suppression of helots is Plut. *Lyc.* 28.1–3 = Arist. fr. 538 Rose. Both Lévy (1988) and Ducat (2006: ch. 9) challenge, in different ways, the historicity of the institutionalized killing of helots in the fifth century. I see, however, no way around taking seriously the claim of Thuc. 4.80.4 that the Spartans "disappeared" 2000 particularly threatening helots at some point in the later fifth century (Hornblower *ad loc.*; Cartledge 2001: 127–30; Harvey 2004).

elite dispensed justice within their own, supposedly "similar" (*homoioi*) ranks in such an authoritarian manner, *a fortiori* such repression must have been much more marked within more "normal" oligarchies.[37] Moreover, the following evidence comes from the fourth century, when increasingly unequal land distribution and the demotion of many Spartiates to sub-citizen status are signs that the constitution was becoming much more conventionally oligarchical.[38]

It appears from Plutarch's *Life of Agesilaus* that in their methods of execution, as in other areas, the Spartans understood the value of secrecy.[39] We learn of two conspiracies in the period after Leuctra.[40] In the first, a group of two hundred "treacherous and worthless [*ponēroi*] men" gather at a shrine of Artemis in Issorium (32.3). The other Spartans want to attack them, but Agesilaus, "fearing mutiny," devises a clever trick. He goes to Issorium accompanied by a single servant and acts as though the men are still under his command, saying that he had not ordered them to gather in one place but to stay at separate locations. The soldiers, considering him ignorant of their plot, do as he commands so as not to arouse suspicion. Agesilaus then captures Issorium when the mutineers are divided and has fifteen of them killed at night (*nuktos*, 32.5).[41] Noteworthy here is Agesilaus's decision not to attack the conspirators directly for fear that they would inspire the other troops to rebel. His handling of the situation at night reflects the Spartan practice, mentioned elsewhere, of carrying out all executions at night, but it also serves to keep the act secret and prevent the further spread of mutiny that might result from popular reaction to the spectacle.[42] Plutarch then mentions a second, even greater conspiracy, this one reported to Agesilaus by informants.[43] Certain men were plotting a revolution secretly at someone's private home, and so Agesilaus, having conferred with the ephors, had them put to death immediately without trial (*akritoi*), although this constituted a violation of normal Spartan practice (32.6). The episode may indicate the ambiguous nature of the Spartan oligarchy: normally, unlike in conventional oligarchies, the Spartiates all enjoyed full judicial rights. It was only under increasing pressure (the loss at Leuctra) that

---

37. On this point—that, despite the Spartan "mirage," there existed considerable social, economic, and political inequality among members of the full Spartiate class—I am in agreement with the revisionist school, particularly Hodkinson (e.g., his 2000, 2009).

38. See esp. Hodkinson 2000: ch. 13.

39. Cf. Thuc. 5.68.2 ("Secrecy [*to krupton*] in government policy rendered the total force of the Lacedaemonians unknown"), with Bradford 1994.

40. See further David 1980; Cartledge 1987: 164; Richer 1998: 473.

41. Cf. Polyaen. *Strat.* 2.1.14 and Ael. *VH* 14.27.

42. For Spartan nocturnal executions, see Hdt. 4.146.2.

43. For informants in oligarchies, see further below, section 3.4.

Agesilaus and the ephors consented to treating subversives extralegally. Even still, Spartan justice in its idealized version was hardly a picture of equality under the law, as Cartledge has established. In fact, he concludes his study of Spartan justice with the statement that "the justice [Sparta] meted out was... oligarchic, that is, non- or rather anti-democratic."[44]

Thus, in stark contrast to democratic acts of "tyrannicide," the purpose of which was to appeal to and draw support from the common people's shared antipathy toward anti-democratic subversion, oligarchic violence tended to be surreptitious, anonymous, and terror-inducing.[45] Oligarchic governments rarely took official credit in such instances for their actions, preferring to leave the author(s) of the act uncertain.[46] In this respect, too, ancient Greek oligarchs resemble modern authoritarian governments, which must attempt to hide or mask much of their repression for fear of democratic mobilization. The political scientists Levitsky and Way, discussing the characteristic institutions of what they call "competitive authoritarian" regimes, observe that these states employ

> informal or "privatized" violence to suppress opposition. When the cost of imposing martial law or banning opposition activity is prohibitively high, incumbents may opt for violence that is "orchestrated by the state... but carried out by nonstate actors, such as paramilitaries, vigilantes, and militias."[47]

With the mention of "informal" or "privatized violence" we are reminded of the shadowy circumstances surrounding Ephialtes's nighttime murder in Athens, as well as the "unidentified men" sent by the Theban oligarchs to murder Androcleidas. Whereas tyrannicidal killings in defense of democracy transpired in daylight, oligarchic violence operated under the cover of darkness.[48]

---

44. Cartledge 2000a: 22, not, however, discussing the examples listed here.

45. On the dynamics involved in tyrannicide legislation and the act of tyrannicide itself, see now Teegarden 2014.

46. There are a few instances that look like exceptions but actually bolster the present argument. First, Sicyonian oligarchs killed the tyrant Euphron in public, in an act of apparent tyrannicide. However, the murder took place, not in Sicyon itself (where demotic resistance might be expected), but in Thebes, where the assassins thought they would have a sympathetic audience (Xen. *Hell.* 7.3.4–6). The demos of Sicyon did not agree with the oligarchs' assessment of Euphron but instead buried him in the agora as a hero (7.3.12; cf. the comments of Riess 2006: 72). Second, Timophanes of (oligarchic) Corinth was killed in the open in the polis itself, perhaps at the hand of his brother Timoleon (Plut. *Tim.* 4.8, Diod. Sic. 14.46.4). However, Timophanes's constituency seems not to have been the demos of Corinth but instead mercenaries the polis had hired (Arist. *Pol.* 5.1306a19–24; Plut. *Tim.* 4.4; Xen. *Hell.* 7.4.6).

47. Levitsky and Way 2010: 28, quoting Roessler 2005: 209.

48. Note description of Schatzberg (1993: 450; quoted by Bratton and van de Walle 1997:

3.1.3 The Avoidance of Public Violence

Surprising as it may seem at first glance, the threat of clandestine violence existed simultaneously with a parallel, public discourse of goodwill toward the demos. In point of fact, this division between the two sides of the curtain—between the "backstage" of elite coercion and the "stage" of agreeable public appearances—was typical of oligarchies. As much as repression was sometimes required to keep the regime in power, oligarchs could never admit this fact, let alone revel in it. In fact, the ancient sources make clear that oligarchies, precisely because they were the less popular constitution, had to be all the more careful not to give the appearance of hubris. Aristotle repeatedly advises oligarchs not to mistreat the demos. In a characteristic passage, he emphasizes that the poor, provided they are not "outraged," will maintain their "quiet" (*hēsuchia*, *Pol.* 4.1297b6–8).[49] Similarly, one of the central recommendations given oligarchs by the author of the *Rhetoric to Alexander* is to leave the demos alone, "for the majority is not so much annoyed by being deprived of office, but rather at the thought that it is being mistreated" (1424b4–6). Isocrates's speech to Nicocles frames the relationship in a more positive way: "when it comes to oligarchies as well as the other types of government, the ones that best serve the majority [*arista to plēthos therapeuōsin*] last the longest" (2.16). In practice, however, this really means ensuring that the "mob" (*ochlos*) is not treated hubristically.

Restraining oneself from hitting a common person might sound like a relatively simple task, but Aristotle is quick to point out that "it is not an easy thing, since those who share in the government do not always turn out to be humane."[50] Indeed, since the lack of accountability afforded by oligarchy

---

76) on the nature of so-called "neopatrimonial" authoritarian regimes in Africa: "A major social and political divide thus occurs between those who can 'eat' and those who cannot; *between those who command the forces of the night and those who are its victims*.... In most cases, the 'winners'... are usually inside the state, while the losers are usually on the outside looking in" (emphasis added). Cf. Demosthenes's homily to the judges at the close of his speech against Meidias: "When the court lets out [*sc.* in the evening], each one of you will head home, one perhaps walking quickly, another more slowly, and you won't give it a second thought or look over your shoulder or be afraid.... Why is this? Because you know this in your heart and have put your trust in the constitution, that no one will grab you or outrage you or strike you" (21.221).

49. See also *Pol.* 5.1305a38, 1307a24–25, 1308a7, 1309a22, 1310a11–12, 1311a13.

50. *Pol.* 4.1297b8–10; cf. the "oligarch's oath" quoted at 5.1310a9–10. (For what this oath might reveal about oligarchic weakness, see chapter 6, section 6.2.2.) We might expect tempers to run high among oligarchs especially at the onset of a new oligarchic regime, when a democracy had just been put down: in that case, the elite would enjoy *carte blanche* to avenge themselves for any abuses they suffered under popular government. This kind of thinking drove Critias, the

presented the elite with seemingly unlimited opportunities to indulge in abusing the common people, we might ask how oligarchy ever worked. The elite themselves seem to have recognized the danger and to have taken measures to check their own worst habits. Both Aristotle and the author of the *Rhetoric to Alexander* advocate heavy penalties for those who mistreat fellow citizens. On Aristotle's recommendation, members of the upper classes (the *euporoi*) who outrage the poor ought to pay more in fines than if they had attacked one of their own number (*Pol.* 5.1309a22–23). The author of the *Rhetoric* says that the "greatest punishments" (*megistai zēmiai*) in the oligarchy ought to await those who attempt to outrage the citizens; indeed, "generally speaking," the most important laws in oligarchies are those that prevent the full members of the constitution from outraging the weaker (1424b3–4, 12–14).

These passages are prescriptive rather than descriptive—they do not guarantee that oligarchs actually implemented the policies advocated. We can recognize, however, their importance for successful oligarchy. Although each member of the oligarchy might personally want to be able to mistreat the demos, he would have appreciated the need to join in sanctioning one of his fellow elites who had endangered the oligarchy by lashing out violently at a member of the demos. With all of the oligarchs aware that their fellow ruling elites had an interest in punishing their excesses, elite-on-mass violence would have been more reliably deterred. The unequal punishment system advocated by Aristotle would have driven the point home even more that mistreating members of the demos was a serious source of weakness for an oligarchy. The explicitly heavier penalties were not so much a deterrent *per se* as a signal, a reminder to oligarchs of the position they were in. Thus I find it likely that at least some oligarchies instituted laws roughly along the lines of the ones proposed by the *Politics* and the *Rhetoric*, and that these institutions helped rather than hurt oligarchic regime longevity.[51] In any case, we know of instances where blatant violence against members of the demos led to the implosion of oligarchies; I address these in chapter 6.

---

ringleader of the Thirty, to be as violent as possible towards the Athenian demos, since, in his words, "it had been reared so long in freedom [*eleutheria*]" (sc. and had thus gotten used to being the outrageous one) (Xen. *Hell.* 2.3.24; cf. Thuc. 8.68.4).

51. These comments apply only to public actions taking place in the central spaces of the polis, where visibility would have been high. If, as I argue in chapter 4, oligarchies encouraged the parcelization of power into local patron-client relations, elite-demos interaction may have looked very different in the oligarchs' own "backyards," as it were, where they would have enjoyed landlord-like status. Herodotus's story of Archaic Media, where the tyrant Deioces came to power, indicates that local control by elites could lead to corruption and exploitation (1.96.3). Peisistratus's deme judges were also presumably instituted in part to usurp legal and political authority (which may have been unpopular) from the local elite ([Arist.] *Ath. Pol.* 16.5).

3.2 Beyond Simple Repression: The Oligarchic Use of Assemblies

The acts of violence studied in the last section were exceptional and not oligarchs' primary tool for securing stability. Starting with this section I turn to more sophisticated instruments of rule, which, while not eschewing the threat of violence completely, incorporated psychological elements as well, designed to thwart collective action. I begin with assemblies. In chapter 1 (sections 1.1–2) I assessed the evidence for general assemblies of citizens within oligarchies in the Classical period and for the sociological makeup of those assemblies. I found that—with a few exceptions—it is safest to say that in most poleis the "demos" in both the Archaic and Classical periods included the adult free male population, and not some subset of the citizenry such as the hoplites. Although the lack of evidence prevents us from saying much more about the Archaic assembly, it appears overall to have been tolerated by the elite. It would be a mistake, however, to apply this conception of assemblies to Classical-era oligarchies. In this section I show that assemblies took on a new and sinister character, as oligarchs consciously worked to prevent the emergence of any democratic alternative to the status quo. If oligarchs could pressure assembly-goers into ratifying the ruling class's preferences, they could precipitate "cascades" of identical behavior, yielding unanimous decisions. These votes would then serve to divide the demos by exaggerating the popularity of the regime and creating confusion about the strength and numbers of the democratic opposition. The section illustrates another survival technique for unpopular oligarchs. It provides an alternative explanation to the theory that oligarchies, while restrictive in citizenship rights, nevertheless roughly tracked "public opinion" in their decision-making.

Classical-era oligarchs generally did not approve of assemblies of the people. The Old Oligarch relishes the thought of "good government" (*eunomia*), under which the "worthy people [*chrēstoi*] will punish the scum [*ponērous*] and will deliberate about the polis and not allow crazy people to serve as councilors or speak or assemble [*ekklēsiazein*]."[52] Xenophon's Chrysantas in the *Cyropaedia* takes the further step of linking mass assemblies (this time of soldiers) with demands for greater equality: "Can it be," he says to Cyrus, "that you think that the majority, when it has come together [*sunelthon*], will not vote that each person get the same things . . . ?"[53] Plato has Socrates note that the rule of the majority is strengthened by its meetings in assemblies, law

---

52. [Xen.] *Ath. Pol.* 1.9.

53. Xen. *Cyr.* 2.2.20. For the importance of this passage in understanding the danger posed to oligarchic regimes by military assemblies, see chapter 6, section 6.1.2.

courts, theaters, military camps, and "any other common gathering of the crowd."[54] All of these sources assume that democracy was bolstered by full meetings of the people, and Xenophon hints at the dangers to oligarchies inherent in popular assemblies. If the members of the demos used the meeting as an opportunity to act on their perceived common interests, they could overwhelm the few with their numbers and forcefully overthrow the oligarchic regime. During the Classical period, therefore, the popular assembly increasingly became a place of unease for oligarchs. The assembly was potentially an instrument for regime stabilization, but the tool could easily turn in the oligarch's hand. The dissolution of oligarchies by popular assembly meetings is discussed in chapter 4 and analyzed in detail in chapter 6.[55]

As we have seen, the solution in some constitutions was to do away with popular assemblies altogether.[56] This method had its problems, however, since the excluded might treat their exclusion as grounds for revolt. One assumption of Alcibiades's imaginary dialogue with Pericles is that the enactments of assembled oligarchs constitute an act of force (*bia*) against the majority.[57] Likewise in Plato an oligarchy is defined as a constitution based on a wealth qualification, in which the rich rule and the poor have no share in the government. The constitution is forced through either by outright violence or by intimidation, and the excluded long for revolution.[58]

On this topic, as with others, Aristotle displays considerably more nuance than his predecessors, yet his pronouncements in the *Politics* are inconsistent. In several places he suggests that the poor, even if they have no role to play in the constitution, will not protest their lot in oligarchies as long as they are not treated violently and are allowed to keep their possessions and make

---

54. Plat. *Rep.* 6.492b-c.

55. Section 6.1. As will become clearer below, institutions were never an ironclad guarantee against subversive activity, and in fact they represented considerable risks for oligarchs. The political scientist Andreas Schedler has well brought out the contingent nature of authoritarian institutions: "On average, authoritarian political institutions seem indeed to fulfill regime-supporting functions. And yet, inevitably, although to variable degrees, they contain seeds of subversion.... Even when authoritarian institutions work as they are supposed to, absorbing, channeling, dampening, deflecting, or dispersing oppositional energies, regime-critical actors may still succeed to some extent in neutralizing these institutions or even appropriating them for their purposes. Even if institutions make autocracy work, and augment the ruler's *probability* of surviving in office and governing effectively, they still contain the *possibility* of eroding authoritarian stability and governance" (2013: 73–74, emphasis in original).

56. See above, chapter 2, section 2.2.1, on the Boeotian *koinon*, and Whibley (1896: 165–66), citing Arist. *Pol.* 2.1273b7–8; Rhodes with Lewis 1997: 502.

57. Xen. *Mem.* 1.2.45.

58. Plat. *Rep.* 8.550c, 551b, 555d.

money.⁵⁹ Elsewhere, however, he contradicts himself by saying that the poor often take offense at exclusion but can be placated by minor concessions.⁶⁰ These can come in the form of co-optation (discussed below, section 3.3), but Aristotle devotes chapter 14 of Book 4 specifically to the topic of assemblies. Here he counsels that oligarchies should either co-opt certain people from the demos, or appoint *probouloi* or *nomophulakes*, officers who control the proceedings of the assembly.⁶¹ The demos can then concern itself with matters that the *probouloi* and *nomophulakes* have deliberated on in advance (*probouleusōsin*, 1298b30). "In this way," Aristotle says, "the demos will have a share [*methexei*] in deliberating, but it will not be able to overthrow any aspect of the constitution." Furthermore, the demos should either affirm policy or at least vote nothing contrary to what has been preformulated, although it should remain possible for them to veto (*apopsēphizomenon*) decisions of the ruling class without appeal.⁶² In other words, the demos in an oligarchy should be invited on occasion to review a given decision of the council.⁶³ It should then either affirm or reject the decision, presumably without debate.⁶⁴

59. e.g., *Pol.* 4.1297b6–8, 5.1308b34–38, 6.1318b16–21.

60. This is clearest in the case of Archaic Erythrae, where the demos "changed the constitution because they were aggrieved at the fact that it was ruled by a few people" (5.1305b18–22). See also 5.1302a29–30, 1304a14–17.

61. *Pol.* 4.1298b26–29. For *probouloi* in Aristotle, see also *Pol.* 4.1299b31–36, 6.1322b16, 1323a7–9. Oligarchic *probouloi* are attested at Corinth (Nic. Dam. *FGrH* 90 F 60.2) and Cnidus (Plut. *QG* 4 = *Mor.* 292a, but the latter is more likely an Archaic elite-led regime). There were *probouloi* at Megara (Ar. *Ach.* 755), but it is unclear whether these should be taken to indicate an oligarchic constitution (as de Ste. Croix [1972: 243n25] thought). *Nomophulakes* appear most famously in the regime of Demetrius of Phalerum (for which see chapter 2, sections 2.3 and 2.4 above): see Jacoby's commentary *ad* Philoch. *FGrH* 328 F 64; Gehrke 1978: 151–62; Williams 1985: 176.; O'Sullivan 2009: 72–86, 154–55 (although she denies their function as *probouloi*-type overseers); Banfi 2010: 142–47, 157–61; Canevaro 2011: 66–69. They also feature in the oligarchic *diagramma* for Cyrene: *SEG* 9.1, line 32. In the *Oeconomicus*, Xenophon's Ischomachus casually remarks that "in well-ordered [*eunomoumenai*] poleis, it is not enough for the citizens that they draft good laws, but they also appoint *nomophulakes*, who inspect the process and praise those who produce lawful/customary things [*nomima*], but punish those who produce legislation contrary to the laws" (9.14).

62. *Pol.* 1298b35–38. The text is slightly unclear here, but I follow Newman *ad loc.*

63. Cf. *Pol.* 3.1275b7–8: "In some constitutions there is no 'demos' [i.e., institutionalized assembly], nor do they hold [regular] meetings of the *ekklēsia* but only extraordinary ones [*sunklētous*]."

64. Aristotle's advice here conforms to his description of the Spartan system in Book 2, where it is said that in Crete, as in Sparta, everyone can attend the assembly, but they can only ratify or reject proposals of the magistrates (1272a10–12). As is known from elsewhere, Spartans

Although such a procedure falls far short of the standards of full ancient democracy, we might nevertheless suppose that it afforded the demos significant influence. The poorer members of a polis, while not being able to propose alternative measures, might still reject any *probouleuma* they found unacceptable.[65] The oligarchs, in turn, anticipating the assembly members' general mood, would have to try to formulate a recommendation that avoids the assembly's veto. Thus, while successful policy would remain considerably more "conservative" than the preferences of the median voter, it would still be constrained to a degree by the opinion of the demos.

This view is logical and attractive, and some scholars have held it up as a potential explanation for how some oligarchies might have survived. Salmon, for example, noting 1) the Classical Corinthian oligarchy's startling longevity, 2) its limited but attested use of the assembly, and 3) its use of *probouloi*, Aristotle's favored oligarchic presiding magistrate, attempts to use Aristotle's remarks in Book 4 to account for what he calls the "remarkable consensus" between rulers and ruled in Corinth.[66] Although he does not spell out the logic of his argument explicitly, Salmon presumably thinks that a schema like that outlined by Aristotle existed in Corinth and kept the oligarchs in tune with mass opinion.

There is, however, a problem with such an approach, one that Salmon himself detects. Salmon hints at something sinister in the whole process, remarking at one point on the Corinthian oligarchs' "long and successful manipulation of public opinion." In his picture, the oligarchs not only recorded the assembly's vote, but also "guided" it (238). This suggestion of tampering muddies his earlier picture of the Corinthian oligarchy as reaching decisions "with a careful eye to what the citizens could be persuaded, rather than forced, to accept" (236), as "ensur[ing] that their decisions coincided with the popular will" (237). Clearly, if the oligarchy's policies strictly *coincided* with preexisting popular opinion there would be very little need for manipu-

---

other than magistrates could not address the floor of the assembly or debate motions (de Ste. Croix 1972: 127–31).

65. Strictly speaking, the "median voter" in the assembly determines policy, since they possess the decisive opinion in a majority vote. If the oligarchy encourages richer members to attend and discourages poorer members (see Arist. *Pol.* 4.1297a17–19), then the median voter's preferences might be quite conservative, since "the assembly" of course comprises not only the demos (defined as the poorer majority) but the whole citizen population.

66. 1984: 238. Longevity: the Corinthian regime "remarkably stable" (236). Sparing use of assembly: Plut. *Dion.* 53.4. Probouloi: Nic. Dam. *FGrH* 90 F 60.2. Note also that Salmon persuasively argues that there was probably no property qualification for attendance in the assembly (237).

lation. Yet Salmon, without fully accounting for it, admits that the manipulation was there.

Here I propose an alternative explanation, with causal mechanisms clearly stated, of how this manipulation worked. I assume that assemblies under oligarchies were not simply ways of registering popular opinion, since democratic institutions performed that task better. Nor were assemblies mere "window dressing" meant to placate the demos by offering a semblance of democratic procedure. That would be a relatively low pay-off for the oligarchs compared to the potentially deadly risk they were taking by convening the people. In my view, the dividends to be had were much greater. A successful oligarchic assembly did not simply mollify the demos, it weakened and divided it. The key to this process lies in the practice of open voting (i.e., by a show of hands) in Greek assemblies, which has profound implications for our understanding of ancient political gatherings' effectiveness at recording "genuine" opinions. In democracies, where (in theory, at least) members of the demos had little reason to mask their true thoughts, open voting might come close to fulfilling the task of aggregating preferences. In oligarchies, by contrast, a little intimidation might go a long way in nudging the individual members of the demos toward accepting the ruling class's policies unopposed.

An episode of Spartan political history reveals the strategic choices at work in this process. As we have seen, Sparta had a unique constitution for an oligarchy. One remarked-upon feature of its assemblies was "the shout," whereby the mass of Spartiates voted by acclamation to decide between competing policies. Thucydides makes this clear ("they decide by shout and not by vote," 1.87.2), and Aristotle mentions the method in the *Politics*, calling it "childish" (*paidariōdes*, 2.1271a10). Modern scholars have often concluded from these descriptions that Sparta was hopelessly backward compared to dynamic Athens. In de Ste. Croix's words, it was a "half-way stage in the evolution of proper voting procedure," an "archaic procedure . . . closely bound up with the absence of any real *isēgoria* or any democratic initiative in the Spartan Assembly."[67] Cartledge agrees, noting that "the Spartans did not recognize the principle of 'one man, one vote,' according to which everyone counts for one and no one for more than one." Aristotle's denigration of the shouting method as "childish" stemmed presumably from the fact that it was "so easily manipulated."[68]

It is striking, however, that neither scholar fully explores the implications of the rest of the Thucydides passage, which actually proves the opposite of what they argue. "The shout" was in fact less prone to manipulation than a

---

67. De Ste. Croix 1972: 349.
68. Cartledge 2001: 51–52; cf. 34–35.

system in which individual preferences were openly displayed. As Thucydides reveals, when the Spartans took a vote on war with Athens using the accustomed shouting procedure, the presiding official Sthenelaidas claimed he could not discern the result. He therefore divided the room in half and ordered the "yeas" to stand on one side, the "nays" on the other. His hope, according to Thucydides, was that "they would incline *more* to war because they had to *deliver their votes openly*"; and the result was in fact that "those [voting yes] *became much greater* in number."[69] In other words, by making the vote open, Sthenelaidas forced the Spartiates into a scenario where the leaders could see their individual decisions. Whereas the shout preserved anonymity, the new method exposed the Spartiates to sanction if they voted the "wrong" way. There was greater motivation now not to stand out. Voting became less about expressing one's conviction and more about choosing the path the majority was likely to follow (which by default was the leadership's position). In social science terms, the vote was a "coordination game" in which individual Spartiates wanted to vote only as others did.[70] The result was greater consensus for the elite's position. The episode confirms Andrewes's observation that normally Sparta "had in some ways a more open constitution than most oligarchies." Lewis agreed with Andrewes against de Ste. Croix and others, noting that "the anonymity of the system might have made it relatively free from external pressure."[71] Sparta was thus backward compared to a democracy like Athens, but less coercive compared to other oligarchies. The institution of open voting had different effects depending on the political context.

Thucydides's account of the beginnings of the Constitution of the Four Hundred in Athens in 411 reveals the same dynamics.[72] In the author's presentation, the assembly continued to meet, but the oligarchic conspirators vetted all proposals. If anyone dared to speak in opposition, "he was quickly put to death in some convenient way, and there was no inquiry into who did it" (8.66.2). As a result, the assembly later voted the democracy out of existence "with no one opposing" (8.69.1). The members of the Athenian demos had come to understand that votes no longer signaled honest policy preferences; instead, they afforded the oligarchs a screening mechanism with which to identify and punish dissidents.[73] The political scientist Beatriz Magaloni, who

---

69. 1.87.2: ἀλλὰ βουλόμενος αὐτοὺς φανερῶς ἀποδεικνυμένους τὴν γνώμην ἐς τὸ πολεμεῖν μᾶλλον ὁρμῆσαι ἔλεξεν... ἀναστάντες δὲ διέστησαν, καὶ πολλῷ πλείους ἐγένοντο οἷς ἐδόκουν αἱ σπονδαὶ λελύσθαι.

70. See chapter 1, section 1.3.

71. Andrewes 1966: 1; Lewis 1977: 42. See also Hornblower *ad* 1.87.2.

72. This episode is also discussed in the section on "secret assassinations" above, 3.1.2.

73. Of course, the decision to launch the Sicilian expedition saw a similar moment of in-

BALANCING COERCION AND CO-OPTATION   127

has studied the history of the authoritarian PRI regime in Mexico during the twentieth century, calls this ability of autocrats to distinguish between supporters and proponents a "punishment regime."[74] The oligarchs of the Four Hundred set up just such a regime in 411. With just a few targeted acts of terror, they were able to push the entire Colonus assembly toward a completely unanimous cascade of "yea" votes.[75]

The processes uncovered in those two cases extend to other poleis as well. For example, Thucydides tells us that the Corcyrean oligarchs, after murdering Peithias, the *prostatēs* of the demos and sixty other councilors and private citizens, "called together the Corcyreans" and "forced them" to ratify a decision to sever ties with Athens.[76] The oligarchs' involvement of the demos is at first puzzling, since they put themselves in danger by convening an assembly of the people whose *prostatēs* they had just killed. One could argue that they felt the need to justify their actions and that they were vulnerable in the period between Peithias's murder and the arrival of Spartan envoys (3.72.2).[77] But if they knew the Spartans were coming, they could have told the Corcyreans anything to pacify them in the meantime; instead, they are said to have forced the demos to vote for an unpopular position. In my view, their action represented more than an attempt at pacification. As with the Spartan and Athenian oligarchs, by dangling an implicit threat over the heads of the majority, they induced the demos to partake in their plan.[78]

Similar events transpired at Mende in 423. Thucydides first describes the inhabitants of the city as "openly coming over [to Brasidas] during the truce" (4.123.1). He goes on to explain, however, that the initiators of the plan were

---

timidation and unanimity (Thuc. 6.24.4 with Samons 2004: 135–37). Elsewhere in Thucydides, however, the Athenian democracy is characterized by narrow votes rather than unanimous ones (1.44.1, 3.36.6, 49.1; cf. Xen. *Hell.* 1.7.7–35). Comedians joked that the Athenians were capricious (*tachubouloi*, Ar. *Ach.* 628, *metabouloi*, 632), not monolithic in their voting patterns. The vote for the Sicilian expedition was a travesty, but it was exceptional.

74. Magaloni 2006: 20, 66–67.

75. For the notion of cascading, in which voters' (and others') decisions unanimously align—often with detrimental results—see Kuran 1995; Lohmann 2000; and, in an ancient context, Ober 2008: 114–15, 180–81.

76. Thuc. 3.71.1. I assume that up to this point Corcyra had been a democracy (Thuc. 3.81.4; Diod. Sic. 12.57.3; *pace* IACP Index 11 and the too-skeptical arguments of Brock 2009: 157–58); cf. Bruce 1971: 68–69.

77. Wilson (1987: 91) claims that it was "natural" for the oligarchs to call the Corcyreans together, "in order to give their explanations and avert any backlash."

78. Thucydides tells us nothing about the numbers who voted for and against the oligarchs' proposal at 3.71.1, but there can be little doubt that the crowd was unanimously in favor, since they were "forced to approve."

actually few, and that they had "coerced the majority contrary to their general opinion" (4.123.2). Although Thucydides does not explicitly say so, it is likely that the Mendaean *oligoi* implicated the *polloi* in the decision by forcing them to vote on it, just as in the Corcyrean case. This would account for Thucydides' description of the Mendaeans as collectively "coming over" to Brasidas.[79]

The truly decisive evidence for oligarchic manipulation of assemblies, however, comes from Megara. In the aftermath of heavy *stasis*, the oligarchs conducted a military review (*exetasis hoplōn*) in which they assembled the regiments in different locations and then picked out their enemies from each, a hundred in total. They then "forced the demos" to pass open judgment on these men and killed them (4.74.3). The members of the demos, coerced into making their decision public, would have gone along with the wishes of the oligarchs to avoid punishment. They would then have seen themselves openly and unanimously condemning their former leaders. The psychological and practical effects of this inter-visibility (to be elaborated below) would have been consequential, and Thucydides hints at their importance when he says that "this change in government arising from *stasis*, although effected by a very small number of men, lasted the longest time."[80]

The events in Megara dovetail with similar actions under the Thirty, which brings us full circle in our exploration of oligarchic techniques in and out of Athens.[81] Both Xenophon and Lysias describe the Thirty's use of the open ballot. In the former, Critias orders the wider oligarchic *politeuma* known as the Three Thousand to "make their vote openly" when condemning select enemies of the regime, with armed Spartans providing the necessary intimidation (*Hell.* 2.4.9–10). Lysias similarly speaks of the Thirty as forcing people to deliver their votes, "not [secretly] into containers, but openly" (13.37), so that there was no chance that any of the defendants would be acquitted. Xenophon's Critias spells out the reasoning behind these methods: "Since you [the Three Thousand] share in the benefits [*timai*] of this constitution, you must

---

79. By contrast, the Acanthians at 4.88.1 debate Brasidas's offer from both sides and then vote secretly. Gomme in *HCT* 3: 557 cites Grote's praise of "the care to protect individual independence of judgment by secret suffrage."

80. Thuc. 4.74.4. An extremely similar episode occurs in fourth-century Corcyra, recorded by Aeneas Tacticus: the wealthy and oligarchic plan a revolt against the demos with the help of the Athenian commander Chares, in which certain members of the Athenian garrison cut themselves and display their wounds in the agora (for the tactic, cf. Hdt. 1.59.4; [Arist.] *Ath. Pol.* 14.1; Plut. *Sol.* 30.1). An assembly is called in which the majority of the Corcyreans, knowing nothing of the plot, condemn the *prostatai* of the demos to death, thinking they were the instigators of the wounding, at which point the oligarchic conspirators established an oligarchy (11.13–15).

81. Spivey (1994: 48) and Larsen (1949: 175–76) also connect the Megarian episode with manipulation under the Thirty.

share in the dangers. [Condemn the defendants,] so that you take heart in and fear the same things that we do" (*Hell.* 2.4.9). Critias's explicit goal is to implicate the others in the regime by forcing them to have a stake in its success.[82] Since he is talking to the Three Thousand, actual members of the constitution who enjoy the benefits (*timai*) of full citizenship, his remarks only partially apply to the case of the excluded under oligarchies—they were often required to implicate themselves in the actions of the regime but received even less for doing so, as in Megara.[83]

The evidence so far has tended to come from instances of oligarchic takeover, when oligarchs were violently overthrowing democratic regimes. One might therefore object to the proposed schema on the grounds that the most it can show is that oligarchs intimidated assemblies in times of crisis but not necessarily that they did so during "normal" circumstances. As it happens, however, there is a good description in the historical sources of assemblies under stable oligarchy operating in the way I describe. The oligarchy of Phocion at Athens, established in 321 and lasting until 319, was notoriously ordered according to a property assessment, with a minimum census of twenty *mnai*. Whether this meant that twelve thousand of the citizens (Plutarch) or twenty-two thousand (Diodorus) were stripped of full citizenship ("disenfranchised" is an unhelpful term, as I explain below), contemporaries and later sources clearly considered the resulting constitution an oligarchy.[84] What I wish to stress here is that it appears incorrect based on the sources to assume that those not meeting the twenty-*mnai* qualification were excluded from voting in the *ekklēsia*. Many of the members of the demos went into exile in Thrace and so would not have been present anyway, it is true, but not all who were excluded emigrated (as Plut. *Phoc.* 28.4 makes clear).[85] In addition, we have several positive pieces of evidence that the demos (understood in the usual

---

82. Cf. Plat. *Ap.* 32c: the Thirty summon Socrates and others and order them to arrest Leon of Salamis, "just as they ordered many times to many people, hoping to implicate as many as possible in their crimes." For more on this particular episode from Xenophon, see chapter 6, section 6.2.2.

83. There would therefore seem to be some justice in the Syracusan demagogue Athenagoras's remark (Thuc. 6.39.2) that oligarchy "gives the majority a share in the dangers but not only takes more of the benefits, it steals away the whole lot for itself."

84. For the figures, see Plutarch *Phoc.* 28.4; Diod. Sic. 18.18.5. I do not wish to wade into the debate concerning the accuracy of these figures; for a review of the scholarship, see van Wees 2011: 107–10. For a contemporary Athenian designation of the Phocion regime as oligarchic, see *IG* II² 448, line 61. For recent studies of this period, see Habicht 1997: 36–53; Dreyer 1999; Poddighe 2002; O'Sullivan 2009; van Wees 2011; Bayliss 2011.

85. As chapter 4 makes clear, acts of expulsion by oligarchies rarely affected the entire demos.

sense as the full native male citizen population of Athens) continued to attend the assembly. First, the epigraphic evidence of the period (thirty-nine known decrees, usefully surveyed by Oliver [2003b]) retains the word "demos" in the enactment formulae.[86] While it is possible that "demos" here now designates a narrower, qualified civic body, it seems unlikely that an oligarchic regime would have retained the ideologically charged title "demos" for itself if the common people were not, in fact, voting in the assembly.[87]

It would be a mistake, however, to think that just because the very poorest were not excluded from the assembly, the regime of Phocion was in fact a kind of democracy. Here I must part ways with Tritle, who sees in the post-321 regime a "moderate democracy."[88] For as Plutarch puts it in a telling formulation, the demos was "moderate and conducting itself with proper decorum in politics *out of fear.*"[89] This "fear" was not simply of the Macedonian garrison at Munichia but, I would argue, fear of the power of the ruling oligarchs. Phocion and the other members of the oligarchic government obtained the outcomes they wanted in the assembly because they controlled the agenda (as many scholars have noted) and, just as importantly, because the demos was cowed and subservient out of fear of persecution.[90] The institution of the assembly had been transformed, as the present model would predict, into a rubber stamp for the authoritarian elite.

Finally, it is worth noting additional evidence for oligarchs' preference for open voting in two literary sources, both dealing with the mythical figure of

---

86. See, e.g., *IG* II² 380, line 7, a decree enacted by Demades.

87. Oliver is agnostic on this point, citing Tritle's analysis (discussed below) without endorsement (2003b: 46). Both Diodorus and Plutarch, however, describe the demos as participating in the assembly under the oligarchy: Diod. Sic. 18.64.2, 64.3, 65.6; Plut. *Phoc.* 30.4 (discussed below). For what it is worth, Diodorus says (18.18.5) that the Athenians were supposed to govern themselves according to Solon's constitution: it is well known that the thetes were allowed to attend the assembly under that dispensation. See [Arist.] *Ath. Pol.* 7.3 with Rhodes's note *ad loc* and Raaflaub 2006a: 404. Tritle is therefore correct when he claims that "[a] careful reading of Plutarch and Diodorus does not suggest that the disfranchised were prohibited from attending the *ekklesia* or law courts" (1988: 134). Cf. Ferguson 1911: 31n1.

88. Tritle 1988: 136. See also Tracy 1995: 18: "the internal workings of the Athenian state, the real indicator of the nature of the government, remained essentially intact and democratic."

89. Plut. *Phoc.* 30.4: σωφρονοῦντα τὸν δῆμον καὶ πολιτευόμενον εὐτάκτως διὰ τὸν φόβον.

90. The oligarchs' agenda control is acknowledged by Ferguson (1911: 22, 32) and Tritle (1988: 135). It is therefore unclear, since the demos's sovereignty in the assembly was compromised, how Tritle can still label the regime a democracy. See also Oliver on the epigraphic record: "The apparent dominance of the *Ekklesia* over the *Boule* . . . may reflect greater confidence in the functioning of the *Ekklesia* or *a greater ease for proposers of decrees to ratify their motions.*" (2003b: 46, emphasis added)

Ajax. In Pindar's eighth Nemean ode, the poetic voice laments the decision of the Achaeans to award Odysseus Achilles's armor over Ajax: "With secret votes (*kruphiaisi... psaphois*) the Danaans paid court to Odysseus" (26). Pindar later seems to suggest that Ajax's worthiness was obvious (the wounds the two men inflicted on the enemy were "not the same," *anomoia*, 27), but Odysseus took advantage of hateful "slander" (*parphasis*) in order to malign Ajax and, in classic rhetorical fashion, make the weaker case the stronger. The secret ballot allowed the Danaans to cast a vote that they would have felt ashamed to make under the watchful eye of the elite in an open vote.[91]

In much the same way, the philosopher Antisthenes has his Ajax argue in a mock courtroom speech that the Achaeans should "cast [their] vote, not in secret, but openly, so that [they will] recognize that justice must be rendered by the judges themselves, should they not vote correctly."[92] Ajax's logic here carries an underlying threat: if the judges vote openly, he will exact retribution (*dikē*) from those who vote "wrongly" (in favor of Odysseus). They should therefore vote openly so that they vote "correctly" and avoid this unpleasant outcome. This threat, coupled with Ajax's disparaging characterizations of the judges elsewhere as ignorant, suggests a brazenly oligarchic personality who cannot accept the possibility of the majority voting secretly against what he perceives to be his rightful due.[93]

It seems clear from the assembled evidence that the open voting characteristic of assemblies proved advantageous for oligarchies. Oligarchs could threaten the demos with violence if they voted the wrong way; this threat provided the necessary motivation to vote for the oligarchs' favored *probou-*

---

91. See Miller 1982: 116: "The point of *kruphiaisi* is not that Odysseus falsified the votes but simply that the Danaans reached their decision by secret ballot—with the additional implication that it was the very secrecy of the process, the freedom from the restraint of public opinion, that encouraged them to indulge their envious spite against Ajax's patent excellence." See further Carey 1976: 3; Pinney and Hamilton 1982: 583 with n24; *pace* Brown 1951: 15n23; Boegehold 1963: 368n6.

92. Antisthenes fr. 14.9 Caizzi: καὶ ταῦτα μὴ κρύβδην [φέρετε], ἀλλὰ φανερῶς, ἵνα γνῶτε ὅτι καὶ αὐτοῖς τοῖς δικάζουσι δοτέα δίκη ἐστίν, ἂν μὴ δικάσωσιν ὀρθῶς. Similarly Plato in the *Laws* has the Athenian Stranger speak scornfully of "lowly" (*phaula*) and "voiceless" (*aphōna*) courts (he has the example of democratic Athens in mind), where dicasts are free to deliver their verdicts in secret (9.876b).

93. Cf. 14.1 ("you who know nothing are judging"), 14.4 ("you who know nothing promise to judge things about which you are ignorant"). At one point, Ajax makes his conception of justice exceptionally clear: "It's impossible to argue in words against an enemy: one must either fight and win, or submit to slavery in silence" (14.7). This brusqueness is indeed "blunt rudeness" on Ajax's part (Worman 2002: 185), but there are deeper political oppositions involved as well. For more on this understudied text, see Hesk 2000: 118–21; Prince 2015 *ad loc.*

leumata. The result in many cases was (the appearance of) unanimity. But, as has been hinted at already, the practical effects of these kinds of outcomes would not end when the votes had been counted. The sight of so many members of the community collectively validating the decisions of the ruling group could weigh profoundly on the strategic calculus of political actors deciding in the future whether to challenge the regime.[94]

The same is true in the modern era, when authoritarian rulers either buy votes or inflate their margins of victory to absurd figures, sometimes ninety percentage points or more. Such elections are clearly fraudulent to the outside world, but they are not simply empty rituals devoid of meaning for those at home. As the political scientist Alberto Simpser has explained,

> Electoral manipulation can potentially yield substantially more than simply winning the election at hand. Specifically, excessive and blatant manipulation has a series of intended effects that include, among other things . . . [discouraging] opposition supporters from turning out to vote or to protest. . . . In other words, I argue that electoral manipulation ought to be understood not merely as a marginal vote-getting technique, but also as an important tool for consolidating and monopolizing political power. (2013: 3–4)

To return to an ancient Greek context, if a member of the demos saw himself and others voting in line with the oligarchy—and others saw him in turn—he might inflate the regime's popularity in his mind and come to think that the potential opposition within the population was small or nonexistent.[95] Others could think the same, even if individually each preferred that the oligarchy fall. All that is necessary to prevent coordination against the regime in such a case is for each person to believe that he would be alone and vulnerable if he took a stand against the oligarchy. Since the members of the demos want to revolt

---

94. One might object that we know the results of several assembly votes from the Hellenistic period, which tend to show large supermajorities. Gauthier analyzed these decrees in an important study (1990). For example, Hellenistic Colophon approved a measure with 1,326 votes in favor, 16 against (*SEG* 39.1244, lines 48–51). Perhaps, then, democracies were just as susceptible to social pressure and cascading. However, as Gauthier points out, these decrees represent a special case, that of bestowing civic honors on foreigners. They were intended by the community to show to the honorand the unanimous or near-unanimous consent of the citizen body. Moreover, they were conducted by secret ballot. Thus, the conditions of a "punishment regime" as I have described it do not obtain. For further examples of this phenomenon published since Gauthier's study see *SEG* 41.929, lines 34–35; *SEG* 57.1046 II, lines 39–41.

95. In other words, there is "common knowledge" of the demos's acquiescence to the oligarchy.

only on the guarantee that others revolt as well, the unanimous votes taken in the assembly would make it less likely for them to take to the streets in the future, since members of the demos would not be able to trust one another not to stick with the regime. As Beatriz Magaloni has said of "hegemonic party" authoritarian regimes (which resemble in certain ways ancient oligarchies), "Hegemonic-party autocracies strive to create an image of invincibility. By winning with [huge] margins of victory . . . a hegemonic party generates a public message that outside of the ruling party there is nothing but limbo."[96] This "image of invincibility" was one of the "indirect effects" produced by unanimous assembly-voting in oligarchies, to use Simpser's terminology once again (2013: 4). Assemblies not only bestowed a veneer of popular legitimacy on oligarchic policies at the time of voting, but—more importantly—they made subsequent acts of resistance less likely. This would have been one of the crucial indirect effects of the assemblies in Corcyra, Megara, and, I would hypothesize, Salmon's "remarkably stable" Corinth.

3.3 Co-optation into the Regime

As we saw above, Aristotle recommends the "selection of certain people from the mass [*plēthos*]" to oversee assembly proceedings as an alternative to the use of *probouloi* and *nomophulakes* (*Pol.* 4.1298b27). The verb used, *proshaireisthai*, denotes the unilateral selection by one agent of another agent for the purpose of association or service.[97] As such, it makes perfect sense as a general tool for oligarchic governance, and again, it finds parallels in the practices of contemporary authoritarian regimes. The political scientist Jennifer Gandhi, in a study of institutions within dictatorships, notes that legislatures often serve as a carefully controlled forum for negotiating policy concessions among a hand-selected group of opposition members. The institutionalized nature of the legislature means that members of society have a clear picture of the criteria necessary to gain entry, with the result that they may individually strive to meet the qualifications rather than work with other members of the excluded opposition to alter the underlying rules of the game. From the ruling elite's perspective, on the other hand, the regularized interaction afforded by

---

96. Magaloni 2006: 46. Cf. Gandhi and Lust-Okar 2009: they countenance the possibility that elections under authoritarianism both "serve as a signal to members of the regime elite that opposition is futile" (405) and "compel people to participate in a ritual that everyone knows is 'fake'" (406).

97. Cf. Hdt. 9.10.3, Thuc. 5.63.4, [Arist.] *Ath. Pol.* 35.1 (the last of which is examined in greater detail below).

the institution lowers the informational costs involved in trying to discover the preferences of the opposition and the price at which they can successfully be bought off. The result, as Gandhi points out, is that "concessions made in response to opposition demands can be revealed within a closed forum rather than on the street. Within the halls of an assembly, demands do not appear to be acts of resistance and concessions do not seem like capitulations."[98]

The situation in ancient Greek oligarchies was comparable, but with a few important modifications. Oligarchies did sometimes establish qualifying criteria for entry to the ranks of full citizenship, and these rules could be counted on to divide and co-opt the members of the demos. Less likely, however, is the idea that members of the demos, once they attained membership in the ruling group, used this position to extract concessions on behalf of the rest of the demos. More plausibly, we should view the acquisition of full citizenship status as its own reward: becoming a member of the oligarchy brought its own material and psychological perquisites, such as connections with wealthy oligarchs and the gratification inherent in exercising full political power.[99] The general purpose of co-optation within Greek oligarchies was not so much to allow the negotiation of demands as to make individual advancement rather than collective action the preferred strategy for members of the demos.[100]

Our evidence for co-optative practices in Classical Greek oligarchies comes largely from Aristotle. For example, he describes the method of directly choosing members of the demos to serve with the ruling elite in accordance with some measure of merit. This device first comes up in a passage from Book 4 of the *Politics* about the kinds of oligarchies: in the second type, the property qualification for citizenship is still high, but oligarchs can fill vacancies of office by "choosing" whomever they wish (*haireisthai* this time instead of *proshaireisthai*, 1292b1–2). If the magistrates thus selected come from the entire male citizen population, the method is "aristocratic," if from a preselected group, "oligarchic." We might think, therefore, that selecting from among the entire population is rare for oligarchies, but elsewhere Aristotle says that oligarchies can better survive if relations between those inside and outside the ruling group are good, with the governing class not "mistreating" the excluded but instead "bringing those fit to command [*hēgemonikoi*] into the constitution" (5.1308a8). We should understand this group as comprising

98. Gandhi 2008: 75–79 (quotation at 79).

99. For political participation as an opportunity to establish connections with influential individuals, see Ober 2008: 147–51, discussing the very different context of the Athenian democratic Council of 500.

100. Cf. Magaloni and Kricheli 2010: 126: "In selectively co-opting the opposition ... dictators ... create divided oppositions and increase coordination costs among their opponents."

those among the demos who stand out as naturally charismatic (and therefore also threatening).[101]

Aristotle gives us a concrete example of this practice in Book 6, when he praises the famously oligarchic Massalians for their habit of "yielding a share of the ruling body [*politeuma*] to the masses" through a process of "selecting those deemed worthy" (1321a26–31).[102] Isocrates might also provide evidence for the technique in his eighth letter, directed to the "rulers" (*archontes*) of Mytilene. Editors are agreed that the rulers in this case are an oligarchic faction that came to power in the city in the mid-fourth century (cf. Dem. 13.8, 15.19). Isocrates begins his letter, in which he beseeches the oligarchs to restore the tutor of his grandchildren to full citizenship, with the observation that they "have been advised well in becoming reconciled to your citizens, and in trying to make the number of exiles few, the number of fellow full citizens [*sumpoliteuomenoi*] many" (3).[103] Isocrates's words suggest that the Mytilinean oligarchs were willing to allow those not normally qualified to partake in such a regime into the ranks of the full citizenry.[104] The oligarchs of Larissa in Thessaly possibly also engaged in the co-option of lower-class citizens into their ranks, but in a biased or otherwise haphazard way. The sophist Gorgias mocked them in a pun recorded by Aristotle (*Pol.* 3.1275b26–30): "just as mortars are made by mortar-makers, the Larissaeans have been made by the magistrates [*dēmiourgoi*]" (= DK 82 A 19: a *larissa* is also a kind of kettle, hence the comparison with mortars; a *dēmiourgos* is both a kind of magistrate and a skilled workman). It seems that the *dēmiourgoi* of Larissa "made" Larissaeans in a manner that looked comically arbitrary to outsiders.[105] Random

---

101. A fragment of a treatise by Theophrastus likewise says that it is "rather old-fashioned" (*archaikōteros*) to choose offices by *timēmata*, since many "born leaders" would be excluded. He agrees, though, that some offices, like the treasury, ought to be performed by the wealthy alone (Aly 1943, Fragment B, 18–46).

102. For the oligarchic constitution of Massalia (modern-day Marseille) see *IACP* no. 3, pp. 166–67. The same passage of Aristotle says that the Thebans extended participation to those who had abstained from "banausic" trades for a certain amount of time (cf. *Pol.* 3.1278a25–26, where this is phrased as "abstained from the agora for ten years").

103. There may be some irony in his tone, as it is on the surface paradoxical that an oligarchy would make their opponents "fewer" and their own ranks "greater."

104. It may be that the oligarchs' opponents are wealthy supporters of the previous democracy, since Isocrates makes a point of praising the oligarchs for restoring the returning exiles' property to them (3). Even so, their incorporation of elements of the democratic faction into the regime would have weakened the potential opposition.

105. See further Wade-Gery 1945: 25 with n4, where the Larissaean *dēmiourgoi* are compared to the *katalogeis* charged with drawing up the citizen list of the "Five Thousand" in Athens during the reign of the Four Hundred in 411. The Athenian process was similarly arbitrary.

co-optation was thus an option, but it threatened to expose oligarchs to charges of favoritism in comparison with the relatively disinterested tool of property qualifications.[106]

Also noteworthy are the ways in which individualized co-optation could serve as a form of implication if the co-opted carried out the "dirty work" of the oligarchy. For example, the Thirty in 404 "selected" (*proshaireisthai* again) three hundred "whip-bearers" (*mastigophoroi*) as their security service.[107] Little is known about these men, but they are described as "young and audacious" by Xenophon and labeled "servants" (*hupēretai*) by the author of the *Ath. Pol.* These men may have been subversive young members of the elite eager to try something different from democracy.[108] More likely, however, they were lower-class men who responded positively to the offer of easy (and violent) work, a theory that grows in probability when we consider the *Ath. Pol.*'s use of the word "servants." In Plato's *Apology* we hear furthermore that the Thirty often ordered people outside the political class to arrest and kill others (such as Leon of Salamis) "in order to infect as many people as possible with their crimes" (32c). The Thirty no doubt hoped that this incrimination would work to divide the opposition, since more and more people would have reason to fear recriminations for their actions should the regime fall.[109]

Finally, a more impersonal form of co-optation existed that was undoubtedly the most common. This was the practice of admitting into the ranks of the oligarchic class those men who had attained a specified level of wealth. As we saw in chapter 1, there were other criteria for determining oligarchic citizenship, such as membership in a specific family or *hetaireia*, but these were considered more "dynastic" and were not likely the norm.[110] The belief that

---

106. Also potentially contentious were instances of throwing open "money-making offices" to members of the demos (Arist. *Pol.* 5.1309a21–22). This is the most blatantly materialistic of the inducements suggested for securing oligarchies, and it is unclear how often it was utilized.

107. [Arist.] *Ath. Pol.* 35.1; cf. Xen. *Hell.* 2.3.23, 55.

108. Note that the Four Hundred in 411 also had an entourage of knife-wielding helpers drawn from Andros, Tenos, Carystos, and Aegina (Thuc. 8.69.3). These were almost certainly likeminded oligarchs, not co-opted commoners. However, they also employed 120 "young Hellenes" (69.4—the second word is omitted in some manuscripts) whose identity remains unclear.

109. Cf. Dem. 15.14: the oligarchs at Rhodes in the mid-fourth century, "in order to overthrow the democracy, enlisted some of the citizens, but when they had accomplished it, they drove these men into exile again." This would have had the long-term strategic effect of weakening the potential opposition by compromising the reputation of the collaborators.

110. For regimes determined according to family, see e.g., Arist. *Pol.* 4.1292b4–7. For mem-

wealth qualified one for citizenship, and the amount of wealth considered sufficient for oligarchic citizenship, are important topics in their own right and have been treated separately in chapter 1. Here I wish to focus on census thresholds as a way of dividing and weakening the democratic opposition, which is clearly how Aristotle understood them. In Book 4 of the *Politics* he notes that the first type of oligarchy is that in which it is "possible for anyone who obtains the required property qualification to share in the constitution," even though most people will not get the chance (1292a39–41; cf. 1293a14–17). We learn how this rule might benefit an oligarchy later in Book 6, when Aristotle explains that the many "desire profit more than honor" (1318b16–17). The "proof" of this is that the people used to tolerate Archaic tyrannies, just as they currently tolerate oligarchies, so long as no one prevents them from working or takes away their earnings. "For some of them quickly become rich, while others are not totally destitute" (1318b17–21). If the poor are left alone, their natural inclination is to work and make more money; the result is that some of them become wealthy, thus attaining the level of wealth necessary to be enrolled among the elite. In other words, if oligarchs can only refrain from outraging the people, the "greediness" of the poor will naturally keep them locked into the oligarchic status quo.[111] Thus the oligarchic response to the demos's collective demand for political rights was often, in the words of the nineteenth-century French minister Guizot, "enrichissez-vous." Work individually to enrich yourself, and you can engage in politics all you want.[112] In the meantime, the poor would safely channel their energy into money-making rather than political organization.[113]

---

bership in a hetaireia or other conspiratorial groups as the qualification, see Arist. *Pol.* 4.1300a16–19 (on Megara), [Arist.] *Rhet. ad Alex.* 1446b26. Lysander's "regimes of ten" or "decarchies," in which hand-selected supporters of Lysander ruled cities, were criticized on the grounds of not respecting either wealth or excellence (*sc.* as genuine oligarchies are supposed to do): Plut. *Lys.* 13.4.

111. Cf. [Arist.] *Rhet. ad Alex.* 1424b4–5, discussed above, section 3.1.3, for its advice that oligarchs not commit *hubris* against the demos.

112. François Guizot (1787–1874), influential politician during the post-1818 period of the Conservative Order in France; quoted in Rapport 2008: 38.

113. There was a long tradition of Archaic tyrants encouraging citizens to engage in labor rather than politics: see [Arist.] *Ath. Pol.* 15.4, 16.3 (Peisistratus of Athens); Nic. Dam. *FGrH* 90 F 58.1; Ephorus *FGrH* 70 F 179; Arist. frr. 516, 611.20 Rose (Periander of Corinth). Oligarchs seem to have taken over this tactic, as Aristotle suggests—or it may be that oligarchic practices from the Classical period have been retrojected back onto the Archaic tyrants. See further chapter 4, section 4.1.

3.4 Implication in the Regime: Rewards for Informants

A final institutional means of co-optation is the use of paid informants. There are generally speaking two purposes behind encouraging informants. The direct purpose is to foil plots against the state through early detection. A further, indirect result of this climate of denunciation is distrust sown among potential subversives so as to deter them from initiating conspiracies in the first place. While an individual plotter might choose to denounce the rest of the group on his or her own private initiative, central authorities can attempt to exacerbate such in-group tendencies by actively publicizing the specific rewards to be had from turning informant. By making the rewards a matter of common knowledge among the wider population, they ensure that conspirators' expectations will be uniform and that they will be forced to participate in the same "game" with each other as they contemplate subversion.

The resulting game is essentially a Prisoner's Dilemma, to return to the language of chapter 1. Imagine *arguendo* that two revolutionaries suffice to undermine the state if they can cooperate. As long as the state can offer each individual a reward for informing that outweighs the benefits to accrue to each from the revolution, he or she will have a reason to renege on any agreement. Of course, if both plotters defect they end up worse off than they would have been cooperating, but the structural incentives in place prevent them from trusting each other. The wider result would be for people not currently in the game to choose not to play in the first place, since they can anticipate that any game will end in failure. The hope of the state is therefore that conspiracies never materialize. Furthermore, when we take the more realistic step of assuming that more than two people are required for an effective revolt, we see that the likelihood of informing (and thus of plot failure) goes up, since the state's reward to an individual can easily outweigh the individual's benefit from the revolution, since the revolution's benefits will be divided among a large group.

Every state arguably depends somewhat on informing for its survival, but the conspiratorial behavior to be denounced differs based on the popularity of the regime and its vulnerability to subversive plotting. Authoritarian regimes, which by definition could not survive a fair election among a majority of the population, are especially reliant on informant networks and the secret police. From notorious cases such as the KGB and the DDR's Stasi to lesser-known entities such as Rafael Trujillo's SIM and the Persian Shah's SAVAK, dictators and ruling parties over the last century have employed a veritable alphabet soup of clandestine security services.[114] In ancient Greece it was no

---

114. The technique is also known from Imperial Rome (Epictetus *Diss.* 4.13.5, discussed by Kyle 1998: 123n154); from medieval Italian oligarchies (the Segreti of fifteenth-century Siena,

different: all types of regime are known to have employed spies and informants. Their use makes sense, since every government in ancient Greece was technically speaking a form of authoritarianism, holding power over a significant majority (made up of women and slaves, especially) that had no formal political privileges. Thus even (especially?) Athens encouraged informants on the domestic scene, particularly after the desecration of the Herms in 415. Citizens, foreigners, and slaves were all called upon to inform and rewards were set at one thousand drachmas by Cleonymus and ten thousand by Peisander.[115] Within the Athenian empire, the need for a spy network was only compounded. The Athenians tried, through oaths, to enforce delation against insurrectionary plots in the cities of the empire, some of which were democracies.[116] They also utilized official observers, the *episkopoi*, who gathered information on the subject cities and oversaw the implementation of imperial decrees. The allies, quite understandably, viewed them as an encroachment on their freedom.[117]

Outside of democratic Athens, it is unsurprising to find notices of secret police within tyrannies. Aristotle points out the need for spies (*kataskopoi*) in tyrannies and cites the examples of the so-called "female informers" (*potagōgides*) in Syracuse under Dionysius and the "eavesdroppers" (*ōtakoustai*) Hieron sent out to meetings and gatherings. "For people will speak their minds less freely," he says, "when they're afraid of such informers, and if they do speak freely, they will escape detection less easily."[118] Similar groups are recorded for the cities of Cyprus, which were dynastically ruled.

---

although Shaw (2006: 108) disputes their status as an "all-powerful secret police"); and from the post-1815 Conservative Order in Europe (Rapport 2008: 9), among countless other examples. For more on the use of spies and the secret police by contemporary authoritarian governments, see Levitsky and Way 2010: 58–59.

115. Thuc. 6.27.2, cf. 53.2, 60.4; And. 1.27–28. I do not have the space to discuss it fully, but the figure of the *sukophantēs* might also represent an "institutionalized" (albeit informal) informant against threats to the democracy (see esp. Ar. *Plut.* 907–19), although the position could be abused and was hotly debated. See Osborne 1990 (= 2010: ch. 10); Harvey 1990; Christ 1998.

116. The most securely attested case is Chalcis (ML 52, line 25), but see also *IG* I³ 39, for Eretria. Osborne (2010: 239–42) discusses an inscription from the period of the Second Athenian Confederacy (RO 40) in which the Athenians encourage Cean slaves to inform on their masters about the use of Cean ruddle. The Athenians count on Cean slaves to inform on free citizens in the service of Athenian power.

117. See *IG* I³ 14, lines 14–15, 34, line 7 (restored); Ar. *Av.* 1020–55; Harp. s.v.; Balcer 1976: 258–69. Balcer 1977 and Raaflaub 2009 draw attention to the similarity between this and other Athenian imperial offices and the Persian king's "eye" (Hdt. 1.114.2, Ar. *Ach.* 91–92, Xen. *Cyr.* 8.2.10–12).

118. *Pol.* 5.1313b12–16. For the Syracusan *potagōgides*, see Plut. *Dion* 28.1, where they are men

Clearchus mentions people called "Gerginoi" and "Promalangas" who served as spies and inquisitors, reporting their findings to the "lords" (*anaktes*).[119] Most of the aforementioned were specialized positions, which tyrants seem to have kept staffed with specific individuals. On a more general level, Isocrates has the tyrant Nicocles (from Salamis, in Cyprus) tell his people that even their secret thoughts will be detected by him (2.51), and he commands them not to keep silent if they see someone acting like a scoundrel (*ponēros*) concerning his rule, but to denounce them (*exelengchete*, 53). Clearly tyrants, as single rulers attempting to control a population full of potential subversives, had good reason to invest in domestic spy networks.

Despite the use of spies and informants by democracies and tyrannies, scholars have paid little attention to informing under oligarchy. Yet it stands to reason that a system which excluded more inhabitants from the exercise of political power than did a democracy would for that very reason need to rely even more heavily on spies. In fact we find several instances of insurrectionary plots against oligarchic regimes being foiled by informants. I begin with Sparta, although the same caveats apply as in the discussion of secret assassination above. Several helots informed against Pausanias's invitation to join him in an uprising against the Spartan state (Thuc. 1.132.5, *mēnutais*); however, when dealing with helots we are on similar ground to the promise of rewards to slaves under democracy. More distinctively oligarchic is the episode in which an unnamed informant (not a helot) foils the conspiracy of Cinadon by revealing the plot to the ephors.[120] Presumably both Cinadon and the informant were men who had somehow fallen out of the full Spartiate class and become *hupomeiones* or member of another sub-citizen group. They were therefore comparable to members of the demos under oligarchies. For whatever reason, the informant chose cooperation with the ephors over revolution with Cinadon and his group. Similarly, Agesilaus learned from an informant (*emēnuthē*) about the supposedly dire conspiracy, which he then suppressed with ruthless efficiency, as we saw above (Plut. *Ages.* 32.6). That so many examples should come from Sparta is unsurprising, since the Spartan constitution excelled at co-opting members of its multiple under-classes into supporting the ruling elite.[121]

(and where they are lynched following the fall of the tyranny). See also Plut. *De Curios.* 16 (= *Mor.* 522f-23b); Polyaen. *Strat.* 5.2.13; and the sources cited at Newman ad Arist. *Pol.* 1313b11.

119. Fr. 19 Wehrli. Cf. Eustathius *Comm. ad Hom. Il.* 3.516, and for a discussion of all these passages, Russell 1999: 107–14.

120. Xen. *Hell.* 3.3.4. See further chapter 6, section 6.1.1, with bibliography cited.

121. Cawkwell 1983: 390–95.

Beyond Sparta, acts of informing characterized oligarchies elsewhere. A Phocian named Nicomachus spoiled a pro-democratic plot hatched in oligarchic Boeotia in 424 (Thuc. 4.89.1, *mēnuthentos tou epibouleumatos*). The plan had been for ringleaders in multiple poleis within the oligarchic *koinon* to initiate popular uprisings, but Nicomachus, for reasons unknown, informed the authorities. He himself was a member of the insurrectionary group, and perhaps the ruling Boeotian oligarchs had instituted rewards for informants that made him nervous that someone else from the group would do the same to him unless he acted first.[122]

There is also the account of the partnership of Themistocles and Ephialtes against the Areopagus at [Arist.] *Ath. Pol.* 25.3–4. As Rhodes has observed (1993: 320), this is a *ben trovato* story with little or no basis in historical truth. It may, however, be informed by oligarchic ideology. The two Athenian leaders conspire to deprive the Areopagus of its leadership, which the author of the *Ath. Pol.* remembers as having flourished in the aftermath of the Persian Wars (23.1). Themistocles, who is himself an Areopagite but wants to prevent an impending trial for treason, tells the Areopagus council that he will reveal to them the identities of certain people "conspiring" (*sunistamenous*) against the "constitution" (*politeia*) (25.3). Meanwhile he tells Ephialtes that the Areopagus is planning to arrest him, and when the two groups confront each other, Ephialtes cries foul and has the Areopagus stripped of its powers. If an antidemocratic source, one that wished to paint Ephialtes as a demagogue and the Areopagus as a redoubt of conservatism, fabricated and inserted the story, it may display what the author thought was a plausible means of plot-detection by an "oligarchic" body like the Areopagus council. The council relies on informers to sniff out conspiracies against its *politeia*.[123]

We read also of situations in which no one actually informs, but the fear of informants renders people suspicious and inactive. Athens under the Four Hundred in 411 is a prime example, as when Thucydides says that the members of the demos approached each other suspiciously out of concern that everyone was potentially involved in the oligarchy. The participation of some unexpected democrats in the new regime "provided the greatest source of mistrust [*apiston*] for the many and did the most to shore up the stability [*asphaleian*] of the few."[124]

---

122. I treat this episode in chapter 2, section 2.5, as well.

123. Cf. the discussion in chapter 4 of Isocrates's picture of the Areopagus Council, in which Athens is divided into wards and villages and informants report subversive activities to the Council (7.46).

124. Thuc. 8.66.5.

The case of Athens under the Thirty further confirms the oligarchic use of informants. The most notable example is that of Agoratus, the target of Lysias's thirteenth oration, who in the prosecutor's version of events conspired with the council, which had been co-opted by oligarchs, in the lead-up to the appointment of the Thirty. Roisman has shown that the prosecutor's argument contains several logical holes and that the case is patently weak.[125] The speaker, however, so takes it for granted that the audience will be familiar with the idea of oligarchic informing as to suggest that he was attempting to make his picture of Agoratus fit a well-known paradigm. Incidentally, his mention of one Menestratus (13.55–56), who, unlike Agoratus, received immunity from the Thirty for his testimony, confirms this suspicion. Elsewhere in the *corpus Lysiacum* (6.45, 12.48) we also meet Batrachus, who along with the otherwise unknown Aeschylides served as an informant under the Thirty. He later went into self-imposed exile, presumably to escape the demos's anger. As Todd has argued, however, the title of a lost speech, *On the Death of Batrachus*, may indicate that the demos later killed Batrachus for his informing.[126]

The strength of the foregoing literary evidence notwithstanding, our best attestation of the practice of informing under oligarchy comes from an epigraphic discovery. This inscription affords a unique view onto informing under oligarchy insofar as it represents the actual law that advertised the rewards to be had for relaying information to the authorities. As a law, and furthermore as a physical monument on display in the civic landscape, it played a crucial role in structuring the expectations of those living under the oligarchy that issued it. By examining the law in detail we can better understand why those who would have benefited from a change in regime often chose instead to support those in power. We also move closer to the lived experience of the demos during periods of oligarchic rule, in that the law was something they would have physically encountered on a daily basis in the public space of the polis.[127]

The piece of evidence in question is an inscription from the island of Thasos first published by Pouilloux in 1954 and included as number 83 in the revised edition of Meiggs and Lewis's *Greek Historical Inscriptions*.[128] The text,

---

125. Roisman 2006: 72–83.

126. Lys. frag. XXX Carey *apud* Harp. s.v. φηγούσιον. For Batrachus's possible murder see Todd 2007: 467 (*ad* Lys. 6.45). As we saw above in the case of Syracuse (Plut. *Dion* 28.1), informants might be lynched when the regime supporting them fell.

127. In addition to the inscription studied here, see the decree from oligarchic Miletus promising rewards for informants (ML 43, discussed in chapter 2, section 2.5).

128. Pouilloux 1954: 139–62, no. 18; see further Koerner no. 70 with commentary.

consisting of two laws of slightly differing date inscribed on a horizontally oriented white marble block, enumerates precise rewards for those who inform on any "revolt being plotted against Thasos." The wording of the two is very similar.[129] The first stipulates that:

> Whoever denounces a revolt [*epanastasis*] being plotted against Thasos and proves it to be true, let him have a thousand staters from the city. And if a slave denounces, let him also be free. If more than one person should denounce, let three hundred men judge the case and decide. If one of those taking part denounces, let him have the money and let him not be under oath against himself, nor let any suit, sacred or profane, be lodged against him about these matters, and may he not be numbered among the accursed, excepting the one person who first plotted the scheme.[130]

The second law further specifies that denunciations should be against "someone of the Thasians or from the settlements [*apoikiai*] who betrays [*prodidonta*] the *polis*" or plots "in the settlements" (lines 7–8).

Historians have disputed the political context of this pair of laws, but scholarly opinion overwhelmingly inclines toward the Thasian oligarchic regime of the late fifth century.[131] While my arguments here cannot decide the issue, I start from the *communis opinio* that the document is oligarchic and show that

---

129. Cf. the translations of Fornara no. 153 and Arnaoutoglou no. 72.

130. ὃς ἂν ἐπανάστασιν βολευομένην ἐπὶ Θάσωι κατείπηι καὶ φανῆι ἐόντα ἀληθέα, χίλιος στατῆρας ἐκ τῆς πόλεως ἰσχέτω. ἢν δὲ δόλος κατείπηι, καὶ ἐλεύθερος ἔστω. ἢμ πλέος ἢ εἷς κατείπωσι, τριηκόσιοι κρινόντων δίκην δικάσαντες. ἢν δέ τις τῶν μετεχόντων κατείπηι, τό τε ἀργύριον ἰσχέτω καὶ κατώμοτος κατ' αὐτὸ μὴ ἔστω μηδὲ δίκη μηδεμία μήτε ἱρὴ μήτε βεβήλη περὶ τότων μηδὲ ἐν τῆι ἐπαρῆι ἔστω πλὴν ἑνός, τὸ πρῶτο βολεύσαντος. The second law further specifies that denunciations should be against "someone of the Thasians or from the settlements [*apoikiai*] who betrays [*prodidonta*] the polis" or plots "in the settlements" (lines 7–8).

131. The factors favoring that particular date and political context, independent of the content of the law (democracies, after all, can encourage informing), are letter forms, alphabet, and political terminology. Jeffery (1990: 303) established that the letter forms will not support a date earlier than the last decades of the fifth century. The text also avoids all mention of the "demos," a typical (though not strictly necessary) indicator of a democracy, and speaks instead in terms of "the polis" and "Thasos." For the introduction of oligarchy at Thasos by the Four Hundred (and the oligarchy's subsequent revolt from the Athenian empire), see Thuc. 8.64.2. The oligarchy probably lasted until 407, when Thrasybulus recovered the island for Athens (Xen. *Hell.* 1.4.9; Diod. Sic. 13.72.1). Oligarchy certainly resurfaced in Thasos later, probably following Athens' loss in the Peloponnesian War (Xen. *Hell.* 2.2.5; *IG* II² 6, 17), but Thasos returned to democracy around 390 (Picard 2000 = *SEG* 51.1096; Grandjean and Salviat 2006 = *SEG* 56.1017; Fournier and Hamon 2007 = *SEG* 57.820).

it strongly conforms to the larger picture of informing under oligarchy developed above.[132]

The laws are clearly aimed against internal subversion. The word used to designate the plot, *epanastasis*, is commonly used in Thucydides and elsewhere to refer to an internal uprising against the reigning order, whether democratic or oligarchic.[133] This terminological point, along with the mention of the possibility of multiple conspirators within Thasos, guarantees that we are dealing with a domestic threat.[134] As for the actual substance of the laws and the rewards promised, they reveal a more sophisticated strategic logic than scholars have previously recognized. The monetary payment and the promise of freedom are not innovations of this document—it is the immunity clause and the rule excepting all but the first conspirator that are the truly interesting points.[135] While only one person could claim the reward promised, multiple people could enjoy immunity as long as the original plotter was identified and apprehended. These aspects of the law would have worked in two directions. In the first case, the law would have triggered a "commitment problem" among preexisting revolutionaries, making continued cooperation extremely risky and unstable.[136] Each conspirator would have to trust all the others individually not to give in to the monetary enticements on offer. But if even just one revealed the plot to the authorities, the rest could end up cursed. With the immunity clause in place, however, each one could hope that, even if he did not win the reward money, he could save himself from punishment. It is therefore easy to see how the publication of the law could trigger a wave of simultaneous defectors from a conspiracy. The new

---

132. Pouilloux in his original commentary on the inscription argued forcefully for an oligarchic context. Chamoux (1959) challenged several of Pouilloux's minor points, but his criticisms did not undermine the basic argument for oligarchy. Others who have agreed with Pouilloux include Mattingly in his review (1972: 79–80) of ML; Graham 1999: 83–84; Graham and Smith 1989: 405–6; Pleket 1963: 75–76; Avery 1979; Meiggs 1972: 575; Arnaoutoglou no. 72; Hornblower *ad* Thuc. 8.64.3; Liddel 2010: 127; Matthaiou 2011: 32. Rubinstein (2003: 103) expresses less certainty. For doubts see ML 83; Gehrke *Stasis*: 16on6; Osborne 2010: 236–37 (citing ML).

133. See *HCT* 5: 45 (*ad* 8.21), citing Steup and Busolt. To Andrewes's citations of 1.115.5, 2.27.2, 3.39.2, 4.56.2, 5.23.3, 8.63.3, 73.2, add 1.132.4. For inscriptional uses see RO 79, line 7; SEG 28.60, line 12 (decree for Callias of Sphettus; Athenian demos starts an uprising); SEG 31.984, lines 10–11 (oath requiring Teans not to plot or carry out an *epanastasis*); ML 30, line b.5 (Teos again); IK Ilion 25, line 118 (oath against joining in an uprising against the democracy). Meiggs (1972: 575) also compares the language of the Thasos delation law to Thuc. 8.21.

134. Chamoux (1959: 352) thought that the concern was about external, rather than internal threats, but see Pleket's convincing rejoinder (1963: 75n9a).

135. Antiph. 5.34; Thuc. 6.27.2, And. 1 *passim* all attest to similar schemes of remuneration.

136. See the discussion in chapter 1, section 1.3.

payoffs presented by the law would foster distrust among the sworn conspirators, leading each to seek immunity based on the fear that one of his fellow conspirators was already giving him up.[137]

On the other hand, the law also works as a check on future revolutionaries. With the "all but the first conspirator" clause, the law ensures that no one will want to be the one to originate the plot. Those dissatisfied with the status quo will prefer to "bandwagon" with others' conspiracies rather than begin one themselves. But with no one wanting to take the initiative to conspire, few if any conspiracies will even get started. Without actually having to pay people a reward, the Thasian oligarchs can be more secure against revolutionary threats through deterrence.

Finally, we should consider the ramifications of the law's place of publication. Pouilloux records in his *editio princeps* that the inscription was discovered in the Thasian agora. This was almost certainly the location where the inscription was originally erected. As we will see in chapter 5, oligarchies often withheld important political information from the wider population and took a manipulative approach to publicizing information generally.[138] In this case, however, the Thasian oligarchs would have wanted the laws to be as widely known as possible. A place of publication in the agora would have ensured that

---

137. One might object that my argument is too "economistic" and that religious and social norms might have helped to overcome collective action problems based strictly on monetary considerations. However, the Thasian authorities thought of that, too: as Graham and Smith have shown, with the clause "let him not be under oath against himself," "the informer is freed from the oath he gave to his fellow-conspirators, calling down annihilation on himself and his family if he should betray the plot" (1989: 41). For a similar clause, see now *SEG* 57.576, lines 82–84 (reconciliation from Dikaia in the Chalcidice, ca. 364/3).

138. Although I cannot address the issue at length, I will note here my agreement with the widely held opinion that oligarchies published decrees on stone much less frequently than democracies: Dow 1942: 119 (an "oligarch only invites unwanted publicity, or even defacement of his inscription, when he publishes an edict"); Bodel 2001: 12; Davies 2003a: 338; Scafuro 2013: 413; *contra* Pébarthe 2006; Liddel 2009. Delphi, which has sometimes been cited as an oligarchy that published numerous decrees (e.g., Liddel 2009: 412n4), was in fact a democracy: *IACP* no. 177, p. 413 (Oulhen). To my knowledge, there are slightly over a dozen known inscriptions published in the Classical period by oligarchies: 1) ML 81 (Athens); 2) ML 82 (Eretria); 3) ML 83 (Thasos); 4) *IG* XII.8 263 (Thasos); 5) *I. Lindos* II 16; 6) *SEG* 34.849 (Mytilene); 7) *SEG* 18.772 (Euhesperides); 8) *PEP Chios* 2; 9) *PEP Chios* 76; 10) *SEG* 35.923 (Chios); 11) RO 56 (Erythrae); 12) *SEG* 31.969 (Erythrae); 13) RO 68 (Erythrae); 14) ML 43 (Miletus). I discuss several of these in detail elsewhere: see chapter 2, section 2.5 for ML 43; chapter 3, section 3.1.1 for *IG* XII.8 263. (ML 80, labeled an "oligarchic decree" by the editors, is an ambiguous case: it may have originated from the intermediate regime following the Four Hundred. Hansen 2013 labels the Thasian inscription *IG* XII.8 264 as emanating from an oligarchy, in my view mistakenly—see Andrewes 1953: 8n26.)

the content of the laws became a matter of common knowledge. Even if the members of the demos were illiterate, they could have their friends or neighbors read the laws to them. As a prominent monument in its own right within the agora, the inscription would have encouraged stories to circulate explaining its existence. Anyone who wanted to know (and probably many who did not) would have learned very quickly about the new laws. This informational dynamic was well-known to the ancients themselves: Aeneas Tacticus advises, "Proclaim that whoever informs on someone plotting against the city, or whoever reports something being plotted, will receive money, and put the proclamation clearly on display *in the agora* or on an altar or in a shrine, so that people will more readily be willing to inform on things being plotted" (10.15). Furthermore, once citizens knew what the law said, its physical presence would have reminded them, whenever they entered the agora, of the laws in place concerning plots and informing. Like a closed-circuit security camera displayed prominently in a modern-day public place, the sight of the Thasian law would have subtly reawakened awareness in passersby that the oligarchic authorities were alert to potential threats.[139]

Overall, the preemptive and preventive nature of the Thasian delation law, as well as its place and function within the civic space of the polis of Thasos, reveal how an oligarchy might preempt internal resistance to its power. Assuming that the document does indeed date to the period between 411 and 407, I find it noteworthy that the regime published the law in the absence of any recorded threat to its existence. Neither Thucydides nor Xenophon nor the Oxyrhynchus historian mentions any conspiracy on Thasos, and democracy was restored only with the outside intervention of the Athenian Thrasybulus in 407. Unlike in the case of the Herms and Mysteries at Athens, the Thasian oligarchs did not react to an unexpected act of subversion but instead appear to have anticipated one. The law might then both "reveal uneasiness on behalf of the oligarchic regime" (Arnaoutoglou no. 72) and show by what sorts of institutional mechanisms this unpopular government managed to survive for several years.

In sum, rewarding informants was one of several methods used by oligarchs to entice (or threaten) otherwise reluctant citizens into supporting the political establishment. Rubinstein has explored this phenomenon from a slightly different perspective, focusing on instances in which what would normally be a "volunteer prosecutor" under a democratic constitution is, in a nondemocratic setting, encouraged to lay information against certain individuals or groups through "carrots" (rewards) or "sticks" (punishments).[140] Rubinstein

---

139. For oligarchic control of public space, see the following chapter.

140. Rubinstein 2003: 100–104. In addition to the Isocrates *Nicocles* passage and the Thasian

provocatively compares this unwilling involvement of the citizenry in each other's lives to the tactics of the East German Stasi, and while Greek authoritarian governments hardly possessed the repressive force of the DDR, the principle involved is indeed similar.[141] Here the Attic orators' damning remarks about oligarchic regimes, which are often distorted by democratic ideology, might actually not be far off the mark. Demosthenes notes the ability of oligarchies (along with tyrannies) to reward a "toady" (*kolakeuonta*) with riches, and he observes that should the capacity to reward the loyal (*eunous*) run out, the security (*phulakē*) of those constitutions would be put in serious jeopardy (20.15–17). Aeschines, meanwhile, depicts tyrants and oligarchs as relying on armed guards and distrust (*apistia*), in contrast to democracies, which depend upon willing adherence to the laws (1.5). These are extreme and politically partisan characterizations, but based on what we have seen in this section it does appear that oligarchies relied to a greater extent than democracies on the ability to bribe or otherwise co-opt citizens, thus creating the atmosphere of *apistia* noted by Aeschines.

---

delation law, she mentions *PEP Chios* 2 (labeled "1" in her account), which prescribes fines for citizens who do not lodge denunciations before the *basileis*. Cf. Plat. *Leg.* 11.914a, where fines are laid down for failing to inform the authorities about theft.

141. Rubinstein 2003: 102.

4

The Politics of Public Space

> The mob must not gather from the countryside into the city: Such meetings cause the masses to combine and overthrow oligarchies.
>
> —RHETORIC TO ALEXANDER[1]

4.0 Introduction: Space and Politics in the Classical Greek World

The previous chapter concluded with an examination of the Thasian delation law (ML 83), in which I pointed to the location of the inscription in the Thasian agora as playing a crucial role in the law's effectiveness. As we will see in the present chapter, the Thasian oligarchs' concern over—and manipulation of—public space was no aberration, but constitutes a recurring theme in the story of Classical oligarchic governance.

Public space was a particular source of anxiety for oligarchic regimes, which had to worry in a way that democracies did not about the movement of bodies within the polis's central spaces. As a survey of Archaic sources will make clear, the Greek elite had always claimed a special relationship with the city-center, often to the exclusion of those deemed "outsiders." Their arrogant attitude was the product of a set of specific cultural values, as well as a reflection of the fact that the elite were in fact the ones in the Archaic period who controlled the polis's central political organs. With the introduction of a democratic constitutional alternative in the Classical period, however, fear replaced snobbery as the primary motivating factor behind oligarchic approaches to public space. Because the large, open areas of the city-center—in

---

1. [Arist.] *Rhet. ad Alex.* 1424b8–10: μηδὲ συνάγειν ἐκ τῆς χώρας τὸν ὄχλον εἰς τὴν πόλιν· ἐκ γὰρ τῶν τοιούτων συνόδων συστρέφεται τὰ πλήθη καὶ καταλύει τὰς ὀλιγαρχίας.

particular the agora—represented the most effective venue for facilitating democratic collective action, oligarchs took a number of precautionary measures to monitor and control such spaces. The history of oligarchic politics in the Classical period thus reveals a gradual hardening not only of the ideological boundary between full, "active" citizens on the one hand and lesser, "passive" ones on the other, but also of the literal, spatial boundary between oligarchs and demos. Socrates's remark in the *Republic*, that the oligarchic city in fact houses two distinct poleis, one of the rich and one of the poor (8.551d), is more apt than has previously been recognized.

At the same time, oligarchs did not rest content with simply patrolling central spaces. Hand-in-hand with monopolization of the center went a sophisticated system of divide and conquer in the polis's periphery. In a more speculative later section of the chapter, I will bring together several historical sources to sketch the outline of what I believe was a common method within oligarchies of decentralized, individualized control of the demos by patron-like elites. Rather than allow the demos the opportunity to gather *en masse* in the *astu*, oligarchs cultivated ties with smaller groups of common people within their traditional spheres of influence. In the manner of tribal "big men" or Mafia bosses, individual oligarchs provided a minimal package of "benefits" to their local constituents in exchange for the latters' political passivity. Faced with the dilemma of accepting this non-ideal arrangement or attempting, at great personal risk, broader collective action, many members of the demos chose acquiescence. The aggregate result of such a series of decisions was an equilibrium state in which politics remained local and democratic mobilization never materialized. Following contemporary political scientists, who have shown how citizen dilemmas along these lines can help to sustain authoritarian regimes, I label this system "clientelism."

In discussing the politics of public space in oligarchies, this chapter seeks to make its own contribution to debates about the meaning and function of "political space" in the ancient Greek world. Important recent studies have highlighted the "spatial politics" of Panhellenic sites such as Delphi and Olympia, the relationship between space and violence, the importance of Athenian democratic spaces in promoting common knowledge, and the use of visual spectacle within public space by Hellenistic elites.[2] As in so many other areas, however, historians have generally neglected oligarchic regimes of the Classical period. A few exceptional studies have examined spatial imagery in

2. Scott 2010, 2013; Riess and Fagan 2016; Ober 2008 (esp. 190–205); Dickenson and van Nijf 2013. Hellenistic and Imperial scholarship in particular has engaged productively with the idea of political space: see further Ma 2013; van Nijf 2011; Viviers 2010.

Classical oligarchic ideology, but they have tended to focus on private domestic space.³ Compounding the problem is the familiar scholarly habit, identified in chapter 1, of conflating oligarchy with the government of the Archaic period. As we have seen, conceptualizing Greek political history along these lines often results in overlooking key differences between Archaic-era elite political practices and the reactionary tactics of Classical oligarchies.

4.1 The Archaic City: Idealizations and Realities

The central spaces of the polis, and in particular the agora, provided the Archaic elite with an early and important forum for their self-fashioning and -promotion. From the Homeric agora, "where men win glory," to Alcaeus's longing to hear the agora ("assembly") summoned, to Xenophanes's thousand perfumed Colophonians promenading through the agora, the Archaic sources make clear that the city-center represented a shared, public space, one in which the members of the highly competitive Greek elite exhibited their achievements and preeminence both to each other and to the wider polis community.⁴ Indeed, scholars have considered the tendency of the Greek elite to cultivate their prestige in the open setting of the city-state, rather than in a monarch's secluded court, a major determinant of subsequent Greek political history.⁵ Even if public competition was originally the preserve of the leisured elite, their choice of the agora as a competitive arena incorporated the broader demos as onlookers and judges early on. Thus Vernant could characterize the Archaic agora as "a centered space—common, public, egalitarian, and symmetrical" (1982: 126). The Archaic agora was, according to this understanding, a forerunner and image *in nuce* of Classical democratic politics, toward which the Archaic world was inexorably developing.

Such a view is in danger, however, of overlooking the sense of contestation in the sources over who would have access to that shared space. Although Classical democracy is indeed impossible to imagine in the absence of such elite Archaic developments, the Greek elite at the time certainly had no conception of themselves as acting for the benefit of future generations of common people. In fact, certain strands of thinking within elite Archaic discourse about the agora could be possessive and exclusionary, seeking to limit participation in the agora to those who "deserved" to be there. We find these statements in fragments of Archaic poetry, as well as in post-Archaic sources that

---

3. See especially Fearn 2009 on "oligarchic Hestia" (by definition hearth-based and thus interior).

4. Hom. *Il.* 6.124; Alcaeus fr. 130b.3–5 Liberman; Xenophanes fr. 3 West.

5. See Raaflaub and Wallace 2007: 24, 28–29; Morris 1996: 27–28, 40–41; Duplouy 2006.

purport to describe Archaic conditions. Often the sources present themselves as politically neutral descriptions of fact, but we should not miss the prescriptive, normative nature of such discourse—they are just as often about *how* society should look as about *what* in fact it looked like. In many cases we are likely seeing reactions to unwanted changes in political practice, attempts to recreate an idealized status quo ante. What I would emphasize is that these Archaic statements do not yet indicate a sense of genuine fear on the part of the elite that the fundamental structure of their rule is under threat. That would have to wait until the emergence of democracy in the late Archaic and early Classical periods. Instead, they represent a feeling of disgust that decorum has been broken—that things are culturally and socially not what they should be. This ideological discourse would continue unbroken into the Classical period, but would be bolstered by a more profound anxiety over maintaining political power.

Consider, to begin, a passage from the Theognidean corpus, which expresses concern over contamination of elite civic space by outsiders. This is the famous description of the "strange new *laoi*," people who "previously knew neither *dikai* nor *nomoi*, but wore out goat-skins around their ribs, and grazed outside this city like deer" (53–56). Whether we think of these savages as social *arrivistes* derided for their supposedly "low" origins, demagogic politicians, or simply the latest rivals to the author's slightly better-established clique, the poet's language suggests a basic division between the cultured, urbane city and the wild hinterland.[6] As several scholars have pointed out, the description of the outsiders as knowing "neither *dikai* nor *nomoi*" echoes the *Odyssey*'s depiction of the Cyclopes, while the center/periphery distinction might also suggest colonists surrounded by hostile natives.[7] In any case, the poetic voice creates a distinction between the cultured center of the polis, inhabited by wealthy elite of good families, and the low-born people beyond the walls, who until recently lived in the manner of animals and thus have no place in city-center politics. The poet of the *Theognidea* is laying the groundwork for a conception of the city according to which the poor, peripheral demos, because of its savagery and low birth, needs to stay where it belongs.

Theognis's division of the polis into the elite center and the demotic outskirts recurs in several other sources that purport to describe Archaic living conditions. Caution is in order here, since the authors are post-Archaic and may be projecting contemporary political ideas onto the past. Nevertheless, the picture is clear and consistent: in a fragment of Aristotle's *Constitution of*

---

6. *Arrivistes:* Lane Fox 2000: 42–45. Demagogues: Robinson 1997: 115–16. Rivals: van Wees 2000: 60–67.

7. Cyclopes (*Od.* 9.215): Nagy 1985: 44, § 29 n4. Colonists: Nagy 1990: 71n96, 267n93.

the Naxians, for example (fr. 558 Rose), "most of the rich men" of Archaic Naxos lived in the town proper, while "the rest" were scattered among the villages.⁸ Similarly, the fourth-century philosopher Heraclides Ponticus records a bout of *stasis* from Archaic Miletus between the rich of the city (*hoi plousioi*) and the poor of the hinterland, whom the rich derisively call "Gergithes," a reference to a nearby non-Greek population.⁹ In Plutarch's description of Archaic Epidaurus, the men in control of the government were 180 in number, while "the majority of the common people [*demos*] spent their time in the countryside."¹⁰ Whenever the demos came to town, says Plutarch, they were recognized by the dust on their feet, whence arose the nickname "dusty-feet" (*konipodes*). These examples conform to a more generalized picture offered by Aristotle and others, according to which early Greece was characterized by dispersed settlement patterns, with the poorer demos living primarily in the countryside.¹¹ If there is any historical truth to these visions of the past, they indicate a discriminatory attitude on the part of the elite as to who belonged where. For the Milesian rich, the rural poor could be equated with barbarians, not fit for city life, while the Epidaurians' epithet for their demos is clearly derogatory.¹² Thus, like Theognis, these pictures of Archaic polis life, while not insisting on the outright expulsion of the lower orders from the city center, nevertheless indicate a strong preference for a specific distribution of rich and poor citizens throughout civic space.

The actual practice of physical expulsion from the city, short of complete exile, seems at first glance to have originated with Archaic tyrants. Once again,

---

8. One of the rich men in the villages, Telestagoras, is honored by the demos, which suggests that the demos had a greater presence in the periphery than in the city-center.

9. Fr. 50 Wehrli, with Suda s.v. Γέργηθες and Gorman 2001: 106–7; van Wees 2008: 29. For the tribe of the Gergithes in the Troad, see Hdt. 5.122.2. Heraclides (as quoted by Athenaeus) does not actually specify that the Gergithes lived in the countryside, but their method of killing the children of the rich—by having them trampled on threshing-floors—indicates their rural origins. For alternative versions of the story, see Plut. *QG* 32=Mor. 298c–d; Hdt. 5.28–29.

10. Plut. *QG* 1 = *Mor.* 291e. For a discussion of the 180 as an oligarchy, see Whibley 1896: 159. I am hesitant to apply the label to the institution if it is genuinely Archaic.

11. e.g., *Pol.* 4.1292b25–29, 5.1305a18–20, 6.1318b9–21, 1319a6–19, 28–32; Philoch. *FGrH* 328 F 2. Cf. Herodotus's description of early Media, in which the people "dwell in villages" (Hdt. 1.96.2).

12. Some scholars have thought that the name "Gergithes" in Miletus indicates an indigenous population that had been reduced to serf-like status by Greek settlers (e.g., Halliday 1928: 146; Berve 1967: 579 ["wohl nichtgriechischer Abstammung"]); but Gorman gives convincing arguments otherwise (2001: 106–107). As for the Epidaurian "dusty-feet," it was common in the Greek world to identify (and denigrate) a country bumpkin by the state of his feet: Ar. *Eq.* 315–21; Theophr. *Char.* 4.2, 13 (on the *agroikos*); Cratinus fr. 77 K-A.

we lack a contemporary source that could confirm these characterizations of tyrannical behavior by Classical and later writers. What these sources describe are various ways in which tyrants, fearing for their own security, kept citizens out of the city-center. As early as Herodotus we read that the Athenians in the time of Peisistratus were "oppressed and scattered" (*katechomenon te kai diespasmenon*, 1.59.1). The author later explains that during Peisistratus's third attempt at power, the tyrant had his sons explain to his routed enemies that they would be left alone if they simply returned to their own homes (1.63.2). Those who disobeyed saw their children kidnapped and sent to Naxos as hostages (1.64.1). Through a combination of forbearance and force, Peisistratus achieved the crucial goal of neutralizing his political opposition. He created a situation in which Athenians preferred to stay home and out of politics rather than risk the punishments associated with attempting collective action.

In the *Athēnaiōn Politeia*, Peisistratus's repertoire of techniques becomes even more sophisticated. He provides loans to small farmers, in order, says the author, "that they not spend time in the *astu* but be scattered [*diesparmenoi* now] throughout the countryside" (16.3). For the same reason he institutes the traveling deme judges, who oversee disputes in the villages of Attica. "He himself often went out into the countryside investigating and putting a stop to quarrels," elaborates the *Ath. Pol.*, "to prevent the people from coming into the city and neglecting their work" (16.5). Other tyrants were accused of using "sticks" rather than "carrots" as means of keeping people out of the city. Periander of Corinth, for example, is said to have fined those who sat in the agora, for fear that they would plot against him.[13] The oligarchic tyrants of Erythrae did not allow any of the common people (*demotai*) within the walls, preferring instead to hear disputes at a special court (*dikastērion*) just in front of the city gates.[14]

We may question the accuracy of these reports. The victims of Archaic tyranny were overwhelmingly more likely to have come from the elite than from the common people. When tyrants attacked these opponents, their methods were typically murder and exile, not internal displacement. Forsdyke has outlined a convincing picture of what she calls "the aristocratic politics of exile." The phenomenon is not limited to tyrants but encompasses both single rulers and the broader Greek elite. Whether it is Polycrates and the elite of Samos, Peisistratus and his rivals in Athens, or Alcaeus and Pittacus in Mytilene, many Archaic elites engaged at one point or another in extralegal

---

13. Nic. Dam. *FGrH* 90 F 58.1 (cf. Ephorus *FGrH* 70 F 179 *apud* Diog. Laert. 1.98; Arist. fr. 611.20 Rose).

14. Hippias of Erythrae *FGrH* 421 F 1. For more on this source, see below, section 4.3.

violence and forced expulsion in order to best their rivals.[15] Both approaches involved the physical removal of opponents from contested civic space. No one, however, neither the elite nor tyrants, appears to have been much concerned with keeping the city-center of the polis permanently cleared of all but their own close supporters.[16] There were, *pace* Aristotle, few institutional attempts on the part of tyrants to maintain rigid spatial divisions among different portions of the polis population. Such measures as there were tended to be *ad hoc* actions taken against elite rivals, not against the wider demos.

My suspicion is that accounts of internal displacement such as those cited above are Classical-era retrojections by democratic sources that draw from experiences under oligarchic regimes. Democrats took their own treatment by oligarchs and grafted it onto traditional elite narratives about expulsion and assassination under tyrants. The effect was to tar oligarchs with associations of tyranny, but at the cost of historical accuracy. Thus when Aristotle says that both tyrannies and oligarchies "mistreat the mob and drive them from the city and disperse them" (*Pol.* 5.1311a13–14), he is inadvertently promoting democratic ideology. Of course, distortion could also work in the opposite direction. Democratic accounts of oligarchy often draw upon narrative tropes from Archaic anti-tyrannical sources, with democrats envisioning themselves as a new elite beset by new tyrants in the form of oligarchs.[17] Historians would be remiss, however, not to acknowledge what is new and distinctively oligarchic in these accounts. Classical-era depictions of Archaic tyranny contain important evidence for contemporary oligarchic practices. My point for now is that these practices were Classical innovations, not attested in the Archaic-era sources. As just surveyed, what good evidence we do possess for the Archaic period suggests that certain members of the elite (Theognis, the Milesians, the Epidaurians) despised the presence of lower-class citizens in the city-center but did little systematically to combat it. They might imagine an idealized picture of spatial divisions between mass and elite, but it remained in the realm of fantasy. The novel threat of democracy in the Classical period, however, helped to bring the Archaic elite's longed-for vision into actual practice. In a

---

15. See Forsdyke 2005: ch. 2 and *passim*. I question some of Forsdyke's arguments about the dangers of exile in chapter 2, section 2.5.

16. A potential exception is to be found in the story of the tyrant Syloson of Samos's ruling over a depopulated island. This state of affairs gave rise to a proverb: "Because of Syloson there is a lot of room" (Arist. fr. 574 Rose; Strabo 14.1.17). The emptying out of the polis was not Syloson's intention, however, but resulted from a "netting" carried out by the Persians, who then installed Syloson as tyrant (Hdt. 3.149).

17. Forsdyke convincingly argues this in her treatment of Athens after the regimes of the Four Hundred and the Thirty (2005: 182, 198–204).

kind of changing of the guard, Classical-era oligarchs became the tyrants of Archaic yore, faced with the problem of how to suppress their more numerous enemies. But because the members of the demos were a different kind of entity, socially and numerically, from the Archaic elite, Classical oligarchs had to devise new ways of dealing with them. They could not simply adopt the methods of their tyrannical counterparts. The particular historical context of Classical oligarchy explains oligarchs' distinctive approach to civic space.

4.2 Oligarchic Anxiety over Civic Space in the Classical Period

So far I have attempted to trace Archaic elite thinking about access to central civic space. The evidence is compromised by the fact that it often derives from Classical-era sources, which have their own agendas. Now we may examine Classical oligarchic authors as they deal with their own times, largely eliminating in the process the problem of distortion. These sources are not involved in a project of reconstructing the past, in which they might be tempted to imagine history as they would have liked it. Instead they deal primarily with political problems of the here-and-now, and offer concrete solutions. What is striking about these sources, which have rarely if ever been considered together, is how frank and uncompromising they are on the topic of civic space. We have already seen Aristotle's matter-of-fact statement that oligarchs "drive the people from the city-center [astu] and disperse them."[18] Theophrastus's Oligarchic Man similarly speaks of the city-center in exclusive, zero-sum terms: "It's either them [the demos] or us [the few] that must occupy the city."[19] Finally, the *Rhetoric to Alexander*, a frequently neglected but crucial source of information for Classical-era oligarchies, states the case most straightforwardly in its advice to oligarchic regimes: "The mob [ochlos] must not be allowed to gather from the countryside [chōra] into the city [polis]."[20] The sources are clear: there must be a strict division between the central spaces of the city (*polis*, *astu*), controlled by the oligarchic class, and the broader countryside (*chōra*), in which the demos will be allowed to live.

As will be demonstrated shortly, these characterizations of oligarchy are accurate and not simply extrapolated from Athenian cases, in particular the

18. *Pol.* 5.1311a13–14, quoted above.

19. Theophr. *Char.* 26.3: ἢ τούτους δεῖ ἢ ἡμᾶς οἰκεῖν τὴν πόλιν. Diggle 2004 *ad loc.* makes clear that οἰκεῖν here literally means "live in," not "govern," the polis. The contest is over who will physically inhabit the city.

20. [Arist.] *Rhet. ad Alex.* 1425b8–9: μηδὲ [χρὴ] συνάγειν ἐκ τῆς χώρας τὸν ὄχλον εἰς τὴν πόλιν.

oligarchy of the Thirty in 404. For now I wish to ask why oligarchs should have taken this extreme stance toward spatial separation. The answer lies in the strength democratic movements derived from having many people concentrated in a central location. Again the *Rhetoric to Alexander* spells out the logic clearly, in the sentence directly following the one quoted above: "for from such gatherings [*sc.* of the demos from the countryside into the city] the masses come together and overthrow oligarchies."[21] Massing in the city-center allowed the common people to utilize their numerical advantage most effectively against the ruling few. A look back at the historical record of the late Archaic and Classical periods provides several examples of this phenomenon in action. Already in the time of Solon, it was a potentially dangerous thing to "gather the people" (*xunēgagon dēmon*, fr. 36.1–2 West); another man, explains Solon, with fewer scruples than he, might not have "restrained the people" (*katesche demon*), with the result that the polis would have been "deprived of many men."[22] Even if a democracy *per se* was not in the offing in 594, Solon's words nevertheless indicate that the demos derived strength from massed gatherings. It was based on their collective numbers at Solon's convocation, presumably, that the members of the demos dared to demand more (which Solon ultimately denied them).[23]

Keeping with Athens, we see that later in the sixth century Cleisthenes also made good use of the city-center of Athens for populist purposes. Although it is nowhere stated unequivocally by the ancient sources, the modern scholarly consensus sees Cleisthenes as enacting his reforms through decrees of the assembly.[24] He must have proposed his tribal reforms to the assembled demos, knowing that they would enjoy broad appeal, with the technicalities

---

21. 1425b9–10: ἐκ γὰρ τῶν τοιούτων συνόδων συστρέφεται τὰ πλήθη καὶ καταλύει τὰς ὀλιγαρχίας. Theophrastus' Oligarchic Man similarly links the agora with demotic power: "We [the oligarchs] must come together on our own and deliberate and be free of the mob and the agora" (26.3).

22. Lines 22, 25; cf. fr. 37.6–7. During the heyday of the Athenian democracy, by contrast, leaders were not in the habit of "restraining the people" when assembled. According to Thucydides, at least, it was the rare politician, such as Pericles (2.65.8) or, on one occasion, Alcibiades (8.86.5), who could manage that. On these Thucydidean echoes of Solon, see Szegedy-Maszak 1998: 208–209; Hornblower 2008 *ad* Thuc. 8.86.5.

23. It is not clear where exactly Solon gathered the people, but presumably it was in the agora, the regular site for assemblies before they moved to the Pnyx in the early fifth century: Camp 2001: 153–54.

24. An assembly context is practically the only one in which we can imagine Cleisthenes saying that "he would hand over the constitution to the masses," [Arist.] *Ath. Pol.* 20.1. See further Rhodes 1993: 244, 248–49 (citing earlier scholarship); Ober 1998: 218.

to be worked out afterward.[25] In any case, the reaction of the demos to Cleisthenes's proposals in the assembly was neither the last nor the most influential of its public actions in 508/7: as Josiah Ober has shown, that distinction goes to the three-day siege that forced Isagoras and Cleomenes off the acropolis.[26] When the majority of the Athenians were "of one mind" (*ta auta phronēsantes*, Hdt. 5.72.2), there was little they could not accomplish, particularly if the spatial context—in this case, the agora and the space around the acropolis—allowed them to make the best use of their superior numbers.[27]

Subsequent actions by the Athenian people suggest that they well understood the advantages afforded by central public space. The statues to Harmodius and Aristogeiton in the agora, if not originally erected for this purpose, later came to be seen as a blueprint for recreating the kind of mass action that brought down Cleomenes and Isagoras.[28] Aristophanes's *Lysistrata* of 411 provides evidence for this mindset. The half-chorus of old men, reacting to the women's takeover of the acropolis, first makes plain at lines 274–82 that they will besiege them like they did Cleomenes in 508/7. At lines 617–35, they once again voice concern over a Spartan-led *coup*, which aims at tyranny; this time, however, their model of anti-tyrannical action shifts from their own performance in 508/7 to the exemplum provided by the statues of the tyrannicides in the agora: "I will stand guard, and I will bear my sword in the future in a branch of myrtle, and I will muster in the agora [*agorasō*] under arms next to Aristogeiton, like this [assumes the statue pose] I will stand beside him." Several scholars have recently drawn attention to the use of the tyrannicides as models for collective action in Aristophanes's comedy.[29] For the purposes of the present argument, the most important feature is the emphasis on the

---

25. Andrewes 1977 (noting that the "break-up of old associations, with the consequent damage to the influence of some great families, was a conscious and deliberate aim," and so the reforms "had to be carried through quickly, while ... feeling still ran high," 243).

26. Ober 1993, 1998, 2007.

27. As the Council met in the agora, this must have been the site of the Council's resistance to Cleomenes's attempts and of the subsequent gathering of the people (*sunathroisthentos tou plēthous*, [Arist.] *Ath. Pol.* 20.3).

28. The original statue group, created by the sculptor Antenor, seems to have been erected in 509, after the expulsion of the Peisistratids but before Cleisthenes' reforms (Pliny *NH* 34.17). The Antenor group, stolen by the Persians during the occupation of Athens, was replaced in 477/6 by the famous Critius and Nesiotes group (Marm. Par. *FGrH* 239 A54, lines 70–71). For the close connection between the tyrannicide statue group, the agora, and democracy, see Azoulay 2014 and Kosmin 2015: 147.

29. See Henderson 2003: 173–74; Ober 2003: 220–21; Osborne 2003: 258; Teegarden 2014: 47n63.

agora as the site of collective resistance to anti-democratic *coups*. As in 508/7, so also in 411 the central space of the agora provided the demos with the launching pad for attacking and overthrowing an authoritarian regime.[30] The assassination of the oligarch Phrynichus in front of the bouleuterion, "when the agora was full," suggests that several democrats tried to put this line of thinking into practice during the regime of the Four Hundred.[31] Although the assassination did not produce a groundswell of democratic resistance right away, it did, as Meiggs and Lewis put it, "herald the fall of the Four Hundred" in the long term (262). Once again, the agora spelled danger for an oligarchy.[32]

Were this connection between central space and anti-oligarchic collective action confined to the case of democratic Athens, it would be of limited use in illuminating the reasoning behind the oligarchic restrictions on space contained in the quotations from Aristotle, Anaximenes, and Theophrastus above. As it happens, however, there are numerous instances from outside Athens of precisely the same phenomenon, in which gatherings of the demos in the city-center lead to the downfall of oligarchic regimes. Thucydides, for example, describes the recovery of democracy in Argos in 417, following a brief oligarchic *coup*, in the following terms: "The Argive demos, *coming together [xunistamenos]* little by little and regaining confidence, attacked the few ... and a battle occurred in the city [*en tēi polei*], and the demos was victorious."[33] Similarly, the demos of Mende recovers its city, and its democratic constitution, when the Spartan commander Polydamidas makes the mistake of striking a democratic partisan in plain view during a military muster. Oligarchs had taken over the city with Spartan help earlier in 423 (Thuc. 4.123.2), but they lose control of the situation when Polydamidas attacks a "man from among those on the demos' side" for talking back. The demos, "enraged" (*periorgēs*) at the sight, picks up its weapons and sets upon the Spartans and the oligarchs (4.130.4). Once they had erred in allowing a member of the demos to be struck in public, the oligarchs could not withstand the assault of a massed demos under arms. If the demos was going to be allowed to re-

---

30. Note too that, according to Thucydides at least, the tyrannicides themselves had counted on the agora—in their case the crowded agora of the Panathenaic festival—to help them in their attempted assassination of the tyrant Hippias: see further chapter 6, section 6.1.1.

31. Thuc. 8.92.2; cf. Lys. 13.70–72; Lycurgus 1.112; Shear 2011: 28–29.

32. Teegarden (2014: 26–30) argues convincingly that Phrynichus's murder set in motion a "revolutionary bandwagon" that eventually brought down the Four Hundred, but he does not discuss the importance of the agora in particular in this episode or in past and future attempts at defending democracy.

33. Thuc. 5.82.2. For the oligarchic takeover leading up to this episode, see below, section 4.3.

main within the city walls, it had to be subjected to subtler techniques, which we will examine in a moment.[34]

Xenophon attests to several further cases. The Sicyonian oligarchy is overthrown in 369 when a defector from the regime, Euphron son of Adeas, calls together the demos in the agora to offer them a democratic constitution.[35] Members of the Tegean oligarchy, unable to pass certain measures in favor of joining the Arcadian *koinon* in the oligarchic magistracies, reckon that if "the demos should assemble, they could overpower their enemies with numbers." They therefore parade in arms in the city, calling out supporters. The ensuing battle takes place within the city walls.[36] The dioecism (political and physical dispersal) imposed on Mantinea by the Spartans in 385 is reversed when the Mantineans "come together" (*sunēlthon*) and vote to reestablish a single, democratic polis in 370/69.[37] In Elis, an attempted oligarchic takeover around 400 is thwarted when the demos gathers "like bees" around the house of the democratic "champion" (*prostatēs*) Thrasydaeus, who leads the demos to victory against the oligarchic plotters assembled in the agora.[38] Outside of Xenophon, we have the Oxyrhynchus Historian's description of the democratic "uprising" (*epanastasis*) at Rhodes in 395, in which democratic conspirators rally the demos in the agora before assassinating members of the oligarchic ruling class.

---

34. See further chapter 6, section 6.1.2, for this episode as a paradigmatic case of oligarchic breakdown. Note also that the armed democrats chase the oligarchs and Spartans up onto the acropolis, "which they had also previously occupied" (4.130.6), just as Cleomenes and Isagoras had done in Athens.

35. Xen. *Hell.* 7.1.45; cf. Diod. Sic. 15.70.3. For Euphron, see Griffin 1982: 70–74; Lewis 2004. The bloodlessness of Euphron's *coup* against the reigning oligarchy is remarkable—apparently it sufficed for a single renegade member of the elite to summon the demos to the agora in order for the oligarchy to collapse.

36. Xen. *Hell. Hell.* 6.5.7. The renegade oligarchs in question, Proxenus and Callibius, choose to ally with the demos only when the normal (oligarchic) means are exhausted: they are "getting the worst of it in the *thearoi*" (some kind of oligarchic magistracy—see Rutherford 2015: 127), ἡττώμενοι . . . ἐν τοῖς θεαροῖς, 6.5.7.

37. Xen. *Hell.* 6.5.3. See further Gehrke *Stasis* 105; Roy 1971: 570, 2000: 308–309; Moggi 1976: 251–56. Mantinea was not actually an oligarchy before the re-synoecism, however, but a dioecized series of villages governed "aristocratically"; see further below, section 4.3.

38. Xen. *Hell.* 3.2.27–29. See Robinson 2011: 30; Gehrke *Stasis* 53–54. For Thrasydaeus, the *prostatēs* of the Elean demos, see further Paus. 3.8.4–5; Plut. *Mor.* 835f. The image of the common people as a swarm of bees goes back to Homer: *Il.* 2.86–90 (and see Brock 2013: 159–60 with 186n130). The leader of the Elean oligarchs in this case was one Xenias, guest-friend (*xenos*) of King Agis and *proxenos* of the Spartans (Paus. 3.8.4). Xenophon provides the gossipy tidbit that he was called "the man who measured out the money from his father by the *medimnos*" (*Hell.* 3.2.27).

They then call together the people in an assembly and establish a democratic constitution.[39]

Interestingly, such movements are rarely spontaneous mobilizations undertaken by the average members of the demos, independent of elite action. Either an elite figure spearheads the movement—a renegade member of the ruling oligarchy, or the champion of the demos—or oligarchic violence provokes a demotic reaction.[40] I explain these patterns in greater detail in chapter 6. For the moment, we can appreciate that the author of the *Rhetoric to Alexander* was correct when he identified the city-center as a site of particular danger for oligarchies. Although the mere presence of common people in the central spaces of the polis was not sufficient on every occasion to bring down an oligarchic regime—if true, no oligarchy would ever have survived—the demos always remained a potential source of instability.

4.3 Oligarchic Control of Civic Space 1: Expulsion

The sources surveyed above reveal the very real danger posed by public space to oligarchies. We can now begin to examine the actual ways in which oligarchs responded to the threat. In this and the following section I argue that two tactics in particular emerge from the historical sources, conceptually distinct but devoted to the same long-term strategy. A straightforward reading of the texts gives evidence of the first, studied in the present section, while the second is more speculative. We have already seen these tactics outlined in Aristotle's description of the similarities between oligarchs and tyrants: "they both mistreat the mob and drive them [*apelaunein*] from the city and disperse them [*dioikizein*]." Expulsion and dispersal: Aristotle is not being repetitive here, but instead distinguishing between two different sets of actions.[41]

---

39. *Hell. Oxy.* 18.1–3 Chambers. See further Simonton 2015, which uses Plutarch's description of the performance of Solon's "Salamis" poem (*Sol.* 8.1–3) to demonstrate that this act conforms to a "common knowledge-coordination" model of democratic revolution. Gottesman 2014: 78 independently identifies the Solon episode as an instance of solving a coordination problem.

40. Only in Argos and in Mantinea do we see spontaneous demotic action, although the laconic descriptions of the events by Thucydides and Xenophon may obscure the actions of pro-democratic elites.

41. Despite the use of the verb *dioikizein*, I do not think that Aristotle is referring specifically to the practice of *dioikismos*, whereby a polis was broken up into dispersed settlements (Moggi 1976). Oligarchs might decry the effects of *sunoikismos*, "synoecism," in that it encouraged centralized, democratic politics (Theophr. *Char.* 26.5), but when in power they did not actually subject their poleis to dioecism (*pace* Whibley 1896: 179–81). The reason was that dioecism would have weakened the community defensively: Hornblower 1982: 81; Demand 1990: 94–95. The most famous example of dioecism, that imposed on Mantinea by the Spartans in

THE POLITICS OF PUBLIC SPACE 161

Expelling the demos from the city-center (*astu*, in Aristotle's words) represents the first step toward consolidating control over civic space within oligarchies. This action, which almost always took place during the foundational moments of a new oligarchy, served several important functions. Most immediately, it was the act that established the new constitution. Changes in government rarely followed a peaceful vote and orderly transfer of power in Classical Greece. Even in those cases where some kind of assembly voted the new regime into existence, violence and intimidation typically overshadowed the procedure.[42] Expulsion served further, more complex ends as well: by beginning a new oligarchy with the act of seizing central space, oligarchs deprived the members of the demos of the very location that could best channel their individual energies into collective resistance. Just as acts of demotic rebellion in the agora frequently brought oligarchies, as we saw in the previous section, so oligarchs often sought to preempt such movements when they were overthrowing democracies. Monopolizing the city-center dissipated the collective strength of the demos by spreading a larger, more disorganized group over a broader, more disconnected terrain. Finally, in temporarily expelling the common people, oligarchs very likely had longer-term considerations in mind. If they seized the city without provoking a counterattack, they presented a *fait accompli* to the common people, discouraging them and causing them to call into question their fellow citizens' devotion to democracy. Successful acts of expulsion could thus pay future returns in a manner similar to the manipulation of assemblies analyzed in the previous chapter.

The Thirty of Athens will serve as a convenient starting point for discussion.[43] Xenophon states that the Thirty decreed that those not included in the

---

385 (Xen. *Hell.* 5.2.1–7, 6.4.18, 6.5.3; Ephorus *FGrH* 70 F 79; Isoc. 8.100; Plat. *Symp.* 193a; Diod. Sic. 15.5.4–5; Polyb. 4.27.6; Paus. 8.8.6), was not at first voluntarily submitted to by the Mantinean elite. Later, however, they came to appreciate the *aristokratia* they now enjoyed, living closer to their holdings in the countryside (Xen. *Hell.* 5.2.7; note that Xenophon never calls the arrangement *oligarchia*).

42. The institution of the Four Hundred at Athens in 411 is a classic instance of this: we should prefer Thucydides's account of the events leading up to the Colonus assembly, full of assassination and confusion (8.65–67), over the *Ath. Pol.*'s description of a more constitutional procedure (29.1–3—but see 29.1, where the author says the Athenians were "forced" to change their democracy, and Arist. *Pol.* 5.1304b12–15, where the transition to the Four Hundred is attributed to fraud). See also Thuc. 4.74.3–4; Aen. Tact. 11.13–15 (for both episodes see above, chapter 3, section 3.2). Changes to democracy were also typically violent. Cf. de Ste. Croix 1981: 288: "I know of no single case in the whole of Greek history in which a ruling oligarchy introduced democracy without compulsion and by simple vote."

43. Newman in his commentary on the passage of Aristotle's *Politics* cited above immediately thought of the Thirty (422–23), but there are more instances than that.

list of the Three Thousand "were not to enter the city-center *(mē eisienai eis to astu),*" a description that finds confirmation in Lysias, Isocrates, and post-Classical sources.[44] They provide sufficient evidence that the Thirty expelled the demos from the city, but not from Attica itself. The move was not only symbolic but practical, in that it kept undesirables out of the physical act of politics, which necessarily took place within the city. As Forsdyke notes, "expulsion from the city proper confirmed in physical terms the exclusion of the mass of Athenian citizens from the political process."[45]

The regime of the Thirty did not last long enough for us to know whether they would have continued to enforce the spatial division of the city into two parts, the regime members in the *astu* and the rest in the *chōra*. It may be that a strategy of permanent exclusion was more feasible in Athens than elsewhere, since Attic territory was exceptionally large for a single polis and more people lived outside of the *astu* than was normally the case. As Hansen has emphasized in his study of polis settlement patterns, for the majority of a polis's population to live within the city walls was quite typical, at least in the case of small- to medium-sized poleis, while the opposite pattern is found only in the largest cities, such as Athens and Sparta.[46] A policy of ongoing exclusion would therefore have affected fewer people in Athens than in other places.[47]

A more obvious explanation, however, is that the Thirty enjoyed the backing of a Spartan garrison, commanded by the harmost Callibius.[48] Originally the Thirty prefaced the request for a garrison with the pledge that it would remain in Athens only until they were able to get rid of the "scum" (*ponēroi*). Once Callibius arrived, however, the Thirty proved unable to restrain themselves: they arrested not only the *ponēroi* and people of little account (most likely sycophants and minor demagogues), but also influential men who were not likely to tolerate being pushed aside by an extremely narrow junta.[49] We

---

44. Xen. *Hell.* 2.4.1; Lys. 12.95, 25.22, 31.8; Isoc. 7.67; Diod. Sic. 14.32.4; Justin 5.9.12. Curiously, the *Ath. Pol.*, while mentioning exile and deprivation of arms (37), does not discuss mass expulsion, although the author speaks in familiar terms of "the men in the city" as a distinct group from the demos (e.g., 38.1–2) and later says that the demos "secured its return by its own efforts" (41.1), implying that the entire demos was exiled, an exaggeration.

45. Forsdyke 2005: 199; cf. Wolpert 2002: 22.

46. Hansen 2006a: 67–72.

47. It is also likely that many of those who did possess real estate within the *astu* of Athens were quite wealthy: Xenophon says that the Thirty "drove them from their lands so that they themselves and their allies might gain possession of their fields" (*Hell.* 2.4.1).

48. Xen. *Hell.* 2.3.13–14. [Arist.] *Ath. Pol.* 37.2 erroneously places the arrival of Callibius after the execution of Theramenes and the disarming of the rest of the population; see Rhodes 1993: 455.

49. Xen. *Hell.* 2.3.14.

should thus expect permanent expulsion only in those cases where a very narrow oligarchy had the services of a foreign garrison at its disposal.

This is in fact precisely what we see in cases of expulsion by oligarchies outside Athens, which are plentiful. The acts come in different forms and different degrees of severity, from the relatively limited tactic of monopolizing the space of the agora to the more extreme move of seizing the acropolis or locking the demos out of the city walls. There is, for example, the case of the attempted oligarchic *coup* at Elis that was eventually defeated by Thrasydaeus and the demos (above, section 4.2). In the opening moves, the oligarchic conspirators murder a man they mistakenly identify as Thrasydaeus under the cover of early-morning darkness. The demos then loses heart (*katēthumēse*), supposing Thrasydaeus to be dead, while the supporters of the oligarchs "carry arms into the agora" (Xen. *Hell.* 3.2.27–28). The oligarchs clearly intended, with their parade of arms in the marketplace, to dissuade the demos from offering any resistance. In terms of the model offered here, their goal was to prevent demotic collective action in the early stages of the takeover. The exclusion of the demos from the Elean agora would not have been an ongoing policy, but was instead used as a temporary shock tactic to preempt the possibility that the demos might assemble in the city-center and launch a counterattack. The oligarchs' plan might have worked, were it not for the fact that Thrasydaeus, the *prostatēs* of the demos, was not actually dead. Once the demos rallies around his house, as we saw, it drives the oligarchic plotters from the agora quite easily.[50]

Sometime after 424, the demos of Leontini enrolled several new citizens and was on the verge of redistributing the land.[51] This proposal was anathema to the "powerful men" (*dunatoi*) of Leontini, who called in the neighboring Syracusans and "expelled [*ekballousi*] the demos, who were scattered in disparate directions [*eplanēthēsan*]" (5.4.3) The *dunatoi*, meanwhile, came to an agreement with the Syracusans and left their city completely deserted, choosing instead to become citizens of Syracuse. The Leontinian oligarchs' decision to leave the polis is surprising, but clearly the initial act of expelling the demos was meant to overthrow the democratic constitution and so prevent the impending land reform. The *dunatoi* presumably could have continued at that point as a new, oligarchic ruling elite, but they chose instead to emigrate to

---

50. For the episode as evidence for oligarchs' use of secretive assassination see chapter 3, section 3.1.2, with comparisons to Thuc. 2.2–3.

51. Thuc. 5.4.2; Berger 1992: 26; Robinson 2011: 104. As the episode actually precedes the Athenian example, it shows that oligarchs already possessed a repertoire of spatially based institutions and did not require the example of the Athenian oligarchic regimes of the late fifth century.

Syracuse. Had they stayed in Leontini, their initial expulsion of the demos likely would have helped to solidify their rule. Yet it is important at the same time to see what this act was not: the Leontinian oligarchs did not drive the demos from the actual territory of the polis, only from the city-center itself. This becomes apparent later on, when a few dissatisfied Leontinian oligarchs decide to leave Syracuse and return to their city. There they are joined by "a majority of those of the demos who had been expelled" (5.4.4) The demos, then, while indeed expelled from the city-center proper, were still living nearby when the oligarchs returned.[52] In fact, they probably would have continued to inhabit their traditional homesteads within the territory of Leontini.[53] It is unlikely that the Leontinian oligarchs and the Syracusans would have had the power (or the desire) to try to force the entire population to move great distances from Leontini.[54]

Argive oligarchs effected a similar *coup*. According to Aeneas Tacticus, when the Argives were celebrating a festival *en masse* outside the city walls, conspirators launched a surprise attack and killed a number of magistrates.[55]

---

52. The *IACP* classes Leontini as having a territory size of "4," or 200–500 km². By contrast, almost 80 percent of recorded poleis had territorial sizes of less than 200 km² (*IACP* 71). Leontini is not included among the "super poleis" of *IACP* 72, but it was still probably large enough to have a polis center along with "second-order nucleated settlements scattered over [its] territory."

53. Cf. Vattuone 1994: 87–88; Berger 1992: 26. Those considered the *prostatai* of the demos in Leontini likely did flee the city entirely and live abroad, some of them in Chalcis: see Franke 1966, cited by Berger 1992: 26n89, and Hornblower *ad* 5.4.3. An honorary decree of Samos for two Chalcidians lists one as Antileon the son of Leontinus; the latter was presumably the son of a Leontinian exile born in Chalcis ca. 420 (*SEG* 57.814). As Thucydides's language makes clear, a minority "of those of the demos who had been expelled" were in exile and did require restoration to the city, which the Athenians (cynically) promoted in their imperial campaign against Sicily: Thuc. 6.50.4, 63.3, 77.1.

54. The Leontinian example is so similar to those of other oligarchies that we should resist thinking of the their actions in terms of the Archaic example of Gelon of Syracuse. Gelon was notorious for uprooting and transferring whole populations of poleis on a whim. He often favored the elite in his policies while deporting or enslaving the demos (Hdt. 7.156.1–3). Several scholars have thus explained the Leontinian oligarchs' actions in specifically Sicilian, tyrannical terms (e.g., Berger 1991: 137; Dreher 2007: 75). The demos of Leontini in 424 was not actually transferred abroad, however; they were simply displaced internally.

55. It was not unusual for a polis to be seized while the community was celebrating an extramural festival: see Hdt. 1.150 (Colophonian exiles take Smyrna while the inhabitants are outside conducting a festival to Dionysus); Thuc. 3.3.3 (the Athenians hope to take advantage of the Mytilineans while they are celebrating an extramural festival to Apollo Maloeis). These are interstate examples, however. Seizures during episodes of intra-state *stasis* tend to be by oligarchs: see further below.

They then fled, arms in tow, into the city, where they used their advantage in position and weaponry to admit only those they approved within the walls (17.2–4). Scholars are in general agreement that Aeneas is referring to the oligarchic takeover of the city in 417, recorded by Thucydides, when the elite "put down the democracy and established an oligarchy loyal to the Spartans."[56] As we have already seen, the Argive oligarchs do not seem to have made their monopolization of the walled city permanent, since the demos was able to regroup and attack the oligarchs "in the city" later that same year.[57] Instead, following the schema developed here, the oligarchs wished to deprive the demos of the coordinating potential of centralized civic space, if only long enough to establish their own regime.

In the fourth century, several attempts by oligarchs to seize control of the *astu*, or at the very least the acropolis, are known from inscriptions.[58] In an Athenian decree for the Ionian polis of Erythrae from the first quarter of the century, the Athenians forbid their generals from coming to terms with "those in the polis" without the Athenian demos's consent.[59] Clearly the Athenian demos and its client, the Erythraean democracy, are in control of the situation, but a dissident group currently occupies "the polis." [60] The dissidents, who had apparently hoped for outside assistance from "barbarians" (lines 13–14), are almost certainly oligarchs, and it is possible that they have not simply fled to the "polis" but attempted to take it over.[61] We should compare a later inscription from the tiny island of Telos, enacted by the demos after

---

56. Thuc. 5.81.2; cf. Diod. Sic. 12.80.2–3; Paus. 2.20.2; Arist. *Pol.* 5.1304a25–27. For the identification, see David 1986, Whitehead 2001 *ad loc*. Note that those outside the plot are called *hoi polloi*, "the majority," a label which suggests that the conspirators were a minority of oligarchs.

57. Thuc. 5.82.2, discussed above, section 4.2.

58. One might hypothesize that the acropolis was, for logistical reasons, easier to seize than the agora or the broader *astu*, but that by the same token it was easier for defenders to resist and besiege those who attempted a takeover, since they could muster in the agora: cf. Hdt. 5.71.1–2; Thuc. 1.126.3–8 (Cylon's attempted takeover of Athens in 632); Hdt. 5.72.2; [Arist.] *Ath. Pol.* 20.3 (Isagoras's seizure of the acropolis and subsequent besiegement). Rosivach 2008 sees no advantage to seizing the acropolis; he argues that it was a frequent target of *coups* in Archaic Athens because it housed the prytaneion, which until the Classical period was the Athenian "seat of government." This perspective ignores the fact that revolutionaries in poleis other than Athens also seized the acropolis during violent takeovers. See the suggestion above that the purpose was to present a *fait accompli* and stun the population into acquiescence.

59. RO 17, lines 3–6.

60. See the discussion at RO 17. I incline toward the meaning "city" for polis, rather than "acropolis." It is unlikely that the Athenians would leave room for ambiguity, especially since this is an interstate rather than local context.

61. As we have seen, Mendaean oligarchs fled to the acropolis with the Spartans in the after-

successful reconciliation with oligarchs.[62] A large section of the inscription is taken up by an oath, in which the swearers promise to "remain in the established constitution and guard the democracy" (lines 92–93). One of the central provisions of the oath is "not to conspire with anyone who is planning to seize the acropolis [*tan akran*]" (96–97); the oligarchs may have initially made such a seizure before the *stasis* was resolved.[63]

These attempts were so frequent that criticizing them became part of the stock-in-trade of anti-oligarchic discourse among democrats. The latter assumed that attacks on the democratic status quo by oligarchs would take this devious, underhanded form and warned against them accordingly. The deployment of these tropes by democrats was important for both ideological and practical reasons. Oligarchs' reliance on these sorts of tactics was reflective of their small, unrepresentative numbers and thus of their inherent illegitimacy; at the same time, identifying these methods made it more likely that instances of them would be met with successful resistance. Relevant in this regard is the recently published Eretrian law against tyranny and oligarchy.[64] At one point the law advises the Eretrian democrats on what to do if "it is impossible to occupy the Agoraion ... or if the demos is locked out of the walls" (fragment B, lines 24–26). Knoepfler, in his *editio princeps*, concludes after a thorough discussion that the "Agoraion" must have been a sanctuary or *temenos* devoted to a god with the epithet "Agoraios" (Zeus or perhaps Artemis). The shrine would have served as the meeting place for the Eretrian democratic council (*boulē*), mentioned in the same line of the inscription ("if it is impossible to occupy the Agoraion right away so that the council can [convene]"). Such a *temenos*, by its very name, must have been located in the Eretrian agora, and so the Eretrian law guards against one

---

math of the democratic uprising in 423 (Thuc. 4.130.6, discussed above), but the acropolis had already been serving as their base of operations.

62. *IG* XII.4 1 132. For more on this inscription, most of which remained unpublished until 2010, see Thür 2011; Gray 2015: 94–98.

63. Cf. the language of the pro-democratic oath contained in *Tit. Cal.* test. xii, line 24 ("I will not seize the *akra*"), as well as that of a recently published inscription from Sagalassos in Pisidia (*SEG* 57.1409, lines 1–3: "no one is to seize the *akra*"). The Cymaean decree outlining the duties of the generals (see below) imagines a situation where someone proposes "handing over the polis [the acropolis?] and receiving a garrison" (*SEG* 59.1407, lines 18–19). In this connection it is notable that Aristotle says that different types of fortification are suitable for different constitutions: "an acropolis is monarchic and oligarchic, while level ground [*homalotēs*] is democratic" (*Pol.* 7.1330b19–20).

64. Knoepfler 2001b/2002 = *SEG* 51.1105 (translation and discussion in Teegarden 2014: ch. 2).

of the eventualities discussed above, in which oligarchs take control of the marketplace.[65]

The second possibility listed in the law is the expulsion of the demos from the city's walls, which, as we have just seen, was an equally common oligarchic tactic. Knoepfler in fact cites the example of Argos from Aeneas Tacticus discussed above, pointing out that the Eretrians celebrated their own extramural festival, which may in the past have provided the opportunity for an oligarchic takeover.[66] An even more recently discovered inscription is pertinent here. An early-third-century decree from Aeolian Cyme issues warnings to the city's generals against various anti-democratic activities. One forbids handing over "the keys" (*sc.* of the gates to the city walls) "to those [attempting to] put down the democracy" (lines 19–20).[67] The decree envisions a scenario in which a renegade general agrees to work with an anti-democratic faction, giving them the keys to the city and thus allowing them control over civic space.[68] Like the Eretrian law, the Cymaean decree treats democracy as the only legitimate constitution (one of the duties of the generals is to "hand over the city in a condition of freedom and democracy" at the end of their term of office, line 13), and it attests to the ongoing concern that oligarchs might take advantage of the polis's walls. Clearly the connection in democrats' minds between oligarchic *coups d'état* and the usurpation of civic space was not an isolated phenomenon confined to the Athenian experience with the Thirty, but a Panhellenic trend that reflected the similar dangers faced by democracies in different poleis. The Eretrian law thus shows the Eretrian demos learning from the oligarchic track record, so to speak, and training themselves, as the Cymaeans later would, to respond appropriately in the face of attempted oligarchic putsches. In ideological terms, their law also furthers the democratic aim of conflating oligarchy and tyranny and establishing the power of the people as the exclusive constitutional "rules of the game."[69]

65. The law's assumption that the demos would normally try to occupy the Agoraion suggests that the agora was a "focal point" of democratic coordination and anti-oligarchic resistance: for this term, see chapter 5, section 5.2.4.

66. Knoepfler 2002: 176. The festival was to Artemis: Strabo 10.1.10. See further the example from Hippias of Erythrae *FGrH* 421 F 1, discussed below.

67. The decree was first published by Manganaro 2004 = *SEG* 54.1229; see now also Hamon 2008 = *SEG* 59.1407. See further the afterword.

68. Cf. RO 83 β, lines 2–3: the tyrants of Eresus in the mid-fourth century "locked [the people] out of the city *en masse.*"

69. For the notion of the institutional "rules of the game," see North 1990: 3. The oligarchic propensity to expel citizens from the city walls features in the local history of Hippias of Erythrae (*FGrH* 421 F 1; early Hellenistic period?). In Hippias's account of Archaic Erythraean history, a clique of "tyrant oligarchs" kills the rightful king Cnopus and takes over the city while

4.4 Oligarchic Control of Civic Space 2: Clientelism

Oligarchic acts of expulsion were both too much and too little. Expulsion was a violent and illegitimate tactic, unlikely to endear the new ruling group to the populace. At the same time, due to lack of resources, oligarchs could not hope to keep the members of the demos permanently excluded from the city-center. Expulsion might be used to establish oligarchic power, but it could not maintain it over the long term. For ongoing stability, a more subtle approach to the problem of central space was needed. This section reconstructs from the available evidence a hypothetical model of what this form of control may have looked like. No historical source straightforwardly states that oligarchic regimes of the Classical period instituted this model, but we glimpse its basic outline in the comments of philosophers and theorists, as well as in historians' reconstructions of the ancient past, which I suggest were influenced by contemporary oligarchic practices.[70]

My label for the set of techniques in question is "clientelism." There is no exact ancient Greek equivalent for this ultimately Latin-derived term, although as we will see, the word *epimeleia*, signifying both "care" and "oversight," comes close to the sense required. Nor is clientelism identical with patronage, another Latinate concept that historians have occasionally applied to the Greek world.[71] Clientelism does involve something like Roman-style patron-client relations, but in a fully institutionalized, politicized context. Clientelism is not a primordial, pre-political social relationship between pairs of isolated actors, but is in fact the intentional product of a political regime. It is a state of affairs coordinated by ruling authorities at the political center and enforced at the periphery. Patronage is a "private" relationship that might even persist under a democratic regime if left untampered-with; clientelism is a political strategy instituted by an authoritarian government to ensure its rule.

---

the citizenry is celebrating an extramural festival to Artemis. The oligarchs then let none of the common people within the city walls but instead hold court outside the gates. The situation is quite similar to the expulsion scenario envisioned by the Eretrian anti-tyranny law. It is noteworthy also that Erythrae had experienced at least one episode of oligarchic takeover of the city-center (RO 17, discussed above). As we will see in chapter 5, section 5.2.4, oligarchs also mistreated a statue in the Erythraean agora. Hippias's work, with its fiercely anti-tyrannical and -oligarchic slant, reflects this local history, as I have argued elsewhere: See Simonton forthcoming and below, chapter 6, section 6.1.1.

70. On the other hand, several post-Classical historical sources do describe explicitly non-democratic regimes engaging in the relevant practices: see the examples of Strabo on Rhodes and Polybius on Elis below.

71. Although see the discussion below of the relationship between the Greek world *pelatēs* and the Latin *cliens*.

What problem occasioned clientelism, and how did it work to solve that problem? As we have seen, oligarchs feared central space, with its capacity to coordinate democratic collective action. They preferred a state of affairs, often extolled in idealizing visions of the past, in which the common people stayed away from city politics and contented themselves with rural life. With their needs at least minimally met in the countryside, poorer citizens would not feel inclined to travel to the city-center to make demands; at the same time, dispersal throughout the hinterland would keep the demos divided and weak. Clientelistic practices attempted to make this vision a reality. Under clientelism, individual oligarchs (the majority of whom would have owned land both in the *astu* and in the *chōra*) brought members of the demos within their country districts under their supervision.[72] The oligarchs provided a bare set of social, legal, and economic "goods"—dispute resolution, money-making opportunities, insurance against poor harvest years—with the understanding that, in exchange, their clients would forswear central, collective politics, leaving it to their oligarchic "betters." This "agreement," whether explicit or left tacit, was backed up with the threat of violence, should the members of the demos ever venture beyond their station. When operationalized across a polis's entire territory, the clientelistic system placed individual members of the demos in a giant collective action problem. While an individual might have preferred that the demos come together in the city-center and overthrow the oligarchy, calculations of individual reward and punishment would argue against taking the initial step of leaving the hinterland. Getting by on their oligarchic patron's limited offerings might be preferable to risking one's life in the pursuit of a potentially more rewarding democratic arrangement.

To begin, we can examine the oligarchic preference for a dispersed, "agricultural" demos. Aristotle is our clearest and most consistent proponent of this arrangement, which he thinks benefits both democracies and oligarchies. In the former case, distance from the city-center and engagement in agricultural labor prevents the common people from spending their time in assemblies and upsetting the laws, activities Aristotle considers characteristic of "agoric" populations.[73] By the same token, he thinks agricultural populations

---

72. Note that the elite of Mantinea had both homes in the city and extra-urban agricultural property: Xen. *Hell.* 5.2.7. Thuc. 2.65.2 says that the Athenian *dunatoi* (elite) had fine possessions (including houses) in the countryside, in addition, presumably, to those they possessed in the city.

73. *Pol.* 4.1292b25–29, 6.1318b9–21, 1319a28–32. Aristotle is either ill-informed or disingenuous if he thinks that a majority of the citizens of the Athenian democracy, which he considered a "final," debased form of democracy, was agoric rather than agricultural (an error committed also by the Old Oligarch; see Rhodes and Marr 2008: 22).

"still today" tolerate oligarchies (as they used to tolerate tyrannies), since their focus is on their work rather than on politics.[74] We have seen already (section 4.1) that Classical sources, including Aristotle, attributed to Archaic tyrants the habit of encouraging labor in the countryside in the hope of keeping the common people out of politics. The present passage lends support to the idea, suggested above, that these images of tyrants are more likely projections back onto the past of contemporary oligarchic practices. Aristotle saw rural populations of his own day tolerating oligarchic regimes and so reasoned that earlier people must have done the same under tyrannies.

Other sources express Aristotle's point about the desirability of an "agricultural demos" in a less systematic fashion. Euripides's description of the poor member of the country demos (put into the mouth of the virulently antidemocratic Theban herald) is a case in point: "A man who must work the soil is poor, and even if he is not ignorant, he is prevented by his labor from casting his eye towards politics."[75] A similar figure graces the same author's *Orestes* (917–22): "He was not fair to look upon in appearance, but a manly man, spending little time in the city or the circle of the agora, a poor farmer, one of those who alone preserve the land." These descriptions cast the yeoman as a necessary part of the polis, a farmer as well as a fighter. Yet there is little doubt that he is expected to keep away from city politics. Carter, in his study of the "quiet Athenian," reviews the *Orestes* and other relevant passages and concludes that "this [farmer] shows a sturdy independence, yet knows his place; he is, in a word, respectable, and it is this which endures him to the oligarchic and fourth-century theorists [*sc.* like Aristotle]."[76] As a final example, Andocides is not happy to see country folk crowding into the city during the Peloponnesian War: "May we never again see the charcoal-burners coming from the mountains into the *astu*."[77] The comment could conceivably come from a lost public oration, but scholars have traditionally ascribed it to Andocides' secretive "Speech to his Companions [*hetairoi*]," in which he was said

---

74. *Pol.* 6.1318b17–21; cf. 5.1305a18–20.

75. *Supp.* 420–22.

76. Carter 1986: 91. There may be a similar ideology at work in Aristophanes's portrayal of farmer protagonists (Dicaeopolis of *Ach.*, Trygaeus of *Peace*) who hate life in the city during the Peloponnesian War, but I cannot address the politics of Old Comedy here.

77. Fr. 4 Blass = *schol. ad* Ar. *Ach.* 477. Note the similarity in language between Andocides's statement and that of the *Rhetoric to Alexander* about mobs and the *astu*, studied above. The "charcoal-burners" are most likely men from the deme of Acharnae, famous for its charcoal (Ar. *Ach. passim*). Kellogg (2013: 136–37) asks why Andocides would direct so much wrath at the Acharnians in particular and speculates that, being numerous, they would have constituted an especially visible and painful reminder of the Athenians' need to abandon the countryside during the Peloponnesian War. I suggest instead that his distaste was class-based and political.

to have "riled up the oligarchs against the people."[78] In that case, the orator, who had a compromised political reputation to begin with, would have been lamenting to his fellow oligarchs about the presence of "undesirables" in the city, country bumpkins whose "natural place" was the hinterland.[79]

For these authors—particularly Aristotle—the nature of the agricultural population was an external condition that affected the character of a polis's constitution. Elsewhere in the *Politics* Aristotle discusses the different kinds of occupations and settlement patterns that made up a city and how these combined in different ways to produce different *politeiai*. A city may be particularly democratic due to its large population of fisherman, as at Byzantium and Tarentum, or its large number of trireme rowers, as at Athens.[80] Along the same lines, a large agricultural demos makes a democracy manageable or an oligarchy more sustainable. For Aristotle, these factors are exogenously given—they are independent variables that determine the dependent variable in question, regime type. By contrast, the present analysis reverses the relationship. The characteristic institutions of different types of regime, democracy and oligarchy, affect in different ways the participation of various polis populations in the politics of the city. That participation then affects regime stability in the long term. In other words, the extent to which a demos was "agricultural" was not set in stone. It was a function of institutional choices made by key regime actors, who faced great pressures to keep the demos as dispersed and de-politicized as possible.

How they did so I will now explain. Some of the evidence that follows has been collected and analyzed in previous studies of "patronage" in the Greek world. While much previous scholarship focuses on Athens, I am more interested in what the Athenian evidence might suggest for oligarchic practice more generally.[81] I begin with a heavily studied passage concerned with the generosity of the Athenian politician Cimon. According to the *Ath. Pol.*,

---

78. Plut. *Them.* 32.3.

79. Cf. Theophrastus's character sketch of the *Agroikos* (Country Bumpkin), *Char.* 4.2–3: He comes to the assembly having just drunk gruel, wears shoes too big for his feet, and prattles on in a loud voice. He also describes the proceedings of the assembly to his wage laborers when he returns to the farm (*sc.* in the countryside). Theophrastus's attitude toward the poor farmer may indicate what thinking lies behind Andocides's statement.

80. *Pol.* 4.1291b22–25.

81. Some things, presumably, Athens cannot show us. Millett 1989, for example, argues convincingly that the Athenian democracy largely eliminated relations of patronage (Jones 2004: 68–85 does not overturn this view). This does not mean that patronage ceased to exist everywhere in Greece, as Zellnick-Abramovitz suggests (2000: 66), citing Millett. Indeed, Millett was convinced that patronage "must have existed" in the wider Greek world (1989: 17). In other poleis, members of the demos may have become debt-bondsmen (*pelatai*) of the elite, as

> Pericles first made the lawcourts sources of income, employing a demagogic tack opposite to that of Cimon's, which was based on personal wealth. Cimon, who possessed wealth on the level of a tyrant, first of all carried out the common liturgies magnificently, and he also furnished many of his fellow demesmen with sustenance. For he allowed any of the demesmen of Laciadae who wished to do so to come to his house every day and take their share of goods, and his land was unfenced, so that it was possible for whoever so desired to enjoy his fruit. Pericles was at a serious loss in terms of wealth when it came to this kind of public beneficence, but Damonides [*sic*] of Oa advised him ... since he was at a disadvantage in terms of private income, to give the majority "their own," and so he devised a system of payment for serving as a judge. (27.3–4)

The story is repeated, with minor variations, twice in Plutarch and again by Theopompus.[82] Most scholars have agreed that the point of the story is to show two competing methods of political influence, one local and "aristocratic" and one public, urban, and democratic.[83] In the more trusted versions of the story, Cimon's munificence extends only to his fellow demesmen, the men of Laciadae, not to the polis as a whole.[84] He attempts to cultivate a specifically local form of authority based on food and, in Plutarch and Theopompus's version of events, donations of money and clothing.[85] Pericles, by contrast, in an attempt to undercut Cimon's local prestige and create a greater audience for himself, provides the demos with a new reason to gather in the city and conduct legal business there. In other words, the answer to Cimon's strategy of keeping politics local is to make it more central, which means in practice more democratic.[86] It is therefore misleading to follow Zelnick-

---

happened in pre-Solonian Athens (see Rhodes *ad* [Arist.] *Ath. Pol.* 2.2). In the early fourth century, an Athenian himself had a *pelatēs* under his control, probably from Naxos (Plat. *Euth.* 4c; cf. Pollux 3.82). Later Greek-speaking Roman historians translate Latin *clientes* into Greek *pelatai* (Plut. *Rom.* 13.5; Dion. Hal. *Ant. Rom.* 2.9.2). On patronage see now also Alwine 2016.

82. Plut. *Cim.* 10.1–8, *Per.* 9.2; Theopomp. *FGrH* 115 F 89. (Cf. Theophrastus F 515 Fortenbaugh *apud* Cic. *Off.* 2.64; Nep. *Cim.* 4.1–3.)

83. Cf. Davies 1971: 312; Rhodes 1993: 339.

84. Plutarch (*Cim.* 10.2) maintains this point, citing Aristotle. Elsewhere Theopompus uses his "whole polis" version to compare Cimon to Peisistratus (*FGrH* 115 F 135), but it is better to see Peisistratus' strategy as an attempt to *undercut* the authority of Cimon-like local elites. Note the similarities between Cimon and Telestagoras of Naxos, mentioned by Arist. fr. 558 Rose: Telestagoras lived in the "village" (*kōmē*) of Lestadae (cf. Cimon's deme of Laciadae) and was held in high regard by the demos, who sent gifts daily.

85. Plut. *Cim.* 10.2–3; Theopomp. *FGrH* 115 F 89.

86. Cf. Millett 1989: 25.

Abramovitz in thinking that "both aspired to political eminence and reached it by benefitting the poor," thus revealing their basic similarity.[87] In a crucial difference, Pericles's tactic is incompatible with oligarchy. Although he no doubt wished to increase his own influence by promoting higher levels of popular participation in government, Pericles effectively conceded to the demos the potential to formulate policies to the detriment of himself and his elite peers.

It is difficult to determine Cimon's exact motives in this case: Plutarch says that his contributions to the poor allowed them to "devote time to public affairs" (*tois dēmosiois scholazōn*, *Cim.* 10.1), but he also quotes the rhetorician Gorgias (DK 82 B 20) to the effect that "Cimon made money so that he might use it, and he used it so that he might be honored" (*timōito*, 10.5), and he denies that Cimon practiced flattery of the mob or demagoguery (10.7). Promoting democracy and amassing greater individual honor are certainly not incompatible, but it is safest to suppose that Cimon was primarily interested in personal glory. His actions, furthermore, while not necessarily rolling back democracy, will have helped to check it. In any case, his particular form of largesse could presumably function under oligarchy. It is probably for this reason that the arch-oligarch Critias praised Cimon's "high-mindedness," praying in his elegiac verses for "the wealth of the Scopadae, the *megalophrosunē* of Cimon, and the victories of Arcesilas the Lacedaemonian" (DK 88 B 8). In fact, Wade-Gery plausibly argued that both Aristotle and Theopompus derived their stories about Cimon's generosity from Critias's writings.[88] Critias probably saw in Cimon's clientelism a tactic that, on a polis-wide scale, could have secured the power of an oligarchic constitution. Cimon's "high-mindedness" coexisted with an already-robust democracy, but in the absence of regular assembly meetings and universally accessible law courts, a network of Cimonian-style "boroughs" could have helped to keep the demos in check.

Cimon's practices are described as keeping his fellow demesmen of Laciadae confined to the village; those of Pericles, by contrast, entice the members of the demos to the law courts. The connection between elite patronage and the control of central space is also strongly pronounced in Isocrates's *Areopagiticus*, a text often cited in discussions of patronage but never through the lens of the model of oligarchy employed here.[89] One difficulty in using the work to gain access to oligarchic ideology is the fact that Isocrates protests that he is in favor of democracy (7.16–17, 27, 60–61) and strongly opposed to

---

87. Zelnick-Abramovitz 2000: 72.

88. Wade-Gery 1938: 133 with n9. Cf. also Critias' interest in Cimon at DK 88 B 52 = Plut. *Cim.* 16.8.

89. See Fuks 1979–80: 51–53; Millett 1989: 25–28.

oligarchy, which he anticipates his opponents will claim he is trying to instate (57, 62, 70). Some scholars, like Markle, have dismissed these attempts at establishing democratic *bona fides* as sophistic ruses meant to obscure the fact that Isocrates was advocating constitutional measures that would entrench the power of the wealthier classes.[90] Others, particularly Wallace, have argued instead that Isocrates was mainly interested in improving Athenian civic and military performance in a manner consistent with roughly "democratic" ideals.[91] I cannot treat this issue at length, but I agree with Markle over Wallace, especially on the ideological viewpoint of the *Areopagiticus*. The dialogue displays inconsistences with other works that indicate a more subversive and anti-democratic undercurrent,[92] and its vision of the Solonian-Cleisthenic "good old days" may fairly be called a fantasy.[93]

The *Areopagiticus*'s chief point of interest for us is its praise of what are arguably oligarchic political practices in the course of its idealized description of Athens' past. I suggest that Isocrates, when it came time to critique the present state of Athenian democracy, used as a point of contrast not simply idealized, abstract models, but institutions known from contemporary oligarchic regimes. Actually existing oligarchies are not cited, but of course it would have severely weakened Isocrates's "reformist" argument had he explicitly mentioned oligarchic examples. His recollections of the Athenian past are not only indicative of clientelistic relationships, as scholars previously have noted, but bring together local patronage with centrally devised disciplinary institutions in such a way that the demos is encouraged to withdraw from the city center and avoid political life.[94] Clientelism interacts with a physically divided "ward system" to ensure that no one will want to make the first move toward

---

90. Baynes 1955: 144–67; Markle 1976 (esp. pp. 98–99); de Ste. Croix 1981: 608n53.

91. Wallace 1989: 145–73. There is another view that treats Isocrates as basically rhetorical and apolitical: Harding 1973 (who cites Baynes but refuses to treat Isocrates as conveying any particular political perspective).

92. In particular, at *Areop.* 7.61 he calls the Lacedaemonians the "most democratically governed people," while in the *Panathenaicus* (12.177–79) he calls them a democracy only in the sense that the ruling class, separate from the mass of the poor, enjoyed equality amongst themselves.

93. As Markle 1976: 98 deems it. The fact that Isocrates separates out the Solonian-Cleisthenic period as a unified "*patrios politeia*," much as Cleitophon had done in the establishment of the Four Hundred ([Arist.] *Ath. Pol.* 29.3), rather than treating the whole period beginning with Solon as a single regime as the democrats did, indicates his divergence from mainstream democratic ideology.

94. See esp. Ober 1998: 283: "The society, and thus the politics, of Isocrates's ideal Athens were grounded in firmly established and universally accepted relationships of patronage and clientage."

holding an assembly (an institution that is completely absent from this supposedly democratic tract).

Beginning in section 31 of the text, Isocrates recounts the "unity" (*homonoia*) that the citizens of the *patrios politeia* felt toward one another, both in public business and in private interactions. The poor respected the property holdings of the elite, considering them a potential source of revenue for themselves, and the rich came to the aid of those in need, "granting some people land to cultivate at reasonable rates, sending out others for the purpose of trade, and providing others the means to enter into various forms of work" (32). Moreover, judges in property and lending disputes sided strictly with owners in accordance with the law, refusing to give in to any sense of "equity" (*epieikeia*, 33). The result was that "possessions were secured as justice demanded, while the use of property was available to all citizens who needed it" (35).

These and other comments (44–45, 55) have rightly led scholars to believe that Isocrates is advocating what Millett has labeled a "neo-Cimonian" program of patronage.[95] The proposals for private beneficence on the part of the elite, however, have not been studied in conjunction with Isocrates's other preferred institutions, despite the fact that the author explicitly says that the different elements work together as causes and effects (36). In particular, the Areopagus council and its supporters function to keep the citizens in a state of "sobriety" (*sōphrosunē*, 37) and "good order" (*eutaxia*, 39) by both swiftly punishing offenders and deterring potential criminals through oversight (*epimeleia*) (47).[96] Although the Council itself did the punishing and threatening, the "disorderly" (*akosmountes*) throughout the city first had to be detected and arrested by other means, and this was achieved through "the division of the urban center into wards [*kōmai*] and the countryside into demes," in which "they" (a subject whose identity is suggested below) "inspected the way of life of each person and brought the unruly before the Council" (46).[97]

---

95. See Fuks 1979–80: 51–54; Millett 1989: 25–28 ("neo-Cimonian" remark at 28); both authors also cite *Archid.* 6.67, in which the young Spartan king laments the distrust between classes in the newly democratic Peloponnese, where before there had been *homonoia* and generosity toward one another.

96. *Epimeleia* can mean both "surveillance," as here, and "care," as in a passage of Aristotle cited below. The concept of clientelism nicely bridges the two connotations, since under patronistic relations the patron both supports the client and keeps him under close watch. Plato, who focuses on the violence and paranoia of oligarchies in the *Republic*, stresses the first sense of *epimeleia* when he says, "The rulers [of oligarchies] forcibly restrain [the discontented] through oversight" (οὓς ἐπιμελείᾳ βίᾳ κατέχουσιν αἱ ἀρχαί, *Rep.* 8.552e).

97. διελόμενοι τὴν μὲν πόλιν κατὰ κώμας τὴν δὲ χώραν κατὰ δήμους ἐθεώρουν τὸν βίον τὸν ἑκάστου, καὶ τοὺς ἀκοσμοῦντας ἀνῆγον εἰς τὴν βουλήν. ἡ δὲ τοὺς μὲν ἐνουθέτει, τοῖς δ' ἠπείλει,

The job of detection, then, is parcelized and distributed among individuals within discrete zones of the polis, who then report back to the Council.

Although Isocrates does not specifically identify the inspectors within the wards and demes (referring to them simply as "those men" or "our forefathers"), it is unlikely that they would be anyone other than those who shared the Areopagus's conception of *akosmia* and were on a friendly basis with its members, in other words the elite themselves.[98] Just as the patronage program can fairly be described as "neo-Cimonian," therefore, so too the "neighborhood watch" system described in *Areopagiticus* 46 is probably best thought of as one in which the Cimons of the city monitor their spheres of influence and then confer with the Areopagus. Although the patronistic part of the system is private, the informing element would be impossible without the existence of a generally agreed upon institutional structure. The city's different "divisions" and their political duties must be common knowledge to at least some of the population, most likely the richer citizens who can have been expected to participate in this constitution (26).[99]

One outcome of this system, Isocrates says, was that the young men did not waste their time with gambling or flutegirls, nor did they frequent the agora or the taverns (48–49). This passage contains more than a hint of the moralizing sentiment found, for example, in Aristophanes's *Clouds* (e.g., 991, 998). As recent scholarly work has shown, however, we should take seriously the idea that the public gathering places of the "lower class" elements—such as the marketplace, barber shops, inns, and brothels: "free spaces" in K. Vlassopoulos's language—often promoted democratic activity.[100] With so many dif-

---

τοὺς δ' ὡς προσῆκεν ἐκόλαζεν. Cf. [Arist.] *Ath. Pol.* 3.6, which does not, however, mention the spatial arrangement.

98. As in the section (chapter 3, 3.4) on informing, however, we might imagine members of the lower classes eventually becoming motivated to follow the actions of the elite and inform on their peers.

99. A similar instance of "dividing up" an oligarchic city can be seen in the case of Larissa (for the oligarchic status of which, see Arist. *Pol.* 5.1305b29–30, 1306a29–30; Bacchyl. fr. 14b S-M with Fearn 2009), as indicated in a fragment (498 Rose) of Aristotle's lost *Constitution of the Thessalians* (apud schol. ad [Eur.] *Rhes.* 307): "Dividing up [*dielōn*, the same verb as at Isoc. 7.46] the city [*tēn polin*], Aleuas commanded that each group supply from their plot [*kata ton klēron*] 40 cavalry members and 80 hoplites." The editor of the *Fragmenta*, Rose, changed "*tēn polin*" in the manuscripts to "*tas poleis*," presumably because he thought all of the cities of Thessaly were being referred to. This would mean, however, that each *tetras* of the Thessalian *tetrarchia* (Dem. 9.26; Hellanicus *FGrH* 4 F 52; Arist. fr. 497 Rose) supplied only 80 hoplites for a total of 320, an absurdly low number. It is better to keep the manuscripts' singular polis and assume that the reference is to Aleuas's hometown of Larissa: see Helly 1995: 153–54.

100. See Davidson 1997a *passim*, 1997b; Lewis 1995, 1996; Vlassopoulos 2007; Gottesman 2014.

ferent kinds of people mixing, mingling, and freely conversing, these spaces of the city greatly facilitated the coordination and collective action of large numbers of ordinary people. When Isocrates speaks of keeping these areas clear, therefore, he is likely invested in a project of preventing the growth of popular power.[101]

Likewise, the speaker relishes the thought that in the olden days the emphasis was on the countryside rather than the city, with the houses and buildings "in the fields" (*epi tōn agrōn*) being much finer and more expensive than those within the walls. Again, the result was that the citizens conspicuously avoided the civic spaces of the city: "many of the citizens never came to the city, not even for the festivals, but chose to keep to their own possessions rather than enjoy the common stock" (52). It is also no surprise that the author should disparage grandiose festivals that encourage the participation of the demos in city life, since conservative critics of democracy understood very well the opportunities these events afforded for increasing the power of the masses. The demos, in fact, often self-consciously utilized them to coordinate against an oligarchic regime or to strengthen a democracy, as we will see in chapter 6.[102]

Within Isocrates's professedly "democratic" proposal, then, we see the outlines of an oligarchic system of division and control, in which local patrons provide their clients with sufficient reason to accept their dispersed and depoliticized lot. Such a scheme is fully consonant with Aristotle's recommendations to oligarchs in the *Politics*, as Fuks and others have noticed.[103] First there is Isocrates's encouragement of *epimeleia* or "oversight" (7.47, 55), which is echoed by the rather vague suggestion in Aristotle that "care" (*epimeleia*) should be taken of the poor in oligarchies (5.1309a20–21). Aristotle returns to the issue in Book 6. His starting point is democracy, but some of his proposals apply equally well to oligarchies and are addressed explicitly to the latter. In a democracy, the rich should provide the poor with work and also pay for their attendance at assemblies (1320a35-b4).[104] Aristotle then switches to a more general tone: "it is characteristic of a generous and wise class of notables [*gnōrimoi*] to divide the poor among themselves [*dialambanontas*] and

101. For parallels, see Theopomp. *FGrH* 115 F 100, 213, 233, and esp. 62 (the Byzantine democracy spent its time in taverns, the agora, and the harbor, and introduced the same practices to the Calchedonians).

102. For conservative complaints about festivals, see [Xen.] *Ath. Pol.* 2.9–10, 3.2; Plat. *Rep.* 6.492b; Arist. fr. 89 Rose; Theopomp. *FGrH* 115 F 213, 233 (cited above); Plut. *Mor.* 818c, 821f (= *Praec. Ger. Reip.* 24, 29).

103. Fuks 1984: 179: "the verbal parallels can hardly be missed."

104. Note that while the methods of poor relief are similar to Isocrates's in the *Areopagiticus*, the paid attendance for assemblies is much more democratic than anything Isocrates proposes.

provide them with the means to pursue work" (1320b7–9). Here the allusions to Isocrates are unmistakable: as in Isoc. 7.32, the rich give the poor an inducement, *aphormē*, to look for *ergasia*. The division of the poor into groups (*dialambanontas*) also mirrors Isocrates's depiction of the polis as "divided up" by the elite (*dielomenoi*, 46).[105] The great nineteenth-century commentator on Aristotle, W. L. Newman, understood the implications of this passage perfectly, some of it from contemporary experience, as his note on the text reveals: "If a rich man took charge of a section of the poor, not only would there be no 'overlapping of charity,' but a cordial relation would spring up between the rich man and those whom he befriended ... '[t]he individualizing of the work [of relief], which assigns to each almoner as limited an area as possible,' is a feature of the Elberfeld system of poor-law administration."[106]

That local elites also offered themselves to their constituents as mediators in disputes is evident in [Aristotle's] description of Peisistratus's institution of deme judges (*Ath. Pol.* 16.5): "thus he also set up judges throughout the demes, and he himself often went out into the countryside, inspecting and reconciling those at odds with each other, so that they would not come down to the city and neglect their work." Although several motives underlie Peisistratus's scheme,[107] Rhodes has pointed out that one major reason would have been to "substitut[e] representatives of the central authority for whatever arbitration the disputants had been able to obtain locally—usually, no doubt, from the local nobility."[108] In other words, Peisistratus sought to supplant local elite influence and control, although he retained structures that would dissuade people from petitioning for their interests at the center. The fact that later incarnations of the deme judges settled disputes dealing with sums up to 10 drachmas (*Ath. Pol.* 53.1) may indicate that they were always meant for small claims among non-elite citizens.[109] For the theme of elite judgment at the

---

105. Fuks (1984: 188n59) compares Aristotle's use of *dialambanontas* (for which he writes "*analambanontas*," surely a misprint) to Strabo's *hupolambanousi* in his description of Rhodes (14.2.5, discussed below), but there it clearly means "support," while Isocrates' *dielomenoi* is much closer in meaning.

106. Newman *ad loc*. The quotation is from "G. Drage, Report on Gemany to the Royal Commission of Labour, p. 87." In addition to the Strabo passage on Rhodes (see below), Newman is also able to cite examples from medieval Venice and Switzerland.

107. It is said that Peisistratus liked to keep the population busy with work so that they not spend time in the city but remain dispersed throughout the countryside (16.2–3). This is a common complaint against tyrants and oligarchs, as we saw above, and is likely to be a contemporary oligarchic practice retrojected onto Archaic tyrants.

108. Rhodes 1993: 216, citing Hignett 1952: 115. Cf. Finley 1983: 46–47; Ober 1989: 66; Forsdyke 2005: 126.

109. The number of judges was thirty at least by the time of their second establishment in

local level, we should also compare Herodotus's Median king Deioces, whose skills were appealing to the demos because there was such injustice and corruption throughout the local districts (*kōmai*). Many other populist figures could be cited.[110] These passages collectively give the impression that, unless a democratic government took steps either to centralize the courts of justice or to undercut elite authority in the hinterland, dispute resolution at the local level would tend to be in the hands of the wealthy and powerful.

Finally, the importance of local clientelistic ties for the stability of oligarchies can be seen indirectly in Aristotle's comments in the *Politics* on the necessity of dissolving old associations and creating new ones in order to strengthen a democracy. "Measures," he says, "such as those which Cleisthenes made use of at Athens when he wanted to increase the power of the democracy, and which those in Cyrene establishing the democracy [used], are useful for an extreme democracy. Numerous new tribes and phratries should be created, and matters of private cult should be consolidated into a few common organizations, and all should be contrived so that everyone is mixed up amongst themselves as much as possible, and previously existing links should be decoupled [*diazeuchthōsin*]" (6.1319b19–27). We see an echo of these words in the *Athēnaiōn Politeia* precisely where we would expect to find them, in the author's description of Cleisthenes's reforms (21.2): "He first divided [the Athenians] into ten tribes instead of four, with the intention of mixing them up so that more people would partake of the *politeia*."[111] These statements are highly elliptical, but the basic meaning behind them can be reconstructed: before democracy, numerous organizations and associations existed throughout Attica, but they were primarily in the hands of local elites. Democratic reformers could either dissolve these ties completely or allow for the construction of parallel organizations, which might then coexist with and provide

---

453/2 (*Ath. Pol.* 26.3), a number which probably maps onto the thirty trittyes (Rhodes 1993: 331). Paga has recently argued that we should probably envision these courts as operating in the deme theaters (2010: 381).

110. Hdt. 1.96.2: κατοικημένων τῶν Μήδων κατὰ κώμας, ἐν τῇ ἑωυτοῦ ἐὼν καὶ πρότερον δόκιμος καὶ μᾶλλόν τι καὶ προθυμότερον δικαιοσύνην ἐπιθέμενος ἤσκεε· καὶ ταῦτα μέντοι ἐούσης ἀνομίης πολλῆς ἀνὰ πᾶσαν τὴν Μηδικὴν ἐποίεε, ἐπιστάμενος ὅτι τῷ δικαίῳ τὸ ἄδικον πολέμιον ἐστί. The presence of unjust local judges is made clear shortly afterward, when it is said that people preferred Deioces because they had suffered from "unjust decisions" (ἀδίκοισι γνώμῃσι, 1.96.3). Recall also Aristotle's Telestagoras of Naxos (fr. 558 R), who lived in a *kōmē* and was honored by the demos with gifts.

111. *Politeia* here means "participation in government," not simply "citizenship": see Rhodes 1993: 250, following Wade-Gery 1933: 25n2. For more on the intentions behind the strategy described, see further in the text above. For more on "mixing," cf. *Ath. Pol.* 21.3.

a counterweight to previously existing associations.[112] Democracies were strengthened both by cross-cutting associations (tribes, trittyes) that fostered communication and participation among local community members, regardless of class status.[113]

The sources surveyed above constitute the best Classical-era evidence for the oligarchic practice of clientelism.[114] Several post-Classical sources are worth mentioning in this context, as they are suggestive of ways in which Hellenistic and Roman-period oligarchies might have continued in the tradition of their Classical forebears. Polybius, for example, at one point describes the political situation of the Eleans of his day, some of whom, he says,

> so love their life in the fields that they have not come to the lawcourt [*halia*] at all for two or three generations, so sufficient are they in their possessions. This has resulted from the fact that those involved in political affairs [*tous politeuomenous*] have great concern and forethought for those who dwell in the countryside, *and they deliver justice to them on the spot* [*epi topou*] *and make sure none of life's necessities are lacking.* (4.73.7–8)[115]

---

112. We are told that Cleisthenes left the gene and phratries the same (*Ath. Pol.* 21.2). It is more difficult to tell what is happening in the Cyrene situation: see Robinson (1997: 105–108), who tentatively suggests connecting Aristotle's statement with the sixth-century reforms of Demonax discussed by Herodotus 4.161.3. Robinson admits that Aristotle may be referring to a fifth-century democracy (mentioned by Arist. fr. 611.17 Rose; Diod. Sic. 14.34.6—to which add schol. *ad* Pind. *Pyth.* 5.12a, schol. *ad* Pind. *Pyth.* 4 inscr. a).

113. See the discussion of Ober 2008: 134–42, who brings out the importance of Cleisthenes's reforms in overcoming what he calls the "the cliquish strong-tie local networks that characterized ordinary Athenian social life" (139).

114. Additional evidence might come from the figure of Ptoeodorus of Megara, a wealthy and powerful man who worked for the interests of Philip of Macedon (Dem. 18.295, 19.295; see also the new fragments of Hyperides's *Against Diondas*). According to Plut. *Dion* 17.9–10, when Dion went to visit Ptoeodorus at his home, he found a "crowd of people and a heap of business" preventing him from meeting the host. He told his friends, however, that they should expect as much, since they used to do the same in Syracuse. Lest we think Plutarch is interpreting the episode through a Roman lens, the story derives from the third-century BCE Peripatetic Ariston of Ceos (fr. 13.2 Wehrli). Megara was likely an oligarchy at the time (Legon 1981: 176–79), and so the Ptoeodorus episode might illustrate the role patronage (if not full clientelism) played in it (as well as in Dion's Syracuse).

115. Interestingly, neither Fuks 1979–80 nor Millett 1989 discusses this passage. Roy (2015: 183; cf. Burford 1993: 63; McInerney 2006: 50) thinks Polybius refers to "wealthy Elean landowning families," but Polybius says only that they possessed "sufficient" (*hikanai*) estates, not considerable ones. Furthermore, if the Eleans mentioned were rich, the central authorities would have no need to ensure them "life's necessities" (*biotikai chreiai*). The Eleans referred to are not members of the elite but average farmers (Hanson 1998: 112–13). Walbank 1957 *ad* 4.73.7

Here once again we see an attempt to address problems locally, with the result that a substantial portion of the population stays out of politics completely. The political class, it should be noted, deals with the administration of justice themselves. This is not simply decentralized power but center-periphery coordination of the type postulated above. The *politeuomenoi* resolve disputes in the countryside itself and furthermore see to the provision of "life's necessities," in other words the "minimal bundle" of social insurance and opportunities for work discussed earlier. The Elean situation mirrors almost precisely the non-democratic "ancestral constitution" described and endorsed by Isocrates in the *Areopagiticus*.[116]

Similar to Polybius's depiction of Elis is a puzzling passage in Strabo purporting to describe the sociopolitical arrangement at Rhodes. "The Rhodians," he says,

> although they are not democratically governed [*dēmokratoumenoi*], are mindful of the demos, and they wish to take care of the mass of the poor. Indeed, the people are supplied with grain, and the wealthy [*euporoi*] support [*hupolambanousin*] the needy according to an ancestral custom of theirs [*ethei tini patriōi*], and there are liturgies that provide rations, so that the poor man has his daily sustenance and the city is not deprived of necessities, especially its navy. But some of the harbors [*naustathma*] are hidden [*krupta*] and forbidden [*aporrhēta*] to the majority, and death has been established as the penalty for anyone spying on them or entering them. (14.2.5)

Modern scholars have typically disagreed with Strabo's labeling of Rhodes as non-democratic,[117] but his description may still hint at an idealizing oligarchic ideology, according to which the beneficent wealthy provide the poor with life's necessities in exchange for the demos's abstention from politics. In particular, the mention of "forbidden" areas such as harbors, which could serve as a source of popular power much as Athens' Piraeus did, suggests that the freedom of movement of the demos was a topic of particular concern to this ideological perspective.[118] It seems that the *euporoi* could maintain the

---

rightly compares the situation to Peisistratus' use of the *dikastai kata dēmous* in Athens, where it was a matter of small farmers, not large landowners ([Arist.] *Ath. Pol.* 16.5).

116. Elis in the Hellenistic period seems to have lost much of its earlier democratic character, for which see Robinson 2011: 28–33.

117. e.g., O'Neil 1981a; Rhodes with Lewis 1997: 274–75; Grieb 2008: 316–20. For further discussion, see Migeotte 1989; Radt 2009: 71.

118. Blackman, Rankov, et al. (2013: 211) cite the Strabo passage in a discussion of the threat of arson at shipsheds, comparing it with other instances in which access to the dockyards was

all-important Rhodian fleet and remain in control of civic affairs by a combination of patronage and threats against massed gatherings. Indeed, we should probably see the two phenomena as related: the rations were distributed, perhaps locally, on the condition that the members of the demos be content with their share and demand nothing further through collective petition.[119]

There is a final hint of clientelistic relations in Plutarch's treatment of the oligarchic regime at Athens headed by Phocion. In the wake of the oligarchic revolution encouraged by Antipater, Phocion stocked the magistracies with "urbane and better sorts of people" (*asteioi ... charientes*), but taught the "troublesome and revolutionary" types (*polupragmonas ... neōteristas*) to "love the countryside and rejoice in farming" (*philochōrein ... agapān geōrgountas*).[120] One might argue that Phocion is here mainly concerned with elites, potential leaders of the demos, but just as likely is the idea that the members of the demos were encouraged to remain on their farms rather than participate in politics. We should note that the phrase "rejoice in farming" (*agapān geōrgountas*) strongly resembles Polybius's description of the Eleans as "loving their life in the fields" (*stergousi ton epi tōn agrōn bion*, 4.73.7). Phocion similarly seems to have tried to induce the Athenian demos to keep away from the *astu*. Certainly, once the regime had fallen, it was in the interest of the resurgent democracy to present the foregoing period as a time in which the entire demos had been in exile. The inscription *IG* II² 448, erected in 318/17, proudly proclaims, "Now, since the demos has returned and has reclaimed the laws and the democracy...."[121] As with earlier episodes of oligarchic rule in Athens, however, the claim of universal exile is more a unifying fiction than a description of reality. While many did go into exile, Phocion's oligarchy did not bother to try to expel the entire demos from Attica, as several sources indicate.[122] Much of the day-to-day work of regulating the Athe-

---

restricted. They miss the fact, however, that in this instance Strabo says access was forbidden to the majority (*hoi polloi*) in particular.

119. Cf. the story that there was a "seller" (*poletēs*) at Epidamnus who prevented people from mingling with foreign merchants out of fear of *ponēria* and *neōterismon* (revolution) spreading through the population (Plut. *Mor.* 297f = *QG* 29; *contra* Robinson 2011: 129, who thinks it is a democratic measure, but see Gehrke *Stasis ad* Epidamnos). Here, too, we should detect antidemocratic undertones and fear of the demos having access to "free spaces" (Vlassopoulos 2007).

120. Plut. *Phoc.* 29.4. For more on this oligarchy's treatment of the demos, particularly when assembled in the *ekklēsia*, see above, chapter 3, section 3.2, citing recent studies of Phocion's regime.

121. Lines 62–64: νῦν δὲ ἐπειδὴ ὅ τε δῆμος [κατελ]|ήλυθε καὶ τοὺς νόμους καὶ τὴν δημοκρατίαν ἀ[πείλη]|φε.

122. Unifying fiction: see Forsdyke 2005: 200; Wolpert 2002: 75–136. For the presence of the

nian demos in the years of Phocion's oligarchy likely involved the local clientelism outlined here.

If Classical Greek oligarchs engaged in these sorts of practices, as the foregoing review of the evidence strongly suggests, they are in good company with contemporary authoritarian governments studied by political scientists. One of the best treatments of clientelism under a modern authoritarian regime comes in Beatriz Magaloni's study of the PRI (Partido Revolucionario Institucional) dictatorship in Mexico, which lasted from 1929 to 2000.[123] During its time in power the PRI actually held elections, albeit uncompetitive ones with little to no chance of opposition victory. Magaloni describes how the PRI kept voters in line through a clientelistic system that worked at the local level to offer rewards and punishments to groups of citizens in exchange for their ongoing support. "The ruling party," says Magaloni, "observes voters' behavior and targets side payments, rewarding supportive voters with patronage funds and punishing defecting voters by withdrawing these funds."[124] Punishments might include "not receiv[ing] land from the government," having "subsidies ... cut," "be[ing] excluded from the government's housing program," or having one's locality "punished by cuts in central government funding."[125]

The system's efficiency derived from both the nature of the goods in question and the ability of the regime to monitor voters' behavior. With targeted private goods, the regime can choose which localities, and sometimes even which individuals, to reward, which to punish. Were the regime to offer *public* goods to all citizens of Mexico (goods which by definition are non-excludable and the use of which by some citizens does not entail less availability to others), the system would lose its effectiveness, since voters could take the public goods and still vote against the PRI in subsequent elections. The use of private goods tied the enjoyment of such goods to the survival of the regime.[126] We should compare a hypothetical scenario in Athens in which elites like Cimon were the exclusive suppliers of income and social insurance to their fellow demesmen. Poorer residents of Laciadae were dependent upon Cimon personally for free fruit and other goods; they thus had reasons to defer to him politically, to keep him in power and prominence so as not to "kill the goose

---

demos under Phocion's regime, see Diod. Sic. 18.64.2, 3, 65.6; Plut. *Phoc.* 29.4, discussed above in chapter 3, section 3.2.

123. Cf. chapter 3, section 3.2.

124. Magaloni 2006: 65.

125. Magaloni 2006: 65–66. Note that while the target audience is local, the agent ultimately ensuring the distribution of goods is the centralized state. For versions of this clientelistic system used by other authoritarian states, see Lust-Okar 2006 (on Jordan) and Blaydes 2010 (on Mubarak-era Egypt).

126. See Magaloni, Diaz-Cayeros, and Estévez 2007.

that lays the golden eggs." Pericles's system of payment for judges, by contrast, broke up elite-demos patronage networks by granting all Athenians, regardless of geographic location or loyalty to a particular member of the elite, the ability to be compensated for their political service.

The lynchpin of clientelistic effectiveness, of course, is the regime's ability to distinguish between supporters and detractors. Were the regime not able to screen voters, voters would have no reason to fear casting ballots for the opposition. Clientelism thus requires an effective screening mechanism on the part of the state, or at least the *perception*, among citizens, that the government possesses such a mechanism. Magaloni explains:

> Vote buying works better when people's votes can be observed. This is the reason why clientelistic networks are far more effective in small rural communities rather than in large impersonal cities. In rural settings, local party brokers and caciques possess more *local knowledge* about voters—with whom voters hang out, what their political opinions are, at which political rallies they show up. The story in the large cities is different because in urban areas it is harder for the ruling party to acquire knowledge about voters' types, monitor their behavior, and target private transfers to its loyal supporters.[127]

Magaloni's comments map neatly on to what we have observed about Classical Greek oligarchies. In Isocrates's decentralized program of demes and wards, for example, supporters of the Areopagus-dominated status quo were more easily able to "inspect the way of life of each person and bring the unruly before the Council" (7.46). Massed groupings in the city-center, on the other hand, were far more difficult to monitor and control. In fact, the ancient Greek situation displays even more starkly than the modern one the importance of geographic proximity. Whereas for modern authoritarian governments the significance of localism lies in the greater ability it affords authoritarians to screen votes, for Greek oligarchs the danger was that rural citizens would literally leave the oligarchs' individual spheres of interest and gather in the center. The average citizen's dilemma under Greek oligarchy was not which party to vote for but *where to go*: to remain within a local patron's zone or to travel to the *astu*.

The forms of clientelism, ancient and modern, are thus varieties, differing in terms of their spatial specifics, of the "collective action problem," in which concerted action that would benefit a large groups fails to take place because each person would prefer to "piggyback" on the efforts of others.[128] The politi-

---

127. Magaloni 2006: 67–68 (emphasis in original).
128. See Olson 1965, discussed in chapter 1, section 1.3.

cal scientist Mona Lyne has shown how clientelism amounts to a variant of the Prisoner's Dilemma, which she calls "the voter's dilemma." As in Magaloni's study, an individual hoping for a win by the opposition can either vote for them or vote for the clientelist status quo candidate. If the person votes for the opposition but others do not, he or she faces the possibility of being singled out and punished by the authorities. If, however, others vote for the opposition and the opposition wins, then the individual receives the benefits of the opposition's policy platform regardless of whether he or she voted for them. The "dominant strategy" for the individual voter is therefore to vote for the establishment, but in the aggregate this pattern of behavior maintains the status quo, since no one votes for the opposition.[129]

In the ancient Greek case, the individual is offered some package of personal benefits from a local elite/oligarch. He can then either reciprocate the offer and keep his nose out of public affairs or attempt to attend an assembly in the *astu*. If no one else attends, however, he can easily be targeted for sanctioning by the local elite. If he stays at home but the rest of the demos converges on the city for an assembly and a democratic revolution, he receives the benefits of democracy anyway. Just as in Lyne's "voter's dilemma," the dominant strategy for the individual member of the demos is to remain at home and content himself with receiving the big man's largesse. Even if the benefits to be had from democracy—more public goods, law courts manned by members of the demos, greater scrutiny and control over elites—were arguably superior to the elite's benefactions, the demos might fail collectively to achieve those benefits through too many individuals choosing not to participate.

129. Lyne 2008: 29–39.

5

The Manipulation Of Information

Sometimes the ways of silence are most reliable.
—PINDAR[1]

5.0 Introduction

Governments have rarely if ever followed a policy of complete transparency. The contemporary United States is no exception, as the controversies surrounding the Church Committee, the Pentagon Papers, and now the Edward Snowden affair reveal.[2] But while there are significant impediments to access of information in the U.S. and other liberal democracies, the leaders of non-democratic regimes often employ restriction of information at a more systematic level. The importance of public information and its methods of circulation for both regime elites and dissidents can be understood in the following terms: First, accurate information about the performance of the regime can fuel dissatisfaction if times are bad or if decisions are unpopular; rulers therefore have reason to suppress such potentially costly information. Second, if the members of the ruling elite control the flow of information, they can more easily target individuals or groups for manipulation and co-optation. When a person does not know all of the facts—what others are thinking and doing, what the level of popularity of the regime is—he or she is in a much weaker bargaining position, and may more readily acquiesce to the regime's wishes. Third, the control of information is important to the ruling elite because its

---

1. Fr. 180 S-M: ἔσθ' ὅτε πιστόταται σιγᾶς ὁδοί.

2. A pair of *Washington Post* reporters published an eye-opening series of articles in a collection titled *Top Secret America: The Rise of the New American Security State* (Priest and Arkin 2011). On the other hand, a conservative commentator has argued for "necessary secrets" (Schoenfeld 2011).

ability to project its power unopposed sends a signal to the opposition about the likelihood of successful coordinated action against the regime. In other words, the propagation of pro-regime ideology creates an image of invincibility that can dissuade people from engaging in resistance.[3]

Overall, then, an authoritarian government is more stable the greater the extent to which it can (1) monopolize important political information, (2) project an idealized image of its own unity and power, and (3) selectively deploy specific information to targeted audiences. In the modern world, the antidote to this state of affairs is freedom of assembly and freedom of information, the logic being that citizens with unobstructed access to accurate news and forums of discussion can more easily coordinate to punish leaders who try to overstep their legal bounds. Of course, citizens may desire those rights independently of specifically *political* aims: they may seek information for narrower instrumental goals, or they may simply value communal gathering as an act in itself, because they are sociable. A democratic polity secures people these rights whatever their ultimate reason for desiring them. In an authoritarian state, on the other hand, leaders cannot afford to let citizens exercise such rights unimpeded, even if people want them for non-political purposes (for what we call "civil society"). The exercise of the rights in question leaves open the possibility that citizens may use them for subversive, anti-state activities. A non-democratic regime therefore has an interest in suppressing those rights to some degree, but, since people value them, it cannot afford to suppress them to the point that the benefits of revolting to obtain the rights outweigh the potential costs. According to the neat formulation of the political scientists Bueno de Mesquita and Smith,

> Leaders can dissipate revolutionary threats via two mechanisms. They can increase the provision of public goods, thereby improving the welfare of the citizens and diminishing their desire for revolutionary change. Alternatively, leaders can suppress the provision of public goods, particularly such goods as a free press, transparency, and easy communication that help people coordinate and organize. Suppressing these goods reduces the probability of revolutionary success. (2010: 936)

The authoritarian approach to the flow and content of information thus usually entails a balance of suppression and concessions.

In this chapter I argue that Classical Greek oligarchs engaged in a similar policy of control of information. We must bear in mind, however, the specific context of the ancient Greek polis. As emphasized in chapter 1, the city-state

---

3. For the importance of information and publicity in authoritarian regimes, see Bhavnani and Ross 2003: 346; Magaloni 2006: 8–9; Simpser 2013; and see chapter 3, section 3.2.

was much smaller than a modern state, and so there were, on the face of it, fewer impediments to information reaching the entire community. The relative weakness of the ancient Greek state also meant that there was less centralized political capacity to record, organize, store, and guard information beyond the direct reach of the majority of the population. On the other hand, communication technology was limited, and many people were illiterate.[4] Information circulated orally, through preexisting social networks and family ties, much more than it did through inscribed decrees, public pronouncements, or any kind of "news" service.[5] Thus "official" information was capable of being monopolized and manipulated, depending upon how many people were present at the site of its original production and circulation. I argue that it was characteristic of a successful oligarchy to restrict this primary audience as much as possible to the members of the political class and to oversee how the information produced at their own secret political meetings was later promulgated. Democracies abandoned all attempts at this on grounds of infeasibility or— what is more likely—welcomed widespread publicity for ideological reasons. Although democratic decisions made in the assembly hardly ever took place before the *entire* citizen community (since assemblies were not expected to house the whole demos), their results could easily be publicized by word of mouth, while the "epigraphic habit" created opportunities for citizens to consult policy outcomes after the fact if they cared to. By contrast, oligarchies not only restricted the political privileges of deliberating and voting to a smaller group, they attempted to limit the ability of the politically excluded even to witness and report on the acts of the ruling elite.[6] Yet in other contexts, oligarchs did allow the demos to receive political messages, highly specific messages that emphasized the unity of the oligarchy and created divisions within the majority population. I assemble examples of each type of manipulation, which I label "secrecy," "projection," and "selectivity," in turn.

5.1 Secrecy

As might be expected, the ancient evidence gives numerous indications of the greater secrecy, exclusivity, and unaccountability of oligarchic political delib-

---

4. There is a potential problem of *petitio principii* here, since it could be that democratic government encouraged more people to read than oligarchy. This problem has not, to my knowledge, been addressed.

5. See Harris 1989; Thomas 1989, 1992, 2009; Lewis 1996; Bresson, Cocula, and Pébarthe 2005; Capdetrey and Nelis-Clément 2006; Pébarthe 2006; Missiou 2011.

6. As I argue in chapter 3, section 3.2, general assemblies within oligarchies were rare and, when they did occur, were orchestrated for specific, pro-regime purposes.

eration. We have already seen (in chapter 2) that restricting attendance to the full members of the regime afforded oligarchs breathing room in which to hash out their personal differences, which might otherwise undermine the stability of the *politeia*. In the present chapter I shift my focus from relations among the elite themselves to interactions between the ruling group and the wider community. Whibley characterized that relationship well in his study of oligarchy: "the powers of the assembly were inconsiderable beside those of the council [in an oligarchy], and the oligarchs carried into effect their theory of specialisation of authority, of *efficiency, secrecy, and dispatch* by delegating the duties of government to small councils or to the magistrates."[7] My purpose here is to flesh out Whibley's picture with historical examples and, more importantly, to show how such institutional processes functioned in the aggregate to stabilize an oligarchic constitution.[8]

It was a truism in ancient Greece that, outside of extraordinary meetings of the assembly, the rulers in an oligarchic polity generally met alone, with the demos not allowed to oversee the proceedings and in some cases entirely ignorant that they were even taking place.[9] As we have already seen, the practice of oligarchic government revealed an imbalance structurally embedded in the notions of democracy and oligarchy: democracy, regardless of whether it was to be understood as "the rule of all" or "the rule of the many," admitted all adult male citizens into the assembly without discrimination, while oligarchy entailed a restriction in the number of citizens exercising political power. Thus while democracy could be derided as the tyranny of the poor majority, the wealthy could not complain of being excluded—it was simply that their opinions were drowned out when everyone was granted an equal vote. The oligarchic minority accordingly could make their voices dominant only by shutting others out.[10] Oligarchic government is thus frequently depicted as the coming

---

7. 1896: 142, emphasis added.

8. One area in which oligarchies might be thought to be relatively open was in their *euthunai*, or the rendering of accounts by magistrates at the end of their tenure. Fröhlich, who has treated *euthunai* in an impressive study, finds that despite popular perceptions (e.g., Hdt. 3.80.6), oligarchies like democracies demanded accounts from their magistrates (2004: 46, 446–47, 529). I would note, however, that this did not typically transpire before the eyes of the demos: the ephors carried out *euthunai* in Sparta (Arist. *Pol.* 2.1271a6–8), while in the oligarchic *diagramma* of Ptolemy for Cyrene the magistrates are indeed "accountable" (*hupeuthunoi*, SEG 9.1, lines 38–39), but almost certainly not to the demos. Aristotle advises magistrates in oligarchies to hold transfers of revenue (*paradoseis*) in public, in the presence of all the citizens (including the demos), but we do not know how often his advice was put into practice, and it may have been atypical (*Pol.* 5.1309a10–14).

9. For assemblies under oligarchy, see chapter 3, section 3.2.

10. Another means of effecting the same result would be weighted voting, but Greek poleis

together of the few and only the few: this is how Xenophon's Alcibiades understands oligarchy ("not the many, but the few come together and decree what is to be done," *Mem.* 1.2.43), as does the Eleatic Stranger in Plato's *Statesman* ("we would call an assembly, either of the entire people or of the wealthy alone," 298c). Theophrastus's "Oligarchic Man" advises his political allies to "be rid of the mob and the agora" and to "come together to deliberate *on our own* [*autoi*]," while the Old Oligarch flatly states that under "good government" (*eunomia*), "the worthy men [*chrēstoi*] will not allow crazy people [*sc.* the demos and its politicians] to serve on the Council or to speak or even to assemble [*ekklēsiazein*]."[11] All of these sources imply that under oligarchy the demos not only lacked voting rights in the most authoritative political institutions, but they were not expected (or even allowed) to attend at all.[12]

If pressed on why they shrouded their meetings in secrecy, oligarchs had a battery of reasons ready. An old and influential excuse, ultimately epistemological in nature, was that small groups of wealthier and more intelligent men were uniquely capable of arriving at true, just, and rational political decisions. The demos, by contrast, was likely to be too ignorant and confused to produce sound policy.[13] Thus Aristotle's advice, in the *Rhetoric*: "[Points of law] left open to the opinion of judges should be minimal, first of all because it is easier to find one man or a few people who are intelligent and capable of establishing laws and judging than it is to find many" (1.1354a31-b3). Furthermore, the dy-

---

never seem to have adopted this practice (although see Aristotle's exploration of the idea at *Pol.* 6.1318a27-b5).

11. Theophr. *Char.* 26.3; [Xen.] *Ath. Pol.* 1.9. See, however, chapter 3, section 3.2, on how oligarchs manipulated select meetings of the demos.

12. It seems that on some occasions these stereotypical characteristics of oligarchs could seep into and color a political community's collective memory of its past: see Plutarch's *Greek Question* 32, in which he answers the query, "Who were the Perpetual Sailors [*aeinautai*] of Miletus?": "When the elite [*hoi dunatoi*] had triumphed and gathered all power into their clique [*hetaireia*], they used to deliberate about the most important political matters by embarking on ships and sailing far from shore. Once they had ratified their decisions, they sailed back again, and for this reason were called the 'Perpetual Sailors'" (*Mor.* 298c-d). Unrelated (and much less sinister) *aeinautai* are found in the epigraphical record (*IG* XII.9 909, 923; *SEG* 34.898), and so it seems likely that partisan historians at Miletus made sense of an unremarkable but oddly named magistracy from the Archaic past using anti-oligarchic ideology. Thus even if Plutarch's account does not give us a reliable account of the functions of the *aeinautai*, it might count as evidence for popular perceptions of oligarchy. For different interpretations of the Plutarch passage see Robertson 1987: 381–84 and Gorman 2001: 108–10.

13. This has been a consistent point of opposition to democracy throughout history. Even John Stuart Mill, who was sympathetic to popular government, argued for weighted voting as "a counterpoise to the numerical weight of the least educated class."

namics of small groups allowed for the possibility of considering all concerns equally, while the massed assembly produced a chaotic environment filled with untrained audiences and competing *rhetores*.[14] Something like this assumption already underlies Agamemnon's complaint in *Iliad* 19: "How among the great noisy throng of men could someone listen or speak? Even if someone is a clear speaker, he is overwhelmed" (81–82). The idea that the people—here the Homeric *laos*—are noisy and inarticulate, while the few are wise, also appears in Pindar's famous threefold division of regimes in the second *Pythian*, with tyranny rounding out the three: the *stratos* or army is *labros*, "boisterous," while in other places the polis is governed by the wise (*sophoi*, 86–88).[15] Megabyzus, one of the participants in Herodotus's "Constitutional Debate," gives this critique of the demos in its canonical form:

> How could the demos, which has not been taught anything and knows nothing noble or fitting, understand anything? It rushes and falls upon political concerns without thought, like a raging river.... Let us pick out a company of the best men and confer power on them: we are among such men, after all, and the best deliberations are likely to arise from the best men. (3.81.2–3)[16]

Over a century later, Menander brings a character onstage despairing of the fact-finding capabilities of the demos (the outcome of a court case decided in an Athenian *dikastērion* is being described):

> A: You're a nonsense-filled pest, you bastard, if you expect a wailing, needy person to argue an honest case. What happened just now is proof that nothing good ever comes of it. That's not how the truth is discovered—for that you need a much smaller [group].
> B: You *are* an *oligarchic* bastard, by Zeus almighty! (*Sicyonius* 150–56)

These assumptions abound in the ancient evidence, especially in the philosophy of Plato and Aristotle, and it would be excessive to list them all.[17] As has

---

14. See chapter 2, section 2.2.2.

15. The scholion *ad* 157a Drachmann sees a reference to democracy, oligarchy, and tyranny; see further Raaflaub 2007: 107–108. For the connotations of the word "*labros*," see Hornblower 2004a: 80–81, citing earlier scholarship.

16. Cf. the oligarchic complaints about demotic stupidity cited in chapter 1, section 1.1. According to Polybius, the historian Timaeus depicted Hermocrates of Syracuse delivering a speech in 424 in which he tells the assembled elite of Sicily at Gela that they are wise "for ensuring that the masses did not deliberate about the peace terms but rather the foremost men of the regimes, who understood the difference between war and peace" (*FGrH* 566 F 22).

17. It is unclear how much the historical Socrates engaged in the sort of anti-democratic philosophizing Plato depicts, but a supposed verse of Socrates quoted by Diogenes Laertius

been repeatedly noted, democrats responded to such critiques by asserting that the freedom of every adult male citizen to speak in the assembly brought useful knowledge to bear on important political matters; that large groups were best at judging speakers' proposals; and that popular participation was one of the most reliable safeguards against abuse and oppression on the part of the elite.[18]

With the last consideration listed above, we reach the point where oligarchic complaints about mass ignorance begin to shade into a more self-serving rationale. Indeed, authoritarian rulers throughout history have never maintained their privileges with only the good of the whole community in mind; they are also worried about losing their grip on power. Ancient Greek oligarchs were no different, and try as they might to justify secrecy on epistemological grounds, their more fundamental concern was to place their political decisions above accountability. Thus a second reason for oligarchic secrecy, less suitable for public consumption, was the need to conceal unpopular policies that might meet with resistance.

This need is on display in a suggestion made by the oligarchic Corinthians to the democratic Argives in 421. Following a meeting of the Peloponnesian poleis, the Corinthians approach some Argive magistrates about a defensive alliance. Pointedly, they advise the Argives to establish a few plenipotentiary ambassadors rather than bring the matter before the demos. Their stated reason is to avoid an awkward situation in which the ambassadors publicly go over the heads of the people to make an alliance, even when the people reject the measure ("should they not persuade the majority," *mē peisantas to plēthos*, Thuc. 5.27.2). The Corinthians believed that the alliance should be cemented no matter what the majority thought and that the demos would likely just get in the way of the process. The Corinthians' advice to the Argives also indirectly suggests that the Corinthians followed the same tack at home with respect to their own demos. There was probably little or no

---

could be taken to indicate that he did indeed criticize the knowledge of the majority (2.42 = Socrates fr. 1 West): "Aesop once told those dwelling in the Corinthian city not to judge virtue according to the people's version of wisdom [λαοδίκῳ σοφίῃ]."

18. Noted by: Raaflaub 1989; Wallace 1996; Herman 2006: 73–76. Useful knowledge: Thuc. 2.37.1; Eur. *Supp.* 438–49; Ar. *Thesm.* 380; Aeschin. 1.27. From a slightly different angle, Plato's Socrates notes that in addition to useful technical knowledge, the Athenians thought every citizen had something to contribute to matters of general political import: *Prot.* 319b-d. On the collection and aggregation of useful knowledge at Athens, see Ober 2008: ch. 4. Large groups the best judges: Thuc. 6.39.1. Safeguard against abuse: Dem. 21.221–22; Isoc. 20.13; Aeschin. 3.233. See Edge 2009 for a thorough discussion of Athenian democrats' conception of liberty and non-domination.

institutionalized role for the majority in the Corinthian decision-making system.[19]

Several other oligarchic poleis are depicted by Thucydides as not allowing the demos to observe political deliberations. At the outset of the Melian Dialogue, Thucydides sets the scene by explaining that the Melians "did not bring the Athenians before the masses, but ordered them to explain their mission before the magistrates and the few" (5.84.3). The Melians' reasoning—or so the Athenians conjecture—is that granting the Athenian ambassadors an audience before the demos would allow the Athenians to deliver an "uninterrupted speech" that would "deceive" the majority through its appealing rhetoric (5.85). As Bosworth has noted, "the oligarchic government deliberately restricted the audience to those most likely to resist the Athenian blandishments."[20]

Similar episodes in Thucydides attest to the oligarchic practice of boxing out the demos during negotiations with Athens. For example, until being armed, the demos of Mytilene was barred from negotiating with the Athenians, a task left to the *"archontes"* (3.27.3). In oligarchic Chios, "oligarchic conspirators" (literally, "the few and informed") who want to city to break from the Athenian empire encourage Alcibiades and Chalcideus to arrive unannounced on a day when the council happens to be in session (8.14.1–2).[21] The majority, who had no idea pro-Spartan overtures were being made (8.9.3), flee in terror, while the council agrees to revolt from Athens.[22] In the Chian case the oligarchs' secrecy helped them in two ways: not only did they avoid bringing up an unpopular position with the populace, but the demos's unpreparedness caused them to run at the terrifying sight of the Peloponnesian ships, making resistance even more difficult. Secrecy therefore both shielded

---

19. Cf. Plut. *Dion* 53.4: the Corinthians of the fourth century "did not do much of their political decision-making in the assembly" (literally "in the demos"). For the Corinthian oligarchy's use of the assembly, see chapter 3, section 3.2.

20. Bosworth 1993: 33; cf. Morrison 2000: 123. After their first attempt at peace fails, the Spartans try a similar technique at Athens (4.22.1), asking the crowd to choose select commissioners (*sunhedroi*) to discuss the matter "in peace" (*kata hēsuchian*), but to no avail.

21. For Chios as oligarchic at this time, see Hornblower *ad* 8.9.3 οἱ δὲ ὀλίγοι καὶ ξυνειδότες, citing *inter alios* Andrewes in *HCT ad loc.*, who adduces *Syll.*³ 986, a fifth-century decree enacted by council alone, with no mention of an assembly. See also Thucydides's judgment at 8.24.4 and the language of 8.38.3 with Hornblower's n.; [Arist.] *Ath. Pol.* 24.2 with Rhodes's n.; *IACP* no. 840, p. 1067 (Rubinstein).

22. I disagree with Quinn 1969 and O'Neil 1978/79, who view the Chian council as "largely if not wholly a popular council" within a generally oligarchic constitution and a body with "final say" in a system dominated by the elite, respectively. It is mistaken to conceive of Greek political institutions as neutral playing fields for competing factions, democratic and oligarchic.

oligarchs from the demos's penetrating eye and put the demos at an informational (and thus organizational) disadvantage.

Finally, secrecy was not simply a means of ensuring the passage of desired legislation: oligarchs very likely feared that if they opened up their deliberations to popular oversight, demands would escalate to the point that the constitution itself, the entire oligarchic order, would be put in danger. Any massed gathering of the people represented an existential threat to the constitution, as we have already learned from the *Rhetoric to Alexander*: "The mob must not gather from the countryside into the city: such meetings cause the masses to combine and overthrow oligarchies" (1424b8–10).[23] This fear of the collective power of the masses was probably the most basic consideration weighing against the regular inclusion of the demos in political deliberations. It goes some way toward explaining the Thessalians' practice, noted by Aristotle, of constructing two agoras, one for trade and one for politics. The former was open to all, while the latter, called the "free" agora, housed the magistrates and was restricted to members of the oligarchic class.[24] One important function of this "separate and unequal" arrangement, in addition to keeping the circulation of important political information limited to a select group of people, would have been to put greater distance between threatening crowds and the center of oligarchic decision-making.[25]

5.2 Projection

If oligarchic meetings were generally kept out of view of the demos, there were other occasions in oligarchic poleis when the greatest concern was publicity. An oligarchic regime in Classical Greece, like authoritarian governments throughout history, increased its power not only through concealment but through revelation. I call this latter practice "projection," or the ability of the regime to broadcast an image of strength and unity that then becomes a matter of common knowledge among the inhabitants of the polis. Projection was the public face of the oligarchy, the smooth surface whose existence was made possible by the opportunities for bargaining and compromise that secretive

---

23. See further chapter 4, section 4.2, above.

24. Arist. *Pol.* 7.1331a30-b4; cf. Xen. *Cyr.* 1.2.3–5.

25. For more on the oligarchic Thessalians, see section 5.3.1 below. A final way of distancing elite and demos, this time horological rather than spatial, was the practice of holding "nocturnal councils" (*nukterinoi sullogoi*). Plato most famously creates a nocturnal council for his utopian polis of Magnesia in the *Laws* (12.961a-b), but there is also a historical example, noted by Plutarch, from Archaic Cyme (*Mor.* 292a = *QG* 2). It is impossible to know how common nocturnal councils were from these scraps of evidence, however.

political meetings afforded to oligarchs.[26] The performance could take many forms: processions, civic festivals, public sacrifices, and choral poetry (in other words, ritual), but also any number of irregular public acts, including the desecration or destruction of monuments, the demolition of houses, and other conspicuous alterations to the civic landscape. Any of these could serve as a means of consolidating the dominant position of the oligarchic elite.

In line with the focus elsewhere in this book on the importance of information for both collective action and inactivity, the approach adopted here has more to do with the delivery and communicative dynamics of acts of projection than with their content. Content-based theories of authoritarian legitimation assume that rulers invest in power projection because the messages conveyed convince their subjects of the rightness of authoritarian rule. On this reading, projection is a kind of brainwashing that inexorably wears down the resistance of the recipient until he or she comes to believe the propaganda's message. It works because it changes the subject's subjective assessment of the regime, from rejection to acceptance.[27] More sophisticated recent accounts of ritual practice, which shift the focus from the passive reception of messages to the active formation of subjectivities through bodily movement and direct participation, add layers of complexity to the traditional picture without, however, altering the basic position of the old view that projection is about ideology.[28] I do not reject the use of these models, which have featured in several important studies of the politics of ancient Greek ritual.[29] The ideological effects of public spectacles and rituals are real and must play some role in conditioning subjects within authoritarian regimes. It seems excessive to deny

26. The political scientist Robert Barros, in his analysis of the Chilean military junta, indicates how the two techniques, secrecy and projection of power, could work together in an authoritarian regime: "[The fact of] secrecy and insulation of debate from public scrutiny was highly functional for the rule of the armed forces, as it allowed the commanders in chief to articulate differences internally without eroding the Junta's capacity to publicly present its power as undivided and monolithic" (2002: 39n5). For the "backstage" and the "front stage" of oligarchies, see further chapter 3, section 3.1.3, on the avoidance of public violence.

27. In popular culture, this view can be found in the statement, often attributed to Goebbels, that "if you repeat a lie often enough, people will believe it." In the press and in some political analysis, it is often assumed that the point of propaganda within authoritarian regimes is to convince subjects of the rightness and truth of the message. A 2014 article in the *Financial Times* quoted an academic as saying the North Koreans "live in the mental walls of their own propaganda" ("Mind your language: N. Korea's self-defeating propaganda," May 12 2014). The political scientist Juan Linz, in his study of totalitarian and authoritarian regimes, says straightforwardly that "ideologies in totalitarian systems are a source of legitimacy" (2000: 77).

28. The forerunner here is Bourdieu (e.g., his 1977); see also Bell 1992; Turner 1995.

29. E.g., Kurke 2005 and 2007; Kowalzig 2007; Fisher 2010, discussed in greater detail below.

the possibility that at least some people within non-democratic states accept the legitimacy of the ruling elite as expressed through public displays of power. At the same time, models that rely heavily on ideological content in explaining authoritarian regime stability encounter several difficulties.

First, assuming that ideological messaging genuinely "works" makes it hard to explain instances of resistance on the part of dominated subjects, particularly when that resistance occurs precisely in the context of the legitimating rituals themselves. As the sociologists Steven Pfaff and Guobin Yang discovered in their study of protests in the tumultuous year 1989, protesters often used existing, state-sanctioned occasions, such as historical anniversaries, funerals, or memorial services, to mobilize citizens against the status quo. Pfaff and Yang therefore labeled political rituals "double-edged," in the sense that while they normally functioned to "reinforce relations of domination," they simultaneously "provid[ed] aggrieved actors with opportunities for dissension."[30] Underlying their study is the assumption that while rituals indeed performed important political "work," that work did not consist in actually persuading subjects of the dominant group's right to rule.

A second, related problem with content-based ideological models derives from considerations of parsimony: with Occam's Razor in mind, we can point to a simpler model that explains political behavior just as well and that, moreover, finds empirical confirmation in real-world accounts of life under authoritarianism. Rather than have recourse to the notoriously slippery concept of ideology, we can conceive of projection working in the now-familiar terms of common knowledge and coordination. In a hotly contested political arrangement, the ability of one group to execute a public spectacle is itself a kind of power. It signals to the community that one faction has the ability to exact desired performances and, by the same token, that the rest are ready to acquiesce. Thus when one group is in the habit of successfully projecting its strength and unity, it can negatively impact the ability of others to coordinate resistance. Engaging subjects in rituals of power is, for the rulers, less about brainwashing them than it is about conditioning their expectations. The projection of power is on this reading about people's "heads" (their strategic assessment of the situation), not their "hearts" (their subjective feelings).[31]

Political scientists working on contemporary authoritarian states have productively utilized this understanding of the power of ritual. Researchers have

---

30. 2001: 542. Recall the political scientist Andreas Schedler's statement, quoted in chapter 3, section 3.2, that authoritarian political institutions (including rituals) contain the "seeds of subversion" (2013: 73).

31. As indicated above, the dynamics are similar to those at work in oligarchic assemblies, analyzed in chapter 3, section 3.2.

found that, in private at least, subjects of authoritarian regimes are often willing to express their dissatisfaction with the government. When the time comes to test their loyalty in public, however, they dutifully deliver the required slogans and gestures. As the political scientist Lisa Wedeen notes in her study of the regime of Hafiz al-Asad in 1980s Syria,

> the official rhetoric in Syria ... consistently include[s] patently absurd statements whose explicit content cannot possibly be intended to produce belief or generate emotional commitment, reactions presupposed by the concepts of legitimacy, charisma, and hegemony. Citizens in Syria are not required to believe the cult [of personality's] flagrantly fictitious statements and, as a rule, do not. But they are required to act *as if* they do. (1998: 506, emphasis in original)

This "acting as if" is itself sufficient to reinforce the power of the Syrian regime, even when both subjects and rulers know that the performances are disingenuous. Wedeen's analysis resembles that of James C. Scott, who has studied the rhetorical strategies of dominant and dominated groups in unequal political societies. Scott ultimately rejects a Gramscian-style analysis that would explain domination through the concept of ideological hegemony.[32] He argues instead that "if rituals of subordination are not convincing in the sense of gaining the consent of subordinates," they are nonetheless "convincing in other ways": "they are ... a means of demonstrating that, like it or not, a given system of domination is stable, effective, and here to stay" (1990: 66). Scott, like Wedeen, draws attention to the fact that the ability to look powerful is itself a kind of power: "Ritual subservience reliably extracted from inferiors signals quite literally that there is no realistic choice other than compliance." And as in al-Asad's Syria, the essential emptiness of rituals of domination, their well-known status as actions of bad faith, leaves open the possibility that they can be used as springboards for resistance. They can be a means of forcing what Scott calls the "hidden transcript" of dissent into the open at the very moment when the dominant group is attempting to reinforce its own image (the "public transcript"). We are now in a position to understand why and how the political rituals studied by Pfaff and Yang's were "double-edged": because public rituals of domination bring into one space people who do not believe the message they are encouraged to participate in and perpetuate, there is always the danger that subordinate groups will use the gathering as an opportunity to express their hidden dissatisfaction.[33]

32. E.g., Gramsci 1971.
33. For further examples of this (common knowledge/coordination-based) understanding

In chapter 6 I show that exactly this outcome befell several oligarchic regimes in ancient Greece, when occasions that normally functioned as mechanisms of political stabilization—specifically, public festivals—exploded into acts of democratic revolution.[34] For now, however, I wish to paint a picture of the system functioning smoothly. We can use the model of projection sketched above to illuminate the workings of oligarchic spectacle in a new way. Instead of focusing on the ideological message of rituals, we can acknowledge that it was sufficient for oligarchic stability that rituals implicate the demos in the political status quo—that the common people be made to act "as if" they believed the content of oligarchic ideology. In making my argument I assume that the Greeks were well aware that public spectacles could serve a narrowly political purpose—we need only note that Xenophon has Cyrus the Great arrange a procession with the express purpose of "making it as fine a spectacle as possible for his well-wishers, but most terrifying to his enemies" (*Cyr.* 8.3.5)—but the greater burden will be to deliver a convincing account of spectacle working this way in a specifically oligarchic context.

5.2.1 *Choral Performances*

Choral performances will serve as an appropriate starting-point, not only because they constitute some of our earliest evidence for public spectacle within Classical-era oligarchies, but also because they have received considerable attention from scholars who would understand ritual in terms of instilling an ideological message.[35] By "choral performance" I mean ancient poetry performed in unison by a group of people, typically all of the same age and gender. There were many different genres of choral poetry, defined primarily by ritual occasion. Whether they were composed for an outstanding individual (as in epinician, or "athletic victory" poetry) or for the entire polis (a host of paeans, dithyrambs, *hyporchēmata*, and other, more specific religious poems), the growing scholarly consensus is that the performance of these poems normally took place within the view of the wider civic community.[36] *Choreia*, the

---

of public ritual, see Chwe 2001: 20–21 (disputing Clifford Geertz on the significance of "royal processions"); Kuran 1995.

34. Chapter 6, section 6.1. This possibility was also foreshadowed in chapter 4, section 4.2, when public space was identified as a source of oligarchic anxiety.

35. The proposition that choral performance had a political function is not modern but goes back to Plato (see *Laws passim* with Peponi 2013) and Polybius (4.20.4–21.3, on the musical training of the Arcadians), among many others.

36. For the relationship between genre and ritual occasions, and the performance contexts involved, see Carey 2009. Most scholars would now agree that epinician poetry was ultimately

act of singing and dancing with others in choral performance, was itself an important component of upper-class Greek life, as Calame (1997) and others have argued, and it constituted a means of socializing young men and women into the world of the polis elite. While I am interested in the use of public spectacle to unify members of the oligarchy, the primary focus will be on choral performance as a link between oligarchs and demos.

The most common approach to understanding the political power of ritual in previous scholarship has involved sophisticated applications of the ideological-hegemony model. For example, Wilson has argued that dithyrambic choruses, a common type of choral performance devoted to the god Dionysus, worked in oligarchic Corinth and elsewhere to "enac[t] and establish[h] a sense of solidarity, of cohesion, often in the face of the real aggressive internal divisions endemic to Greek polis-life."[37] The "social work" of dithyramb, in Wilson's phrasing (he is playing upon a fragment of the poet Pindar that mentions the "labors of choruses"), resides in putting citizens from different classes and political persuasions on the same ideological page. Similarly, Fisher, in what he admits is an "avowedly functionalist and idealizing" treatment, suggests that "widespread citizen participation in the festival contests [sc. choruses] . . . may have fostered political good will and positive evaluations across formerly strong class and/or geographical divides."[38] Again, the assumption is that choral performance, in its capacity as public spectacle and community ritual, was not only political in nature, but also accomplished its political goal through the attainment of ideological assent.[39]

This picture gains plausibility from the fact that many of the poleis from which extant choral poetry originates remained *stasis*-free for long periods of time. The absence of political conflict has been considered evidence for acceptance of the status quo by the majority of the population, even in oligarchic poleis where the demos was deprived of political equality. This line of thinking in turn rests on the further assumption that constitutions, particularly minority-run constitutions like oligarchies, are likely to be stable only

---

meant for public consumption: even if reperformance scenarios can be imagined for private homes and sanctuaries, the primary audience was the victor's community (see Kurke 1991: 5; Currie 2011: 270–72; Eckerman 2012: 359–60). Indeed, one of the primary functions of epinician, it has been established, was to reintegrate the triumphant *laudandus* into the community of the polis (Crotty 1982: 112–22; Kurke 1991: 6–7).

37. Wilson 2003: 179.

38. Fisher 2010: 72.

39. For similar approaches to Greek public ritual, see Kowalzig 2007; Stehle 1997 (who speaks of the "psychological efficacy" of choral song at p. 19); Hornblower 2009; D'Alessio 2009; Fearn 2010; Athanassaki and Bowie 2011; Nicholson 2015.

when they enjoy widespread consent. It is difficult, on this view, to conceive of how a regime would survive for long if it were truly unpopular. However, as this book has endeavored to show, regime longevity in the absence of a popular mandate is perfectly possible when backed by well-crafted institutions. In that same vein, we can see that the persistence of the oligarchic regimes that produced our choral poetry need not imply that the poetry actually won over hearts and minds. Indeed, a very different dynamic from that predicted by the ideological model may have been at work. In what follows, it will become apparent that I agree with proponents of an ideological approach to ancient poetry that we should be looking to choral performance as an explanation for political outcomes. Greek song, far from being purely for "entertainment's sake," was deeply enmeshed in, even constitutive of, relations of political power—but I differ in my understanding of how the processes of domination operated.

The distinctiveness of the view adopted here emerges from an examination of the Theban Daphnephoria ritual, the politics of which have been brilliantly analyzed by Kurke. The components of the Daphnephoria ("laurel-bearing") festival are known to us from two post-Classical accounts, but it was definitely celebrated already by the post-447 Boeotian *koinon*—the oligarchic federal state, dominated by Thebes, that emerged after a brief period of Athenian-backed democracy in Boeotia.[40] As best we can understand from the late and not-entirely-consistent sources for the festival, it involved a procession of singing and dancing maidens, at the head of which was a young man from one of Thebes' elite families. This youth was made priest of the cult for a year and called the *daphnēphoros* ("laurel-bearer"). It is said that the ritual had its *aition* (origin) in a military alliance supposedly forged between two groups of early Aeolian immigrants to Central Greece when they were sacking Pelasgian-controlled Thebes. As both groups already had festivals to Apollo, they merged their customs and jointly offered laurel branches to the god; following their victory over the Pelasgians, the practice of bearing laurel crystallized into a specific festival for Apollo, the Daphnephoria, celebrated every year. Whatever the true origins of the ritual, by the mid-fifth century it fulfilled multiple political functions within the *koinon*: it was a source of power and prestige shared by the families of the Theban oligarchic ruling class; it represented an attempt by Thebes, the hegemonic polis of the wider Boeotian *koinon*, to identify itself as a traditional site of pan-Boeotian unity; and it was a spectacle presented to the wider (politically excluded) community of the

---

40. Sources for Daphnephoria: Paus. 9.10.4; Proclus *apud* Phot. *Bibl.* cod. 239, pp. 321a35-b32 Bekker. For the political history of the *koinon*, see chapter 2, section 2.2.1.

demos.[41] Mackil has illuminated the workings of the second function in her recent study of Greek federal states. I wish to focus on the first and last functions, evidence for which is significantly enhanced by our possession of a fragmentary poem by Pindar, composed to be sung by the maidens of the Daphnephoria (fr. 94b S-M). The poem was likely performed sometime after 447 and honors Agasicles, the *daphnēphoros* on that particular occasion, as well as his father, Pagondas, and his grandfather, Aeoladas.[42] Although the poem as we have it is not complete, several portions are continuous enough to permit interpretation.

One of the passages (lines 61–72) fulfills perfectly the need in acts of political projection to present the ruling group as harmonious and united. The religious office of *daphnēphoros* was a preserve of the elite that brought glory to the family that possessed it for the year, and it was for that reason an important component of oligarchic power-sharing and equality in Thebes (see chapter 2), but it was also fraught with danger. An elite family that desired more than an equal share in the oligarchic circle of privilege might attempt to use the prestigious office as a stepping stone to tyrannical power. The combination of material resources, personal networks, and cultural capital that attached to political and religious magistracies frequently made them stepping-stones to individual dominance and the dissolution of the oligarchic ruling coalition.[43] The public therefore watched the magistrates carefully to see how they would perform while in office: the elite were guarding against peers who might dare transgress oligarchic norms of power-sharing, while the demos searched for divisions among the oligarchs, which they could exploit in the struggle for democratization. The choral voice of Pindar's Daphnephoria poem, however, is quick to put any such suspicions to rest. At a key moment, the chorus of maidens highlights the civic responsibility that has always characterized the family of Agasicles, even in the face of intra-elite jealousy and spite:

> Then, too, malicious rage brought forth hateful, unpreventable [?] strife [*eris*] on account of the moderate ambitions [*merimna sōphrōn*] of these men, but they loved the trusty paths of justice [*dikē*]. Father of Damaena [Pagondas is likely meant], going forth now lead me with a calm [*hēsuchos*] foot; for your merry daughter will follow you first along the way, stepping with her sandals near the leafy laurel (61–70).

---

41. For the *aition* and fifth-century functions of the festival, see Kurke 2007: 71–74; Mackil 2013: 168–72.

42. Probably the same Pagondas as at Thuc. 4.91.

43. See Aristotle's warnings at *Pol.* 5.1308a18–24, 1310b20–23.

Although adorned with the language of poetry, the passage nonetheless clearly expresses the idea that the elite family of Agasicles and Pagondas has consistently hewn to the ideals of moderation, peace, and justice. Although their civic ambitions have always been "moderate" (*sōphrōn*, an oligarchic slogan) and thus within the boundaries of legitimate elite self-promotion, they have encountered inevitable hostility from their peers. Nevertheless, this strife has always been met with equanimity and adherence to justice. As Kurke has shown, the language of this passage functions as a kind of performative antidote to the oligarchic weaknesses diagnosed in Herodotus's "Constitutional Debate." There, Darius of Persia notes that intra-elite competition within oligarchies tends toward hateful feuds, *stasis*, and the rise of a tyrant (3.82.3; see further chapter 2, section 2.1).[44] Pindar's Daphnephoria poem answers Darius's worries essentially point-by-point, showing that this particular family possesses the qualities necessary for avoiding civic strife and maintaining stable oligarchy. The history of Agasicles's clan is a chronicle of ideal oligarchic behavior, which is exemplified and perpetuated in the present moment by the father Pagondas's "calm" (*hēsuchos*) leading of the procession.[45] The choral language is thus a commentary on, and an amplification of, the civic virtues displayed in the family's leading of the Daphnephoria ritual, virtues which serve both to bind the ruling elite together and to present the wider community with an image of competent and unified elite leadership.

But did oligarchic stability at Thebes require that the demos, which was presumably present to witness the Daphnephoria ritual, actually accept the ideological message of Pindar's poem? Kurke, in her analysis of the political function of the Daphnephoria, argues that regime stability called for "consensus- and community-building at several different levels," including "between the Theban elite and the civic population at large."[46] There is thus an assumption that regime longevity requires active consent on the part of the demos. Kurke therefore detects consensus in the workings of the spectacle: "the ritual spotlighting of a single noble family ... speaks to the broader community of Thebes, *affirming—even staging—*the cosmic propriety of oligarchic leadership."[47] However, while some spectators may indeed have been convinced by

---

44. Kurke 2007: 92–93, noting the close similarities in language between Herodotus and Pindar.

45. For *hēsuchos* and *hēsuchia* as political values in Pindar (particularly in oligarchic and tyrannical scenarios) cf. *Pyth.* 1.70, 4.296, 11.55, 8.1 (where *hēsuchia* is personified as a goddess overseeing oligarchic Aegina), *Nem.* 9.48, fr. 109.2 S-M.

46. Kurke 2007: 71.

47. Kurke 2007: 79, emphasis added. Cf. 99: the family's "leadership of the city, as of the procession ... came to seem cosmically right and proper."

the ideological message of the poem, this need not have been the only process at work. Adopting a perspective based on practical reasoning provides a further, complementary explanation as to how ritual could be used to secure control. It also allows us to reconcile the picture of peace and harmony voiced by the poem with the evidence for political discord in Boeotia in the fifth century. Despite Pindar's protestations to the contrary, several sources point to considerable unrest brewing beneath the surface.

The first thing to consider is that the post-447 *koinon* was born in turbulent political times. Following the Battle of Oenophyta in 457/6, the Athenian empire set up democratic constitutions in the poleis of Boeotia. These regimes, far from simply being hated foreign impositions, seem to have exacerbated existing social and political tensions between mass and elite in Boeotia. Aristotle states that the disorder and anarchy (*ataxia kai anarchia*) of the democracy at Thebes, for example, caused the downfall of the government when the rich got fed up with the demos's lack of control (*Pol.* 5.1302b27–30). The incident reads like a purely internal affair, independent of Athenian meddling. The Old Oligarch likewise makes clear that when the oligarchs came back into power in Thebes, their hostility toward the common people was unrelenting: the demos was quickly "enslaved" (3.11). It is difficult to believe that ideological messaging could mend rifts in the body politic of this depth and intensity.

Furthermore, we know that there were subversive elements in the cities of the Boeotian *koinon* during the Peloponnesian War. In chapter 2, section 2.5, we met the Thespian exile Ptoeodorus. In 424 he organized an attempted democratic uprising with the help of the Athenian generals Demosthenes and Hippocrates. His express aim was to change the constitution (*kosmos*) of Boeotia to a democracy on the Athenian model. Dissidents from Siphae and Orchomenos were also involved (Thuc. 4.76.2–3). The plot failed for logistical reasons, but the attempt shows that renegade elites like Ptoeodorus thought they could count on domestic support during an anti-oligarchic revolt.[48] The Athenian epigraphic record also reveals the existence of exiled Orchomenians who asked for and obtained support from the Athenian demos following the Battle of Delium in 424 (*IG* I³ 73: Potamodorus and his son Eurytion); these men had likely been supporters of democracy within the *koinon*. Finally, the demos of Thespiae actually attempted a democratic revolution in 414. The threat was suppressed by the ruling Thespian oligarchs, who had support from the Thebans (Thuc. 6.95.2). Thespiae is of course not Thebes, and so it is possible that the Thebans had managed to convince their demos of the rightness

---

48. For this episode, see further chapter 2, section 2.5; chapter 3, section 3.5.

of oligarchy in a way that other poleis of the Boeotian *koinon* had not. However, in light of the evidence above, I find it more likely that the Thespian democrats were simply the most proactive out of several pockets of democratic resistance spread throughout the Boeotian cities, including Thebes. In sum, this extensive record of democratic dissatisfaction and insurrection makes it impossible to accept that rituals such as the Theban Daphnephoria necessarily guaranteed oligarchic ideological hegemony. While they may have convinced some people, they do not appear to have fully convinced the common people of the cosmic propriety of the ruling oligarchy.

If, then, the Daphnephoria and other such politicized rituals in oligarchic Thebes were not primarily about winning the allegiance of the subjects of the oligarchy, the coordination/common-knowledge model of ritual emerges as a more plausible way of understanding the dynamics of choral performance and of public spectacle in general. The members of the demos among the audience at the performance of Pindar's Daphnephoria poem did not have to believe the message of the song and dance they witnessed. It was enough that they were there, assembled and thus collectively powerful, but nevertheless observing the spectacle in subservient silence. The striking spectacle of so many citizens, rich and poor, passively receiving what was patently a message of oligarchic power and unity would have sent a signal to the people that opportunities for resistance were nonexistent. The Daphnephoria therefore likely did accomplish the crucial stabilizing task that Kurke proposes, but not solely by ideological means. The mechanisms at work dealt instead with the strategic calculations of the different political actors within Theban society: members of the oligarchic elite, would-be popular revolutionaries, and the mass of the demos.

We can conjecture that the coordination/common knowledge model of stability was similarly at play in other instances of choral performance and public ritual.[49] For example, in one of our earliest extant epinician poems, that of Simonides (*PMG* 511) for the sons of Aeatius, members of the Thessalian elite, we read at one point that [something] occurs "with happiness for the whole demos of the Thessalians" (fr. I.b.7–8). This reads as a self-justifying pronouncement, meant to impress upon the audience's mind the connection between elite athletic success and community flourishing.[50] Similarly, Pindar's

---

49. Luraghi 2011: 43 (citing the political scientists Boix and Svolik 2008) has already noted the working of this dynamic in tyrannical contexts, but he emphasizes the relationship between the tyrant and his inner circle rather than regime and populace. In an oligarchic context, I argue, intra-elite cooperation is highly important, just as that between tyrant and entourage; the relationship between elite and demos is just as crucial, however.

50. See further Molyneux 1992: 129–30. Unlike Simonides, when Pindar and Bacchylides praise victors from oligarchic polies such as Aegina, Corinth, and Thebes, they never use the

tenth *Pythian*, also for a Thessalian victor, closes with the thought that "the solemn, ancestral governing [lit. 'steering'] of cities resides in noble men [*agathoi*]" (71–72). Thus, the dominance of the Thessalian oligarchy, of which the *laudandus* is a member, is again signaled to the populace through choral poetry.[51] In the same author's fragmentary first *Paean*, written for the Theban festival of Apollo Ismenius, the *persona loquens* of the poem counsels the elite Theban citizen to "shade his wrath-free mind with tranquility in accordance with moderate things [*metra*], content with seeing his power stored up at home" (fr. 52a.2–4 S-M). As in the Daphnephoria poem, the message is as much a piece of advice for the oligarchs' consideration as it is a projection of power and unity to the excluded demos. At the end of the extant fragment, the personified completion of the year (Eniautos) and the Horai are imagined as coming to Thebes and bringing a feast for Apollo, with the concluding wish that the god might "shower the race of peoples [*laoi*] with blooms of moderate good order [*sōphrōn eunomia*]" (9–10). This same collocation, so redolent of oligarchic images and ideas, also appears in Bacchylides's thirteenth ode, for a victor in oligarchic Aegina: "Indeed, [Excellence] honors the glory-bearing island of Aeacus, and steers the city with Euclea, lover of crowns, and *sōphrōn Eunomia*, who has received as her portion festivities, and guards the cities of pious men in peace" (182–89).[52] From other songs, mainly Pindaric ones, we also know that choral lyric could address the issue of *stasis*, counseling harmony instead of strife. A Pindaric *hyporchema* (song set to dance) for Thebes (fr. 109 S-M), which recalls the language of the aforementioned *Paean* 1, exhorts one of the citizens (*astoi*) to "set the community at peace" and "seek out the bright light of great-hearted Hesuchia, removing wrathful *stasis* from his mind, giver of poverty, a hateful nurse."[53] There is no *a priori* reason for assuming that the *stasis* mentioned in such instances was necessarily intra-elite,

---

word "demos." They do use it when praising victories from democracies, e.g., Camarina (Pind. *Ol.* 5.14 with Robinson 2011: 96–100) and Argos (*Nem.* 10.23), as well as tyrannies (*Ol.* 3.16, *Pyth.* 1.70). This change may reflect the increased antagonism between democracy and oligarchy in Pindar and Bacchylides's time compared with Simonides's time.

51. For this poem, see also Rose 1992: 172–73 and Hornblower 2004a: 173. The root of the word "government," *kubernēsis*, literally means "steering" (of a ship).

52. For the political terminology, see chapter 1, section 1.2.4. For *eunomia* in epinician generally, as an oligarchic catchphrase, Hornblower 2004a: 169n154. For Aegina as an oligarchic polis, see de Ste. Croix 2004: 371–411; Figueira 1981: 299–305, 314–21; Fearn 2011, esp. 216–17 (citing this ode). Like Thebes, Aegina had a history of oligarchic-democratic strife: see Hdt. (6.88–91), on the attempted democratic *coup* of Nicodromus in the early fifth century.

53. For *stasis* in Thebes see also Paean 9, fr. 52k S-M, where "baleful *stasis*" is portended by a solar eclipse. See further Hornblower 2004a: 76–78, who rightly emphasizes the plentiful evidence for fifth-century *stasis* to be found in Pindar.

rather than intra-polis. The poetry is very likely guarding against democratization as much as the threat of tyranny. Choral lyric thus both promotes the status quo while remaining cautiously aware of the possibility of civil conflict.

In all of these examples, choreia puts the inherent rightness of elite political control on display before what is presumably the wider community, delivering a message of ruling-class accomplishment, social harmony, and overall civic prosperity. Without insisting that the inter-audience dynamics outlined above are *the* central function of such performances, we can say that there are good reasons for suspecting that considerations of that sort factored into the intentions of patrons, performers, and poets, in addition to what would undeniably have been aesthetic, generic, and local/epichoric concerns.[54] Since we know, from examples to be studied below, that song and festivity were put to consciously oligarchic use at the end of the fifth century, it is only through a denial of politics that we can skirt the issue of oligarchic power projection in early fifth-century choral lyric.[55]

5.2.2 Aristotle on Sacrifices and Public Banquets in Oligarchies

The foregoing section was necessarily speculative, since we know so little about the original performance context—let alone political function(s)—of choral lyric. The argument gains credibility, however, when we compare the comments of Aristotle writing in the later fourth century. In Book 6 of the *Politics*, he describes ways to placate the demos's frustration at being excluded from the major political offices of oligarchies. After discussing methods of co-optation (see further chapter 3, section 3.3), he says that it is

> appropriate for incoming magistrates to perform lavish sacrifices and make improvements on some object of public property, so that the demos, partaking of the elements of the feast and *seeing* [ὁρῶν] the polis beautified in its dedications and buildings, is glad to *see* [ὁρᾷ] the regime persist; another result is that the members of the upper class will have memorials [μνημεῖα] of their expenditure.[56]

The passage at first seems to describe a straightforwardly transactional relationship between oligarchs and demos: the demos is feasted and treated to the

---

54. Lewis (1996: 4) straightforwardly labels epinician "propaganda"; I would not go so far.

55. Cf. Kurke 1991: 260: "Pindar's era was heir to the crisis of the aristocracy, the last flowering of tyranny, the rise of the democratic polis, and the shift from a premonetary to a money economy. Such social turbulence demands sophisticated poetic strategies."

56. 1321a35–40 (emphasis added). Treatments of this passage are few: de Ste. Croix 1981: 305–306; Veyne 1990: 92–93.

sight of a beautified city, and in return the oligarchs are allowed to remain in power. The oligarchs also enjoy the opportunity to have their individual names associated with public buildings, such as temples, civic administration centers, or porticoes. They might also dedicate memorials celebrating military victories or other achievements.[57] In Greek history two of the most heavily studied examples of such "political building" are those of the Archaic tyrants and of Periclean Athens; the passage from Aristotle suggests that oligarchies engaged in this kind of behavior as well.[58] He implies that in oligarchies the direct association of specific buildings with well-known (*gnōrimoi*) members of the elite was important for solidifying in viewers' minds the connection between their city's prosperity and the regime in power. Again, we should understand these structures and their dedications in terms of populated (but controlled) public space (see chapter 4), in which rulers made their beneficence clear to the assembled ruled. Both sacrifices and dedications, then, transpired in public view, like the choral performances of the previous section.

We can now turn from the content of the dedications to their practical effects. As I have emphasized, Aristotle repeatedly uses visual terms in the passage. Although he does not draw the inference explicitly, we should extrapolate from this fact of visibility (and, more importantly, *inter*-visibility) just the sorts of strategic dynamics outlined above. When the members of the demos collectively *see* one another compliantly enjoying the regime's offerings, they will indeed continue to *see* the oligarchy in power. This is not only because they individually enjoy their present privileges, as Aristotle says, but also because they achieve common knowledge of their collective acquiescence to the rule of the few.[59] In this case, the focus is more on the enticements being

---

57. As in ML 11, a dedication of Peisistratus, son of Hippias, which identifies itself as a "*mnēma*"; ML 18, the memorial of Callimachus, again (probably) a *mnēma aretēs* (restored). More pertinent for our purposes is *Syll.*³ 274, the well-known dedication of the Daochid family from Pharsalus in Thessaly. It contains a set of six dedicatory epigrams outlining both athletic and political accomplishments. The inscription is from a Panhellenic context, Delphi, but it is a copy of a bronze original by Lysippus from Pharsalus: see Jacquemin and Laroche 2001; Geominy 1998. The Daochid family would therefore have been on prominent display in the civic landscape of their oligarchic polis.

58. On Athenian building projects generally, see Boersma 1970. On tyrannical/elite building projects: Forsdyke 2005: 18–29; Anderson 2005: 192–94. On the Periclean building program: Kallet 1998: 48–52; Hölscher 1998; Camp 2001: 71–116. Note that the demos refuses to let Pericles fund the construction himself and so earn the right to inscribe his name on the buildings (Plut. *Per.* 14.1–2). Aristotle's comments make it clear that such an action was more common under an oligarchy.

59. Note that the collective nature of the viewing is inherent in Aristotle's phrase "the demos sees."

offered by the oligarchs to the demos rather than on threats, but here, as in the choral lyric scenario, both elements are at play. Poetic performances and civic sacrifices under oligarchy were presented as public benefactions, but they were at the same time symbols of the oligarchs' power. If feasting and poetry represented a gift, this was because the oligarchic class was in a position to bestow it as they saw fit.

Aristotle thus gives us an example that we can readily re-describe in terms of informational effects and coordination problems. His recommendations in the *Politics* appear at first glance to be about simply bribing the individual members of the demos with enticements: feasts and beautifying civic projects will buy the oligarchs time by periodically gratifying the people's desire for food and spectacle ("bread and circuses," as it was known to a later time).[60] A strategy along these lines certainly makes sense, and it has parallels in modern dictators' tendency to target poorer members of the population with bribes and patronage in order to secure their favor. As the political scientists Magaloni and Kricheli note,

> In many one-party regimes, the party controls land titles, fertilizers, subsidized housing, scholarships, food, construction materials, and many other privileges, which are distributed to the most loyal members of the party. One-party regimes therefore virtually create a market for privileges that are allocated based on degrees of loyalty. When they are well institutionalized, ruling parties should thus be understood as giant patronage systems that give the citizens a vested interest in the perpetuation of the regime. (2010: 128, references omitted)

This is not the whole story of the Aristotle passage, however. Present also is an emphasis on the public, visible character of the presentation of the desired goods and, by extension, on the ways in which the visual dynamics of the spectacle bolster stability all on their own. The practice is thus not just a matter of securing each individual member of the demos a piece of the pie, but also of ensuring that the entire civic body collectively sees itself receiving the inducements.

5.2.3 *The Samian Oligarchs' Worship of Lysander*

If Aristotle treats public spectacle as a form of bribery, another example reveals the more threatening side of the coin. It also proves oligarchs' willingness to manipulate the religious and cultural institutions of the polis for political

---

60. Veyne 1990: 93–93 discusses the Aristotle passage but sees it more as a prefiguration of euergetistic practices from the Hellenistic period.

ends. When, in 404, the Spartan commander Lysander finally defeated the besieged Samians, he appointed an oligarchic "decarchy" of ten men, loyal to him, to rule Samos.[61] The other Samians, the "free men", were given the opportunity to leave. As in many of the examples of exile studied in chapter 4, it is safest to see here an expulsion of the champions (*prostatai*) of the demos, not a wholesale forced migration of the entire population. The small group of restored oligarchs would not have been economically self-sufficient, and the presence of the garrison suggests that potentially disruptive "lower elements" were still present, requiring control. A large portion of the Samian demos therefore would have remained in the polis and the surrounding territory.[62]

In return for his benefactions to the Samian oligarchs, Lysander received cult honors from them. As Plutarch tells us, citing the historian Duris of Samos, the Samians renamed their festival for Hera, traditionally called the Heraea, the Lysandreia.[63] The event attracted famous poets from all over the Greek world, including Antimachus of Colophon and Niceratus of Heraclea, as well as homegrown stars like Choerilus of Samos.[64] Lysander had his achievements memorialized in verse by Choerilus and a certain Antilochus, and there was even a paean in his honor, recorded by Plutarch.[65] Some scholars once considered Duris's report fanciful, distrusting him on account of his apparent excesses and fabrications elsewhere; however, an inscription was published in 1965 recording a victory at the Lysandreia, proving its historicity.[66] It is now certain that there was an entire festival devoted to Lysander, treating him at least as a hero and perhaps as a living god.[67]

If there were still many members of the Samian demos living on Samos, we should assume that the Lysandreia was as much for their consumption as it

---

61. See Xen. *Hell.* 2.2.6, 2.3.6–7; Diod. Sic. 14.3.5. Lysander had in his corner several oligarchic exiles from Samos (Thuc. 8.21; *IG* I^3 96; ML 94).

62. Shipley 1987: 132–33. RO 2 reveals that some exiled Samians were in Ephesus and Notium.

63. Plut. *Lys.* 18.3–4 = Duris *FGrH* 76 F 71.

64. Plut. ibid.; cf. Duris F 83.

65. Cf. Duris F 26. Abroad, he dedicated a set of statues at Delphi, which have been discovered, adorned with elegiac couplets by Ion of Samos: Plut. *Lys.* 18.1; Paus. 10.9.7–10; ML 95. The Samian oligarchs also dedicated a statue of Lysander at Olympia, with a verse inscription, at "public expense" (*dēmosiai*) (Paus. 6.3.14).

66. *IG* XII.6 1 334.

67. Despite the testimony of Plutarch/Duris, the first person to receive cult while alive was probably Euthymus of Epizephyrian Locri (Currie 2002). The Spartan leader Brasidas was posthumously heroized: Thuc. 5.11.1. For the bestowal of cult on contemporary figures in general and Lysander in particular see Habicht 1970; Flower 1988; Cartledge 1982: 264; Currie 2005: 159–63.

was for the ruling elite's. While it lasted (and we know from the inscription that it occurred at least four times), the Lysandreia served as a powerful reminder of the oligarchs' dominance and the demos's subordination, with the literary world's leading lights focusing their talents on celebrating a man who had dealt ruthlessly with the demos of Samos.[68] With the *prostatai* of the demos banished and the Spartan garrison all too visible, the average Samian would have lacked the courage to voice his complaints or to try to initiate a popular uprising against the oligarchs. At the same time, whatever concrete benefits the members of the demos did receive from the Lysandreian festivities would have given them at least a small individual stake in the regime, in line with the processes explicated by Aristotle in the *Politics* passaged examined above.[69]

5.2.4 *The Manipulation and Destruction of Monuments*

So far we have seen examples of oligarchs projecting their power through the creation of new objects of culture. The appearance of strength could be cultivated just as easily, however, through the conspicuous *destruction* of monuments that had once stood as symbols of democracy. Especially in the immediate aftermath of the revolutionary overthrow of a democracy, acts of alteration or demolition could serve as forceful assertions of newfound oligarchic authority. As with the other instances of power projection studied above, however, we must recognize that the process was about more than simply delivering a message to each member of the demos considered in isolation; in the case of destruction, too, there were important practical dynamics at work. Acts of destruction could discourage potential subversives by publicizing the reigning regime's control over what had previously been sources of unity and coordination.

The introduction of the concept of a "focal point" will make this idea clearer. The economist Thomas Schelling created the term as a way to explain the phenomenon of spontaneous coordination. He considered situations in which people know they must meet but have no prearranged meeting place or time. For instance, he told two students that they must meet in New York City but have no means of communicating beforehand. The students indepen-

---

68. e.g., Miletus (Plut. *Lys.* 8.1–3, 19.2; Diod. Sic. 13.104.5; Polyaen. *Strat.* 1.45.1), Thasos (Polyaen. *Strat.* 1.45.4), Sestos (Plut. *Lys.* 14.2).

69. This technique may not have been limited to Samos. The language of Plut. *Lys.* 18.3 (Duris F 71) implies that other Greek poleis followed a similar route, instituting altars and sacrifices to Lysander. Cf. Paus. 6.3.15: the Samians "and the Ionians" dedicated to Lysander at Olympia, and the Ephesians set up a statue of him at their sanctuary of Artemis.

dently wrote down a place and time they thought the other might also guess: in many cases, both said "noon at Grand Central Station." The secret to the successful coordination was knowledge of what features and landmarks were "salient." In the 1960s, when Schelling performed the experiment, the likeliest meeting place for a general encounter in New York was Grand Central Station. The station possessed "salience" in most people's minds; thus, a person could anticipate with some degree of certainty that another person would also pick it as a meeting place. Grand Central Station could therefore serve as a "focal point" or "focal solution" for an act of successful spontaneous coordination.[70]

As Ober has shown, such focal points existed in the Athenian civic landscape. He singles out the statue group of the tyrannicides Harmodius and Aristogeiton, the threatening stance of which the chorus members of Aristophanes's *Lysistrata* explicitly mimic, saying they will "gather in the agora" beside the tyrannicides in order to defend the polis against tyranny.[71] In other words, in the event of an attempted *coup* the Athenians possessed sufficient common knowledge of the salience of the tyrannicide monument to muster there spontaneously in defense of democracy.[72] By the same token, any successful alteration or destruction of the monument by tyrants or oligarchs would have served as both a symbolic victory (a kind of *damnatio memoriae*) and an impediment to future democratic coordination around the statue.[73] Not only would the focal point be gone, but the oligarchs would have raised an unsettling question in the people's minds: if the demos could not successfully defend the very monument meant to rally them in times of civil unrest,

---

70. Schelling 1980. "Salience" is a subtle concept, since some minimal set of shared cultural assumptions must exist for it to obtain. Thus we can expect that different groups possess different points of salience.

71. See esp. lines 631–34. Analysis: Ober 2005: 220–21, 2008: 198–99 and n43; cf. Azoulay 2014. I discuss the importance of the statue group for coordinating democratic behavior in the agora in chapter 4, section 4.2.

72. In a similar manner, the Eretrian law against tyranny and oligarchy instructs the demos on what to do if "it is not possible to secure the Agoraion immediately so that the Council can hold a lawful session" (see Knoepfler 2002: 171 for the restorations to the text). The Eretrian Agoraion is likely to have been a sanctuary in the agora where the council met (Knoepfler *ibid*: 172–74), and so it seems that the sanctuary was expected to serve as a focal point for democratic coordination in the case of a tyrannical or oligarchic *coup*. In other words, it was common knowledge that the members of the demos would head for the Agoraion in the event of an attempted takeover; the law therefore spells out what to do if this turns out to be impossible.

73. For the applicability of the Roman term *damnatio memoriae* to Greek history see Flower 2006, ch. 2; Savalli-Lestrade 2009. I assume that was is accomplished in such acts is not literally a forgetting but rather the consignment of the affected individual to public infamy.

what really was the likelihood that an opposition movement capable of overthrowing the oligarchy existed that there existed an opposition movement capable of overthrowing the oligarchy?

Considered in this light, the decision by newly installed oligarchs to deface democratic tyrannicide monuments makes good sense. To attack and damage these monuments, which, in their exaggerated poses and gestures, constituted veritable "instruction manuals" on how to resist conspiracies against democracy, was to make the loudest possible statement that you were now in control. We possess at least two instances of this behavior in the historical record. The first, from early Hellenistic Erythrae, has received considerable attention lately.[74] The political situation at Erythrae is known to us from a single inscription, numbered 503 in Engelmann and Merkelbach's *Die Inschriften von Erythrai und Klazomenai* (= *IK Erythrai*).[75] The decree, issued by a democratic regime, contains its own, politically slanted version of recent events in the city. The first part of the inscription—the only part that will concern us here—reads,

> Resolved by the Council and the Demos. Zoilus the son of Chiades spoke: since those in the oligarchy removed the sword from the statue in the likeness of Philites the tyrant-killer, thinking that its position [*stasis*] was completely aimed at them; in order that the demos clearly show much concern for and always remember its benefactors, both living and dead, with good fortune be it decided by the Council and the Demos . . . . (lines 1–10)[76]

---

74. Teegarden, in his recent study of democratic anti-tyranny legislation, devotes an entire chapter to the incident, employing a similar methodology to the one used here (2014: ch. 5). However, while Teegarden is interested in understanding democratic responses to both oligarchic and tyrannical takeovers, this book's focus is on oligarchic actions and their propensity to perpetuate oligarchic rule.

75. The provenance of the stone was disputed for many years—by, amongst others, Wilamowitz—and generally believed to have been Clazomenae. However, Heisserer (1979) provided convincing arguments that Erythrae makes the most sense as the origin of the decree; the inscription has for the most part been considered Erythraean ever since. The date has been placed in the first quarter of the third century. Those accepting Heisserer's proposal or otherwise considering the inscription to be of Erythraean origin include Ober 2003: 227; Chaniotis 2005a: 38; Ma 2009: 249; Teegarden 2014: 142–43.

76. This is one of the few extant instances of the word "oligarchy" on stone. Lewis would restore it at *IG* I³ 96, line 3, but this seems too uncertain. Secure instances include the Theozotides decree of post-404 (Stroud 1971; perhaps post-411: Matthaiou 2011); RO 41, line 26 (Athens, 362/1 [plausibly restored]); *SEG* 51.1096 *passim* (Thasos, early fourth century); *SEG* 51.1105, line 21 (Eretria, mid-fourth century); RO 84 B, line 17 (Chios, late fourth century); *IG* II² 448, line 61 (318/17 [spelled *oliarchia*]); *IK Erythrai* 503, line 2 (ca. 280); *SEG* 28.60, line 81 (Athens, 270/69 [*oliarchia*]); *Tit. Cal.* test. xii, line 21 (Cos, mid-third century); *IK Ilion* 25 *pas-*

The decree describes a situation in which the demos of Erythrae was overthrown and the resulting oligarchy removed the sword of Philites, the demos's champion, from its statue. The existence of the decree itself, meanwhile, indicates that the demos reclaimed power, perhaps with Zoilus at its forefront, and restored the statue to its original state.[77] While this reconstruction of the context of the decree seems certain, the original intention of the oligarchs in disfiguring the statue is more difficult to grasp. The democratic interpretation contained in the decree rather self-servingly implies fear on the part of the oligarchs, and it conveniently associates oligarchs with tyrants in its assumption that the oligarchs thought the tyrant-killer's sword was aimed at them. They might, however, have had alternative motives. Ober has tentatively suggested that the oligarchs were "symbolically proclaiming an end to an era of citizen-on-citizen violence, the end of *stasis*" (2003: 228). By removing the sword, the oligarchs were anointing themselves as the guardians of order and peace. Their decision should thus perhaps be interpreted as a genuinely conciliatory gesture. Ma, on the other hand, thinks that the oligarchs were attempting to make the threatening connotations of the statue fade into oblivion: "The honorific statue of a tyrannicide was considered so potent that an oligarchy tried to neutralize it by removing its characteristic attribute, the avenging sword, in the hope that the statue would simply become another artwork" (2009: 250).[78]

I argue, by contrast, that we should read the act as a conscious attempt at intimidation by the oligarchs. By denuding the statue of its sword, the oligarchs were sending a very public signal that they had appropriated a powerful symbol of the democracy. More importantly, if the tyrannicide monument was regarded by the demos as a potential focal point for mass coordination, like the statues of Harmodius and Aristogeiton in Athens, the oligarchs' success in openly desecrating it would have emphasized that the demos had failed in the event to prevent an oligarchic takeover. In other words, by successfully attacking the very object that might have organized the demos against them, the oligarchs ultimately rendered the demos weaker, by making its conspicuous failure to unite a matter of common knowledge.[79] Finally, the location of

---

sim (early third century). See also the decree for Demosthenes preserved at Plut. *Mor.* 850f-51c. The references are all negative in tone.

77. Heisserer 1979: 284. Engelmann and Merkelbach suggested a much more convoluted sequence in which one faction, the oligarchs, pitted two other factions, the democratic and the tyrannical, against one another through manipulation of the statue in order to secure their own supremacy.

78. Quite similar is the interpretation of Gauthier 1982: 215–21.

79. Cf. Teegarden 2014: 150: "[The oligarchs] advertised [by removing the sword] that tyran-

the statue in the agora (a fact made plain by the mention of *agoranomoi* [market regulators] later in the decree) would have further rubbed salt in the demos's wound. As we saw in chapter 4, section 4.2, the agora was a site of demotic power and therefore typically a source of anxiety for oligarchs. The demos's inability to assemble in the agora during an emergency betokened a lack of commitment to democracy on the part of the common people. The oligarchs had revealed them to be more interested in individual self-preservation than collective action.

Oligarchic plotters utilized a similar strategy in late-fourth-century Ephesus. Arrian tells us that the oligarchs, during their brief takeover of the polis, had "plundered the temple of Artemis and pulled down the statue of Philip [of Macedon] in the shrine and dug up the grave of Heropythes, the liberator of the city, from the agora."[80] This Heropythes, as we know from Polyaenus (*Strat.* 7.23.2), was an opponent of Mausolus, the satrap of Caria, in the mid-fourth century. His interment in the agora must therefore have been fairly recent in 334, the year of the attempted oligarchic *coup*. It is unclear why precisely Heropythes was called "liberator" of the city. Ephesus had fallen under Persian control following the Peace of Antalcidas in 387, so it seems likely that sometime before the episode related by Polyaenus, Heropythes (whom Polyaenus called "Herophytus") had led an uprising against the Persians and thus incurred the enmity of Mausolus. He therefore could have received the title "liberator" before his death pre-334.[81] In any case, Heropythes received special dispensation to be buried in the Ephesian agora, typically reserved for founders and tyrannicides. Indeed, there is considerable conceptual slippage in the sources between *ktistai* or *archēgetai* (founders), tyrant-killers, and liberators.[82] Thus even if Heropythes was not technically a tyrant-killer, his tomb

---

nicide, qua rebellion that ushers in a democracy, will fail.... [H]istory 'backed up' the statue's new symbolic significance: the democracy ushered in by Philites did, in fact, fail." I am in substantial agreement with Teegarden's analysis, but I would emphasize more the spatial factors at play in the episode: the statue was likely intended to be the focal point, the precise location, where citizens were expected to coordinate resistance in the event of an oligarchic takeover.

80. *Anab.* 1.17.11: τοὺς τὸ ἱερὸν συλήσαντας τῆς Ἀρτέμιδος καὶ τοὺς τὴν εἰκόνα τὴν Φιλίππου τὴν ἐν τῷ ἱερῷ καταβαλόντας καὶ τὸν τάφον ἐκ τῆς ἀγορᾶς ἀνορύξαντας τὸν Ἡροπύθου τοῦ ἐλευθερώσαντος τὴν πόλιν.

81. See Judeich 1892: 261 for the sequence of events adopted here.

82. The Spartan commander Brasidas, who is buried by the Amphipolitans in their agora following his death in 422, is considered a "founder hero" because he was their "savior" (*sōtēr*) (Thuc. 5.11.1). The Sicyonian tyrant Euphron, who had initially led a democratic uprising against the Sicyonian oligarchy, was buried by the demos in the agora and worshiped as *archēgetēs* (Xen. *Hell.* 7.3.12); one could quite plausibly speculate that the demos regarded him as their liberator. And of course the tyrannicides Harmodius and Aristogeiton were (very probably)

in the agora (complete with statue?) would likely have evoked the same sorts of emotions in the minds of Ephesians, and could have served as a focal point for democratic resistance no less than a tyrannicide monument. Like a tyrant-killer, Heropythes as "liberator" provided a model of how to combat anti-democratic takeovers.[83] By attacking this civic landmark, then, the Ephesian oligarchs were attempting to advertise the demos's weakness and their own strength. Just as in the Erythraean example, the action took place in the political heart of the polis, the agora, an area that usually afforded the demos a numerical advantage. Rather than resist in concert, however, the democrats had scattered in fear (*phobos*, in Arrian's words).

The Erythraean and Ephesian episodes constitute the clearest examples of oligarchs attacking politically charged monuments. The list of destructive acts does not end there, however. In addition to the more spectacular practice of defacing graves and tyrannicide statues, there was a whole host of subtler but no less meaningful transgressions against objects of democratic value. One such target was *stēlai*, the vertical stone slabs on which the Greeks inscribed their laws and decrees. That *stēlai* were objects of political contestation is unsurprising, since they recorded in permanent form the decisions of the ruling body of the polis. If one was not in sympathy with those decisions, *stēlai* might serve as a hateful reminder of the enemy's political dominance. The Greeks had long been aware that dissenters might try to alter decrees physically, whether out of spite or because they hoped to nullify the laws in question. We possess several examples of Archaic Greek inscriptions proscribing the removal or alteration of the physical decree.[84] There are also hints in the sources that the subjects of the Athenian empire might desecrate imperial *stēlai* in displays of resistance.[85] We know of instances where poleis physically

---

remembered as having "liberated" the polis: *eleutheria* ("freedom") has been restored in the epigram from the Critius and Nesiotes statue that celebrated them in the Athenian agora (Lebedev 1996: 267).

83. The Ephesian oligarchs' treatment of the grave makes one wonder what the Sicyonian oligarchs would have liked to do to Euphron's monument. Here was the grave of a "patent tyrant" (Xen. *Hell.* 7.1.46), which, moreover, the demos worshipped annually with founder's rites (7.3.12) in the same place, the agora, where Euphron had originally called together the demos in an act of revolution (7.1.45). Like Heropythes' grave at Ephesus, it seems a likely target for oligarchic abuse.

84. ML 17, lines 7–8 (see also *Nomima* I.52); *Nomima* I.56, line 19 (see also Koerner no. 44); *Nomima* I.100, line 2 (see also Koerner no. 29); Solon fr. 22 Ruschenbusch *apud* Dem. 23.62. ML 30, lines 35–41, from early-fifth-century (democratic) Teos, specifies that "whoever takes down the *stēlai* on which the curses are written or cuts out the letters or makes them illegible, that man is to be destroyed, both him and his family."

85. At Ar. *Av.* 1049–54, an exchange between the comic hero Peisetaerus, an Athenian *epis-*

demolished their agreements with other states, as well.[86] Of greater interest, however, are times when oligarchic revolutionaries destroyed the decrees of their democratic opponents. There was likely a strong sense of hostility at play here, as well as a desire to do away with the laws of the old constitution. I would argue, however, that the destruction of *stēlai* also served a function similar to that of the attacks on monuments studied above.

Most notoriously, the Thirty at Athens "took down the laws of Ephialtes and Archestratus concerning the Areopagites from the Areopagus" ([Arist.] *Ath. Pol.* 35.2); they are also described in a less reliable scholium to Aeschines (*ad* 1.39) as "mistreating (*lumēnanto*) the laws of Draco and Solon." As Shear has shown, these actions "allowed the Thirty to claim these spaces as their own ... [and] further served to begin to erase the control of the *demos* from the topography."[87] Taking down the laws of Ephialtes, who had supposedly opened the floodgates to radical democracy, would have sent an especially clear message that the Thirty were attempting to roll back democratic advances. The oligarchs also destroyed several proxeny decrees that were subsequently re-inscribed (with democratic pride) by the restored democracy.[88] As Mack has recently pointed out, "as the privileges which *proxenoi* received were to an extent modeled on the rights citizens possessed ... it is hard to believe that this action was unrelated to the well-documented activities of the Thirty in restricting citizenship and civic participation."[89] The destruction of the

---

kopos (inspector), and a "decree seller," Peisetaerus is accused of "not receiving the magistrates [into Cloudcuckooland] according to the *stēlē*," and later of "crapping on the *stēlē*" (as a bird would appropriately do, but also revealing something about the subjects' attitudes towards the empire). Dunbar in her commentary (*ad loc.*) quotes Meiggs (1972: 587): "there must have been a strong temptation to oligarchs as well as dogs to deface or foul decree stones"; see further Liddel 2010: 115–16. In several versions of the Athenian decree imposing weights and measures, it is specified at one point (e.g., at ML 45, line 10) that the Athenians will ensure that a *stēlē* is set up in the agora of each polis in front of the mint and will do it themselves, "if they [the allied cities] *are not themselves willing*." N.b. that this decree is the very one introduced by the "decree seller" in Ar. *Av.* and comically rejected by Peisetaerus.

86. E.g., *IG* II² 116, lines 39–40 (Athenian agreement with Alexander of Pherae, 361/0); Philoch. *FGrH* 328 F 55a, b (Athenian agreement with Philip of Macedon). On the afterlife of Greek treaties see further Bolmarcich 2007.

87. Shear 2011: 179. Shear also accepts (177) Plutarch's statement (*Them.* 19.4) that the Thirty also reconstructed the Pnyx so that it would face away from the sea, "thinking that the naval empire was the source of democracy, but that farmers would be less opposed to oligarchy."

88. *IG* I³ 229; *IG* II² 6, 52; *Agora* xvi. 37; Walbank *Proxenies* no. 26. See Shear 2011: 176–77 for a discussion. Shear also suggests that the same fate befell ML 94, following the remarks of ML pp. 286–87.

89. Mack 2015: 95.

stēlai rewarding proxeny signaled loud and clear that Athens now operated according to a restricted definition of citizenship.

The Thirty was not the last oligarchic regime in Athens to manipulate decrees. A fourth-century inscription (*IG* II² 448) honoring Euphron of Sicyon, grandson of the very Euphron heroized by the Sicyonians, explains that the demos had previously decreed privileges for Euphron, but that "those in charge during the oligarchy [*sc.* of Phocion and Antipater] withdrew his gifts and took down the *stēlai*."[90] The decree then orders that they be re-inscribed and set up on the acropolis beside Zeus the Savior (lines 66–70).[91] Euphron's heroic example is to be (re)publicized for all to see and emulate, despite the best efforts of the oligarchs.

We know from other sources that oligarchs elsewhere did the same, as at Iulis on the island of Ceos in 363/2. An inscription tells us that oligarchic exiles returned to the city and "overthrew (ἐξέβαλο[ν]) the *stēlai* on which had been written the agreements with Athens and the names of those transgressing the oaths and the agreements" (RO 39, lines 30–33). They subsequently killed the allies of the Athenians whom the demos of Iulis had restored earlier, sentenced others to death, and confiscated their property (33–35).[92] The *stēlai* on which the agreements with Athens were written were objects of hatred for the exiled Iulietans, who had opposed the specific policy of allying with Athens, but more than likely they also constituted symbols of the democratic regime that made that alliance possible. To overthrow the decrees was to mark the ascendance of a new political order.

As a final example of conspicuous destruction, this time targeting a different object, we turn to the island of Thasos during its period of oligarchy in the late-fifth and early-fourth centuries. The constitutional history of Thasos around this time is fraught with episodes of civil strife and violence, for the island was buffeted by both Athenian democrats and Spartan oligarchs (and sometimes by Athenian oligarchs!).[93] The Athenian oligarch Diitrephes

---

90. lines 60–62: ἀφείλοντο [αὐτὸν] / τὰς δωρεὰς οἱ ἐν τεῖ ὀλιαρχίαι [sic] πολιτευόμεν[οι καὶ / τὰς στήλας καθεῖλον. (This is another one of the rare epigraphical instances of "oligarchy," together with the reference in *IK Erythrai* 503 discussed above.)

91. See Oliver 2003a for a convincing restoration of the text at this point.

92. The targets of the oligarchs had spoken against one Antipater, who was condemned to death by the Athenians for killing their *proxenos* Aesion contrary to the decrees of the demos of Athens (37–40). We possess decrees similar to the one protecting Aesion from the first Delian League (e.g., *IG* I³ 19, 27, 28, 57). The decree is admittedly therefore deeply enmeshed in Athenian imperial-style politics, but Rhodes and Osborne comment that the instance falls squarely into the general category of "returning exiles try[ing] to change the political stance of their state" (RO p. 202).

93. See *IACP* no. 526 (Reger); Robinson 2011: 180–81. (But see below on the dating of *SEG* 38.851.)

overthrew the democracy there in 411 (Thuc. 8.64.2), establishing the oligarchy that probably published the law announcing rewards for informants (ML 83) discussed above in chapter 3, section 3.4. Thrasybulus won back the island for Athens in 407 and probably restored democracy there (Xen. *Hell.* 1.4.9; Diod. Sic. 13.72.1), but the Spartans reclaimed it following their victory over Athens in the Peloponnesian War (Xen. *Hell.* 2.2.5). The reconstituted oligarchy exiled several democrats, who appear in the Athenian epigraphic record (*IG* II² 6, 17). Thanks to further intervention by Thrasybulus in 390, however, Thasos returned to democracy once again (Xen. *Hell.* 4.8.26; Dem. 20.59; *IG* II² 24; *SEG* 56.1017).

It is in this context that Picard places a Thasian inscription documenting extensive procedures of reconciliation enacted under the restored democracy.[94] Toward the end of the first fragment (A) of the inscription we read a series of punishments for anyone "who would not follow" the terms of reconciliation (line 12): he is to be cursed, exiled (?) "for all time," and his possessions are to be "[made public]" (τὰ χρήμ[α|τα δημόσια, lines 14–15). There is then a separate segment stating "let them tear down to the foundations" (κ] ατασκαψάντων ἐς ἔ[δαφ|ος, lines 16–17), something about the Dionysia festival, and then a further command to "[re]build the [houses] of these men" (ἀνοι]κοδομῆσαι τὰς τούτω[ν ο|ἰκίας, lines 18–19). Reger (1990: 399) shows that the later lines should fit into a context of "problems arising from the abolition of the old regime." Therefore, the lines "enjoin not the destruction of houses of the oligarchs—whose disposition has already been foreseen in the previous line [lines 16–17]—but the reconstruction of houses of the 'victims of the previous regime'" (Reger is quoting a suggestion, ultimately rejected, by Salviat and Grandjean). Picard follows suit on this point, equating τούτω[ν in line 18 with the "victimes de l'oligarchie" (2000: 1070). So, there are two separate commandments about tearing down houses. The first specifies the punishments to be meted out against transgressors of the reconciliation, while the second guarantees the rebuilding of the houses of democratic exiles destroyed under the oligarchy. We therefore have an instance of oligarchs tearing down democrats' houses.[95] We should understand this action in terms of an

---

94. Picard 2000 = *SEG* 51.1096. Original inscription: *IG* XII.8 262 + *Suppl.* p. 150. Hicks (1887) thought from this fragment that an oligarchy was publicly referring to itself as such, an act otherwise unattested (Picard 2000: 1061, following Pouilloux). Salviat and Grandjean 1988 (= *SEG* 38.851), reconsidering the original in light of the new fragment, concluded it was from 407, when Thrasybulus recovered Thasos. (Reger 1990 adds important notes, including a more plausible interpretation of lines A.16–19 [see below], but accepts Salviat and Grandjean's dating.) Picard, noting the complete absence of references in the extant text to the Athenians, convincingly makes the document a purely internal affair, with the polis of Acanthus arbitrating.

95. As we have seen, the Mantineans in 385 had to tear down some of their houses (Xen. *Hell.*

attempt by the oligarchs not simply to punish their individual enemies, but to send a message to the wider community that they now possessed the power to restructure the polis as they saw fit. The demos would have borne silent witness to the destruction of their leaders' homes and possessions, much as the populations did at Erythrae and Ephesus in the case of the defaced heroic monuments, and from this experience they would have taken away the lesson that they were powerless to resist the oligarchic takeover.[96] Furthermore, it is possible to think of the democrats' houses as focal points for democratic coordination, and therefore of the oligarchs' actions as measures for neutralizing potential resistance. As we saw in chapter 4, section 4.2, an attempted oligarchic *coup* at Elis around 400 was thwarted when the demos rallied to the house of its *prostatēs* Thrasydaeus. The members of the demos were at first demoralized when they thought Thrasydaeus was dead, but upon learning that he was alive and asleep in his house (he had gotten drunk the night before and was sleeping off his hangover), "the house was crowded by people here and there like the leader of bees is by the swarm" (Xen. *Hell.* 3.2.28). It seems that the members of the demos were able to mass spontaneously around the house, without any rallying cry on Thrasydaeus's part (Xenophon's language suggests that the assembled demos woke Thrasydaeus up from his nap). The champion's house might thus function as a locus for collective action in a democratic polity; destroying it could alert the population to the fact that oligarchs were now closely monitoring the demos's usual haunts.[97]

The strategies studied in this section should not be regarded as falling exclusively within the repertoire of oligarchic political actors. In fact, the dynamics of public spectacle analyzed here were probably much more common in Classical democratic regimes or in episodes throughout Greek history of

---

5.2.7), but this was because they were experiencing a dioecism, and the elite had to raze their own houses just as much as (perhaps more than) the exiled leaders of the demos.

96. The incident necessitates a qualification to the views of Connor 1985 and Forsdyke 2012, who interpret episodes of house-razing as "spectacular communal events" (Forsdyke 2012: 159–64) in which the entire community enforces its norms in an extralegal fashion. The fact that oligarchs had torn down houses shows that unpopular groups could also harness public spectacle for their own political ends.

97. Cf. the circumstances surrounding the assassination of the Athenian oligarch Phrynichus in 411: Thucydides says that the Four Hundred, putting one of the assassins to torture, learned that "many people had come together in the house of the peripolarch [the leader of the border patrol] and in other houses" (8.92.2). The accuracy of the assassin's account is called into question by the fact that multiple versions of the event existed in antiquity, but the story was at least considered plausible and shows the importance of private houses for conspiratorial activity, in this case against an oligarchy.

populist outcry against tyrant-like figures.[98] Triumphant democrats often paraded their victories over their opponents in a manner that would ensure the widest possible public reception. We see this tactic on display in the punishments meted out to the oligarchs after the restoration of democracy in Athens in 410 and 403, and in similar scenarios.[99] There are, moreover, far more examples in the historical record of democracies propagating explicit political messages in festival contexts than of oligarchies doing the same.[100] This holds for both Athens and other poleis,[101] and it is unsurprising. The public projec-

---

98. This assumption underlies the studies of Connor 1985 and Forsdyke 2012, cited above.

99. Note, for example, the razing of the oligarch Antiphon's house and the erection of a plaque commemorating his infamy on the spot (Craterus *FGrH* 342 F 5b), as well as the sale of the property of the Thirty (*SEG* 32.161), all analyzed by Shear 2011. Sometimes victors could put the vanquished's property to creative reuse: at Plut. *Tim.* 22.1–3 Timoleon and the Syracusans destroy the tyrant Dionysius's fortress and tomb and build a law court on the site. Philoch. *FGrH* 328 F 181 says that the Athenians used the property of the Thirty as implements in their processions (on this act see Fornara and Yates 2007; Kindt 2009: 239–44). The Athenians' melted down Hipparchus's statue to make a *stēlē* announcing the names of traitors: Lyc. 1.117–19, with analysis by Ober 2008: 187–89. They also supposedly pulled down Demetrius of Phalerum's honorary statues after his political downfall and melted some of them down into chamber pots (Diog. Laert. 5.77 with Azoulay 2009, esp. 324–32). Note also the desecration of the statue of Mausolus of Caria, likely meant as a subversive act: RO 54, lines 21–22.

100. I cannot discuss the whole complex issue of the relationship between Athenian tragic drama and democracy (for which see, most recently, Carter 2004; Rhodes 2003, 2011; Wilson 2009, 2011). As Wilson 2009 shows, however, the triumphant democratic return at the Dionysia of 410/9, with its reward for the assassins of Phrynichus (ML 85), surely made a strong impression upon those who had served under the oligarchy. The democrats used the festival setting for pro-regime purposes.

101. Explicit promotion of one regime type over another during a festival seems to be limited to democracies, which frequently glorified themselves and sometimes castigated oligarchy. (Oligarchies might advertise their own power implicitly, as in section 5.2.1 above.) The festival of the Artemisia at Eretria, for example, was reconstituted in c. 340 with provisions ensuring that "as many people as possible may sacrifice"; the closing lines of the inscription in question (enacted with a democratic formula) proclaim that the Eretrians are "free and prosperous and in control of themselves" (RO 73, lines 44–45). A later Eretrian inscription (*IG* XII.9 192) sets up a Dionysian festival "so that there might be a memorial of this day . . . when the garrison left and the demos was freed and re-established the ancestral laws and the democracy." In the Erythraean decree about the statue of Philites (*IK Erythrai* 503, discussed above), the demos takes steps to ensure that the statue will be crowned at the Noumenia and at the other civic festivals. In the law against oligarchy and tyranny edited by Knoepfler (2001b/2002, = *SEG* 51.1105), curses against subversives are to be read out at the Dionysia and Artemisia. See also RO 85A, lines 10–12 (a democratic reconciliation agreement from Mytilene ca. 334): "perform a sacrifice and procession . . . as the demos decides." And in the democratic reconciliation decree from

tion of power was easier where the message being conveyed was favored by more rather than fewer people. By the same token, however, we might speculate that the frequency and facility of these kinds of acts under democracy entailed a decrease in the importance of any individual act at the margin. In the Athenian democracy, as Ober (2008) has shown, public information was plentiful but the stakes for day-to-day political stability were relatively low.[102] In oligarchies, by contrast, the comparatively precarious position of the elite meant that the select messages that were disseminated took on a correspondingly pivotal character. Even if poetic performances, sacrifices, building projects, and the manipulation of objects in the civic landscape were rarer under oligarchies, their successful execution could have a greater impact on the overall strength of the regime.

5.3 Selectivity: The Oligarchs of Pharsalus

This closing section addresses selectivity, the method of deploying information to specific audiences. Just as in modern autocratic states monopolization of the media can convince the population that there is no viable alternative to the prevailing government, so in ancient Greece oligarchs could attempt to specify which messages were received by whom and when. The result was failure to coordinate against the regime: as the political scientist Beatriz Magaloni says of Mexico under the PRI,

> Information dissemination about the preferences of the other players, and the relative standing of the alternatives . . . is necessary for coordination to take place. Yet in hegemonic-party autocracies, there are normally no independent sources of information because the government controls the mass media. Control of the media is an important tool autocrats employ to prevent voter coordination. (2006: 76, references omitted)

There are many places one could turn to find examples of oligarchic selectivity in action. We possess several examples of oligarchs swearing false oaths, manipulating important political documents, and in general sending mixed

---

early-fourth-century Thasos just discussed (Picard 2000 = *SEG* 51.1096), some part of the process takes place "during the contest at the Dionysia" (A. 17). See also *SEG* 58.1220 (discussed in the afterword), lines 11–14. For festival celebrating political anniversaries in the Hellenistic period, see Chaniotis 1995.

102. This helps to explain, in part, why democratic Athens held so many festivals—"more than any other Greek city," in the Old Oligarch's words (*Ath. Pol.* 3.2; cf. 2.9–10). For the danger of festival contexts to oligarchies, see chapter 6, section 6.1.1.

messages to the demos.[103] I will limit my focus, however, to one particularly striking instance of selectivity, which has so far not received the scholarly attention it deserves. Thanks to two pieces of evidence, we catch a glimpse of one oligarchic polis, the Thessalian city of Pharsalus, deploying selectivity to its long-term advantage.[104]

In the *Politics*, Aristotle explains that an oligarchy "in agreement with itself" (*homonoousa*) is not likely to be undermined from within (5.1306a9–10). As an example he cites Pharsalus, where the rulers, "although few, have power over many people because they treat each other well."[105] In the fourth-century pseudo-Platonic dialogue *Sisyphus*, meanwhile, we learn of a law that this unified oligarchy employed to gather important information from citizens.[106] At the beginning of the dialogue, the Pharsalian interlocutor Sisyphus explains to Socrates that he was busy the previous day because "our [Pharsalian] leaders [*archontes*] were deliberating, [and] they compelled me to deliberate with them; for we Pharsalians have a law that we must obey the leaders if they order one of us to join in deliberation with them" (387b-c).[107]

Assuming that the *archontes* here belong to the same regime described by Aristotle, we can make good sense of this particular law by analyzing it under the rubric of selectivity.[108] The rulers are clearly a class apart, whose decisions

---

103. For false oaths and empty promises of good will, see Thuc. 4.74.2 (the oligarchs of Megara); Thuc. 8.67.1 and [Arist.] *Ath. Pol.* 29.2 (the Four Hundred at Athens in 411); Xen. *Hell.* 2.3.11 and [Arist.] *Ath. Pol.* 35.2–3 (the Thirty in 404). Regarding important documents, the Four Hundred were notorious for withholding the list of the Five Thousand: Thuc. 8.65.3, 86.3, 89.2, 93.2. Thucydides makes clear that their intent was to sow confusion and division among the hoplites (8.92.11).

104. See also Kent 1904: appendix II: 16. On the stable oligarchy at Pharsalus, see now de Luna 2011, although she does not adduce the pseudo-Platonic dialogue I discuss here.

105. *Pol.* 5.1306a10–12: σημεῖον δὲ ἡ ἐν Φαρσάλῳ πολιτεία· ἐκεῖνοι γὰρ ὀλίγοι ὄντες πολλῶν κύριοί εἰσι διὰ τὸ χρῆσθαι σφίσιν αὐτοῖς καλῶς. Aristotle's statement attests to the importance of internal unity among oligarchs: see chapter 2.

106. Date: Hutchinson in Cooper 1997: 1707–1708.

107. This Sisyphus is perhaps to be identified with the member of the famous Daochid family (listed in *Syll.*³ 274, discussed above). Theopomp. *FGrH* 115 F 18 mentions a Pharsalian Sisyphus who employed a full-time flatterer or *kolax*, a luxury that suggests wealth and power. In any case it can be taken for granted that the Platonic interlocutor is from the elite; the law he cites, however, probably applies to the whole citizen body.

108. Given the similar dating of the two texts and the strong tradition of oligarchy at Pharsalus (see *IACP* no. 413, p. 703), we are on safe grounds with this assumption. Note also that Sisyphus's statement that "we must obey the leaders if they order one of us to join them" echoes Aristotle's description, in his discussion of the "free agora" of the Thessalians (see the section on "secrecy" above, 5.1), that members of the demos are excluded from the free agora, "unless they are summoned by the *archontes*" (*Pol.* 7.1331a35).

are insulated from wider public scrutiny except by official invitation. Sisyphus's description of the law implies that those summonses that did go out were targeted toward individual members of the Pharsalian community, thereby allowing the *archontes* to isolate those they considered useful sources of information. What actually transpired at such meetings is unknown, but we might imagine that in addition to consulting people genuinely thought to be helpful advisors, the Pharsalian oligarchs could use the forum as an opportunity to extract information about subversive activity, perhaps threatening or rewarding informants in a manner consistent with our other evidence for delation in oligarchies (see chapter 3, section 3.4). The Pharsalians summoned to the meeting of the rulers would have been limited in their own strategic options by what private information they personally possessed and by the front being presented to them by the *archontes*. Cut off from broader sources of information and from the potential aid afforded by public onlookers, they would have been more easily manipulated by the leaders. From pseudo-Plato's description, therefore, we start to understand just how, in Aristotle's words, the "few" oligarchs of Pharsalus retained "power over many people."

6

Processes of Regime Breakdown

Democracy appears to be safer and less liable to revolution than oligarchy. For in oligarchies there are two forms of stasis, that of the oligarchs towards each other and that again of the oligarchs towards the people.

—ARISTOTLE[1]

6.0 Introduction: Explaining Change as Well as Stability

Chapters 2 through 5 brought theoretical perspectives to bear on the available historical evidence in order to reconstruct the institutional repertoire that Classical Greek oligarchies used to resist their own overthrow. The basic thesis was that, all else being equal, oligarchies that employed such institutions could expect to remain in a state of stable equilibrium. A satisfactory political history, however, must explain regime change as well as stability. And, notoriously, the ancient Greek world was full of political change. Civil war, or *stasis*, constituted a significant problem for the poleis of Greece, particularly during the Classical period.[2] Although some scholars speak of the polis in highly communitarian terms, as a place of unity and strong civic identity, the ancient evidence suggests that sedition, treason, factional infighting, and all-out social conflict were common in ancient Greece, in fact to a degree that would shock the modern world. Moreover, *stasis* was not confined to a particular kind of polis (large or small, rich or poor), but seems to have affected most of them. As Hansen states, "there can be no doubt that discord among the citizens and civil war were problems which most of the time affected most of the Greek

---

1. *Pol.* 5.1302a8–11: ὅμως δὲ ἀσφαλεστέρα καὶ ἀστασίαστος μᾶλλον ἡ δημοκρατία τῆς ὀλιγαρχίας. ἐν μὲν γὰρ ταῖς ὀλιγαρχίαις ἐγγίγνονται δύο, ἥ τε πρὸς ἀλλήλους στάσις καὶ ἔτι ἡ πρὸς τὸν δῆμον.

2. For previous treatments of *stasis*, see Lintott 1982; Gehrke *Stasis passim*; Berger 1992 (covering areas in Sicily and Magna Graecia omitted by Gehrke); Fisher 2000a. For *stasis* in the Archaic period, see van Wees 2008.

poleis from Massalia [in the west] to Herakleia Pontike [in the east]."[3] Recent epigraphical discoveries have further contributed to our knowledge of *stasis* in the late Classical and early Hellenistic periods.[4]

While it is clear that *stasis* was endemic in Classical Greece, I show in this chapter that it affected the different types of political regime in distinctive ways. *Stasis* was not necessarily as likely to erupt, nor the ensuing civil war likely to follow the same dynamic path, in a democracy as in an oligarchy. Moreover, the general effects of *stasis* changed over time. As scholars are increasingly coming to acknowledge, oligarchy proved unsustainable as a viable alternative to democracy over the course of the Classical period, leaving government "by the people" the sole legitimate political form in Hellenistic times.[5] Thus there seem to have been certain tendencies inherent in oligarchic government that not only encouraged civil war but also discouraged the successful reinstitution of stable oligarchy afterward. What those tendencies might have been, however, has not been treated systematically. We know how the Classical period started out (with a competitive ecology of tyrannies, oligarchies, and democracies), and we know how the high Hellenistic period (ca. 150 BCE) ended (with democracy as the institutional "rules of the game"), but we do not understand the process whereby the situation changed.[6] The present and final chapter contributes to such an understanding by analyzing the strategic dynamics of oligarchic breakdown.

6.1 Unguarded Public Space and the Breakdown of Oligarchies

We saw in chapter 4 that public space was particularly dangerous to oligarchies. Here I expand upon examples of oligarchic overthrow that occurred in public space and clarify their internal logic. What I hope to make apparent is the extent to which these revolutions were dependent upon considerations of

---

3. *IACP*, p. 125. N.b. the title of the section: "*Stasis* as an *essential* aspect of the polis" (emphasis added).

4. See, e.g., the reconciliation agreement from mid-fourth-century Dikaia in the Chalcidice (*SEG* 57.576; Gray 2013); a late-fourth-century decree from the tiny island of Telos for foreign judges from Cos, who helped to resolve *stasis* at Telos (*IG* XII.4 1 132); an early-Hellenistic reconciliation agreement from the Pisidian community of Sagalassos (*SEG* 50.1304, 57.1409); a decree from early-third-century Aeolian Cyme forbidding generals from betraying the city to enemies (Hamon 2008 = *SEG* 59.1407). For late Classical and early Hellenistic *stasis* and reconciliation, see Gray 2015.

5. See the bibliography discussed below in the afterword.

6. For the notion of institutional "rules of the game," see North 1990: 3. For the term "high Hellenistic period," see the afterword.

space, visibility, and the dissemination of information. The sources indicate that political actors took advantage of the opportunities afforded by large gatherings within public space in order to effect revolutionary uprisings. These practical conditions obtained in a variety of contexts, whether festival or military. Thus it is not so much the *content* as the *frame* of the situation that promotes revolution. While shared cultural connotations also played an important role in directing collective action, the most fundamental driver of revolutionary mobility in such scenarios was the opportunity created by the space itself. This finding holds important implications for our understanding of the "politics of Greek festivals," a topic that has received extensive study in recent years.

Oligarchies frequently collapsed following uprisings that began in the central spaces of the city. In chapter 4 we saw the examples of Rhodes, Sicyon, Tegea, Argos, Elis, and Mantinea.[7] These cases illustrate perfectly the *Rhetoric to Alexander*'s warning, examined in chapter 4, that the mob not be allowed to gather from the countryside into the city.[8] The author of the *Rhetoric* makes clear that there are in fact two steps to the process: first come the initial "meetings" (*sunodoi*), following which the masses "combine" (*sustrephetai*) and attack the oligarchy. Gatherings of the people do not necessarily start out politicized. Instead, I would argue that the members of the demos first require an opportunity to witness and thus collectively understand their shared antipathy to the ruling oligarchy. The bringing together of so many demotic bodies in one place provides a safe space in which citizens can air their grievances. This dialogue then allows the common people to overcome their previous disinclination to oppose the regime, which had characterized them when they were atomized and isolated. A concern to divide and therefore conquer the people was of course one of the primary drivers of oligarchic institutions, as we saw in chapters 3 through 5. The political tools of the elite served to engender problems of collective action and coordination among the populace, such that the individual members of the demos found it more rational to acquiesce to the ruling class than to risk their lives in collective resistance. The public spaces of the polis served as an open forum in and through which to solve these problems of group action.

From the above examples it is clear that the agora was an ideal location from which to launch a democratic uprising. Precisely how best to gather the people together in the first place was another question. In the cases of Rhodes, Sicyon, and Tegea, renegade members of the elite assemble the people. In Argos, Mantinea, and Elis, the common people spontaneously gather. There

---

7. See the references cited in section 4.2.
8. 1424b8–10.

were specific occasions, however, on which large numbers of people could be counted on to be in the city-center. Plato has Socrates list them in the course of a discussion on the contexts considered mostly likely to lead to trouble between rulers and ruled in an oligarchy: "On journeys or in other kinds of joint ventures, during spectacles (*theōriai*) or on military campaign (*strateia*), when they sail together or are fellow soldiers."[9] It is in these situations, Socrates explains, that the excluded poor realize to what extent they outnumber the ruling few. Moreover, they not only witness the comparative weakness of the oligarchy, but they are able—thanks to the public forum—to see that the observation is shared by their fellow common people. In the course of the gathering, the demos begins to comprehend, and thus to act upon, its own strength. From there, Socrates explains, all the "sick body" of the polis needs to fall into outright *stasis* is a "tiny imbalance" (*mikra rhopē*, 556e). Plato was right. As I now show, "spectacles" like civic festivals and military contexts like armed reviews proved equally good opportunities for attacking oligarchic regimes. Moreover, in stressing the role of "tiny imbalances" in initiating *stasis*, Plato got the means as well as the contexts of oligarchic downfall correct. As contemporary political scientists have observed, sometimes an individual act of courage or outspokenness, if carried out in the right circumstances, is all that is required to precipitate a wave of collective action sufficient to bring down an authoritarian regime.

6.1.1 Festivals

I begin with festivals, which were already identified in antiquity as potentially dangerous sites of civil disturbance. As Aeneas Tacticus puts it, "those plotting a revolution very often make their attempt during festivals [*heortai*]" (22.17).[10] It was already understood in antiquity that festivals were disproportionately dangerous for certain kinds of regime, the most commonly cited being tyrannies. In Xenophon's dialogue *Hiero*, the Sicilian tyrant tells the poet Simonides that "it is not safe for [tyrants] to go where they will not be stronger than those present." He explicitly mentions *theōriai*, spectacle events.[11] As an illustration we might cite the defacement of Dionysius of Syracuse's tents at the Olympics, supposedly at the orator Lysias's instigation.[12] The third-century

---

9. *Rep.* 8.556c: ἢ ἐν ὁδῶν πορείαις ἢ ἐν ἄλλαις τισὶ κοινωνίαις, ἢ κατὰ θεωρίας ἢ κατὰ στρατείας, ἢ σύμπλοι γιγνόμενοι ἢ συστρατιῶται.

10. Cf. 17.1, where Aeneas, like Plato above, pairs festivals with armed processions as sites of likely unrest.

11. *Hier.* 1.12.

12. Diod. Sic. 14.109.1–6; cf. Lys. 33. Dionysius himself remained at Syracuse, but we can

tyrant Aristodemus of Argos, says Plutarch, slept with his bed barring the only entrance to his bedroom—how much more, then, must he have shuddered at the thought of the theater and the political meeting places.[13] In fact, we know of several instances where tyrants were murdered at festivals: Hipparchus of Athens is perhaps the most famous example (see further below), but we can also list Aristodemus of Cyme, Clearchus of Heraclea Pontica, and (should we choose to label him a tyrant) Philip II of Macedon.[14]

Did Classical oligarchs face similar dangers at festivals? We have already seen (chapter 5) that rituals, sacrifices, processions, and similar civic-religious events represented both opportunities and risks for oligarchic governments. On the one hand, they were excellent contexts in which to stage regime-affirming messages, which served to dissuade potential revolutionaries from taking action. As I noted earlier, however, there was a concomitant danger that a festival might be used as a facilitator for a democratic uprising. It depended upon the willingness of enterprising individuals to utilize the informational dynamics afforded by the public context of the festival to advertise the fact that a revolt was now underway. If they successfully managed to propagate their message, there was a good chance that those observing others' positive responses to the invitation would join in bringing down the oligarchy.[15]

The template for this kind of insurrectionary act is the assassination of Hipparchus of Athens as described by Thucydides.[16] The earliest sources on the killing of the Peisistratid ruler, the Attic skolia or drinking songs, already inform us that the murder took place at the Panathenaea, "the sacrifices of Athena."[17] Herodotus likewise mentions the festival context but does not spell out the plan of the tyrannicides, Harmodius and Aristogeiton, in detail.[18]

---

easily imagine that violence might have been attempted on him had he actually attended the games.

13. *Mor.* 781e.

14. Hipparchus: Hdt. 5.55–62; Thuc. 6.54–58; [Arist.] *Ath. Pol.* 18.2–6. Aristodemus of Cyme: Dion. Hal. *Ant. Rom.* 7.11.3–4. Clearchus: Memnon *FGrH* 434 F 1 (though Justin says simply that he was killed in his citadel: 16.5.15). Philip: Arist. *Pol.* 5.1311b2–3, Diod. Sic. 16.93.3–94.3. A failed attempt was made on Mausolus of Caria's life at the festival of Zeus Lambraundos: RO 54, lines 33–38. For the deaths of tyrants, see Riess 2006; Luraghi 2013b.

15. Teegarden wonders whether the Erythraean oligarchy of the early third century "sought to atomize the population by having few festivals" (2014: 152). This section suggests that he was on to something about oligarchic regimes more generally.

16. For a discussion of how this episode helps to explain the Rhodian democratic uprising of 395 (*Hell. Oxy.* 18.1–3 Chambers), see Simonton 2015.

17. Athen. 15.695b = *PMG* 895.

18. 5.56.2.

It is Thucydides who gives us the most intricate and rationalizing account of the murder.[19] Notoriously, he also attempts to denigrate the motives of the participants and deflate their importance, calling the whole affair a "romantic mishap."[20] Yet despite Thucydides's cynical reading of the episode, certain details of his account seem to represent an attempt by the author to make sense of the legend using language culled from the political struggles of his own day. While he would prefer to label it a farce, Thucydides cannot help but explain certain undeniable facts of the tale in terms of strategy and rationality. These elements of the story, I suggest, point to contemporary democrats' exploitation of festival events as arenas for common knowledge and coordination.

Thucydides initially does his best to make both the Athenians and the tyrannicides themselves appear far from heroic, even shabby. The tyrannicides' plan evolved following Hipparchus's sexual attempt upon Harmodius. Harmodius reported the incident to Aristogeiton, who, "feeling a lover's anguish and fearing the power [*dunamis*] of Hipparchus to take away [Harmodius] by force, immediately began plotting for a dissolution of the tyranny based on his present social standing [*axiōsis*]."[21] There are two points to note here. First, Hipparchus's "power" stems from his familiar relationship with the tyrant, such that, were he a private citizen, the dispute might have been resolved by other means. Since he does enjoy a powerful political position in the polis, however, Aristogeiton must deal with this fact. He and Harmodius thus decide to attack Hippias himself, the source of Hipparchus's power, so as to cut out the root of the problem. The second point to note is Thucydides's mention of Aristogeiton's *axiōsis*, his "influence" or "social standing." The author had already noted Aristogeiton's status as a *mesos politēs*, a "middle citizen," at 6.54.2.[22] Now that he has entered into a dangerous situation from which political assassination appears the only feasible means of escape, Aristogeiton must kill a tyrant, but he must do it from the position of an ordinary citizen, an even greater challenge. By drawing attention to Aristogeiton's *axiōsis*, Thucydides signals that the plot to follow will exemplify the asymmetrical social and

---

19. For the significance of the story for the larger structural arc of Thucydides's narrative, see Connor 1984: 176–80; Rood 1998: 180–82; Meyer 2008. For the act, as described by Thucydides, as a paradigm for acts of tyrannicide more generally, see Taylor 1991; Raaflaub 2003: 63–70; Ober 2003; Anderson 2003: 199–206; Teegarden 2014: 32–34; Azoulay 2014.

20. 6.54.1 (*erōtikē xuntuchia*).

21. 6.54.3.

22. Davidson (2006) suggests that *mesos* designates age group rather than social status, and while we should think of Aristogeiton as being older than Harmodius, Thucydides is also contrasting their status, as his use of *axiōsis* shortly afterward confirms.

political relationship he has posited between the Peisistratids and the tyrannicides. Thus we ought to think of the conspiracy as a paradigm of how weaker, socially "inferior" political actors could expect to succeed against a narrower, more entrenched opponent.

Thucydides's description of the actual plan helps to make the foregoing argument clear, and so deserves a close reading:

> They were waiting for the Great Panathenaea, the one day when it was not considered suspicious for the citizens to gather together in arms, as long as they were taking part in the procession. The plan called for [Harmodius and Aristogeiton] to begin the attack, while the others would immediately join in fending off the bodyguards. Out of concern for security, there were not many conspirators; but they hoped, you see, that if they, even being so few in number, made a bold move [*tolmēseian*], those not in on the plot to begin with, who were in possession of weapons, after all, would immediately want to join in freeing themselves [*xuneleutheroun*].[23]

The strategic logic of common knowledge and coordination here is impeccable. The festival setting provides an opportunity to gain easy access to the ruler, and the ability of citizens to carry arms boosts the conspirators' prospects of success. Initially, the plot does not require a particularly large group of insiders. The expectation is that the show of daring in a public space, with many onlookers simultaneously in view of one another, will tap the latent resentment of the individual members of the crowd against the Peisistratid regime. Thucydides's description implies a situation in which each procession participant sees the act, knows that all the others have seen it as well, and can therefore join in the attack with the knowledge that others will in all likelihood support him. It is when they share common knowledge of the act of tyrannicide that all can be said to want to participate in the liberation.

Of course, the plan failed horribly in the event. Harmodius was killed immediately, and Aristogeiton was captured, tortured, and eventually killed.[24] Based purely on the way he has described the situation, however, not even Thucydides can claim to know that the plot was inevitably doomed to failure, or that the conspirators were wrong in their assessment of their fellow citizens' discontent. The plan is foiled when one of the group appears to inform

---

23. 6.56.2–3: περιέμενον δὲ Παναθήναια τὰ μεγάλα, ἐν ᾗ μόνον ἡμέρᾳ οὐχ ὕποπτον ἐγίγνετο ἐν ὅπλοις τῶν πολιτῶν τοὺς τὴν πομπὴν πέμψοντας ἀθρόους γενέσθαι· καὶ ἔδει ἄρξαι μὲν αὐτούς, ξυνεπαμύνειν δὲ εὐθὺς τὰ πρὸς τοὺς δορυφόρους ἐκείνους. ἦσαν δὲ οὐ πολλοὶ οἱ ξυνομωμοκότες ἀσφαλείας ἕνεκα· ἤλπιζον γὰρ καὶ τοὺς μὴ προειδότας, εἰ καὶ ὁποσοιοῦν τολμήσειαν, ἐκ τοῦ παραχρῆμα ἔχοντάς γε ὅπλα ἐθελήσειν σφᾶς αὐτοὺς ξυνελευθεροῦν.

24. Thuc. 6.57.4. [Arist.] *Ath. Pol.* 18.4–6 reports competing narratives about Aristogeiton's death.

on the plot to Hipparchus. Had the original scheme gone as planned, there is no telling how the armed members of the procession would have reacted.[25] Furthermore, since the citizens were disarmed by Hippias before they heard about Hipparchus's murder, they were in no position to attempt a revolution when the news was disclosed. As Rhodes has noted, Thucydides "protests too much" in his caustic treatment of the tyrannicides, which actually allows for many more possibilities than he seems willing to countenance.[26]

Thucydides thus gives us a textbook description of the use of common knowledge generated by festivals as a coordinating device for popular action against a narrow regime.[27] We can now compare Thucydides's paradigm with a later, explicitly oligarchic example. It will emerge that the story Thucydides pieced together through inference was likely based upon political struggles of his own time.

Both Xenophon and Diodorus inform us of a bloody episode of *stasis* that took place in Corinth in the middle of the Corinthian War, probably in 393.[28]

---

25. For informing as a means of preventing pro-democratic revolutions, see chapter 3, section 3.4.

26. Rhodes in Hammond 2009, note *ad* 6.53.3. See also Hornblower in his commentary *ad* 6.54.3: "[Thucydides] here suggests an ideological motive was present after all."

27. I reserve for a footnote another example, that of the Partheniae's attempted *coup* against Sparta, as described by a fragment of the lost historian Antiochus of Syracuse (*FGrH* 555 F 13 = Strabo 6.3.2; Antiochus was writing at the time of Thucydides, in the late fifth century, and may in fact have served as one of the latter's sources for his excursus on Sicily). Antiochus describes the aftermath of the First Messenian War in the eighth century: the children of those born to non-participants in the war were called Partheniae (literally "virgin-children") and were deprived of citizen rights at Sparta. "Being numerous" (*polloi*), they plotted against the full citizenry. The uprising was to take place at the festival of the Hyacinthia, in Amyclae, and the signal was to be when the ringleader (*prostatēs*) of the group, Phalanthus, put on his leather cap (*kunē*). Once again, a festival setting is put in the service of coordinating a large-scale attack on a small ruling elite. Phalanthus, however, had turned informer and alerted the Spartan authorities to the plot. They therefore have the herald (*kērux*) come forward during the festival and publicly forbid Phalanthus from donning his cap. The conspirators are thereby alerted to the fact that the plot is foiled and give themselves up. The story closely resembles that of the conspiracy of Cinadon as related by Xenophon (*Hell.* 3.3.4–11; Arist. *Pol.* 5.1306b34–36; Polyaen. *Strat.* 2.14.1 with David 1979; Hamilton 1979: 125–28; Cartledge 1987: 233–35; Lazenby 1997; Gish 2009). That, too, was a situation in which a small number of conspirators (3.3.6) hoped to spark a general uprising of the lower orders against the ruling class. Note especially the detail that within the agora it was possible to see that the helots, perioikoi, and other subordinate classes outnumbered the Spartiates 100-to-1 (3.3.5): this suggests that it would have been quite easy to launch a general uprising against the regime from within the marketplace, in line with what we have examined above.

28. Xen. *Hell.* 4.4.1–13; Diod. Sic. 14.86. For earlier treatments, see Griffith 1950; Kagan 1962;

While it is clear that a general slaughter took place on the last day of the festival of Artemis Euclea, there is little agreement among scholars as to the political ideology of the chief participants, or of the ensuing constitutional ramifications of the massacre. This uncertainty is due in large part to the fact that Xenophon never uses explicit political language (e.g., *dēmokratia* or *oligarchia*) in describing the *stasis*. Furthermore, the text of Diodorus has been made to mention democracy only through an influential emendation of Wurm, which cannot ultimately stand.[29] Yet even if Diodorus's text supplies no direct testimony for democracy, there is sufficient evidence outside of his wording to suggest that many members of the wider Corinthian demos took part in the festival massacre and that its ultimate result was democratic government in Corinth.

The most parsimonious and coherent reading of Xenophon's description of the civil war is that a minority of those within Corinth's governing oligarchy, sensing that they would soon be unable to sustain their anti-Spartan policy through the usual constitutional channels, were willing to turn to the Corinthian demos and acquiesce to the establishment of a democracy in order to secure their desired ends. To do so they hatched a plot to effect a general rout of the ruling majority during the festival of Artemis Euclea.[30] If the present argument is correct that festivals were excellent opportunities for the demos to coordinate against an oligarchic regime, the revolutionaries' plan makes good sense. They staged a democratic-style uprising, which they correctly supposed would meet with popular enthusiasm, in order to overpower opponents whom they would be ineffectual at removing by themselves.[31]

To understand the constitutional impasse faced by the conspirators, we first need to grasp the nature of the early-fourth-century Corinthian oligarchy. Salmon has reconstructed the constitution insofar as this is possible.[32] It is

---

Hamilton 1979: ch. 9; Tuplin 1982; Whitby 1984; Salmon 1984: 354–62; Gehrke *Stasis* 82–87; Cartledge 1987: 255–57; Robinson 2011: 22–23.

29. At 14.86.1, the corrupt τινὲς τῶν ἐπιθυμίᾳ κρατούντων, "certain of those in power due to desire," was emended by Wurm to read τινὲς τῶν ἐπιθυμούντων δημοκρατίας, "certain of those desiring democracy." This reading was accepted by Hamilton 1979: 267 and Gehrke *Stasis* 83n9. Wurm's solution, however, begs the question of whether the conspirators actually desired democracy, and cannot be used as evidence that the uprising was democratic in nature (Salmon 1984: 355). Buckler (1999: 211) suggests τινὲς τῶν ἐπιθυμούντων κράτους, "certain of those desiring power."

30. For the cult, see Plut. *Arist.* 20.6; Paus. 1.14.5; *SEG* 33.556. It may be significant that Euclea is paired with Eunomia in Bacchyl. 13.183–86; see further below.

31. For further instances of oligarchic defection in which part of the ruling class attacks the other, see below, section 6.2.3.

32. 1984: 231–39.

likely that there was a pool of candidates, determined by a high property census, who filled the magistracies and the authoritative political bodies, including the eight *probouloi* (advisors) and the *boulē* (council) of seventy-two (and the *gerousia* [council of elders], if this was a distinct institution); the assembly was probably open to all but was weak and rarely utilized.[33] It was in this complex of political institutions that the following disagreements emerged: We read in Xenophon of two Corinthians, Timolaus and Polyanthes, who were part of a larger group of leading statesmen from the major poleis who took money from the Persian King in 396/5 in order to start a war with Sparta.[34] The Oxyrhynchus historian likewise mentions them (*Hell. Oxy.* 10.2–3 Chambers) and notes further than Timolaus was hostile to Sparta on personal grounds despite his previous Laconophilia. The author calls Timolaus one of those Corinthians "seeking to change *ta pragmata*," and while some scholars have interpreted this as a reference to a faction at Corinth in favor of democracy, the "policies" (*pragmata*) in question clearly refer to Corinth's policy of peace toward Sparta.[35] Timolaus, Polyanthes, and people who shared their policy preferences got their way through the usual constitutional channels in Corinth and (following the Battle of Haliartus, in which the Corinthians took no part) established a common council of themselves, the Argives, the Boeotians, and the Athenians.[36]

Next we read that in the aftermath of the Battle of Nemea in 394 the Corinthian survivors and their allies were shut out of the city by those inside. Demosthenes adds that the Corinthians in the city intended to make peace overtures to the Spartans, but that those outside somehow forced them to open the gates.[37] This act marks the first indication of serious internal dissension and probably put the prowar contingent within Corinth on alert that their reigning political coalition was in danger.

Following the Battle of Coronea later in 394, we get Xenophon's description of the Corinthians' "change of heart." They "saw their own land being

---

33. For possible manipulation of the assembly by Corinthian oligarchs, see the reconstruction above in chapter 3, section 3.2.

34. Xen. *Hell.* 3.5.1. Paus. 3.9.8 says they "favored Argos's interests," a factor not related elsewhere but which strengthens the thesis that some sort of political alliance or unification with Argos was considered before the revolution of 393.

35. Bruce 1967 *ad loc.*, McKechnie and Kern 1988 *ad loc.*, Gehrke *Stasis* 83n9, and Robinson 2011: 23 all think the language means "favored democracy," but it is safer and less question-begging to assume that the decision to remain at peace with Sparta or declare war was at first purely a matter of policy difference within the Corinthian oligarchy: cf. Buckler 1999: 211 (though I disagree with him on several other points of interpretation); Perlman 1964: 68–69.

36. Diod. Sic. 14.82.2; Polyaen. *Strat.* 1.48.3.

37. Xen. *Hell.* 4.2.23; Dem. 20.52–53.

ravaged and people dying through their constant close proximity to the enemy, while the other allies were at peace and their fields were being worked." Therefore "the majority (*pleistoi*) of them, who were the outstanding citizens (*beltistoi*), came to desire peace" (*Hell.* 4.4.1). Previous treatments have expressed perplexity at the identification of this group. The grammatical construction implies not two separate groups ("both the majority and also the best Corinthians"), but a hendiadys pointing to one group with both characteristics ("the majority who were the best"). Kagan and Hamilton postulate the existence of a land-owning "aristocratic party," whose numbers Xenophon inflates for ideological reasons. These *beltistoi* are to be distinguished from the other members of the ruling oligarchy, who were wealthy traders and in favor of war with Sparta.[38] Kagan and Hamilton are right that *pleistoi* describes members of the oligarchy itself rather than the population as a whole, but it is probably not an exaggeration, nor does it pick out a readily identifiable "aristocratic" party. Instead, it means that a majority of the ruling oligarchy, which previously had been persuaded by Timolaus, was now swinging back toward a peaceful position. The hardcore peace contingent was prevailing upon those they saw as potential allies to join with them and change Corinthian policy, and the recent failures at Nemea and Coronea no doubt provided them with strong arguments.[39] Xenophon calls the newly emerging majority *hoi beltistoi* not because they represented the most traditional, conservative, landowning element of the state, but because they took a pro-Spartan line; he is paying a compliment in hindsight to those who took the "best" stance. The entire struggle takes place within Corinth's traditional ruling oligarchy, and there is no need to introduce any sort of "party" system, least of all a "democratic party."

What happened next, however, requires careful unpacking. Xenophon tells us that the Argives, Athenians, Boeotians, and Corinthians "who took money from the King" realized that unless they eliminated those who were turning to a policy of peace, the city was in danger of again favoring the Spartans (lit. "laconizing," 4.4.2). It seems that Timolaus was so devoted to his policy of war that he would rather kill his political opponents than suffer a reversal. He might have feared future recriminations against himself for initiating the war policy in the first place. Xenophon calls the plot concocted by him and the other anti-Spartan politicians "the most sacrilegious of all": "For other people, even if a person is condemned by law, do not execute him on a festival day. But those men chose the last day of the Euclea, because they thought they would catch and kill more people in the agora."[40] According to Xenophon, the con-

---

38. Kagan 1962: 450–51; Hamilton 1979: 262–66.

39. Cf. Buckler 1999: 213.

40. *Hell.* 4.4.2. Diodorus, if we accept Buckler's emendation, similarly says, "In Corinth

spirators chose the festival day purely out of concern for the greater numbers they would be able to kill. Yet as we have seen, considerations of surprise, publicity, the creation of common knowledge, and the potential spontaneous coordination of large numbers of onlookers in the agora could also have factored into the decision. Xenophon declines to say whether any outsiders joined in the massacre (he may have found the participation of the demos distasteful), but he does say *hoi beltistoi* fled the city *en masse*, by which he probably means the pro-peace majority within the ruling oligarchy.[41] The anti-Spartan members of the Corinthian elite then (on this reading) remained in the city and promoted themselves as the people's champions.

Whatever the precise details, what seems undeniable is that Corinth, as part of the greater state of democratic Argos, then became a democracy. The strongest evidence comes from Xenophon's description of the *beltistoi* who were persuaded to return to the city after the slaughter. These men

> [s]aw [those in power] acting as tyrants, and when they realized that the polis was disappearing through the removal of the boundary-stones [*horoi*] and Argos was being called their fatherland instead of Corinth, and when they were forced to partake in the constitution [*politeia*] of Argos, which they didn't want, and had less power in the polis than metics, there were some of them who thought this state of affairs was unlivable. They thought that if they tried to make their fatherland Corinth again, as it had been from the beginning, and to establish it as free and purged of the accursed murderers, and to make it enjoy good government [*eunomia*], it would be a worthy endeavor. (4.4.6)

The recently returned exiles complain that the rulers are tyrants, but this cannot literally be true.[42] They hyperbolically bewail their status as inferior to that of metics, but this means only that they had lost the prominence they once enjoyed and now had to be counted on an equal basis with members of the

---

those desiring power banded together and effected a slaughter when contests were being held in the theater, and they filled the city with civil war" (14.86.1). For Xenophon's "piety" in his treatment of this episode, see Pownall 1998: 254–55, with good comments about the politics of festivals at n16.

41. See further the discussion in chapter 1, section 1.2, about the total number of oligarchs within the Corinthian ruling group.

42. Oligarchs often described democrats and democratic constitutions as "tyrannical," in the sense that they forced oligarchs to do what they did not want to do: see Xen. *Mem*. 1.2.40–46 and Xenophon's treatment of Euphron of Sicyon, discussed by Lewis 2004. It is important to note that it is certain that Argos was a democracy at this time: see Robinson 2011: 6–21. If Corinthians were forced to "partake in the Argive constitution," then they were partaking in a democracy. Robinson agrees that they became a democracy: 2011: 22–25.

demos.⁴³ Most obviously, they wish to return Corinth to a state of *eunomia*, that consummately oligarchic rallying cry. Since the city was not a tyranny or *dunasteia*, this must mean it was now a democracy.⁴⁴

Given what we know about the democratic outcome of the Corinthian festival revolt, we can now return to the event itself and see how it does appear to be the work of men who felt they had to initiate a democracy. As with the Athenian tyrannicides, it began with a relatively small group of conspirators, with the majority population kept in the dark. The uprising appears to have grown so great, however, that the oligarchs led by Pasimelus on Acrocorinth decide not to attack those in the city but instead go into exile.⁴⁵ It is therefore highly likely that Timolaus and the other conspiratorial insiders thought they could count on the widespread support of the Corinthian demos in an attack against the most visibly pro-Spartan members of the oligarchy, and they calculated that one of the most efficacious ways of accomplishing this would be to make their move during a public gathering like the Euclea festival.⁴⁶ The incident at the Corinthian Euclea thus suggests a pattern of democratic action against tyrannical and oligarchic regimes devised for public festival settings. The initial murder of prominent pro-Spartan members of the Corinthian oligarchic regime served as the flashpoint of common knowledge that sparked the ensuing popular attack and establishment of a democratic regime. Even though the chief perpetrators were not themselves ideological democrats but only reluctant, pragmatic ones, they understood well enough the strategic advantages afforded by the dense crowds, high levels of publicity, and direct access to political figures that characterized the celebration of the goddess.⁴⁷

---

43. They do not mean that they have been excluded from government and literally have less power than the metics living in Corinth (for which meaning we should expect the definite article with metics, "the metics"), but that they now practically have less power than metics generally, in any Greek city. On this point I disagree with Robinson 2011: 22, 24.

44. Salmon (1984: 355) admits that "the word has a strong oligarchic flavor" but claims that "it shows only that those who used it were oligarchs." However, there had to be some constitutional regime against which they were employing the term.

45. *Hell.* 4.4.5. This same Pasimelus later conspired with the Spartan polemarch Praxitas to bring a Spartan contingent into the harbor of Lechaeum (4.4.7). He is also later found serving as an intermediary between Euphron of Sicyon and the Spartans (7.3.2). He was probably a Laconophile even before the events of 393.

46. Timolaus and company almost certainly received advice from the Athenians, Argives, and Boeotians on how best to carry out the massacre (Xen. *Hell.* 4.4.2). Might the Athenians have told them the story of Harmodius and Aristogeiton at the Panathenaea?

47. The episode also serves as a nice illustration of the fact that festivals, far from rigidly determining social order in a mechanistic, functionalist way, represented *opportunities* for competing political groups, which could be harnessed for both stabilizing and revolutionary pur-

Xenophon may have decried their impiety, but this was neither the first nor the last time a festival provided the setting for democratic political upheaval.[48]

6.1.2 Military Settings

Along with "spectacles" (*theōriai*), Plato names "military campaigns" (*strateiai*) as a setting where rulers and ruled in an oligarchy are likely to encounter one another.[49] Martial contexts like army camps, military reviews, and processions could serve, like festivals, as venues of common knowledge where citizens could quickly and effectively coordinate their action. Contributing to the possibility of such mass movements was the fact that the typical Greek army of the Classical period was much more unstructured and egalitarian than the professional military forces of the present day. The Greek state had little to no monopoly on violence and could not hope to discipline the armed forces through pure repression, and so military relations were largely voluntaristic. The roughly equal capacities of individual Greek troops, coupled with the aforementioned egalitarian ethos and the weak sanctioning power of centralized authorities, made the military campaign a potential testing ground for intra-polis sociopolitical tensions.[50]

---

poses. Corinth was famous for its musical culture, its *mousikē*, and scholars have pointed to its use of choreia and Dionysiac ritual to maintain stability within the oligarchy (Wilson 2003; Fisher 2010: 87). Pindar's thirteenth Olympian ode, for Xenophon of Corinth (no relation to the historian), proudly proclaims the city's affiliation with personified Eunomia (line 6), an oligarchic catchword. The revolution of 393 turned the tables on all this.

48. For a further instance of democratic attacks on non-democratic regimes during a festival, see Hippias of Erythrae *FGrH* 421 F 1 (describing, admittedly, the early Archaic period, but heavily influenced by contemporary—late fourth/early third century—language): Hippotes, the brother of the murdered king Cnopus, returns to Erythrae from exile *during a festival* (*heortēs ousēs*) and, with the rest of the Erythraeans assisting him, kills the tyrants who have taken over the city. (Note that the tyrants had themselves taken over the city during a festival, that of Artemis Strophaea. A cynical reader might assume that both sides in the *stasis* use festivals as it suits their interests. However, the two parties take advantage of festivals in distinctive ways: the tyrants use an extra-mural festival as an opportunity to seize the city while the demos is outside the walls; Hippotes uses what is presumably an intra-mural festival, with the populace gathered *en masse*, as a means of attacking the tyrants. The relative popularity and numbers of each side determine *how* they utilize festivals.) See further Simonton forthcoming.

49. *Rep.* 8.556c.

50. For the egalitarianism of Greek armies, see Pritchett 1971–79 vol. 2, chapter 12; van Wees 2004: 108–13, 2007; Hunt 2007: 127–32; Hornblower 2004b. Greek armies, such as Xenophon's Ten Thousand in the *Anabasis*, have sometimes been compared to miniature poleis, but Lee

"Potential" is the operative term here, since other factors simultaneously worked to mitigate against the likelihood of outright mutiny or political revolt. From Homer to Thucydides, figures appear warning that political dissension plays directly into opponents' wishes.[51] Faced with the existential threat of military defeat, soldiers on the march understandably tended to obey their superiors and maintain discipline. Of course, home governments still had to face grievances when armies returned home to the polis, and Gehrke has identified the time immediately following battle as the primary context for episodes of *stasis*. Yet revolutionary situations could also arise on campaign itself. Marches, sieges, and troop reviews frequently provided the stage for popular political movements to attack reigning oligarchic regimes.

Consider first the famous incident of the Mytilinean demos's mutiny during the Athenian siege of 427. According to Thucydides, the city was running out of food, and the Spartan commander Salaethus, when he no longer expected reinforcements to arrive, "armed the demos which had previously been unarmed [or 'lightly armed'—*psilos*]" with the intention that they would fight the Athenians. Instead, the members of the demos refused to obey their commanders, gathered in informal assemblies (*kata xullogous . . . gignomenoi*), and demanded that the "powerful" (*dunatoi*) openly produce the remaining food and distribute it to all. The *dunatoi*, realizing that they were powerless, entered into an agreement with the Athenian general Paches rather than face internal subversion.[52] Some scholars have refused to see any sort of deep-seated sociopolitical tensions at play in the situation. They assume that the demos's grievances are based exclusively on the food shortage and that, had this issue been honestly dealt with from the beginning, the demos might have "continued" to support Mytilene's ruling oligarchy.[53] However, several features of the narrative point to internal tension, especially the refusal of the oligarchs to arm the demos up to this point.[54] It may in fact be that they were not so poor as to not

---

(2007: 9–11) gives good reasons for qualifying this view. I prefer to think, not that armies functioned consistently like poleis, but that they sometimes provided opportunities for political, indeed sometimes democratic, decision-making and collective action.

51. See Nestor's lament at Hom. *Il*. 1.255–58 that "Priam and the sons of Priam and the other Trojans would rejoice" seeing the Achaeans at odds. In Thucydides, one Thucydides of Pharsalus (Pharsalus's *proxenos* or "foreign consul" in Athens) warns the oligarchs of the Four Hundred not to "destroy their fatherland" through *stasis* when the enemy were watching and waiting nearby (8.92.8).

52. Thuc. 3.27.1–28.1.

53. See, e.g., Bradeen 1960; Andrewes 1962: 78 (but disagreeing with Bradeen's overall argument at n34); Quinn 1971. Hornblower in his commentary favors these views over those of de Ste. Croix 1954, 1972: 40–41, 1981: 603–4 with n26; and Gillis 1971.

54. De Ste. Croix 1972: 40–41.

possess arms but had been intentionally deprived of their weapons by the oligarchs during the siege.[55] Such an act would suggest relations of extreme mistrust between rulers and ruled in Mytilene.

The sequence of events at Mytilene points to processes of common knowledge and coordination along the lines of those outlined above. Salaethus's "arming" of the demos probably took place in the open and at the general invitation of the Spartan commander and the other authorities (*archontes*), 3.27.3), rather than by private, individual summonses. This, for example, is how Xenophon's Cyrus arms the Persian lower classes: he places the arms "in the open" (*eis to meson*) and "calls together" (*sunkalesas*) all the Persians to be armed.[56] In the Mytilenean case, a general arming assembly also makes sense as the most convenient opportunity for Salaethus to give the demos their marching orders ("so that they march out against the Athenians," 3.27.2). If, then, we are to imagine the arming of the Mytilenean demos as a public call-up of troops, it would represent an instance of mass assembly and common knowledge. The members of the demos would not only individually be in possession of arms, they would see each other armed and furthermore know that everyone else was similarly aware of their combined numbers and power. If they were dissatisfied with the policies of the oligarchy but had been previously too disorganized to act in opposition, it is no wonder that they now spontaneously refuse to obey and initiate a serious of impromptu meetings (*xullogoi*, 3.27.3).[57]

Thucydides gives us another vivid picture of a military force revolting along these lines in his description of the Athenian fleet at Samos during the reign of the Four Hundred. The fleet had first been stunned into submission by the unexpected news that they would receive money from the Persian King if they recalled Alcibiades and altered the constitution from democracy to

---

55. Gillis 1971: 43–44; Wilson 1981: 146–48; Lavelle 1989: 39.

56. Xenophon's language recalls instances of democratization: in Herodotus, Maeandrius of Samos, having inherited power from the tyrant Polycrates, gathers (*sunageiras*) an assembly of all the Samians and announces, "I set power in the middle (*es meson*) and proclaim equality (*isonomia*) to you" (3.142.2–3; cf. Cadmus of Cos at 7.164.1). Similarly, Euphron of Sicyon "calls together" (*sunekalei*) the demos in the agora, the physical and symbolic "middle space" of the polis, to proclaim "fair and equal" shares for them (Xen. *Hell.* 7.1.45).

57. Such assemblies are a common feature of politically charged mutinies. In 404/3, Dionysius the tyrant of Syracuse attempted a siege of the city of Herbessus, but when his soldiers gained possession of arms, they gathered in groups (*sustaseis*) and began to mutiny (Diod. Sic. 14.7.6). In 411 the common soldiers of the Peloponnesian army as well as some of the officers "gather in groups" (*xunistamenoi kat' allēlous*) to discuss their missing pay (Thuc. 8.83.3). When the Spartan commander Astyochus raises his stick at their leader Dorieus of Rhodes, the mass of the soldiers, "as sailors are wont to do," are furious and rush at Astyochus as though to strike him down (84.2–3); cf. the case of Polydamidas in Mende, discussed in detail below.

oligarchy. "And the crowd," says Thucydides, "even if they were immediately incensed at what was being done, kept quiet, taking the easy path of holding out hope for wages from the King."[58] Later, however, the demos surges back into action through an act of joint resistance against an attempted oligarchic *coup* on Samos. Some prominent Athenians, Leon, Diomedon, Thrasyboulus, and Thrasyllus, go around to each of the soldiers individually and beg them not to give way in the event of an attack. The result is that everyone they contact comes to their aid when the Samian oligarchs attempt their counter-*coup*.[59] Even after an oath not to abandon the democracy, however, the troops are still suspicious of subversive oligarchic activity.[60] They therefore convene an assembly where they depose the former generals and trierarchs and elect new ones, and in general take turns standing and encouraging the assembled group.[61] Thucydides appears to be presenting us with an instance of institutional learning. Whereas at first the assembled troops do not use their superior numbers to oppose the turn to oligarchy, they later come to see that they can more decisively defeat oligarchy through frequent assemblies where common knowledge of their united commitment to democracy is constantly maintained. Later the troops become so emboldened that they threaten to kill "the destroyers of democracy" (i.e., the envoys sent by the Four Hundred) and are restrained only by the intervention of Alcibiades.[62] The military assembly has become a democratic hothouse.

It might be objected that while the examples just discussed do indeed illustrate the danger posed by some military assemblies to oligarchic regimes, they cannot necessarily be generalized so as to apply to all cases of military assembly. This is because a) the Mytilenean demos and the Athenian fleet represent the unarmed, thetic class of citizens and are therefore the most dedi-

---

58. 8.48.3. Taylor, in a strongly revisionist assessment of the oligarchic *coup* (2002), claims that this passage shows that the "mass of men cares ... only about pay" (95) and that they do not "perceive [democracy] to hold many benefits for them" (96). These statements ignore the fact that Thucydides says the men were upset. *Pace* Taylor, we should countenance other possible explanations for the soldiers' inaction, for example the "fear combined with hope of future reversal" ascribed by Thucydides to the Athenians in the city at 8.54.1. As the present study shows, oligarchs relied heavily on such moments of confusion and collective acquiescence in order to divide and weaken the demos. For additional arguments against Taylor's position, see Bearzot 2006: 53–54; Teegarden 2014: 24–25n21.

59. 8.73.5–6.

60. Oaths: 8.75.3. They swear that they will "govern themselves democratically and remain of one mind [*homonoēsein*]." The terms prefigure those found in later oaths of reconciliation, e.g., *SEG* 30.1119; *Tit. Cal.* test. xvi; *SEG* 57.576; *IG* XII.4 1 132.

61. 8.76.2–3.

62. 8.86.2–5.

cated to democracy, while an assembly of members of the so-called "hoplite class" might be more sympathetic to oligarchy[63]; and/or b) the Athenian case is a special one, coming as it does from a city-state with a long, unique history of expanding democratic practice and ideology that is not typical of Greek poleis on the whole.[64]

While one should certainly not discount the importance of context and local history, however, these concerns seem largely misplaced. First, it is important to note that when Thucydides speaks of the pro-democratic elements among the fleet at Samos, he often includes the hoplite marines (*epibatai*) and even sometimes the lower-level officers. Thrasyllus "the hoplite" (*hopliteuonti*, 8.73.4) is in fact one of the primary leaders of the anti-oligarchic movement.[65] Second, and more important, we can point to instances in which hoplites (and non-Athenian hoplites, at that) defended democracy in broadly similar ways to their naval counterparts.[66] For example, the city of Mende in the Chalcidice was one of the subject states of the Athenian empire approached by Brasidas and enticed to revolt during his northern campaign. Specifically, Thucydides tells us that in 423 Mende defected, but that this act came at the instigation of a small number of conspirators within the city who forced the majority to go against its wishes.[67] This act of "forcing" also entailed a change of constitution, since we later learn that after the Athenian recovery of the city the Mendaeans were instructed to restore their customary constitution.[68] During the brief oligarchy, as the Athenians besiege the town, the Mendaeans at first take no action because of political discord within the city.[69] Eventually, however, the Spartan commander Polydamidas, on "loan" from the Spartans to the newly ascendant Mendaean oligarchs, draws up the Mendaean troops for battle and

63. See the remarks of Hornblower (2004b: 244), discussing the politics of the Ten Thousand in Xenophon's *Anabasis* and comparing them to a "broad-based oligarchy."

64. This position has been most vigorously argued for by Hanson 1995: ch. 9, 1996; cf. Strauss 1996 and Raaflaub 2007.

65. Hornblower *ad loc.* perceptively notes that Thucydides' designation of Thrasyllus as a hoplite "make[s] the point that the Athenian democratic movement on Samos was not just the work of the 'naval crowd.'"

66. Cf. chapter 1, section 1.2.2.

67. 4.123.2; cf. Gehrke *Stasis* 111–12. Hornblower *ad loc.* refers the reader to Connor 1984: 137n76, who asks whether the factionalism on view in Mende suggests less general enthusiasm for Brasidas in the cities of the Chalcidice than Thucydides lets on. For the act of "forcing" see chapter 3, section 3.2.

68. Such moments of "forcing" in foreign policy often came with constitutional changes: see Thuc. 3.71.1 (Corcyra); Aen. Tact. 11.13–15 (Corcyra on another occasion).

69. 4.130.1. Thucydides elsewhere explains inactivity as being due to *stasis* and mutual suspicion: cf. 8.63.2 (Athenians), 8.38.3 (Chians).

exhorts them to go out and fight.[70] At this point "one of the men from the demos" talks back to Polydamidas "in a spirit of faction" (*kata to stasiōtikon*), an act of insubordination that leads the Spartan to manhandle the speaker. "The demos," says Thucydides, "immediately took up their arms in anger (*periorgēs*) and attacked the Peloponnesians and the men who along with them had pursued an opposing policy."[71] The rout leads to the retreat of the oligarchs and Spartans and the admittance of the Athenians in Mende.

This extremely important passage reveals how a military review might serve as a sort of open forum in which actions transpire before the eyes of an engaged audience. Polydamidas, in a manner typical of a Spartan commander, does not understand the effect his violent actions might have on the observing crowd.[72] His act of hubris against a rank-and-file soldier becomes a matter of common knowledge, with all of the troops witnessing the abuse and knowing that the others have seen it as well. They therefore have the confidence to initiate an attack on their enemies: each soldier is assured that every other soldier, seeing the same outrageous behavior as he and being similarly infuriated, is willing to act simultaneously with the rest. The soldiers of the Mendaean demos thus spontaneously effect just the sort of response that Thucydides says Harmodius and Aristogeiton hoped would materialize when they appeared with swords drawn at the Panathenaea. Polydamidas's mistreatment of the soldier serves as the trigger that coordinates the actions of people who hitherto possessed no explicit plan of revolt.[73] Had the Mendaean oligarchs

---

70. 4.130.3. Note the similarities with the situation at Mytilene in 427, when Salaethus ordered the newly armed demos to march out against the Athenians (3.27.2). In this case, however, we are dealing with citizens who have always been hoplites, not newly armed poor men.

71. 4.130.4. Compare the situation in Archaic Naxos described by Aristotle (fr. 558 Rose), in which the demos, enraged, picks up their weapons and attacks members of the oligarchy who had abused one of their patrons. I discuss this example in greater detail below, section 6.2.2.

72. For this habit of Spartans see Hornblower 2000, who mentions *inter alia* Thuc. 3.93.2 (Spartan harshness at the new colony of Heraclea Trachinia), 8.84.2 (Astyochus and Dorieus, examined above). The Spartans learned this behavior in their treatment of helots and other subordinate groups in Lacedaemon. Hornblower seems to me to underappreciate, however, the extent to which the Spartan actions he catalogues interact with broader social and political structures, such as constitutional regimes.

73. Cf. the extremely similar incident described at Diod. Sic. 14.7.6–7, where newly armed Syracusan troops meet in groups and rebuke each other for not opposing Dionysius's tyranny. Their commander, the aptly named Doricus, threatens one of these "free-speaking men" (*parrhēsiazomenoi*), who then talks back, prompting a violent response from Doricus. The rest of the troops, "outraged" (*paroxuthentes*; cf. *periorgēs* at Thuc. 4.130.4), kill Doricus and rally the citizens to freedom. The similarity of this incident to that of Thucydides's Mendaeans shows once again the close connection between oligarchs and tyrants.

known of Polydamidas's intention in advance, they might have warned him against it: in striking a member of the common people, the Spartan was breaking one of the cardinal rules of oligarchy, not to abuse the demos in public. We see here, through a concrete historical example, the wisdom of Aristotle and the *Rhetoric to Alexander*'s warnings not to commit hubris against the people.[74] In Mende, oligarchic errors and the publicity of the troop assembly combined to spark a democratic uprising and the end of the oligarchy.

We possess additional evidence for thinking that oligarchs recognized the danger to their rule inherent in the military. The best illustration comes not from a work of history but from the odd text that is Xenophon's *Cyropaedia*. Despite its self-presentation as a "factual" account of the Persian King Cyrus's upbringing and reign, it contains didactic material, philosophy-inspired dialogue, explorations of political and military leadership, and an interest in what are clearly Greek social questions.[75] The episode that concerns us here comes early in the work, when Cyrus decides to arm the poor, agricultural Persian demos and thus make them equals of the elite "peers in honor" (*homotimoi*).[76] The initial arming goes without incident, but later, during a banquet of the commanding officers, the Persian leader Chrysantas raises the issue of the distribution of spoils and other honors.[77] "Some of us are better [*beltiones*], others are worthy of less [*meionos axioi*]," he says, "but if we are victorious, all of these men will think themselves worthy of enjoying equal shares [*isomoirein*]. And yet I consider nothing to be more unfair than the bad and the good obtaining equal results."[78] Chrysantas's concern turns on one of the oldest problems in Greek social and political thought, the question of desert. The notion figures into Achilles's complaint against Agamemnon that he takes more despite doing less of the fighting, but an especially close parallel is Solon's insistence that he did not want "the good and the bad to have an equal portion [*isomoiriē*] of the rich fatherland."[79] It was a common justification of oligarchies in the Classical period that those who were "better" or otherwise

---

74. Arist. *Pol.* 5.1309a20–23; [Arist.] *Rhet. ad Alex.* 1424b13–14; see further chapter 3, section 3.1.3. Aeneas Tacticus, discussing the problem of disciplining troops during a siege, says that "if it is necessary to discipline people who are careless and out of line, make it the wealthiest and most powerful people in the polis, since this can serve as an example to the rest" (38.4–5). See the discussion of Whitehead *ad loc.*

75. For the literary genre of the *Cyropaedia* and its various functions, see Tatum 1989, Due 1989, Gera 1993, Nadon 2001, Azoulay 2004, and most recently Gray 2011.

76. *Cyr.* 2.1.14–19.

77. For more on this episode see Gera 1993: 163–64 and Gray 2011: 283–89, although neither explores the issue of shared space and collective action as I do here.

78. 2.2.18. For the episode that follows, cf. Johnstone 2011: 141–46.

79. Hom. *Il.* 1.163–68; Solon fr. 34.8–9 West.

contributed more to the polis deserved unequal, that is to say more, political rights, one that democrats countered with the argument that the polis functioned best when all partook equally of citizenship.[80] In this instance, therefore, we should view Chrysantas's worry about *isomoiria* as touching not only on the issue of the distribution of spoils but also on political power more generally.[81]

Cyrus's reply to Chrysantas is hardly comforting. He proposes putting the question up for debate before a general assembly of the troops, thus making the rank-and-file participants in a deliberation about their own deserts.[82] "Why not send out a message that you have decided to do it a certain way?" Chrysantas nervously suggests, hoping to keep the masses dispersed and ineffectual.[83] Cyrus, however, insists that it is only fair that the troops have a say in their own earnings. Here Chrysantas finally makes the explicit connection between the assembled troops and political power: "Can it be that you think the majority [*plēthos*], when it has come together [*sunelthon*], will vote not that each person gets the same things [*isa*], but that the most powerful [*kratistoi*] have a greater share [*pleonektein*] of honors and gifts?"[84] For Chrysantas, it is impossible to imagine a situation in which a mass of people assembled for the express purpose of discussing their distributive outcomes would not take advantage of their numerical superiority and vote for what is in their collective interest, namely equality. He no doubt recognizes that a general assembly of the troops would grant them a perfect opportunity for collectively seeing and recognizing their mass power.[85]

---

80. See especially Thuc. 6.39.1, where the Syracusan democrat Athenagoras insists that the rich, "the wise" (*xunetoi*), and the majority all "have an equal share" (*isomoirein*) in a democracy. For the oligarchic thought that those with more to contribute (and thus more at stake) ought to have more political rights, see e.g., Thuc. 3.65.3 (the Thebans to the Plataeans) and Ostwald 1995.

81. Cf. Due 1989: 182–83; Hunt 1998: 203–5; Gray 2011: 284–85 (although I would question her assertion [285 with n61] that Xenophon comports with the "mainstream" view that *isomoiria* is "preposterous"—in democratic Athens it was a way of life).

82. 2.2.18.

83. 2.2.19.

84. 2.2.20. Xenophon seems exceptionally attuned to the problem of the assembled masses. In the *Hellenica*, the *dēmos* or *plēthos* is frequently depicted as achieving political power when it "comes together" (*sunelthein*): 6.5.3 (Mantinea), 6.5.7 (Tegea), 7.1.44–45 (Sicyon).

85. As it turns out, Chrysantas's fears are misplaced: The assembled soldiers accept a "meritocratic" scheme rather than a strictly egalitarian one. In Xenophon's fantasy of leadership, the delicate problem of military participation and political power is sidestepped by imagining a demos that willingly, even eagerly, allows itself to be co-opted into a desert-based spoils system limited strictly to the military sphere. Nonetheless, I see in the entire exchange

Plato imagines just such a situation leading to the breakdown of an oligarchy in the *Republic*. When rich and poor are stationed next to each other on the battlefield (*paratachtheis en machēi*), the poor man sees that he is lean and suntanned, while the rich are overweight, short of breath, and generally useless.[86] When the poor notice this, they realize that it is only their own cowardice that keeps the rich in power, and they exhort one another with the words, "These men are ours—for they are nothing."[87] It is the open forum of the military campaign that first generates the common knowledge necessary for galvanizing democratic forces within an oligarchy.[88]

In many of the examples examined above, whether festival or military, the success of a democratic uprising depends upon the actions of an initial few who commit to instigating the movement. Widespread participation emerges (or is expected to emerge) from the interplay between individual actors and a large, public, centrally assembled audience. This pattern can serve as an opportunity to make some broader observations about individuals and groups in history. The ancient Greek cases point to a fact that has been well documented and explored by contemporary social scientists: that although broader ideas, identities, and structures are crucial for the "making" of history, ultimately human society comprises discrete individuals who make their own choices.[89] At the very least, this fact necessitates that we recognize that human beings are not psychic: we cannot know the content of one another's thoughts simply because we may share certain traits or other markers of identity. In turn, this gives rise to the problem of collective action: groups of individuals

---

an acknowledgment on Xenophon's part that the armed demos posed a significant threat to oligarchic rule.

86. *Rep.* 8.556d. Note that, for Plato, both rich and poor participate in the hoplite phalanx. Political tension does erupt along military lines (wealthier hoplites vs. poorer light-armed) but within the phalanx itself. See the discussion in chapter 1, section 1.2.2.

87. 556d-e. The poor "gather privately in groups" (ἰδίᾳ συγγίγνωνται) in the same manner as the armed demos of Mytilene (Thuc. 3.27.3: κατὰ ξυλλόγους τε γιγνόμενοι).

88. The danger of the demos taking part in the hoplite phalanx seems to have induced many oligarchies to hire mercenaries: for oligarchic use of hired soldiers, see Arist. *Pol.* 5.1306a21–22; Isoc. 10.32, 19.38; Thuc. 1.24.5, 1.115.4, 3.18.1, 3.34.2, 3.73; Diod. Sic. 14.34.3–6. Note especially the story episode related by Aen. Tact. 11.7–10: the Argive "rich" (*plousioi*) were trying to make a "second attempt" upon the democracy (probably the abortive *coup* described by Thuc. 5.83.1: Stylianou *ad* Diod. Sic. 15.57.3). They were planning to bring in mercenaries to accomplish this, but the *prostatēs* of the Argive demos, catching wind of the plot, foiled it. See further chapter 1, section 1.2.2.

89. Cf. chapter 1, section 1.3. For the importance of individuals in effecting revolutions, see, e.g., the work of Kuran (1989, 1995), cited below (and discussed in detail by Teegarden 2014: 21–24).

with shared interests may fail to act upon those interests, for any number of reasons. The above examples were attempts to bridge this epistemological gap between what the subjects of an authoritarian each individually think and what they collectively know about the thoughts and behavior of their fellow citizens. Just as democratic resistance fails under oligarchy because of the aggregate decisions of acquiescent individuals, so revolution succeeds when some individuals choose to break the silence. Revolution requires collective action, but that action never just spontaneously "happens," nor is it the automatic outcome of structural determinants. Collective action must begin somewhere, and this is with the choices of specific people. They must decide to act; moreover, their failure to act can mean that resistance in general will fail. Revolutions are never guaranteed by history. They may be derailed by any number of uncontrollable contingencies. Yet when they do occur, we can be sure that they are traceable to an immediate cause.

The ancient Greeks were themselves aware of this. We have seen that Plato recognized that in an oligarchic regime, all it takes is a "tiny imbalance" (*mikra rhopē*, Rep. 8.556e) to tip the scales in favor of civil war. This trigger can come from practically anywhere—it may be all but guaranteed to occur—but it nonetheless has to happen for *stasis* to break out. Some individual or small group of individuals must make the decision to act. Similarly, Aristotle points in the *Politics* to the importance of "trivial causes" in precipitating political, and in particular oligarchic, breakdown.[90] Though seemingly insignificant, small acts could, like a spark, ignite a general conflagration.[91] This insight was not only recognized, it was the organizing principle behind the festival and military uprisings against oligarchies studied here.[92] Individuals thus have an indispensable role to play in mass movements. However, this is emphatically not an attempt to rehabilitate the "Great Man" as the chief protagonist of his-

---

90. *Pol.* 5.1303b18–1304a18.

91. Cf. Solon fr. 13.14–15 West: "like fire, it [*sc. atē* or 'ruin'] arises from an insignificant origin, trivial [*phlaurē*] at first, but in the end terrible." Completely independently, Fisher notes that assaults on people's honor "serious enough to be called *hybris*" could act as "sparks that brought conflicts to a head, or *tipped the balance* [cf. Plato's weight metaphor] into violence" (2000a: 89).The language of sparks and fires finds a parallel in the revolutionary saying of Mao Zedong that "a single spark can start a prairie fire" and serves as the organizing metaphor for the political scientist Timur Kuran's study of unanticipated revolutions: "Just as a normally ephemeral spark can, given the right combination of physical conditions, touch off a wildfire, an event that would normally lead to mere grumbling can, given the right combination of social conditions, touch off a revolutionary uprising" (1989: 60).

92. The Rhodian democratic uprising of 395 was organized with similar considerations of common knowledge and collective action in mind: Simonton 2015.

tory.[93] If anything, the present model of revolution encourages us to ascribe considerable responsibility to non-elite actors, such as Thucydides's anonymous Mendaean hoplite. The political scientists O'Donnell and Schmitter, in their seminal study of transitions from authoritarian rule, put the relationship between revolutionary "first movers" and mass uprisings in the following, quite evocative, terms, which will serve as the conclusion to the present section:

> Our personal experience in having lived through several of these moments [*sc.* of authoritarian breakdown] indicates that the catalyst in this transformation comes first by gestures from exemplary individuals, who begin testing the boundaries of behavior initially imposed by the incumbent regime. This leads to mutual discoveries of common ideals, which acquire enormous political significance just because they are articulated publicly after such a long period of prohibition, privation, and privatization. In the precarious public spaces of the first stages of transition, these individual gestures are astonishingly successful in provoking or reviving collective identifications and actions; they, in turn, help forge broad identifications which embody the explosion of a highly repoliticized and angry society. (1986: 49)

6.2 Games Oligarchs Play: Breakdown Dynamics within the Ruling Elite

Since the focus of the previous section was on the interaction between revolutionary individuals and the larger mass of the demos within public space, relatively little was said about the actions of the oligarchs themselves. In fact, there was little to say: Most of the above examples resulted in swift, violent changes in regime, with the oligarchic class having little or no opportunity to defend itself. That deadly efficacy is one of the reasons revolutionaries chose festivals and other mass events as the backdrop for attacks on the regime. Unguarded public space could help to bring down an oligarchy of even very long standing.

In other scenarios, however, the process of breakdown was more drawn out. Here the individual choices of the members of the oligarchic ruling group could be extremely important, and could in fact mean the difference between regime survival and implosion. Everything hinged on the decisions of a few

---

93. For an intellectual history of the "Great Man" idea in Classical Greece, see now Ferrario 2014.

powerful men.[94] In this section I examine various kinds of strategic decisions facing oligarchs in situations of constitutional crisis, elucidating the reasons why members of the oligarchic class made the choices they did. I model the oligarchs' dilemmas using game theory, the study of strategic interaction between individuals operating under binding and commonly known constraints.[95] Game theory usefully captures the essential features of intra-oligarchic breakdown. It also yields predictions, which can then be tested against the available evidence of history.[96]

Political scientists have similarly utilized game theory to explain the processes of breakdown within contemporary authoritarian regimes. The work of Barbara Geddes has been pioneering in this respect.[97] Geddes hypothesizes that different types of authoritarian regime will break down in different ways, since participants in each kind face particular pressures. For example, she claims that minority and majority factions in a military regime are locked in a so-called "coordination game," in which it is better for them in every case

---

94. Cf. Plat. *Rep.* 8.545d (quoted repeatedly by Hawke 2011): "Every constitution changes beginning with the element that holds power, if *stasis* arises within it; but it is impossible for a unified regime to be disturbed, even if it is very small." Plato thus thinks regime change is entirely a matter of the decisions made by individuals within the elite. Things are not so simple, however: Newman (*ad* Arist. *Pol.* 5.1306a9) notes that Aristotle complicates Plato's picture by showing that pressure from below can overthrow an oligarchy. A similar debate on "top-down" vs. "bottom-up" political change has taken place among political scientists studying contemporary regimes. O'Donnell and Schmitter, for all their emphasis on the role of exemplary gestures by regime outsiders (quoted above), are more famous for their statement that "there is no transition whose beginning is not the consequence—direct or indirect—of important divisions within the authoritarian regime itself" (1986: 19). Others have contested this thesis, particularly Bratton and van de Walle (1997 on democratic transitions in Africa. Sometimes authoritarian breakdown originates in demands from civil society, which then trigger defections among the ruling elite.

95. For accessible introductions to game theory, see Kreps 1990, Morrow 1994. Previous applications of game theory to the ancient world include Herman 2006: 398–414 and Ober 2012.

96. There are some potential objections to using a modern theory like that of games to understand the politics of the ancient world, but they do not withstand scrutiny. For example, it might be objected that game theory assumes egotistical individuals interested solely in maximizing "cash value" (a "*homo economicus*" model of human behavior). However, this is not the case. Game theory assumes only that individuals have stable, consistently ordered preferences; the content of the preferences themselves can be anything, including altruism or group behavior. Moreover, these preferences are absolutely influenced by culture and historical context—they are not assumed to be the same for all people at all times. It is the job of the historian to reconstruct from the evidence the preferences people possessed at any given time. On this issue see further chapter 1, section 1.3.

97. See, e.g., her 2003.

to converge on the same action rather than take different ones.[98] This conceptualization gives rise to several predictions which Geddes then tests. By contrast, Geddes thinks of "personalist" autocracies (those in which power revolves around a single individual) as playing a different game, with different tendencies.

I adopt a slightly different tack here. I treat only one type of ancient Greek authoritarian regime, oligarchy, and I will assume there is only one kind of oligarchy. Furthermore, in my analysis oligarchy breaks down when confronted with different types of shocks to the stable cooperative equilibrium, shocks that force oligarchs to act upon their preexisting preferences in different ways. I organize the different shocks into two types: exogenous (external) shocks and endogenous (internal) ones. The former arise from circumstances outside of the oligarchs' control, while the latter stem from mistakes of governance on the part of the oligarchs themselves. I find that the different shocks, and the different games that went with them, tended to produce distinctive constitutional outcomes. Exogenous shocks largely resulted in tyranny, while endogenous ones favored democratization.

6.2.1 Exogenous Shocks

Chapter 1 conceptualized stable oligarchic rule as the long-term solution to an iterated Prisoner's Dilemma.[99] If oligarchs recognize that they are locked in a potential war of all against all, but that the game is likely to go on for the foreseeable future, they have reasons to favor peaceful cooperation over destructive civil war. The system works only so long as the oligarchs are able to monitor one another's individual resources and maintain an equilibrium of rough parity. If any one member of the oligarchy becomes too powerful, suspicions arise that he will use his power base to establish a tyranny. Oligarchs then fall into mutually destructive distrust and betrayal. Much of the time, however, oligarchs succeeded in establishing effective self-monitoring institutions (see chapter 2).

Sometimes, however, new sources of power appeared unexpectedly, from without. An increase in an oligarch's individual power due to negligence on the part of his fellow oligarchs would count as an "endogenous" change, one that was itself the product of (failed) institutions. With exogenous shocks,

---

98. This is because members of the military, according to Geddes, value unity over individual gain—i.e., she posits actor preferences based on observed cultural behaviors in society. This is an important example of game theory not requiring maximized individual utility in terms of cash value.

99. See chapter 1, section 1.3.

we are looking at changes beyond the oligarchs' control. Exogenous shocks ought to disrupt the cooperative equilibrium. When new means of dominating one's rivals appear, the oligarchs should not be able to restrain themselves from breaking ranks and trying to be the first to acquire the new form of power. This is because each still wants to be tyrant above all (this is his highest preference), but he has simply not had an opportunity under the oligarchic status quo.

Exogenous power sources, then, ought to shorten oligarchs' "time horizons" (the point at which game play is expected to end) from indefinite to immediate. They are plunged back into a one-off Prisoner's Dilemma, with the expected result of ongoing *stasis*. Each oligarch tries to grab the new source of power, even though he would prefer sustained cooperation, because he cannot trust his peer not to; "defect" is the dominant strategy, and "defect" becomes the new equilibrium. (Consult chapter 1, section 1.3, fig. 1, where a "defect"—"defect" becomes the new equilibrium is represented by the upper left corner.) There is another possibility, however. If knowledge of the new power source is asymmetrical, that is, if some oligarchs become aware of it before the others, then those oligarchs would be in a position to take advantage of this insider information and "sucker" the others. They could establish themselves as tyrant or as a tyrannical oligarchic clique, a *dunasteia*.[100]

This result is precisely what we see in the sources. The introduction of new, untapped sources of power almost always destabilizes the oligarchic status quo in the direction of tyranny. In the ancient world, such sources of power included unexpected increases in wealth for individual oligarchs; powerful Greek hegemons willing to back their clients as tyrants; and, in particular, the support of the Persian Empire.[101] To begin with the last example, as the Greek poleis came into contact with the Persians, it was impossible in many cases for elites to restrain themselves from pledging allegiance to the Great King in exchange for tyrannical power.[102] We can start, for example, with the case of

---

100. A mythological parallel for such a situation is Plato's parable of the ring of Gyges (*Rep.* 2.359a-360d): it is of course a story of using an unexpected power source to make oneself tyrant. One of Plato's points is that not even a lowly shepherd (to say nothing of a member of the elite) could pass up such an opportunity.

101. Aristotle recognizes the importance of sudden changes in relative power for explaining constitutional change, especially in oligarchies: "When the number of rich men increases or property grows, constitutions change into oligarchies or *dunasteiai*" (*Pol.* 5.1303a11–13); "most of all one must order people through the laws such that no one becomes superior in power, whether that is through friends [*philoi*] or possessions [*chrēmata*]; but if this is impossible, to remove such people from the community" (*Pol.* 5.1308b16–19).

102. I agree with Graf 1985, who argues that Persia did not pursue a fixed policy of installing

Coes, a general (*stratēgos*) of the Mytileneans (and so very likely a member of the elite), who gives King Darius useful advice.[103] Darius promises him a reward for his help, and we later read that Coes asked for a tyranny and received it.[104] Very similar are the cases of Theomestor of Samos, who was made tyrant of the island in exchange for his service to the King; Euphorbus and Philagrus of Eretria; and of course the Ionian tyrants who guard the bridge to Scythia for the King.[105] Herodotus has Histiaeus say of them that "each of them holds a tyranny over their poleis thanks to Darius." We cannot know for certain, but most of the men named probably would have achieved their position through personal initiative.[106]

A famous incident of eliciting Persian support for political power comes from Thebes. A small faction of elites "medized" by accepting the authority of the invading Persian army in the late 480s. Herodotus calls the two chief members of the elite responsible, Attaginus and Timagenides, "leaders [*archēgetai*] from amongst the foremost men."[107] Later, when the Thebans are being besieged by the Greeks for medizing, Herodotus has Timagenides say to the inhabitants that "it was with the consent of the whole community [*koinon*] that we medized and not ourselves alone" (9.87.2), but this is a likely excuse for someone in Timagenides's position.[108] In fact a number of later Greek authors excused the Boeotians of medism, blaming it on a small faction of unrepresentative oligarchs.[109] It thus seems likely that the actions of

---

tyrants in the Greek city-states; instead, the Persians were happy to let individual members of the elite come to them. Cf. Austin 1990: 291.

103. Hdt. 4.97.2. He is called a *dēmotes* ("commoner"?—see Osborne 2007: 91) at 5.11.2, but when we observe the context we see that this is simply in contrast to Histiaeus of Miletus, who is a tyrant. Thus *dēmotes* should mean something like "private citizen." The fact that Coes is a general and is given a patronymic ("son of Erxander") by Herodotus indicates that he is not a member of the lower classes.

104. 5.11.2, 5.37.1. Coes is later stoned to death by the Mytileneans (5.38.1).

105. Theomestor: Hdt. 8.85.3, 9.90.1. Euphorbus and Philagrus: 6.101.2–3 (where they are called "prominent men [*dokimoi*] from among the citizens"). Tyrants at bridge: 4.137–138.

106. 4.137.2. Gorman points out (2001: 132) that Histiaeus's statement does not require that the King actively imposed them in power, but only that they held their power thanks to Darius's backing.

107. 9.86.1. Herodotus contradicts himself at one point by saying that the "whole population [*plēthos*] of Boeotia medized" (8.34), but this is either carelessness or a bit of personal bias on his part belied by evidence that he supplies elsewhere (9.16 and, as we have just seen, 9.86.1).

108. As Marincola and Flower 2002 point out in their n. *ad loc.*

109. Thuc. 3.62.3 (where the speakers are, however, similarly interested in excusing their behavior); Plut. *Arist.* 18.6; Paus. 9.6.2.

Timagenides and Attaginus follow the pattern predicted by the game-theoretic model.[110]

Thebes is also the site of another case of oligarchic breakdown that took place almost exactly one hundred years later. Life in Thebes in the late fifth and early fourth centuries was characterized by political competition between two main factions within the ruling oligarchy, that of Ismenias (pro-Athenian) and that of Leontiades (pro-Spartan).[111] A truly decisive tipping of the balance in favor of Leontiades came in 382, when the Spartan commander Phoebidas was leading a body of troops south through Boeotia. The Spartans' appearance was quite unexpected to the Thebans, and it presented Leontiades with the opportunity to "flatter" Phoebidas and work his way into the Spartan's good graces (Xen. *Hell.* 5.2.25). Once he had obtained a private audience with Phoebidas, Leontiades offered him complete loyalty from Thebes in exchange for placing the polis under the tyrannical control of his faction. Phoebidas, for whom this was likewise a completely unexpected opportunity, accompanied Leontiades to the Theban acropolis and established him and his friends as dynasts with the backing of a Spartan garrison. The resulting *dunasteia* lasted until 379.[112] The sequence of events accords well with the behavior predicted by the Prisoner's Dilemma: the new source of power is unantici-

---

110. Plut. *de Her. mal.* 31 adds the detail that the exiled Spartan king Demaratus was a guest-friend of Attaginus and introduced him to the Persian King. This would represent a way in which Attaginus enjoyed insider information and special access not available to other members of the Theban elite.

111. *Hell. Oxy.* 20.1–2 Chambers; Xen. *Hell.* 5.2.25; Plut. *Pel.* 5.1–2. For this political rivalry, see esp. Cook 1988, also Lendon 1989 and Bearzot 2009. The differences between the two groups centered around foreign policy disputes and should not be seen as reflecting ideological preferences for oligarchy and democracy, despite Plutarch's too-easy depiction of Ismenias's faction as "freedom-loving and populist," Leontiades's as "oligarchic, rich, and immoderate" (*Pel.* 5.1–2). All members of the Theban governing class were no doubt rich and—by definition—oligarchic. The *hetaireiai* (factions) of Ismenias and Leontiades resemble the intra-oligarchic Corinthian groups discussed above, section 6.1.

112. Xen. *Hell.* 5.2.29; Plut. *Pel.* 5.2–3, 6.1. As in Corinth in 393, the aggressive faction in this case may have been the minority one: Androtion (*FGrH* 324 F 50) says four hundred refugees fled Thebes when Phoebidas seized the Cadmea. Jacoby is probably right that Androtion's number should be trusted over the three hundred of Xen. *Hell.* 5.2.31 and Diod. Sic. 15.20.2. If these four hundred were all members of the federal council of 660 (*Hell. Oxy.* 19.3–4 Chambers), they would represent a majority. Note, however, that the Corinthian and Theban factions were playing different "games," with different possible moves: when presented with an external source of power, Leontiades's faction could avoid using the demos as a source of support and could establish itself directly as a tyrannical clique (what I have posited as one of the highest preferences of an oligarch). The Corinthian faction, having no such advantage, had to call upon the demos and establish a democracy, a much less desirable outcome for them, presumably, but one

pated; it is taken advantage of by one of the parties currently in "cooperative" equilibrium, rather than being imposed from without by the source of power itself; and there seems to be an informational asymmetry that allows Leontiades to take advantage of the Spartans' presence without the other faction realizing the danger they are in.[113] Ismenias and his faction accordingly receive the "sucker's payoff."

We should note that in this and in all previous bouts of internal dissension, the Theban oligarchs had scrupulously avoided appeals to the demos. Leontiades' recourse to the Spartans appears to confirm the general axiom that oligarchs preferred overcoming their rivals through the establishment of tyrannies and dynasties rather than democracies, all else being equal. In fact, it was the desperate situation created by the dynasty and the Spartan garrison that finally forced other members of the traditional Theban ruling class—including Pelopidas, Epaminondas, and others—to reach out to the wider populace as allies against the usurpers.[114] This signal, revealing to the members of the Theban demos that it had reliable collaborators within the ranks of the oligarchs, authorized the ensuing collective action and mass contention that reconstituted the Theban politeia as a democracy.[115] The liberators needed the demos to accomplish their plan, and so they accepted the political consequences of an energized and organized populace, even if they would ideally have preferred to maintain their traditional oligarchy. The Theban democracy of the fourth century was thus conceded rather than willingly bestowed.[116]

---

that served to save their own skins. It is important to distinguish between what oligarchs do when they can get away with it and what they do out of necessity.

113. Xenophon makes it clear that Ismenias and his faction did not expect Leontiades's proposition to Phoebidas, since they are holding a session of the council when Phoebidas attacks, as though nothing were amiss.

114. Xen. *Hell.* 5.4.1–12; Plut. *Pel.* 11–12, *de genio Socratis* 34 (= *Mor.* 598c-f); Diod. Sic. 15.25. Pelopidas was a member of the faction of Ismenias (Plut. *Pel.* 5.1; Nep. *Pel.* 1.4) and so, presumably, had been a participant in the oligarchic *koinon* down to Leontiades's coup.

115. For democracy as the constitution in post-liberation Thebes, see Buckler 1980: 30; *IACP* no. 221, p. 455; Robinson 2011: 56–57. Recently published decrees of the *koinon*, enacted in the name of the demos, include *SEG* 55.564bis, 58.447.

116. The situation in Thebes in 379 was thus quite similar to that of Athens in 508: one member or faction of the elite (Pelopidas and company/Cleisthenes), dominated by another member or faction (Leontiades and company/Isagoras), reached out to the demos in order to overcome their position of weakness. The insurgent demos, which welcomed the appeal, was further galvanized by the appearance of a foreign enemy (the Spartans in both cases). See further below, section 6.2.3.

6.2.2 Endogenous Shocks

As stated above, endogenous shocks are those that are internal by-products of the decisions of the oligarchs themselves. They emerge from the interactions between fellow oligarchs or between oligarchs and demos. Normally such encounters were tightly regulated by oligarchic institutions, which were designed to produce a cooperative political equilibrium. The endogenous shocks analyzed here thus represent moments of breakdown and failure within oligarchic institutions. They are the mistakes that somehow slipped through the cracks of institutional design. Such errors do not necessarily mean that the institutions in question were poorly constructed, or that the oligarchs could have done a better job—some "noise" (random error) is inevitable in any large system. What will become clear, however, is the degree to which oligarchic institutions were inherently weaker and less capable of sustaining "noise" than their democratic counterparts. The particularly precarious situation of oligarchs, even when enjoying a cooperative equilibrium, meant that their favored constitution was comparatively bad at handling deviations from the set "script."[117] Moreover, these mistakes exposed oligarchs to a specific set of possible moves and strategies, which can be represented by a game-theoretic model.

I begin with cases singled out by Aristotle as a principal cause of revolution in oligarchies: "When the oligarchs oppress the people . . . ." (*Pol.* 5.1305a38). What happens in such cases is that the oligarchs' oppressiveness solves what had formerly been a coordination problem among the members of the demos, as in the case of Polydamidas at Mende studied above.[118] Blatant oligarchic injustice toward the demos serves as a focal point for overcoming this dilemma.[119] When oligarchic oppression is a matter of common knowledge, the members of the demos have adequate grounds for acting upon their shared (but hitherto tacit) anti-oligarchic feelings. However, their banding together is not in itself sufficient to bring down the oligarchy. The demos also requires a leader from among the ranks of the elite itself, one who has the political savvy to organize the demos effectively and lead them against the regime.[120]

---

117. See above, chapter 2, sections 2.3–4.

118. Recall that this coordination problem (really, a kind of collective action problem) was one of the intended by-products of such oligarchic institutions as rewards for informants (chapter 3, section 3.4) and the projection of a united front (chapter 5, section 5.2).

119. For the idea of a focal point, see chapter 5, section 5.2.4.

120. One might suppose that demotic self-organization was enough, and that a leaderless mob could bring down an oligarchy, as the Athenians did in 508 according to the influential argument of Ober 1996. Even in that case, however, the collective action carried out by the

PROCESSES OF REGIME BREAKDOWN

Aristotle attests to this process in the same passage: "Then anyone [*pas*] is good enough [*hikanos*] to be the champion [*prostatēs*] of the people, especially if he himself is a member of the ruling class" (*Pol.* 5.1305a39–40). Aristotle recognizes that the problem for an oligarchy at this point is structural rather than individualistic. Any oligarch, whatever his individual personality, suffices to fulfill the role of leader of the people.

The oligarchs' dilemma at this point resembles a scenario from game theory known as the Stag Hunt.[121] An informal version of the game was formulated by Jean-Jacques Rousseau, who provided the following allegorical story in his *Discourse on Inequality*: "If it was a matter of hunting deer, everyone well realized that he must remain faithful to his post; but if a hare happened to pass within reach of one of them, we cannot doubt that he would have gone off in pursuit of it without scruple."[122] In other words: A group of people (we can simplify to a pair) can hunt a stag together, in which case they will acquire quite a lot of meat (10 pounds each). In order to track down the stag successfully they must remain quiet, so as not to startle their quarry. It turns out, however, that the forest is also full of hares, which the participants could choose to catch at any time, but which represent much less meat than a stag (5 pounds). By going after a hare, however, one hunter ruins the stag hunt for the other by scaring away the stag. The game can be represented graphically as follows:

		Hunter B	
		Stag	Hare
Hunter A	Stag	(10, 10)	(0, 5)
	Hare	(5, 0)	(5, 5)

FIGURE 2. The Stag Hunt

---

demos required the prior leadership of Cleisthenes, who first "made the demos part of his faction" (Hdt. 5.66.2). Similarly, the Mendaean case studied above is exceptional in that the populace was under arms at the time of Polydamidas's assault on the democratic partisan. Cf. de Ste. Croix 1981: 288: "no democratic revolution had much chance of success, or of leading to a stable democracy, unless the impoverished masses received leadership from some members of the governing class."

121. On the Stag Hunt and its relevance for the evolution of social structure, see Skyrms 2004.

122. Quoted in Skyrms 2004: 1.

The Stag Hunt differs in important ways from the Prisoner's Dilemma. In the latter, there are overriding incentives not to cooperate. The result is a suboptimal equilibrium in which the two parties defect from one another. In the Stag Hunt, by contrast, the players' highest preference (to catch a stag and thus acquire the most meat) can be achieved by sustained coordination along a "stag"-"stag" strategy, but the players have to trust each other. They cannot let themselves be distracted by the readily available but much less satisfying hare, nor can they pursue a hare preemptively, out of fear that their partner will abandon them in their joint stag hunt, the worst possible outcome (represented by the bottom-left and top-right boxes). There are thus two possible "Nash equilibria" in the Stag Hunt game, unlike the single "defect"-"defect" equilibrium of the Prisoner's Dilemma: either both players hunt the stag or both players go after hares.[123] The former equilibrium is known as a "payoff-dominant" strategy, because it nets the best possible outcome (the stag), while the latter is a "risk-dominant" strategy, in which players, having less certainty about each other's preferences, choose the less risky option (in this case, of hunting hares.) Presumably, Stag Hunt games will result in a payoff-dominant set of strategies if the players have established trust and assurance beforehand.

Oligarchs, when one of them has oppressed the demos, find themselves in the condition of a Stag Hunt game. If the oligarchs each refuse to make themselves the demos's champion, the demos's uprising fails and the oligarchs get to retain their oligarchy, the best possible outcome for them in this game (represented by the upper left box). If even one oligarch, however, decides to accept the demos's invitation, his defection is sufficient to create a revolution that brings down the oligarchy and establishes a democracy.[124] The other oligarchs are punished, while the defecting oligarch is allowed to live (perhaps even thrive) under the new democracy. (This outcome is represented by the

---

123. A Nash equilibrium, named after the late mathematician and game theorist John Nash, is a situation in game theory in which, given the other players' moves, no player can improve his or her situation by unilaterally changing strategies. (This is just to say that, in the Prisoner's Dilemma, for example, no player would ever change from a "defect" to a "cooperate" strategy if the other player were playing "defect." Such a move would entail a worse outcome rather than a better.)

124. Democracy is the outcome here because the demos is in a strong enough bargaining position to demand nothing less than democracy. In the Archaic period, the demos was not strong enough to insist on something like democracy but instead allowed themselves to be used by oligarchs as a means of establishing a tyranny (what they received in exchange was less oppression than under the oligarchic status quo). It is important to understand that, unlike in the Prisoner's Dilemma game, tyranny is not a possible outcome, at least as I am arguing, in the Stag Hunt game.

upper right or lower left boxes). This is not the oligarch's highest preference (he always prefers to live under oligarchy than under democracy, all else being equal), but it is his safest choice. After all, how much can he trust his fellow oligarchs not to accept the demos's petition? The disgruntled demos represents a powerful weapon, one which a renegade oligarch could use to punish his enemies. In order not to accept the demos's appeal, an oligarch has to be certain that none of his peers has a reason to do so. The oligarchs' level of trust among themselves therefore determines which strategy will be followed, the payoff-dominant one of all of the oligarchs presenting a united front to the demos, or the risk-dominant one of all of the oligarchs rushing to be *prostatēs* of the demos out of fear that some other oligarch will get there first.

The ancient sources bear out this model of endogenous oligarchic breakdown. For example, Thucydides provides a near-perfect example of Stag Hunt dynamics in action when he describes internal problems besetting the oligarchy of the Four Hundred at Athens in 411:

> Thanks to their private ambitions [*philotimia*], they inclined toward the thing that most often destroys an oligarchy that arises out of a democracy: for they all immediately wanted, not to be equal [*isoi*], but that each one actually be foremost [*polu prōtos*]. [. . .] The things that most obviously threatened them were the strong position of Alcibiades at Samos and the thought that the oligarchy was not going to persist [*monimon*]. Accordingly each one [was] struggling to be the first to be champion [*prostatēs*] of the people.[125]

Thucydides suggests that the inexperience of the oligarchy of the Four Hundred meant that its members had not had the time to cultivate a proper sense of oligarchic equality. Instead, they were eager to surpass one another now that they were not constrained by the old democratic system. In other words, interoligarchic trust of a level necessary to ensure the payoff-dominant strategy was lacking. Furthermore, the threat of Alcibiades and of the fervently democratic fleet at Samos here performs the function of the demos's appeal (the "hare") in the Stag Hunt model. The oligarchs of the Four Hundred could potentially have defused the threat had they remained united. Instead, each assumes that the other is already planning to defect to the other side. It is a foregone conclusion to them that the oligarchy will collapse. Thucydides intimates that it was within the Four Hundred's collective power to preserve the oligarchy, but that strong individual pressures to develop a contingency plan as *prostates* of the

---

125. 8.89.3–4. For the importance of this passage for understanding the value of equality within an oligarchy, see chapter 2, section 2.1.

demos (that is, to "chase the hare" in the risk-dominant strategy) worked in the aggregate to bring down the regime.[126]

We see another example of Stag Hunt dynamics at work in a fragment of Aristotle. Interestingly, the story is connected with his remarks in the *Politics*, quoted above, on oligarchic abuse of the demos. There he identified mistreatment as something that gave rise to the demos's demand for a champion. He then immediately provides an empirical example: "[Consider] Lygdamis of Naxos, who afterwards came to be tyrant" (*Pol.* 5.1305a40–42). This reads at first glance like an example of another type of game, since tyranny is not one of the possible outcomes of the Stag Hunt scenario as I have constructed it. We know from additional evidence, however, that Aristotle's remarks in the *Politics* are not the whole story. It seems that Naxos did in fact democratize first, before Lygdamis was established as tyrant. We possess this information thanks to a fragment of Aristotle's own *Constitution of the Naxians* (fr. 558 Rose) preserved in Athenaeus. The fragment is worth quoting in full. Aristotle is describing Naxos in the second half of the sixth century:

> Most of the rich men in Naxos lived in the town, while the rest were scattered among the villages. Now in one of the villages, called Leistadae, there lived Telestagoras, a very rich man with a good reputation who was honored by the people [*dēmos*] in various ways including the daily sending of gifts. And when they came down from the town and haggled over anything being sold, the sellers used to say that they would rather give it to

---

[126]. Similar weaknesses worked to bring down the regime of the Thirty in 404–3; moreover, several of the participants in that oligarchy seem to have understood the nature of their dilemma. Xenophon reports a remark by the arch-oligarch Critias, who is criticizing his fellow oligarch Theramenes for vacillating between supporting the Thirty and joining the democratic resistance: "[A man], like a person on a ship, should persist in his efforts, until they come to a fair wind. If he didn't, how would the crew ever arrive where they're supposed to, if whenever there was a complication they sailed in the opposite direction?" (*Hell.* 2.3.31) Critias recognizes that the oligarchic "voyage" depends upon the united effort of the "sailors" in charge of it, and that if they work together, they will reach their destination safely. Remarkably, Critias's metaphor is identical to the one David Hume used to formulate his own version of the Stag Hunt game: "Two men who pull at the oars of a boat, do it by agreement or convention, tho' they have never given promises to each other" (Hume 1738: III, p. 490, quoted in Skyrms 2004: 2). Rowing together is the payoff-dominant strategy, while for everyone simply to cease to row is the risk-dominant strategy. The worst thing would be to row in the boat (in circles, presumably) while the other person does nothing. Of course, Critias's ship metaphor belongs to a long tradition of "ship of state" imagery (e.g., Archilochus fr. 105 West; Alc. fr. 6 Liberman; Thgn. 667–82; Soph. *OT* 25). In this case, however, he explicitly refers to the cooperation among sailors required to bring a voyage to completion, rather than, e.g., the social class of the sailors (as in Theognis). He seems well attuned to the problem of intra-oligarchic unity.

Telestagoras than sell it at such a price. Now some young men were buying a large fish, and when the fisherman made the usual remark they were annoyed at hearing it so often; so, being tipsy, they roistered round to his house. Telestagoras received them civilly; but the young men assaulted him [*hubrisan*] and his two daughters, who were of marriageable age. The Naxians were enraged at that, took up arms, and attacked the young men. And there was then serious unrest [*stasis*], the Naxians being led by Lygdamis, who from this generalship became tyrant of his country. (trans. Barnes and Lawrence)[127]

There are several fascinating aspects of this fragment, but I will concentrate on its close adherence to the Stag Hunt model.[128] Here the object of the oligarchs' mistreatment (for the young men are clearly members of the ruling elite) is not a member of the demos, but rather the demos's patron, the rich Telestagoras. The act of hubris nevertheless serves as a focal point for democratic coordination, as the members of the demos treat it as the last straw. The attack on Telestagoras and his daughters is the spark that ignites a fire of political grievances and demands in the form of *stasis*.[129]

At this juncture the oligarchs of Naxos could have remained united (the payoff-dominant strategy) and beaten back the flames of democracy. Lygdamis, one of their number, chooses instead to side with the demos and so pours fuel on the fire, ending the oligarchic regime. We do not know why Lygdamis chose to do this. We might be tempted to speculate that he planned to make himself tyrant all along, since that was the eventual outcome. This was not an assured result in the beginning, however, and in fact both Herodotus and the author of the *Athenaion Politeia* state that Peisistratus, the tyrant of Athens,

---

127. = Athen. 8.348a-d.

128. For example, we might note the socioeconomic and physical division of the city between rich/city and poor/countryside (see chapter 4, sections 4.3); the patronage-like relations between Telestagoras and the demos (see chapter Four, section 4.4); and the way in which Telestagoras's generosity serves as a kind of standard in the demos's "moral economy" (for application of this term, first devised by Thompson (1971), to the ancient world, see Forsdyke 2012: 118, 140–41 and Johnstone 2011: 21 [citing this example]).

129. For the "spark-wildfire" imagery of civil war and revolution, made famous by Kuran (1989), see above, section 6.1.2. Note also the close similarity between the Telestagoras episode and the democratic counter-revolution at Mende, discussed above, again at section 6.1.2. There the members of the demos, "angered" (*periorgēs*), "immediately took up their arms . . . and attacked the Peloponnesians and the men who along with them had pursued an opposing policy" (ὁ δῆμος εὐθὺς ἀναλαβὼν τὰ ὅπλα περιοργὴς ἐχώρει ἐπί τε Πελοποννησίους καὶ τοὺς τὰ ἐναντία σφίσι μετ' αὐτῶν πράξαντας, Thuc. 4.130.4). In Naxos, the Naxians "enraged . . . took up arms and attacked the young men" (ἀγανακτήσαντες . . . τὰ ὅπλα ἀναλαβόντες ἐπῆλθον τοῖς νεανίσκοις).

was responsible for establishing Lygdamis as tyrant.[130] There must therefore have been a period during which Naxos was no longer an oligarchy but not yet a tyranny under Lygdamis—in all probability, it was a democracy.[131] In the beginning, at least, Lygdamis's decision to support the demos must have been a begrudging one, but he likely thought this choice was safer than waiting to see what his fellow oligarchs would do. Had the oligarchs of Naxos been on better terms with each other, Lygdamis might not have felt sufficiently pressured to side with the demos during the *stasis*. As it was, he chose the risk-dominant strategy, which later paid off considerably when Peisistratus made him tyrant.

One useful aspect of models is their propensity to yield non-obvious predictions, which can then be tested against the empirical evidence. If the events of history align with the predictions, the model gains in validity; also, thanks to the model, we now possess a new means of explaining phenomena whose causal mechanisms were previously unclear.[132] In the case of the Stag Hunt, we can predict from the model that oligarchs would work very hard to build assurance among themselves, so that challenges to their rule would result in their choosing the payoff-dominant strategy of unity rather than the risk-dominant strategy of defecting. As it happens, the ancient sources were already attuned to the importance of assurance and trust within oligarchies. As Aristotle notes, "An oligarchy which is of one mind [*homonoousa*] is not easily overthrown from within."[133] How best to achieve like-mindedness, however, was a difficult question. We saw in chapter 2 the ways in which oligarchs attempted to build up good relations and trust with one another. Such long-term network-building, however, could be tedious and costly. (Recall that the oligarchs of the Four Hundred in Thucydides could not tolerate being each other's equals.) A more immediate way of achieving assurance was the tech-

---

130. Hdt. 1.64.2; [Arist]. *Ath. Pol.* 15.3. For further references to Lygdamis, see [Arist.] *Oec.* 1346b6–12; Plut. *Mor.* 859d; *schol. ad* Aeschin. 2.77. The role of Peisistratus in making Lygdamis tyrant aligns with the Prisoner's Dilemma model of tyranny outlined above, in which it is primarily external sources of power that establish members of the elite as tyrants.

131. Naxos seems to have become a democracy again sometime after the fall of Lygdamis at the hands of Sparta in the later sixth century (Plut. *Mor.* 859d; Hdt. 5.30.1); see further Robinson 1997: 117–18. Robinson does not consider the possibility that Naxos became a democracy following the assault on Telestagoras.

132. See Quillin 2002: 76.

133. *Pol.* 5.1306a9–10. (His historical example is Pharsalus in Thessaly, for which see chapter 5, section 5.3.1.) The participle *homonoousa* evokes the idea of *homonoia*, or "like-mindedness," a concept that was of great importance for oligarchs and oligarchies: Isoc. 6.67; Xen. *Mem.* 4.4.16; Antiph. FF 45–71 Pendrick. For the idea of *homonoia* in general, see Funke 1980; Thériault 1996.

nique of mutual implication, often in a shared crime. Rather than invest in the long-term strategy of "positive" trust, oligarchs made a kind of quick-and-easy suicide pact, in which the "negative" motivation of shared fear kept them cooperative.

There are several examples of this in the sources. Sometimes the circumstances of the pact were relatively harmless, as when oligarchs swore binding oaths of hostility against the demos. Aristotle tells us of the "oligarchs' oath" that members of the ruling elite sometimes swore, to the effect that "I will be hateful towards the demos and devise whatever evil against it I can."[134] Scholars have traditionally treated this as evidence for the implacable class hatred and snobbery of the oligarchs toward the common people.[135] Yet it could just easily be a sign of the oligarchs' *weakness*, of their tendency to desert each other in extremis, and thus of their need to overcome problems of internal unity using sacred (in this case, oath-based) means. We have further evidence that oligarchs made oaths with each other against democracy. In a recently published reconciliation agreement from Dikaia in the Chalcidice, the reintegrated members of the community are to proclaim: "If I swore another oath, I dissolve it, and I will consider this one the most important."[136] The oligarchs, who are now being reincorporated into the democratic civic body, are freed from the oaths they swore to one another when they pledged to overthrow the constitution.[137] Of course, conspirators in general, whether oligarchic or democratic, are often called *sunōmotai* by the sources, "fellow swearers." Their devotion to their common cause, cemented with curses brought down on their own heads should they defect, would presumably have

---

134. *Pol.* 5.1310a9–10. Aristotle mentions an oligarchic regime at Megara in which only those were allowed citizenship who had "returned from exile and fought the demos together" (*Pol.* 4.1300a18). The ruling group would thus all have been equally compromised and so unlikely to break ranks against each other. Unfortunately we cannot date this Megarian oligarchic regime (see Newman *ad loc.*, discussing further passages in Aristotle—*Pol.* 5.1302b30–31, 1304b35–39— and their potential relationship to Thuc. 4.66–74).

135. De Ste. Croix 1981: 73; Teegarden 2014: 3.

136. *SEG* 57.576, lines 82–84. Of course, democrats living under an oligarchy might similarly swear oaths of loyalty to one another when attempting an uprising against the regime. This seems to be the import of the lines in ML 83 (the delation law from oligarchic Thasos, studied above, chapter 3, section 3.4) in which it is said that a conspirator "shall not be under oath against himself." That is, the oath the conspirator swore, to the effect that he submits to be destroyed by the gods should he betray his allies, is annulled: see the study of Graham and Smith 1989.

137. Cf. *SEG* 51.1096 B, lines 13–16; also Andoc. 1.98, quoting the decree of Demophantus to the effect that "as many oaths as were sworn at Athens or in the army or elsewhere against the demos, I dissolve and annul." Canevaro and Harris (2012) argue that the documents preserved in Andocides 1 are forgeries, but even if so the forgeries would be based on Classical examples.

carried over into whatever regime they instituted and would have helped to keep them cooperative.[138]

A far more extreme means of creating assurance was to participate in an illegal act together, frequently murder. The Athenian oligarchs of the late fifth century cemented their pact this way: Thucydides describes the killing of the demagogue Hyberbolus by oligarchs explicitly as a *pistis*, or "pledge."[139] Their shared responsibility for the murder would bind the oligarchs together in the future.[140] Such acts were not always undertaken voluntarily by all parties. More fanatical oligarchs might try to implicate the less willing by forcing them to participate. Thus Critias requires that the Three Thousand at Eleusis cast their ballots openly for the condemnation of the capture Eleusinians. This stratagem procured him his desired outcome (a unanimous death sentence), but it also linked the Three Thousand with the crimes of the Thirty.[141] As Critias puts it, "Since you [the Three Thousand] share in the benefits [*timai*] of this constitution, you must share in the dangers. [Condemn the defendants,] so that you take heart in and fear the same things that we do."[142] After the *coups* of 411 and 404 it was common for compromised members of the elite to argue that they had been forced to participate in the oligarchies. In some cases, like that of Eratosthenes, a member of the Thirty, the claim beggared belief, but in others we can imagine that the speakers actually had been coerced against their will.[143]

Thus, somewhat paradoxically, it may be that oligarchs gained a reputation for violence more through their weakness than through their strength. In trying to overcome their own worst tendencies of mistrust in order to coordinate on a payoff-dominant strategy, they made short-term choices that doomed the

---

138. Democratic or otherwise populist *sunōmotai* include the Athenian tyrannicides (Thuc. 6.56.3). Interestingly, neither the Rhodian conspirators of 395 (*Hell. Oxy.* 18.2 Chambers) nor the participants in the conspiracy of Cinadon (Xen. *Hell.* 3.3.6) are called *sunōmotai*, but instead *suneidotes* ("those privy to the plot") and *sumprattontes* ("confederates"). Oligarchic *sunōmotai* are mentioned at Thuc. 8.54.4, 8.81.2; Ar. *Eq.* 476, 862; *IosPE* I² 401.36–37, 44–47; *IC* III.iv.8.16–18. On *sunōmosiai/sunōmotai*, see Roisman 2006: 66–94; Rhodes 2007: 17–19; Sommerstein and Bayliss 2013: 120–28.

139. Thuc. 8.73.3. Hammond (2009) translates "as a guarantee of their complicity," which is superior to Jowett's "to whom they pledged their faith." Cf. Andoc. 1.67.

140. In this case, they bloodied their hands in order to "tie their hands," to use a phrase from social science. For the importance of "hands-tying" (i.e., credibly committing to cooperation), see Root 1989.

141. For this episode, see further chapter 3, section 3.2.

142. Xen. *Hell.* 2.4.9.

143. Eratosthenes: Lys. 12.28. The speaker of Isoc. 18.17 says that many Athenians were forced by the Thirty to commit crimes.

oligarchic project in the long run.[144] When oligarchs left themselves no room for escape, when they bound themselves together in ways that prevented one or more of them from defecting to the demos, they guaranteed that their eventual downfall would be all the more decisive and spectacular.[145] When they went down, they all went down together.[146]

6.2.3 Intra-Oligarchic Feuds

A final category of endogenous breakdown is that in which oligarchs abuse each other, leading to the willingness of some of them to appeal to the demos as an escape route.[147] Instances of this phenomenon represent failures to mediate oligarchic disputes properly through the institutional channels examined in chapter 2. Feuds, lawsuits, and familial squabbles that were left "undiagnosed" and "untreated" by the wider oligarchic community could easily lead to *stasis* and breakdown, and frequently did. The cause of such disputes lay ultimately in the fiercely competitive ethos of the elite, in the *philoneikia* (love of strife) and *philotimia* (love of honor) that figure in the earliest ac-

---

144. Note Aristotle's repeated emphasis that oligarchs swear the oligarchs' oath *now* (*nun*: *Pol.* 5.1310a8 [twice]), i.e., during his time in the later fourth century. Elsewhere he is similarly pessimistic about contemporary oligarchs' likelihood of success (*Pol.* 6.1321a40–42). For the increasing instability of oligarchy in the later fourth century, see the afterword below.

145. Consider the fates of the ringleaders of the Four Hundred at Athens: Phrynichus was murdered in broad daylight and afterward had his bones removed from Attica (Thuc. 8.92.2; Lyc. 1.113; Craterus *FGrH* 423 F 17); Antiphon and Archeptolemus were tried by the democracy, condemned, executed, had their property confiscated, and were refused burial (Thuc. 8.68.2; Craterus F 5b); and Alexicles and Aristarchus were likewise tried, put to death, and refused burial by the restored democracy (Xen. *Hell.* 1.7.28; Lyc. 1.115). They had chosen, however, the path of no return: Thucydides makes clear that they knew well before the regime fell that they would be tried and killed "before all others" if the demos regained power (Thuc. 8.91.3).

146. This occurred at Heraclea Pontica in the mid-fourth century, where the ruling oligarchy of three hundred stubbornly refused to grant any concessions to the demos (Justin 16.4.2; Polyaen. *Strat.* 2.30.2). The oligarchs then sought help from Clearchus, one of their number, whom they had previously exiled (Justin 16.4.4; Suda s.v. Κλέαρχος). Clearchus betrayed their trust and appealed to the populace. He became the *prostatēs* of the demos (Latin: *patronus plebis*) and persecuted the oligarchs, according to some sources torturing them to death (Polyaen. *Strat.* 2.30.2; other sources for his tyrannical behavior include Memnon *FGrHist* 434 F1; Diod. Sic. 15.81.5). For the episode, see Berve 1967 I: 315–18; Burstein 1976 47–54; Riess 2006: 72–73; Robinson 2011: 159.

147. Arist. *Pol.* 5.1305b22–23: "oligarchies are made unstable through the oligarchs themselves playing the demagogue due to their rivalry [*philoneikia*] with each other." For Aristotle, this is the second major cause of oligarchic breakdown after abuse of the demos (1305a37–40, examine above). For what follows, see the more in-depth arguments of Simonton 2017: 6–17.

counts of oligarchy and which had played such an important role even earlier, during the Archaic period.[148]

Examples of oligarchic breakdown along these lines are extremely numerous, to the point of almost defying a complete catalogue. What I hope to clarify here are the slightly different dynamics according to which these changes of constitution unfolded. In some cases, oligarchs chose to appeal to the people because they had their "backs against the wall": their disputes had either come to the point where they feared for their lives, or they saw no viable political future for themselves if they remained within the oligarchic status quo. Democratization in these cases represented an act of desperation, chosen *faute de mieux*. In other, more complex cases, the sources point to an actual change of preferences on the part of the oligarchs, due primarily to the influence of the emotions. Oligarchs in this case are not faced with a life-or-death dilemma; instead, based on their sense of wounded pride, their extreme outrage at mistreatment, or for some other emotional reason, they reorder their political preferences (their *prohairēsis*) and rank democracy above oligarchy.[149] This set of cases is interesting for the light it casts on the role of the emotions in political life.

Examples of the first type of breakdown abound. Cleisthenes of Athens presents an early and prominent instance.[150] The cases discussed above of Tegea, Corinth, and Thebes in 379 fit the bill as well.[151] Aristotle, however,

---

148. See the sources discussed in chapter 2, section 2.1. *Philotimia* is not considered a positive force until the Athenian democracy of the fourth century, in which elites channel their love of honor toward the public good: see Whitehead 1983.

149. For an ancient quotation that nicely illustrates the two forms of change, those arising from fear and those arising from a sense of vengeance, see Antiph. fr. 1a Caizzi: "Most people desire a constitution [*politeia*] different from the established one for the following reasons, either so that they not pay the penalty [*dikē*] for the crime they have been convicted of, or so that they have their revenge [*timōrōntai*] for the wrongs they have suffered."

150. For Cleisthenes's decision to ally with the demos, see chapter 1, section 1.1.2.

151. Note the close similarity, discussed by Bultrighini (2005: 81–82), between the Tegean episode (the faction of Proxenus and Callibius are "defeated in the *thearoi*," ἡττώμενοι... ἐν τοῖς θεαροῖς, and thus seek to establish democracy, Xen. *Hell.* 6.5.7) and the case of Cleisthenes ("getting the worst of it," he reached out to the demos, ἑσσούμενος, Hdt. 5.66.2; ἡττώμενος, [Arist.] *Ath. Pol.* 20.1). Aristagoras of Miletus was similarly a democrat *malgré lui*. He promised *isonomia* to the Milesians only because he needed to extricate himself from his feud with the Persian Megabates, thus sparking the Ionian Revolt (Hdt. 5.30–37; Baragwanath [2008: 185] compares Aristagoras with Cleisthenes). Some scholars have thought that Herodotus's focus on Aristagoras is misplaced and that there were deeper causes of the Revolt: Burn 1984: 193; Evans 1963: 118; Munson 2007: 167. As we will see, however (section 6.2.4), seemingly "private" conflict between elites could lead to large-scale political crises.

devotes an entire section of Book 5 of the *Politics* exclusively to this type.[152] The initial causes of the destructive disputes are multiple, from love affairs to inheritance to personal insult. Disputes over such matters led to constitutional change in Syracuse, Hestiaea, Delphi, Mytilene, Phocis, and Epidamnus—all, it seems, oligarchic regimes.[153] He lists additional cases further on in Book Five, in the section properly devoted to oligarchic breakdown. Here the causes of *stasis* are largely the same: marriages and inter-family strife.[154] Aristotle's point is that the beginnings of such disputes often appear trifling. They start out small, but because of the extremely fraught political atmosphere of oligarchies, in which multiple parties are hoping to exploit private affairs for political purposes, the whole community is quickly involved. Moreover, this is as likely to happen in intra-family disputes as in conflicts between different families. As Aristotle says, "The civil strife of the upper classes gets the whole city completely involved."[155] This is important evidence that oligarchies were comparatively more fragile than democracies and

---

152. Interestingly, the section falls not under the general heading of oligarchy but under the category of "*stasis* caused by trivial matters" (*ek mikrōn, Pol.* 5.1303b18). It is telling that nearly all of the examples given come from oligarchies. This point was noted by Newman in his commentary on Aristotle's *Politics, ad loc.*: "The instances which Aristotle gives in what follows of *staseis* arising from small causes seem all to be taken from oligarchies ... [q]uarrels would be especially frequent and mischievous in oligarchies."

153. Love interest: Syracuse in the late Archaic period (*Pol.* 5.1303b20–26; cf. Plut. *Mor.* 825c-d). Inheritance: Hestiaea after the Persian Wars, Delphi, Mytilene (cf. Thuc. 3.2.3), Phocis (1303b31–1304a13). Personal insult: Epidamnus (1304a13–17; cf. Thuc. 1.24.5).

154. 1306a31–36, covering Elis and Eretria (Aristotle explicitly ties in his new examples with those discussed earlier in Book 5). For women under oligarchy, see chapter 2, section 2.3.

155. *Pol.* 5.1303b31–32. Literary evidence provides some fascinating parallels to the phenomenon Aristotle describes. Pindar, for example, speaks of the conflict between the brothers Zeus and Poseidon (cf. Aristotle's Hestiaean example) over who will marry Thetis (*I.* 8.26–27). The strife threatens to tear apart the gods' political world, but Themis "of good counsel" (*euboulos*) speaks "in the middle" (*en mesoisi*, line 31) in order to reconcile them. Another paradigm case of feuding elite brothers is Polynices and Eteocles of Thebes. In Euripides's treatment of the myth in the *Phoenissae*, their mother Jocasta urges them to respect personified *Isotēs* (Equality), rather than *Philotimia* (531–61). Eteocles instead chooses *Tyrannis*, thus shattering the normatively sanctioned sharing of power among the elite. The political ideals espoused in the tragedy are not necessarily, or even primarily, democratic, and seem to point instead to the importance of equality within the ruling elite of an oligarchy (see further de Romilly 1965; Balot 2001: 207–10; McHardy 2008: 101–2; Papadodima 2011: 31–35). Intriguingly, the *Phoenissae* was probably staged around 408, just a few years after the oligarchic interlude of 411 that saw members of the elite fall prey to destructive *philotimia* (Thuc. 8.89.3, cited by Mastronarde 1994 *ad* 532—see the discussion above).

required greater policing, a point Aristotle makes elsewhere and which we have observed already.[156]

Even more important for our purposes is the role played by the demos during periods of intra-oligarchic discord. As has been emphasized throughout this study, the excluded demos in an oligarchy always constituted a "reserve army" of the politically discontent. In times of *stasis*, it became a cudgel with which a desperate oligarch could beat his peers. The losing parties in the disputes listed by Aristotle are frequently described as "enlisting the help of the *dēmotikoi* [populists]" or "reaching out to those outside the constitution."[157] At Cnidus the demos itself sensed that members of the oligarchy were at odds with each other and so used the opportunity to demand a champion (*prostatēs*), triggering the Stag Hunt scenario discussed above and gaining a democracy for themselves. The story represented for Aristotle an object lesson in the importance of internal oligarchic unity: "dissension [*to stasiazon*] means weakness."[158] The story of Cnidus nicely illustrates the two-way nature of political action during periods of oligarchic regime implosion: the members of the demos are never simply passive spectators to the intrigue and high drama of the elite. Instead, they are constantly looking for weaknesses in the oligarchs' unified façade that might lead to the much-sought-after prize of democracy. As we saw in chapter 5, the projection of power and unity by the oligarchs might successfully deter would-be democratic revolutionaries for a time, but a temporary acquiescence by the demos to the oligarchs did not mean that the common people had ceased despising the oligarchy. As Aristotle recognized, they needed only the merest hint of weakness and they could "catch the oligarchs by surprise [*epilambanein*]."

6.2.4 Emotions and Preferences

I now explore in greater detail a new factor that was hinted at in the preceding discussion, the role of the emotions. Scholars have long noted that any study of ancient Greek political and social life that neglects the emotions—passions such as shame, anger, pride, and jealousy—is woefully incomplete.[159] Following the lead of Konstan and others who have recently deepened our apprecia-

---

156. *Pol.* 4.1296a13–14, 5.1302a8–9, 1315b11–12, 6.1321a1–4. See further chapters 1 and 2, especially section 2.4.

157. 5.1303b36, 1304a16–17. Presumably Diagoras of Eretria, who overthrew the oligarchy of the "knights" (*hippeis*) there when he was wronged in a marriage, enlisted the help of the demos (1306a35–36).

158. 5.1305b12–18.

159. See Dodds 1963, esp. 26n106, citing the anthropologist Ruth Benedict for the notion of

tion of the ancient emotions, political theorists have stressed that spontaneous feelings, such as visceral responses to perceived virtue and vice, played an integral part in the politics of the Greeks.[160] Finally, and most importantly, any investigation into oligarchic politics has to take into account the centrality, noted time and again, of competition and zealous striving for superiority among the ancient Greek elite, issues which in some studies verge on being the only important factors at play in ancient politics.[161]

By introducing the emotions, and especially the rivalrous emotions, this section will therefore demonstrate that the "strategic" approach adopted here complements emotion-based accounts of ancient Greek politics rather than contradicts them. In particular, I show that "strategic" thinking should not be confused with the model of self-interested, individualistic utility maximization commonly referred to as "*homo economicus.*"[162] Instead, the social and cultural context of strategic interaction influences the motivations in individual actors' minds that give rise to those actors' preferences, which they then pursue by means-ends reasoning. In other words, the cultural milieu affects the types of emotions likely to arise in situations, while the emotions in question give rise to different "games" or interaction possibilities where different actors have different preference orderings.[163] One upshot of this approach is that it allows us to see how culturally embedded political agents, anticipating the emotions that might flare up in a given political system, might be inspired to design institutions to contain those emotions. More immediately, this approach helps to account for what we see in the historical record when institutions designed to prevent insulting behavior break down, emotions do erupt, and events take their course. The outcome in the case of oligarchies was typically regime collapse and a spiral into democracy.

In addition, by incorporating the emotions this account bridges the gap noted by Fisher (2000a) in much of the literature on ancient *stasis*, namely,

---

"shame culture"; Adkins 1960 *passim*; Walcot 1978; Dover 1974, esp. section V.B; Williams 1993; Cairns 1993.

160. Works on the emotions of the Greeks: Konstan 2006; Konstan and Rutter 2003; Harris 2001; Sternberg 2005. The connections between the emotions, virtues, and Greek political thought has long been noted by Balot: 2004, 2006 (esp. 263–65 and 298–302), 2014; see further Sissa 2009; Ludwig 2009; Sanders 2014; Eidinow 2016.

161. Stein-Hölkeskamp 1989; van Wees 1992; Osborne 1996: 189–90; Foxhall 1997; Thalmann 2004; Forsdyke 2005: ch. 1; Duplouy 2006; Fisher and van Wees 2011.

162. See chapter 1, section 1.3.

163. For much more complete statements of the relationship between motivations, preferences, and actions, which I cannot fully delve into here, see Elster 2007: ch. 8, and the articles contained in Katznelson and Weingast 2005.

the disconnect between modern studies that stress wider sociopolitical contexts (economic exploitation, political ideology, elite competition, foreign intervention) and the evidence in the ancient sources for the importance of individual honor (*timē*). As Fisher correctly points out, assaults on people's honor "serious enough to be called hubris" could act as "sparks that brought conflicts to a head, or tipped the balance into violence."[164] Rather than see these incidents as separate from issues of social struggle and political structure, I would say that individuals reacted to hubris differently in different institutional settings. The available repertoire of responses to hubristic assaults depended in part upon the political-constitutional environment. While Fisher himself identifies "horizontal" and "vertical" relationships of honor in city-states (basically those between classes and those between competing members of the ruling class) as important sources of social conflict (87), he does not explore the ways in which the interaction between the two kinds of honor-seekers could be especially explosive. I show, by contrast, that it was the partnership between renegade elites and the politically aspirant demos that was distinctively dangerous for oligarchies.

As we have just seen, a new source of power (exogenous factor) or a disgruntled demos (endogenous factor) could tempt oligarchs to break away from the reigning constitution. In reviewing these scenarios I took as given some basic assumptions about oligarchs' preferences and actions. Specifically, I assumed that their actions remained instrumentally rational (i.e., they pursued those means that they thought had the greatest chance of achieving their desired ends), that their preferences were stable and consistent over a number of possible outcomes (i.e., they preferred to be a tyrant to an oligarch, and an oligarch to a member of a democracy). What changed in the situations outlined above were the available means, to which the oligarchs adjusted their actions accordingly. In other words, given a stable oligarchic constitution with normally functioning institutions, it was assumed that the oligarchs' behavior would remain the same until new factors were introduced. The oligarchs then were expected to react to the new circumstances as their preferences dictated. The extant evidence, particularly from Aristotle, appeared to bear out this model.

Heightened emotions, however, could change all that. If a man was insulted or otherwise mistreated by a rival, he might, in his passion and rage, undergo an alteration of preferences. Suddenly, living under a democracy might be seen as more desirable than enduring continued hubris, since the change in constitution would afford him an opportunity to punish the offender. This was

---

164. 2000a: 89. (See the discussion above, section 6.1.2, on he relationship between Fisher's spark imagery and the model of political revolution developed by Kuran 1989.)

not simply a matter of life-or-death survival: it was a burning need for revenge. The process is nowhere better described than in a later source, Dionysius of Halicarnassus, whose subject matter is admittedly Roman; nevertheless, the relevant attitudinal phenomenon is perfectly descibed and would seem to apply equally to a Classical Greek oligarchic context. Dionysius is discussing the establishment of the dictatorship in Rome, in which the Senate considered bestowing the power upon one of the two consuls, Titus Larcius. That course of action would, however, leave the other consul, Cloelius, without an office while bestowing an even greater privilege on his peer. In this scenario, says Dionysius, they were worried that "Cloelius would take his removal from office badly and consider himself to have been treated dishonorably [*ētimasmenos*] by the Senate, in which case he would change [*metathētai*] his political way of life [*prohairesis tou biou*], become champion of the people, and overthrow the whole state."[165] Here Dionysius makes clear that a political decision might be deemed an act of deliberate dishonor by the affected member of the elite, in which case his habits, his ideals, and his whole political orientation might shift (presumably in a way outside of his direct rational control) and lead him to challenge what he had previously accepted.[166]

I suggest that the political situation in oligarchies in the Classical period was not so different from that of the Roman Cloelius as imagined by Dionysius. Heated arguments and acts of perceived shaming could alter an oligarch's usual preferences so as to make him prefer democracy over the status quo. For example, we learn that the excessive punishment of individuals at Heraclea and Thebes led to *stasis* and, to judge from the context of Aristotle's *Politics* in which these incidents come up, the destruction of the regime. Both cases arose from punishments meted out after trials (*ek dikastēriou kriseōs*), and both were strictly speaking in accordance with the letter of the law (*dikaiōs*). The victims, however, felt the mode of punishment to be excessive (the men were pilloried in the agora for adultery—note the *public* character of the humiliation). They also resented the participation of their personal enemies in the execution of the punishment.[167] From the victims' point of view,

---

165. *Ant. Rom.* 5.71.2.

166. I take *metatithēmi* here to mean "change" only in the loosest intentional sense (see *LSJ* s.v., II.3.a, "adopt"). *Prohairesis* too is to be understood in a general way, "a course of life," "a principle" (*LSJ* s.v., 2), not the more technical Aristotelian sense, "deliberational desire for things in our power" (see the discussion in Broadie and Rowe 2002: 42–46, discussing Arist. *NE* 3.2–3, 6.2). For a discussion of the relationship between Aristotle's definition and popular usage, see Allen 2006.

167. Arist. *Pol.* 5.1306a36-b2. The method of punishment—binding in the stocks (*kuphōn*)—may have usually been reserved for petty criminals and lower-class people: see Newman's note *ad loc.*, citing Suda s.v.; schol. *ad* Ar. *Plut.* 476; Poll. 10.177; Dem. 24.114; Plut. *Nic.* 11.4 (applied

therefore, the issue was not so much the justice of the verdict as the spiteful and partisan manner in which it was carried out (*stasiastikōs, ephiloneikēsan*). Had the procedure been more obviously neutral and the rivals less involved, Eurytion and Archias, the two men in question, might have accepted their fate and contented themselves with eventual reintegration into the regime.[168]

Aristotle thus provides good evidence for the potential political and emotional ramifications of shaming and outrage, and he gives reasons for believing that these problems posed a greater threat to oligarchic governments than to democracies.[169] Yet some scholars have remained skeptical of the general applicability of Aristotle's claims, preferring to see view his comments in the "empirical" books of the *Politics* (4–6) as highly conditioned by his own (distorting) theoretical framework.[170] Yet there is good historical evidence for the contrary position that Aristotle accurately reflects, albeit in his own idiosyncratic way, general truths about Classical (even Archaic) Greek political conflict.

To begin with Herodotus, this is nowhere more evident than in the episode of Nicodromus of Aegina, surveyed already above in chapter 2.[171] Recall that Nicodromus led an unsuccessful uprising of the Aeginetan demos against the island's oligarchic elite. Herodotus makes it clear that Nicodromus was numbered among the Aeginetan ruling class (he was *dokimos* and his name sug-

---

to Hyberbolus); add Lucian *Pseudol.* 17; Callisthenes *FGrH* 124 F 5.15. Forsdyke (2012: 149, discussing Dem. 24.114), notes that the penalty, a form of "public shaming," is one of many in which "'formal' legal procedures and 'informal' collective sanctions operate side by side as modes of punishing offenders against social norms." If I am right about oligarchs' sensitivity to issues like shame and publicity, it may be that the combination of formal and informal Forsdyke detects was more common in democracies. Certainly Aristotle's description makes these sorts of punishments appear exceptional for their contexts. See also Allen 2000: 200 with 388n6–8.

168. Recall what was said in chapter 2, section 2.5, about the need in oligarchies for swift, impartial, and communally sanctioned punishment.

169. I do not discuss tyrannies, but Aristotle gives several examples of similar conflicts bringing down tyrants: *Pol.* 5.1304a29–31, 1311a39-b36; cf. 1315b11–39. Tyrannies were probably even less stable than oligarchies, since in the majority of cases, the elite detested them in addition to the demos. This is not surprising: modern research finds that "sultanistic" and "neo-patrimonial" (i.e., highly exclusionary) authoritarian regimes are shorter-lived than party autocracies: see esp. Goodwin 2001: 49–50.

170. See Frost 1968: 11; Davies 2004: 21; Blok 2005: 35. It is certainly true that Aristotle was prone to forcing facts onto his Procrustean bed of theory, but from what follows it should be clear that Aristotle was not alone in seeing shame and outrage as dangerous for oligarchies. If anything shame and outrage have traditionally been considered non-"Aristotelian" political categories (since they are less focused on justice and equality).

171. Chapter 2, section 2.5.

gests athletic victories on his father's part), and it is highly doubtful that he was ideologically attracted to democracy.[172] Instead, he was seeking revenge on his elite peers for subjecting him to exile in the past. Herodotus's use of the phrase "holding his exile against them" (*memphomenos ... exelasin*) indicates that it was the fact of his exile that angered Nicodromus against the Aeginetan oligarchs and not some preexisting political agenda. If we go back to the original infraction that earned him a period of banishment, it is not likely to have been sedition.[173] Instead, it is better to suppose that Nicodromus's exile originated in a private dispute or rivalry along the lines of the examples listed by Aristotle above.[174] Especially pertinent for us here is that Nicodromus blamed the Aeginetan ruling class as a whole for his condition. This suggests that he had not fled for his life out of fear of his personal enemies but had been officially exiled by some authoritative oligarchic body operating through generally agreed-upon political procedure.[175] It is possible that Nicodromus's rivals were also banished, but a more likely hypothesis is that the rest of the oligarchs, whether due to bias or out of a genuine sense of justice, had sided with Nicodromus's enemies and singled him out for punishment. What is remarkable from a modern perspective, and what serves to emphasize once again the centrality of honor and emotion in the political processes of the ancient world, is Nicodromus's willingness, even after he had been reintegrated into the oligarchic community, to engage in potentially costly violence in order to satisfy his sense of self-worth. As Calchas said of Agamemnon, "even if he should choke down his rage for the time being, he still retains his anger afterwards, until he can bring it to fulfillment."[176]

Further examples can be cited in abundance from Classical and later sources, which confirm Aristotle and Herodotus's emphasis upon honor and emotion as drivers of *stasis*. Euphron of Sicyon, a by-now familiar figure,

---

172. For Nicodromus's elite stateus, see Hornblower 2004a: 220 and Fearn 2011: 222.

173. If the crime had been so serious we should not expect to see him back in the ranks of the oligarchic elite at the time of his attempted uprising.

174. In this I follow Scott *ad* 6.88, citing Figueira 1981: 306–10 to question "whether Nicodromus was exiled because he had been advocating constitutional change, or from partisan politics within the aristocracy, so that his 'alliance' with Athens was a marriage of convenience rather than ideology."

175. Unfortunately, we know almost nothing about oligarchic Aegina's political structures: see Figueira 1981: 299–305, 314–21 for a thorough discussion of the little evidence we possess. One board was apparently the *theōroi*, mentioned at Pind. *Nem*. 3.70 with scholl.; cf. the similarly named body at Tegea, Xen. *Hell*. 6.5.7, discussed above, section 6.1. On the Aeginetan board, see Rutherford 2015: 131–35.

176. Hom. *Il*. 1.81–82: εἴ περ γάρ τε χόλον γε καὶ αὐτῆμαρ καταπέψῃ, / ἀλλά τε καὶ μετόπισθεν ἔχει κότον, ὄφρα τελέσσῃ.

offered the excuse to the Spartans that he had established a democracy in his polis "out of a desire to *avenge himself* on his betrayers."[177] Xenophon is unsure how many people believed him, not because the story was inherently implausible, but because everyone had seen him blatantly acting otherwise. The fact that Euphron chooses this excuse implies that it must have been considered a believable account of democratization. Iamblichus, admittedly a late source, reports in his *Life of Pythagoras* that trouble began for the Pythagoreans at Croton in the late sixth century when they rejected from their school a man named Cylon, "foremost among the citizens for his reputation and wealth." He then plotted against the Pythagoreans out of a sense of "unadulterated rivalry" (*philotimia*). He eventually appealed to the Crotoniate demos and established a democracy.[178]

The historical examples are buttressed, moreover, by numerous gnomological sayings stretching back to Homer. It would be impossible to catalogue all of the aphorisms about honor and emotion in Greek literature, but we should note especially the philosopher Democritus's denunciation of strife: "Love of strife [*philoneikiē*] is completely mindless [*anoētos*, lacking *nous*], because in constantly seeking out ways to damage one's opponent, it pays no attention to one's own personal advantage."[179] Democritus seems to have been a proponent of democracy over oligarchy, but these remarks are plainly directed toward the Greek elite, with their love of competition.[180] One can read them as a warning to oligarchs not to forget their individual interest (maintaining the oligarchic status quo) in the pursuit of short-term gain. Plato, meanwhile, devotes a section of the *Laws* to the topic of insult (*kakēgoria*), emphasizing that thanks to mere words a "trifling matter" (*kouphon pragma*) could soon devolve into genuine hatred and serious enmity, and that there was no place in a city of well-ordered people (*eunomoi*) for a slanderer.[181] By "gratifying an ungracious emotion, anger," continues Plato, a person "feasts his

---

177. Xen. *Hell.* 7.3.3: ἔπειτα δὲ τοὺς προδόντας ἑαυτὸν βουλόμενος τιμωρήσασθαι δῆμον καταστῆσαι.

178. Iamb. *VP* 248–249. For this episode, see Minar 1942: 50–94; Dunbabin 1948: 359, 366 with n9, 371; Robinson 1997: 76–77. The tradition dates back to Timaeus of Tauromenium. Robinson (77) aptly compares Cylon with Cleisthenes of Athens.

179. Democritus DK 68 B 237, reading *philoneikiē* (preserved in Stobaeus and Arsenius) rather than *philonikiē*, "love of victory."

180. For Democritus' democratic leanings, see DK 68 B 251 with Procopé 1989; Mejer 2004.

181. For the idea of a "trivial cause" leading to a widespread social problem, cf. Arist. *Pol.* 5.1303b17–1304a17 and Plut. *Mor.* 824f-825a, discussed above. *Eunomoi* recalls oligarchies' emphasis on *eunomia*.

passion on a banquet of evils" and is deprived of everything he has learned, his *paideia*, reverting again to the condition of a beast.[182]

While these emotions might have been widespread among all men within ancient Greek society, the rich would have been particularly well placed to act upon them. With these sorts of values being encouraged among the elite, putting an end to disputes between them and convincing them to relinquish their anger in favor of cooperation was often a considerable endeavor. I showed in chapter 2 how oligarchs did sometimes manage, through institutional means, to overcome their own worst tendencies and secure stable government. As this section has shown, however, that equilibrium could be dangerously brittle. Over time, even the most carefully thought out and robust constitutions could succumb to error, from which there could be no return to oligarchic business as usual. Collapsed oligarchies were stymied in their attempts at recrudescence not only by the opposition of the local majority population, who, once they had tasted democracy, had little reason to go back to the *ancien régime*. Re-oligarchization was also made difficult by the norms of the "international" milieu, which from the mid-fourth century onward was growing more and more favorable toward democracy. Domestic and interstate trends were steadily closing the window of opportunity for oligarchy in its strong form. It is to these trends that I now turn in conclusion.

[182]. Plat. *Leg.* 11.934d-35a. See further Pindar fr. 210 S-M: "those men in cities who strive excessively after *philotimia* create a manifest pain"; Xen. *Mem.* 2.6.20; and the passages from Herodotus (3.82.3) and Thucydides (8.89.3-4) discussed earlier. For the need among the Greek elite to channel strife in nondestructive ways, see Thalmann 2004.

AFTERWORD

The Eclipse of *Oligarchia*

In August 2002 an inscription was discovered in the vicinity of the ancient theater of Aeolian Cyme.[1] The decree, which dates to the mid-third century, was proposed by one Euhippus the son of Laonicus with the express purpose of "maintaining the polis in a state of freedom and autonomy [*eleuthera kai autonomos*], as is traditional [*patrion*] for us" (lines 4–5).[2] The body of the decree sets out a series of "duties" for the city's generals (*doveri* in the formulation of the author of the *editio princeps*, Manganaro). "If one of the generals, whom the demos elects [*cheirotonēsēi*], during his generalship ... does not hand over the city in a state of freedom and democratic governance [*damokratēmenē*]," he is to be subject to a number of criminal indictments (lines 11–13).[3] The decree expresses concern over those who would "put down the demos" (line 14), as well as the possibility that the generals might cooperate with them for the purpose of "putting down the democracy" (line 20). Any general who does so is in fact liable to charges of "treason" (*prodosia*) and "putting down the people" (*katalusis tō damō*) (line 23).

A few decades later, in the second half of the third century, the polis of Mylasa in Caria passed a decree honoring a foreign benefactor, the local dynast Olympichus. In an inscription published in 2008, the demos of Mylasa praises Olympichus for his role in the events of 14 [month], on which day "the demos regained its [freedom] and its democracy" (line 14).[4] To make clear their gratitude towards the *euergetēs*, the people order the construction of a

---

1. *Ed. pr.* Manganaro 2004 = SEG 54.1229. See further Hamon 2008 = SEG 59.1407, combining Manganaro's decree with an earlier known inscription from Cyme (SEG 47.1660).

2. The proposer is known from a further inscription, *IK Kyme* 12.

3. For the idea of a general "handing over" the city in a state of freedom and democracy at the end of his term, see *IG* II² 682, lines 38–40; *IK Erythrai* 9.

4. *Ed. pr.* Isager and Karlsson 2008 = SEG 58.1220. A further inscription, this time a letter from Olympichus to Mylasa, has since been discovered: Carless Unwin and Henry 2016.

bronze image of Olympichus, to be placed in the [agora?], in the "most conspicuous location" (lines 3–5). The public statuary program is not complete, however: "erect also an image of the People [Demos] in bronze, five *pecheis* [around seven feet] in height, crowning the image of Olympichus; and inscribe on the base: 'The People [Demos] crowns Olympichus the son of Olympichus as its benefactor'" (lines 5–8). The people of Mylasa, in a practice stretching back to the heyday of democracy in Athens, think of themselves as a corporate figure, united in will and power, possessing the sole authority within the community to bestow civic honors.[5]

The Cymaean and Mylasan decrees evince powerful devotion to and vigilance over the polis's democracy on the part of the common people. Here, in the heart of the early Hellenistic period, we have new and significant evidence for the continuing importance of democratic government in the Greek world. To be sure, democracy now exists within a complex matrix of competing kings and local powers, whose influence might be thought to constitute an impediment to internal self-governance. In both the Cymaean and Mylasan cases the interstate situation is in fact more complex than it first appears. We know from a separate dossier of Cymaean documents that the city had applied for military support from the Pergamene dynast Philetaerus around 270.[6] The Cymaeans indicate in an initial decree that Philetaerus had "consistently been well-minded towards the democracy on all previous occasions" (lines 5–6). To a request for six hundred shields he had responded with a gift of one thousand, prompting effusive praise from the demos. In their honorary decree for him, they reveal that he already enjoys divine honors at Cyme: he has a religious precinct, the Philetaireion, which includes a "sacred house" (*hieros oikos*), and a fragmentary passage later in the decree suggests that the Cymaeans also already celebrate a festival of the Philetaireia (lines 27, 42).[7] In the Mylasan case, Olympichus had served as an intermediary between the polis and Seleucus II, who had decided to grant Mylasa freedom and democracy.[8] The decree ordering the erection of the two statues, as well as many other

---

5. For depictions of the personified Demos in democratic Athens, see Glowacki 2003, analyzing a previously unpublished document relief and providing an appendix listing 31 known instances; Blanshard 2004. These are document reliefs, however; the practice of erecting an actual statue of the Demos is known from the later Hellenistic period, making the Mylasan example an early instance (later examples listed by Isager and Karlsson 2008: 45). For the lack of a corresponding artistic program from oligarchs, see chapter 1, section 1.2.4.

6. Manganaro 2000 = *SEG* 50.1195 with *Bull. ép.* 2001 no. 373; Gauthier 2003. The dossier includes an initial decree of the Cymaeans, a letter from Philetaerus to the polis, and a follow-up Cymaean decree honoring the dynast.

7. See further Thonemann 2013: 88–90; Chaniotis 2005a: 68–69.

8. *IK Labraunda* 3 lines 8, 30.

honors for Olympichus, is thus a community's grateful response to a warlord who had carried out a distant potentate's request.[9] In both cases, democracy was clearly important, but its existence was also precarious.

The combined content and context of the two decrees gives a good indication of the status of democracy in the Hellenistic period, as a (perhaps the) prominent constitutional form, but one frequently constrained in various ways in practice. The scholarly consensus on this point has shifted considerably since the early 1980s, when de Ste. Croix could speak of the "destruction of Greek democracy" during the Hellenistic period (1981: 300). A sustained reexamination of the fourth-century and later sources reveals, however, precisely the opposite state of affairs. Democracy did not retreat, it expanded during the fourth century, as both Robinson (2011: ch. 4 with figs. 4.1–4) and Teegarden (2014: 2 and appendix) have independently demonstrated.[10] Specifically, Teegarden counts 52 out of the 112 cities for which data is available as having experienced democracy in the second half of the fourth century, or 46 percent. The number for the end of the fifth century is 40 percent. By contrast, the number of oligarchies fell, from 59 percent of cities in the second half of the fifth century, to 50 percent in the first half of the fourth, to 37 percent in the second half.[11] (Democracies thus outnumber oligarchies at the end of the fourth century, at least in the data available to us.) For the early Hellenistic period, a largely Francophone tradition of epigraphic research beginning with Robert has shown that democracy flourished in the centuries after Chaeronea. Strong citizen assemblies, allotted magistracies, and the epigraphic habit known from Athens spread throughout the Greek-speaking world, even (especially) in the newly Hellenizing poleis of Asia Minor and the East.[12] In

---

9. In addition to the statue, Olympichus receives an altar, "similar to the one for Mausolus located in the sanctuary of Zeus Labraundos" (lines. 8–11); a yearly procession and an offering on the day when the Mylasans regained their democracy; hymns sung in his honor at the four-year Taureian games, "as for the founders [*ktistai*, restored] of the polis"; and proclamation as civic benefactor at the athletic games for Zeus Osogos. For more on Olympichus see Isager 2011; Aubriet 2012.

10. To be precise, Robinson sees net positive growth over the near-century from 400 to 323, with a few dips in between. By contrast, de Ste. Croix thought democracy "barely held its own" during the fourth century (1981: 295); see further O'Neil 1995: 85, 99, 101.

11. See his Figure A1 at 2014: 223. He speaks of a "Hellenistic democratic revolution" at 213–14.

12. Scholars often distinguish these "moderate" democracies (Chaniotis 2005a: 37) from the "radical" democracy of Classical Athens (Brélaz 2009: 44). While most Hellenistic democracies were no doubt less intensely democratic than Athens, it is important to note that the "radical"/"moderate" distinction is a modern one with no corresponding set of terms in the ancient sources.

Robert's influential formulation, further developed by Gauthier, the "high Hellenistic period" (*haute époque hellénistique*) of the late-fourth to mid-second century represented the apogee of democracy in the ancient Greek world, while a diminution of citizen participation came only in the "low Hellenistic period" (*basse époque hellénistique*) and in connection with the involvement of Rome in the eastern Mediterranean.[13] We see beginning around that time the gradual "oligarchization" of the Greek polis (the term is modern, not ancient) as the Romans encouraged permanent boards of elite magistrates, who evolved into a more or less hereditary order of notables.[14] Before that, however, democracy had represented the Hellenistic "rules of the game" when it came to political type.[15]

---

13. The rule is not absolute, of course; there were oligarchic exceptions, such as Messene in the late third century (Polyb. 4.31.2, 32.1; Fröhlich [2013: 297–98] views the Messenians' practice of burying elite families within the city walls as emblematic of their oligarchic constitution).

14. Pausanias reports that after the Battle of Corinth in 146 BCE the Roman commander Lucius Mummius "put down democracies" in mainland Greece and "set up magistracies [*archai*] based on property requirements [*apo timēmatōn*]," 7.16.9; presumably the Greeks had previously selected magistrates from the whole citizen body, either through election or lottery. The so-called "Stadiasmus Patarensis," an inscription from the Lycian city of Patara that serves as a road map of the territory, provides evidence for the oligachization of the council in the first century CE. It states at the beginning that "the constitution [*politeia*] was entrusted to councilors [*bouleutai*] selected from the best men [*aristoi*], instead of [the meaning is certain] from the undiscerning majority [*akriton plēthos*]" (*SEG* 51.1832, lines 25–29). For the disparaging language about the demos, see chapter 1, section 1.1.3. For much of the Hellenistic period, however, we possess evidence for continuing popular control of institutions like the law courts (Crowther 1992; Walser 2012). As late as the first century CE some communities were still utilizing sortition for selecting judges (*SEG* 55.838, from Tauric Chersonesus). The assembly of the demos remained symbolically important even in Imperial times, when its power was admittedly much diminished: Fernoux 2011. The poleis never speak openly about practicing *oligarchia*, which had become an unacceptable term in mainstream political discourse.

15. Robert insisted early and often that "the Greek city did not die at Chaeronea" ("la cité grecque n'est pas morte à Chéronée," e.g., 1969: 603). His distinction between high and low Hellenistic: 1960: 325–26. Gauthier's work (e.g., 1984, 1985, 1993) shows the spread and normalization of democracy during the high Hellenistic period, where he sees a "*koinè démocratique*" (a kind of democratic lingua franca; 1993: 217–18). On Hellenistic democracy, see also Quass 1979; Gruen 1993; Rhodes with Lewis 1997: 531–49; Ma 2000: 108–9, 115; Grieb 2008; Carlsson 2010 (and on these last two see the review article of Hamon 2009); van Nijf and Alston 2011; Mann and Scholz 2012. Fröhlich 2004 and Feyel 2009 show the largely (but not exclusively) democratic workings of *euthuna* and *dokimasia* procedures during the Hellenistic period (see the comment of Fröhlich p. 3: "La démocratie paraît même avoir été le régime dominant à l'époque hellénistique"). For oligarchization during the low Hellenistic period (sometimes even later) see Fröhlich and Müller 2005; Hamon on the late Hellenistic council (e.g., 2005, 2007);

The stigmatization of oligarchy during this period is remarkable and requires explanation.[16] One contributing factor may have been the persistence of democracy at Athens, which, notwithstanding two oligarchic interludes in the late fourth century, continued largely unchanged into the early Hellenistic period.[17] Athens made a point during the wars against Macedon and the Diadochi not merely of respecting other poleis' constitutions, as they were capable of doing when diplomacy required it, but of actively applauding and encouraging specifically democratic uprisings.[18] Certainly the inscriptional formulae found in the decrees of many Hellenistic democracies owe their existence to the Athenian model, as Lewis showed (1997). Teegarden has argued convincingly in a recent study that democracy was also aided by the spread of anti-tyranny legislation in the style of the Athenian decree of Demophantus and the law of Eucrates. As he puts it, a "diffusion of institutions" stemming from Athens encouraged a common culture of democracy.[19]

Another turning point in the struggle against oligarchy was the decision by Alexander the Great to support democratic regimes in Asia Minor, beginning in the mid-330s. Already in 336 and 334, the Macedonian King had ordered democratic regimes restored at Eresus, Chios, and Mytilene; in 334, however, following his takeover of Ephesus, he explicitly ordered that "the oligarchies everywhere be put down, and democracies instated."[20] A great number of new

---

contra Habicht 1995, arguing for continuity of moderate democratic rule; Quass 1993, who does not distinguish between high and low Hellenistic period.

16. Veyne is largely correct that in the Hellenistic period "the epoch of the militant oligarchy which tried to seize power by force had been left behind" (1990: 83), but his explanation for democracy's success—"oligarchy was an idea that conflicted with the spirit of the age" (84)—is vague. There was nothing natural or inevitable about democracy becoming the hegemonic regime type during the Hellenistic period: this state of affairs had to be achieved, and I try to give some idea how in what follows.

17. For the oligarchies of Phocion (321–318) and Demetrius of Phalerum (317–307), see above, chapter 1, section 1.2.1; chapter 2, section 2.3; chapter 3, section 3.2; chapter 4, section 4.4; chapter 5, section 5.2.4. For democracy at Athens in the Hellenistic period, see Habicht 1997: 2; Rhodes with Lewis 1997: 35–61; Oliver 2007: 266.

18. They had paid lip service to the notion of constitutional autonomy in the charter of the Second Athenian League of 378 (RO 22.19–21). In the decree for Euphron of Sicyon, by contrast (*IG* II² 448), they praise the honorand's willingness to "die struggling on behalf of democracy rather than see his *patris* enslaved" (lines 53–56.)

19. 2014: 220. I agree that anti-tyranny legislation contributed substantially to democratization, but just as important were local popular movements in the Greek poleis and internecine struggles within the oligarchic class, as described below.

20. Arr. *Anab*. 1.18.2. Eresus: RO 83; Chios: RO 84; Mytilene: RO 85; Ephesus: Arr. *Anab*. 1.18.2.

or reconstituted democracies in Asia Minor resulted, the genuine nature of which we have no good reason to question. Nawotka in fact has shown, in a survey of the epigraphic evidence, that the post-Alexander regimes of Asia Minor not only adopted democratic enactment formulae in their decrees, but they also published decrees more frequently than in previous periods. The change in regime type renewed civic pride and with it the desire to publish the community's decisions on stone.[21]

Athens and Alexander were thus two possible drivers of democratic growth in the late-Classical period, to the detriment of existing oligarchies. There is no reason to doubt that they both played a part in spreading democracy, albeit on the "supply" side: they provided opportunities for adopting democracy where previously there had been none. We should also inquire, however, about the "demand" side of the equation: might the growth of democracy have come as a result of more and more communities of everyday citizens requiring accountability from their ruling elite?[22]

Chapter 6 provides us with good reasons for thinking so. I would describe it more specifically as a cyclical process. As oligarchies committed the mistakes of governance—many of them completely unintended—surveyed above, leading to regime implosion and the institution of democratic constitutions, the members of the demos gained relevant experience of self-government. Previously, in poleis where *dēmokratia* had never been tried, we can imagine that common people faced great uncertainties: Just how much more preferable was democracy to oligarchy? Was it worth risking one's life for? What if it did not meet their expectations? When poleis were forced to experiment with democracy, however, it must on the whole have assuaged the people's concerns. With democracy proven to be not so disruptive as they perhaps feared, oligarchs would have a more difficult time in the future

---

21. Nawotka 2003. See further Bosworth 1988: 192–94; Robinson 2011: 160, 169, 172, 173, 175, 178, 206. Gauthier further observes that the policies of Alexander's immediate successors (Antipater, Cassander, Lysimachus), which involved installing garrisons and non-democratic regimes, made oligarchy and tyranny appear as "twins" (*jumeaux*), equally "detestable" because they represented outside impositions. Democracy thus became the sole regime type that was desirable for a polis, while oligarchy and democracy were "hateful and pernicious" (1984: 100). I would only add that the Diadochi consolidated growing feelings of popular disgust against oligarchies, already known from the fifth and earlier fourth centuries, but did not create them.

22. For an alternative account of the spread of democratic practice during the Classical period, see Robinson 2011: ch. 4. In contrast to older studies that posited Athens as the main driver of democratization, Robinson emphasizes regional democratic powers (Argos, Syracuse, Miletus) and the role of the sophists in spreading democratic ideas through peer-polity interaction. I focus instead on the interplay between local communities and the oligarchs who ran them, showing how democratic norms gained ground through oligarchic failure.

arguing for the "normalcy" of their preferred political setup.[23] When they did return to power, their rule would be much more likely to exhibit paranoia and violence, as they sought to preempt the democratic resistance they anticipated.[24]

This is precisely what we see in microcosm in the two different experiences of oligarchic rule in Athens in 411 and 404. The Four Hundred had engaged in selective violence, as other oligarchies were accustomed to do. They had subtly coerced the population through intimidation and clandestine terror, rather than through outward displays of brute force. Even they could not hold onto power, however, largely because of the ruling elite's inexperience with oligarchic cooperation. The lesson for Critias and the Thirty was clear: eliminate any potential opposition in advance via large-scale killings; govern the city like conquered enemy territory, through the use of a garrison; and cultivate an ever-smaller circle of trustworthy followers, whose loyalty can be bought through incrimination if not through genuine allegiance. The Thirty (in fact, the Three Thousand) risked everything on a reign of terror, and it ended in spectacular failure.[25] Other oligarchs watching the debacle might have attempted to draw lessons from the example in the direction of moderation and tolerance, but direct experience would confound their best-laid plans. When faced with life-or-death crises in their conflicts with the demos, they could not restrain themselves from choosing the more tempting path of reliance on violence.

Aristotle indicates that the oligarchs of his day had placed themselves in such a quandary. As we have seen, in his discussion of the "oligarchs' oath"

23. Tellingly, we read of no demos that regretted its experimentation with democracy and longed for a return to elite rule.

24. This thesis receives some (very rough) quantitative support from a look at oligarchic regime duration. (The following points make no claim to statistical "proof" and are simply meant as suggestive.) It seems that stability begat stability: those regimes that had never experienced democracy and entered the Classical period (ca. 500 BCE) as oligarchies tended to last a long time (5 cases or 9 cases: average 117.4 or 87.66 years). By contrast, when a polis does have at least one instance of a democratic regime in its past, oligarchies are much shorter-lived on average within it (34 cases or 26 cases: average 21.97 or 28.42 years). Using the four different figures, we see an average decrease of 81.3, 75.8, 74.9 or 67.6 percent. Within individual poleis, we can see a shortening of subsequent oligarchic regimes when the polis has experienced at least one democracy. For example, Mytilene's second oligarchy was 38 years shorter than the first; Miletus's was 41 years shorter. Oligarchies following democracies experience on average 11.87 fewer years than previous oligarchic regimes in the same polis, representing a percentage decrease of 48.8 percent (eight cases). See the appendix.

25. For the violence of the Thirty and its causes, see Wolpert 2006 (and cf. Shear 2011: 180–85, who, while acknowledging the Thirty's violence, accords the Thirty too much initial popularity among the demos).

against the common people, he emphasizes that the few of his own day ("now," [*nun*], *Pol.* 5.1310a8) fall back on this tactic far more often than they should. There was a time, Aristotle suggests, when ruling oligarchs could make *bona fide* displays of good will toward the demos, but those days are past. Similarly, the oligarchs of the mid-fourth century refuse to engage in the kinds of civic display—sacrifices, building programs—that in earlier periods had secured the demos's acquiescence, if not through willing obedience then at least through dissuasion. Aristotle faults them for being "like democracies" in their love of petty gain, but late-Classical oligarchs' neglect of public expenditure may reflect their more predatory nature: fearing a revolt of the demos, they did not bother trying to placate it with *panem et circenses* but instead grabbed as much power as they could. With re-democratization looming like a specter over the oligarchic project, their "discount rate" (the rate at which they discount potential future gains to be made in favor of present certainties) would have risen, leading to strategies of short-term gain. As the political scientist Margaret Levi has shown, rulers unsure of their basic security are much more exploitative (Levi 1988: 32–33).[26]

One might counter that the same sort of mounting security worries would have driven democracies to be just as oppressive, and thus just as short-lived, as the Classical period wore on. The two regime types might have been locked in a deadly struggle that eventually saw the disappearance of both of them in favor of some new, more stable regime. We know that democrats were perfectly capable of abusing the elite: the *Athēnaiōn Politeia* notes that in cities other than Athens, triumphant democratic factions often carried out wholesale redistributions of the land in the wake of victories against oligarchs (40.3). As concrete examples we have the numerous incidents cited in Book 5 of the *Politics*, as well as the grisly episode from Argos known as the *skutalismos* ("clubbing"), in which demagogues goaded the populace into bludgeoning to

26. Compare the actions of the oligarchs at Rhodes in the mid-fourth century. These men likely came to power during the Social War with the support of Mausolus, satrap of Caria (Berve 1967: 339; Shrimpton 1991: 74). According to the description by Theopompus preserved in Athenaeus (*FGrH* 115 F 121 *apud* Athen. 10.444e-445a), this oligarchy, and especially its ringleader Hegesilochus, spent their time in drinking and dicing, and "disgraced" free wives and youths. Hegesilochus had a terrible reputation, not only among the citizens, but even within his faction (*hetairoi*). The actions of this regime seem short-sighted, careless, and extremely predatory. They seem to have survived until the 330s, but only through the support of a garrison (see *IACP* no. 1000, p. 1206 [Nielsen and Gabrielsen]). The nature of this regime is quite similar to that of the polemarchs in Thebes who ruled as a *dunasteia* with Spartan support from 382–79 (Hobden 2013: 174). Cf. also the description of the Archaic Erythraean "oligarchic tyrants" by the local historian Hippias (*FGrH* 421 F 1), which may be based on contemporary oligarchies.

death over a thousand supposed oligarchs.[27] Was not uncontrolled populism (mob rule [*ochlokratia*]) the mirror image of violent oligarchy?

In fact, several structural factors prevented democracy from spiraling out of control in the manner of oligarchies. First, democracies' lack of concentrated power—the very thing that allowed oligarchs comparatively greater facility of coordination—kept them from acting on powerful impulses as frequently. Even elite critics of democracy like Plato and Aristotle admitted that, of the "perverted" constitutions, it did the least harm. In the *Statesman* (303a-b), the Eleatic Stranger phrases this in terms of the distribution—and thus the dissipation—of political power, in that the magistracies in a democracy are dispersed among a wide mass of people, rendering them less effective. Aristotle says that democracy is the most "moderate" (*metriōtatē*) compared with oligarchy and tyranny; in a separate passage, he labels democracies the more "lax" (*aneimenai*) and "gentle" (*malakai*), while oligarchies are "taut" (*suntonōterai*) and despotic (4.1290a27–29).[28] The author of the *Ath. Pol.* speaks of the "accustomed gentleness [*praotēs*] of the demos" in allowing associates of the tyranny to remain in Athens without being ostracized (22.4; cf. 16.10 on the "gentle" laws against tyranny), and we have just seen the author's praise of the restored democrats' moderation in their handling of the oligarchs (40.3).[29] Proponents of democracy were happy to repeat this claim: as Christ has recently shown, the Athenian orators, and in particular Demosthenes, refashioned values like "gentleness" (*praotēs*) and "humaneness" (*philanthrōpia*) as specifically democratic traits.[30] This greater leniency likely has more to do, in point of fact, with the number of individuals involved than with their ethical character.[31] Oligarchs' small numbers allowed them to act quickly and effectively in concert, often with violent intent. The greater number of common people made it more difficult for them to coordinate their actions, so that in many instances their moderate treatment of oligarchs was more the result of

---

27. Diod. Sic. 15.57.3–58. See further Isoc. 5.52; Dion. Hal. *Ant. Rom.* 7.66.5; Plut. *Mor.* 814b; Ael. Arist. 13.273d, 311d.

28. "Lax" and "taut" come from the language of musical tuning—cf. *Pol.* 5.1304a20–21, in which the domination of the Areopagus made the Athenian *politeia* "more taut" (*suntonōterē*), and [Arist.] *Ath. Pol.* 26.1, in which the constitution "slackened" (*aniesthai*) after the decline of the same institution.

29. See Rhodes 1993: 272; Forsdyke 2012: 133.

30. Christ 2013, discussing *inter alia* Dem. 20.109, 24.24, 40.32, 22.51. Cf. [Lys.] 6.34; Hyp. col. 25. Christ observes that if toleration and gentleness are "natural" to the members of the Athenian demos, this is not independent of their democratic constitution, which has shaped them in that direction (217–18).

31. Still, there is a case to be made that the average oligarch was a man of more violent passion than the average member of the demos (see, e.g., Arist. *Pol.* 5.1302a9–13).

a collective action problem than of any ethical considerations: many could not be bothered to retaliate violently against oligarchs and left it to others to do so. Oligarchs, because they often conceived of "the demos" as a corporate person, thought of it as an unintelligent brute, usually docile but prone to violent outbursts. This paternalistic image both assured them of the rightness of their rule over "inferiors" and helped them to make sense of the seemingly haphazard actions of the common people.[32] In point of fact, democratic movements only appeared more capricious, and that was because they were made up of more individuals.[33]

Another factor that accelerated the downfall of oligarchies was, ironically, the competitiveness of the oligarchs themselves, the opposite tendency to the singleness of purpose they exhibited much of the time. More specifically, when renegade oligarchs reached out to the demos in order to punish their enemies, as we saw above in chapter 6, they were often tempted to paint their opponents as tyrants. This figure of public hatred, equally opposed by elite and demos, served to unite the disparate groups against a common enemy. We see oligarchs' willingness to label their fellow elite "tyrannical" already in 427, when the Thebans, according to Thucydides, call the government that medized during the Persian Wars a "*dunasteia* of a few men ... closest in form to a tyranny" (3.62.3). In later instances oligarchs actually call on support from the common people using similar language. The Rhodian conspirators of 395, who almost certainly came from the elite, rally the populace in the agora with the cry of "let us attack the tyrants!" (*Hell. Oxy.* 18.2 Chambers). The Thebans revolutionaries led by Epaminondas and Pelopidas, once they have murdered the members of the ruling *dunasteia*, similarly call out to the people that "the tyrants are dead" (Xen. *Hell.* 5.4.9). Even though these are sub-sets of the oligarchic elite attacking dynastic cliques, over time the language of tyrannicide would come to be more and more associated with democratic uprisings

---

32. We saw in chapter 1, section 1.1, Megabyzus's early and influential characterization of the demos as completely thoughtless (*aneu noou*), a river bursting forth (3.81.2). Plato memorably depicted it as a great and powerful beast that required taming (*Rep.* 6.493a). Even in the case of the Argive *skutalismos*, Diodorus depicts the episode basically as a crazed aberration: after much senseless killing (including of the demagogues who originally incited them), the demos snaps out of its "frenzy" (*luttē*) and "returns to its senses" (*eis ... ennoian apokatestē*, 15.58.4). For elite critics, the demos was not normally vicious, only occasionally, but those instances were abrupt, unexpected, and spectacularly violent.

33. The comments of Rhodes about the demos in the Athenian assembly apply equally here: "The assembly was perfectly capable of taking one decision at one meeting, and then at its next meeting ... taking another ... not because the mob was fickle ... but simply because different proposals attracted the support of different collections of men within an unregulated body of voters" (2000: 474).

against oligarchies more generally. Thus the growing trend of conflating oligarchy with tyranny, mentioned throughout this book, was furthered in many cases by the oligarchs themselves.[34] Many democratic opponents of oligarchy had tarred it as tyrannical from the beginning, and democratic anti-tyranny legislation over time would increasingly list both tyranny and oligarchy as unacceptable alternatives to the *patrios politeia* of democracy.[35] By introducing intra-oligarchic rivalry into the picture, we see what is perhaps an unexpected reason why this rhetorical move gained ground.

Thus, through a dialectical development of democratization, re-oligarchization, and re-democratization, oligarchy gradually sank into disrepute. Oligarchies had never offered a political program of any real mass appeal, and what legitimate criticisms they did level against democracies proved incorporable into the latter without undermining the basic principles of government by the people.[36] As experiments in democracy increased across poleis, oligarchs had few persuasive arguments for re-instituting their rule, and more often than not turned even more oppressive in response. This trend, coupled with oligarchs' tendency to betray each other in the heat of political crises, slowly dismantled the planks undergirding the possibility of stable oligarchic

34. See further the intra-oligarchic dispute between Theramenes and Critias as reported by Xenophon: Critias says the Thirty should not be so naïve as to think they are not a tyranny, while Theramenes opposes a regime that comes close to tyrannical rule (2.3.16, 48).

35. Note the accusations of Chaereas against the Four Hundred (Thuc. 8.74.3), and the historian Hippias's discussion of "tyrannical oligarchs" in his treatment of Archaic Erythrae, *FGrH* 421 F1. For conflation of oligarchs with tyrants in anti-tyranny and other kinds of legislation, see RO 41, lines 25–26; *SEG* 51.1105 (Eretria, mid-fourth century); *IK Ilion* 25 (early third century); *Tit. Cal.* test. xii (Cos/Calymna, mid-third century). For discussion of these and other passages, see chapter 1, section 1.2.4 and Teegarden 2014: *passim* and esp. ch. 6. Finally, see the philosophical discussion of Pseudo-Archytas, probably writing in the early Hellenistic period: while democracy utilizes the "geometric mean" in distributing justice, giving equal portions to both "greater" and "lesser" parties, both oligarchies and tyrannies utilize the arithmetic mean, with the greater portion of justice going to the lesser party (fr. 34.6–8 Thesleff). (This is an interesting inversion of the usual distinction between "arithmetical" and "geometric" equality in democracy and oligarchy, respectively). This is elite philosophical discourse, but it picks out an important feature of oligarchy that popular audiences likely would have acknowledged as well: that anything less than democracy disproportionately favors a narrow group of the citizenry, whether a tyrant or an oligarchy.

36. For example, the distinction in Athens in the fourth century between laws (*nomoi*) and decrees (*psēphismata*), and the institution of the *graphē paranomōn* (Hansen 1979), are clearly the product of reformist thinking following the disturbances of the later fifth century. The Athenians wished to establish a system in which some legislation could not be superseded by a vote in the assembly. As several scholars have shown, the reforms did not undermine democracy but strengthened it (Harris 2005; Rhodes 1995).

government. Well-designed institutions kept oligarchies afloat for considerable periods of time; recovering after collapse was another matter, however, and even the best institutions proved ineffective in a world where the power of the people was becoming the norm. It would take an enormous external shock to the Greek polis system, in the form of Rome, to revitalize the oligarchic project, and even then the few understood that all outward talk of *oligarchia* had been finally, irreversibly silenced.

APPENDIX

For what follows, compare Appendix 11 of *IACP*, and the sources cited in the individual polis entries. Departures from *IACP*'s designations are indicated by a footnote. The temporal boundaries are 500–300 BCE except in two cases (Croton, Caulonia). A beginning date of 500 may represent an even older regime.

KEY: Polis (Possible starting and ending dates, where "C 5/4 l/e/m/f/s= Century, Fifth or Fourth, late/early/middle/first half/second half; total number of years if known; regime type preceding, regime type proceeding: D[emocracy], T[yranny], O[ligarchy]).

Western Greece

1. Acragas   450s; D, D
2. Leontini   C5l; D, D
3. Syracuse   C6l; ?, D
4. Syracuse   –316; D, D
5. Croton   –510; ?, D
6. Croton   C5m; T, ?
7. Cyme   –504; ?, T
8. Cyme   490–?; T, ?
9. Locri   500–352; 148; ?, T
10. Rhegium   –494; ?, T
11. Thurii   413–?; D, D?

Eastern Mainland Greece

12. Epidamnus   ?–437; ?, D
13. Epidamnus   433–C4; D, ?
14. Ambracia   –C5; T, D)
15. Ambracia   338–336; 2; D, D
16. Corcyra   361–?; D, ?
17. Zacynthus   404–C4e; D, D
18. Zacynthus   380s–?; D, ?

Central Greece

19. Acraephia   446–386; 40; D, D
20. Chaeronea   446–386; 40; D, D
21. Haliartus   446–386; 40; D, D
22. Hyettus   446–386; 40; D, D
23. Copae   446–386; 40; D, D
24. Coronea   446–386; 40; D, D
25. Orchomenos   446–364; 82; D, D
26. Siphae   C5s; ?, ?
27. Tanagra   446–386; 40; D, D
28. Thebes   446–382; 67; D, O

Peloponnese

29. Corinth   500–393; 107; T, D
30. Corinth   386–366; 20; D, T
31. Megara   424–?; D, D
32. Sicyon   500–367; 133; T, D
33. Aegae   417–366; 51; ?, D
34. Aegae   365–; D, ?
35. Aegira   417–366; 51; ?, D
36. Aegira   365–; D, ?

287

Peloponnese (con't.)

37. Aegium	417–366; 51; ?, D
38. Aegium	365–; D, ?
39. Aschium	417–366; 51; ?, D
40. Aschium	365–; D, ?
41. Dyme	417–366; 51; ?, D
42. Dyme	365–; D, ?
43. Cerynea	417–366; 51; ?, D
44. Cerynea	365–; D, ?
45. Leontium	417–366; 51; ?, D
46. Leontium	365–; D, ?
47. Olenus	417–366; 51; ?, D
48. Olenus	365–; D, ?
49. Patrae	417–366; 51; ?, D
50. Patrae	365–; D, ?
51. Pellene	417–366; 51; ?, D
52. Pellene	365–; D, ?
53. Pherae	417–366; 51; ?, D
54. Pherae	365–; D, ?
55. Phelloe	417–366; 51; ?, D
56. Phelloe	365–; D, ?
57. Rhypae	417–366; 51; ?, D
58. Rhypae	365–; D, ?
59. Tritaea	417–366; 51; ?, D
60. Tritaea	365–; D, ?
61. Elis	365–350?; D, D
62. Elis	343–?; D, ?
63. Tegea	500–370; 130; ?, D
64. Argos	417; 1; D, D
65. Phlius	379–?; D, ?

Saronic Gulf, Attica, Euboea

66. Aegina	500–431; 69; ?, D
67. Aegina	405–?; D, ?
68. Athens	411; 1; D, D
69. Athens	404–403; 1; D, D
70. Eleusis	403–401; 2; D, D
71. Eretria	411; 1; D, D

Thessaly

72. Pharsalus	C4m; ?, ?

Aegean Islands

73. Andros	411–C4e; D, D
74. Cos	C4m–332; D, D
75. Melos	–415; ?, ?
76. Paros	?–410/9; ?, D
77. Paros	404–394; 10; D, D
78. Siphnos	404–394; 10; D, D
79. Tenos	411–?; D, D
80. Thasos	411–407; 4; D, D
81. Thasos	404–390; 14; D, D

Thrace, Chersonese, Black Sea

82. Mende	423; 1; D, D
83. Torone	423–?; D, ?
84. Calchedon	–C4m; ?, D
85. Byzantium	404–390; 14; D, D
86. Olbia	–ca. 480; foundation, T
86. Heraclea Pontica	–364; D, T
88. Abydus	411–ca. 360; ca. 51; ?, T

Lesbos, Aeolis, Ionia

89. Methymna	C4m; D, T
90. Mytilene	479–427; 52; T, D
91. Mytilene	405–389; D, 16; D, D
92. Mytilene[1]	353/2–ca. 347; ca. 6; D, T

---

1. *IACP* does not follow the contents of the city entry in Index 11. An oligarchy was installed around 353/2 (Isoc. *Ep.* 8; Dem 15.19) and lasted until the tyranny of Cammys, whose regime, *at the shortest* (and thus most favorable to oligarchic regime length), was less than a year.

93. Aeolian Cyme	c5–c4?; D, ?	
94. Chios	479?–412; <u>67</u>; T, O	*Rhodes and Caria*
95. Chios	C4–C4l; D, D	105. Cnidus ?–C4; ?, D
96. Ephesus	334; <u>1</u>; D, D	106. Ialysus 411–395; <u>16</u>; D, D
97. Erythrae	C5m; <u>1</u>; D, D	107. Camirus 411–395; <u>16</u>; D, D
98. Erythrae	C4s–330s; D, D	108. Lindos 411–395; <u>16</u>; D, D
99. Colophon	C4–334; D, D	109. Rhodes 408–395; <u>13</u>; foundation, D
100. Miletus	479–434?; <u>45</u>?; refoundation, D	110. Rhodes 391–90; <u>1</u>; D, D
101. Miletus	405–401; <u>4</u>; D, D	111. Rhodes 355–332; <u>23</u>; D, D
102. Samos	479–441; <u>38</u>; T, D	*North Africa*
103. Samos	440–412; <u>28</u>; D, D	
104. Samos[2]	404–394; <u>10</u>; D, D	112. Euhesperides C4; ?, ?
		113. Cyrene C4m–322; ?, D

Averages and Comparisons

Poleis beginning in 500 with oligarchy:

Locri, Corinth, Sicyon, Tegea, Aegina (5 cases)
= 587 years/5 cases
= **avg. 117.4 years**

Including poleis with oligarchy beginning first half fifth century (Mytilene, Chios, Miletus, Samos, total 9 cases)
= 789 years/9 cases
= **avg. 87.66 years**

Poleis with at least one instance of democracy in the past:

Ambracia, Boeotian cities, Corinth, Argos, Athens (x2), Eleusis, Eretria, Paros, Siphnos, Thasos (x2), Mende, Byzantium, Mytilene (x2), Ephesus, Erythrae, Miletus, Samos (x2), Ialysus, Camirus, Lindos, Rhodes (x2)
= 747 years/34 cases
= **avg. 21.97 years**

Minus 1-year regimes (8 cases)
= 739/26
= **avg. 28.42 years**

---

2. There is little reason for thinking democracy was not restored after Cnidus in 394, *pace IACP*.

Percentage Decreases

Between poleis with no democracy in past and those with at least one democracy in past (different possibilities using four figures): **81.3%; 75.8%; 74.9%; 67.6%**

Within poleis:

Thasos	4 years	–14 years	= –10
Mytilene	52 years	–14 years	= 38
	14 years	–6 years	= 8
Miletus	45 years	–4 years	= 41
Samos	38 years	–28 years	= 10
	28 years	–10 years	= 18
Rhodes	13 years	–1 year	= 12
	1 year	–23 years	= –22
TOTAL			= –95

Average result: 95 fewer years / 8 cases = **11.87 fewer years**
Average percentage: 24.37 years (195/8) to 12.5 years (100/8) = **48.8% decrease**
(Note that in the case of Mytilene and Samos, each regime is shorter than the last)

WORKS CITED

Acemoglu, D. and J. Robinson. 2006. *Economic Origins of Dictatorship and Democracy.* Cambridge.
Adkins, A.W.H. 1960. *Merit and Responsibility: A Study in Greek Values.* Oxford.
Allen, D. 2000. *The World of Prometheus: The Politics of Punishing in Democratic Athens.* Princeton.
———. 2006. "Talking about revolution: On political change in fourth-century Athens and historiographic method." In S. Goldhill and R. Osborne, eds., *Rethinking Revolutions through Ancient Greece.* Cambridge: 183–217.
Alwine, A. T. 2016. "Freedom and patronage in the Athenian democracy." *JHS* 136: 1–17.
Aly, W. 1943. *Fragmentum Vaticanum de elegendis magistratibus = Studi e Testi* 104.
Ampolo, C. 1983. "La boule demosie di Chio: un consiglio 'popolare'?" *PP* 38: 401–16.
Anderson, G. 2003. *The Athenian Experiment: Building an Imagined Political Community in Ancient Attica, 508–490 B.C.* Ann Arbor.
———. 2005. "Before turannoi were tyrants: Rethinking a chapter of early Greek history." *CA* 24: 173–222.
———. 2007. "Why the Athenians forgot Cleisthenes: Literacy and the politics of remembrance in ancient Athens." In C. Cooper, ed., *The Politics of Orality* (Orality and Literacy in Ancient Greece, vol. 6). Leiden: 104–27.
———. 2009. "The personality of the Greek state." *JHS* 129: 1–22.
———. 2015. "Retrieving the lost worlds of the past: the case for an ontological turn." *AHR* 120: 787–810.
Andreev, J. 1979. "Die politischen Funktionen der Volksversammlung im homerischen Zeitalter." *Klio* 61: 385–405.
Andrewes, A. 1938. "Eunomia." *CQ* 32: 89–102.
———. 1953. "The generals in the Hellespont, 410–407 B.C." *JHS* 73: 2–9.
———. 1956. *The Greek Tyrants.* London.
———. 1962. "The Mytilene debate: Thucydides 3.36–49." *Phoenix* 16: 64–85.
———. 1966. "The government of classical Sparta." In E. Badian, ed., *Ancient Society and Institutions.* Oxford: 1–20.
———. 1977. "Kleisthenes' reform bill." *CQ* 27: 241–48.
———. 1981. "The hoplite katalogos." In G. S. Shrimpton and D. J. McCargar, eds., *Classical Contributions: Studies in Honor of Malcolm Francis McGregor.* Locust Valley, NY: 1–3.
Asheri, D. et al., eds. 2007. *A Commentary on Herodotus Books I–IV.* Oxford.
Athanassaki, L. and E. Bowie, eds. 2011. *Archaic and Classical Choral Song: Performance, Politics, and Dissemination.* Berlin.
Aubriet, D. 2012. "Olympichos et le sanctuaire de Zeus à Labraunda (Carie): Autour de

quelques documents épigraphiques." In C. Feyel, ed., *Entités locales et pouvoir central: La cité dominée dans l'Orient hellénistique*. Nancy: 185–209.

Austin, M. 1990. "Greek tyrants and the Persians, 546–479 B.C." *CQ* 40: 289–306.

Avery, H. C. 1979. "The Three Hundred at Thasos, 411 B.C." *CP* 74: 234–42.

Axelrod, R. 1984. *The Evolution of Cooperation*. New York.

Azoulay, V. 2004. *Xénophon et les grâces du pouvoir: De la charis au charisma*. Paris.

———. 2009. "La gloire et l'outrage: Heurs et malheurs des statues honorifiques de Démétrios de Phalère." *Annales HHS* 2: 303–40.

———. 2014. *Les Tyrannicides d'Athènes: vie et mort de deux statues*. L'Univers historique. Paris.

Azoulay, V. and P. Ismard. 2007. "Les lieux du politique dans l'Athènes classique. Entre structures institutionnelles, idéologie civique, et pratiques sociales." In P. Schmitt Pantel and F. de Polignac, eds., *Athènes et le politique. Dans le sillage de Claude Mossé*. Paris: 271–309.

Bakewell, G. 2007. "Written lists of military personnel in Classical Athens." In C. Cooper, ed., *Politics of Orality (Orality and Literacy in Ancient Greece*, vol. 6.). Brill: 89–102.

Balcer, J. 1976. "Imperial magistrates in the Athenian empire." *Historia* 25: 257–87.

———. 1977. "The Athenian episkopos and the Achaemenid 'King's Eye.'" *AJP* 98: 252–63.

Balot, R. K. 2001. *Greed and Injustice in Classical Athens*. Princeton.

———. 2004. "Courage in the democratic polis." *CQ* 54: 406–23.

———. 2006. *Greek Political Thought*. Oxford.

———. 2014. *Courage in the Democratic Polis: Ideology and Critique in Classical Athens*. Oxford.

Banfi, A. 2007. "'GYNAIKONOMEIN': Intorno ad una magistratura ateniese del IV secolo ed alla sua presenza nelle fonti teatrali greche e romane." In E. Cantarella and L. Gagliardi, eds., *Diritto e Teatro in Grecia e a Roma*. Milan: 17–29.

———. 2010. *Sovranità della legge. La legislazione di Demetrio del Falero ad Atene (317–307 a.C.)*. Milan.

Baragwanath, E. 2008. *Motivation and Narrative in Herodotus*. Oxford.

Barceló, P. 1993. *Basileia, Monarchia, Tyrannis*. Stuttgart.

Barker, E.T.E. 2009. *Entering the Agon: Dissent and Authority in Homer, Historiography and Tragedy*. Oxford.

Barros, R. 2002. *Constitutionalism and Dictatorship: Pinochet, the Junta, and the 1980 Constitution*. Cambridge.

Bates, R. 1988. "Contra contractarianism: Some reflections on the New Institutionalism." *Politics & Society* 16: 387–401.

Bayliss, A. 2011. *After Demosthenes: The Politics of Early Hellenistic Athens*. London.

Baynes, N. H. 1955. *Byzantine Studies and Other Essays*. London.

Bearzot, C. 2006. "Atene nel 411 e nel 404: Tecniche del colpo di stato." In G. Urso, ed., *Terror et pavor: Violenza, intimidazione, clandestinità nel mondo antico*. Pisa: 21–54.

———. 2007. "Political murder in classical Greece." *AncSoc* 37: 37–61.

———. 2009. "'Partis politiques,' cités, états fédéraux: Le témoignage de l'historien d'Oxyrhynchos." *Mouseion* 9: 239–56.

———. 2013. *Come si abbatte una democrazia: Tecniche di colpo di Stato nell'Atene antica*. Rome.

Beck, H. 1997. "Das Attentat auf Lykomedes von Mantineia." *Tekmeria* 3: 1–5.

———. 1999. "Ostlokris und die 'Tausend Opuntier': Neue Überlegungen zum Siedlergesetz für Naupaktos." *ZPE* 124: 53–62.

Becker, G. 1976. *The Economic Approach to Human Behavior*. Chicago.

Bell, C. 1992. *Ritual Theory, Ritual Practice*. Oxford.

Berger, S. 1991. "Great and small poleis in Sicily: Syracuse and Leontini." *Historia* 40: 129–42.

———. 1992. *Revolution and Society in Greek Sicily and Southern Italy*. Stuttgart.

Berent, M. 1996. "Hobbes and the 'Greek tongues.'" *History of Political Thought* 17: 36–59.

Bernhardt, R. 2003. *Luxuskritik und Aufwandsbeschränkungen in der griechischen Welt*. Stuttgart.

Berve, H. 1967. *Die Tyrannis bei den Griechen*. 2 vols. Munich.

Bhavnani, R. and M. Ross. 2003. "Announcement, credibility, and turnout in popular rebellions." *Journal of Conflict Resolution* 47: 340–66.

Black, D. 1958. *The Theory of Committees and Elections*. Cambridge.

Blackman, D., B. Rankov, et al. 2013. *Shipsheds of the Ancient Mediterranean*. Cambridge.

Blanshard, A. J. L. 2004. "Depicting democracy: An exploration of art and text in the law of Eukrates." *JHS* 124: 1–15.

Blaydes, L. 2010. *Elections and Distributive Politics in Mubarak's Egypt*. Cambridge.

Bleicken, J. 1979. "Zur Entstehung der Verfassungstypologie im 5. Jahrhundert v. Chr. (Monarchie, Aristokratie, Demokratie)." *Historia* 28: 148–72.

Blok, J. 2005. "Becoming citizens: Some notes on the semantics of 'citizen' in Archaic Greece and Classical Athens." *Klio* 87: 7–40.

———. 2006. "Solon's funerary laws: Questions of authenticity and function." In J. Blok and A. Lardinois, eds., *Solon of Athens: New Historical and Philological Approaches*. Leiden: 197–247.

———. 2013. "Citizenship, the citizen body, and its assemblies." In H. Beck, ed., *A Companion to Ancient Greek Government*. London: 162–75.

Blösel, W. 2000. "Der Wandel der oligarchischen Verfassungskonzeption vom fünften zum vierten Jahrhundert v. Chr." In A. Haltenhoff and F.-H. Mutschler, eds., *Hortus litterarum antiquarum: Festschrift für Hans Armin Gärtner zum 70. Geburtstag*. Heidelberg: 79–91.

———. 2014. "Zensusgrenzen für die Ämterbekleidung im klassischen Griechenland: Wie gross war der verfassungsrechtliche Abstand gemässigter Oligarchien von der athenischen Demokratie?" In W. Blösel, W. Schmitz, and G. Seelentag, eds. Stuttgart: 71–93.

Bodel, J. 2001. "Epigraphy and the ancient historian." In J. Bodel, ed., *Epigraphic Evidence: Ancient History from Inscriptions*. London and New York: 1–56.

Boegehold, A. 1963. "Toward a study of Athenian voting procedure." *Hesperia* 32: 366–74.

Boersma, J. 1970. *Athenian Building Policy from 561/0 to 405/4 B.C.* Groningen.

Boix, C., and M. Svolik. 2008. "The foundations of limited authoritarian government: Institutions and power-sharing in dictatorships." Manuscript, Princeton.

Bolmarcich, S. 2005. "Thucydides 1.19.1 and the Peloponnesian League." *GRBS* 45: 5–34.

———. 2007. "The afterlife of a treaty." *CQ* 57: 477–89.

Bosworth, A. B. 1988. *Conquest and Empire: The Reign of Alexander the Great*. Cambridge.

———. 1993. "The humanitarian aspect of the Melian dialogue." *JHS* 113: 30–44.

Bourdieu, P. 1977. *Outline of a Theory of Practice*. Cambridge.

Bourriot, F. 1995. *Kalos kagathos, kalokagathia.* Hildesheim.
Bowie, E. 2008. "Sex and politics in Archilochos' poetry." In D. Katsonopoulou, I. Petropoulos, and S. Katsarou, eds., *Archilochus and his Age.* Athens: 133–141.
Bradeen, D. 1960. "The popularity of the Athenian empire." *Historia* 9: 257–69.
Bradford, A. S. 1994. "The duplicitous Spartan." In A. Powell and S. Hodkinson, eds., *The Shadow of Sparta.* London: 59–85.
Bratton, M., and N. van der Walle. 1997. *Democratic Experiments in Africa: Regime Transitions in Comparative Perspective.* Cambridge.
Braun, T. 1994. "ΧΡΗΣΤΟΥΣ ΠΟΙΕΙΝ." *CQ* 44: 40–45.
Brélaz, C. 2009. "Les bienfaiteurs, 'sauveurs' et 'fossoyeurs' de la cité hellénistique? Une approche historiographique de l'évergétisme." In O. Curty, ed., *L'huile et l'argent. Gymnasiarchie et évergétisme dans la Grèce hellénistique.* Fribourg: 37–56.
Brenne, S. 2002. "Die Ostraka (487-ca. 416 v. Chr.) als Testimonien (T 1)." In P. Siewert, ed, *Ostrakismos—Testimonien* I. Stuttgart: 36–166.
Bresson, A. 2016. *The Making of the Ancient Greek Economy: Institutions, Markets, and Growth in the City-States.* Princeton.
Bresson, A., A.-M. Cocula, and C. Pébarthe, eds. 2005. *L'écriture publique du pouvoir.* Paris.
Broadie, S., and C. Rowe, eds. 2002. *Aristotle: Nicomachean Ethics.* Oxford.
Brock, R. 1989. "Athenian oligarchs: The numbers game." *JHS* 109: 160–64.
———. 1991. "The emergence of democratic ideology." *Historia* 40: 160–69.
———. 2009. "Did the Athenian empire promote democracy?" In J. Ma, N. Papazarkadas, and R. Parker, eds. *Interpreting the Athenian Empire.* London: 149–66.
———. 2013. *Greek Political Imagery from Homer to Aristotle.* London.
Brock, R. and S. Hodkinson, eds. 2000. *Alternatives to Athens: Varieties of Political Organization and Community in Ancient Greece.* Oxford.
Brown, N. O. 1951. "Pindar, Sophocles, and the Thirty Years' Peace." *TAPA* 82: 1–28.
Brownlee, J. 2007. *Authoritarianism in an Age of Democratization.* Cambridge.
Bruce, I.A.F. 1967. *An Historical Commentary on the "Hellenica Oxyrhynchia."* Cambridge.
———. 1971. "The Corcyraean Civil War of 427 B.C." *Phoenix* 25: 108–17.
Buck, R. J. 1994. *Boiotia and the Boiotian League, 423–371 B.C.* Edmonton.
Buckler, J. 1980. *The Theban Hegemony, 371–362 BC.* Cambridge, MA.
———. 1999. "A note on Diodorus 14.86.1." *CP* 94: 210–14.
Bueno de Mesquita, B. and A. Smith. 2010. "Leader survival, revolutions, and the nature of government finance." *American Journal of Political Science* 54: 936–50.
Bugh, G. R. 1988. *The Horsemen of Athens.* Princeton.
Bultrighini, U. 1999. *"Maledetta democrazia": Studi su Crizia.* Alexandria.
Bultrighini, U., ed. 2005. *Democrazia e antidemocrazia nel mondo Greco. Atti del convegno internazionale di studi, Chieti 9011 aprile 2003.* Alessandria.
Bundy, E. L. 1962. *Studia Pindarica.* Berkeley.
Burckhardt, L. A. 1999. "Katalogos." In H. Cancik and H. Schneider, eds., *Der neue Pauly: Enzyklopädie der Antike,* Bd. 6, col. 337. Stuttgart.
Burford, A. 1993. *Land and Labor in the Greek World.* Baltimore.
Burke, E. M. 2005. "The habit of subsidization in classical Athens: Toward a thetic ideology." *C&M* 56: 5–47.

Burn, A. R. 1984. *Persia and the Greeks: The Defense of the West, c. 546–478 B.C.* Rev. ed., D. M. Lewis. London.

Burstein, S. M. 1976. *Outpost of Hellenism: The Emergence of Heraclea on the Black Sea.* Berkeley and Los Angeles.

Busolt, G. 1920. *Griechische Staatskunde* I. Munich.

Caire, E. 2016. *Penser l'oligarchie à Athènes aux Ve et IVe siècles. Aspects d'une idéologie.* Paris.

Cairns, D. 1993. *Aidōs: The Psychology and Ethics of Honour and Shame in Ancient Greek Literature.* Oxford.

Calame, C. 1997. *Choruses of Young Women in Ancient Greece: Their Morphology, Religious Role, and Social Functions.* Lanham, MD.

Camerer, C. and E. Fehr. 2006. "When does 'economic man' dominate social behavior?" *Science* 311: 47–52.

Camp, J. 2001. *The Archaeology of Athens.* New Haven.

Canevaro, M. 2011. "The twilight of nomothesia: Legislation in early-Hellenistic Athens." *Dike* 14: 55–85.

Canevaro, M. and E. Harris. 2012. "The documents in Andocides' *On the Mysteries*." *CQ* 62: 98–129.

Capdetrey, L., and J. Nelis-Clément, eds. 2006. *La circulation de l'information dans les états antiques.* Paris.

Carey, C. 1976. *A Commentary on Five Odes of Pindar.* New York.

———. 1993. "Return of the radish, or just when you thought it was safe to go back into the kitchen." *LCM* 18: 53–55.

———. 2009. "Genre, occasion and performance." In F. Budelmann, ed., *The Cambridge Companion to Greek Lyric.* Cambridge: 21–38.

Carless Unwin, N. and O. Henry. 2016. "A new Olympichos inscription from Labraunda: I. Labraunda 137*." *EA* 49: 27–45.

Carlier, P. 1984. *La Royauté en Grèce avant Alexandre.* Strasbourg.

———. 1998. "Observations sur la décision politique en Grèce, de l'époque mycénienne à l'époque archaïque." In W. Schuller, ed., *Politische Theorie und Praxis im Altertum.* Darmstadt: 1–18.

Carlsson, S. 2010. *Hellenistic Democracies.* Stuttgart.

Carter, D. 2004. "Was Attic tragedy democratic?" *Polis* 21: 1–25.

Carter, L. B. 1986. *The Quiet Athenian.* Oxford.

Cartledge, P. 1977. "Hoplites and heroes: Sparta's contribution to the technique of ancient warfare." *JHS* 97: 11–27.

———. 1982. "Sparta and Samos: A special relationship?" *CQ* 32: 243–65.

———. 1987. *Agesilaos and the Crisis of Sparta.* London.

———. 2000a. "Spartan justice? Or the 'state of the ephors'?" *Dike* 3: 5–26.

———. 2000b. "Boiotian swine f(or)ever? The Boiotian superstate, 395 BC." In P. Flensted-Jensen, T. H. Nielsen, and L. Rubinstein, eds., *Polis and Politics.* Copenhagen: 397–418.

———. 2001. *Spartan Reflections.* Berkeley.

———. 2007. "Democracy, origins of: Contribution to a debate." In K. Raaflaub, J. Ober, and R. W. Wallace, eds., *Origins of Democracy in Ancient Greece.* Berkeley: 155–69.

———. 2009. *Ancient Greek Political Thought in Practice.* Cambridge.

———. 2016. *Democracy: A Life*. Oxford.
Cawkwell, G. L. 1983. "The decline of Sparta." *CQ* 33: 385–400.
———. 1995. "Early Greek tyranny and the people." *CQ* 45: 73–86.
Chamoux, F. 1959. "L'île de Thasos et son histoire." *REG* 72: 348–69.
Chaniotis, A. 1995. "Sich selbst feiern? Städtischen Feste des Hellenismus im Spannungsfeld von Religion und Politik." In M. Wörrle and P. Zanker, eds., *Stadtbild und Bürgerbild im Hellenismus*. Munich: 147–72.
———. 1999. "Milking the mountains: Economic activities on the Cretan uplands in the classical and Hellenistic period." In A. Chaniotis, ed., *From Minoan Farmers to Roman Traders*. Stuttgart: 181–220.
———. 2005a. *War in the Hellenistic World: A Social and Cultural History*. Oxford.
———. 2005b. "The Great Insription, its political and social institutions and the common institutions of the Cretans." In E. Greco and M. Lombardo, eds., *La Grande Iscrizione di Gortyna: Centoventi anni dopo la scoperta*. Athens: 175–94.
———. 2011. "Greek festivals and contests: definition and general characteristics." *Thesaurus cultus et rituum antiquorum* (ThesCRA), vol. VII. Los Angeles: 5–43.
Chankowski, A. 2010. *L'Éphébie hellénistique. Étude d'une institution civique dans les cités grecques des îles de la Mer Égée et de l'Asie Mineure*. Athens.
Christ, M. R. 1998. *The Litigious Athenian*. Baltimore.
———. 2001. "Conscription of hoplites in classical Athens." *CQ* 51: 398–422.
———. 2006. *The Bad Citizen in Classical Athens*. Cambridge.
———. 2007. "The evolution of the eisphora in Classical Athens." *CQ* 57: 53–69.
———. 2012. *The Limits of Altruism in Democratic Athens*. Cambridge.
———. 2013. "Demosthenes on philanthrōpia as a democratic virtue." *CP* 108: 202–22.
Chwe, M. S.-Y. 2001. *Rational Ritual: Culture, Coordination, and Common Knowledge*. Princeton.
Cichorius, C. 1894. "Zu den Namen der attischen Steuerklassen." In *Griechische Studien Hermann Lipsius zum sechzigsten Geburtstag dargebracht*. Leipzig: 135–40.
Clemens, E. and J. Cook. 1999. "Politics and institutionalism: Explaining durability and change." *Ann. Rev. Sociol.* 25: 441–66.
Cloché, P. 1952. *Thèbes de Béotie*. Namur.
Cohen, D. 1995. *Law, Violence and Community in Classical Athens*. Cambridge.
Coleman, J. S. 1990. *Foundations of Social Theory*. Cambridge, MA.
Connor, W. R. 1984. *Thucydides*. Princeton.
———. 1985. "The razing of the house in Greek society." *TAPA* 115: 79–102.
———. 1992 [first published 1971]. *The New Politicians of Fifth-Century Athens*. Princeton.
Cook, M. 1988. "Ancient political factions: Boiotia 404 to 395." *TAPA* 118: 57–85.
Cooper, C. 2011. "Oligarchy and the rule of law." In *Tabachnick and Koivukoski* 2011: 196–216.
Cooper, J., ed. 1997. *Plato: Complete Works*. Indianapolis.
Corner, S. 2010. "Transcendent drinking: The symposium at sea reconsidered." *CQ* 60: 352–80.
Crotty, K. 1982. *Song and Action: The Victory Odes of Pindar*. Baltimore.
Crowther, C. 1992. "The decline of Greek democracy?" *JAC* 7: 13–48.
Currie, B. 2002. "Euthymos of Locri: A case study in heroization in the classical period." *JHS* 122: 24–44.

———. 2011. "Epinician choregia: Funding a Pindaric chorus." In L. Athanassaki and E. L. Bowie, eds., *Archaic and Classical Choral Song: Performance, Politics and Dissemination*. Berlin: 269–310.

D'Alessio, G.-B. 2009. "Defining local identities in Greek lyric poetry." In R. L. Hunter and I. Rutherford, eds., *Wandering Poets in Ancient Greek Culture: Travel, Locality and Pan-Hellenism*. Cambridge: 137–67.

David, E. 1979. "The conspiracy of Cinadon." *Athenaeum* 57: 239–59.

———. 1980. "Revolutionary agitation in Sparta after Leuctra." *Athenaeum* n.s. 58: 299–308.

———. 1986. "The oligarchic revolution in Argos, 417 B.C.". *AC* 55: 113–24.

Davidson, J. 1997a. *Courtesans and Fishcakes: The Consuming Passions of Classical Athens*. New York.

———. 1997b. "A ban on public bars in Thasos?" *CQ* 47: 392–95.

———. 2006. "Revolutions in human time: Age-class in Athens and the Greekness of Greek revolutions." In S. Goldhill and R. Osborne, eds., *Rethinking Revolutions through Ancient Greece*. Cambridge: 29–67.

Davies, J. K. 1971. *Athenian Propertied Families*. Oxford.

———. 1981. *Wealth and the Power of Wealth in Classical Athens*. New York.

———. 2003a. "Greek archives: From record to monument." In M. Brosius, ed., *Ancient Archives and Archival Traditions*. Oxford: 323–43.

———. 2003b. "Democracy without theory." In P. Derow and R. Parker, eds., *Herodotus and His World*. Oxford: 319–35.

———. 2004. "The concept of the 'citizen.'" In S. Cataldi, ed., *Poleis e Politeiai: Atti del Convegno Internazionale di Storia Greca*. Alessandria: 19–30.

de Libero, L. 1996. *Die archaische Tyrannis*. Stuttgart.

de Luna, M. E. 2011. "Un' oligarchia concorde: Il case di Farsalo (Aristotele, Politica, 5.6.10)." In B. Badoud, ed., *Philologos Dionysios*. Geneva: 467–77.

Demand, N. 1990. *Urban Relocation in Archaic and Classical Greece*. Bristol.

Denyer, N., ed. 2008. *Plato: Protagoras*. Cambridge.

de Romilly, J. 1965. "Les Phéniciennes d'Euripide ou l'actualité dans la tragédie grecque." *Rev. phil.* 39: 28–47.

de Ste. Croix, G. E. M. 1953. "Demosthenes' TIMHMA and the Athenian eisphora in the fourth century B.C." *C&M* 14: 30–70.

———. 1954. "The character of the Athenian empire." *Historia* 3: 1–41.

———. 1956. "The constitution of the Five Thousand." *Historia* 5: 1–23.

———. 1972. *The Origins of the Peloponnesian War*. London.

———1981. *The Class Struggle in the Ancient Greek World*. London.

———. 2004. *Athenian Democratic Origins and Other Essays*. Oxford.

Deshours, N. 2006. *Les mystères d'Andania. Étude d'épigraphie et d'histoire religieuses*. Pessac.

Detienne, M. 1996. *The Masters of Truth in Archaic Greece*. New York.

Dickenson, C., and O. van Nijf, eds. 2013. *Public Space in the Post-Classical City*. Leuven.

Diggle, J., ed. 2004. *Theophrastus: Characters*. Cambridge.

Dodds, E. R. 1963. *The Greeks and the Irrational*. Berkeley and Los Angeles.

Domínguez Monedero, A. J. 2013. "The late Archaic Period." In J. Pascual and M.-F. Papakonstantinou, eds., *Topography and History of Ancient Epicnemidian Locris*. Leiden: 445–70.

Donlan, W. 1978. "Social vocabulary and its relationship to political propaganda in fifth-century Athens." *QUCC* 27: 95–111.

———. 1999. *The Aristocratic Ideal and Selected Papers*. Wauconda, IL.

Dover, K. J. 1974. *Greek Popular Morality in the Time of Plato and Aristotle*. Berkeley and Los Angeles.

Dow, S. 1942. "Corinthiaca." *HSCP* 53: 89–119.

Dreher, M. 2007. "Das Bürgerrecht im Griechischen Sizilien zwischen Recht und Politik." *Symposion* 2005: 57–78.

Drews, R. 1983. *Basileus: The Evidence for Kingship in Geometric Greece*. New Haven.

Dreyer, B. 1999. *Untersuchungen zur Geschichte des spätklassischen Athen (322-ca.230 v. Chr.)*. Stuttgart.

Ducat, J. 1997a. "La cryptie en question." In P. Brulé and J. Oulhen, eds., *Ésclavage, guerre, économie en Grèce ancienne*. Rennes: 43–74.

———. 1997b. "Crypties." *Cahiers du Centre Gustave Glotz* 8: 9–38.

———. 2006. *Spartan Education: Youth and Society in the Classical Period*. Swansea.

Due, B. 1989. *The Cyropaedia: Xenophon's Aims and Methods*. Aarhus.

Dunbabin, T. J. 1948. *The Western Greeks: A History of the Greek Colonies in Sicily and South Italy from their Foundation to the Death of Gelon (c. 750–478 BC)*. Oxford.

Duplouy, A. 2006. *Le prestige des élites: Recherches sur les modes de reconnaissance sociale en Grèce entre les Xe et Ve siècles avant J.-C.* Paris.

Eckerman, C. 2012. "Was epinician poetry performed at Panhellenic sanctuaries?" *GRBS* 52: 338–60.

Edge, M. 2009. "Athens and the spectrum of liberty." *History of Political Thought* 30: 1–45.

Ehrenberg, V. 1950. "Origins of democracy." *Historia* 1: 515–48.

Eidinow, E. 2016. *Envy, Poison, and Death: Women on Trial in Ancient Athens*. Oxford.

Elmer, D. 2013. *The Poetics of Consent: Collective Decision Making and the Iliad*. Baltimore.

Elster, J. 2007. *Explaining Social Behavior: More Nuts and Bolts for the Social Sciences*. Cambridge.

Epstein, S. 2011. "Direct democracy and minority rule: The Athenian assembly and its relation to the demos." In G. Herman, ed., *Stability and Crisis in the Athenian Democracy*. Stuttgart: 87–102.

Evans, J.A.S. 1963. "Histiaeus and Aristagoras: Notes on the Ionian Revolt." *AJP* 84: 113–28.

Evrigenis, I. D. 2007. *Fear of Enemies and Collective Action*. Cambridge.

Fearn, D. 2009. "Oligarchic Hestia: Bacchylides 14b and Pindar, Nemean 11." *JHS* 129: 23–38.

———. 2011. "Aeginetan epinician culture: Naming, ritual, and politics." In D. Fearn, ed., *Aegina: Contexts for Choral Lyric Poetry*. Oxford: 175–226.

Ferguson, W. S. 1911. *Hellenistic Athens: An Historical Essay*. London.

Fernoux, H. 2011. *Le Demos et la Cité: Communautés et assemblées populaires en Asie Mineure à l'époque impériale*. Rennes.

Fernoux, H. and C. Stein, eds. 2007. *Aristocratie antique: Modèles et exemplarité sociale*. Dijon.

Ferrario, S. B. 2014. *Historical Agency and the 'Great Man' in Classical Greece*. Cambridge.

Feyel, C. 2009. *Dokimasia: La place et le rôle de l'examen préliminaire dans les institutions des cités grecques*. Nancy.

Figueira, T. J. 1981. *Aegina: Society and Politics*. New York.

Finley, M.I. 1983. *Politics in the Ancient World*. Cambridge.
———. 1985. *Democracy Ancient and Modern*. Revised ed. Rutgers.
Fischer-Bovet, C. 2014. *Army and Society in Ptolemaic Egypt*. Cambridge.
Fisher, N. R. E. 1992. *Hybris*. Warminster.
———. 1998. "Violence, masculinity and the law in classical Athens." In L. Foxhall and J. Salmon, eds., *When Men Were Men: Masculinity, Power and Identity in Classical Antiquity*. London: 6897.
———. 2000a. "Hybris, revenge and stasis in the Greek city-states." In H. van Wees, ed., *War and Violence in Ancient Greece*. Swansea: 83–123.
———. 2000b. "Symposiasts, fish-eaters, and flatterers: Social mobility and moral concerns." In D. Harvey and J. Wilkins, eds., *The Rivals of Aristophanes*. London: 355–96.
———. 2010. "Kharis, kharites, festivals, and social peace in the classical Greek city." In R. Rosen and I. Sluiter, eds., *Valuing Others in Classical Antiquity*. Leiden: 71–112.
Fisher, N. R. E. and H. van Wees, eds. 2011. *Competition in the Ancient World*. Swansea.
———. 2015. *'Aristocracy' in Antiquity: Redefining Greek and Roman Elites*. Swansea.
Flaig, E. 2013. *Die Mehrheitsentscheidung: Entstehung und kulturelle Dynamik*. Paderborn.
Fleck, R. and A. Hanssen. 2006. "The origins of democracy: A model with application to ancient Greece." *Journal of Law and Economics* 49: 115–45.
Flower, H. 2006. *The Art of Forgetting: Disgrace and Oblivion in Roman Political Culture*. Chapel Hill.
Flower, M. A. 1988. "Agesilaus of Sparta and the origins of the ruler cult." *CQ* 38: 123–34.
Fornara, C. 1970. "The diapsephismos of Ath. Pol. 13.5." *CP* 65: 243–46.
Fornara, C. and D. C. Yates. 2007. "FGrH 328 (Philochorus) F 181." *GRBS* 47: 31–37.
Forsdyke, S. 2000. "Exile, ostracism, and the Athenian democracy." *CA* 19: 232–63.
———. 2005. *Exile, Ostracism, and Democracy: The Politics of Expulsion in Ancient Greece*. Princeton.
———. 2009. "Civic institutions." In G. Boys-Stones, B. Graziosi, and P. Vasunia, eds., *The Oxford Handbook of Hellenic Studies*. Oxford: 197–210.
———. 2012. *Slaves Tell Tales: And Other Episodes in the Politics of Popular Culture in Ancient Greece*. Princeton.
Fournier, J., and P. Hamon. 2007. "Les orphelins de guerre de Thasos: un nouveau fragment de la stèle des Braves (ca. 360–350 av. J.-C.)." *BCH* 131: 309–81.
Foxhall, L. 1997. "The Solonian tele: A view from the top." In L. Mitchell and P. J. Rhodes, eds., *The Development of the Polis in Archaic Greece*. London: 113–36.
———. "Can we see the 'Hoplite Revolution' on the ground? Archaeological landscapes, material culture, and social status in early Greece." In Kagan and Viggiano 2013: 194–221.
Franke, P. R. 1966. "Leontinische Phygades in Chalkis?" *Archäologischer Anzeiger* 81: 395–407.
Frier, B. W. and D. P. Kehoe. 2007. "Law and economic institutions." In W. Scheidel, I. Morris, and R. Saller, eds., *The Cambridge Economic History of the Greco-Roman World*. Cambridge: 113–43.
Fröhlich, P. 2004. *Les cités grecques et le contrôle des magistrats*. Geneva.
———. 2010. "L'inventaire du monde des cités grecques. Une somme, une méthode et une conception de l'histoire." [Review of *IACP*.] *Revue historique* 655: 637–77.
———. 2013. "Funérailles publiques et tombeaux monumentaux intra-muros dans les cités

grecques à l'époque hellénistique." In M.-C. Ferriès, M. P. Castiglioni, and F. Létoublon, eds., *Forgerons, élites et voyageurs d'Homère à nos jours*. Grenoble: 227–309.

———. 2014. Review of Martzavou and Papazarkadas 2013. *REA* 116: 745–60.

Fröhlich, P. and C. Müller, eds. 2005. *Citoyenneté et participation à la basse époque hellénistique*. Geneva.

Frost, F. J. 1964. "Pericles, Thucydides, son of Melesias, and Athenian politics before the war." *Historia* 13: 385–99.

———. 1968. "Themistocles' place in Athenian politics." *CSCA* 1: 105–24.

———. 1984. "The Athenian military before Cleisthenes." *Historia* 33: 283–94.

Fuks, A. 1984. *Social Conflict in Ancient Greece*. Leiden.

Fukuyama, F. 1995. *Trust: The Social Virtues and the Creation of Prosperity*. New York.

Funke, P. 1980. *Homonoia und Arche: Athen und die griechische Staatenwelt vom Ende des peloponnesischen Krieges bis zum Königsfrieden (404/3–387/6 v. Chr.)* Wiesbaden.

Gabrielsen, V. 2002a. "Socio-economic classes and ancient Greek warfare." In J. E. Skydsgaard and K. Ascani, eds., *Ancient History Matters*. Rome: 203–20.

———. 2002b. "The impact of armed forces on government and politics in archaic and classical Greek poleis: A response to Hans van Wees." In A. Chaniotis and P. Ducrey, eds, *Army and Power in the Ancient World*. Stuttgart: 83–98.

Gaertner, J. F., ed. 2007. Writing Exile: *The Discourse of Displacement in Greco-Roman Antiquity and Beyond*. Leiden.

Gagarin, M. 2002. *Antiphon the Athenian: Oratory, Law, and Justice in the Age of the Sophists*. Austin, TX.

———. 2008. *Writing Greek Law*. Cambridge.

Gagarin, M., and P. Perlman, eds., 2016. *The Laws of Ancient Crete c. 650–400 BCE*. Oxford.

Gandhi, J. 2008. *Political Institutions under Dictatorship*. Cambridge.

Gandhi, J. and E. Lust-Okar. 2009. "Elections under authoritarianism." *Annual Review of Political Science* 12: 403–22.

Gandhi, J., and A. Przeworski. 2006. "Cooperation, cooptation, and rebellion under dictatorships." *Economics & Politics* 18: 1–26.

Garland, R. 1985. *The Greek Way of Death*. London.

———. 1989. "The well-ordered corpse: An investigation into the motives behind Greek funerary legislation." *BICS* 36: 1–15.

———. 2014. *Wandering Greeks: The Ancient Greek Diaspora from the Age of Homer to the Death of Alexander the Great*. Princeton.

Gauthier, Ph. 1982. "Notes sur trois décrets honorant des citoyens bienfaiteurs." *RPh* 108: 215–31.

———. 1984. "Les cités hellénistiques: épigraphie et histoire des institutions et des régimes politiques." *Actes du VIIIe Congr. int. épigr. 1982*: 82–107.

———. 1985. *Les cités grecques et leurs bienfaiteurs*. Paris.

———. 1990. "Quorum et participation civique dans les démocraties grecques." In C. Nicolet, ed., *Du pouvoir dans l'Antiquité: mots et réalités*. Geneva: 73–99.

———. 1993. "Les cités hellénistiques." In M. H. Hansen, ed., *The Ancient Greek City-State*. Copenhagen: 211–31.

———. 2003. 'De nouveaux honneurs cultuels pour Philétairos de Pergame: A propos de deux inscriptions récemment publiées." In B. Virgilio, ed., *Studi Ellenistici*. Pisa: 9–23.

Gauthier, Ph., and M. Hatzopoulos. 1993. *La loi gymnasiarchique de Béroia*. Athens.
Gawlinski, L. 2012. *The Sacred Law of Andania: A New Text with Commentary*. Boston.
Geddes, A. 2007. "Ion of Chios and politics." In V. Jennings and A. Katsaros, eds., *The World of Ion of Chios*. Leiden: 110–38.
Geddes, B. 2003. *Paradigms and Sand Castles: Theory Building and Research Design in Comparative Politics*. Ann Arbor.
Gehrke, H.-J. 1978. "Das Verhältnis von Politik und Philosophie im Wirken des Demetrios von Phaleron." *Chiron* 8: 149–93.
———. 1997. "Gewalt und Gesetz: Die soziale und politische Ordnung Kretas in der Archaischen und Klassischen Zeit." *Klio* 79: 23–68.
———. 2009. "States." In K. A. Raaflaub and H. van Wees, eds., *A Companion to Archaic Greece*. Oxford: 395–410.
Geominy, W. 1998. "Zum Daochos-Weihgeschenk." *Klio* 80: 369–402.
Georges, P. 1993. "Review article: Athenian democracy and Athenian empire." *International History Review* 15: 84–105.
Gera, D. L. 1993. *Xenophon's Cyropaedia: Style, Genre, and Literary Technique*. Oxford.
Gernet, L. 1981. *The Anthropology of Ancient Greece*. Baltimore.
Gilens, M. and B. I. Page. 2014. "Testing theories of American politics: Elites, interest groups, and average citizens." *Perspectives on Politics* 12: 564–81.
Gillis, D. 1971. "The revolt at Mytilene." *AJP* 92: 38–47.
Gish, D. A. 2009. "Spartan justice: The conspiracy of Kinadon in Xenophon's *Hellenika*." *Polis* 26: 339–69.
Glotz, G. 1908. "Le conseil fédéral des Béotiens." *BCH* 32: 271–78.
Glowacki, K. 2003. "A personification of Demos on a new Attic document relief." *Hesperia* 72: 447–66.
Gomme, A. W. 1951. "Notes on Thucydides." *CR* 1: 135–38.
Goodwin, J. 2001. *No Other Way Out: States and Revolutionary Movements, 1945–1991*. Cambridge.
Gorman, V. B. 2001. *Miletos, the Ornament of Ionia: A History of the City to 400 B.C.E.* Ann Arbor.
Gottesman, A. 2014. *Politics and the Street in Democratic Athens*. Cambridge.
Graf, D. F. 1985. "Greek tyrants and Achaemenid politics." In J. W. Eadie and J. Ober, eds., *The Craft of the Ancient Historian*. Lanham, MD: 79–123.
Graham, A. J. 1999 [1964]. *Colony and Mother City in Ancient Greece*. Manchester.
Graham, A. J., and G. Forsythe. 1984. "A new slogan for oligarchy in Thucydides III.82.8." *HSCP* 88: 24–45.
Graham, A. J., and R. A. Smith. 1989. "An ellipse in the Thasian decree about delation (ML 83)?" *AJP* 110: 405–12.
Graham, D. W. 2010. *The Texts of Early Greek Philosophy: The Complete Fragments and Selected Testimonies of the Major Presocratics*. Cambridge.
Gramsci, A. 1971. *Selections from the Prison Notebooks*. New York.
Grandjean, Y., and F. Salviat. 2006. "Règlements du Délion de Thasos." *BCH* 130: 296–327.
Graninger, D. 2011. *Cult and Koinon in Hellenistic Thessaly*. Leiden.
Gray, B. 2013. "Justice or harmony? Reconciliation after stasis at Dikaia and the fourth-century BC polis." *REA* 115: 369–401.

———. 2015. *Stasis and Stability: Exile, the Polis, and Political Thought, c. 404–146 BC.* Oxford.
Gray, V. 2011. *Xenophon's Mirror of Princes: Reading the Reflections.* Oxford.
Grieb, V. 2008. *Hellenistische Demokratie.* Stuttgart.
Griffin, A. 1982. *Sikyon.* Oxford.
Griffith, G. T. 1950. "The union of Corinth and Argos (392–386 B.C.)." *Historia* 1: 236–56.
Gruen, E. 1993. "The polis in the Hellenistic world." In R. Rosen and J. Farrell, eds., *Nomodeiktes: Greek Studies in Honor of Martin Ostwald.* Ann Arbor: 339–54.
Guia, M. V. and J. Gallego. 2010. "Athenian zeugitai and the Solonian census classes: New reflections and perspectives." *Historia* 59: 257–81.
Habicht, C. 1970. *Gottmenschentum und griechische Städte.* 2nd edition. Munich.
———. 1995. "Ist ein 'Honoratiorenregime' das Kennzeichen der Stadt im späteren Hellenismus?" In M. Wörrle and P. Zanker, eds., *Stadtbild und Bürgerbild im Hellenismus.* Munich: 87–92.
———. 1997. *Athens from Alexander to Anthony.* Cambridge, MA.
Hall, P. and R. Taylor. 1996. "Political science and the three new institutionalisms." *Political Studies* 44: 936–57.
Halliday, W. R. 1928. *The Greek Questions of Plutarch.* Oxford.
Hamilton, C. D. 1979. *Sparta's Bitter Victories: Politics and Diplomacy in the Corinthian War.* Ithaca.
Hammer, D. 2002. *The Iliad as Politics: The Performance of Political Thought.* Norman, OK.
———. 2005. "Plebiscitary politics in archaic Greece." *Historia* 54: 107–31.
Hammond, N.G.L. 1989. *The Macedonian State.* Oxford.
———. 2000. "Political developments in Boeotia." *CQ* 50: 80–93.
Hammond, M., trans. 2009. *Thucydides: The Peloponnesian War.* Oxford.
Hamon, P. 2005. "La Conseil et la participation de citoyens: Les mutations de la basse époque hellénistique." In P. Fröhlich and C. Müller, eds., *Citoyenneté et participation à la basse époque hellénistique.* Geneva: 121–44.
———. 2007. "Élites dirigeantes et processus d'aristocratisation à l'époque hellénistique." In H.-L. Fernoux and Chr. Stein, eds., *Aristocratie antique.* Dijon: 79–100.
———. 2008. "Kymè d'Éolide, cité libre et démocratique, et le pouvoir des stratèges." *Chiron* 38: 63–106.
———. 2009. "Démocraties grecques après Alexandre: à propos de trois ouvrages récents." *Topoi* 16: 347–82.
Hansen, M. H. 1979. "Did the Athenian ecclesia legislate after 403/2 B.C.?" *GRBS* 20: 27–53.
———. 1983. *The Athenian Ecclesia: A Collection of Articles, 1976–83.* Copenhagen.
———. 1985. *Demography and Democracy: The Number of Athenian Citizens in the Fourth Century B.C.* Herning.
———. 1989. *The Athenian Ecclesia II: A Collection of Articles, 1983–89.* Copenhagen.
———. 1994. "The 2500th anniversary of Cleisthenes' reforms and the tradition of Athenian democracy." In R. Osborne and S. Hornblower, eds., *Ritual, Finance, Politics: Athenian Democratic Accounts Presented to David Lewis.* Oxford: 25–38.
———. 1999. *The Athenian Democracy in the Age of Demosthenes: Structure, Principles, and Ideology.* Norman, OK.

———. 2002. "Was the *polis* a state or a stateless society?" In T. H. Nielsen, ed., *Even More Studies in the Ancient Greek Polis*. Stuttgart: 17–47.
———. 2006a. *Polis: An Introduction to the Ancient Greek City-State*. Oxford.
———. 2006b. Review of Samons 2004. BMCR 2006.01.32.
———. 2006c. *Studies in the Population of Aigina, Athens and Eretria*. Copenhagen.
———. 2011. "How to convert an army figure into a population figure." *GRBS* 51: 239–53.
———. 2013. Review of Robinson 2011. BMCR 2013.01.17.
Hanson, V. D. 1995. *The Other Greeks: The Family Farm and the Agrarian Roots of Western Civilization*. Berkeley and Los Angeles.
———. 1996. "Hoplites into democrats: The changing ideology of Athenian infantry." In J. Ober and C. Hedrick, eds., *Dēmokratia: A Conversation on Democracies, Ancient and Modern*. Princeton: 289–312.
———. 1998. *Warfare and Agriculture in Classical Greece*. Revised edition. Berkeley.
———, ed. 1991. *Hoplites: The Classical Greek Battle Experience*. London.
Hardin, R. 1982. *Collective Action*. Baltimore.
Harding, P. 1973. "The purpose of Isokrates' Archidamos and On the Peace." *CSCA* 6: 137–49.
———. 2007. *The Story of Athens: The Fragments of the Local Chronicles of Attika*. London.
Harris, E. 2005. "Was all criticism of Athenian democracy necessarily anti-democratic?" In U. Bultrighini, ed., *Democrazia e antidemocrazia nel mondo Greco. Atti del convegno internazionale di studi, Chieti 9011 aprile 2003*. Alessandria: 11–23.
———. 2006. "Solon and the spirit of the laws in archaic and classical Greece." In J. Blok and A. Lardinois, eds., *Solon of Athens: New Historical and Philological Perspectives*. Leiden: 290–318.
———. 2007. "Who enforced the law in classical Athens?" In E. Cantarella, ed., *Symposion 2005: Vorträge zur griechischen und hellenistischen Rechtsgeschichte*. Vienna: 159–76.
Harris, W. V. 1989. *Ancient Literacy*. Cambridge, MA.
———. 2001. *Restraining Rage: The Ideology of Anger Control in Classical Antiquity*. Cambridge, MA.
Harvey, D. H. 2004. "The clandestine massacre of helots (Thucydides 4.80)." In T. J. Figueira, ed., *Spartan Society*. Swansea: 199–218.
Harvey, F. D. 1965. "Two kinds of equality." *C&M* 26: 101–46.
———. 1990. "The sykophant and sykophancy: Vexatious redefinition." In P. Cartledge, P. Millett, and S. Todd, eds., *Nomos: Essays in Athenian Law, Politics, and Society*. Cambridge: 103–21.
Hatzopoulos, M. 1996. *Macedonian Institutions under the Kings*. Athens.
Haubold, J. 2000. *Homer's People*. Cambridge.
Hawke, J. 2011. *Writing Authority: Elite Competition and Written Law in Early Greece*. Chapel Hill.
Heftner, H. 2001. *Der oligarchische Umsturz des Jahres 411 v. Chr. und die Herrschaft der Vierhundert in Athen*. Frankfurt am Main.
———. 2003. "Oligarchen, Mesoi, Autokraten: Bemerkungen zur antidemokratischen Bewegung des späten 5. Jh. v. Chr. in Athen." *Chiron* 33: 1–41.
Heisserer, A. J. 1979. "The Philites stele (SIG³ 284 = IEK 503)." *Hesperia* 48: 281–93.
Helly, B. 1995. *L'État thessalien: Aleuas le Roux, les tétrades et les tagoi*. Lyon.

Henderson, J. 2003. "Demos, demagogue, tyrant in Attic Old Comedy." In K. Morgan, ed., *Popular Tyranny: Sovereignty and its Discontents in Ancient Greece*. Austin, TX: 155–79.

Henrich, J. et al. 2005. "'Economic man' in cross-cultural perspective: Behaviorial experiments in 150 small-scale societies." *Behavioral and Brain Sciences* 28: 295–855.

Herman, G. 2006. *Morality and Behaviour in Democratic Athens*. Cambridge.

Hesk, J. 2000. *Deception and Democracy in Classical Athens*. Cambridge.

Hicks, E. L. 1887. "A Thasian decree." *JHS* 8: 401–8.

Hignett, C. 1952. *A History of the Athenian Constitution to the End of the Fifth Century B.C.* Oxford.

———. 1963. *Xerxes' Invasion of Greece*. Oxford.

Hobden, F. 2013. *The Symposion in Ancient Greek Society and Thought*. Cambridge.

Hodkinson, S. 2000. *Property and Wealth in Classical Sparta*. Swansea.

———. 2005. "The imaginary Spartan politeia." In M. H. Hansen, ed., *The Imaginary Polis*. Copenhagen: 222–81.

———, ed. 2009. *Sparta: Comparative Perspectives*. Swansea.

Hölkeskamp, K.-J. 1998. "Parteiungen und politische Willensbildung im demokratischen Athen: Perikles und Thukydides, Sohn des Melesias." *HZ* 267: 1–27.

———. 1999. *Schiedsrichter, Gesetzgeber und Gesetzgebung im archaischen Griechenland*. Stuttgart.

———. 2002. "Ptolis and agore: Homer and the archaeology of the city-state." In F. Montanari, ed., *Omero. Tremila anni dopo*. Rome: 297–342.

Hölscher, T. 1998. "Images and political identity: The case of Athens." In D. Boedeker and K. A. Raaflaub, eds. 1998. *Democracy, Empire, and the Arts in Fifth-Century Athens*. Cambridge, MA: 153–83.

Hornblower, S. 1982. *Mausolus*. Oxford.

———. 1992. "Creation and development of democratic institutions in ancient Greece." In J. Dunn, ed., *Democracy: The Unfinished Journey 508 BC to AD 1993*. Oxford: 1–16.

———. 2000. "Sticks, stones and Spartans: The sociology of Spartan violence." In H. van Wees, ed., *War and Violence in Ancient Greece*. Swansea: 57–82.

———. 2004a. *Thucydides and Pindar: Historical Narrative and the World of Epinikian Poetry*. Oxford.

———. 2004b. "'This was decided' (*edoxe tauta*): The army as polis in Xenophon's Anabasis—and elsewhere." In R. Lane Fox, ed., *Xenophon and the Ten Thousand*. New Haven: 243–63.

———. 2009. "Greek lyric and the politics and sociologies of archaic and classical Greek communities." In F. Budelmann, ed., *The Cambridge Companion to Greek Lyric*. Cambridge: 39–57.

Hunt, P. 2007. "Military forces." In P. Sabin, H. van Wees, and M. Whitby, eds., *The Cambridge History of Greek and Roman Warfare*, vol. I: *Greece, the Hellenistic World, and the Rise of Rome*. Cambridge: 108–46.

Hunter, V. 1994. *Policing Athens: Social Control in the Attic Lawsuits, 420–320 B.C.* Princeton.

Isager, S. 2011. "The epigraphic tradition at Labraunda seen in the light of Labraunda inscription no. 134: A recent addition to the Olympichos file." In L. Karlsson and S. Carlsson, eds., *Labraunda and Karia*. Uppsala: 121–31.

Isager, S. and L. Karlsson. 2008. "A new inscription from Labraunda: Honorary decree for Olympichos: I. Labraunda no. 134 (and no. 49)." *Epigraphica Anatolica* 41: 39–52.
Jacoby, F. 1944. "ΧΡΗΣΤΟΥΣ ΠΟΙΕΙΝ (Aristotle fr. 592 R.)." *CQ* 38: 15–16.
Jacquemin, A., and D. Laroche. 2001. "Le monument de Daochos ou le trésor des Thessaliens." *BCH* 125: 305–32.
Jameson, M. 1963. "The provisions for mobilization in the decree of Themistokles." *Historia* 12: 385–404.
———. 1997. "Women and democracy in fourth-century Athens." In P. Brulé and J. Oulhen, eds., *Esclavage, guerre, économie en Grèce ancienne. Hommages à Yvon Garlan*. Rennes: 95–107.
Jeffery, L. H. 1956. "The courts of justice in archaic Chios." *ABSA* 51: 157–67.
———. 1990. *The Local Scripts of Archaic Greece: A Study of the Origin of the Greek Alphabet and Its Development from the Eighth to the Fifth Centuries B.C.* Revised edition. Oxford.
Johnstone, S. 2011. *A History of Trust in Ancient Greece*. Chicago.
Jones, A.H.M. 1957. *The Athenian Democracy*. Baltimore.
Jones, N. F. 2004. *Rural Athens under the Democracy*. Philadelphia.
Judeich, W. 1892. *Kleinasiatische Studien: Untersuchungen zur Griechisch-Persischen Geschichte des IV. Jahrhunderts v. Chr.* Marburg.
Kagan, D. 1962. "Corinthian politics and the revolution of 392 B.C." *Historia* 11: 447–57.
Kagan, D. and G. Viggiano, eds. 2013. *Men of Bronze: Hoplite Warfare in Ancient Greece*. Princeton.
Kahn, C. 1981. *The Art and Thought of Heraclitus*. Cambridge.
Kahneman, D. and A. Tversky. 1979. "Prospect Theory: An analysis of decision under risk." *Econometrica* 47: 263–91.
Kallet, L. 1998. "Accounting for culture in fifth-century Athens." In D. Boedeker and K. A. Raaflaub, eds., *Democracy, Empire, and the Arts*. Cambridge, MA: 43–58.
Karachalios, F. 2013. The Politics of Judgment in Early Greece: Dispute Resolution and State Formation from the Homeric World to Solon's Athens. Diss. Stanford.
Katznelson, I., and B. Weingast, eds. 2005. *Preferences and Situations: Points of Intersection between Historical and Rational Choice Institutionalism*. New York.
Keaney, J. J. 1974. "Theophrastus on Greek judicial procedure." *TAPA* 104: 179–94.
Kellogg, D. 2013. *Marathon Fighters & Men of Maple: Ancient Acharnai*. Oxford.
Kent, R. G. 1904. *A History of Thessaly from the Earliest Times to the Accession of Philip V. of Macedonia*. Leicester, PA.
Kierstead, J. 2013. A Community of Communities: Associations and Democracy in Classical Athens. Diss. Stanford.
Kindt, J. 2009. "On tyrant property turned ritual object: Political power and sacred symbols in ancient Greece and in social anthropology." *Arethusa* 42: 211–50.
King, G., R. Keohane, and S. Verba. 1994. *Designing Social Inquiry: Scientific Inference in Qualitative Research*. Princeton.
Knight, J. 1992. *Institutions and Social Conflict*. Cambridge.
Knoepfler, D. 2001a. *Eretria. Fouilles et recherches XI. Décrets érétriens de proxénie et de citoyenneté*. Lausanne.

———. 2001b. "Loi d'Érétrie contre la tyrannie et l'oligarchie (première partie)." *BCH* 125: 195–238.
———. 2002. "Loi d'Érétrie contre la tyrannie et l'oligarchie (deuxième partie)." *BCH* 126: 149–204.
Koerner, R. 1981. "Vier frühe Verträge zwischen Gemeinwesen und Privatleuten auf griechischen Inschriften." *Klio* 63: 179–206.
———. 1985. "Tiryns als Beispiel einer frühen dorischen Polis." *Klio* 67: 452–57.
Konstan, D. 2006. *The Emotions of the Ancient Greeks: Studies in Aristotle and Ancient Literature*. Toronto.
Konstan, D. and N. K. Rutter, eds. 2003. *Envy, Spite and Jealousy: The Rivalrous Emotions in Ancient Greece*. Edinburgh.
Kosmin, P. J. 2014. *The Land of the Elephant Kings*. Cambridge, MA.
———. 2015. "A phenomenology of democracy: Ostracism as political ritual." *CA* 34: 121–61.
Kowalzig, B. 2007. *Singing for the Gods: Performance of Myth and Ritual in Archaic and Classical Greece*. Oxford.
Krehbiel, K. 1988. "Spatial models of legislative choice." *Legislative Studies Quarterly* 13: 259–319.
Krentz, P. 1982. *The Thirty at Athens*. Ithaca.
———. 1985. "Casualties in hoplite battles." *GRBS* 26: 13–20.
Kreps, D. 1990. *Game Theory and Economic Modeling*. Cambridge.
Kuran, T. 1989. "Sparks and prairie fires: A theory of unanticipated political revolution." *Public Choice* 61: 41–74.
———. 1995. *Private Truths, Public Lies: The Social Consequences of Preference Falsification*. Cambridge, MA.
Kurke, L. 1991. *The Traffic in Praise: Pindar and the Poetics of Social Economy*. Ithaca.
———. 1999. *Coins, Bodies, Games, and Gold: The Politics of Meaning in Archaic Greece*. Princeton.
———. 2005. "Choral lyric as 'ritualization': Poetic sacrifice and poetic ego in Pindar's sixth paian." *CA* 24: 81–130.
———. 2007. "Visualizing the choral: Epichoric poetry, ritual, and elite negotiation in fifth-century Thebes." In C. Kraus, S. Goldhill, H. Foley, and J. Elsner, eds., *Visualizing the Tragic: Drama, Myth, and Ritual in Greek Art and Literature*. Oxford: 63–101.
Kyle, D. G. 1998. *Spectacles of Death in Ancient Rome*. London.
Lalonde, G. V., M. K. Langdon, and M. B. Walbank. 1991. *The Athenian Agora XIX: Inscriptions: Horoi, Poletai Records, Leases of Public Land*. Princeton.
Lane Fox, R. 2000. "Theognis: An alternative to democracy." In R. Brock and S. Hodkinson, eds., *Alternatives to Athens*. Oxford: 35–51.
Lanni, A. 1997. "Spectator sport or serious politics? οἱ περιεστηκότες and the Athenian lawsuits." *JHS* 117: 183–89.
———. 2006. *Law and Justice in the Courts of Athens*. Cambridge.
Lape, S. 2004. *Reproducing Athens: Menander's Comedy, Democratic Culture, and the Hellenistic City*. Princeton.
Larsen, J.A.O. 1949. "The origin and significance of the counting of votes." *CP* 44: 164–81.

———. 1955. "The Boeotian confederacy and fifth-century oligarchic theory." *TAPA* 86: 40–50.
Latacz, J. 1977. *Kampfparänese, Kampfdarstellung, und Kampfwirklichkeit in der Ilias, bei Kallinos und Tyrtaios*. Munich.
Lavelle, B. 1989. "Epikouroi in Thucydides." *AJP* 110: 36–39.
———. 2004. *Fame, Money, and Power: The Rise of Peisistratos and "Democratic" Tyranny at Athens*. Ann Arbor.
Lazenby, J. F. 1997. "The conspiracy of Kinadon reconsidered.." *Athenaeum* 85: 437–47.
Lebedev, A. 1996. "A new epigram for Harmodios and Aristogeiton." *ZPE* 112: 263–68.
Lee, J. W. I. 2007. *A Greek Army on the March: Soldiers and Survival in Xenophon's Anabasis*. Cambridge.
Legon, R. P. 1967. "Phliasian politics and policy in the early fourth century B.C." *Historia* 16: 324–337.
———. 1968. "Megara and Mytilene." *Phoenix* 22: 200–25.
———. 1981. *Megara: The Political History of a Greek City-State to 336 B.C.* Ithaca.
Lehmann, G. 1997. *Oligarchische Herrschaft im klassischen Athen: Zu den Krisen und Katastrophen der attischen Demokratie im 5. und 4. Jahrhundert v. Chr.* Opladen.
Lendon, J. E. 1989. "The Oxyrhynchus Historian and the origins of the Corinthian War." *Historia* 38: 300–13.
Leppin, H. 1999. *Thukydides und die Verfassung der Polis: ein Beitrag zur politischen Ideengeschichte des 5. Jahrhunderts v. Chr.* Berlin.
———. 2013. "Unlike(ly) twins? Democracy and oligarchy in context." In H. Beck, ed., *A Companion to Ancient Greek Government*. London: 146–58.
Le Roy Ladurie, E. 1979. *Carnival in Romans*. New York.
Levi, M. 1988. *Of Rule and Revenue*. Berkeley.
Levitsky, S. and L. Way. 2010. *Competitive Authoritarianism: Hybrid Regimes after the Cold War*. Cambridge.
Lévy, E. 1988. "La kryptie et ses contradictions." *Ktema* 13: 245–52.
Lewis, D. K. 1969. *Convention: A Philosophical Study*. Cambridge, MA.
Lewis, D. M. 1963. "Cleisthenes and Attica." *Historia* 12: 22–40.
———. 1967. "A note on IG I² 114." *JHS* 87: 132.
———. 1977. *Sparta and Persia*. Leiden.
———. 1993. "Oligarchic thinking in the late fifth century." In R. Rosen and J. Farrell, eds., *Nomodeiktes: Greek Studies in Honor of Martin Ostwald*. Ann Arbor: 207–12.
———. 1997. "Democratic institutions and their diffusion." In P. J. Rhodes, ed., *Collected Papers in Greek and Near-Eastern History*. Cambridge: 51–59.
Lewis, S. 1995. "Barbers' shops and perfume shops: 'Symposia without wine.'" In A. Powell, ed., *The Greek World*. London and New York: 432–41.
———. 1996. *News and Society in the Greek Polis*. Chapel Hill.
———. 2004. "Καὶ σαφῶς τύραννος ἦν: Xenophon's account of Euphron of Sicyon." *JHS* 124: 65–74.
———. 2006. *Ancient Tyranny*. Edinburgh.
Liddel, P. 2009. "The decree cultures of the ancient Megarid." *CQ* 59: 411–36.

———. 2010. "Epigraphy, legislation, and power within the Athenian empire." *BICS* 53: 99–128.

Lintott, A. 1982. *Violence, Civil Strife, and Revolution in the Classical City, 750–330 B.C.* Baltimore.

Linz, J. 2000. *Totalitarian and Authoritarian Regimes*. Boulder.

Lohmann, S. 2000. "Collective action cascades: An informational rationale for the power in numbers." *Journal of Economic Surveys* 14: 655–84.

Loraux, N. 2002. *The Divided City: On Memory and Forgetting in Ancient Athens*. New York.

Lorimer, H. 1947. "The hoplite phalanx with special reference to the poems of Archilochus and Tyrtaeus." *ABSA* 42: 76–138.

Ludwig, P. 2009. "Anger, eros, and other political passions in ancient Greek thought." In R. K. Balot, ed. *A Companion to Greek and Roman Political Thought*. Oxford: 294–308.

Lukes, S. 2006. *Individualism*. Colchester, UK.

Luraghi, N. 2011. "Hieron agonistes or the masks of the tyrant." In G. Urso, ed., *Dicere Laudes: Elogio, comunicazione, creazione del consenso*. Pisa: 27–47.

———, ed. 2013a. *The Splendors and Miseries of Ruling Alone: Encounters with Monarchy from Archaic Greece to the Hellenistic Mediterranean*. Stuttgart.

———. 2013b. "To die like a tyrant." In Luraghi, ed. 2013a. Stuttgart: 49–72.

———. 2015. "Anatomy of the monster: The discourse of tyranny in ancient Greece." In H. Börm, ed., *Antimonarchic Discourse in Antiquity*. Stuttgart: 67–84.

Lust-Okar, E. 2006. "Elections under authoritarianism: Preliminary lessons from Jordan." *Democratization* 13: 456–71.

Lyne, M. 2008. *The Voter's Dilemma and Democratic Accountability*. University Park, PA.

Ma, J. 1999. *Antiochos III and the Cities of Western Asia Minor*. Oxford.

———. 2000. "The epigraphy of Hellenistic Asia Minor: A survey of recent research (1992–1999)." *AJA* 104: 95–121.

———. 2009. "The city as memory." In G. Boys-Stones, B. Graziosi, P. Vasunia, eds., *The Oxford Handbook of Hellenic Studies*. Oxford: 248–59.

———. 2013. *Statues and Cities: Honorific Portraits and Civic Identity in the Hellenistic World*. Oxford.

MacDowell, D. M. 1991. "The Athenian procedure of phasis." *Symposion* 1990: 187–98.

Mack, W. 2015. *Proxeny and Polis: Institutional Networks in the Ancient Greek World*. Oxford.

Mackil, E. 2013. *Creating a Common Polity: Religion, Economy, and Politics in the Making of the Greek Koinon*. Berkeley.

Macleod, C. W. 1974. "Form and meaning in the Melian Dialogue." *Historia* 23: 385–400.

Magaloni, B. 2006. *Voting for Autocracy: Hegemonic Party Survival and Its Demise in Mexico*. Cambridge.

Magaloni, B. and R. Kricheli. 2010. "Political order and one-party rule." *Annual Review of Political Science* 13: 123–43.

Magaloni, B., A. Diaz-Cayeros, and F. Estévez. 2007. "Clientelism and portfolio diversification: A model of electoral investment with applications to Mexico." In H. Kitschelt and S. Wilkinson, eds., *Patrons, Clients and Policies: Patterns of Democratic Accountability and Political Competition*. Cambridge: 183–202.

Malkin, I. 1994. *Myth and Territory in the Spartan Mediterranean*. Cambridge.

Manganaro, G. 2004. "Doveri dello stratego nella Kyme eolica, a regime democratico, nel III sec. a.C." *Epigraphica Anatolica* 37: 63–68.
Manin, B. 1997. *The Principles of Representative Government*. Cambridge.
Mann, C. 2007. *Die Demagogen und das Volk: Zur politischen Kommunikation im Athen des 5. Jahrhunderts v. Chr.* Berlin.
Mann, C. and P. Scholz, eds. 2012. *"Demokratie" im Hellenismus: Von der Herrschaft des Volkes zur Herrschaft der Honoratioren?* Mainz.
Mann, M. 1986. *The Sources of Social Power*. Vol. 1: *A History of Power from the Beginning to A.D. 1760*. Cambridge.
Manville, P. B. 1990. *The Origins of Citizenship in Ancient Athens*. Princeton.
Marincola, J. and M. Flower, eds. 2002. *Herodotus: Histories Book IX*. Cambridge.
Markle, M. M. 1976. "Support of Athenian intellectuals for Philip: A study of Isocrates' *Philippus* and Speusippus' *Letter to Philip*." *JHS* 96: 80–99.
Marr, J. L. 1993. "Ephialtes the moderate?" *G&R* 40: 11–19.
Martzavou, P. and N. Papazarkadas, eds. 2012. *Epigraphical Approaches to the Post-Classical Polis: Fourth Century BC to Second Century AD*. Oxford.
Matthaiou, A. 2011. *Ta en tēi stēlēi gegrammena: Six Greek Historical Inscriptions of the Fifth Century B.C.* Athens.
———. 2014. "Four inscribed bronze tablets from Thebes: Preliminary notes." In N. Papazarkadas, ed., *The Epigraphy and History of Boeotia: New Finds, New Prospects*. Leiden: 211–22.
Mattingly, H. 1972. "Review of Meiggs and Lewis, *Greek Historical Inscriptions*." *CR* 33: 75–80.
McGlew, J. 1993. *Tyranny and Political Culture in Ancient Greece*. Ithaca.
McHardy, F. 2008. *Revenge in Athenian Culture*. London.
McInerney, J. 2006. "On the border: Sacred land and the margins of the community." In R. Rosen and I. Sluiter, eds. *City, Countryside and the Spatial Organisation of Value in Classical Antiquity*. Leiden: 33–69.
McKechnie, P. 1989. *Outsiders in the Greek Cities in the Fourth Century B.C.* London.
McKechnie, P. and S. Kern, eds. 1988. *Hellenica Oxyrhynchia*. Warminster.
Meier, M. 1998. *Aristokraten und Damoden*. Stuttgart.
———. 2002. "Tyrtaios fr. 1B G/P bzw. fr. 14 G/P (= fr. 4 W) und die grosse Rhetra—kein Zusammenhang?" *GFA* 5: 65–87.
Meier, M., B. Patzek, and U. Walter, eds. 2004. *Deiokes, König der Meder: Eine Herodot-Episode in ihren Kontexten*. Stuttgart.
Meiggs, R. 1972. *The Athenian Empire*. Oxford.
Mejer, J. 2004. "Democritus and democracy." *Apeiron* 37: 1–9.
Merkelbach, R. 1949. "Politischer Dialog in einem Florentiner Papyrus." *Aegyptus* 29: 56–58.
Messerschmidt, W. 2003. *Prosopopoiia: Personifikationen politischen Charakters in spätklassischer und hellenistischer Kunst*. Cologne.
Meyer, E. A. 2008. "Thucydides on Harmodius and Aristogeiton: Tyranny and history." *CQ* 58: 13–34.
Michels, R. 1962. *Political Parties*. New York.
Migeotte, L. 1989. "Démocratie et entretien du peuple à Rhodes d'après Strabon, XIV, 2, 5." *REG* 102: 515–28.

———. 2005. "Les pouvoirs des agoranomes dans les cités grecques." In R. W. Wallace and M. Gagarin, eds., *Symposion 2001*. Vienna: 287–301.

Mikalson, J. D. 1998. *Religion in Hellenistic Athens*. Berkeley.

Mili, M. 2015. *Religion and Society in Ancient Thessaly*. Oxford.

Miller, A. M. 1982. "*Phthonos* and *parphasis*: The argument of Nemean 8.19–34." *GRBS* 23: 111–20.

Millett, P. 1989. "Patronage and its avoidance in classical Athens." In A. Wallace-Hadrill, ed., *Patronage in Ancient Society*. Leicester: 15–48.

Minar, E. L. 1942. *Early Pythagorean Politics in Practice and Theory*. Baltimore.

Minon, S. 2007. *Les inscriptions éléennes dialectales (Vie-IIe siècle avant J.-C.), I-II*. Geneva.

Missiou, A. 2011. *Literacy and Democracy in Fifth-Century Athens*. Cambridge.

Mitchell, L. G. 2013. *The Heroic Rulers of Archaic and Classical Greece*. London.

Moe, T. 2005. "Power and political institutions." *Perspectives on Politics* 3: 215–33.

Moggi, M. 1976. *Sinecismi interstatali greci*. 1: *Dalle origine al 338 a.C.* Pisa.

Molyneux, J. 1992. *Simonides: A Historical Study*. Wauconda, IL.

Monson, A. 2012. *From the Ptolemies to the Romans: Political and Economic Change in Egypt*. Cambridge.

Moore, J. M. 1975. *Aristotle and Xenophon on Democracy and Oligarchy*. Berkeley.

Morgan, C. 2003. *Early Greek States Beyond the Polis*. London.

Morgan, K. 2015. *Pindar and the Construction of Syracusan Monarchy in the Fifth Century B.C.* Oxford.

Morris, I. 1987. *Burial and Ancient Society*. Cambridge.

———. 1996. "The Strong Principle of Equality and the archaic origins of Greek democracy." In J. Ober and C. Hedrick, eds., *Dēmokratia: A Conversation on Democracies, Ancient and Modern*. Princeton: 19–48.

———. 2004. "Economic growth in ancient Greece." *Journal of Institutional and Theoretical Economics* 160: 709–42.

Morrison, J. V. 2000. "Historical lessons in the Melian dialogue." *TAPA* 130: 119–48.

Morrow, J. D. 1994. *Game Theory for Political Scientists*. Princeton.

Mossé, C. 1969. *La tyrannie dans la Grèce antique*. Paris.

———. 1979. "Citoyens actifs et citoyens 'passifs' dans les cités grecques: une approche théoretique du problème." *REA* 81: 241–49.

Mulgan, R. 1991. "Aristotle's Analysis of Oligarchy and Democracy." In D. Keyt and F. D. Miller, Jr., eds., *A Companion to Aristotle's Politics*. Cambridge, MA: 307–22.

Müller, C. 2010. "Les élites béotiens et la richesse du IVe au IIe s. a.C.: quelques pistes de réflexion." In L. Capdetrey and Y. Lafond, eds., *La Cité et ses élites: Pratiques et répresentation des formes de domination et de contrôle social dans les cités grecques*. Bordeaux: 225–44.

———. 2011. "Évertétisme et pratiques financières dans les cités de la Grèce hellénistique." *REA* 113: 345–63.

Munson, R. V. 2007. "The trouble with the Ionians: Herodotus and the beginning of the Ionian Revolt (5.28–38.1)." In E. Irwin and E. Greenwood, eds., *Reading Herodotus: A Study of the Logoi in Book 5 of Herodotus' Histories*. Cambridge: 146–67.

Nadon, C. 2001. *Xenophon's Prince: Republic and Empire in the* Cyropaedia. Berkeley and Los Angeles.

Nafissi, M. 2015. "Le iscrizioni del monumento per gli Ecatomnidi: edizione e commento storico." *SCO* 61: 63–99.

Nagy, G. 1985. "Theognis and Megara: A poet's vision of his city." In G. Nagy and T. Figueira, eds., *Theognis of Megara*. Baltimore: 8–40.

———. 1990. *Pindar's Homer: The Lyric Possession of an Epic Past*. Baltimore.

Nawotka, K. 2003. "Freedom of the Greek cities of Asia Minor in the age of Alexander the Great." *Klio* 85: 15–41.

Neils, J. 2013. "Monumental representations of government." In H. Beck, ed., *A Companion to Ancient Greek Government*. London: 417–31.

Németh, G. 2006. *Kritias und die Dreissig Tyrannen: Untersuchungen zur Politik und Prosopographie der Führungselite in Athen 404/403 v. Chr.* Stuttgart.

Nicholson, N. 2015. *The Poetics of Victory in the Greek West: Epinician, Oral Tradition, and the Deinomenid Empire*. Oxford.

Nielsen, T. H. 2000. "Epiknemidian, Hypoknemidian, and Opountian Lokrians. Reflections on the political organization of East Lokris in the classical period." In P. Flensted-Jensen, ed., *Further Studies in the Ancient Greek Polis*. Stuttgart: 91–120.

———. 2002. *Arkadia and Its Poleis in the Archaic and Classical Periods*. Göttingen.

Nightingale, A. W. 1995. *Genres in Dialogue: Plato and the Construct of Philosophy*. Cambridge.

North, D. 1990. *Institutions, Institutional Change, and Economic Performance*. Cambridge.

North, D., J. Wallis, and B. Weingast, eds. 2009. *Violence and Social Orders: A Conceptual Framework for Interpreting Recorded Human History*. Cambridge.

North, H. 1966. *Sophrosyne: Self-Knowledge and Self-Restraint in Greek Literature*. Ithaca.

Ober, J. 1989. *Mass and Elite in Democratic Athens: Rhetoric, Ideology, and the Power of the People*. Princeton.

———. 1993. "Thucydides' criticism of democratic knowledge." In R. Rosen and J. Farrell, eds., *Nomodeiktes: Greek Studies in Honor of Martin Ostwald*. Ann Arbor: 81–98.

———. 1996. "The Athenian revolution of 508/7 B.C.: Violence, authority, and the origins of democracy." In *The Athenian Revolution*. Princeton: 32–52.

———. 1998. *Political Dissent in Democratic Athens: Intellectual Critics of Popular Rule*. Princeton.

———. 2003. "Tyrant killing as therapeutic *stasis*: A political debate in images and texts." In K. Morgan, ed., *Popular Tyranny: Sovereignty and its Discontents in Ancient Greece*. Austin: 215–50.

———. 2007. "'I besieged that man': Democracy's revolutionary start." In K. A. Raaflaub, J. Ober, and R. W. Wallace, eds., *Origins of Democracy in Ancient Greece*. Berkeley and Los Angeles: 83–104.

———. 2008. *Democracy and Knowledge: Innovation and Learning in Classical Athens*. Princeton.

———. 2012. "Democracy's dignity." *American Political Science Review* 106: 827–46.

———. 2015. *The Rise and Fall of Classical Greece*. Princeton.

O'Donnell, G. and P. Schmitter. 1986. *Transitions from Authoritarian Rule: Tentative Conclusions about Uncertain Democracies*. Baltimore.

Oliver, G. 2003a. "(Re-)locating Athenian decrees in the Agora: *IG* II^2 448." In J. S. Traill and D. Jordan, eds., *Lettered Attica*. Athens and Toronto: 94–110.

———. 2003b. "Oligarchy at Athens after the Lamian War: Epigraphic evidence for the boule and the ekklesia." In O. Palagia and S. V. Tracy, eds., *The Macedonians in Athens, 323–229 B.C.* Oxford: 40–51.

———. 2007. *War, Food, and Politics in Early Hellenistic Athens.* Oxford.

Oliver, J. 1977. "The Vatican fragments of Greek political theory." *GRBS* 18: 321–39.

Olson, M. 1965. *The Logic of Collective Action.* Cambridge, MA.

O'Neil, J. 1978/79. "The constitution of Chios in the fifth century BC." *Talanta* 10–11: 66–73.

———. 1981a. "How democratic was Hellenistic Rhodes?" *Athenaeum* 59: 468–73.

———. 1981b. "The exile of Themistokles and democracy in the Peloponnese." *CQ* 31: 335–46.

———. 1995. *The Origins and Development of Ancient Greek Democracy.* Lanham, MD.

Osborne, R. 1990. "Vexatious litigation in classical Athens: Sykophancy and the sykophant." In P. Cartledge, P. Millett, S. Todd, eds., *Nomos: Essays in Athenian Law, Politics, and Society.* Cambridge: 83–102.

———. 1996. *Greece in the Making 1200–479 BC.* New York.

———. 1997. "Law and laws: How we join up the dots." In L. Mitchell and P. J. Rhodes, eds., *The Development of the Polis in Archaic Greece.* London: 74–82.

———. 2003. "Changing the discourse." In K. Morgan, ed. 2003. *Popular Tyranny: Sovereignty and Its Discontents in Ancient Greece.* Austin, TX: 251–72.

———. 2007. "The Paeonians (5.11–16)." In E. Irwin and E. Greenwood, eds., *Reading Herodotus: A Study of the Logoi in Book 5 of Herodotus' Histories.* Cambridge: 88–97.

———. 2010. *Athens and Athenian Democracy.* Cambridge.

Ostrom, E. 1990. *Governing the Commons.* Cambridge.

———. 1998. "A behavioral approach to the rational choice theory of collective action." *American Political Science Review* 92: 1–22.

———. 2000. "Collective action and the evolution of social norms." *Journal of Economic Perspectives* 14: 137–58.

Ostwald, M. 1973. "Isokratia as a political concept (Herodotus 5.92a.1)." In S. M. Stern, A. Hourani, and V. Brown, eds., *Islamic Philosophy and the Classical Tradition.* Columbia, SC: 277–91.

———. 1986. *From Popular Sovereignty to the Sovereignty of Law: Law, Society, and Politics in Fifth-Century Athens.* Berkeley.

———. 1993. "*Stasis* and *autonomia* in Samos: A comment on an ideological fallacy." *SCI* 12: 51–66.

———. 1995. "Public expense: Whose obligation? Athens 600–454 B.C.E." *TAPA* 139: 368–79.

———. 2000. *Oligarchia: The Development of a Constitutional Form in Ancient Greece.* Stuttgart.

———. 2002. "Athens and Chalkis: A study in imperial control." *JHS* 122: 134–43.

———. 2009. *Language and History in Ancient Greek Culture.* Philadelphia.

O'Sullivan, L. 2009. *The Regime of Demetrius of Phalerum in Athens, 317–307 B.C.* Leiden.

Paga, J. 2010. "Deme theaters in Attica and the *trittys* system." *Hesperia* 79: 351–84.

Page, D. L. 1955. *Sappho and Alcaeus.* Oxford.

Papadodima, E. 2011. "Forms and conceptions of *dike* in Euripides' *Heracleidae, Suppliants,* and *Phoenissae*." *Philologae* 155: 14–38.

Papakonstantinou, Z. 2002. "Justice of the 'kakoi': Law and social crisis in Theognis." *Dike* 5: 5–17.
———. 2008. *Lawmaking and Adjudication in Archaic Greece*. London.
Pébarthe, C. 2006. *Cité, démocratie et écriture: Histoire de l'alphabétisation d'Athènes à l'époque classique*. Paris.
Peponi, A.-E., ed. 2013. *Performance and Culture in Plato's Laws*. Cambridge.
Perlman, P. 1992. "One hundred-citied Crete and the 'Cretan politeia.'" *CP* 87: 193–205.
———. 2004. "Tinker, tailor, soldier, sailor: The economies of archaic Eleutherna, Crete." *CA* 23: 95–127.
———. 2014. "Reading and writing Archaic Cretan society." In G. Seelentag and O. Pilz, eds., *Cultural Practices and Material Culture in Archaic and Classical Crete: Proceedings of the International Conference, Mainz, May 20–21, 2011*. Berlin: 177–206.
Perlman, S. 1964. "The causes and the outbreak of the Corinthian War." *CQ* 14: 64–81.
Pfaff, S. and G. Yang. 2001. "Double-edged rituals and the symbolic resources of collective action: Political commemorations and the mobilization of protest in 1989." *Theory and Society* 30: 539–89.
Picard, O. 2000. "Le retour des émigrés et le monnayage de Thasos (390)." *CRAI* 144: 1057–84.
Piérart, M. 2000. "Argos. Une autre démocratie." In P. Flensted-Jensen, T. H. Nielsen, and L. Rubinstein, eds. *Polis & Politics*. Copenhagen: 297–314.
Pierson, P. and T. Skocpol. 2002. "Historical institutionalism in contemporary politics." In I. Katznelson and H. Milner, eds. *Political Science: The State of the Discipline*. New York: 693–721.
Pinney, G. F. and R. Hamilton. 1982. "Secret ballot." *AJA* 86: 581–84.
Piolot, L. 2009. "À l'ombre des maris." In L. Bodiou et al., eds., *Chemin faisant. Mythes, cultes et société en Grèce ancienne*. Rennes: 87–113.
Pleket, H. W. 1963. "Thasos and the popularity of the Athenian empire." *Historia* 12: 70–77.
Poddighe, E. 1997. "La natura del tetto censitario stabilito da Antipatro per l'accesso al *politeuma* di Atene nel 322 a.C." *DHA* 23: 47–82.
———. 2002. *Nel segno di Antipatro: L'eclissi della democrazia ateniese dal 323/2 al 319/8 a. C*. Rome.
Pouilloux, J. 1954. *Recherches sur l'histoire et les cultes de Thasos I*. Paris.
Pownall, F. 1998. "Condemnation of the impious in Xenophon's *Hellenica*." *Harvard Theological Review* 91: 251–77.
Price, J. 2001. *Thucydides and Internal War*. Cambridge.
Priest, D. and W. M. Arkin. 2011. *Top Secret America: The Rise of the New American Security State*. New York, Boston, and London.
Prince, S. 2015. *Antisthenes of Athens: Texts, Translations, and Commentary*. Ann Arbor.
Pritchard, D. 2010. "The symbiosis between democracy and war: The case of ancient Athens." In D. Pritchard, ed., *War, Democracy and Culture in Classical Athens*. Oxford: 1–62.
———. 2013. *Sport, Democracy and War in Classical Athens*. Cambridge.
———. 2015. *Public Spending and Democracy in Classical Athens*. Austin, TX.
Pritchett, W. K. 1971–79. *The Greek State at War*. 5 vols. Berkeley.
Procopé, J. F. 1989. "Democritus on politics the care of the soul." *CQ* 39: 307–31.

Putnam, R. D. 1993. *Making Democracy Work: Civic Traditions in Modern Italy.* Princeton.
Pyzyk, M. unpublished manuscript. "Onerous burdens: Liturgies and the Athenian elite."
Quass, F. 1979. "Zur Verfassung der griechischen Städte im Hellenismus." *Chiron* 9: 37–52.
———. 1993. *Die Honoratiorenschicht in den Städten des griechischen Ostens.* Stuttgart.
Quillin, J. 2002. "Achieving amnesty: The role of events, institutions, and ideas." *TAPA* 132: 71–107.
Quinn, T. J. 1969. "Political groups at Chios: 412 B.C." *Historia* 18: 22–30.
———. 1971. "Political groups in Lesbos during the Peloponnesian War." *Historia* 20: 405–17.
Raaflaub, K. A. 1983. "Democracy, oligarchy, and the concept of the 'free citizen' in late fifth-century Athens." *Political Theory* 11: 517–44.
———. 1989. "Contemporary perceptions of democracy in fifth-century Athens." *C&M* 40: 33–70.
———. 1996. "Equalities and inequalities in Athenian democracy." In J. Ober and H. Hedrick, eds., *Demokratia: A Conversation on Democracies, Ancient and Modern.* Princeton: 139–74.
———. 1997. "Soldiers, citizens, and the evolution of the early Greek *polis*." In L. Mitchell and P. J. Rhodes, eds., *The Development of the* Polis *in Archaic Greece.* London: 49–59.
———. 1998. "A historian's headache: How to read 'Homeric society'?" In N.R.E. Fisher and H. van Wees, eds., *Archaic Greece: New Approaches and New Evidence.* London: 169–93.
———. 2003. "Stick and glue: The function of tyranny in fifth-century Athenian democracy." In K. Morgan, ed., *Popular Tyranny: Sovereignty and Its Discontents in Ancient Greece.* Austin, TX: 59–93.
———. 2004. *The Discovery of Freedom in Ancient Greece.* Chicago.
———. 2006a. "Athenian and Spartan *eunomia*, or: What to do with Solon's timocracy?" In J. Blok and A. Lardinois, eds., *Solon of Athens: New Historical and Philological Approaches.* Leiden: 390–428.
———. 2006b. "Thucydides on democracy and oligarchy." In A. Rengakos and A. Tsakmakis, eds., *Brill's Companion to Thucydides.* Leiden: 189–222.
———. 2007. "The breakthrough of *dēmokratia* in mid-fifth-century Athens." In K. A. Raaflaub, J. Ober, and R. W. Wallace, eds., *Origins of Democracy in Ancient Greece.* Berkeley and Los Angeles: 105–54.
———. 2008. "Homeric warriors and battles: Trying to resolve old problems." 101: 469–83.
———. 2009. "Learning from the enemy: Athenian and Persian 'instruments of empire.'" In J. Ma, N. Papazarkadas, and R. Parker, eds., *Interpreting the Athenian Empire.* London: 89–124.
Raaflaub, K. A. and R. Wallace. 2007. "'People's power' and egalitarian trends in archaic Greece." In K. Raaflaub, J. Ober, and R. W. Wallace, eds., *Origins of Democracy in Ancient Greece.* Berkeley: 22–48.
Radt, S., ed. 2009. *Strabons Geographika, Band 8. Buch XIV-XVII.* Göttingen.
Rapport, M. 2008. *1848: Year of Revolution.* New York.
Raubitschek, A. 1962. "Demokratia." *Hesperia* 31: 238–43.
Redfield, J. 2003. *The Locrian Maidens: Love and Death in Greek Italy.* Princeton.
Reger, G. 1990. "Some remarks on '*IG* XII 8, 262 complété' and the restoration of Thasian democracy." *Klio* 72: 396–401.
Rhodes, P. J. 1972a. *The Athenian Boule.* Oxford.

---. 1972b. "The Five Thousand in the Athenian revolutions of 411 B.C." *JHS* 92: 115–27.
---. 1982a. "Problems in Athenian *eisphora* and liturgies." *AJAH* 7: 1–19.
---. 1982b. *The Athenian Boule*. Oxford.
---. 1993. *A Commentary on the Aristotelian* Athenaion Politeia. 2nd edition. Oxford.
---. 1995. "Judicial procedures in fourth-century Athens: Improvement or simply change?" In W. Eder, ed., *Die athenische Demokratie im 4. Jahrhundert v. Chr.* Sturttgart: 303–19.
---. 2000. "Oligarchs in Athens." In R. Brock and S. Hodkinson, eds., *Alternatives to Athens*. Oxford: 119–36.
---. 2003. "Nothing to do with democracy: Athenian drama and the polis." *JHS* 123: 104–19.
---. 2006. "Milesian *stephanephoroi*: Applying Cavaignac correctly." *ZPE* 157: 116.
---. 2007. "Oaths in political life." In A. Sommerstein and J. Fletcher, eds., *Horkos: The Oath in Greek Society*. Exeter: 1–25.
---. 2011. "The Dionysia and democracy again." *CQ* 61: 71–74.
Rhodes, P. J. with D. M. Lewis. 1997. *The Decrees of the Greek States*. Oxford.
Rhodes, P. J. and J. L. Marr, eds. 2008. *The 'Old Oligarch': The Constitution of the Athenians Attributed to Xenophon*. Oxford.
Richer, N. 1998. *Les éphores: études sur l'histoire et sur l'image de Sparte (VIIIe-IIIe siècle avant Jésus-Christ)*. Paris.
Riess, W. 2006. "How tyrants and dynasts die." In G. Urso, ed., *Terror et Pavor: Violenza, intimidazione, clandestinita nel mondo antico*. Pisa: 65–88.
---. 2012. *Performing Interpersonal Violence: Court, Curse, and Comedy in Fourth-Century BCE Athens*. Berlin.
Riess, W. and G. Fagan, eds. 2016. *The Topography of Violence in the Greco-Roman World*. Ann Arbor.
Robert, L. 1960. "Recherches épigraphiques." *REA* 62: 276–361.
---. 1969. "Théophane de Mytilène à Constantinople." *CRAI* 52: 42–64.
Robertson, N. 1987. "Government and society at Miletus, 525–442 B.C." *Phoenix* 41: 356–98.
Robinson, E. W. 1997. *The First Democracies: Early Popular Government Outside Athens*. Stuttgart.
---. 2011. *Democracy Beyond Athens: Popular Government in the Greek Classical Age*. Cambridge.
Roesch, P. 1965. *Thespies et la Confédération béotienne*. Paris.
Roessler, P. G. 2005. "Donor-induced democratization and the privatization of state violence in Kenya and Rwanda." *Comparative Politics* 37: 207–27.
Roisman, J. 2006. *The Rhetoric of Conspiracy in Ancient Athens*. Berkeley.
Roller, D. W. 1989. "Who murdered Ephialtes?" *Historia* 38: 257–66.
Romer, F. E. 1982. "The *aesymnetia*: A problem in Aristotle's historic method." *AJP* 103: 25–46.
Rood, T. 1998. *Thucydides: Narrative and Explanation*. Oxford.
Root, H. 1989. "Tying the King's hands: Credible commitments and royal fiscal policy during the Old Regime." *Rationality and Society* 1: 240–58.
Rose, P. W. 1992. *Sons of the Gods, Children of the Earth: Ideology and Literary Form in Ancient Greece*. Ithaca.
---. 2012. *Class in Archaic Greece*. Cambridge.

Rosivach, V. 2002a. "The requirements for the Solonic classes in Aristotle, *A.P.* 7.4." *Hermes* 130: 36–47.
———. 2002b. "*Zeugitai* and hoplites." *AHB* 16: 33–43.
———. 2008. "Why seize the acropolis?" *Historia* 57: 125–33.
Roubineau, J.-M. 2012. "La main cruelle de l'agoranome." In L. Capdetrey and C. Hasenohr, eds., *Agoranomes et édiles. Institutions des marchés antiques.* Bordeaux: 47–59.
Roy, J. 1971. "Arcadia and Boeotia in Peloponnesian affairs, 370–362 B.C." *Historia* 20: 569–99.
———. 1991. "Traditional jokes about the punishment of adulterers in ancient Greek literature." *LCM* 16: 73–76.
———. 2000. "Problems of democracy in the Arcadian Confederacy 370–362 BC." In R. Brock and S. Hodkinson, eds., *Alternatives to Athens: Varieties of Political Organization and Community in Ancient Greece.* Oxford: 308–26.
———. 2015. "The distribution of cult in the landscape of Eleia." In L. Käppel and V. Pothou, eds., *Human Development in Sacred Landscapes: Between Ritual Tradition, Creativity and Emotionality.* Goettingen: 173–88.
Rubinstein, L. 2003. "Volunteer prosecutors in the Greek world." *Dike* 6: 87–113.
Runciman, W. G. 1990. "Doomed to extinction: The *polis* as an evolutionary dead end." In O. Murray and S. Price, eds., *The Greek City: From Homer to Alexander.* Oxford: 347–67.
Ruschenbusch, E. 1978. *Untersuchungen zu Staat und Politik in Griechenland vom 7.-4. Jh. v. Chr.* Bamburg.
Russell, D. 1983. *Greek Declamation.* Cambridge.
Russell, F. S. 1999. *Information Gathering in Classical Greece.* Ann Arbor.
Rutherford, I. 2015. *State Pilgrims and Sacred Observers in Ancient Greece: A Study of Theōria and Theōroi.* Cambridge.
Ruzé, F. 1984. "*Plethos*: aux origins de la majorité politique." In *Aux origins de l'Hellénisme: Hommage à Henri van Effenterre.* Paris: 247–63.
———. 1997. *Délibération et pouvoir dans la cité grecque: de Nestor à Socrate.* Paris.
Ryan, F. X. 1994. "The original date of the *demos plethuon* provisions of *IG* I^3 105." *JHS* 114: 120–34.
Salmon, J. B. 1977. "Political hoplites?" *JHS* 97: 84–101.
———. 1984. *Wealthy Corinth: A History of the City to 338 B.C.* Oxford.
———. 1997. "Lopping off the heads? Tyrants, politics, and the *polis*." In L. Mitchell and P. J. Rhodes, eds., *The Development of the Polis in Archaic Greece.* London: 60–73.
Salviat, F. and Y. Grandjean. 1988. "Décret d'Athènes, restaurant la démocratie à Thasos en 407 av. J.-C.: *IG* XII 8, 262 complété." *BCH* 112: 259–78.
Samons, Jr., L. J. 2004. *What's Wrong with Democracy? From Athenian Practice to American Worship.* Berkeley.
Sancho Rocher, L. 2007. "*Athenaion Politeia* 34.3, about oligarchs, democrats and moderates in the late fifth century BC." *Polis* 24: 298–327.
Sanders, E. 2014. *Envy and Jealousy in Classical Athens: A Socio-Psychological Approach.* Oxford.
Savalli-Lestrade, I. 2003. "Remarques sur les élites dans les *poleis* hellénistiques." In M. Cébeillac-Gervasoni and L. Lamoine, eds., *Les élites et leurs facettes: Les élites locales dans le monde hellénistique et romain.* Rome: 52–64.

———. 2009. "Usages civiques et usages dynamiques de la *damnatio memoriae* dans le monde hellénistique (323–30 av. J.-C.)." In S. Benoist, A. Daguet-Gagey, C. Hoët-van Cauwenberghe, and S. Lefebvre, eds., *Mémoires partagées, mémoires disputées: écriture et réécriture de l'histoire*. Metz: 127–58.

Scafuro, A. 2013. "Keeping record, making public: The epigraphy of government." In H. Beck, ed., *A Companion to Ancient Greek Government*. London: 400–416.

Schaefer, H. 1961. "Πόλις μυρίανδρος." *Historia* 10: 292–317.

Schatzberg, M. G. 1993. "Power, legitimacy, and 'democratisation' in Africa." *Africa* 63: 445–61.

Schedler, A. 2013. *The Politics of Uncertainty: Sustaining and Subverting Electoral Authoritarianism*. Oxford.

Schelling, T. 1980. *The Strategy of Conflict*. Cambridge, MA.

Schmitt Pantel, P. 1990. "Sacrificial meal and *symposion*: Two models of civic institutions in the Archaic city." In O. Murray, ed., *Sympotica: A Symposium on the Symposion*. Oxford: 14–33.

Schoenfeld, G. 2011. *Necessary Secrets: National Security, the Media, and the Rule of Law*. New York and London.

Schwartz, A. 2009. *Reinstating the Hoplite*. Stuttgart.

Schwartzberg, M. 2010. "Shouts, murmurs and votes: Acclamation and Aggregation in Ancient Greece." *Journal of Political Philosophy* 18: 448–68.

Scott, J. C. 1990. *Domination and the Arts of Resistance: Hidden Transcripts*. New Haven.

Scott, L. 2005. *Historical Commentary on Herodotus Book 6*. Leiden.

Scott, M. 2010. *Delphi and Olympia: The Spatial Politics of Panhellenism in the Archaic and Classical Periods*. Cambridge.

———. 2013. *Space and Society in the Greek and Roman Worlds*. Cambridge.

Scullion, S. 2002. "Tragic dates." *CQ* 52: 81–101.

Seelentag, G. 2015. *Das archaische Kreta. Institutionalisierung im frühen Griechenland*. Berlin.

Seibert, J. 1979. *Die politischen Flüchtlinge und Verbannten in der griechischen Geschichte*. 2 vols. Darmstadt.

Sen, A. 1967. "Isolation, assurance and the social rate of discount." *Quarterly Journal of Economics* 81: 112–24.

Seubert, S. 2009. *Das Konzept des Sozialkapitals*. Frankfurt.

Shaw, C. 2006. *Popular Government and Oligarchy in Renaissance Italy*. Leiden.

Shear, J. L. 2011. *Polis and Revolution: Responding to Oligarchy in Classical Athens*. Cambridge.

Shepsle, K. 1986. "Institutional equilibrium and equilibrium institutions." In H. F. Weisberg, ed., *Political Science: The Science of Politics*. New York: 51–81.

Shipley, G. 1987. *A History of Samos, 800–188 B.C.* Oxford.

Shrimpton, G. 1991. *Theopompus the Historian*. Montreal.

Sickinger, J. 1999. *Public Records and Archives in Classical Athens*. Chapel Hill.

Siewert, P. et al., eds. 2002. *Ostrakismos-Testimonien I*. Stuttgart.

Simonton, M. 2015. "The cry from the herald's stone: The revolutionary logic behind the Rhodian democratic uprising of 395 B.C.E." *TAPA* 145: 281–324.

———. 2017. "Stability and violence in Classical Greek democracies and oligarchies." *CA* 36: 1–52.

———. "The local history of Hippias of Erythrai: Politics, place, memory, and monumentality." Forthcoming in *Hesperia*.

Simpser, A. 2013. *Why Governments and Parties Manipulate Elections: Theory, Practice, and Implications*. Cambridge.

Simpson, P. 2011. "A corruption of oligarchs." In Tabachnick and Koivukoski 2011: 70–89.

Singor, H. 2000. "The military side of the Peisistratean tyranny." In H. Sancisi-Weerdenburg, ed., *Peisistratos and the Tyranny: A Reappraisal of the Evidence*. Amsterdam: 107–29.

Sissa, G. 2009. "Political animals: Pathetic animals." In R. K. Balot, ed., *A Companion to Greek and Roman Political Thought*. Oxford: 283–93.

Skultety, S. C. 2011. "The threat of misguided elites: Aristotle on oligarchy." In Tabachnick and Koivukoski 2011: 90–109.

Skyrms, B. 2004. *The Stag Hunt and the Evolution of Social Structure*. Cambridge.

Slater, D. 2010. *Ordering Power: Contentious Politics and Authoritarian Leviathans in Southeast Asia*. Cambridge.

Smith, B. 2005. "Life of the party: The origins of regime breakdown and persistence under single-party rule." *World Politics* 57: 421–51.

Snodgrass, A. 1980. *Archaic Greece: The Age of Experiment*. Berkeley.

Sommerstein, A. and A. Bayliss. 2013. *Oath and State in Ancient Greece*. Berlin.

Sourvinou-Inwood, C. 1995. *'Reading' Greek Death: To the End of the Classical Period*. Oxford.

Spence, I. G. 1993. *The Cavalry of Classical Greece: A Social and Military History*. Oxford.

Spivey, N. 1994. "Psephological heroes." In R. Osborne and S. Hornblower, eds., *Ritual, Finance, Politics: Athenian Democratic Accounts Presented to David Lewis*. Oxford: 39–52.

Stahl, M. and U. Walter. 2009. "Athens." In K. Raaflaub and H. van Wees, eds., *A Companion to Archaic Greece*. Blackwell: 138–61.

Stehle, E. 1997. *Performance and Gender in Ancient Greece: Non-dramatic Poetry in Its Setting*. Princeton.

Stein-Hölkeskamp, E. 1989. *Adelskultur und Polisgesellschaft: Studien zum griechischen Adel in archaischer und klassischer Zeit*. Stuttgart.

Steiner, D. 1994. *The Tyrant's Writ: Myths and Images of Writing in Ancient Greece*. Princeton.

Sternberg, R., ed. 2005. *Pity and Power in Ancient Athens*. Cambridge.

Stockton, D. 1982. "The death of Ephialtes." *CQ* 32: 227–28.

Stokes, S. 2005. "Perverse accountability: A formal model of machine politics with evidence from Argentina." *American Political Science Review* 99: 315–25.

Strauss, B. 1987. "Athenian democracy: Neither radical, extreme, nor moderate." *AHB* 1: 127–29.

———. 1996. "The Athenian trireme, school of democracy." In J. Ober and C. Hedrick, eds., *Dēmokratia: A Conversation on Democracies, Ancient and Modern*. Princeton: 313–26.

Stroud, R. S. 1971. "Greek inscriptions: Theozotides and the Athenian orphans." *Hesperia* 40: 280–301.

Stylianou, P. J. 1998. *A Historical Commentary on Diodorus Siculus: Book 15*. Oxford.

Svolik, M. W. 2012. *The Politics of Authoritarian Rule*. Cambridge.

Swoboda, H. 1910. "Studien zur Verfassung Boiotiens." *Klio* 10: 315–34.

Szegedy-Maszak, A. 1998. "Thucydides' Solonian reflections." In C. Dougherty and L. Kurke, eds., *Cultural Poetics in Archaic Greece*. Cambridge: 201–14.

Tabachnick, D. and T. Koivukoski, eds. 2011. *On Oligarchy: Ancient Lessons for Global Politics.* Toronto.

Tamiolaki, M. 2013. "A citizen as a slave of the state? Oligarchic perceptions of democracy in Xenophon." *GRBS* 53: 31–50.

Tatum, J. 1989. *Xenophon's Imperial Fiction: On the Education of Cyrus.* Princeton.

Taylor, M. 1991. *The Tyrant Slayers.* 2nd Ed. Salem, NH.

Taylor, M. C. 2002. "Implicating the *demos*: A reading of Thucydides on the rise of the Four Hundred." *JHS* 122: 91–108.

Teegarden, D. 2014. *Death to Tyrants! Ancient Greek Democracy and the Struggle against Tyranny.* Princeton.

Thalmann, W. 2004. "'The most divinely approved and political discord': Thinking about conflict in the developing polis." *CA* 23: 359–99.

Thelen, K. 1999. "Historical institutionalism in comparative politics." *Ann.. Rev. Pol. Sci.* 2: 369–404.

Thelen, K. and S. Steinmo. 1992. "Historical institutionalism in comparative politics." In S. Steinmo, ed. *Structuring Politics: Historical Institutionalism in Comparative Analysis.* Cambridge: 1–32.

Thériault, G. 1996. *Le culte d'Homonoia dans les cités grecques.* Lyon.

Thomas, R. 1989. *Oral Tradition and Written Record in Classical Athens.* Cambridge.

———. 1992. *Literacy and Orality in Ancient Greece.* Cambridge.

———. 2009. "Functional literacy and democratic literacy in Greece." In W. A. Johnson and H. N. Parker, eds., *Ancient Literacies: The Culture of Reading in Greece and Rome.* Oxford: 13–45.

Thommen, L. 1996. *Lakedaimonion Politeia: Die Entstehung der spartanischen Varfassung.* Stuttgart.

———. 2003. *Sparta: Verfassungs- und Sozialgeschichte einer griechischen Polis.* Stuttgart.

Thompson, E. P. 1971. "The moral economy of the English crowd in the eighteenth century." *P&P* 50: 76–136.

Thomsen, R. 1964. *Eisphora: A Study of Direct Taxation in Ancient Athens.* Copenhagen.

Thonemann, P. 2013. *Attalid Asia Minor: Money, International Relations and the State.* Oxford.

Thür, G. 2011. "Amnestie in Telos (*IG* XII 4/1, 132)." *ZRG* 128: 339–51.

Todd, S. C. 1993. *The Shape of Athenian Law.* Oxford.

———. 2007. *A Commentary on Lysias, Speeches 1–11.* Oxford.

Toher, M. 1991. "Greek funerary legislation and the two Spartan funerals." In M. A. Flower and M. Toher, eds., *Georgika: Greek Studies in Honor of George Cawkwell.* London: 159–75.

Tracy, S. V. 1995. *Athenian Democracy in Transition: Attic Letter-Cutters of 340 to 290 B.C.* Berkeley.

———. 2000. "Demetrius of Phalerum: Who was he and who was he not?" In W. W. Fortenbaugh and E. Schütrumpf, eds., *Demetrius of Phalerum: Text, Translation and Discussion.* New Brunswick: 331–45.

Trampedach, K. 1994. *Platon, die Akademie und die zeitgenössische Politik.* Stuttgart.

Tritle, L. 1988. *Phocion the Good.* London.

Tsebelis, G. 2002. *Veto Players: How Political Institutions Work.* Princeton.

Tuplin, C. 1982. "The date of the union of Corinth and Argos." *CQ* 32: 75–83.
Turner, V. 1995. *The Ritual Process: Structure and Anti-Structure.* New York.
van Nijf, O. 2011. "Public space and the political culture of Roman Termessos." In van Nijf and Alston 2011: 215–42.
van Nijf, O. and R. Alston, eds. 2011. *Political Culture in the Greek City after the Classical Age.* Leuven.
van Wees, H. 1992. *Status Warriors: War, Violence and Society in Homer and History.* Amsterdam.
———. 1994. "The Homeric way of war: The *Iliad* and the hoplite phalanx." *G&R* 41: 1–18, 131–55.
———. 1995. "Politics and the battlefield: Ideology in Greek warfare." In A. Powell, ed., *The Greek World.* London: 153–73.
———. 1999. "Tyrtaeus' *Eunomia*: Nothing to do with the Great Rhetra." In S. Hodkinson and A. Powell, eds., *Sparta: New Perspectives.* Swansea: 1–41.
———. 2000. "Megara's Mafiosi: Timocracy and violence in Theognis." In Brock and Hodkinson 2000: 53–67.
———. 2001. "The myth of the middle class army." In T. Bekker-Nielsen and L. Hannestad, eds., *War as a Cultural and Social Force.* Copenhagen: 45–71.
———. 2002. "Tyrants, oligarchs and citizen militias." In A. Chaniotis and P. Ducrey, eds., *Army and Power in the Ancient World.* Stuttgart: 61–82.
———. 2004. *Greek Warfare: Myths and Realities.* London.
———. 2006. "Mass and elite in Solon's Athens." In J. Blok and A. Lardinois, eds., *Solon of Athens: New Historical and Philological Approaches.* Leiden: 351–89.
———. 2007. "War and society." In P. Sabin, H. van Wees, and M. Whitby, eds., *The Cambridge History of Greek and Roman Warfare*, vol. I: *Greece, the Hellenistic World, and the Rise of Rome.* Cambridge: 273–99.
———. 2008. "'*Stasis*, destroyer of men': Mass, elite, political violence and security in archaic Greece." In C. Brélaz and P. Ducrey, eds., *Sécurité collective et ordre public dans les sociétés anciennes.* Geneva: 1–39.
———. 2009. "The Economy." In K. A. Raaflaub and H. van Wees, eds., *A Companion to Archaic Greece.* Oxford: 444–67.
———. 2011. "Demetrius and Draco: Athens' property classes and population in and before 317 BC." *JHS* 131: 95–114.
———. 2013a. *Ships and Silver, Taxes and Tribute: A Fiscal History of Archaic Athens.* London and New York.
———. 2013b. "Farmers and hoplites: Models of historical development." In D. Kagan and G. Viggiano, eds., *Men of Bronze: Hoplite Warfare in Ancient Greece.* Princeton: 222–55.
Vattuone, R. 1994. "'Metoikesis': Trapianti di popolazione nella Sicilia greca fra VI e IV sec. a.C." In M. Sordi, ed., *Emigrazione e immigrazione nel mondo antico.* Milan: 81–114.
Vernant, J.-P. 1982. *The Origins of Greek Thought.* Ithaca.
Veyne, P. 1990. *Bread and Circuses: Historical Sociology and Political Pluralism.* London.
Viviers, D. 2010. "Élites et processions dans les cités grecques: Une géométrique variable?" In L. Capdetrey and Y. Lafond, eds., *Le cité et ses élites: Pratiques et représentation des formes de domination et de contrôle social dans les cités grecques.* Bordeux: 163–83.

Vlassopoulos, K. 2007. "Free spaces: Identity, experience and democracy in classical Athens." *CQ* 57: 33–52.
Vlastos, G. 1952. "The constitution of the Five Thousand." *AJP* 73: 189–98.
———. 1953. "Isonomia." *AJP* 74: 337–66.
Wade-Gery, H. T. 1933. "Studies in the structure of Attic society: II. The laws of Kleisthenes." *CQ* 27: 17–29.
———. 1938. "Two notes on Theopompos, *Philippika*, X." *AJP* 59: 129–34.
———. 1945. "Kritias and Herodes." *CQ* 39: 19–33.
———. 1958. *Essays in Greek History*. Oxford.
Walbank, F. 1957. *A Historical Commentary on Polybius*, vol. I: *Commentary on Books I-VI*. Oxford.
Walcot, P. 1978. *Envy and the Greeks: A Study of Human Behaviour*. Oxford.
Wallace, M. B. 1970. "Early Greek *proxenoi*." *Phoenix* 24: 189–208.
Wallace, R. W. 1989. *The Areopagos Council, to 307 B.C.* Baltimore.
———. 1996. "Law, freedom, and the concept of citizens' rights in democratic Athens." In J. Ober and C. Hedrick, eds., *Demokratia: A Conversation on Democracies, Ancient And Modern*. Princeton: 105–120.
———. 2009. "Charismatic leaders." In K. Raaflaub and H. van Wees, eds., *A Companion to Archaic Greece*. Blackwell: 411–26.
———. 2013. "Councils in Greek oligarchies and democracies." In H. Beck, ed., *A Companion to Ancient Greek Government*. London: 191–204.
Wallace, S. 2010. *Ancient Crete: From Successful Collapse to Democracy's Alternatives, Twelfth to Fifth Centuries BC*. Cambridge.
Walser, A. 2012. "ΔΙΚΑΣΤΗΡΙΑ: Rechtsprechung und Demokratie in den hellenistischen Poleis." In Mann and Scholz 2012: 74–108.
Walter, U. 1993. *An der Polis teilhaben*. Stuttgart.
Weber, M. 1978. *Economy and Society: An Outline of Interpretive Sociology*. 2 vols. G. Roth and C. Wittich, eds. Berkeley.
Wecowski, M. 2011. "On the historicity of the 'Homeric World': Some methodological considerations." In A. Ainian, ed., *The "Dark Ages" Revisited*. Thessaly: 73–82.
———. 2014. *The Rise of the Greek Aristocratic Banquet*. Oxford.
Wedeen, L. 1998. *Ambiguities of Domination: Power, Rhetoric, and Symbols in Contemporary Syria*. Chicago.
Weingast, B. 2002. "Rational-choice institutionalism." In I. Katznelson and H. V. Milner, eds. *Political Science: The State of the Discipline*. New York and London: 660–92.
Werlings, M.-J. 2010. *Le dèmos avant la démocratie: Mots, concepts, réalités historiques*. Paris.
Whibley, L. 1896. *Greek Oligarchies: Their Character and Organisation*. Cambridge.
Whitby, M. 1984. "The union of Corinth and Argos: A reconsideration." *Historia* 33: 295–308.
Whitehead, D. 1981. "The Archaic Athenian *zeugitai*." *CQ* 31: 282–86.
———. 1983. "Competitive outlay and community profit: *Philotimia* in democratic Athens." *C&M* 34: 55–74.
———. 1986. *The Demes of Attica*. Princeton.
———. 2001. *Aineias the Tactician: How to Survive under Siege. A Historical Commentary, with Translation and Introduction*. London.

Whitley, J. 1997. "Cretan laws and Cretan literacy." *AJA* 101: 635–61.

Whitman, C. H. 1958. *Homer and the Heroic Tradition*. Cambridge, MA.

Wiles, D. 1984. "Menander's *Dyskolos* and Demetrios and Phaleron's dilemma: A study of the play and its historical context—the trial of Phokion, the ideals of a moderate oligarch, and the rancour of the disfranchised." *G&R* 31: 170–80.

Willetts, R. 1955. *Aristocratic Society in Ancient Crete*. London.

Williams, B. 1993. *Shame and Necessity*. Berkeley and Los Angeles.

Williams, J. M. 1985. *Athens without Democracy: The Oligarchy of Phocion and the Tyranny of Demetrius of Phalerum, 322–307 B.C.* Ann Arbor.

Wilson, J. 1981. "Strategy and tactics in the Mytilene campaign." *Historia* 30: 144–63.

———. 1987. *Athens and Corcyra: Strategy and Tactics in the Peloponnesian War*. Bristol.

Wilson, P. J. 2003. "The politics of dance: Dithyrambic contest and social order in ancient Greece." In D. Phillips and D. Pritchard, eds., *Sport and Festival in the Ancient Greek World*. Swansea: 163–96.

———. 2009. "Tragic honours and democracy: Neglected evidence for the politics of the Athenian Dionysia." *CQ* 59: 8–29.

———. 2011. "The glue of democracy? Tragedy, structure, finance." In D. Carter, ed., *Why Athens?* Oxford: 19–43.

Winters, J. A. 2011. *Oligarchy*. Cambridge.

Winters, J. A. and B. I. Page. 2009. "Oligarchy in the United States?" *Perspectives on Politics* 7: 731–51.

Wohl, V. 2002. *Love Among the Ruins: The Erotics of Democracy in Classical Athens*. Princeton.

Wolpert, A. 2002. *Remembering Defeat: Civil War and Civic Memory in Ancient Athens*.

———. 2006. "The violence of the Thirty Tyrants." In S. Lewis, ed., *Ancient Tyranny*. Edinburgh: 213–33.

Worman, N. 2002. *The Cast of Character: Style in Greek Literature*. Austin, TX.

Yates, D. C. 2005. "The archaic treaties between the Spartans and their allies." *CQ* 55: 65–76.

Zelnick-Abramovitz, R. 2000. "Did patronage exist in classical Athens?" *L'Ant. Class.* 69: 65–80.

INDEX LOCORUM

Literary Sources

Adespota Elegiaca (West)
  fr. 27: 85n48
Aelian
  Varia Historia
  6.1: 37n152
  14.27: 117n41
Aelius Aristides
  13.273d: 283n27
  13.311d: 283n27
Aeneas Tacticus
  10.15: 146
  11.7: 53n228
  11.7–10: 35, 245n88
  11.10bis: 35
  11.13–15: 35, 128n80, 161n42, 241n68
  17.1: 227n10
  17.2–4: 53n226, 165
  17.3: 53n227
  22.17: 227
  38.4–5: 243n74
Aeschines
  1.4–5: 109n6
  1.5: 147
  1.8: 90n72
  1.27: 192n18
  3.6: 109n6
  3.233: 192n18
Aeschylus
  Suppliants
  368–69: 22n87
  398: 22n87
  517–18: 22n87
  600–1: 22n87
  604: 22
  605–7: 22n87
  699: 22n87
Alcaeus (Liberman)
  fr. 6: 258n126
  fr. 70: 16n61
  fr. 129: 16n61
  fr. 130b: 16n60, 150n4
  fr. 348: 16n60, 16n62
Andocides
  1.27–28: 139n115
  1.67: 262n139
  1.96: 32n134
  1.96–98: 110n10
  Fragments (Blass)
  fr. 4: 170n77
Androtion (*FGrH* 324)
  F 50: 252n112
Antiochus (*FGrH* 555)
  F 13: 231n27
Antiphon
  5.34: 144n135
  5.68: 114n25
  Fragments (Nicole)
  fr. 1a: 47n200, 98, 264n149
  Fragments (Pendrick)
  F 45–71: 260n133
  F 70: 30n125
  F 73: 91n76
Antisthenes (Caizzi)
  fr. 14: 131n92, 131n93
Archilochus (West)
  fr. 14: 16n63
  fr. 19: 68n292

Archilochus (West) (*cont.*)
    fr. 105: 258n126
    fr. 182: 16
    fr. 242: 17n64
[Archytus] (Thesleff)
    fr. 34.6–8: 285n35
    fr. 34.11–13: 111n12
    fr. 34.15–20: 56n245
Ariston (Wehrli)
    fr. 13: 180n114
Aristophanes
    Acharnenses (*Acharnians*)
        91–92: 139n117
        628, 632: 127n73
        755: 123n61
    Aves (*Birds*)
        40–41: 97n105
        125: 8n22, 59n262
        1020–55: 139n117
        1049–54: 215n85
        1280–85: 57n248
    Ecclesiazusae (*Assemblywomen*)
        453: 32n135
    Equites (*Knights*)
        315–21: 152n12
        476: 262n138
        579–80: 57n247
        862: 262n138
        924: 33n139
        1111–19: 68n292
    Lysistrata
        273–82: 23, 157
        617–35: 157
        631–34: 211n71
    Nubes (*Clouds*)
        991, 998: 176s
    Pax (*Peace*)
        505: 97n105
    Plutus (*Wealth*)
        907–19: 139n115
    Thesmophoriazusae
        380: 192n18
    Vespae (*Wasps*)
        464–65: 57n248
        474–76: 57n248
    Fragments (K-A)
        fr. 110 (*Farmers*): 57n248
Aristotle
    [*Athēnaiōn Politeia*]
        3.6: 176n97
        4.2: 38n160, 42n173, 45
        7.3: 15n58, 130n87
        7.4: 43n181
        8.1: 38n160
        9.1–2: 33n139
        13.5: 23n96
        14.1: 128n80
        15.2: 25n105, 36n152
        15.3: 260n130
        15.4: 137n113
        16.2–3: 178n107
        16.3: 137n113, 153
        16.5: 120n51, 153, 178, 181n115
        16.10: 283
        18.2–6: 228n14
        18.4–6: 230n24
        20.1: 21n84, 22, 156n24, 264n151
        20.3: 24n98, 157n27, 165n58
        20.4: 21n84
        21.2: 179, 180n112
        21.3: 179n111
        22.3: 26n108
        22.4: 283
        22.7: 26n108
        23.1: 26n108, 141
        24.2: 193n21
        25.3: 141
        25.3–4: 141
        25.4: 114n25
        26.1: 33n139, 43n183, 283n28
        26.3: 179n109
        27.3–4: 172
        28.2: 27n111
        28.3: 33n139
        29.1: 161n42
        29.1–3: 161n42
        29.2: 222n103
        29.3: 174n93
        29.5: 46n193, 48n201
        30: 82n31

33.1: 45
34.1: 47n199
35.1: 133n97, 136n107
35.2: 216
35.2–3: 33n139, 222n103
35.3: 115n29
37: 162n44
37.2: 162n48
38.1: 82n31
38.1–2: 162n44
38.2: 116n33
40.3: 33n139, 92n79, 282, 283
41.1: 162n44
41.2: 33n139
45.1: 111n13
53.1: 178

Nicomachean Ethics
   8.1160a31–b22: 37n154

Politics
   1.1253a9–15: 64n281
   2.1265b33–35: 56n245
   2.1266a12–14: 39n165
   2.1270b6–17: 57
   2.1271a6–8: 189n8
   2.1271a10: 125
   2.1272a10–12: 123n64
   2.1273b7–8: 122n56
   2.1274a18–21: 43n183
   3.1275a2–5: 39n166
   3.1275b5–7: 39n166
   3.1275b7–8: 123n63
   3.1275b26–30: 153
   3.1276a8–13: 61n268
   3.1278a25–26: 135n102
   3.1278b8–11: 40n167
   3.1278b11–13: 40n167
   3.1279b5: 59n262
   3.1280b8–12: 64n280
   3.1280b30–32: 64n280
   3.1280b39: 64n280
   3.1281a34–37: 77n6
   3.1281a42–b7: 77n6
   3.1282a29–31: 40n169
   3.1283b30–33: 77n6
   3.1286b20–21: 21n81

4.1289a8–9: 35n145
4.1289b36–38: 5n17
4.1289b39: 36n152, 37n152
4.1290a13–16: 35n145
4.1290a27–29: 93n80, 112, 283
4.1290a28: 71n304
4.1290b1–3: 35n147
4.1291b22–25: 171n80
4.1292a13–15: 114n27
4.1292a39–31: 137
4.1292a39–b10: 35n144
4.1292a41: 39n163
4.1292b1–2: 134
4.1292b4–7: 136n110
4.1292b25–29: 152n11, 169n73
4.1293a1: 35n146
4.1293a10–34: 35n144
4.1293a14–17: 137
4.1294b3–4: 40n169
4.1294b10: 38n161
4.1294b13–34: 57
4.1294b33–34: 110n12
4.1296a13–14: 266n156
4.1296a22–23: 35n145
4.1296a36–38: 48n201
4.1297a17–19: 124n65
4.1297b2: 38n161
4.1297b6–8: 119, 123n59
4.1297b8–10: 119n50
4.1297b12–16: 45
4.1297b16–28: 42n173
4.1298a26–29: 123n61
4.1298a27: 133
4.1298a30: 123
4.1298a30–31: 40n169
4.1298a35–38: 123n62
4.1299b25–26: 36n150
4.1299b31–36: 123n61
4.1300a6–8: 90n70, 91n77
4.1300a8: 3n8
4.1300a16–19: 137n110
4.1300a18: 261n134
4.1300b1–3: 39n165
4.1301a12–13: 110
5.1301b25–26: 95n95

Aristotle (*cont.*)
    Politics (*cont.*)
        5.1302a8–9: 266n156
        5.1302a8–11: 71n302, 224n1
        5.1302a9–13: 283n31
        5.1302a29–30: 123n60
        5.1302b23–25: 33n139
        5.1302b27–30: 203
        5.1302b29–30: 81n23
        5.1302b30–31: 261n134
        5.1302b31–32: 105n133
        5.1303a11–13: 250n101
        5.1303a23: 38n161
        5.1303b7–10: 29n121
        5.1303b17–1304a17: 272n181
        5.1303b18: 265n152
        5.1303b18–1304a18: 246n90
        5.1303b20–26: 27n113, 105n133, 265n153
        5.1303b26–28: 94n87
        5.1303b31–1304a13: 265n153
        5.1303b33–38: 94n86
        5.1303b36: 266n157
        5.1304a13–17: 28, 123n60, 265n153
        5.1304a16–17: 266n157
        5.1304a20–21: 283n28
        5.1304a25–27: 53n224, 165n56
        5.1304a29–31: 270n169
        5.1304b12–15: 161n42
        5.1304b23–24: 33n138
        5.1304b35–39: 261n134
        5.1305a15–18: 95n95
        5.1305a18–20: 152n11, 170n74
        5.1305a37–40: 263n147
        5.1305a38: 119n49, 254
        5.1305a39–40: 255
        5.1305a40–42: 258
        5.1305b2–16: 62n271
        5.1305b12–18: 266n158
        5.1305b18–22: 123n60
        5.1305b22–23: 263n147
        5.1305b29–30: 176n99
        5.1305b39–1306a9: 91n76
        5.1306a9–10: 222, 260n133
        5.1306a10–12: 222n105

5.1306a19–24: 118n46
5.1306a21–22: 245n88
5.1306a29–30: 176n99
5.1306a31–32: 265n155
5.1306a35–36: 25n105, 36n152, 266n157
5.1306a36–b2: 101n119, 269n167
5.1306b7–16: 37n161
5.1306b34–36: 231n27
5.1306b39–1307a1: 8n22
5.1307a24–25: 119n49
5.1307a27–29: 38n161
5.1307b22–24: 57, 58n253
5.1308a8: 134, 263n144, 282
5.1308a15: 95n95
5.1308a18–24: 201n43
5.1308a31–35: 94n87
5.1308a35–b10: 38n161
5.1308b2–6: 38n159
5.1308b16–19: 250n101
5.1308b19: 105n132
5.1308b20–22: 95n93
5.1308b34–38: 123n59
5.1309a9–10: 34n141, 189
5.1309a10–14: 189n8
5.1309a15–20: 33n139
5.1309a20–21: 177
5.1309a20–23: 243n74
5.1309a21–22: 135n106
5.1309a22: 119n49
5.1309a22–23: 120
5.1310a3–6: 33n139
5.1310a9–10: 119n50, 261n134
5.1310a11–12: 119n49
5.1310a16–17: 73m309
5.1310b20–22: 95n95, 201n43
5.1311a13: 119n49
5.1311a13–14: 154, 155n18
5.1311b2–3: 228n14
5.1311a39–b36: 270n169
5.1311b11–39: 270n169
5.1313b5–6: 65n285
5.1313b12–16: 139n118
5.1313b32–38: 91n77
5.1315b11–12: 266n156

6.1317b11–12: 93n80
6.1317b25–26: 95n95
6.1318a27–b5: 190n10
6.1318b9–21: 152n11, 169n73
6.1318b12–21: 123n59
6.1318b16–17: 137
6.1318b17–21: 137, 170n74
6.1318b35: 33n139
6.1319a6–19: 152n11
6.1319a28–32: 152n11, 169n73
6.1319b1–2: 35n146
6.1319b15: 33n139
6.1319b19–27: 179
6.1320a4–16: 33n139
6.1320a20–33: 33n139
6.1320a35–b4: 177
6.1320b7–9: 178
6.1320b22–25: 38n161
6.1321a1–4: 96n96, 266n156
6.1321a26–31: 135
6.1321a35–40: 206n56
6.1321a40–42: 263n144
6.1322b16: 123n61
6.1322b37–1323a6: 90n70, 96n97
6.1323a7–9: 123n61
7.1330b19–10: 166n63
7.1331a30–b4: 194n24
7.1331a35: 222n108
[*Oeconomica*]
    1346b6–12: 278n130
Rhetoric
    1.1354a16–21: 98
    1.1354a31–b3: 190
    1.1365b33: 37
    3.1407a2–6: 82n37
[*Rhetorica ad Alexandrum*]
    1424a15–16: 88n63
    1424a22–24: 94n90
    1424a24–25: 33n139
    1424a34–35: 33n139
    1424a35–38: 33n139
    1424a40–24b3: 39n165
    1424b1–3: 88n63
    1424b3–4: 120
    1424b3–6: 39n166, 119, 137n111
    1424b6–7: 94n89
    1424b8–9: 155n20
    1424b8–10: 148n1, 194, 226n8
    1424b9–10: 156n21
    1424b11–12: 33n139, 94n90
    1424b12–14: 120
    1424b13–14: 243n74
    1446b24–25: 33n139
    1446b25–26: 37
    1446b26: 137n110
    Fragments (Rose)
    fr. 89: 177n102
    fr. 497: 187n99
    fr. 498: 176n99
    fr. 516: 137n113
    fr. 538: 116n36
    fr. 558: 152, 172n84, 179n110, 242n71, 258–60
    fr. 566: 48n204
    fr. 574: 154n16
    fr. 586: 27n113
    fr. 592: 24n102
    fr. 603: 37n152
    fr. 611.17: 180n112
    fr. 611.18: 97n103
    fr. 611.20: 137n113, 153n13
    fr. 611.39: 36n151
    fr. 611.40: 25n105
Arrian
    Anabasis
    1.17.11: 214n80
    1.18.2: 279n20
Athenaeus
    6.245a–c
    8.348a–d: 259n127
    10.444e–445a: 282n26
    15.695b: 228n17

Bacchylides
    13.182–89: 205
    13.186: 59n261
    13.183–86: 232n30
    Fragments (Snell-Maehler)
    fr. 14b: 176n99

Callisthenes (*FGrH* 124)
    F 5: 270n167
Cicero
    Brutus
        46: 98n106
    De legibus
        2.66: 91n74
    De officiis
        2.64: 172n82
Clearchus (Wehrli)
    fr. 19: 140n119
Comica Adespota (K-A)
    fr. 700: 29n125
Craterus (*FGrH* 342)
    F 5b: 47n200, 98n108, 220n99, 263n145
    F 17: 263n145
Cratinus (K-A)
    fr. 77: 152n12
Critias (DK 88)
    A 13: 29n124, 34n141, 59n259
    B 5: 18n70
    B 6–9: 58n252
    B 8: 173
    B 32–37: 58n252
    B 52: 173n88

Democritus (DK 68)
    B 237: 272n179
    B 251: 60n264, 272n180
Demosthenes
    9.26: 176n99
    9.60–61: 115n29
    13.8: 135
    14.19: 38n161
    15.14: 136n109
    15.19: 135, 288n1
    17.3: 112n20
    18.295: 180n114
    19.239: 88n61
    19.295: 180n114
    20.15–17: 147
    20.52–53: 233n37
    20.59: 218
    20.108: 57, 78n15
    20.109: 283n30
    20.159: 110n10
    21.140: 76n6
    21.221: 119n48
    21.221–22: 192n18
    22.51: 283n30
    24.24: 283n30
    24.114: 269n167
    25.9: 90n72
    40.32: 283n30
Dinarchus
    Fragments (Conomis)
        Or. 6 fr. 12: 91n74
Dio of Prusa
    3.48: 1, 61n270
    3.49: 61n270
Diodorus Siculus
    11.4.7: 44n188
    11.54.1: 24n101
    11.77.6: 114n25
    12.57.3: 127n76
    12.75.7: 53n224
    12.80.2: 25n104, 53n224, 165n56
    13.72.1: 143n131, 218
    13.104.5: 114n27, 210n68
    14.3.5: 209n61
    14.7.6: 239n57
    14.7.6–7: 242n73
    14.32.4: 162n44
    14.34.3–6: 245n88
    14.34.6: 180n112
    14.46.4: 118n46
    14.82.2: 233n36
    14.86: 84n43, 231n28
    14.86.1: 50, 232n29, 235n40
    14.109.1: 227n12
    15.5.4–12: 25n104, 161n41
    15.20.2: 252n112
    15.25: 253n114
    15.57.3–58: 283n27
    15.58.4: 284n32
    15.70.3: 159n35
    15.79.3: 37n153, 59n262

15.81.5: 263n146
16.93.3–94.3: 228n14
18.18.4: 38n156, 38n162, 39n163
18.18.5: 129n84, 130n87
18.64.2–3: 130n87, 183n122
18.65.6: 130n87, 183n122
18.74.3: 38n162
19.4.3: 51n216
Diogenes Laertius
   1.88: 27n114
   1.98: 153n13
   5.77: 220n99
   8.66: 51n216
Dionysius of Halicarnassus
   Antiquitates Romanae
      2.9.2: 172n81
      5.71.2: 269n165
      7.11.3–4: 228n14
      7.66.5: 283n27
Dissoi Logoi (DK 90)
   B 1.8: 31n133
   B 7.5–6: 32
Duris (*FGrH* 76)
   F 10: 91n74
   F 26: 209n65
   F 71: 209n63, 210n69
   F 83: 209n64

Ephorus (*FGrH* 70)
   F 79: 161n41
   F 149: 90n71
   F 179: 137n113, 153n13
Epictetus
   Dissertationes
      4.13.5: 138n114
Euripides
   Hecuba
      607: 29n125
   Hippolytus
      983–1035: 59n261
   Orestes
      917–22: 170
   Phoenissae
      531–61: 265n155

   Suppliants
      420–22: 30n126, 170n74
      438–49: 192n18
   Fragments (Nauck)
      fr. 21: 47n197
      fr. 275: 60n264
      fr. 626: 36n150, 115n29
Eustathius
   Comm. Ad Hom. Il.
      3.516: 140n119

Gorgias (DK 82)
   A 19: 135
   B 20: 173

Harpocration
   ἐπίσκοπος: 139n117
   εὐηνιώτατα: 30n125
   ὅτι χιλίας: 91n75
   φηγούσιον: 142n126
Hellanicus (*FGrH* 4)
   F 52: 176n99
   F 81: 81n23
Hellenica Oxyrhynchia (Chambers)
   10.2–3: 84n43, 233
   17.1: 84n43
   18.1–3: 160n39, 228n16
   18.2: 41n171, 60n264, 262n138, 284
   18.3: 59n260
   19.2: 39n164, 39n166, 48n202, 81n25
   19.3–4: 252n112
   20.1–2: 252n111
Heniochus (K-A)
   fr. 5: 59n262, 61n267
Heraclides Ponticus (Wehrli)
   fr. 50: 152n9
Heraclitus (DK 22)
   B 121: 27n114
   B 104: 27n114, 29n124, 30n127
[Herodes]
   On the Constitution
      31: 45

Herodotus
- 1.59.1: 153
- 1.59.4: 128n80
- 1.63.2: 153
- 1.64.1: 153
- 1.64.2: 260n130
- 1.65.2: 55n238
- 1.65.5: 55n238
- 1.96.2: 152n11, 179n110
- 1.96.3: 120n51, 179n110
- 1.114.2: 139n117
- 1.150: 164n55
- 3.80.5: 112n20
- 3.80.6: 40n170, 189n8
- 3.81: 29n123
- 3.81.1–2: 34n141
- 3.81.2: 30n127, 284n32
- 3.81.2–3: 191
- 3.81.3: 30n128, 31n131
- 3.82.3: 33n138, 77n8, 202, 273n182
- 3.136.2: 105n131
- 3.138.1–3: 105n131
- 3.142.2–3: 239n56
- 3.149: 154n16
- 4.97.2: 251n103
- 4.137–38: 251n105
- 4.137.2: 251n106
- 4.146.2: 117n42
- 5.11.2: 251n103, 251n104
- 5.28–29: 152n9
- 5.30–37: 264n151
- 5.30.1: 27n113, 28n119, 260n131
- 5.37.1: 251n104
- 5.38.1: 251n104
- 5.55–62: 228n14
- 5.56.2: 228n18
- 5.66.2: 21n84, 22, 255n120, 264n151
- 5.69.2: 21n84, 22
- 5.70.1: 25n105
- 5.71.1–2: 165n58
- 5.72.1–2: 24n98
- 5.72.2: 157, 165n58
- 5.77.2: 37n152
- 5.78: 21n84
- 5.79.2: 81n27
- 5.91.2: 21n86, 26n107
- 5.92a: 79n16
- 5.97.2: 21n85, 26n108
- 5.122.2: 152n9
- 6.43.3: 28n115
- 6.88: 103n126, 104n127
- 6.88–91: 27n113, 205n52
- 6.91.1–2: 104n128
- 6.100.1: 37n152
- 6.101.2–3: 251n105
- 6.103.3: 114
- 6.109: 32n134
- 6.131.1: 21n84
- 7.137.3: 112n21
- 7.142.1: 21n85, 26n108
- 7.155.2: 27n113, 105n133
- 7.156.1–3: 164n54
- 7.156.3: 26n107
- 7.164.1: 239n56
- 7.203.1: 44n188
- 8.34: 251n107
- 8.85.3: 251n105
- 9.5.1: 21n85, 26n108
- 9.10.3: 133n97
- 9.16: 251n107
- 9.28.3: 50n211
- 9.37.1: 25n105
- 9.86.1: 251n107
- 9.87.2: 251
- 9.90.1: 251n105

Hesiod
Theogony
- 89: 11n31, 17n67
- 230: 8n22
- 902: 8n22

Hesychius
- γαμόροι: 38n157
- ἐπαρίτοι: 54n230

Hippias (*FGrH* 421)
- F 1: 114, 153n14, 167n66, 167n69, 237n48, 282n26, 285n35

INDEX LOCORUM 331

Hipponax (West)
    fr. 128: 17n65
Homer
    Iliad
        1.81–82: 271n176
        1.163–68: 243n79
        1.255–58: 238n51
        2.73: 11n33
        2.86–90: 159n38
        2.198–202: 109n5
        2.203: 114n27
        6.124: 150n4
        9.460: 12n34
        9.632–36: 101n116
        19.81–82: 191
    Odyssey
        9.215: 151n7
        14.239: 12n34
        15.468: 12n34
        16.361–62: 113
        16.371–84: 113
        17.487: 8n22
        23.118–20: 101n115

Iamblichus
    De vita pythagorica
        248–49: 272n178
Idomeneus (*FGrH* 338)
    F 8: 114n25
Ion (*FGrH* 392)
    F 6: 86n55
    F 13: 26n108, 86n55
    F 15: 26n108
Isocrates
    2.16: 119
    2.51: 140
    2.53: 140
    3.15: 78n14
    3.18: 78n14
    3.19: 78n14
    3.24: 57n246
    5.52: 283n27
    6.67: 175, 260n133
    7.16–17: 173
    7.20: 29n125
    7.26: 176
    7.27: 173
    7.31–35: 175
    7.32: 178
    7.36–39: 175
    7.44–45: 175
    7.46: 96n99, 141n123, 175, 178, 184
    7.47: 92n80, 97n100, 175, 177
    7.48–49: 176
    7.51: 97n101
    7.52: 177
    7.55: 175, 177
    7.57: 174
    7.60–61: 173
    7.61: 174n92
    7.62: 174
    7.67: 162n44
    7.70: 174
    8.100: 161n41
    10.32: 39n166, 245n88
    12.131: 60n263
    12.177–79: 174n92
    12.220: 58n255
    15.172: 30n127
    18.17: 262n143
    19.38: 95n95, 245n38
    20.11: 109n5
    20.13: 192n18
    Ep. 8.3: 135

Justin
    5.9.12: 162n44
    16.4.1: 41n171
    16.4.2: 263n146
    16.4.4: 263n146
    16.5.15: 228n14

Lucian
    Jupiter Tragoedus
        7: 38n157
    Pseudologista
        17: 270n167

Lycurgus
 1.112: 158n31
 1.113: 263n145
 1.115: 263n145
 1.117–19: 220n99
 1.124–27: 110n10

Lysias
 6.34: 283n30
 6.45: 142
 12.5: 73n309
 12.17: 112
 12.28: 262n143
 12.48: 142
 12.58–59: 57
 12.95: 162n44
 13.37: 128
 13.55–56: 142
 13.70–72: 158n31
 20.13: 46n193
 25.8: 3n8
 25.22: 162n44
 25.27: 33n139
 31.8: 162n44
 33: 227n12
 Fragments (Carey)
  fr. XXX: 142n126

Memnon (*FGrH* 434)
 F 1: 228n14, 263n146

Menander
 Sicyonius
  150–56: 191
 Fragments (K-A)
  fr. 208: 91n75

Menander Rhetor (Spengel)
 p. 359: 36
 p. 360: 59n262

Nepos
 Cimon
  4.1–3: 172n72
 Dio
  7.1: 114

Pelopidas
 1.4: 253n114

Nicolaus (*FGrH* 90)
 F 58: 137n113, 153n13
 F 60: 82n30, 123n61, 124n66

Pausanias
 1.14.5: 232n30;2.20.2: 25n104,
  53n224, 165n56
 3.5.2: 88n65
 3.8.4: 25n104
 3.8.4–5: 159n38
 3.9.8: 233n34
 5.4.8: 25n104
 6.3.14: 209n65
 6.3.15: 210n69
 7.16.9: 38n157, 278n14
 8.8.6: 161n41
 9.6.2: 251n109
 9.10.4: 200n40
 10.9.7–10: 209n65

Philochorus (*FGrH* 328)
 F 2: 152n11
 F 55a–b: 216n86
 F 64: 91n74, 96n97, 123n61
 F 65: 91n75
 F 181: 220n99

Photius
 Καλλικύριοι: 27n113

Pindar
 Olympian
  3.16: 205n50
  5.14: 205n50
  7.90–92: 77n10
  13.6: 237n47
 Pythian
  1.70: 202n45, 205n50
  2.86–88: 1n2, 191
  4.296: 202n45
  8.1: 202n45
  8.1–13: 77n10
  10.71–72: 205
  11.5–58: 77n10
  11.55: 202n45

Nemean
   3.70: 271n175
   8.26–27: 131
   9.48: 202n45
   10.23: 205n50

Isthmian
   1.34–40: 103n125
   6.71: 77n10
   8.26–27, 31: 265n155

Fragments (Snell-Maehler)
   fr. 52a: 59n261, 77n10, 205
   fr. 52k: 205n53
   fr. 94b: 201–202
   fr. 109: 77n10, 97n101, 202n45, 205
   fr. 180: 186n1
   fr. 210: 273n182

Plato

Apology
   32c: 129n82, 136

[Axiochus]
   369a: 26n107

Euthyphro
   4c: 172n81

Gorgias
   471a–d: 68n292
   491e–92c: 68n292

Leges (Laws)
   4.710e: 71n304
   4.712d–13a: 56n244
   6.764b: 96n99
   11.914a: 147n140
   11.934d–35a: 273n182
   12.961a–b: 194n25

Menexenus
   238c–d: 60n263

Politicus (Statesman)
   298c: 190
   303a–b: 283

Protagoras
   317d: 86n51
   319b–d: 192n18
   329a: 86n52
   338b: 86n53

Republic
   2.359a–360d: 250n100
   6.492b–c: 122n54, 177n102
   6.493a: 284n32
   8.545d: 248n94
   8.550c: 37, 122n58
   8.551b: 39n163, 49n205, 71n304, 122n58
   8.551d: 149
   8.551d–e: 49n205
   8.551e: 52n220
   8.552e: 71n304, 97n100, 175n96
   8.553a: 37
   8.555c: 29n125
   8.555d: 122n58
   8.556c: 227n9, 237n49
   8.556d: 49n205, 245n86
   8.556d–e: 245n87
   8.556e: 227, 246
   8.563b: 91n77
   8.566b: 115n29
   8.568b–c: 68n292

Symposium
   193a: 161n41

[Sisyphus]
   287b–c: 222

Pliny

Naturalis Historia
   34.17: 157n28

Plutarch

Agesilaus
   26.5: 55n234
   32.3: 117
   32.5: 117
   32.6: 117, 140

Agis
   11.1

Aristides
   13.1: 26n108, 33n139
   18.6: 251n109
   20.6: 232n30

Cimon
   10.1: 173
   10.1–8: 172n82

Plutarch (cont.)
    Cimon (cont.)
        10.2: 172n84
        10.2–3: 172n85
        10.5: 173
        10.7: 173
        16.8: 173n88
    Demetrius
        10.2: 90n73
    Dion
        17.9–10: 180n114
        28.1: 139n118, 142n126
        37.5: 114
        38.5: 26n107
        42.1: 26n107
        53.3: 114
        53.4: 124n66, 193n19
        53.5: 114n27
    Lycurgus
        6.1–4: 18n74
        28.1–3: 116n36
    Lysander
        8.1–3: 210n68
        13.4: 137n110
        14.2: 210n68
        18.1: 209n65
        18.3: 210n69
        18.3–4: 209n63
        19.2: 210n68
        21.4: 29n125
    Moralia
        214a: 55n234
        277b–c: 24n102
        291e: 152n10
        292a: 123n61; 194n25
        292b: 24n102
        295d: 29n125
        297f: 182n119
        298c–d: 152n9, 190n12
        301c: 80n21
        304e–f: 29n125
        447e: 98n107
        522f–23b: 140n118

        598c–f: 253n114
        781e: 228n13
        814b: 283n27
        818c: 177n102
        821f: 177n102
        824f–825a: 272n181
        825c–d: 105n134, 265n153
        825d: 27n113
        827b: 75n1, 79n16
        835f: 159n38
        850f–51c: 213n76
        851c: 60n266
        851f: 40n167
        859d: 260n130, 260n131
    Nicias
        11.4: 269n167
    Pelopidas
        5.1: 253n114
        5.1–2: 84n43, 252n111
        5.2–3: 252n112
        5.3: 25n105
        6.1: 252n112
        6.2: 116n32
        11–12: 253n114
    [Peri Homerou B] (Kindstrand)
        2272–73: 113n24
    Pericles
        7.6: 29n125
        9.2: 172n82
        10.6–7: 114n25
        11.1–3: 27n111
        14.1–2: 207n58
        23.2: 37n152
    Phocion
        27.3: 38n156
        28.4: 129, 129n84
        29.4: 182n120, 183n122
        30.4: 130n87, 130n89
    Romulus
        13.5: 172n81
    Solon
        8.1–3: 160n39
        21.4–5: 89n69

INDEX LOCORUM

Themistocles
   19.4: 216n87
   32.3: 171n78
Timoleon
   4.4: 118n46
   4.8: 118n46
   22.1–3: 220n99

Pollux
   3.82: 172n81
   8.112: 91n75
   10.165: 48n204
   10.177: 269n167

Polyaenus
   Stratagemata
     1.41.2: 28n117
     1.45.1: 210n68
     1.45.4: 210n68
     1.48.3: 233n36
     2.1.7: 55n234
     2.1.14: 117n41
     2.10.3: 28n117
     2.14.1: 231n27
     2.30.2: 41n171, 51n216, 263n146
     5.2.13: 140n118
     7.23.2: 214

Polybius
   2.62.6–7: 38n161
   4.20.4–21.3: 198n35
   4.27.6: 161n41
   4.31.2: 278n13
   4.32.1: 278n13
   4.73.7: 182
   4.73.7–8: 180
   6.53.7: 38n161
   12.16.10: 51n216

Proclus
   200n40

Scholia
   ad Aeschin. 1.39: 59n259, 216
   ad Aeschin. 2.77: 260n130
   ad Ar. *Ach* 477: 170n77
   ad Ar. *Plut.* 476: 269n167

   ad [Eur.] *Rhes.* 307: 176n99
   ad Pind. *Pyth.* 2.157a: 191n15
   ad Pind. *Pyth.* 4. inscr. a: 180n112
   ad Pind. *Pyth.* 5.12a: 180n112
   ad Pind. *Nem.* 3.70: 271n175

Simonides
   fr. 86 West: 22n89
   PMG 511 fr. 1: 204

Socrates (West)
   fr. 1: 192n17

Solon
   fr. 4 West: 8n22
   fr. 9 West: 18n72
   fr. 13 West: 246n91
   fr. 33 West: 68n292
   fr. 34 West: 18n72, 243n79
   fr. 36 West: 18n72, 156
   fr. 37 West: 18n72, 23n94, 156n22
   fr. 22 Ruschenbusch: 215n84

Sophocles
   Oedipus Tyrannus
     25: 258n126

Stesimbrotus (*FGrH* 1002)
   F 4: 26n108

Stobaeus
   4.1.135: 111n12
   4.1.138: 56n245

Strabo
   4.1.5: 51n216
   6.3.2: 231n27
   8.3.2: 24n101
   10.1.8: 37n152
   10.1.10: 167n66
   14.1.17: 154n16
   14.2.5: 178n105, 181

Suda
   Γέργηθες: 152n9
   Κλέαρχος: 263n146

Themistius (Harduin)
   Oration 2, p. 35b: 38

Theognis (West)
   39–52: 18n72

Theognis (West) (*cont.*)
    45: 17n68
    53–56: 151
    53–68: 17n69
    233–34: 17n70
    266–69: 17n66
    493–96: 85
    667–82: 258n126
    847–50: 17n70
    947–48: 18n71
Theophrastus
    Characters
        4.2, 13: 152n12
        4.2–3: 171n79
        26.2: 95n95, 114n27
        26.3: 34n141, 155n19, 156n21, 190n11
        26.4: 26n107
        26.5: 33n139, 160n41
    De elegendis magistratibus
        fr. A: 94n88
        fr. B: 135n101
    Fragments (Fortenbaugh)
        F 515: 172n82
        F 624: 80n21
Theopompus (*FGrH* 115)
    F 18: 222n107
    F 62: 29n125, 177n101
    F 89: 172n82, 172n85
    F 96a: 115n30
    F 100: 177n101
    F 121: 282n26
    F 135: 172n84
    F 213: 177n101, 177n102
    F 233: 177n101, 177n102
Thucydides
    1.18.1: 56n239
    1.19: 24n103, 55n238, 56n239
    1.24.5: 28n119, 245n88, 265n153
    1.44.1: 127n73
    1.68.1: 56
    1.77.1: 97n105
    1.87.2: 125, 126n69
    1.107.4: 27n111
    1.108.3: 81n23
    1.113.2: 81n23
    1.113.2–4: 80n22
    1.114.1–3: 37n152
    1.115.2–3: 26n106
    1.115.4: 245n88
    1.115.5: 144n133
    1.126.3–8: 165n58
    1.132.4: 144n133
    1.132.5: 140
    2.2–3: 163n50
    2.2.1: 81n24, 114n26
    2.2.4: 114n26
    2.2.2: 29n121
    2.4.2: 92n77
    2.21.1: 101n117
    2.25.3: 54n229
    2.27.2: 144n133
    2.37.1: 192n18
    2.37.2: 93n80
    2.46.1: 33n139
    2.61.2: 87n59
    2.65.2: 169n72
    2.65.8: 156n22
    2.67.4: 112n21
    3.2.3: 265n153
    3.3.3: 164n55
    3.18.1: 245n88
    3.19.1: 46n195
    3.27.1–28.1: 238n52
    3.27.2: 239
    3.27.3: 41n171, 193, 239, 245n87
    3.34.1: 29n121
    3.34.2: 245n88
    3.35.1: 49n207
    3.36.6: 127n73
    3.39.2: 144n133
    3.49.1: 127n73
    3.50.1: 49n207
    3.62.3: 59n259, 60n264, 77n11, 81n24, 251n109, 284
    3.65.3: 34n141, 59n261, 244n80
    3.68.3: 29n121
    3.70: 33n139

3.70.4: 36n150
3.71.1: 127n76, 127n78, 241n68
3.72.2: 127
3.73: 245n88
3.74.1: 50n210, 92n77
3.75.3: 50n210
3.75.5: 50n210
3.81: 50n210
3.81.4: 32n135, 127n76
3.82.1: 28n118, 58n253
3.82.8: 8n22, 59n261, 59n262
3.85.2: 50n210
3.93.2: 242n72
4.1.3: 29n121
4.22.1: 193n20
4.48.5: 50
4.56.2: 144n133
4.66.1: 29n121
4.74.2: 53n223, 222n103
4.74.3: 128
4.74.3–4: 161n42
4.74.4: 51n216, 128n80
4.76.2: 104n129
4.76.2–3: 203
4.80.4: 116n36
4.88.1: 88n61, 128n79
4.89.1: 104n129, 141
4.91: 81n24, 201n42
4.92.6: 28n118, 83n37
4.123.1: 127
4.123.2: 128, 158, 241n67
4.126.2: 56n240
4.130.3: 242n70
4.130.4: 158, 242n71, 242n73, 259n129
4.130.6: 159n34, 166n61
5.4.2: 163n51
5.4.2–3: 29n121
5.4.3: 33n139, 36n150
5.4.4: 164
5.11.1: 209n67, 214n82
5.16.1–2: 101n117
5.23.3: 144n133
5.27.2: 192

5.31.6: 47n198, 48, 56, 81n24
5.38.2: 81n24
5.63.4: 133n97
5.67.2: 53n224
5.68.2: 117n39
5.76.2: 32n135, 53n224
5.81–82: 28, 56n239
5.81.2: 25n104, 53n223, 165n56
5.82.2: 36n150, 53n225, 158n33, 165n57
5.82.6: 92n77
5.83.1: 53n228, 245n88
5.84–85: 86n55
5.84.3: 36n150, 41n171, 193
5.85: 193
6.11.7: 56n241
6.17.4: 28n118
6.24.4: 127n73
6.27.2: 157n115, 144n135
6.38.2: 116n33
6.38.3: 28n118
6.38.5: 77n11
6.39.1: 29n124, 38n161, 39n163, 192n18, 244n80
6.39.2: 34n141, 129n83
6.43.1: 61n182
6.50.4: 164n53
6.53.2: 139n115
6.54–58: 228n14
6.54.1: 105n133, 229n20
6.54.2: 229
6.54.3: 229n21
6.56.2–3: 230n23
6.56.3: 262n138
6.57.4: 230n24
6.60.1: 57n248, 60n264
6.60.4: 139n115
6.63.3: 164n53
6.77.1: 164n53
6.89.6: 56n240
6.95.2: 29n121, 83n38, 203
7.30.3: 81n24
8.1.1: 87n59
8.9.3: 193

Thucydides (cont.)
    8.14.1–2: 193
    8.21: 29n121, 36n150, 144n133, 209n61
    8.24.4: 41n171, 56, 59n261, 193n21
    8.38.3: 111n18, 193n21, 241n69
    8.47.2: 36n150
    8.48.1: 33n139, 46n196
    8.48.3: 240n58
    8.48.4–5: 59n259
    8.48.6: 112n22
    8.53.3: 40n170
    8.54.1: 240n58
    8.54.4: 33n139, 262n138
    8.63.2: 241n69
    8.63.3: 144n133
    8.63.4: 33n139, 36n150, 46n196
    8.64.2: 143n131, 218
    8.64.2–65.1: 41n171
    8.64.3: 59n262
    8.65–67: 161n42
    8.64.5: 59n261
    8.65.1: 33n139
    8.65.2: 115n30
    8.65.3: 45n191, 222n103
    8.66: 115
    8.66.1: 32n134
    8.66.2: 112, 116n33, 126
    8.66.5: 141n124
    8.67.1: 222n103
    8.68.1: 98n108
    8.68.2: 47n200, 98n108
    8.68.4: 120n50
    8.69.1: 126
    8.69.3: 136n108
    8.69.4: 32n134, 136n108
    8.72.1: 45n192
    8.73.2: 144n133
    8.73.3: 115n30, 262n139
    8.73.4: 241
    8.73.5–6: 240n59
    8.74.3: 109n4, 285n35
    8.75.3: 240n60
    8.76.2–3: 240n61
    8.83.3: 239n57
    8.84.2: 242n72
    8.84.2–3: 239n57
    8.86.2–5: 240n62
    8.86.3: 222n103
    8.86.5: 156n22
    8.89.2: 222n103
    8.89.3: 34n141, 78n12, 78n13, 88n64, 265n155
    8.89.3–4: 257n125, 273n182
    8.91.3: 263n145
    8.92.2: 60n264, 158n31, 219n97, 263m145
    8.92.8: 238n51
    8.92.11: 45n192, 52n221, 82n32, 222n103
    8.93.1: 47n200
    8.93.2: 222n103
    8.97.1: 42n173, 45, 46
    8.97.2: 47
    8.98.4: 46, 48
Timaeus (*FGrH* 566)
    F 22: 191n16
Timocles (K-A)
    fr. 34: 91n75
Tyrtaeus (West)
    frr. 1–4: 8n22

Valerius Maximus
    2.6.7: 51n216

Xenophanes (West)
    fr. 2: 8n22
    fr. 3: 150n4
Xenophon
    Agesilaus
        1.4: 56n243
    Anabasis
        7.6.4: 94n86
    [*Athēnaiōn Politeia*]
        1.5: 29n125, 31n132
        1.8: 59n261
        1.9: 59n261, 121n52, 190n11
        1.13: 33n139

INDEX LOCORUM 339

1.14: 33n139
2.9–10: 33n139, 177n102, 221n102
2.17: 87n58, 87n59
2.20: 59n259, 92n80
3.2: 177n102, 221n102
3.6: 97n105
3.11: 32n135, 81n23, 102n121, 203

Cyropaedia
1.2.3–5: 194n24
2.1.14–19: 243n76
2.2.18: 244n82
2.2.19: 244n83
2.2.20: 121n53, 244n84
8.2.10–12: 139n117
8.3.5: 198

Hellenica
1.1.32: 58n254
1.3.19: 25n105
1.4.9: 143n131, 218
1.7.7–35: 127n73
1.7.28: 263n145
2.2.5: 143n131, 218
2.2.6: 209n61
2.3.2: 112n18
2.3.6–7: 209n61
2.3.11: 222n103
2.3.12: 33n139
2.3.13–14: 162n48
2.3.14: 162n49
2.3.16: 285n34
2.3.17: 59n259
2.3.18: 30n127
2.3.22: 33n139
2.3.23: 136n107
2.3.24: 59n259, 120n50
2.3.24–25: 58n250
2.3.24–26: 73n309
2.3.25: 33n139
2.3.26: 59n259
2.3.27: 33n139
2.3.31: 258n126
2.3.34: 84n44
2.3.47: 59n262
2.3.48: 34n141, 45n189, 285n34

2.3.55: 136n107
2.4.1: 162n44, 162n47
2.4.9: 129, 262n142
2.4.9–10: 128
3.2.23: 59n261
3.2.27: 114n26
3.2.27–28: 163
3.2.27–29: 25n104, 159n38
3.2.28: 219
3.3.4: 140n120
3.3.4–11: 231n27
3.3.6: 262n138
3.3.8: 92n77
3.5.1: 233n34
3.5.19: 49n206
4.2.17: 50n211
4.2.23: 233n37
4.4.1: 50, 234
4.4.1–13: 84n43, 231n28
4.4.2: 234, 234n40, 236n46
4.4.5: 236n45
4.4.6: 235
4.4.7: 236n45
4.8.20: 35, 58n254
4.8.26: 218
5.1.22: 49n206
5.2.1–7: 25n104, 161n41
5.2.7: 33n139, 161n41, 169n72, 219n95
5.2.25: 84n43, 252, 252n111
5.2.29: 252n112
5.2.31: 252n112
5.3.10–13: 58n254
5.3.16: 51n214
5.3.25: 112n18
5.4.1–12: 253n114
5.4.9: 49n206, 60n264, 284
6.4.18: 58n254, 161n41
6.5.3: 159n37, 161n41, 244n84
6.5.7: 159n36, 244n84, 264n151, 271n175
6.5.10: 50n212, 58n254
7.1.42: 59n260
7.1.44: 35, 58n254

Xenophon (*cont.*)
    Hellenica (*cont.*)
        7.1.44–45: 244n84
        7.1.45: 159n35, 239n56
        7.1.46: 215n83
        7.2.9: 92n77
        7.3.1: 35n148
        7.3.2: 236n45
        7.3.3: 272n177
        7.3.4–6: 118n46
        7.3.12: 118n46, 214n82, 215n83
        7.4.3: 115n29
        7.4.6: 118n46
        7.4.13: 53n229
        7.4.16: 53n229
        7.4.18: 51n216
        7.4.31: 53n229
        7.4.34: 54n231
        7.5.3: 54n232, 58n254
    Hiero
        1.9: 68n292
        1.12: 227n11
    Lacedaemonion Politeia
        2.2: 90n71
        8.4: 97n102
    Memorabilia
        1.2.31: 99n109
        1.2.40–46: 61n269, 235n42
        1.2.43: 190
        1.2.45: 33n139, 122n57
        1.2.58–59: 109n5
        3.5.16: 97n105
        4.4.16: 260n133
        4.6.12: 36n149
    Oeconomicus
        2.3: 46n194
        9.14: 123n61
    Symposium
        2.4: 18n70
        4.31–32: 33n139

Inscriptions

Agora
    xvi: 216n88

F. Delphes
    III.4.163: 61n267

I Lindos II
    16: 41n171, 145n138
    16 appendix: 41n171

IC
    III.iv.8: 262n138

IG
    I^3 1: 22n88
    I^3 4: 22n88
    I^3 5: 22n88
    I^3 14: 139n117
    I^3 19: 217n92
    I^3 21: 102n121
    I^3 27: 217n92
    I^3 27: 217n92
    I^3 39: 139n116
    I^3 57: 217n92
    I^3 73: 203
    I^3 96: 209n61, 212n76
    I^3 105: 15n58
    I^3 229: 216n88
    II^2 6: 111n17, 143n131, 216n88, 218
    II^2 17: 143n131, 218
    II^2 24: 218
    II^2 33: 111n17
    II^2 52: 216n88
    II^2 116: 216n86
    II^2 380: 96n99, 130n86
    II^2 448: 60n266, 129n84, 182, 212n76, 217, 279n18
    II^2 682: 275n3
    II^2 1496: 60n267
    II^2 1606: 61n267
    II^3 306: 90n72
    IV^2 1 128: 60n263
    V.1 1390: 90n71, 96n99
    $IX\ 1^2$ 3 717: 44n188
    XII.4 1 132: 166n62, 225n4, 240n60
    XII.6 1 334: 209n66
    XII.6 1 461: 90n71
    XII.8 262 + *Suppl.* p. 150: 218n94
    XII.8 263: 101n115, 111n15, 145n138

XII.8 264: 145n138
XII.9 192: 220n101
XII.9 245–47: 45n189
XII.9 909: 190n12
XII.9 923: 190n12
XII *Suppl.* 549a: 25n105
IG Bulg. I^2
   320: 61n267
IK Erythrai
   9: 275n3
   503: 60n266, 212, 212n76, 217n90,
      220n101
IK Ilion
   25: 60n265, 144n133, 212n76, '
      285n35
IK Kyme
   12: 275n2
   13: 61n267
IK Labraunda
   3: 276n8
IK Magnesia
   98: 90n71
IK Sinope
   1: 32n135
IosPE I^2
   401: 262n138
IPArk
   7: 14n45
IvO
   7: 15
   9: 15
Koerner
   24: 19n78
   25: 19n78
   27: 19n78
   29: 19n78, 101n115, 215n84
   31: 12n37, 19n78
   35: 19n78
   37: 101n115
   39: 16n59
   44: 215n84
   47: 19n78
   60: 89n68
   61: 13n43
   70: 142n128

Marmor Parium (*FGrH* 239)
   A.52: 27n113
   A.54: 157n28
ML
   2: 19
   4: 13n40
   8: 13n43, 13, 14, 17n65, 19n78
   11: 207n57
   17: 15n50, 215n84
   18: 207n57
   20: 16n59, 44n188
   30: 215n84
   32: 101n115
   43: 101n115, 102, 142n127,
      145n138
   45: 216n85
   47: 29n121
   52: 139n116
   80: 145n138
   81: 41n171, 145n138
   82: 41n171, 145n138
   83: 51n216, 107n1, 142–43, 145n138,
      148, 218, 261n136
   85: 220n100
   86: 101n116
   94: 209n61, 216n88
   95: 209n65
Nomima
   I.18: 19n78
   I.21: 12n38
   I.24: 16n59
   I.32: 16n59
   I.34: 13n40
   I.36: 15n54
   I.44: 19n78
   I.52: 15n50, 215n84
   I.56: 215n84
   I.58: 16n59
   I.62: 13n43
   I.72: 19n78
   I.78: 12n37, 19n78
   I.80: 17n63
   I.100: 101n115, 215n84
   I.101: 19n78
   I.102: 16n59

Nomima (cont.)
- I.107: 19n78, 101n115
- I.108: 15n52
- I.109: 15n53
- I.109: 14n45

PEP Chios
- 2: 41n171, 145n138, 147n140
- 76: 41n171, 145n138

RO
- 2: 209n62
- 17: 165n59, 168n69
- 22: 279n18
- 39: 217
- 40: 139n116
- 41: 59n260, 60n265, 212n76, 285n35
- 54: 220n99, 228n14
- 56: 41n171, 145n138
- 68: 145n138
- 73: 220n101
- 79: 60n267, 110n10, 144n133
- 83: 168n68, 279n20
- 84: 14n48, 40n167, 212n76, 279n20
- 85: 220n101, 279n20

SEG
- 9.1: 38n161, 40n167, 51n216, 82n31, 97n103, 189n8
- 11.1112: 89n69
- 18.772: 145n138
- 25.149: 60n267
- 28.60: 60n266, 144n133, 212n76
- 30.1119: 240n60
- 31.969: 41n171, 145n138
- 31.984: 144n133
- 32.161: 3n8, 220n99
- 33.556: 232n30
- 34.849: 145n138
- 34.898: 190n12
- 34.1238: 90n71
- 35.923: 41n171, 145n138
- 38.851: 217n93, 218n94
- 39.1244: 132n94
- 41.929: 132n94
- 47.1660: 275n1
- 50.1195: 276n6
- 50.1304: 225n4
- 51.1096: 143n131, 212n76, 218n94, 221n101, 261n137
- 51.1105: 32n135, 41n171, 60n265, 166n64, 212n76, 220n101, 285n35
- 51.1832: 29n124, 278n14
- 54.1229: 167n67, 275n1
- 55.564bis: 253n115
- 55.838: 278n14
- 56.1017: 143n131, 218
- 57.576: 145n137, 225n4, 240n60, 261n136
- 57.814: 164n53
- 57.820: 33n139, 90n71, 143n131
- 57.1046: 132n94
- 57.1409: 166n63, 225n4
- 58.447: 253n115
- 58.1220: 61n267, 221n101, 275n4
- 59.1407: 166n63, 167n67, 225n4, 275n1

Syll.[3]
- 274: 207n57, 222n107
- 986: 193n21

Tit. Cal.
- test. xii: 60n265, 166n63, 212n76, 285n35
- test. xvi: 240n60

GENERAL INDEX

Acanthus, 88n61, 128n79, 218n94
Aceratus of Paros and Thasos, 17n63
Achaea, 28, 56n239, 59n260
Acharnae, 170n77
Achilles, 101n115, 131, 243
Acragas, 51n216
acropolis, 17, 23, 53, 157, 159n34, 163, 165, 165n58, 165n60, 166, 217, 252
Aeatius of Thessaly, 204
Aegina: 27, 77n20, 103–4, 136n108, 202, 204n50, 205, 205n50, 270–71, 271n175
aeinautai ("Perpetual Sailors," supposed oligarchic regime at Miletus), 190n12
Aeneas of Stymphalus, 35n148
Aeoladas of Thebes, 201
Aesimides of Paros, 16
Aesion of Iulis, 217
Aesop, 192n17
Africa, 248n94
Agamemnon, 11, 191, 243, 271
Agasias of Lamptrae, 26
Agasicles of Thebes, 201–2
Agesilaus, king of Sparta, 54, 117–18, 140
Agis, king of Sparta, 159n38
agora, 16, 17, 17n67, 60n267, 96n99, 101n119, 113, 118n46, 128n80, 135n102, 145–46, 148–50, 153, 156n21 156n23, 157–59, 159n35, 161, 163, 165n58, 166, 168n69, 170, 176, 177n101, 190, 211, 211n72, 214–15, 215n83, 226, 231n27, 234–35, 269, 284; "free agora" of Thessalians, 194, 222n108
Agoraion, sanctuary in Eretrian agora, 166, 211n72

agoranomos (magistrate, market official), 96n99, 214
Agoratus of Athens, 142
Ajax, 101n116, 131
al-Asad, Hafiz, 197
Alcaeus of Mytilene, 16, 150, 153
Alcibiades of Athens, 18n70, 56, 61n269, 122, 156n22, 190, 193, 239–40, 257
Aleuas of Larissa, 176n99
Alexander of Pherae, 216n86
Alexander the Great, 7, 40n167, 279–80, 280n21
Alexicles of Athens, 263n145
Alkimos of Miletus, 102
Anaximenes of Lampsacus, 88
Andania, 90n71
Androcleidas of Thebes, 116, 118
Androcles of Athens, 115
Andros, 42n173, 136n108
Antileon the son of Leontinus of Chalcis, 164n53
Antimachus of Colophon, 209
Antinous, 113
Antipater of Iulis, 217n92
Antipater of Macedon, 38, 182, 217
Antiphon of Athens, 47n200, 98, 220n99, 263n145
Apemantus of Thasos, 111n17
Apollo, 60n263, 164n55, 200, 205
Arcadia, 19n78, 54, 59n260, 89n69, 198n35
Arcesilas of Sparta, 173
archai. *See* magistrates/magistracies
Archeptolemus of Athens, 263n145

343

Archestratus of Athens, 216
Archias of Thebes, 270
Archidamus II, king of Sparta, 28n117
Archidamus III, king of Sparta, 175n95
Archilochus of Paros, 16–17
Areopagus Council of Athens, 96–97, 141, 175–76, 184, 216, 283n28
Argentina, 72n308
Argos, 19n78, 24–25, 35, 42n175, 512–53, 56, 92n77, 95n95, 101n115, 158, 160n40, 167, 192, 205n50, 226, 228, 233–34, 233n34, 245n88, 280n22, 282, 284n32
Aristagoras of Miletus, 21, 264n151
Aristarchus of Athens, 46, 263n145
Aristocrates of Athens, 59n262
Aristodemus of Argos, 228
Aristodemus of Cyme, 228
Aristodicus of Tanagra, 114n25
aristokratia (aristocracy), 8n22, 36n149, 37n154, 59, 60, 134, 159n37, 161n41
Aristophilides of Tarentum, 105n131
Aristotle, 9, 10n28, 34–35, 39n166, 41, 48n201, 61, 119–20, 122–23, 171, 206–8, 270, 270n170
arms (weapons), 45–46, 49, 53, 53n227, 157–59, 162n44, 162n48, 163, 165, 193, 230–31, 238–39, 242, 242n70, 243, 255n120, 259, 259n129
army, 11, 43, 43n183, 47, 50n211, 52, 52n220, 53, 53n223, 54, 94n86, 191, 237, 239n57, 261n137
Artemis, 117, 166, 167n66, 168n69, 210n69, 214, 220n101, 232, 237n48
Asclepius, 60n263
Asopodorus of Thebes, 103n125
assassination. *See* killing
assembly (*ekklēsia*), 11, 15–18, 40, 54, 76, 81–82, 86, 96n97, 109, 113, 121–33, 156, 160, 182n120, 185, 188, 188n6, 190–92, 193n19, 193n21, 233, 240, 244, 277, 284n33, 285n36
astu (city-center), 148, 150–56, 158, 160–62, 164–65, 168–69, 174, 177n104, 182, 185
Astyochus of Sparta, 239n57, 242n72
Athenagoras of Syracuse, 29n124, 129n83, 244n80

Athens, 1–2, 4, 9, 12, 15–16, 21–29, 31–32, 36, 38, 41, 43, 46, 48–49, 51–52, 56–58, 60, 80–82, 87, 89–90, 92–93, 95–100, 104, 109–12, 114–18, 125–30, 139, 141–42, 146, 149, 153, 155–58, 161–63, 165, 167, 170–84, 191, 193, 200, 203, 207, 211, 213, 215–18, 220–21, 228–29, 233–35, 236, 238–42, 252, 257, 259, 262, 264, 276–77, 279–83
Athenian empire, 6n17, 26n106, 49, 80, 88n61, 112, 139, 139n117, 143n131, 164n53, 193, 203, 215, 216n85, 217n92, 241
athletics/athletes, 77, 198, 204, 207n57, 271, 277n9
Atrax, 16n59
Attaginus of Thebes, 251–52
Aulon, 92n77
authoritarianism/authoritarian regime, 3, 6, 7, 33n138, 65–66, 70–73, 79n19, 85n45, 108, 116–18, 119n48, 122n55, 127, 132–33, 138–39, 147, 149, 168, 183–84, 186–87, 195–97, 195n26, 208, 221, 227, 247, 248–49, 270n169

Bacchylides, 204n50, 205
ballot, secret, 39, 75, 87–88, 131, 132n94
barbarian(s), 152, 165
basileus (magistrate at Chios), 14
Batrachus of Athens, 142
Bias of Priene, 27n114
Boeotarchs, 81, 83
Boeotia, 24, 26n106, 39, 46, 48, 80–83, 104, 140, 200–204, 233–34, 251n107
boulē. *See* council
bouleuterion (council house), 158
Bourdieu, Pierre, 32
Brasidas of Sparta, 56n240, 57, 127–28, 209n67, 214n82, 241
bribe(s), 101n117, 147, 208, 233–34
Burke, Edmund, 84n41
Byzantium, 171, 177n101

Cadmus of Cos, 239n56
Calchedon, 177n101
Callias son of Hipponicus of Athens, 86
Callias of Sphettus, 60n266, 144n133

Callibius of Sparta, 162
Callibius of Tegea, 51, 159n36, 264n151
Callimachus of Athens, 207n57
Camarina, 205n50
Caria, 275
Carystus, 136n108
cascading, phenomenon of voting, 121, 127, 127n75
Casmenae, 19n78
census, 38n161, 41, 48. *See also timēma/timēmata* (property requirements/assessments)
Ceos, 89, 139n116, 217
Chaeronea, Battle of, 277
Chalcideus of Sparta, 193
Chalcidice, 145n137, 225n4, 261
Chalcis, 24, 36, 139n116, 164n53
Chares of Athens, 128n80
children, 33n139, 90, 90n71, 109, 135, 152n9, 153, 259
Chile, 85n45, 195n26
Chios, 13–14, 17n65, 19n78, 40n167, 41n171, 56, 111n18, 145n138, 193, 212n76, 241n69, 279
Choerilus of Samos, 209
Chrysantas, Persian noble, 121, 243–44
Cimon of Athens, 26n108, 86n55, 171–73, 175, 183
Cimon the son of Stesagoras, 113
Cinadon of Sparta, 140, 231n27, 262n138
circulation of information, 187–88
class, 5n16, 62n274
Clazomenae, 212n75
Cleandridas of Sparta, 28n117
Clearchus of Heraclea Pontica, 228, 263n146
Cleisthenes of Athens, 21–23, 25n105, 43–44, 156, 174, 179, 180n112, 180n113, 253n116, 255n120, 264, 264n151, 272n178
Cleitophon of Athens, 174n93
Cleomenes, king of Sparta, 23–24, 55n238, 157
Cleonymus of Athens, 139
clientelism, 71n304, 149, 168–85
Cloelius, 269
Cnidus, 105, 123n61, 266

Cnopus, king of Erythrae, 114, 167n69, 237n48
co-optation into oligarchies, 51, 109, 123, 133–37
coercion. *See* violence
Coes of Mytilene, 251, 251n103, 251n104
collective action problem, 9, 64, 65–68, 73, 121, 134, 169, 184–85, 226, 284
Colophon, 29, 132n94, 150, 164n55, 209
commitment problem, 144
common knowledge, 9, 65–66, 102, 108, 132n95, 138, 160n39, 196, 204, 207, 227, 230–31, 236, 237, 242, 245, 254
competition among elite, 33n137, 33n138, 73, 75, 77, 78, 80, 91, 100, 150, 202, 252, 263, 267–68, 272, 284
confiscation of property, 33, 33n139, 101n115, 102, 111, 135n104, 217, 218, 263n145
consensus, 75, 84–86, 126, 127n73, 132, 202
"Constitutional Debate" of Herodotus, 29–30, 77, 112, 191, 202
coordination problem, 9, 64–65, 108, 126, 132, 160n39, 177, 196, 204, 226, 230–31, 254
Corax. *See* Tisias and Corax
Corcyra, 13, 35, 42n173, 50, 92n77, 127, 128n80, 241n69
Corinth, 13, 25n105, 28n117, 42, 50, 52n219, 79n16, 82n30, 84n43, 100, 114, 118n46, 123n61, 124, 192–93, 199, 204n50, 231–37, 252n111, 252n112, 264; Battle of, 278n14
Corinthian War, 231
Coronea, Battle of, of 447, 80; of 394, 233–34
Cos, 60n265, 212n76, 226n4, 239n56
council(s) (*boulē*), 13–16, 19, 19n78, 21, 38n161, 39–40, 40n171, 48n203, 51n216, 60n263, 69n296, 81–84, 82n30, 85n49, 86, 88n63, 96n97, 105, 111, 121, 123, 127, 130n90, 134n99, 142, 157n27, 166, 189, 190, 193, 193n21, 193n22, 211n72, 233, 252n112, 278n14, 278n15; of the Areopagus. *See* Areopagus Council of Athens
court(s) of law, 93, 94n86, 96n97, 97–99, 110–11, 119n48, 122, 130n87, 131, 131n92, 153,

court(s) of law (*cont.*)
    168n69, 172, 179n109, 179, 179n109, 180,
    185, 191, 220n99, 269, 278n14
credible commitment, 19, 262n140
Cresphontes of Miletus, 102
Crete, 12n36, 74n312, 123n64
Critias of Athens, 18n70, 29n124, 45n190, 58,
    59n259, 61n267, 73n309, 84, 99n109,
    119n50, 128–29, 173, 173n88, 258, 262, 281,
    285n34
Croton, 272
curse(s), 29n124, 143–44, 215n84, 218,
    220n101, 261
Cyclopes, 151
Cylon of Athens, 165n58
Cylon of Croton, 272
Cyme, Aeolian, 36, 61n267, 167, 194n25,
    225n4, 275–76
Cyme, Italian, 228
Cyprus, 139
Cyrene, 38n161, 40n167, 51n216, 82n31, 97,
    123n61, 179, 180n112
Cyrus, king of Persia, 121, 198, 243
Cyzicus, 16n59

Damonides [Damon] of Athens, 172
Daochids of Pharsalus, 207n57, 222n107
Daphnephoria festival, 200–204
Darius, king of Persia, 77, 105, 202, 251
decarchies (ruling groups of ten men),
    137n110, 209
Deioces of Media, 120n51, 179
delation law of Thasos, 142–46, 218, 261n136
Delian League, 29n122, 217n92
Delium, Battle of, 203
Delphi, 19n78, 61n267, 95n95, 145n138, 149,
    207, 209n65, 265
Delphic oracle. *See* oracle
demagogue(s), 29n124, 33, 33n139, 61n270,
    86, 94n86, 114, 115n30, 129n83, 141, 151, 162,
    172–73, 262, 263n147, 282, 284n32
dēmarchos, 14
Demaretus of Athens, 116
Demaretus, king of Sparta, 252n110
deme(s), 12n38, 44n187, 120n51, 153, 170n77,
    172, 172n84, 173, 175–76, 178, 179n109, 183,
    184
Demetrius of Phalerum, 38, 45n190, 46n194,
    49n204, 90–91, 96n97, 123n61, 220n99,
    279n17
Demetrius Poliorcetes, 60n267
dēmiourgoi (magistrates of Larissa), 135
Demochares of Athens, 60n266
democracy (*dēmokratia*), *oligarchia* as reaction to, 1, 3–10, 18, 20–34; as institutional rules of the game in the Hellenistic period, 4–5, 7, 225, 276–78, 285–86
Demonax of Cyrene, 180n112
demos, definition of, 3, 10n28
Demosthenes of Athens (general), 104n129
Demosthenes of Athens (orator), 60n266,
    213n76, 283
Diagoras of Eretria, 25, 266n157
Diitrephes of Athens, 217
Dikaia, 145n137, 225n4, 261
Dinon of Tarentum, 80n21
dioecism, 25n104, 159, 159n37, 160n41,
    219n95
Diomedon of Athens, 240
Dion of Syracuse, 114, 180
Dionysia festival, 90, 218, 220n100, 220n101
Dionysius of Syracuse, 139, 220n99, 227,
    227n12, 239n57, 242n73
Dionysus, 90, 96n99, 164n55, 199, 218,
    220n100, 220n101, 237n47
disputes, 153, 178; as leading to *stasis* in oligarchies, 93–94, 105, 263–65, 271; resolution of in oligarchic regimes, 93–99, 110
Doricus of Syracuse, 242n73
Dorieus of Rhodes, 239n57, 242n72
Draco of Athens, 45, 101n116, 216
Dreros, 19
dunasteia (narrow junta), 9, 77, 116, 236, 250,
    250n101, 252–53, 282n26, 284
dunatoi (powerful people), 36n150, 163,
    169n72, 190n12, 238

education (*paideia*), 30, 37n154, 73n309,
    273
Egypt, 183n125

GENERAL INDEX 347

eisphora. See tax(es)
elders (*gerontes*), office in Sparta, 18, 88n65; in Corinth, 233
election(s), 17n63, 39, 57, 70, 78n13, 81n27, 83, 84n41, 88n63, 113n95, 132, 133n96, 138, 183, 240, 275, 278n14
Eleusis, 262
eleutheria (freedom), 93, 95, 120n50, 167, 215n82, 275
Elis, 12n38, 15–16, 16n59, 25, 53, 59n260, 114, 159, 163, 168n70, 180–81, 219, 226
elite-led regimes of Archaic period, as distinct from Classical oligarchy, 8, 9–20, 32–33, 150
elite, analytical usefulness of as term, 8n22
emotion(s), 98n107, 99, 264, 266–73
Empedocles of Acragas, 51n215
enemy/enemies, 77, 85, 87–89, 91, 93, 98, 101, 101n117, 101n119, 128, 202, 257, 263, 264n151, 269, 271–72, 284
enmity. See enemy/enemies
Epaminondas of Thebes, 59n260, 253
eparitoi (elite troops of Arcadian *koinon*), 54
Ephesus, 17, 27–28, 209n62, 210n69 214, 219, 279
Ephialtes of Athens, 26n106, 114, 118, 141, 216
ephor(s), magistrate in Sparta and other cities, 55n238, 57–58, 78n15, 84–85, 92n77, 97, 117–18, 140, 189n8
Epidamnus, 28, 182n119, 265
Epidaurus, 60n263, 152, 154
epimeleia (care, oversight), 71, 97, 168, 175, 175n96, 177
epimēnioi (board at oligarchic Miletus), 102–3
Epizephyrian Locri, 51n216
equality, 75, 76–79, 87, 89, 93, 99, 201, 265n155, 270n170
equilibrium, 6, 7, 9, 70, 149, 224, 249–50, 253, 254, 256, 273; Nash equilibrium, 256, 256n123
Eratosthenes of Athens, 262
Eresus, 67n68, 279

Eretria, 25, 36, 41n171, 45n189, 60n265, 139n116, 145n138, 166, 168n69, 211n72, 212n76, 220n101, 251, 266n157
Erythrae, 41n171, 42n173, 60, 114, 123n60, 145n138, 165, 167n69, 212, 212n76, 215, 219, 220n101, 228n15, 237n48, 282n26
Eteocles of Thebes, 265n155
Eteonicus of Sparta, 58n254
Euboea, 30n125, 115n29
Euclea festival, 232, 232n30, 234
Euhesperides, 145n138
Euhippus of Cyme, 275
Eumelides of Athens, 111
eunomia (good order), 8n22, 55, 59, 59n261, 71, 98, 110, 121, 123n61, 190, 205, 205n52, 232n30, 235–36, 237n47, 272n181
Euphorbus of Eretria, 251
Euphraeus of Oreus, 115
Euphron I of Sicyon, 118n46, 159, 214n82, 215n83, 235n42, 239n56, 271–72
Euphron II of Sicyon, grandson of above, 217, 279n18
Eurytion of Heraclea Pontica, 270
Eurytion of Orchomenos, 203
euthuna (rendering of account at end of magistracy), 69n296, 189n8, 278n15
Euthymus of Locri, 209n67
execution. See killing
exile, 50, 56, 60n266, 76, 99–106, 135, 136n109, 142, 152, 162n47, 164n53, 182, 209, 209n61, 209n62, 217, 218, 235, 261n134, 263n145, 271
expulsion, from city-center, 160–67

farmer(s), 30n126, 41, 41n172, 43, 55n235, 153, 170, 170n76, 171n79, 180n115, 182, 216n87
festival(s), 90, 96n99, 158n30, 164, 164n55, 177, 177n102, 195, 198–99, 209–10, 218, 220, 220n100, 220n101, 226–37, 237n48, 245, 246, 276, 277n9
feud. See enemy/enemies
fine(s), 96n99, 97, 102–3, 111, 120, 147n140, 153
Finley, Moses, 3, 3n9, 4

First Messenian War, 231n27
fishermen, 171, 259
Five Thousand, proposed regime at Athens, 45–46, 47n200, 49, 52, 52n219, 82, 135n105, 222n103
focal point, 33, 167n65, 210–11, 211n72, 213, 214n79, 215, 219, 254, 259
force. *See* violence
Forsdyke, Sara, 100
Four Hundred, oligarchy at Athens, 45–46, 52, 77–78, 82, 98–99, 112, 115, 116n33, 126, 135n105, 136n108, 141, 143n131, 145n138, 158, 161n42, 174n93, 219n97, 222n103, 239–40, 257, 260, 263n145, 281, 285n35; select group of soldiers at Elis, 53n229
funeral(s), 89, 89n69, 91, 196

gambling, 176, 282n26
game theory, 7, 9, 66, 248–49, 254
gamoroi/geomoroi (landholders), 19n78, 27n113, 105
garrison(s), 128n80, 130, 162–63, 166n63, 209–10, 220n101, 252–53, 280n21, 281, 282n26
Gauthier, Philippe, 278
Geddes, Barbara, 248–49
Gela, 191n16
Gelon, tyrant of Gela and Syracuse, 26n107, 164n54
general (*stratēgos*), 44n187, 49, 80n21, 104n129, 165, 167, 203, 225n4, 238, 240, 251, 259, 275, 275n3
genos/gene, 180n112
Gerginoi (spies in Cyprus), 140
Gergithes (name for demos in Miletus), 152
Gillus of Tarentum, 105
Goebbels, Joseph, 195n27
Gorgias of Leontini, 135
Gramsci, Antonio, 197
"Great Man" view of history, 246–47
Great Rhetra, 18
Guizot, François, 137
gunaikonomos (magistracy, regulator of women), 90n71, 91, 91n74, 91n75, 91n77

Gyges, myth of, 250n100
gymnasium, 90

Haliartus, Battle of, 233
Halicarnassus, 101n115
Halieis, 19n78, 101n115
harbor(s), 177, 181, 236n45
Harmodius and Aristogeiton. *See* tyrannicides
Hegesilochus of Rhodes, 282n26
Hellenistic period, 7, 69n296, 149, 180, 181n116, 208n60, 221n101, 225, 276–80
Helorus River, Battle of, 27n113
helots, 55, 59n256, 116, 116n36, 140, 231n27, 242n72
Hera, 209
Heraclea Pontica, 35, 41n171, 51n216, 101n119, 225, 228, 263n146, 269
Heraclea Trachinia, 242n72
Heraclides of Syracuse, 114
Heraclitus of Ephesus, philosopher, 27–28
Hermocrates of Syracuse, 191n16
Hermodorus of Ephesus, 27
hero/heroic cult, 118n46, 209, 209n67, 214n82, 217
Heropythes of Ephesus, 214
Hestia, 150n3
Hestiaea, 265
hēsuchia (quietude), 78, 97, 97n101, 119, 193n20, 202, 202n45, 205
hetaireia (political club), 37, 136, 252n111
Hieron of Syracuse, 139, 227
Hipparchus the son of Charmus of Athens, 220n99
Hipparchus the son of Peisistratus of Athens, 228
hippeis (cavalry), 36–37, 45n189, 49n206, 53, 57, 176n99; ruling class of in Archaic Eretria, 25n105, 36, 266n157
Hippias of Athens, 158n30
Hippias of Elis, 86
hippobotai, elite of Chalcis, 36
Hippocrates of Athens, 104n129
Hipponax of Ephesus, 17

GENERAL INDEX 349

Hippotes of Erythrae, 237n48
Histiaeus of Miletus, 251n103
Historical Institutionalism. *See* institutions
home(s). *See* house(s)
Homer, 10n28, 11, 18, 42, 150, 272
homo economicus, 63, 248n96, 267
homonoia (likeminded-ness, unity), 30n125, 78, 175, 175n95, 222, 240, 260n133
honor (*timē*), individual, 269, 271–72
hoplite constitution, 2n6, 4n10, 9, 41–54
Hoplitenpoliteia. See hoplite constitution
hoplite(s), 2n6, 4n10, 9, 10n28, 41–54, 55, 55n235, 58, 81, 94n86, 121, 176n99, 222n103, 241, 241n65, 242n70, 245n86, 247
Horai, 205
house(s), 114, 115n28, 117, 159, 163, 195, 199n36, 218–19, 218n95, 219n96, 219n97, 220n99, 276
hubris, 29, 77, 107–9, 119, 137n111, 242–43, 259, 268
Hume, David, 258n126
Hyacinthia festival, 231n27
Hyperbolus of Athens, 115n30, 262

Iasos, 59n261
ideology, 2, 6, 7, 22, 25, 26n111, 31, 34, 41, 42, 44n186, 45n189, 47n200, 63, 71, 72, 74, 149, 150, 187, 190n12, 195, 198–200, 202–4, 232, 234, 236, 241, 252n111, 268, 271n174
Idrieus son of Hecatomnus, 59n261
Ilion, 60n265, 212n76
imagery, animal, 30n125, 151, 159, 219, 284n32; medical, 227; natural, 191, 246, 246n91, 259n129, 284n32
implication in an oligarchic regime, 108, 129n82, 136, 138–47, 261–62
inequality, 72, 77, 117n37
informant(s), 67, 104, 107, 109, 117, 138–47, 176n98, 218, 223, 230, 231n25, 254n118
inn(s), 176
inscription(s), 60, 142, 145n138, 188, 277
institutions, 5, 6, 7, 69–74, 75–76, 108–9, 122n55, 138, 200, 224–25, 249, 254, 263, 267, 273, 279, 286; definition of, 70; Historical Institutionalism, 69–70; New Institutionalism, 6, 7, 69
intelligence, lack of as reason for excluding demos, 190
intermediate regime at Athens, 411–10 BCE, 45, 47
intoxication, as encouraging of oligarchic *stasis*, 76n76, 259, 282n26
Ionian Revolt, 28n119, 264n151
Isagoras of Athens, 21, 23, 55n238, 157, 165n58, 253n116
Ismenias of Thebes, 252–53, 253n113, 253,114
isonomia (equality before the law), 29n123, 77, 77n11, 81, 239n56, 264n151
Issorium, 117
Isyllus of Epidaurus, 60n263
Iulis, 89, 217

Jocasta, 265n155
Jordan, 183n125
judge (*dikastēs*), 47n200, 78n13, 87, 93, 94n86, 110, 119n48, 120n51, 131, 143, 153, 172, 175, 178, 178n109, 184, 190, 225n4, 278n14

Kallyrioi, slave population of Syracuse, 27n113, 105n133
KGB, 138
killing, state-backed, 101, 102, 111, 117, 230, 263n145; private, 101n116, 102–3, 229; extra-judicial, 112–18, 126, 127, 142, 161n42, 162n48, 163, 217, 262, 281, 282
kingship/kingdoms, 37n154, 72, 74n312, 78, 105n131, 150
koinon (federal state), of Arcadia, 54, 58, 159; of Boeotia, 39, 40n171, 48, 80–83, 104, 140, 200–204, 252n112, 253n114, 253n115
Kurke, Leslie, 200, 202–4

Laciadae, 172, 183
land, 27n114, 43, 72, 72n306, 92n79, 105, 114, 117, 162n47, 163, 169, 169n72, 172, 175, 180n115, 234, 282. *See also* redistribution of land

Larcius, Titus, 269
Larissa, 135, 176n99
lawsuit(s), 17, 33, 76, 93–94, 97, 98, 99, 263, 269
Leon of Athens, 240
Leon of Salamis, 129n82, 136
Leontiades of Thebes, 116, 252–53, 253n113, 253n114, 253n116
Leontini, 29, 163
Lesbos, 16, 49
Leuctra, Battle of, 117
light-armed troops, 44
Lindos, 145n138
literacy, 146, 188
liturgy, 33, 172, 181
Locri, Epizephyrian, 51n216, 209n67
Locris, Opuntian, 16n59, 44n188
lottery, 31, 37n154, 39, 41n171, 88, 277, 278n14
Lycides of Athens, 21
Lycomedes of Mantinea, 115n29
Lygdamis of Naxos, 258–60, 260n130, 260n131
Lysander of Sparta, 90n71, 137n110, 209
Lysias, speechwriter, 227
Lysimachus of Athens, 111
Lysippus, 207

Macedon, 74n312, 130, 180, 279
Maeandrius of Samos, 239n56
Magaloni, Beatriz, 126, 133, 183–84, 208, 221
magistrates/magistracies (*archai*), 18, 19, 36n149, 37–40, 85, 88, 89n69, 90–91, 94–97, 98n107, 110n8, 111, 119, 135, 164, 182, 192–93, 206, 222, 277, 283; individual vs. collegial, 95n95
Magnesia, 90n71
majority vote, 79, 82, 87
Malis, 45
Mantinea, 24, 25, 42n173, 42n175, 54, 115n29, 159, 160n40, 161n41, 169n72, 226, 244n84
Marathon, Battle of, 22
Mardonius of Persia, 28n115
marriage, 25n105, 28, 265, 266n157
Massalia, 51n216, 135, 225

Mausolus of Caria, 214, 220n99, 228n14, 277n9, 2882n26
Marxism. *See* class
Media, 120n51, 152n9, 179
median voter, 83, 124n65
medism, charge of, 251, 284
Megabates of Persia, 264n151
Megabyzus of Persia, 29–31, 191, 284n32
Megara, 16n62, 29, 47, 51n216, 56, 100, 123n61, 128–29, 180n114, 222n103, 261n134
Melos, 86n55, 193
memory, collective, 190n12
Mende, 55n233, 127–28, 158, 165n61, 241–43, 247, 254, 255n120, 259n129
Menecrates son of Tlasias of Oianthea, 13
Menestratus of Athens, 142
mercenaries, 53, 118n46, 245n88
Messene, 278n13
Messenia, 55, 231n27
methodological individualism, 62–64, 74, 245–46
metic(s), 5n16, 235, 236n43
Mexico, 72n308, 127, 183
Michels, Robert, 3, 4
Miletus, 101n115, 102, 114n27, 142n127, 145n138, 152, 154, 190, 210n68, 280n22, 281n24
Mill, John Stuart, 190n13
monarch/monarchy. *See* kingship/kingdoms
monitoring among oligarchs, 69n294, 86, 89, 91, 92n80, 95–96, 106n135, 249
monuments, destruction of, 195, 210–21
Mubarak, Hosni, 183n125
Mummius, Lucius, 278n14
mutiny, 117, 238, 239n57
Mycenae, 19n78
Mylasa, 275–76
Mytilene, 16, 49–50, 52n219, 100, 135, 145n138, 164n55, 193, 220n101, 238, 240, 242n70, 245n87, 251, 265, 279, 281n24

Nash equilibrium. *See* equilibrium
Naucleides of Plataea, 114n26

GENERAL INDEX 351

Naupactus, 19n78
navy, 181–82, 216n87, 241, 241n65
Naxos, 24, 27, 28n119, 152, 172n81, 172n84, 179n10, 242n71, 258–60
Nemea, Battle of, 50n211, 51, 233–34
New Institutionalism. *See* institutions
Niceratus of Heraclea, 209
Nicias of Athens, 56
Nicocles of Salamis, 78n15, 140
Nicodromus of Aegina, 27n113, 103–4, 205n52, 270–71
Nicomachus of Phocis, 104, 140
night, 53, 108, 114, 114n26, 115n28, 116–18, 119n48, 194n25
nomophulakes (magistracy, guardians of the laws), 91, 96n97, 123, 133
North Korea, 195n27
Notium, 209n62
Nympharetus of Miletus, 102

oath(s), 87, 88, 119n50, 139, 143, 144n133, 145n137, 166, 217, 221, 222n103, 240, 240n60, 261, 261n136, 263n144, 281; of Demophantus, 100, 261n137, 279
Ober, Josiah, 3
O'Donnell, Guillermo, 247, 248n94
Odysseus, 109n5, 131
Oenophyta, Battle of, 26n105, 80, 203
Oianthea, 13
oikos (household), 62n271
oligarch, lack of a Greek noun for, 3n8
oligarchia, definition of, 40
Olympia, 14, 149, 209n65, 227
Olympichus, 275–76
oracle, of Delphi, 101n117
Orchomenos, 37n153, 48n204, 103n125, 203
Oreus, 115n29
organization, greater capacity for within small groups, 73; obstacles to in large groups, 73, 115, 194
ostracism, 24, 24n99, 26, 26n108, 100, 115n30, 283
Ostrom, Elinor, 63

ōtakoustai (eavesdroppers during tyranny of Hieron of Syracuse), 139

pachees ("fatcats," oligarchs), 27n113, 28n119, 104n128
Paches of Athens, 49, 238
Pagondas of Thebes, 83, 201–2
paidonomos (magistracy, regulator of children), 90n71
Panathenaea festival, 228, 230, 236n46, 242
paradosis (transfer of revenue), 189n8
Paros, 16
Partheniae of Sparta, 231n27
Pasimelus of Corinth, 236
Patara, 278n14
patronage, 70, 120n51, 149, 168, 171, 171n81, 174, 174n94, 175–77, 180n114, 182–84, 208, 259
Pausanias, king of Sparta, 29n125, 88n65
Pausanias "the regent" of Sparta, 140
Peace of Antalcidas, 214
Peisander of Athens, 46, 139
Peisistratus of Athens, 20n80, 23, 25n105, 114, 120n51, 137n113, 153, 172n84, 178, 259–60, 260n130
Peisistratus son of Hippias of Athens, 207n57
Peithias of Corcyra, 127
Pellene, 51n216
Pelopidas of Thebes, 253
Peloponnesian League, 55
Peloponnesian War, 6n17, 9, 28, 29n123, 31n133, 57, 58, 143n131, 170, 203, 218
Pergamum, 276
Periander of Corinth, 137n113
Pericles of Athens, 26n111, 61n269, 86, 122, 156n22, 172–73, 207, 207n58
Persia/Persians, 154n16, 157n28, 214, 233, 239, 250–51, 264n151
Persian Wars, 77n11, 141, 284
personification, of Aristokratia, 59n262, 60, 61n267; of Demokratia, 59n262, 60; of the Demos, 60, 79n18, 276, 276n5; of Oligarchia, 59n259, 60, 61n267

Phalanthus of Sparta, 231n27
Pharsalus, 207n57, 222, 260n133
Pheidon of Cyme, 36
Philagrus of Eretria, 251
Philetaerus of Pergamum, 276
Philetaireia festival, 276
Philip of Macedon, 180n114, 214, 216n86, 228
Philites of Erythrae, 212–13, 220n101
philoneikia (love of strife), 94n87, 101n119, 263, 263n147, 270, 272
philotimia (ambition, love of honor), 78, 257, 263, 264n148, 265n155, 272, 273n182
Phlius, 51, 58, 92n77, 112n18
Phocion of Athens, 37, 38, 60n266, 96n99, 129, 182, 217, 279n17
Phocis, 104, 140, 265
Phoebidas of Sparta, 252, 252n112, 253n113
phratry/phatries, 179, 180n112
Phrynichus of Athens, 60n264, 112, 158, 219n97, 220n100, 263n145
Pindar, 199, 201–5
Pinochet, Augusto, 85n45
Piraeus, port of Athens, 181
Pisidia, 225n4
Pittacus of Mytilene, 16, 153
Plataea, 29, 92n77, 244n80; Battle of, 50n211
Pleistoanax, king of Sparta, 101n117
ploutokratia (plutocracy), 35–37, 36n149, 59n262
Pnyx, 216n87
poetry, lyric, 77; choral, 195, 198–206, 208, 237n47
politeuma (ruling citizen body), 39n166, 40, 40n167, 40n171, 41, 47, 82n31, 128, 135
Polyanthes of Corinth, 233
Polycrates of Samos, 153, 239n56
Polydamidas of Sparta, 158, 239n57, 241–43, 254, 255n120
Polynices of Thebes, 265n155
Polystratus of Athens, 46n193
Poseidon, 265n155
potagōgides (female informers during tyranny of Dionysius of Syracuse), 139

Potamodorus of Orchomenos, 203
poverty, 17, 17n67, 20, 26, 137, 205
Praximenes of Oianthea, 13
Praxitas of Sparta, 236
preferences, ordering of in game theory, 66–67, 68n292, 248n96, 252n112, 256–57, 264, 267, 267n163, 268
PRI, Mexican political party, 72, 127, 183
priestess/priest, 200–201
Prisoner's Dilemma game, 66–68, 138, 185, 249–50, 252–53, 256, 260n130
probouleusis (deliberation in advance), 81, 123
probouloi (preliminary councilors), 82, 123, 123n61, 124, 133, 233
procession(s), 96n99, 195, 198, 200–202, 220n99, 220n101, 227n10, 228, 230–31, 237, 277n9
projection, of an image of power, 194–219, 254n118
Promalangas (spies in Cyprus), 140
property requirements/qualifications. *See* timēma/timēmata
prostatēs (champion), 53, 114, 115, 127, 128n80, 159, 160, 163, 209–10, 219, 231n27, 255–57, 263n146, 266, 269
prostitute(s), 17, 61n267
Protagoras of Abdera, 86
proxenos (representative of another polis's interests), 13, 43n105, 159n38, 216, 217, 217n92, 238n51
Proxenus of Tegea, 51, 159, 264n151
prytaneion (town hall), 165n58
Ptoeodorus of Megara, 180n114
Ptoeodorus of Thespiae, 104, 203
Ptolemy, Hellenistic king, 38n161, 40n167, 97n103, 189n8
punishment, 99–102, 108, 109–10, 120, 146, 175, 181, 183, 269
Pythagoreans, 272

redistribution of land, 92n79, 114, 163, 282
repression. *See* violence
revolution, 7, 21–23, 28, 33, 43–44, 50,

GENERAL INDEX   353

53n227, 59n260, 60, 65–66, 69n294, 73n310, 87, 96n99, 101n119, 104, 117, 122, 138, 140, 145, 158n32, 160n39, 165n58, 182, 182n119, 185, 187, 198, 203–4, 210, 215n83, 216, 224, 225–28, 231–32, 233n34, 236n47, 238, 245n89, 246, 246n91, 247, 254–56, 259n129, 266, 268n164, 284

reward(s) for cooperation with oligarchic regime, 102–3, 104, 107, 109, 138–47, 218, 223, 254n118

Rhegium, 29

rhetoric/rhetorical ability, 57, 98–99, 110

Rhetoric to Alexander, importance of for understanding oligarchy, 88n62

rhetra (ordinance), 15

Rhodes, 35, 41n171, 58, 59n260, 60n264, 77n10, 95n95, 159, 168n70, 178n105, 181–82, 226, 228, 239n57, 262n138, 282n26

ritual(s), 132, 133n96, 195–204, 228, 237n47

Robert, Louis, 277–78

Rome, 52n219, 72, 95, 138n114, 168, 172n81, 180n114, 211n73, 269, 278, 286

Rousseau, Jean-Jacques, 255

rowers, of triremes. *See* sailors

sacrifice(s), 53, 195, 206–8, 210n69, 220n101, 221, 228, 282

Sagalassos, 225n4

sailors, 171, 190n12, 239n57, 258n126

Salaethus of Sparta, 238, 242n70

Samos, 26n106, 29, 42n173, 90n71, 100, 153, 154n16, 164n53, 209, 239n56, 239, 251, 257

Schelling, Thomas, 210

Schmitter, Philippe, 247, 248n94

Scopadae, 173

Scott, James C., 197

Scythia, 251

Second Athenian Naval League, 279n18

secrecy, 46n192, 84n42, 115, 117, 117n39, 163n50, 188–94

Sestos, 210n68

Shah of Persia, 138

shock(s), to the oligarchic cooperative equilibrium; exogenous, 249–53, 268; endogenous, 254–63, 268

Sicily, 19n78, 56, 127n73, 164n53, 164n54, 191n16, 227

Sicyon, 28, 35, 42n173, 56n239, 58, 118n46, 159, 226, 235n42, 239n56, 244n84, 271

Simonides, 205, 227

Siphnos, 95n95

Sisyphus of Pharsalus, 222

Six Hundred, oligarchic regime at Syracuse, 51n216

skolia, Attic (drinking songs), 228

slaves/slavery, 5n16, 27n113, 34n141, 55, 91n77, 96n99, 105n133, 109, 139, 139n116, 140, 143, 203, 279n18

Smyrna, 164n55

"social capital," 63, 65

Social War, 282

Socrates of Athens, 35, 37, 46n194, 57, 58n249, 86, 99n109, 109n5, 121, 129n82, 149, 191n17, 192n18, 222, 226

Solon of Athens, 15, 16, 19, 20n80, 23, 36, 41, 43–44, 46n194, 47n200, 89, 130n87, 156, 160n39, 174, 216, 243

Sophocles of Athens, 86n55

sōphrosunē (moderation), 59n261, 71, 110, 175, 202, 205

sortition. *See* lottery

space, public, 108, 120n51, 142, 146, 148–50, 155, 160, 207, 225–26, 230, 247,

Sparta, 18, 23–24, 25n105, 28, 45, 50–51, 54–58, 78n15, 84–85, 92n77, 97, 104, 105n131, 110n12, 111n18, 112n18, 114, 116–18, 123n64, 125, 127, 140, 157–59, 160n41, 162, 165, 165n61, 174n92, 175n95, 189n8, 193n20, 209, 217–18, 231n7, 232–34, 236, 238, 239n57, 241–43, 252–53, 253n116, 260n131, 272, 282n26

spectacle, public, 109, 149, 195–96, 198, 204, 227, 237

spy/spies, 139

Stadiasmus Patarensis, 29n124, 278n14

Stag Hunt game, 255–60, 266

Stasi, 138, 147

stasis (civil war), 2n7, 7, 19n77, 53, 58, 76, 83–84, 89, 91, 94, 101n119, 128, 202, 205, 205n53, 213, 224–25, 232, 248n94, 250, 259, 263, 265, 265n152, 266–67, 270–71
statue/statue base, 59n261, 157, 157n28, 207n57, 209n65, 211–14, 214n82, 215, 220n99, 220n101, 275–76
stēlē/stēlai (stone slabs for inscriptions), 215–17, 220n99
Sthenelaidas of Sparta, 126
stoning, 17, 251n104
Stratolas of Elis, 54n229
Stratonax of Miletus, 102
Strophaea festival, 237n48
suitors of Penelope in the *Odyssey*, 113
sumptuary legislation, 75, 89–93
Svolik, Milan, 71
sycophants (vexatious litigators), 33, 33n139, 99n109, 115n29, 139n115, 162
Syloson of Samos, 154n16
symposium, 17n70, 85–86, 89, 91
synoecism, 24n101, 41n171, 159n37, 160n41
Syracuse, 24, 27, 29n124, 42n175, 51n216, 98, 105, 129n83, 139, 142n126, 163, 180n114, 220n99, 227, 227n12, 239n57, 242n73, 265, 280n22
Syria, 197

Tanagra, 114n25; Battle of, 27n111, 31n133
Tarentum, 80n21, 105, 171
tavern(s), 176, 177n101
tax(es), 10n26, 33, 33n139, 46, 46n196
Teegarden, David, 34, 277
Tegea, 24n102, 28n117, 50–51, 58, 159, 226, 244n84, 263, 264n151, 271n175
Telemachus, 113
Telestagoras of Naxos, 152n9, 172n84, 179n110, 258–59, 260n131
Telos, 165, 225n4
temenos (sanctuary), 166, 210n69, 211n72, 276, 277n9
temple(s), 50n210, 207, 214
Ten Thousand, assembly of in Arcadian *koinon*, 54; Greek mercenary army of, 237n50, 241n63; ruling body of in Cyrene, 82n31
Tenos, 95n95, 136n108
Teos, 144n133, 215n84
term of office, 76n3, 95n95
Thasos, 19n78, 51n216, 58, 90n71, 101n115, 107, 111, 142–46, 148, 209n68, 212n76, 217–19, 221n101, 261n136. *See also* delation law of Thasos
thearoi/theōroi (magistracy), 159n36, 271n175
theater(s), 12, 57, 90n72, 122, 179n109, 228, 235n40, 275
Thebes, 42, 47–49, 56, 59n260, 60n264, 77n20, 81n23, 81n27, 84n43, 101n115, 101n119, 116, 118, 118n46, 135n102, 200–204, 204n50, 205, 244n80, 251–53, 264, 269, 282n26, 284
Themis, 265n155
Themistocles of Athens, 141
Theognis, elegiac poet, 17–18, 151, 154
Theomestor of Samos, 251
Theozotides of Athens, 212n76
Theramenes of Athens, 45n189, 52, 58, 84, 162n48, 258n126, 285n34
Thespiae, 29, 83n38, 104, 203–4
Thessaly, 74n312, 176n99, 204, 222, 260n133
thetes, fourth and lowest Solonian census class, 44n186, 46n194, 47n200, 130n87, 240
Thetis, 265n155
Thirty, oligarchic regime at Athens, 24n98, 29n125, 38n201, 58, 73n309, 84, 109, 112, 116, 120n50, 128, 136, 142, 156, 161, 167, 216, 220n99, 258n126, 262n143, 281, 281n25, 285n34
Thousand, oligarchic regime at Acragas, 51n216; oligarchic regime at Cyrene, 61n216; oligarchic regime at Epizephyrian Locri, 51n216; supposed oligarchic regime at Opuntian Locris, 62n188
Thrace, 129
Thrasybulus of Athens, 143n131, 146, 218, 240
Thrasydaeus of Elis, 114, 159, 159n38, 163, 219
Thrasyllus of Athens, 240–41

threat(s) of violence, used by oligarchies, 33, 47n200, 67, 99, 105, 108–9, 119, 121, 127, 131, 146, 169, 175, 182, 208, 223

Three Hundred, oligarchic regime at Thasos, 51n216; select infantry of Elis, 53

Three Thousand, full citizens during the reign of the Thirty at Athens, 82n31, 128–29, 162, 262, 281

Thucydides the son of Melesias of Athens, 27n111

Thucydides of Athens, historian, 229–31

Timagenides of Thebes, 251–52

time horizon(s), 250

timēma/timēmata (property requirements/assessments), 36n149, 37–40, 46n194, 48–49, 122, 124n65, 129, 135n101, 136–37, 233, 278n14

timēsis (rating based on property assessment), 38

timētēs/timētēr (censor), 38n161

timokratia (regime based either on honor or on property requirement), 8n22, 37n154

Timolaus of Corinth, 233–34, 236n46

Timoleon of Corinth, 118n46, 220n99

Timon of Phlius, 27n114

Timophanes of Corinth, 118n46

Tiryns, 12, 15n54, 19n78

Tisias and Corax, inventors of rhetoric, 98n106

totalitarianism/totalitarian regimes, 71n303, 195n27

tragedy of the commons, 68n294

tribe(s), 179–80

trierarch(s), 240

trittys, 179n109, 180

Trujillo, Rafael, 138

trust, 65, 68, 85, 94, 133, 138, 141, 144–45, 147, 175n95, 249–50, 256–57, 260–62, 281

Tydeus of Chios, 111n18

tyrannicides of Athens (Harmodius and Aristogeiton), 24n99, 105n133, 157, 158n30, 211, 228–31, 236, 236n46, 242, 262n138

tyranny/tyrants, 1, 2n4, 8, 16–18, 20n80, 29, 60–61, 68, 72, 77, 89, 95n95, 105n131, 109n6, 110, 118, 137, 139–40, 147, 152–55, 160, 167, 167n69, 170, 172, 178n107, 189, 191, 202, 204, 205n50, 206–7, 207n58, 211, 213, 214n82, 220, 227–28, 229–31, 235–36, 235n42, 237n48, 249–53, 256n124, 259–60, 263n146, 265n155, 270n169, 280n21, 283–85

unanimity. *See* consensus

urbanization, 20

veto points, 75, 80, 83, 123–24

violence, 71, 79, 99–100, 107–8, 109–11, 118–19, 122, 128, 131, 149, 153, 158, 161, 169, 262, 281, 281n25, 283

visibility, 207–8

voting, by acclamation, 125–26; by open ballot, 262; by show of hands, 125, 131. *See also* ballot, secret

walls, of a city, 159, 162–67, 177, 237n48, 278n13

wealth, 9, 19, 20, 35–40, 43, 47, 72, 173, 250, 250n101, 272

weapons. *See* arms

Weber, Max, 63

Whibley, Leonard, 2, 2n5, 3, 34, 189

women, 89n69, 90–91, 90n70, 90n71, 91n77, 105, 139, 176, 200–201, 259, 265n154, 265n155, 282n26

Xenias of Elis, 159n38

Xenophon of Corinth, 237n47

xenos/xenia (guest-friend, guest-friendship), 159n38

Zancle, 16n59

zeugitai (third-highest Solonian census class), 41, 43

Zeus, 96n99, 166, 217, 228n14, 265n155, 277n9

Zoilus of Erythrae, 212–13

A NOTE ON THE TYPE

This book has been composed in Arno, an Old-style serif typeface in the classic Venetian tradition, designed by Robert Slimbach at Adobe.